THE COMPLETE SERMONS OF RALPH WALDO EMERSON

VOLUME 2

THE COMPLETE SERMONS OF RALPH WALDO EMERSON
IN FOUR VOLUMES

Chief Editor: Albert J. von Frank

Editors: Ronald A. Bosco
Andrew Delbanco
Wesley T. Mott
Teresa Toulouse

Contributing Editors: David M. Robinson
Wallace E. Williams

THE COMPLETE SERMONS OF RALPH WALDO EMERSON

VOLUME 2

Edited by Teresa Toulouse
and Andrew Delbanco

UNIVERSITY OF MISSOURI PRESS
COLUMBIA AND LONDON

The publication of this volume was made possible in part by a grant from the Programs for Editions and Publications of the National Endowment for the Humanities, an independent Federal agency.

5 4 3 2 1   94 93 92 91 90

Library of Congress Cataloging-in-Publication Data
(Revised for volume 2)

Emerson, Ralph Waldo, 1803-1882.
    The complete sermons of Ralph Waldo Emerson.

    Vol. 2: Edited by Teresa Toulouse and Andrew H. Delbanco.
    Includes index.
    1. Unitarian churches—Sermons.   2. Sermons, American.
I. Von Frank, Albert J.   II. Title.
BX9843.E487C66   1989   v. 252 .091   88-4834
ISBN 0-8262-0746-4 (v. 2 : alk. paper)

∞™ This paper meets the minimum requirements of the American National Standard for Permanence of Paper for Printed Library Materials, Z39.48, 1984.

COMMITTEE ON
SCHOLARLY EDITIONS

AN APPROVED EDITION

MODERN LANGUAGE
ASSOCIATION OF AMERICA

In Memoriam

As this volume goes to press, we receive word of the death of our friend and colleague Wallace E. Williams. As Contributing Editor, Professor Williams gave crucial advice at the planning stage of this edition and assisted in resolving difficulties that arose during the preparation of the first and second volumes. A sensitive reader of Emerson's works, coeditor of *The Early Lectures of Ralph Waldo Emerson,* and a highly regarded figure in the community of Emerson scholars, Professor Williams will be sorely missed.

A. J. v. F.
July 1990

Preface

Many friends and colleagues have given us guidance and encouragement during the course of our work on this volume. At Harvard, William Bond, Rodney Dennis, and Dennis Marnon of the Houghton Library, and Joel Porte of the Department of English, helped us to get the project off to a good start. For permission to publish the sermons, we are indebted to the Ralph Waldo Emerson Memorial Association and the Houghton Library. The staffs of the Houghton and Widener Libraries at Harvard University, of the Butler Library at Columbia University, and of the Howard-Tilton Library at Tulane University, were unfailingly cooperative. At various stages of the editing process, Linda Ainsworth, Michael Kaufmann, Cybele Merrick, Gwen du Mauriac, Paula Rault, and Hongbo Tan gave valuable assistance. John Klause, Robert A. Ferguson, Graham Hutchins, and Kathy Eden were willing consultants on questions of annotation. The pioneering work of William Barton, Kenneth Cameron, and Gene Irey was of great value to us, as were the numerous works of scholars devoted to the ongoing collective aim of understanding Emerson.

The editors are grateful to Professor Eleanor M. Tilton, who generously made available for inclusion in the present edition the manuscript pages from Sermon LXXXI that she owns.

We would also like to thank Professor Alan Heimert and the Friends of the Matthiessen Room for providing a place to stay while the editors worked with the Emerson manuscripts in Cambridge.

Professor Toulouse would like to thank Provost Francis Lawrence, the Tulane Committee on Research, and the American Philosophical Association for research grants in aid.

By far our greatest debt is to Albert J. von Frank, whose close and patient supervision of our work—from the first stages of transcription to the search for elusive references—has been characteristic of his extraordinary devotion not only to this project, but to the larger enterprise of bringing Emerson's creative process to light.

T.T.
A.D.
January 1990

CONTENTS

Preface   vii

Abbreviations of Works Frequently Cited   xv

Textual Introduction   1

An Emerson Chronology: July 1829 to October 1830   7

SERMON XLIII
For in him we live, and move, and have our being. Acts 17:28   19

SERMON XLIV
Martha thou art careful and troubled about many things; but one thing is needful. Luke 10:41–42   25

SERMON XLV
The statutes of the Lord are right, rejoicing the heart.
Psalms 19:8   30

SERMON XLVI
—to lay hold upon the hope set before us; which hope we have as an anchor of the soul both sure and steadfast. Hebrews 6:18–19   36

SERMON XLVII
He that ruleth his spirit is better than he that taketh a city.
Proverbs 16:32   41

SERMON XLVIII
Ye shall know them by their fruits. Matthew 7:16   46

SERMON XLIX
Wherefore let him that thinketh he standeth, take heed lest he fall.
I Corinthians 10:12   51

SERMON L
This do in remembrance of me. Luke 22:19   56

SERMON LI
Blessed are the pure in heart for they shall see God. Matthew 5:8   61

SERMON LII
If any man offend not in word the same is a perfect man.
James 3:2   66

SERMON LIII
So then every one of us shall give account of himself to God.
Romans 14:12   71

SERMON LIV
*Can the Ethiopian change his skin, or the leopard his spots? Then may ye
also do good, that are accustomed to do evil.* Jeremiah 13:23   76

SERMON LV
*But thou, when thou prayest, enter into thy closet, and when thou hast
shut the door, pray to thy Father, which is in secret, and thy Father which
seeth in secret, shall reward thee openly.*
Matthew 6:6   82

SERMON LVI
*If our gospel be hid it is hid to them that are lost, in whom the God of this
world hath blinded the eyes of them that believe not, lest the light of the
glorious gospel of Christ who is the image of God should shine unto them.*
II Corinthians 4:3–4   87

SERMON LVII
Bless the Lord o my soul and forget not all his benefits.
Psalms 103:2   92

SERMON LVIII
For where your treasure is there will your heart be also.
Matthew 6:21   97

SERMON LIX
*Let us not be weary in well doing, for, in due season we shall reap, if we
faint not.* Galatians 6:9   102

SERMON LX
But when the fulness of time was come, God sent forth his son, made of a woman. Galatians 4:4   108

SERMON LXI
The night is far spent, the day is at hand, let us therefore cast off the works of darkness and let us put on the armor of light.
Romans 13:12   112

SERMON LXII
Henceforth I call you not servants, for the servant knoweth not what his Lord doeth; but I have called you friends, for all things that I have heard of my Father, I have made known unto you. John 15:15   118

SERMON LXIII
Be not conformed to this world, but be ye transformed by the renewing of your mind, that ye may prove what is that good and acceptable and perfect will of God. Romans 12:2   124

NOTE ON SERMON LXIV   131

SERMON LXV
And as ye would that men should do to you do ye also to them likewise. Luke 6:31   132

SERMON LXVI
Are not five sparrows sold for two farthings and not one of them is forgotten before God? But even the hairs of your head are all numbered. Luke 12:6–7   138

SERMON LXVII
There is a spirit in man and the inspiration of the Almighty giveth them understanding. Job 32:8   144

SERMON LXVIII
Thou hast been faithful over a few things: I will make thee ruler over many things. Enter thou into the joy of thy Lord. Matthew 25:23   151

SERMON LXIX
We then as workers together with him beseech you that ye receive not the grace of God in vain. II Corinthians 6:1   156

SERMON LXX
Happy is that people whose God is the Lord. Psalms 144:15   162

SERMON LXXI
Keep thy heart with all diligence, for out of it are the issues of life.
Proverbs 4:23   166

SERMON LXXII
*Suffer little children and forbid them not to come unto me for, of such is
the kingdom of heaven.* Mark 10:14   171

SERMON LXXIII
*Now we see through a glass darkly, but then face to face; now I know in
part but then shall I know even as also I am known.*
I Corinthians 13:12   176

SERMON LXXIV
The last enemy that shall be destroyed is death.
I Corinthians 15:26   181

SERMON LXXV
*Let every man prove his own work and then shall he have rejoicing in
himself alone and not in another, for every man shall bear his own burden.*
 Galatians 6:4–5   186

SERMON LXXVI
He taught them as one having authority and not as the scribes.
Matthew 7:29   192

SERMON LXXVII
Let no man seek his own, but every man another's wealth.
I Corinthians 10:24   196

SERMON LXXVIII
Now is the accepted time, now is the day of Salvation.
II Corinthians 6:2   201

SERMON LXXIX
To do good, and to communicate forget not. Hebrews 13:16   206

SERMON LXXX
*We have heard with our ears, O God, our fathers have told us what work
thou didst in their days in the times of old.* Psalms 44:1   212

SERMON LXXXI
By their fruits, ye shall know them. Matthew 7:20 216

SERMON LXXXII
Whosoever shall exalt himself shall be abased; and he that humbleth himself shall be exalted. Matthew 23:12 222

SERMON LXXXIII
Add to your faith, virtue, and to virtue knowledge. II Peter 1:5 227

SERMON LXXXIV
He that getteth wisdom, loveth his own soul. Proverbs 19:8 232

SERMON LXXXV
It is not a vain thing for you because it is your life. Deuteronomy 32:47 237

SERMON LXXXVI
And he spake a parable unto them, to this end, that men ought always to pray and not to faint. Luke 18:1 242

SERMON LXXXVII
I beseech you therefore brethren by the mercies of God that ye present your bodies a living sacrifice, holy, acceptable unto God, which is your reasonable service. Romans 12:1 246

SERMON LXXXVIII
What! know ye not that your body is the temple of the Holy Ghost, which is in you, which ye have of God, and ye are not your own? For ye are bought with a price, therefore glorify God in your body, and in your spirit which are God's. I Corinthians 6:19–20 251

SERMON LXXXIX
In a little wrath I hid my face from thee for a moment, but in everlasting kindness will I have mercy on thee. Isaiah 54:8 256

SERMON XC
For what is a man profited, if he gain the whole world and lose his own soul? Matthew 16:26 263

Appendix: Sermon XLVII [A] 269

Textual and Manuscript Notes 271

Index 407

Abbreviations of Works Frequently Cited

CW   *The Complete Works of Ralph Waldo Emerson.* Edited by Joseph
       Slater, et al. 5 vols. to date. Cambridge: Harvard University, 1971-.

EL   *The Early Lectures of Ralph Waldo Emerson.* Edited by Stephen E.
       Whicher, Robert E. Spiller, and Wallace E. Williams. 3 vols. Cam-
       bridge: Harvard University Press, 1959-1972.

J   *Journals of Ralph Waldo Emerson.* Edited by Edward Waldo Emer-
       son and Waldo Emerson Forbes. 10 vols. Boston and New York:
       Houghton Mifflin Co., 1909-1914.

JMN   *The Journals and Miscellaneous Notebooks of Ralph Waldo Emer-
       son.* Edited by William H. Gilman et al. 16 vols. Cambridge: Har-
       vard University Press, 1960-1982.

L   *The Letters of Ralph Waldo Emerson.* Edited by Ralph L. Rusk. 6
       vols. New York: Columbia University Press, 1939.

Life   Ralph L. Rusk. *The Life of Ralph Waldo Emerson.* New York:
       Charles Scribner's Sons, 1949.

MHS   Massachusetts Historical Society. Papers of the Second Church,
       Boston.

OFL   *One First Love: The Letters of Ellen Louisa Tucker to Ralph Waldo
       Emerson.* Edited by Edith W. Gregg. Cambridge: Harvard Univer-
       sity Press, 1962.

Pommer Henry F. Pommer. *Emerson's First Marriage.* Carbondale and Ed-
       wardsville: Southern Illinois University Press, 1967.

W   *The Complete Works of Ralph Waldo Emerson.* Edited by Edward
       Waldo Emerson. Centenary Edition. 12 vols. Boston and New York:
       Houghton Mifflin Co., 1903-1904.

The Complete Sermons of Ralph Waldo Emerson

_____ Volume 2

TEXTUAL INTRODUCTION

The sermons of Ralph Waldo Emerson are presented in this edition in an annotated, clear-text format with full textual notes in the back matter. Andrew Delbanco has been chiefly responsible for the editing of Sermons XLIII through LXVII (with the exception of Sermon LXIV, the manuscript of which is missing from the series), and Teresa Toulouse for Sermons LXVIII through XC, though each has checked the work of the other. Albert von Frank, as general editor, has verified the accuracy of the entire volume and assisted with the annotations. Since the editorial principles announced in the first volume have been followed in the preparation of the present volume, the reader is referred to the original Textual Introduction for a full discussion of the issues.

One aspect of editorial policy relating to the occurrence of multiple manuscript versions of particular sermons requires amplification. The policy set forth in the first volume was in each instance to adopt the second or later version as copy-text and to provide a full genetic transcription of the first version in the textual notes. Although we recognize the slight inconsistency of this policy with the general aim of offering the first delivered version of each sermon, we are also conscious of the limits of our ability to determine first-delivery form; specifically, in the case of multiple versions, the first or earlier manuscript is often too contaminated with revisions made for the sake of producing the second manuscript to allow such a reconstruction with any degree of confidence. In other words, where two or more manuscripts exist, the first manuscript is generally more indicative of the revised second manuscript than it is of its own original form. While this policy of adopting the later manuscript as the basis for the clear-text presentation remains sufficient for most such situations, important exceptions have emerged which require a more detailed statement on the matter of copy-text selection.

Among the forty-eight sermons represented in the present volume, there are nine instances of multiple manuscripts; in four of these instances the editors have *not* chosen the later of two manuscripts as copy-text. The reasons in each case illustrate the hazards of an inflexible editorial method:

1. In the case of Sermon XLVII, the two manuscripts do not comprise an earlier and later version of the "same" sermon: the first, designated XLVII [A] (catalogued as 47A by the Houghton Library), is the abandoned draft of a sermon (never delivered) occasioned by Emerson's attendance at the Harvard commencement exercises in August, 1829; the second, XLVII (catalogued as

1

47B by the Houghton Library), is altogether unrelated, though it was inscribed with the same number by Emerson. Since neither is logically a pendant to the other, they have been treated editorially as separate sermons. We give the text of the fragmentary XLVII [A] in an appendix.

2. Sermon LXXVI is represented in three manuscripts: an early abandoned draft, a complete manuscript (the source of the first delivery), and a second complete manuscript, a revised and reorganized version. In this case, the revision that produced the second complete manuscript was so thoroughgoing that Emerson found it inexpedient to do much preliminary rewriting on the first complete manuscript. Consequently, that first manuscript survives in nearly its original condition, and therefore, as the source of the first delivery, it was chosen as copy-text. The second version, delivered seven times, is given in full genetic transcription, along with the first-draft fragment, in the textual notes.

3. Sermon LXXXI presents an exceptional case because of the incompleteness of the manuscripts. The lost pages torn from the Harvard manuscript—torn, perhaps, by Emerson himself—appear to represent about half the sermon text. The editors were therefore delighted on learning that Professor Eleanor M. Tilton had come into possession of four leaves of manuscript clearly from Sermon LXXXI. These leaves, however, turned out not to be from the mutilated Harvard manuscript as we had first supposed, but from a previously unsuspected revised manuscript, of which they represent, again, about half the text. Since the Harvard manuscript included the opening and the Tilton manuscript the close of the sermon, with little overlap and a few lacunae, no solution to the difficulty seemed to the editors more plausible than the presentation of a conjoined text; so the two manuscripts have been edited seriatim.

4. Finally, Sermon LXXXV is represented in two manuscripts, one marked "Princeps Edit." and the other "Palimpsest." In this case, the earlier manuscript is chosen as copy-text, both because it is only lightly revised and because the later manuscript is incomplete.

Apart from these exceptional cases, the editorial policy remains as stated in the first volume.

The present edition, it should be noted, does not in general adopt the system of reference employed by the Houghton Library in referring to multiple manuscripts by letter (as in Sermon 47A and 47B). These designations, necessary for cataloguing purposes, do not appear to represent any actual judgment about chronological ordering, and in fact often prove misleading if taken as an indication of priority (Houghton's 79A, for example, is a revision of 79B). We have in most instances found it both clearer and more accurate to refer to the "earlier" or "later" manuscript.

Textual Notes

The textual notes give the manuscript reading in every case of authorial insertion, deletion, substitution, transposition, and variant reading. With the exception of the categories of silent emendation listed below, the notes also record every instance in which a word or part of a word has been editorially supplied or deleted (for example, to correct Emerson's accidental doubling of words), or in which punctuation has been altered for clarity. No editorial emendations, silent or otherwise, occur in the textual notes, the purpose of which in each instance is to give the manuscript form using such standard symbols as are necessary to describe the situation. (A key to these symbols appears at the head of the Textual and Manuscript Notes.) Thus, a textual note might take this form:

our ⟨beliefs⟩ ↑Xty↓.

The symbols indicate that Emerson canceled "beliefs" and inserted "Xty". Although abbreviations in the edited text are regularly and silently expanded (the clear text would in this instance read "our Christianity."), the textual note is always bound to reproduce the manuscript form. Because the expansion of abbreviations is treated in this edition as a *silent* emendation (see the list below), no textual note is provided when Emerson uses "Xty" or any other abbreviation in the course of a sentence he did not revise. Put another way, the occasion for the textual note in the example above is not the abbreviation, but Emerson's substitution of one word for another.

Silent Emendations

1. Citations for biblical texts at the head of each sermon are given in regularized form, spelling out the book of the Bible, which Emerson often abbreviates, and giving chapter and verse in arabic numerals, which Emerson does not consistently use. Emerson often quotes the Bible, as indeed he quotes other sources, from memory; inexact quotations are not corrected.

2. The following abbreviations are expanded: altho' (although), amt. (amount), & (and), bro't (brought), Xt (Christ), Xdom (Christendom), Xn or Chr^n (Christian), Xty (Christianity), ch. (church), cd. (could), eveg. (evening), gov^t (government), hereaf. (hereafter), hist. (history), incor. (incorrect), mt. (might), m.f. (my friends), nt. (not), pd. (paid), relig. (religious), Rev. (Revelation), sd. (said), servt (servant), shd. (should), y^e (the), y^{r}s (there's), tho't (thought), Wm (William), wd. (would), yrself (yourself).

3. Numbers and numerical terms are spelled out: e.g., 1 (one), 3^d (third).

4. Missing punctuation is supplied when undoubtedly called for, as periods at the ends of sentences, commas or semi-colons in series, commas or colons to introduce quotations, and question marks at the ends of rhetorical questions (silently emended from a period when necessary). Emerson's use of single and double quotation marks is preserved without imposing uniformity, but omitted marks in a pair are supplied (a textual note describes the situation if there is any doubt about where a quotation ends). Apostrophes have been supplied where necessary; if there is any doubt whether singular or plural possessive is intended, the manuscript form is given in a note.

5. Words beginning a sentence (following Emerson's period) have been cap-

italized; capitalized words following Emerson's semicolons (but not his colons) have been reduced to lowercase.

6. Terminal punctuation consisting of a period followed by a dash has been retained within paragraphs when it seems to have the force of a semicolon. The dash is silently omitted when it falls at the end of a paragraph.

7. Emerson's usual practice is to put commas and periods inside his quotation marks. Contrary instances in the manuscript seem to be the result of haste and carelessness, and are therefore silently regularized.

Variants, Transpositions, and Other Reported Emendations

1. Emerson occasionally inserts an alternate word or phrase above the uncanceled corresponding word or phrase in his initial inscription. This situation is always reported in the textual notes, where it takes the form /first/ second/. The clear text regularly adopts the second inscription in a pair of variants unless doing so results in a reading that is objectionable on the grounds of grammar or sense.

2. Emerson's usual method of indicating transposition is to label the relevant sentences, phrases, or words with subscript numbers 1 and 2 (or, more rarely, a and b) and to mark off the material to be transposed with square brackets. In a few instances, three elements are designated for transposition. The clear text reflects the transposed order; the original order is given (with Emerson's numbers or letters represented as superscript) in a textual note.

3. Misspelled words are corrected and the misspellings reported in the textual notes. Inconsistency in the use of British and American forms is not regularized. No attempt has been made to revise odd spellings when Emerson's version occurs in dictionaries of the period or when contemporary authority for it has been found in the *Oxford English Dictionary*.

4. Emerson's erratic punctuation has been altered in the few instances when it is likely to cause confusion. All such instances are recorded in the textual notes. All ambiguous instances in which *missing* punctuation has been supplied are recorded in the textual notes.

5. Words that Emerson accidentally omitted or that are illegible or lost through damage to the manuscript are supplied without editorial brackets in the clear text and the situation described in the textual notes. Accidentally doubled words (as well as a few deliberately used catchwords) are corrected and reported in the textual notes.

6. Notes by Emerson—either footnotes or parenthetical notes—that briefly identify the source of a quotation are given in the editor's explanatory footnotes, where they are identified as Emerson's; they do not otherwise appear in the text or textual notes. Emerson's notations of hymn and scripture selections, often appearing at the top of the first manuscript page, will be reported in tabular form as an appendix to the final volume of this edition. Emerson's notations concerning the date and place of delivery, irregularly given on the last manuscript page, are incorporated in the information supplied in the first

explanatory footnote for each sermon as well as in the Chronology; they do not otherwise appear in the text or textual notes.

7. Emerson's square brackets are always given in the textual notes (where they are indicated by curved brackets to distinguish them from editorial remarks), though they do not appear in the clear text. In addition to setting off the elements in a transposition, they frequently identify the limits of an inserted passage. Emerson also used them to set off paragraphs or larger blocks of text, most likely to indicate that the portions thus bracketed could be omitted in a particular delivery. Emerson was not consistent in the form of his square brackets, and while we believe we have consistently been able to distinguish them from Emerson's parentheses, we have freely interpreted as square brackets a range of crooked and angled lines that manifestly serve the same function.

Editorial Annotations

Editorial annotations, which appear as footnotes to the text, have been kept to a minimum. For each sermon, the unnumbered first note supplies what is known about its composition and, drawing on Emerson's manuscript Preaching Record and notations on the sermon manuscript itself, information about when and where it was delivered. If substantial draft passages relating to the sermon exist in the *Journals and Miscellaneous Notebooks,* that fact is given in the first note; otherwise, the existence of briefer draft passages is indicated in the appropriate place in subsequent notes. Biblical and other allusions are identified in the numbered notes, as are Emerson's uses of sermon material in lectures and other later compositions.

Emerson's repetitions of the main Bible text in each sermon are not annotated. Phrases of common occurrence in the King James Version of the Bible, such as "strange gods," "the ends of the earth," and "the heaven of heavens," for example, belong to Emerson's generally biblical rhetoric in the sermons and are not annotated. An effort has also been made to annotate passages that occur only in the textual notes, primarily to have as full a record as possible of Emerson's use of the Bible; these allusions have been included in the index along with the other annotations.

An Emerson Chronology

July 1829 to October 1830

Note: When two sermons are listed as having been preached on a particular day, the first is the morning sermon, the second the afternoon sermon. A third sermon indicates a special Sunday evening service. It should be kept in mind that Emerson's preaching was not entirely confined to the Sabbath: he also delivered sermons for Thursday (or other weekday) lectures, Fast Days, Thanksgiving, and Christmas.

While Emerson (and others) often referred to Boston's Second Church as the "North Church" or the "Old North Church," it is here always identified as the Second Church. It should not be confused with another "Old North," the Anglican church associated with Paul Revere's ride; that church, which Emerson referred to as the "New North," was at this time led by Francis Parkman, father of the historian. Similarly, Nathaniel Frothingham's First Church was popularly known as "Chauncy (or Chauncey) Place"; to avoid confusion, it is regularly identified in the following Chronology as the First Church.

1829

July 1	Henry Ware's salary from Second Church terminated; Emerson's salary increased to $1800 (*L* 1:267, n. 28). Responds to further criticism from Ware, who continues to doubt the importance of scripture in Emerson's views (*L* 1:273).
July 2	Completes XLI.
July 4	Completes XLII.
July 5	Preaches XLII and XLI (Second Church).
July 11	Completes XLIII.
July 12	Preaches XLIII (Second Church) and XXXIV (Pine Street).
July 19	Preaches XXXI and XXXIII (Roxbury).
July 24	Completes XLIV.
July 25	Emerson and his brother Charles visit their childhood home in the rural Canterbury section of Boston (*L* 1:274-75 and *OFL* 81-82).
July 26	Preaches XLIV and XIX (Second Church). Charles Emerson joins the Second Church (MHS).
July 28	Pays Mr. Whitney $10.00 for preaching (Account Books).

July 31   "I am striving hard today to establish the sovereignty and self-existent excellence of the moral law in popular argument" (i.e., working on XLV) (F. B. Sanborn, *Recollection of Seventy Years* [Boston, 1909], 2:374).

Aug. 2   Preaches XLV (Second Church) and XLIII (Brattle Street).

Aug. 3   Receipt for $280 "for my Salary to July 1, 1829" (MHS). Mrs. Kent, Ellen's mother, arrives in Boston for a visit (*OFL* 81).

Aug. 5   Emerson travels with Mrs. Kent to Concord, N.H. (*OFL* 81).

Aug. 7   Emerson travels with Ellen and her mother from Concord, N.H., to the Shaker Community at nearby Canterbury (*L* 1:275; *JMN* 3:159).

Aug. 8   The party leaves Canterbury at 7 A.M., travels to Meredith Village, where they dine, and continues on to Centre Harbor (*L* 1:276).

Aug. 9   Emerson attends church in Meredith, N.H., and hears the Rev. Reuben Porter preach (*L* 1:277).

Aug. 10   The party leaves Centre Harbor for Conway (*L* 1:277), where they stay at the Ossipee House (*JMN* 3:161).

Aug. 11   In Conway, Emerson is encouraged by Ellen's apparently better health and believes that a Caribbean voyage will not be necessary (*L* 1:277-78). The party fords the Saco in order to explore Mt. Agiocochook, and Emerson visits the site of the Willey disaster (*JMN* 3:161).

Aug. 16   The party reaches Hanover, N.H., having traveled through Crawford's Notch and Bartlett, back to Conway and Centre Harbor, then through Plymouth, Rumny, Wentworth, and Orford (*L* 1:279; *JMN* 3:161).

Aug. 19   Emerson returns to Boston (*OFL* 86).

Aug. 22   Completes XLVI at Chardon Street.

Aug. 23   Preaches XLVI and XV (Second Church).

Aug. 25   Attends Harvard Commencement; sits with Charles W. Upham (*L* 1:280).

Aug. 28   Composing XLVII, Emerson writes to William: "I am in the roots & seeds of a sermon this A.M. & cant write another word more than to say that I shall preach in town doubtless all day tho' probably at home only in ye morn^g" (*L* 1:281).

Aug. 29   Completes XLVII.

Aug. 30   Preaches XLVII (Second Church) and XLV (Twelfth Church); Emerson drafts the fragmentary XLVII [A] (see Appendix).

Sept. 5   Completes XLVIII.

Sept. 6	Preaches XLVIII and XVI (Second Church).
Sept. 7	Emerson goes to Concord, N.H., to pick up Ellen, her mother, and sister (*OFL* 100).
Sept. 9	Emerson and Ellen, together with Ellen's mother and sister Margaret, begin a trip to Springfield, stopping the first night at Merrimack (*L* 1:282).
Sept. 10	Emerson writes two poems to Ellen at Pepperell along the way (*OFL* 101–2). The party stays overnight in Worcester.
Sept. 11	The party arrives in Springfield.
Sept. 12	Emerson writes from Springfield: "I think I shall get home to Boston next Friday or Saturday night tho peradventure (wh. being interpreted is—in all probability) sermonless" (*L* 1:282). CCE writes to RWE in Worcester: "Now every body is engaged preaching as a candidate, somewhere or other,—& it is really with some considerable difficulty, that I have procured Mr. Jesse Chickering to supply the pulpit tomorrow. . . . I saw Mr. Sampson today & he thought it would be very imprudent & unadvised in you to spend another Sabbath from Boston" (MHS).
Sept. 13	Preaches XXXI and XLV (Springfield, Third Congregational Church, for William B. O. Peabody) (*L* 1:282).
Sept. 14	The party travels to Hartford along the west bank of the Connecticut River (*L* 1:284).
Sept. 15	They travel from Hartford to Worcester by way of Vernon, Ct.; Emerson complains of a lame knee (*L* 1:283–84).
Sept. 17	They return to Concord, N.H.
Sept. 18	Emerson returns to Boston (*OFL* 103).
Sept. 20	Preaches XLIX and XX (Second Church).
Sept. 24	Preaches XXXV, Thursday Lecture (Second Church).
Sept. 26	Completes L at Chardon Street.
Sept. 27	Preaches L (Second Church) and XXXV (Harvard College Chapel).
Sept. 30	Emerson and Ellen L. Tucker are married at the Kent mansion in Concord, N.H.
Oct. 4	Preaches XLIX and XLV (Concord, Mass.).
Oct. 5	They move to Mrs. Keating's house on Chardon St., Boston; Ellen's two sisters and their parents board in the same house (Pommer, 34; *L* 1:285).
Oct. 6	Receipt for $450 "for my Salary to Octo 1st" (MHS). Pays Abel Adams $208.00 for half a year's boarding (Account Books).
Oct. 8	Pays $30.00 for supply of pulpit for three days (Account Books).
Oct. 11	Preaches LI and XXII (Second Church).

Oct. 18	Preaches LII and XXI (Second Church).
Oct. 20	Edward Emerson admitted to the Massachusetts Bar and offered a place in Samuel Hoar's office (*L* 1:285).
Oct. 21	"I am very lame not being able to walk a step without a cane—& Sundays I preach sitting" (*L* 1:285).
Oct. 24	Completes LIII at Chardon Street.
Oct. 25	Preaches LIII (Second Church).
Oct. 31	Writes draft passage for LIV (*JMN* 3:167–68).
Nov. 1	Emerson does not preach.
Nov. 6	Completes LIV at Chardon Street.
Nov. 8	Preaches LIV and XIV (Second Church).
Nov. 11	Emerson participates in the dedication of the Unitarian Church in Concord, N.H., while Ellen stays at home in Boston (*L* 1:286, n. 97).
Nov. 12	Returns to Boston (*L* 1:286).
Nov. 14	Completes LV at Chardon Street.
Nov. 15	Preaches LV and XXIII (Second Church).
Nov. 21	Completes LVI at Chardon Street.
Nov. 22	Preaches LVI and VIII (Second Church).
Nov. 25	Completes LVII at Chardon Street.
Nov. 26	Thanksgiving; preaches LVII (Second Church). "A meeting of the brethren of the Church having been called by the Pastor at the Table Nov. 25, it was holden this evening & the question submitted to their consideration, whether the fund of this Church should go on accumulating or whether its interest shd. be expended for the poor. It was determined that at present it was inexpedient to act thereon. ¶ It was proposed that in future the old quarterly meetings of the Church for mutual religious improvement by conversation & other means should be renewed and that the Pastor shd. give notice of such meeting from the Communion table on the last Sunday in January. ¶ At this meeting Deacon Mackintosh requested that some one be appointed to audit his Church accounts on the first of January next. Brother George A. Sampson was accordingly chosen" (MHS).
Nov. 29	Preaches LVIII and X (Second Church).
Dec. 1	Emerson is elected to Boston School Committee, to serve on the subcommittee for the Boston Latin and Mayhew Schools. He is visited by "the quack doctor [Simon] Hewitt" who cures the knee ailment in "two hours" after several other doctors had failed (*L* 1:287–88).
Dec. 6	Emerson does not preach.
Dec. 7	Writes draft passage for LIX (*JMN* 3:169).

Dec. 10	Emerson is reading Coleridge's *The Friend* "with great interest" (*J* 2:276).
Dec. 13	Preaches LIX (Second Church) and XLIX (First Church).
Dec. 20	Preaches XLIX and LIV (Cambridge).
Dec. 26	Completes LX at Chardon Street.
Dec. 27	Preaches LX (Second Church) and XLIX (West Church).
Dec. 31	Preaches LXI, Thursday Lecture (Second Church, in the evening).

1830

Jan. 3	Preaches XV (Cambridgeport).
Jan. 4	Emerson reports that he is reading Coleridge's *The Friend* and *Aids to Reflection,* Degerando's *Histoire Comparée des Systèmes de Philosophie,* and Combe's *Constitution of Man* (*L* 1:291). Pays Dr. Hewitt $50.00 (Account Books).
Jan. 5	Receives $450 quarterly salary payment (MHS).
Jan. 6	Pays W. Barry $10.00 for supplying pulpit (Account Books).
Jan. 10	Preaches LXII (Second Church) and XIX (New North, for Francis Parkman).
Jan. 16	Completes revised version of LXII at Chardon St.
Jan. 17	Preaches XLIX and LXII (Beverly).
Jan. 22	Emerson attends a ministerial meeting where the morality of the theatre is discussed; Emerson's notes on it find their way into LXIII (*JMN* 3:175).
Jan. 24	Preaches LXIII (Second Church) and XXI (Federal Street Church).
Jan. 29	Emerson gives Friday Lecture; sermon not indicated.
Jan. 30	Charles Emerson lectures at Concord on "The Constitution of Man as Affected by Outward Circumstances" (*L* 1:292).
Jan. 31	Preaches LXIV and XXIV (Second Church).
Feb. 6	Completes LXV at Chardon Street.
Feb. 7	Preaches LXV in the morning (First Church) and again in the afternoon (Second Church); in the evening preaches LXII (South Congregational Church, for Mellish Motte).
Feb. 10	"Is there not the sublime always in religion? I go down to the vestry & I find a few plain men & women there come together not to eat or drink or get money or mirth but drawn by a great thought—come thither to conceive and form a connexion with an infinite Person. I thought it was sublime & not mean as others suppose" (*JMN* 3:178).
Feb. 11	Writes draft passage for LXVI (*JMN* 3:179–80).

Feb. 14	Preaches LXVI (Second Church) and LXV (East Cambridge).
Feb. 17	Ordination of Hersey Bradford Goodwin as colleague pastor to Ezra Ripley at Concord; Emerson delivers the "Right Hand of Fellowship."
Feb. 18	Preaches LXIV, Thursday Lecture (Second Church).
Feb. 21	Preaches LXV (New South) and XXV (Second Church).
Feb. 27	Completes LXVII at Chardon Street.
Feb. 28	Preaches LXVII (Second Church and Purchase Street).
Mar. 2	Writes passage on prayer used in LXXXVI (*JMN* 3:182–83).
Mar. 3	Reads Webster's Reply to Hayne (*JMN* 3:184).
Mar. 7	Preaches LXVIII and XXVI (Second Church); preaches XXVI as an evening lecture (Charlestown).
Mar. 9	Leaves Boston with Ellen and her sister Margaret, heading for Philadelphia (*JMN* 3:343, n. 18; 3:344, n. 29). Lodges at Framingham, Mass. (*JMN* 3:341, n. 14; *OFL* 116).
Mar. 10	Leaving Framingham at 5 A.M., the party arrives at Worcester by 10. After spending most of the day in Worcester, they arrive late in the evening in Springfield (*OFL* 116).
Mar. 13	Emerson rides out from Hartford to Weathersfield to escort Mary Moody Emerson into town; Ellen meets Aunt Mary for the first time (*OFL* 116).
Mar. 14	Preaches XXVI, XLIX, and LXIV (in Hartford at Allynes Hall, "since the Church was forbid" [*OFL* 117]); "I preached in Hartford three times on Sunday to a small but attentive congregation" (*L* 1:293).
Mar. 15	Emerson, traveling with his wife and sister-in-law, Margaret Tucker, arrives at New Haven at 6 P.M. (*L* 1:293). Mary Moody Emerson writes to Charles about Ellen: "I like her better than I dreamt—but not near so handsome—genius and loveliness are enough" (*OFL* 115).
Mar. 16	Emerson visits his cousin, Charles U. Shepard, who gives him and Ellen a tour of the College and the sculpture gallery of Hezekiah Augur; they meet the poet James Gates Percival (*L* 1:294; *OFL* 117–18).
Mar. 17	They depart New Haven at 7 A.M. by steamboat for New York (*L* 1:294), but are forced by a storm to anchor overnight in Norwalk roads (*L* 1:295; *OFL* 118–19).
Mar. 18	Emerson, Ellen, and Margaret arrive at the American Hotel, New York, at 2 P.M. (*L* 1:295). Ellen is coughing up blood (*L* 1:296).
Mar. 19	"Ellen is quite weak today." They rest in the hotel. Emerson writes Charles concerning the Second Church services

for March 28: "If you can, engage a young man from C[ambridge] with the request from me that he . . . exchange with Mr Ripley of Waltham (who promised to gratify me on such an occasion recently) or with Dr Ware or any of the Boston ministers half or the whole day, he will gratify our people's love for old preachg" (*L* 1:295).

Mar. 20   The party embarks early in the morning on "The Thistle" to Philadelphia, where they stay at the United States Hotel, receiving guests in the evening (*L* 1:296; *OFL* 121).

Mar. 21   Preaches XXVI and LXIV (Philadelphia).

Mar. 22   They arrange to take rooms at Mrs. Sarah McElroy's boarding house at Chestnut and Eleventh Streets (*OFL* 122; *L* 1:297).

Mar. 25   Emerson is doubtful about the timing of his return to Boston. Ellen writes: "I have given him leave yea have urged his going away now—for he is every whit as much out of his element as at Concord N H—and (oh tell it not) not a text has he expounded not a skeleton of a sarmint has he formed not a sonnet has he perpetrated since he turned his back B ward" (*L* 1:297, n. 26). Emerson is reading a volume of Jefferson's letters (*L* 1:297, 298, 300).

Mar. 28   Preaches LXV (Philadelphia). Ellen writes: "I have heard two sermons today—Waldo's 'Golden rule' sermon and a sermon by a stranger" (*OFL* 126).

Mar. 31   Emerson leaves Philadelphia (*JMN* 3:343; *OFL* 126).

Apr. 1   Spends the day in New York (*L* 1:299).

Apr. 4   Preaches LXIX (Second Church) and LXIV (Brattle Street).

Apr. 5   Writes to William asking about Johann Gottfried Eichhorn's arguments against the divine authority of the New Testament (Rusk, *Life,* 152). Receives $450 quarterly salary payment (MHS).

Apr. 8   Fast Day; preaches LXX (New North and Second Church).

Apr. 11   Preaches LXXI and VI (Second Church).

Apr. 16   "I am going to Concord tomorrow for Sunday" (*L* 1:300).

Apr. 18   Preaches XXVI and LXIV (Concord, Mass.).

Apr. 24   Completes LXXII at Chardon Street.

Apr. 25   Preaches LXXII and XXVII (Second Church); preaches LXIV as an evening lecture (South Congregational Church, for Mellish Motte).

May 2   Preaches LXXIII (Second Church and First Church, Cambridge).

May 8   Completes LXXIV at Chardon St.

May 9   Preaches LXXIV (Second Church and Hollis Street).

May 11   "I have been sonneteering now ever since March opened
                  . . ." (*L* 1:302).

May 16   Completes LXXV at Chardon St. Preaches LXXV and XI
                  (Second Church).

c. May 20   Moves to new lodgings in Brookline (Mrs. Perry's) in prep-
                  aration for Ellen's return; Emerson's mother will also live
                  with them (*L* 1:302, n. 45).

May 23   Emerson does not preach, having gone to Philadelphia to
                  retrieve Ellen.

May 26   Election Day; Charles writes to William: "Waldo was
                  chaplain on Election day. I envied him his comfortable seat
                  in the Pulpit." Emerson reports that Channing's Election
                  Sermon, "Spiritual Freedom," lasted "one hour thirty five
                  minutes" (*L* 1:302–3).

May 30   Preaches LXXVI and XXX (Second Church).

June 2   "Conversion from a moral to a religious character is like
                  day after twilight" (*JMN* 3:186).

June 6   Preaches LXIV and XLIX (Waltham); in the evening deliv-
                  ers LXXVII (Charity Lecture at the Old South).

June 9   Pays G. Leonard $10.00 for supplying pulpit (Account
                  Books).

June 12   Completes LXXVIII at Brookline.

June 13   Preaches LXXVIII (Second Church and South Congrega-
                  tional Church, for Mellish Motte).

June 20   Preaches XXXI and XXXIV (Second Church).

June 24   Writes draft passage for LXXXI (*JMN* 3:188–89).

June 27   Preaches LXXIX (Second Church) and LIX (Harvard Col-
                  lege Chapel).

July 2   Receives $450 quarterly salary payment (MHS).

July 3   Completes LXXX at Brookline.

July 4   Preaches LXXX and LXXXI (Second Church).

July 11   Preaches XXXV and LXXVIII (New Bedford).

July 15   Writes draft passage for LXXXII (*JMN* 3:190).

July 18   Preaches LXXXII (Second Church) and LXIV (New North).

July 23   Preaches XXXIII, Friday Evening Lecture (Second Church).

July 25   Completes LXXXIII at Brookline. Preaches LXXXIII and
                  XLIII (Second Church).

Aug. 1   Preaches LXXXIV (Second Church) and XLVII (New
                  South).

Aug. 8   Preaches XXI and XXXIII (Charlestown).

Aug. 11   Ellen coughing blood again (*L* 1:307, n. 71).

Aug. 15   Preaches LXXXV (Second Church).

Aug. 22   Preaches LXXXV and LXXVIII (Brookline).

Aug. 23	Edward Emerson arrives from New York for a visit (*L* 1:307).
Aug. 28	Completes LXXXVI at Brookline.
Aug. 29	Preaches LXXXVI (Second Church) and XLIII (First Church).
Sept. 2	Emerson escorts Ellen as far as Lexington on her trip to Concord, N.H. (*L* 1:307).
Sept. 4	Edward returns by boat to New York (*L* 1:307).
Sept. 5	Preaches LXXXVII and XXXV (Second Church). In the Preaching Record, Emerson notes that Henry Ware, Jr., has returned from Europe.
Sept. 10	"It is my purpose to methodize my days. I wish to study the scriptures, in a part of every day, that I may be able to explain them to others & that their light may flow into my life. . . . God grant me persistency enough, so soon as I leave Brookline & come to my books, to do as I intend" (*JMN* 3:198).
Sept. 11	Completes LXXXVIII at Brookline.
Sept. 12	Preaches LXXXVIII (Second Church) and LIX (Purchase Street).
Sept. 19	Preaches LIV, LIX, and LXXV (Concord, N.H.).
Sept. 24	Preaches LXII, Friday Lecture (Second Church).
Sept. 25	Completes LXXXIX at Brookline.
Sept. 26	Preaches LXXXIX (Second Church) and XXXIII (Twelfth Church).
Oct. 3	Preaches XC (Second Church).

The Sermons

XLIII

For in him we live, and move, and have our being.
ACTS 17:28

The difference of sects is much less than the difference of practice. Men who hold a sterner theology than ours charge what is called the Unitarian Church with giving something like the privilege of sanctuary to reprobates of every sect. Indolence and Pleasure, it is said, are the missionaries which bring in proselytes to the milder views of the divine character, which the lovers of sloth and pleasure think will give a cloak, an apology, to their loose thinking and loose practice. I suppose there is too much foundation in fact for this charge. I suppose, brethren, there are many among us who try to find in their religious views some colour for their own indifference to religion—who having heard that their master was not a hard man, reaping where he had not sown, conclude him to be a very easy man who will bear much and forgive much.[1]

We have found out that God is merciful and we presume on his mercy. We have grown wiser than to fear the *materialism* of the Calvinists, no longer interpret literally the figurative language of the Scriptures which surrounded God with clouds and darkness—and thunders. We have found out that fire and worm cannot touch the soul,[2]—and so we brave the rest, we brave the terrors of the spiritual world,—and hug our vices under the name of liberal Christianity. My brethren, this is a dangerous mistake. Wo unto you that laugh now, for ye shall weep.[3] If this were really the tendency of truth,—deeply as I feel the meanness and the harm of falsehood, I had rather the hand were put back on the dial,—it were better that the mind should retrograde again, that we should go back not only to what modern Calvinists believe, but to the dark impossibilities of Calvin himself, if they would put a bridle on the heart and help us to lead a godly life,—so the heart should be right, if the head were wrong. The moment we admit the immortality of man, the least risk becomes tremendous risk, and it

---

Manuscript dated July 11, 1829, at Chardon Street. Preached ten times: July 12, 1829, at the Second Church, Boston; August 2 at the Brattle Street Church; July 25, 1830, at the Second Church; August 29 at the First Church, Boston; October 10 at King's Chapel; April 16, 1837, in East Lexington; April 30 in Watertown; July 23 in Framingham; October 8 in Waltham; and February 11, 1838, in Concord, Mass.

   1. Cf. Matthew 25:24.
   2. Cf. Isaiah 66:24.
   3. Luke 6:25.

19

were better beyond comparison to wear out life with the poor Hindoo in wildest desarts, and fiercest penances, than to live under the broad glory of Christianity an unworthy sensualist, a hard cunning worldling, a false teacher, or a hypocrite.

But, brethren, this laxity does not belong to true Christianity, but to bad men. All views of Christianity, all who, with any claim to the character of candid disciples, hold on to the name, keep enough truth in their creed to alarm guilt, and arouse indifference, if only they will reason rightly.

For Christianity is only the Interpreter of Natural Religion. Christianity only confirms from God the suggestions of the human mind before and since— perhaps only anticipated the conclusions to which the human mind in the progress of society would come. And as the religious character is a development of the human mind, and not the fruit of external doctrines, it is not the particular speculations we run into about God's simple or twofold or threefold nature or about the preexistence of the Saviour or about atonement and justification and conversion, it is not these that make the difference between men,—but something prior to all these and independent of all, namely the relation which the soul bears to God,—a relation of the faculties and the affections, and so, of all the actions,—a relation so holy and natural and rapid that the poor fences of human sects are no barrier to it; are indifferent to it. Fenelon and Calvin and Taylor, and Priestley, kneel and worship side by side, and Christianity forgets in her love of these holy men that they were champions of four arrogant churches.[4]

It is well that we should keep in mind those views of the gospel which make us feel that our faith has height and depth enough to ravish the saint and to shake the sinner, or rather it has such power, that if we will open our hearts to its influence, we shall sin no more and suffer no more.

It seems to me the whole difference between a religious and an irreligious man, the index by which every man's progress in goodness is marked, common to all sects and utterly regardless of their demarcations, is, the perception of God. All practical religion is the perception of God, for the more distinctly the mind beholds him, the more faithfully will it adopt his will and execute his commands. My brethren, do you know any emblem of order, any sign of elevation, any stimulus to the senses or to the mind—whatever it be, it is but a faint type of the power of this idea upon the soul of man. Many of you have witnessed the common experiment of the loadstone.[5] If you introduce a magnet into a heap of steel-filings the rubbish becomes instantly instinct with life and order. Every particle at once finds its own place, is found to have a north and a

4. François de Selignac de la Mothe-Fénelon (1651-1715), Catholic mystic, archbishop of Cambrai, and author of *Explication des maximes des saints sur la vie intérieure* and *Télémaque;* John Calvin (1509-1564), French Protestant reformer and theologian resident in Geneva; Jeremy Taylor (1613-1667), Anglican religious leader and author of such popular works as *The Rule and Exercises of Holy Living* and *The Rule and Exercises of Holy Dying;* Joseph Priestley (1733-1804), renowned Unitarian clergyman and scientist, discoverer of oxygen.

5. Emerson witnessed the experiment in the summer of 1827 (*JMN* 3:93) and worked out the spiritual analogy in a letter of December 17, 1827, to Mary Moody Emerson (*J* 2:223-25).

south pole, and all arrange themselves in regular curves about the magnet. The same is true of the earth itself in the common theory of magnetism; the globe is a great magnet, and all the magnetic needles upon its surface arrange themselves as the particles of iron dust by its poles. All nature is full of symbols of its Author. I see in this familiar fact an emblem of God's moral action. The mind is that mass of rubbish. The mind is one dull miscellany of actions and passions and wandering affections and purposes—until its hidden virtue is called forth when God is revealed.

The moment the soul becomes aware of the presence of God—not by the hearing of the ear but by its own belief,[6] all its knowledge, all its active powers, throw themselves into irresistible arrangement, the riddle of human life is explained, and all things lose at once their solitary independent value and are thenceforward regarded in a new light as parts of God's agency—nothing is insignificant, for every thing is a part of the mighty whole.

There are three ways in which the connexion of the soul with God may be regarded; as he manifests himself in the material world; as he manifests himself in the history of man; as he manifests himself in our own experience. I know, brethren, this subject is a very high and difficult one. It needs more lights than men have. It is one we shall eagerly explore when the body sleeps in dust. Still my sense of weakness shall not deter me from calling your attention to a theme which, as each man's own breast is the best instructer, may suggest far stronger views of God's agency from your own experience to your conscience than I could hope to unfold.

I. The material Creation is God's work. The most exquisite design is shown in its parts, and our admiration is wakened at every step by the order, and the glory, and the pleasure of the results, and the wiser we grow the more they astonish.

Still this is gazing at a distance.

But men are ever disposed to view God from afar, to look back to a distant period, put back his agency at the Creation 6000 years ago, a notion which all sound philosophy combats. It is imagined that at that time God established the laws of Nature and left it to itself as an Artist winds up a machine and leaves it to perform its work. But this is very unsound analogy. If God leaves his work it will fall asunder. For consider the difference of the two cases. The artist who constructs a watch avails himself of powers perpetually afforded him by nature, that is, by God—as the force of gravity or the elasticity of steel. If these powers should be withdrawn his machine would stop. But God has no such powers out of himself.[7]

The same power is needed this moment as was needed the first moment to produce the same effect. To him it is the same to uphold as to establish. It is a creation of each instant. I look then at my present being as now received, as now

6. Job 42:5.
7. Cf. John 1:3.

sustained by the Omnipresent Father. Therefore, when I look abroad I receive directly from him these impressions of earth and sea and sun and stars and man and beast. All that we behold is not an ancient primeval work, covered with the moss of many an age, but fresh with life, God's immediate act upon each of our minds, at this instant of time. And thus in a most emphatic sense, "In him we live and move and have our being."

II. But a very different and far nobler manifestation of the Divine mind is made in the moral creation, in the history of man, the powers of all intelligent agents, the Providence exhibited in their history, the course of events and the vindication afforded by them of virtue and the punishment of vice. To this view belongs the revelation of God's will in former and in latter times to his children.

But I leave this expanding subject for the more particular consideration of that which really involves all, the *individual experience*.

III. I come to the third consideration, which in its importance swallows up all other speculations. God manifests himself in our own experience. The idea of existing in immediate connexion with the Deity is the most grand that can influence the actions of a human being. The very fact that so stupendous a faith can enter naturally into the soul and become a principle of action is of itself a mighty argument for the truth of Religion. Living in connexion with God, adopting his will, identifying the soul with him is *perfection*. I do not think the man lives that comes up to this celestial mark. But I believe desires and glimpses of this beatitude are constantly attained; degrees of it are the law of millions whose names are not known in the history of man, in a boundless amount of good deeds, prompting pious prayers and thanksgivings and confessions, animating difficult exertions, profuse sacrifices; consoling the extremities of disaster and worldly disgrace and causing anthems of praise to sound up from depths of sorrow and hopeless defeats. I read in the Book of the Acts one of the sublimest passages in human history. At midnight in the prison Paul and Silas prayed and sang praises to God.[8]

My brethren, let us not turn our eyes from these mountain heights of piety. It is good to be here; let us bridge over the gulf between our frailty and this perfection. Let us arrive at this feeling by natural steps. The Christian regards God not as the cold unintelligent Cause of the order of things but as the Energetic Benefactor who pours forth his creation in unmeasured bounty, who is the infinite lover and friend of all he hath made, and who in all things consults the interest of Mind. All knowledge is but the copy of his being, all virtue but the shadow of his perfections. In him is no darkness.[9]

His sight is infinite. And it is his omnipresent energy imparted to us by which we exist.

He believes that God has directed all the great series of events with which his mind is conversant, as a lesson, as an address to his mind; that it comes to him

8. Acts 16:25.
9. I John 1:5.

with a mighty moral. He sees that Jesus Christ was sent to him to assure him of the character and Providence of God and of his own likeness to him and therefore of his own immortality.

He runs over the history of his own life. He feels the filth of sin, the indescribable elevation and delight each act of virtue gives, that each act of virtue opened the soul's eye to new heights; giving visions of unknown and interminable progress. He feels the sympathy with God the father that belongs to all good acts. In his urgent danger he has felt the efficacy of Prayer on his own mind. In his giddy prosperity he has felt the security that only gratitude can give. In his sorrow, he has found that trust a fountain of health.

Out of this faith and this experience grows his view of his own relation to God. He considers himself a part of his work, having a certain place to fill, certain duties assigned to him in the great order of the whole. This appointed part he strives with his might to perform. But greatness and lowness of place are of no account to him when he feels that God acts with him, and he with God; when he feels himself one in will and desire with him; when he rejoices in the assurance whose exultations he cannot keep down that by every step he makes in goodness, the love of God more richly is fallen upon him. The Universe is then lighted by the smile of the Father; all the melodies of nature are the audible token of his approbation. All that is beautiful is only a revelation to him of that which is fairer. All that is solemn and thrilling is only more deeply touched with the power of the Omnipresent Soul. Through every image of poetry, of Art, of Science, through all the advantages of his condition, he worships the great Source, of whose existence these are proofs, through a higher medium, through all the objects on earth that awaken his affections, through his love of mankind, his love of country, his holiest friendships, he worships the Supreme object of all affection.

And still through a higher medium than these his exalted faith can worship, through clouds and darkness, through penury and bereavement and defeat and pain. Here is the highest measure, the sublimest power, in human nature. The soul learned the great lesson of Jesus of Nazareth, the man of sorrows,[10] who nursed his soul alone and "unsupported by the sympathy of a single mind" sought aid above and embodied the sentiment for every age for all souls, "Father not my will but thine be done."[11]

My brethren, it is easy in the day of youth and prosperity when friends are numerous and kind, and the voice of society cheers us on to the objects of honourable ambition, and the eye is dazzled by hope, it is easy in that hour to indulge an emotion of gratitude to God and to please ourselves with our own enthusiasm and contentment with his will. But when the ways in which we walked are blocked up; when the prayers we uttered are not answered; when the face of society is averted; when lover and friend are dead or are hostile;

10. Isaiah 53:3.
11. Luke 22:42.

when poverty pinches, and sickness and age steal on us, and obstruct the action of the mind,—then—in the ruins of the constitution and the ruins of fortune to send up the soul in aspirations of total love and submission to God—it seems to me it is the triumph of man, it is not man, it is God in the soul.

Yet this is the power which Religion imparts. This grandeur of design and success vindicate the divine origin of the gospel. O many a martyr now forgotten in the busy world and known to few whilst yet they lived in it, has borne this unfainting testimony to his faith. I please myself in contemplating such an one whose youth was a transport of hope and enterprize for the Cause of humanity, but afflicted, disappointed, he consoles himself and exults as the welcome shadows of the evening of life fall over him as he languishes alone in obscurity, in disease. Peace, he saith, my doubting heart; by failures, by sorrow of sins even, by these heavy hours, my God is preparing me for brighter scenes, is rooting out my vanity and pride. Had I succeeded in life, I should have loved him less; I should have loved myself.

Here in these despised solitudes of life, the heart still beats with the idea of God, of eternity, and every moment and every object is pleasant. Am I wretched? Yet is not one so mean but he can depend upon and glory in the divine attributes. Forsaken of all, my existence is present to his mind, is remembered in his counsels. Scathed and mildewed by age without one illusion of hope left, I unite myself to this first of Beings. Luxury or comfort I do not ask— cold, hungry, sick, I can praise him; the faster the days go by, the more I praise him, waiting till it shall please him in his high will, to remand my dust to dust,[12] release my spirit into the Communion with him for which it aspires.

My brethren, can we gain any better preparation for life or death, than this lofty relation to the Most High? This is the feeling proper to each of us. This it is "to have our being in God." Is this lax? Will this excuse our sins? He to whom these feelings are habitual is furnished for all duty,[13] is armed against disaster. But it is high, it is hard of attainment.[14] All existence is the School in which we may learn it. God is everywhere and everywhere may be felt and worshipped. In all our ways let us acknowledge him and he shall direct our paths.[15] Let us so use the world that it shall be the passage to a better.[16] Let us be afraid of offending our own sense of right. Let us feel how grand and beautiful is this connexion of which we are made capable, this life within life, this literal Emmanuel *God within us.*[17] Every moment of virtuous endeavour will more and more open that inward revelation until the soul shall be filled with peace and joy and strength and zeal.

12. Cf. "The Order for the Burial of the Dead," *Book of Common Prayer.*

13. Cf. II Timothy 3:17.

14. Cf. Psalms 139:6.

15. Proverbs 3:6.

16. Cf. I Corinthians 7:31.

17. Cf. Isaiah 7:14 and Matthew 1:23; also influenced by Luke 17:21. See the letter of December 17, 1827, to Mary Moody Emerson (*J* 2:225).

XLIV

Martha thou art careful and troubled about many things; but one thing is needful.

LUKE 10:41–42

We derive very solid advantages from society. The greater number of men you collect together the greater is the chance of finding great talents and virtues. And the presence of great men always elevates the tone of feeling of a whole community. So the larger the population the greater is the division of labour, and as this takes place in the production of the refinements as well as in the necessaries of life, civilization is pushed farther on, the means of knowledge are multiplied, generous projects meet attention, the means of religious improvement, the excitements of religious sympathy abound and exalt themselves. A solitary man of an ardent spirit who has felt all the inconvenience of remote residence in limiting his knowledge and depriving him of sympathy looks with delight and desire at these advantages and wonders that they are so little regarded by those who have them. He contrasts with his own confined means the ease of procuring information. There is hardly any town on the globe so remote, no institution so obscure, almost no private individual living or dead— but in the next street or within sight of your door is some man able to give ample satisfaction to your curiosity.

But these advantages are purchased by some considerable disadvantages. One of the evils of social life is its tendency to give importance to trifles. When man dwells in solitude, he attends only to the supply of real wants, and consults no opinion but his own. So in the country, where intercourse is less frequent and plain fare is procured by plain labour—men are very independent of appearances, and are little disposed to give undue importance to little things. The farmer looks upon clothes as things of use, and not of ornament. He puts on woolens in the cold, and cottons in the heat, without much regard to the shape or the colour of his dress. But as you approach cities, and as people are crowded together, they naturally come to regard each other's opinion much more. *Fashion* becomes a consideration of importance. People live so near, and

---

Manuscript dated July 24, 1829, at Chardon Street. Preached twice: July 26, 1829, at the Second Church, Boston, and December 11, 1831, again at the Second Church. Emerson's first choice for the sermon text, canceled in favor of the present text, was I Corinthians 6:2 ("Are ye unworthy to judge the smallest matters?").

in such continual familiarity, that the eye seems to grow microscopic. Dress and ceremony and a most exaggerated regard to opinion take the place of the former simplicity. Vice, at least in its more refined forms, begins to be thought a less enormity than aukwardness and vulgarity, and the soul is beset with new temptations.

It is a very remarkable property of the human mind, its range of action. It is capable of the most comprehensive views that regard God and eternity, and it can dedicate its whole force to the merest straws. It is like the range of vision of the eye that explores the atmosphere and catches the dim outline of a mountain a hundred miles distant and examines the anatomy of the smallest insect. And this extent of power often resides in the same individual to a remarkable degree. It is related of Frederic of Prussia, that so minute was his love of order and his economy that whilst he marshalled the armies of Europe, he knew the situation of every bottle in his cellar.[1] This range of which the mind is capable, from the most grand to the most minute objects, is a valuable power and exceedingly useful to us in our condition in the world. It gives body and certainty to our knowledge, and at the same time gives it a great extent. It seems to us borrowed of that Power which in the preservation of the whole Universe, is ever mindful of the parts, which cuts the fine notches in the petal of a dandelion and hurls the globe in its orbit.[2]

But it is full of danger, very liable to abuse. If you busy the natural eye too exclusively on minute objects, it gradually loses its powers of distant vision; and more surely will the eye of the mind grow dull and incapable of great contemplation which is daily degraded to little studies. If you are careful about many small things, you cannot fix your thoughts upon the one thing needful.

That this is a strong tendency of social life I think none will deny. Men cease to regard great principles, they turn from looking after truth itself, they turn from seeking simple duty, to consider *what is agreeable to other people.* What will offend others, is more avoided than what is injurious to one's self. Men become studious of whatever the eyes of others will notice, they are very careful of their dress, of their manners, of their house, and are not easily convinced that these are not really matters of gravest consequence. There are many parents who would discover much more emotion if their children appear in soiled or ragged clothes, than if they had shown stupidity or gross ignorance, and be more disturbed by the aukwardness of a boy before a well-bred acquaintance than at detecting him in an untruth. Indeed so strong is this tendency of society to magnify trifles, that there is something that excites derision as hopeless and romantic in persevering attempts to denounce them. Scarcely any man you meet but has his foible of this kind, and (which is worse) is vain of his foible. One man is curious in trinkets, another in the texture of his garments, a third in his horse, a fourth in his furniture, or the binding of his books. There is nothing

1. *JMN* 2:411 suggests a source in Dugald Stewart, though the anecdote has not been located.
2. Cf. *JMN* 2:412.

so absurd or insignificant, but you shall find men of respectable powers who are agitated and piqued about it. You shall see it in loathsome calculations of self-ishness. You shall see a person of a capacity for great and generous views who will sit and meditate on the means of getting his chair nearer to the fire than his who sits next him. And many a man who would unhesitatingly risk his life on a generous cause is afraid of being surprized in the performance of some little menial office. "Ah! what will people think?" is the voice that is heard in our houses;—a low-lived rule of action! They forget in this snug, accommodated, well reputed way of life that they were made for sublime attainments. They forget that the watch is only a measure of time, that clothes are only for a covering, that a house is only a shelter, and that these are all the mere supply of the labourer's outward necessities so that he may go forward with his labour for moral excellence, and that it is the wildest perversion to decline from the straight path of the great end and waste his energies on these toys of petty comforts.

To feel what nothings they are, consider how they appear, when great occasions come, wherever the soul is strongly excited. If one were introduced into the presence of a man of great powers of mind, would he feel it to be of any importance to that person, that his clothes should be rich? On the other hand, every body knows what pleasure men find in describing the contrasts between the plain or mean appearance of any very celebrated man and their heated expectation. Who cares whether Columbus was rich or poor, aukward or grace-ful, when he opened his eyes upon the New World? or who does not feel the superiority of great simplicity of living, and dress, and simplicity of character, whenever it is coupled with real greatness, over ostentation and luxury?

Go into a company of strangers. The eye is caught by the fine personal appearance and tasteful dress of different individuals, and makes its guesses of their merits by their shows. But the moment conversation begins, and let one of the company discover a surpassing wit and rich information, and the most unerring and weighty sense, all those shows are forgotten. A respect is felt for that person which throws all these appearances of others utterly into the shade. Can graceful form or costly dress protect a fool from your pity or contempt? And who does not remember in his own history hours of great diligence or concentrated thought, or of ardent piety when he rose above the low region where these insect influences reign? For a few blessed hours, or days, perchance weeks, the soul was so exercised within, that the world without was slightly esteemed; he did not accurately know the articles of his food, or the times of taking it, the colour of the walls, the trifles of more or less attention he chanced to receive.

The folly and the danger of this overestimate will be felt when 'tis considered that you must degrade them from their importance or they will degrade you. If you give yourself up to the habit of exaggerating their value, of supposing certain indifferent things essential to your comfort, they unman and enslave you. Nothing so small an annoyance but give it attention enough and it will become insupportable. If the buzz of a fly or the step of a person in a neigh-bouring room disturbs you, and you give up to it, it will presently master the whole attention of your ear and eye and mind till the trivial sound swells on your trembling nerves, to the noise of thunder, and produces the most uncontrollable vexation.

And so it is with all trivial things. The man that calculates too nicely on comfort will find the habit too strong for him. He is sowing thistles. He is embarrassing the path of life with additional perplexities, multiplying the sources of his own chagrin. He that observeth the wind shall not sow; he that regardeth the clouds shall not reap.[3]

It becomes a Christian to despise trifles. The first mark and stamp of a great soul is a contempt of them. It should be our prayer that we might give every being and thing in the universe its just measure of importance. Do not be ravished with a little success or a poor jest or a feast or a frolic nor depressed by a rainy day or an affront or a headache. Let the soul feel its dignity and duties; feel that it is God's beloved child, made for the contemplation of himself,—his works, his moral perfections; made for continual self improvement, made to love worthy minds, and so let the soul stay at home in its holy rest, and not hurry out to every sounding brass and tinkling cymbal.[4] It would ill become the general of an army to take a furious part in every chance scuffle that fell out between stragglers on the lines, and surely it is more indecent for the soul, the lord of an immense inheritance of life and power in earth and in heaven, to be thrown into extasies of joy or grief for nothing. The Christian is not too curious about the course of unimportant events, nor too anxious about their convenience or inconvenience to himself. He lets the world go on—satisfied that it is ordered by Wisdom, and that good shall result from all its arrangements. He gives his strength to his great duties, knowing that the less will easily follow. Jesus rebuked the officiousness of Martha, too careful of trifles, too careless of instruction; Martha, thou art troubled about many things but Mary has chosen the good part.

In urging this small esteem of small matters, I am far from wishing to praise an eccentricity which sometimes has been affected under colour of this very magnanimity. It is mere pretence. It is very different to slight trifles and to go studiously wrong in trifles.

Our Saviour was ever graceful and decent in his deportment. And the highest minds have been marked by their simplicity. Newton never did any thing odd; had no tricks; it is recorded of him that he was not distinguished by any sin-gularity natural or affected from any other individual.[5]

Especially should this subject interest those who have the education of a child intrusted to them. A great principle that should be early impressed on the child's mind is to *despise trifles*. And do not destroy the effect of this rule by

3. Ecclesiastes 11:40.
4. I Corinthians 13:1.
5. The remark is attributed to Bernard le Bovier de Fontenelle in *JMN* 6:65.

your own example. Do not confound the guilt of selfishness or of deception in his mind with that of carelessness. If your son has soiled his coat, or spilled his supper, do not let him imagine by your deportment that 'tis all one as if he had broken his word. Do not let this child in his first faltering steps on the world he is entering, and which should be opened before him as a place of conflict on which highest things are depending as presenting the means and occasions of the laborious exercise of the intellect, and of heroic virtue, as a world of which he may be made a guide and a benefactor—do not teach him to be dainty in his food or nice of his dress. Show him the world as God's work; as the house in which wise and great and brave men have dwelled, that with all the evil, almost every spot of it is made venerable by their history—the theatre of their virtues; show him its science; show him it as the platform on which Newton and the astronomers have measured in miles the magnitude of the sun, the pathway of the planets, and written down the changes of the system for a thousand years to come. Show him the sacrifices that have been made; how low men have been born, and how high they have risen by the force of a good life. Let him trace in the earth then with glowing reverence the footsteps of the Maker. Let him know that in this earth the unseen God has spoken to men. Then show him the glory, the moral interest to men and spirits which the death of Jesus Christ has shed over its history—and the Resurrection and its hope. Show him the great images of the Reformers of mankind, Numa[6] and Socrates and the Stoics and the Christian Church and Alfred and Luther—and thus having given him an idea of the great purposes to which life may be spent, do not suffer him to fritter away his energies with such casual or wretched motives as children are permitted to act upon. Don't let him say, 'What will people think?' Don't let him be ashamed of poor dress, of mean occupation or obscure acquaintance or a deformed person, but let him feel that there is that in him which can rear into respect all without him. Let his young heart beat to his maker's name. O quench not his hope, and do not repress one impulse of enthusiasm by the meanspirited apprehensions of vulgar ridicule.

My friends, the question of the value we attach to trifles is not itself trifling. If we will steadily try to keep our attention on things truly great we shall find a great many things are trifling which now we think are important. I know it is difficult to walk in the world with these lofty views, for life is cast among little things, and society is full of superstitions and makes an outcry when its forms or its idols are contemned. And no general rules can be given that can apply to all practice as to what is to be slighted and what observed. But one central rule of life there is, which will guide us safe; the reference in every action of life, to God; the constant acknowledgment of his presence. In the words of our Saviour, Love the Lord your God with all your strength and your neighbour as yourself.[7]

6. Numa Pompilius, legendary Roman king and lawgiver, successor of Romulus.
7. Matthew 22:37–39, Mark 12:30–31, and Luke 10:27.

The statutes of the Lord are right, rejoicing the heart.

PSALMS 19:8

It is always painful to observe those changes in man which seem to unite the soul to the body. The observation that the mind loses its powers when age is crippling the frame and dulling the senses, suggested to the mind, before the immortality of the soul was distinctly revealed, the dark belief of eternal sleep. This union between the mind and matter is undeniably very intimate. Certain derangements of the physical system produce mental derangement: an indigestion fills the soul with gloomy and distressing images, and drunkenness destroys both soul and body. Hence arose the belief of the materialists, that, the mind was only a finer matter—or that more refined notion that the soul was only the relation or the result of a certain arrangement of matter as a tune is the result of the vibrations of a musical instrument; and as, when you break the harp, the tune not only is not heard, but does not exist, so when the bodily system was broken up, the soul deceased, and would not again exist, until a resurrection of the body should reproduce the old result.[1]

The answer to these difficulties lies in the fact that presently appears to any one who speculates on these questions that we have a far more direct and intimate knowledge of mind than we have of matter; that we ourselves are *mind*, the observer is mind, that matter is something separate from us, perceived by the senses, and the senses may deceive us; but leaving this subtle question, for a view that has a deeper interest for all men, I wish to say that the great practical answer to be given to every skeptical objection, it seems to me, must always be the existence of our moral power, *the perception of right and wrong, the perception of duty.* This part of our nature is the sovereign part. It is the distinctive part. He that had it not, would not be man.

Preached six times: August 2, 1829, at the Second Church, Boston; August 30 at the Twelfth Church, Boston; September 13 in Springfield, Mass.; October 4 in Concord, Mass.; October 3, 1830, at the Second Church, Boston; and March 12, 1837, in East Lexington. Emerson's first choice for the sermon text, canceled in favor of the present text, was Matthew 5:8 ("Blessed are the pure in heart for they shall see God"), which he later used for Sermon LI.

1. Emerson refers to the mortalist heresy, the doctrine that the soul dies or "sleeps" until the Last Judgment, most commonly associated with such seventeenth-century figures as John Milton, Thomas Hobbes, Richard Overton, and Sir Thomas Browne.

There can be no ignorance or misconception in any mind as to what is meant by the perception of duty. When you are asked a question about a fact which being affirmed makes against you, why do you say Yes instead of No?—from this feeling of duty. When in secret you abstain from doing any action which you desire to do whilst at the same time you believe that the violation would never be known, why do you abstain?—from the feeling of duty. What is it when you have done wrong, when you have borne false witness, when you have defrauded, when you have criminally gratified your passions—what is it that produces this uneasy mind, this disposition to hide your head, this fear, this condemnation, yourself condemning yourself?—why still this feeling of duty, the perception of duty violated.

There never was a man and there is no situation on earth so forlorn, so insulated, that can expel or alter this perception. You cannot conceive yourself as existing in any future age, in any part of God's Universe, absolved from this law which you carry within you. It can't be defined but it is understood by us all; but as I have said enough to show every one what amount of meaning I affix to the terms, I proceed now to make some remarks on this primitive perception of the soul.

I. And, first, I say, that this perception of duty, or, which is the same thing, this love of virtue doth exist in the mind of man *for itself*. It should be felt that God has made us capable of perceiving and loving the *beauty* of virtue apart from its *utility;* that our minds feel a degradation in admitting the charge that because God has made the order of things consent to virtue, because honesty will be trusted again, because the temperate eater can eat longer, because the advantage we do to our country will redound to our own fame or profit, and because piety to God is graceful among men, that for these reasons alone we desire to be just, and temperate, and benevolent, and holy.

It is an old objection that has been made by the scoffer in every age against the virtues of good men that they were done from the same self-love that led the bad man to a different course of action; that they were done not from the love of God or of goodness but for the sake of the advantages of virtue, as the other is vicious from a view of the supposed advantages of vice. There is a certain smartness in this generalization which is very apt to give it a currency among young reasoners, who are not sorry to give so specious a reason for their own indulgences, a reason which compounds all virtue and vice.

It is most true that holding the belief of the immortality of the soul, we cannot sever our interest from our duty; that this feeling of duty does guide us to our well-being. We cannot well see how this could be avoided, and therefore the moralist properly appeals to the consequences of virtue as motives to all reasonable beings for the practice of virtue. To be sure a man seeks the *advantages* of virtue. But one of the advantages of virtue is that it makes the soul superior to what an evil man calls *advantages* and fills the heart with the love of God's law. And there is no elevated mind that does not disclaim all unworthiness in its pursuit of duty, does not feel that Virtue is its own reward in a far higher sense than that it secures great enjoyment to its votary.

The defender of the selfish system, says that we love and practise virtue simply because we think it will be our interest to do so. But here are multitudes of people who in every age have bravely sacrificed their interest, pleasure, health, or their life to the feeling of duty. The answer made by the objector to this practical argument is, that the Christian faith in the immortality of the soul, makes it the undoubted interest of the believer to undergo any degree of temporal hardship or torment and loss of life—rather than run the smallest risk of failing of this infinite inheritance.

We reply that it is plain that we are capable of perceiving the sovereign and selfexistent excellence of duty apart from any consideration of consequences—from two facts—first, our sympathy with every difficult act of virtue in another; and secondly, that it has been taught and practised by those who had no hope of obtaining these future rewards.

The heart leaps to virtue in another with a mighty affection. And this eager sympathy with virtue, is it not an incontrovertible proof that we see more charm in goodness than the benefit it will bring to us? You cannot read the story of any man's self devotion though a thousand years ago without quickening your blood. What good—what sordid good—do I derive from the heroism of Leonidas, the patience of Socrates, the chastity of Lucretia, from the indomitable independence of Cato?[2] Yet these old-world stories make the heart glow after the passage of centuries and in these remote ends of the earth. Now is there any account to be given of their effect except that virtue itself is supremely beautiful? If we cannot appeal to the heroic story of all that has been done and suffered in the Christian Church without any hope of earthly reward and with the certain assurance of poverty and reproach because the hope of immortality may be said to have sustained these exertions, yet we know there have been wide nations where no such belief prevailed, and yet where self-denying virtues have been practised. And there is no fiction that presents to the mind the image of hopeless devotion to a sentiment, that does not on this account appear beautiful. There are anecdotes of those who without a belief in the future state have died for their country or for their opinion. Among the wild fables of the Indian mythology it is related that the God Vishnu, being pursued by his enemies, the evil spirits, came down to the Lotus islands, and there finding Tamur, a holy hermit, commanded him to deceive his pursuers by denying that he had seen him when they should make inquiry of him and threatened him with annihilation in case of disobedience. When the pursuers arrive and ask Tamur if he have seen the god, he communed with himself and answered Yea, and Vishnu returned and destroyed him. Out of this poor fable of a most gross and ignorant Superstition comes a voice of instruction that could not issue from a purer faith. For we see that this is a representation of the sublimest act of a moral agent, the giving up life for the love of truth when the giving up life is all. Now, carry it where you will, the eye that reads this idle tale, approves this supposed sacrifice

2. Leonidas, Spartan king who defended the pass of Thermopylae against Xerxes in 480 B.C.; Lucretia, noblewoman of Rome, whose rape by Sextus led to the downfall of the Tarquins; Marcus Porcius Cato (95–46 B.C.), called by Livy "the conscience of Rome," opposed Caesar and conspired for the Republican cause.

for the truth. But if we honoured virtue only as the highway to *advantages,* should we not condemn an integrity or a patriotism so desperate as fruitless and absurd?

But why need we go so far to show the native charm of the sentiment? Is there nothing moving in the story of the widow's mite but so much advantage to the treasury?[3] Is there nothing that gratifies us in the story of the Samaritan beyond the fact that a certain amount of suffering in the world was removed?[4]

What is highest, what we reverence in human nature is its ineradicable love of virtue. And say what you will of human depravity, repeat any anecdote of exalted self-devotion, the heart of a multitude will throb to it as the heart of one man. Samuel Hopkins taught that the soul in the true Christian became suscep-tible of a disinterested love of God, the source and author of Virtue, so that it resigned itself with utter self-abandonment to his Will and was content to lie in torment or to perish forever so that his glory and the good of the Universe was thereby promoted.[5]

This is an extravagance: I don't know but it may be said to involve a contra-diction, but there is something so generous and sublime in its absurdity, that good men will forgive it. I honour the Hopkinsian who can pray and act by so lofty a creed, and I wish in the history of human error there were many lines as glorious as this.

I present these views because we hear every day so much suspicion of the motives of men. All goodness is ascribed with a sneer to *mixed motives,* by which is commonly implied a much larger share of reference to this world than to another. Now there is something dangerous in this low and cynical penetra-tion. It has a tendency to degrade your own purposes, to quench your religious fervour, to stop the mouth of prayer, and to hide the face of our Heavenly Father from us.

Far be it from us, to surrender our views of the highest elevation of man to any lower and debasing ones. Let us cherish in our souls this pure image God has put there and lift ourselves to the height of its infinite contemplations. I would that we might feel that Virtue may be dear to us though it neither embel-lishes our manners nor augments our influence nor makes our life of any kind of apparent utility, that struggling against the wind and tide of life, in obscure solitude, where are none to sympathize or be benefitted, its majesty may be shown: there, in prayer and holy thought, its direct connexion with God may be realized; it may learn to contemn external advantages; itself obscure or defeated may love the glory of those whom God dignifies with genius and usefulness, and sing hallelujah for glories, it doth not ask to partake.

Whilst we rejoice in this truth we feel on the other hand that if there is any

---

3. Mark 12:42–44 and Luke 21:2–4.

4. Luke 10:30–37.

5. See *A Dialogue Between a Calvinist and a Semi-Calvinist* (1805), in *The Works of Samuel Hopkins* (Boston, 1852), 3:147: "But to him who loves God supremely, and desires his glory above all things, it is so far from being impossible to be willing to be damned, on the supposition that this is most for God's glory, that he could not will or choose anything else."

object of complete disgust, it is he who makes a creeping calculation of his merits, the *niggardly devotee,* if devotion can be coupled with his name who grasps at heaven through fear of the torments of hell,—who approaches God with professions—yet loves not virtue, listens not to its commands; is cold to every thing in earth and eternity, but his own interest, and to crown his deformities is a fierce exclusive saint, passing judgement on others and insisting much and often on the small number of the saved. It seems to me that this is a miser worse than the hoarder of gold. A bad citizen he is not; his farm, his merchandize, his studies go on in God's order better than those of the sot and the prodigal but if the word of our Lord be true that Thou shalt love the Lord with all thy heart,[6] then in the day of final account many a poor publican shall go up to his house justified rather than he.[7]

II. The next consideration to which I wish very briefly to ask your attention is this: that such is the constitution of the world that something very like disinterested benevolence may be nourished in it. God hides himself from the common eye. Men have doubted whether there was a God. The bad prosper, the good fail of success and are cut off in the beginning of life. An enemy hath sown tares in the field of the world,[8] diseases rage, misfortunes fly thick, and sin abounds. It has seemed to men that this is so much ground to believe that God doth not exist or exists without such a Providence as we impute to him. But I behold in this skepticism its own antidote. I see God behind this present cloud. It seems to me a part of his wisdom that his footsteps *should not be too apparent* in the earth. If every virtue and every sin met with quick retribution, if every place and time and event were blazing with evidence, what room would be left us for choice in our conduct? By fear and by hope we should be bribed to good actions, and the trial by which vigorous virtue is trained would not be. But now there is some room for doubt; there is the choice between present enjoyments and the uncertainties of the future. You make Virtue your friend *at some risk,* at least, at risk enough to prove your attachment. And this makes the glory of virtue, that 'tis never cheap; that 'tis always obtained in the world, at the high price of much exertion and loss and sacrifice.

III. One more consideration offers itself upon this subject, and that is, the eternal nature of Virtue or the feeling of duty. The actor and the actions alter, but the principle remains and what at this moment is right to do in the same circumstances would be right to do a million years hence. Our habits change, our tastes, our appetites, our manners change, we outgrow our vices even, and grow old to new ones,—but the feeling of duty remains the same in the child, in the old man, in the Seraph. Your prosperity may be clouded: Your opinions may be altered: You may repine at the events of God's Providence: Your faith may be shaken. But the tossing mind comes back to this feeling. There still is Duty,

6. Matthew 22:37, Mark 12:30, and Luke 10:27.
7. Luke 18:14.
8. The allusion is to the parable of the sower, which is given in Matthew 13:24-30, followed by Christ's explanation in verses 37-43.

calm, cheerful, distinct, immoveable, sitting sovereign in the soul, and pouring consolation over life precisely in the measure that her dictates are done. Infidelity is staggered and Faith is comforted.

What is there of materialism in this feeling? What is there in it, that smells of death? It seems to me that the more steadily we look at this power of the soul the less do we think it possible that we shall perish. When you calmly contemplate this one perception which has animated every man since the creation of the world, does it seem to you that you who have felt it can die like a beast, die out of the Universe, die out of this perception and die forever?

It seems to me it is our hold on the eternal world. It is the breath of angels and immortal natures for it appears to extend its own eternity to every mind it governs. In the immensity of the future here is our anchor.[9] This is the presence of God to our minds which is more intimate, more fully unfolded, the more piously it is reverenced.

9. Evidently an allusion to Hebrews 6:19, which is the text of Sermon XLVI.

XLVI

—to lay hold upon the hope set before us;
which hope we have as an anchor of the soul
both sure and steadfast.

HEBREWS 6:18–19

Again we assemble, my friends, in the Lord's house. Is it not a pleasant reflexion that its gates are always open to us,[1] that whilst life lasts, this is our proper and honourable resort, that to every condition in life, to every character, the sanctuary opens its generous doors; its day of grace is never past; its sweet intercessions never cease; its psalms of praise are always sung; its divine admonitions and words of comfort, and uplifting encouragements are never mute? The individuals are changed, new tenants fill the pews which our fathers filled, but still from year to year and generation to generation the holy custom survives and the church is filled. We who minister at the altar may perish from it; our strength is withered; our hearts are sad; we die in our place; but the service goes on; God replenishes his house with the breath of praise. In the simple words of the children's hymn

> I have been there and still would go
> 'Tis like a little heaven below.[2]

The church saith to you in that language of its Head and Founder, Come to me all ye that labour and are heavy laden, and I will give you rest.[3] Welcome, it saith, whosoever thou art, and whencesoever thou comest to my spiritual peace, from the giddy merriments of health and prosperity, from the toils of successful industry, from the cunning of the hand and the scheming of the head—come hither to sanctify your hearts, to smooth the irritations of the perturbed soul, to see if you keep the commandments, to remember your relation to the unsuccessful, to remember the Source of prosperity and adversity.

Manuscript dated August 22, 1829, at Chardon Street. Preached twice: August 23, 1829, at the Second Church, Boston, and March 12, 1837, in East Lexington.

    1. Cf. Isaiah 60:11 and Revelation 21:25.

    2. Isaac Watts, "An Hymn for the Lord's Day Evening," *Divine Songs, Attempted in Easy Language, for the Use of Children* (London, 1828), 48.

    3. Matthew 11:28.

Come hither, thou afflicted brother, whom the world does not befriend, whom society frowns upon, whose schemes of worldly gain and aggrandizement have all failed, whose honest exertions are suspected and who seem to be marked to suffer by other men's fault rather than by your own,—come hither to another tribunal than the world's; come hither to a tribunal where not the success, but the intention is weighed; to a tribunal where often the hasty judgments of this world are reversed by a pure and sovereign law of everlasting efficacy. And you who are wounded in your affections, whose domestic happiness has been clouded, who have been bereaved of the life that made your own life pleasant, or who have been disappointed in your friends—your friend has betrayed you. Your children have forgotten the debt of nature and neglected or injured you, or your children have perished from your arms. Come hither to an undeceiving love that folds the Universe in its arms and celebrate in the multitude of the people the parental affection of God.

Come you that have sorrowed for your sins, whose souls have been penetrated with the irresistible convictions of God's presence and government, who know the charm of virtue and the foulness of sin, who know the unspeakable dignity of a living union between God and the heart, come hither to repair your fainting strength; to impart the light and joy of your own breasts; come, for this is your home; it is the field of your pure victories; it is the place of pleasing recollections and unspotted triumphs.

And you that have pawned your soul to your sensual gratifications; who have plunged desperately into vice; who have made the principles of other men the prey of your avarice; who have taken perjury upon your soul; who have abused the ear of individuals or communities with deliberate slanders of the good whom their country should have trusted; who have ground the faces of the poor;[4] who have abased yourself by unworthy compliances to the rich; whose cowardly tyranny has turned into bitterness the peace and hope of your own house; who have braved the angry eye of the Future and disregarded the loud warnings of the world without and the conscience within; who have sinned and mean to sin again—oh welcome, welcome hither! whatever motive has brought you, be it curiosity, or fashion, or indolence, or a momentary good desire,—you are welcome here; abstain for God's hour, at least, from impurity and selfishness; and oh! perchance some sincere word may reach your heart, with wholesome conviction; if you are a sinner, yet you are a man; you are a subject of God's mercy, and the glorious nature he gave you is not wholly corrupt; the evil heart of unbelief is never wholly unbelieving.[5] It may please God in his temple to scatter the malignant fogs which wrap your soul and redeem you with a ray of truth. His goodness may touch your hard heart; some gracious drops of penitence may fall, and the saints and angels in heaven shall rejoice.

My friends, I use the language of exhortation, not that of argument or

4. Isaiah 3:15.
5. Cf. Hebrews 3:12.

illustration of obscure truth. I desired to call your thoughts to this beneficent institution of the Christian Sabbath, this stable ordinance of public worship, the inextinguishable torch which guides the feet of successive generations with the light of another world. I do not now pretend to instruct, for it is not so much that we do not know as that we will not do the commandments of Heaven. Our hearts are always wise, for the law is plain, and those that run may read it;[6] but it seems reasonable and human sometimes to rejoice together that such things stand in the earth. I congratulate you that there is a Sabbath to be kept, that we are now in the house of God, that the Maker's name is written on his work, and that the infinite secrets of the future have been and are from day to day revealed. The particular truth which suggested these reflexions and to which I would call your attention, is, the peculiar attitude in which God has placed man as the object of these influences, the Sabbath keeper, the student of religious truth, the centre and mark, whereon so many causes act. In this respect we are alone among all beings whose existence we know. No influences act on other beings to amend their condition. The vegetable creation is very little susceptible of improvement from our art; the animal creation very little,—and from other causes, as far as appears, not at all. The horse and the elephant gain no increase of sagacity from age to age; no improvement takes place in the web of the spider, or the wild beast's arts of hunting his prey or the swimming of the fish. They soon attain the boundary of their improvement, and they never pass it. But man improves on himself. Man hopes. His hopes are infinite, and with innumerable miscarriages, and defeats, and mortifications, his progress is yet certain, if it be slow.

> "Man's heart is to the future set,
> By secret and inviolable springs."[7]

Man's heart, man's eye is on the future by a divine necessity. All the experience of the past cannot daunt us. What are we that are come up hither? We have been all our life long the servants in succession of different expectations. Consider how often the wariest of us has been deceived. Now we have thought *this* pursuit would give us happiness, and now another. Every new scheme of education, every new application of the powers of nature, every new art, every new political theory, every new church and its interpretation of Scripture, that springs up seems to us fraught with incalculable benefit to mankind. We adopt this as the last capital discovery, and when we find out that it is false or superficial, we quit it only for some new pretension. And now that we are here with all the advantages of our past observation, with all the distrust we have acquired of fine novelties, and all romancing about the perfectibility of man, with all our

---

6. Habakkuk 2:2.

7. Edward Young, *Night Thoughts,* "Night VII," lines 119–20. Used in "The Young American" (*CW* 1:232) and "Immortality" (*W* 8:344). See *JMN* 6:49 and *JMN* 5:284.

sad consciousness of broken resolutions, and shortlived enthusiasm, and the force of temptation, and the omission of prayer—which of us does not know that at this moment he is capable of being convinced that all the future is radiant with glory for him, that the impediments of frailty and passion are now departed from him; which of us is not hungry for that eloquence which quickens the soul in her inmost retirements and persuades it of its own force and undervalues obstacles that always lie in its path?

I can speak for myself. I believe that those minds are now in the earth who can touch my spirit with that force as to rebuild in me the hope I have seen a thousand times overthrown, that henceforward the soul shall pass on from duty to duty with such serenity and elevation, that passion and appetite, that indolence and trifles shall not affect its composure, shall not shake its faith or cool the fervour of its love to God. Who does not know that our judgements are ever warped by our wishes; that however mighty the hope we this moment entertain, there is a mightier hope behind it; that no prosperity, no knowledge, no faith, no action, can fill and satisfy the craving human heart, but all the past is regarded by us as only the little *seed* of what is to come. Nothing is more remarkable in man than this readiness for great things. The soul that inhabits these little bodies is a vast abyss. Who has computed its power? Who has gauged its capacity? Who has measured out its duration? Which of us knows what any other one is capable of doing? It is itself an emblem of the eternity it inhabits.

What is ambition—what is avarice, but the perversions of the same glorious principle? Napoleon is as much an evidence of the great destiny of the human mind as Socrates and St. Paul. What was it that troublesome man was after, as he marched his hundreds of thousands over the cornfields and vineyards of Europe? What mighty insanity disturbs his bosom as he cuts a military road through the white precipices of the Alps and his innumerable train of baggage and artillery are creeping through over the giddy avalanches of the mountains? He thought he was aiming to humiliate the pope in Italy or the emperor in Russia, but if he had succeeded in his purpose, he would soon have found his mistake. He would have found that the gratification he expected to find in conquest was not found in conquest, that the famine of the soul was yet unfed, and would have looked further to the conquest of England, of Asia, of America with the same fruitless and unquenched because unquenchable desire.

It is just so with the man of peaceful and lawful enterprizes. Here is a merchant whose credit is respected by governments as well as individuals. What is he seeking with this navy of ships that line the wharves or are skimming with their white wings the surges of the ocean under every zone? He modestly tells you and he believes it at first that he is barely aiming to obtain for himself and his family a decent or liberal support. But when his cargoes come home and he has put the community under contribution to pay the profits of his skill and enterprize and his modest purpose is attained, does he close the account and furl his canvass and lock up his warehouses? Oh no, he refits and enlarges his floating city and sends it forth on a wider and more ambitious circuit. Remind him of his first intentions and now he tells you that he has just got into a good way of doing business and that he wishes of course to accumulate an ample fortune that shall make him easy as to the future and allow him to provide well for his large family and numerous friends, and he means to endow the college or the hospital or the churches if he shall prosper. And still he thinks that the hour will come when he shall be content but the hour will never come.

For these all grasping desires are but a mis-direction of that instinct in man, that law of progress, that on-look of human nature,[8] which is its distinguishing and beautiful characteristic. The human soul cannot be satisfied. The fame, pleasures, empires of the earth have nothing in material good that is worthy of it. It is born of God. It is his child and it inherits a portion of the infinity of its Sire. Only mind, only love, only truth and virtue, only those things that are infinite like itself, can ever gratify and fix it.

Therefore brethren, I rejoice in the sanguine anticipations of youth which prudence rebukes in that simplicity of the public that makes it credulous in every scheme of improvement; in the faith of our own hearts, which disposes us to expect an eternity of happiness after many a shipwreck of peace and virtue. I rejoice in the feeling that brings us to the Church and the expectations we attach to the Sabbath. I rejoice in that mysterious feeling with which we lay the dead in the dust; in the solemn confidence with which we lie down ourselves in the funeral shroud. I venerate them as good omens, as symptoms of an immortal health in the blood of man, as indications of the sublimest destiny. We have failed often—let us return to our homes and once more try to keep the commandments.

8. *JMN* 6:91; cf. Sermon XXXVII, n. 1.

XLVII

*He that ruleth his spirit is better than
he that taketh a city.*

PROVERBS 16:32

All the virtues are so connected together that the faithful obedience to any one
to the last tittle of observance seems to involve the practice of all. I have sometimes thought that it would be complained of those engaged in the office of
public preachers that they exaggerate the importance of each virtue in turn as it
comes under their notice till it would appear all other commandments were
superfluous, and the hearer would begin to distrust the judgement that was thus
carried away with admiration of the latest object. But this is not the fault of the
preacher but the nature of virtue. Moral excellence is the one thing required,[1]
and this may be viewed under various aspects, and under any aspect will appear
infinite. Now we are directed to use well our time, and told that all duty is
wrapped up in that precept, and it is true; and now we are taught to be perfectly
just, and we need no other rule, and that is true too, for, that will be a proper
improvement of time; and then we are instructed to fulfil our duties as *social*
beings, that God is *love* and virtue is the *law of love,* and that the golden rule of
life is, to do unto others, as we would have others do unto us;[2] and this also is
true, and identical with the other rules, for it would be *just* to do so, and a
proper use of life; and so, when virtue is said to consist mainly in a good
conversation, or in good *action* or in good *thinking,* each of these propositions
is true, because each implies necessarily the one thing needful, that, moral
principle should be the governor of the man. So among the ancients, the wise
men were accustomed to condense the whole duty of man,[3] each into some one
aphorism, which he bequeathed to mankind as a precious treasure, and whose
truth is attested by the fact of their popularity through all ages. Solon said,
Know thyself. Chilo—Regard thy end. Pittacus said, Watch occasions. Cleobulus said 'Moderation.' Periander said Industry conquers all things. Another

---

Manuscript dated August 29, 1829, at Chardon Street. Preached four times: August 30, 1829, at
the Second Church, Boston; August 1, 1830, at the New South Church, Boston; October 24 at the
Second Church; and October 16, 1836, at East Lexington. For the fragmentary text of the abandoned Sermon XLVII [A], see the Appendix.

1. Cf. Luke 10:42.
2. I John 4:8, Matthew 7:12, and Luke 6:31.
3. Ecclesiastes 12:13.

41

said all wisdom lay in the doctrine to Bear and forbear.[4] Now when these propositions are considered they don't contradict each other; each is true and an important truth and if observed in its fullest import, would imply the observation of all the rest. And to know the whole of man it is desirable that we should in succession consider our condition under all its various relations.

One of the most attractive and comprehensive of these views of man that religion has been accustomed to take is that favourite one of the ancient wisdom which is suggested in the words of Solomon, just now repeated, the duty of self-command. And it is to some remarks upon our duty as seen under this regard, that I wish to invite your attention.

He that ruleth his spirit is better than he that taketh a city. Let us leave to others the ambition of an extensive influence, the irksome care of parties and communities, the administration of the Church and the State. Let us remember that the province of the Christian is narrow and single; the guardianship of one spirit. Our duty is like that of the pilot of a ship who, though surrounded by contending navies, has no attention to spare to their various manoeuvres, or to the astounding noise of the battle, or the tempest, but studies only his own compass, and dedicates himself to the direction of a single helm. And as each ship is guided by its own pilot, in so doing he best consults the safety of the whole; so we shall best fulfil our *social* duties by this incessant attention to the virtue of self, for when you are called to act as a parent, as a son, as a citizen, then this sole regard to your own virtue, will make you discharge to the utmost those duties.

What is self-command? It is hardly necessary to clear the duty from the cavils of the skeptic who says The good and the bad alike are the servants of the last and strongest motive—one is governed by pride, and one by hunger, and one by love, and one by truth; how can you say that any commands himself, or give preference to one course of conduct over another and call it self-controul? If a man really sees no difference between the rank of different motives, it were useless to recommend this virtue to him. If he feels that it is just as right to follow one as another, if he says hunger and love of gold and love of power are as much parts of my natural constitution as the perception of right, and I am as much entitled to give one of them the preference and obey it, as to give the perception of right the preference and obey that, all argument is at an end. But there is no such man. There is not only a perception of right in the soul of man but there is with it an instinctive obedience to that perception, a feeling that that is the rightful sovereign and judge of all other principles within us, and, what

4. A variety of aphorisms were indiscriminately attributed throughout antiquity to the "Seven Sages": Solon, Periander, Cleobulus, Chilo (or Chilon), Pittacus, Thales, and Bias. Solon is particularly associated with the sayings, "Know thyself" and "Nothing too much" (i.e., "moderation"), which were engraved on the temple at Delphi; Emerson may have encountered the latter in Diogenes Laertius, *Lives of Eminent Philosophers* (bk. 1, sec. 63). The same source (bk. 1, sec. 79) assigns a version of "Watch occasions" to Pittacus. The phrase "Bear and forbear" is from Vicesimus Knox, *Elegant Extracts . . . in Prose* (London, 1797), 2:1027 (see *JMN* 6:156); it is also used in Sermon XXIV and "Reforms" (*EL* 3:268).

we mean by *self command* is *the complete subjection of every other power to this power so that its feeblest volition is never transgressed.*

This is the law of human nature; this is Natural religion, and in aid of this the gospel came into the world.

It is a singularly safe and honorable accomplishment, or rather, in this consists the safety and honor of the mind. There are numberless illustrations of its value in ordinary life—cases where degrees of it are attained under the influence of ordinary motives. Put a man in what circumstances you will, however ridiculous, however dangerous, so long as he retains his self-command, he is respectable, and inspires you, though in the most forlorn condition, with a confidence for his safety;—the moment he loses it, all seems lost. (The Spartan general said of the mouse that bit his finger so that he threw it from him; See there is no creature so mean but if he use all his powers he shall escape danger; so you cannot put a man where he shall not seem formidable as long as he doth not despair of himself.)[5] There are common risks continually encountered by men engaged on the seas and in war, that appear desperate to any inexperienced eye that sees them for the first time. And that would really be so, but for this discipline of themselves which has been learned by these men in many an hour of tremendous necessity. But in the worst of these dangers, the mind conceives some hope for the adventurer though no way of escape is seen, so long as his self-possession is unshaken; there is still the hope in the most desperate odds that in the course of Providence some fetch, some unexpected turn, shall yet bring him off, who has this dexterity to turn every thing to account. And so we see the survivor of fifty battles and the mariner of twice so many voyages die peacefully in his bed.

Another illustration of it falls under the observation of every one much conversant in society. Go into the brilliant assemblies of fashionable life and see the young aspirant for its honours and mark what progress in manners he will make in a few short months. I speak now of that character which the modern novelist delights to portray, namely the highbred fashionist; what it exhibits of this power of self command makes all that is respectable in a person so fascinating to the young and the idle. The fashionist too is a sort of hero. He leads his giddy train of imitators. Even for those local and fleeting honours serious sacrifices will freely be made, ease, property, health and the rigour of principle. The finished man of the world as 'tis termed must be to all the purposes of fashion a ruler of himself. He must be able to meet unbounded mirth without a smile; to keep his elegant equanimity through all the turns and surprizes of conversation unsurprized; to face all events of joy, of astonishment, of horror, with the same graceful presence of mind. He is to divest himself wholly of all the vulgar good feelings or expressions of feeling and as a cold and low selfishness is the motive of all his action, he is to make and break acquaintance with others with simple

5. Plutarch, "How a Man May Be Sensible of His Progress in Virtue," *Moralia* (Boston, 1871), 3:458.

regard to convenience and without a blush and without pleasure. His control over others has no other foundation than his control over himself. For if he lose this he is no longer admired. And who knows not the powerful influence of this character upon all the young and upon the mature and upon grey hairs in this and in all parts of the civilized world simply from the awe that always attaches to habits of self command.

Well then, ambition and avarice and health and fashion all have their heroes who have forborne every pleasant gratification, who have attained wonderful degrees of self-command, in the pursuit of their several objects. And now the gospel of Christ, the message of God, comes to us, comes to his reasonable children, and demands of us the same sacrifices for motives infinitely higher. Motives so low and poor and short-lived as the desire of a little praise, the desire of a little gain, the preservation of bodily life, the love of power, have prompted and sustained these brave martyrdoms from year to year; and now the greatest considerations that can be proposed to rational beings are brought to urge us to similar fortitude. These exertions were made for partial advantages. Religion proposes to seek in the same way the chief good. Religion asks you to strive earnestly, now that God has given us being, to make that being happy. All the history of man, and of each individual man has been one great struggle between reason set up in the soul and these mutinous passions that draw us aside to injurious gratifications; a war, as the apostle calls it, between the law of the members and the law of the mind,⁶ a struggle of reason for dominion over pride, reason over interest, reason over indolence; and God has sent the Saviour into the world, to confirm the claim of reason.

Religion desires you always to seek the chief good, and never prefer for a single moment a minor good, and points you to all that is sublime in the movement of a man over whom duty holds an undivided dominion, over whom pleasure has no power and fear none, who braves all consequences, and travels on a straight line in defiance of the violence and ridicule and persuasion of the whole world.

My brethren, there is nothing impracticable and nothing of uncertain advantage or reward in the difficult duty of self-command. The atheist and the Christian will alike acknowledge its reasonableness. If the wildest visions of skepticism were probable, if God's existence were unassured, and we were left in dreadful uncertainty about the mode of future being, it would still be far better to stand up in this our span of life, on the shore of a dark unexplored being—with all composure self-collected and disciplined powers than to add to the boundless hazard by a licentious want of preparation and anarchy and disagreement among the principles of action in our own bosom.

We only repeat to you the commandment of Jesus—Watch and pray lest ye enter into temptation.⁷ That you may have the good of your being here, that you

6. Romans 7:23.
7. Matthew 26:41 and Mark 14:38.

may enjoy the noble powers of thought and action that God has given you in their highest perfection; much more on the strong presumptions of an eternal life, keep a guard upon your lips, upon your hands, upon your thoughts. To every one is his own temptation his own darling indulgence. You perhaps are prone to the indulgence of a sulky and selfish humour. Some men do not have this trial. There is a complexional goodness, a native temper that is right, which is called *good nature*. It is something to thank God for, just as we would for good parents, or for a large sphere of action, or if we had been made angels. Who has this, to him are appointed some other trials than yours. Your temptations are not his temptations. His innocence, in that particular, is his fortune, not his virtue.

And in view of this natural disparity I would remark that there are limits to the claim of duty upon the choleric man who by long and painful effort has got the mastery. When this man is provoked, though conscience keep the command of him, sometimes his uneasiness will betray itself, in spite of all he can do. There will be tones that will falter in his voice; there will be rebellion in the muscles of his face; there will be tumult, unsteadiness in his manners, even though his soul sits firm in her seat, and his purpose is immoveably fixed. All that he is required to do, is, in these perilous moments, to keep ceaseless guard upon his tongue and his hand. Let the blood boil if it will; let the unruly will almost choke the utterance and the struggle appear in his unsteady step. Reason yet asserts her paramount authority, not one intemperate syllable drops from his tongue, not one rash impulse breaks out into action. By and by you shall see the blessed influence of that commanding principle calm down these outward extravagances as oil that is poured on the stormy sea. You shall see what respect and wholesome influences the majesty of wisdom will always command.

I have left myself no time to enlarge on the exercise of self-command over other temptations, the sin of intemperance, of unchastity, avarice, of vanity.

But in brief when your conscience by unceasing care and pains is exalted over your actions so that nothing can seduce or alarm you, then my brother, you are prepared for all the events of this world and the next. No terrors, no anxieties can ruffle your immortal serenity. Fear not thou the cherubim, the ministers of God's vengeance, or the day of his judgements. You are free of a law that is higher than theirs. By Him thou art protected. His being itself is pledged for your safety. He has made thee strong in thyself.

I do not indulge in any arrogant views of human power. I know how inconsistent with our frail and offending nature is the boastful spirit of a stoical philosophy. I urge you to assert your strength, because just in proportion as man does command himself, God seems to impart his aid, to come into nearer connexion with him. O no, I do not boast. I know how frail we are. We need every support and every affection; we need the intercession of the faithful, and of the Saviour; we need the kind monition of the Lord's supper, and all the encouragement of each other's faith and example, and we need the effort of every moment.

XLVIII

Ye shall know them by their fruits.
MATTHEW 7:16

There has been a controversy which is as old as Christianity concerning the comparative importance of Faith and Works to the salvation of the human soul. It has been debated from age to age and is still agitated in our own day. It has often been the real point in debate in controversies where these words were not used. Thus the oft repeated doctrine of Regeneration (which seems at the present day to be the partition wall between classes of Christians) I believe is substantially the same question. Now whenever a question remains at issue so long and survives persons and local interests and nations and still continues to animate not only the ignorant to hot debate but to divide the opinions of intelligent and serious men, it becomes plain that it must touch some great and radical doubt which is suggested to the human mind in all circumstances.

When the needle is observed to take a particular direction in any spot, it is readily ascribed to some local disturbing cause; but when on innumerable trials, in every degree of latitude and of longitude, it is found to take one and the same direction, it is then concluded that this is not an accidental effect, but that in that direction must lie the magnetic axis of the globe. So when the speculations of inquiring men are at issue on the same point from age to age, it is fair to conclude that here lies a great question, to settle which the human understanding is perhaps inadequate. (Such is the question touching the origin of evil; such an one too is that of human liberty and such an one in a less degree is this of Faith and Works.) In approaching this question I do not imagine that I shall be able to settle in an hour, a question which the discussion of centuries has left in doubt. Still I shall be glad to present it as it appears to me, and if I can awaken inquiry upon this head in a single mind, or through this topic quicken the sense of duty in any mind, the time will not be lost.

I believe this difference of opinion grows from the observation that good actions may be done from bad motives. It is the same important distinction that is made when we treat of the importance of principles as separated from actions.

Manuscript dated September 5, 1829, at Chardon Street. Preached three times: September 6, 1829, at the Second Church, Boston; April 24, 1831, at the Second Church; and April 9, 1837, in East Lexington. For one or both of the later deliveries, Emerson used Psalms 24:3–5 as his text.

The question is whether any thing more is necessary to our salvation than simple obedience to the moral laws.

The doctrine of one class of Christians, is, that an obedience to the commandments—the doing of Works, is the sum of all religion.

The doctrine of the other class is, that there is something more than obedience and prior to obedience in Religion, a certain state of mind which is called *faith,* and which being once obtained, all is safe. All the rest will follow of course.

This question divides men into two great classes as Christians, among us. The defender of each party takes its departure from one of these two points; one viewing Christianity in the light of a *system of belief,* and the other as a *practical system.* Each naturally magnifies the importance of his own view and depreciates the other. But it is easy to see that truth is not at variance with itself, when its defenders are. Each teacher gives to his doctrine, whether he commend *faith,* or *works,* an extent of meaning which embraces all that is contended for by the other. By *faith* is not meant, a mere assent to certain statements of doctrine on the one hand, neither on the other, by *Works,* is meant any imperfect or merely formal discharge of decent duties. But both terms are often used to cover the same ground. One Christian means by faith such a living conviction as shall influence the acts of every moment, and the other, by works, means that steadfast holiness of life which can spring from no principle less broad than a Christian faith.

I believe that these principles cannot be divorced. Either is imperfect without the other. It is a very partial view of human nature, a very imperfect theory of duty which leaves either of them out of consideration. Still if one is to be commended there are reasons which seem to me good and sufficient why it is better to insist on one of these views of our religion rather than the other, why it is safer to commend works to men rather than faith. Of the two it is very much the safest, very much less liable to mistake or any manner of delusion.

I do not make any abatement of the demands of Christianity; I plead for no pharisaic observance: I feel and press its claim upon the heart; but I know of no index by which it is possible to determine your progress in goodness to others or to yourself, but your good works, nor do I mean by Works, any *stint* of goodness, any partial or outward or ostentatious activity, or any thing that has resting place or end. The doctrine of good works embraces the actions of the poor and helpless as well as of the useful. Good works are done, not only under man's eye, but unto God's, where man cannot behold. An abstinence from the luxury of unnecessary food, is a good work. The forbearance of a harsh or profane or complaining word; the mercy sometimes of a kind look; the exertion even to suppress a bad thought—*Every act of the will,* in short, *in obedience to the conscience,* is a *good work.*

In this broad interpretation of the doctrine of good works, I wish to be its advocate to your consciences. No man's religion that rests itself on the goodness of what he believes about God, or the amount of mystery that he admits, or the fervour of his prayers or of his wishes,—is any thing worth, if it rest on these alone. By their fruits, by their fruits, said the Saviour, ye shall know them.

No pretension can be more utterly destitute of colour than the setting up *faith* as a principle of the heart *in opposition* to good works. It has no claim in reason or in any true interpretation of Scripture, to such distinction.

But every body knows the extremes of absurdity to which the heat of party will push even intelligent and well disposed men, and therefore there is nothing surprizing in the history of opinions upon this point. There was long a persuasion that there was a virtue in believing a great deal and this doctrine gained such ground that at the Reformation it kept its footing when the other Dagons in the temple of Error were shaken down.[1] Luther even took great offence at the eloquence and plainness with which St. James in his Catholic epistle sets forth the worth of good works and called it "an Epistle of Straw" and himself maintained with tenacity that good works were not essential to salvation.[2] One of his followers, Amsdorff, went one step farther and taught that good works were an *impediment* to salvation.[3] These extravagances need no comment. He that has grown up in the belief that the worship of God consists in an acceptance of articles of belief, or in any temporary state of the mind, may grow used and so, insensible to these absurdities; but to a mind once liberated from them, no faith, no feelings in the least degree hostile to good works or that speaks of any merit independent of them, will find any respect. The upright and healthy mind will give for a little virtue at the bottom of the heart, a little pure and humble love of what is right, all the strictness of faith, all the sounding pretensions of all the Churches. (It is not a church but an individual that goes to heaven or to hell.) Intervals of sense return to the most wandering mind, to the most prejudiced community. There are great truths that no skepticism can steadily deny. And if in any assertions we do see our way plain before us we may speak with confidence here. All the theology in the world that disparages good works must melt away,—as smoke before their everlasting beauty. As we understand the language of the human face, so we apprehend the meaning of *Works*. There is no mistake about them. There is no hypocrisy about them. A man that uniformly does good works is good, and a man that uniformly does bad works is bad, let him say what he will, let him believe what he can. For works, cheerful faithful works, I cannot hide my reverence. I pay to them unfeigned love and honour. A man may say he believes what he does not believe—you cannot contradict him. He cannot say he does what he does not, for you can contradict him. Good works are the body of virtue. They are the signs of God's presence;

1. Cf. I Samuel 5.
2. Luther makes this remark at the conclusion of his preface to the New Testament (1522). Emerson's source is probably Luther's *Divine Discourses . . . Table Talk,* trans. H. Bell (London, 1652), 368. For a more recent edition, see *Reformation Writings of Martin Luther,* ed. Bertram Lee Woolf (London, 1956), 2:283. See also "Martin Luther" (*EL* 1:121).
3. Nicholas von Amsdorf (1483–1565), bishop of Magdesburg, sponsor of Luther's writings, and opponent of modifications in the doctrine of justification by faith. See *JMN* 1:188.

they are pledges of his blessing. They bless the doer, and the receiver, and the beholder, and the hearer.

I should feel in maintaining the excellence of good works like one who should say, the sun shines or the fire burns, were it not for the headstrong opposition this simple law has encountered in religious controversy and for another and far more important reason namely, that we are all apt to measure our virtue by our dispositions rather than by our performance. If we are capable of a momentary glow of pious feeling, we think we are nothing less than martyrs. But our experience may show us that these feelings are very subject to ebb and to flow.

Let us apply to them a sure test. The *works* they will prompt, the amount of good action they will sustain, is an unerring index of their intensity. Precisely so great a sacrifice as you can make, precisely so fervent is your faith. Then again we estimate ourselves by our best hours, and for what once we have done we praise ourselves now. But works of this day are the mercury of this day's merit. Tell me not what you did or said in months or years long past. You point at a highwater mark where the sea washed up a month ago; but perhaps the tides of this day do not rise so high; let me see the newly wet marks of this very hour's flood upon the shore. Let me see your conquest of your passions today. Let me see the closeness of your imitation of your Master. It is better than any Confession of faith.

It is the glory of Christianity and the evidence of its truth that beyond all systems of faith, it maintains the cause of good works. We bring to this cause the clear unambiguous testimony of Jesus Christ. 'Not every one,' he said, 'that saith to me, Lord, Lord, shall enter into the kingdom of heaven, but he that doeth the will of my Father.'[4] We bring also the unambiguous testimony of his own works. It was not the tongue of cloven flame that spoke so loudly for him, as the works which he did of charity and of power.[5]

Still the subject is imperfect when all has been said for Virtue: the human heart yet demands its author, its source; yet gropes for the Great Intelligence whereon the affections may rest, and gratify the longing that is in the soul of man to love and to adore. In the society of the Universe the mind is yet solitary that has not found God. Here then is the aid, here the necessity of faith. Faith is the Comforter. Faith adds to the sense of duty the idea of God. Faith teaches us to *pray* and teaches us to *trust.* Man is made of two parts, Reason and Affection. Reason dictates works: Affection teaches faith: reason prescribes duty, Affection makes it pleasant. Works prepare the mind to receive the idea of God; and, as I believe, with every good work, a juster idea of God is entertained; but Faith must come in to perfect the man, by connecting him and his works to God.

4. Matthew 7:21.
5. Cf. Acts 2:3.

Let us understand then that faith and works must live blended in one character to exhibit the perfection of man. Therefore Christianity, which was preached to the poor, to the ignorant, exhibits a better adaptation to man's nature and a better effect upon him than did ever any religion. The effect of Christianity on the common mind, the perfectness it gives to the character in narrow and obscure circumstances, can not be too much considered.

A proficient in Ethics does not always know that the height of virtue may be often studied at the low bedside of almshouses; or in a wretched hovel where faith and works have been united together; in the arm chair of age and poverty he may find demonstration of a virtue that Plutarch and Seneca overlooked, that Hume and Voltaire left out of their reasonings. There you may find a patience which not wrongs nor acute pains have been able to conquer; truth which interest or malice have not had force to shake; honesty that fair offers could not bribe, nor sophistry deceive, nor fears cause to waver; benevolence, that sprung with joy amid its own misery, at the prospect of another's good, at the tale of suffering relieved, and requited exertion. You shall find the rags of poverty speaking to your heart with an eloquence of duty which the careful argument of the pulpit can never attain. The gospel itself with its pages illuminated with light from heaven shall not speak so persuasively as this *practice* of the gospel, this unsuspected testimony to the glory of religion, where life calls unto life, one that has been sorely tried and has prevailed, to you that are sorely tried. It bids you be of good cheer. It shows you the song of angels and the joys of heaven breaking in upon the despised habitation of the poor.

My brethren, let us not trust for a moment a good thought, a good desire, that bears no fruit. 'Tis a sandy foundation;[6] and, oh, let us not trust, when we remember our sins, in the poor merits of what we have done. Let us refer all to God, and live in a faith which shall be a continued effort of good works; a continued effort to do his Will.

6. Cf. Matthew 7:26.

XLIX

Wherefore let him that thinketh he standeth,
take heed lest he fall.

I Corinthians 10:12

The goodness of God affords us this day another opportunity of keeping his Sabbath. That we may do it well and wisely let us ask ourselves what is the object that has assembled us here? What is the reason of all our religious ordinances, our solemn meetings, our pastors, our prayers, our psalms? It is answered—because a Revelation has come into the world, and opened to our eyes the knowledge of a future world,—and these are all remembrancers of that knowledge. See then that ye walk circumspectly not as fools but as wise— redeeming the time.[1]

But why came the Revelation? What is the bearing and intent of this provision and of all the provisions by which our condition in the world is affected? What is the object of all the institutions under whose shadow we are born and live and die? of the schools in which our youth is trained? of the books we read? of the arts and professions into the exercise of which we are disciplined and by which we act upon each other? of the political relations, the social connexions, the private friendships by which each man is anchored to his place in the agitations of human society? All look to one great and plain purpose. All seem to say, that, man, that the soul, is not brutish, is not passive like the plant or the animal body to the influences amidst which it is set, but is made itself to use all, is made capable of unceasing change from bad to good, from good to better. There is one great and common end of all we see and hear and think—The improvement of Man.

For this suns rise, and seasons change; for this, the earth is stored with good; for this we are sent into the earth naked, and feeble and poor;[2] and every good is held out to our labour; for this our fate is entrusted to our own keeping. For this the world is filled with wisdom, which comes to our minds by ten thousand

---

Preached ten times: September 20, 1829, at the Second Church, Boston; October 4 in Concord, Mass.; December 13 at the First Church, Boston; December 20 in Cambridge; December 27 at the West Church, Boston; January 17, 1830, in Beverly, Mass.; March 14 in Hartford; June 6 in Waltham; December 26 at the Second Church; and October 29, 1837, in East Lexington. For one or more later deliveries, Emerson used Philippians 3:13 as his text.

1. Eph[esians] V. 15 [Emerson's note].
2. Cf. Job 1:21.

51

avenues; for this are set before us the elements of so many arts, the idioms of so many languages; for this we are introduced to all this variety of character, and the solemn array of moral influence encompasses us; for this prophets spoke, and good men acted; and for this Christ died. For this, finally, came all the passages of our personal history,—for this sometimes we are put into society, and sometimes we are put apart, sometimes afflicted, and sometimes rejoiced.

All these things speak to each of us—and command us every moment to feel that we are not creatures of necessity, but creatures of free will,—improvable beings—not moving like the silent orb we tread upon, in one eternal round,—but going backward or going forward in our moral career, at our own free choice, and just as far and as fast as we will.

Yet who remembers this when he rises in the morning and when he lies down at night? Who remembers that he is made to be improved by every hour of his life? Who carries this thought with him, as his motive, as his one dear and constant solace—when he begins his work, when he goes to his store, when he enters his family, when he retires to his chamber; when he is excited, and tempted, and bereaved, and prospered? I do not deny that there are such men, but they are few.

It seems to me it is of great practical importance that our views of what Religion means should be sound. For it is our opinion of what is the healthy state of the faculties. Though our own practice may be faulty, yet so long as we are not atheists, we must yet regard the religious life as the perfection of man. And it will not do to have a low standard, for the level of the actions will always be lower.

But in general, both our views of religion are full of error, and our practice full of imperfection. We do indeed yield a heedless approbation to pure views of religion when we hear them expressed. We are willing to believe that Religion is that state of the mind which looks not to our limited but to our infinite well-being;—it is the acknowledgement of unseen things;[3] it is faith in God and in the immortality of the soul, which Jesus was sent to reveal; it is an acknowledgement of these things not verbal, but so true and so deep, as to make the whole life an expression of this belief.

If you can get the attention of a sensible man to the subject, he will probably signify his entire assent to the reasonableness of this account of Religion. But this is not the account that goes current in our common speculations. It is not felt, it is not remembered that the only Religion is a progressive religion, a religion of every moment, not an occasional rule, for sick days or Sabbaths, but a religion that opens upon the heart as the faculties unfold, and lasts as long as life lasts in this world, or in all worlds.

But see in our practice what are our thoughts. When a severe disease confines us in our house; when the physician shakes his head at our low and declining pulse; when the whole head is disordered, and the powers of attention well nigh

3. Cf. II Corinthians 4:18.

gone; when the lessons of the school of life are done for us, and the God of nature gives us this signal to put up our tasks and come away—then men take down from the shelf their religious books, then they go to prayer and try to give to these devout exercises the bewildered attention of a broken mind, and now that life is just coming to its end, set their hearts to the question, *What is the object of life,* and how has it been answered by us? It seems needless to insist on the vanity of these tardy attempts not at obedience but at penitence, not at expiation but remorse.

But I am afraid that very many persons who value themselves a good deal upon their religious character, who often address themselves to God in prayer, and who reason very justly upon the folly of leaving the thoughts of religion to the few worthless hours at the end of life, who neglect no ordinance, and are punctual in their charities, and read the bible and other good books, do hold and cherish the error that this is the sum of religion to do these things, and I think it a very unhappy error and productive of much harm in society because such persons being esteemed the votaries of religion—the world naturally looks to them to find the effects of a principle that makes such lofty pretensions as religion certainly does. And if it finds them ordinary persons, without any remarkable attainments, of no higher standing in the community for intelligence or industry than others, and not more scrupulously honest than others who have not their professions to support; and not more,—perhaps—not so much devoted to objects of general interest and utility to their country, as others,—why then,—men say—if this is all that religion can do, do not even the publicans the same?[4] They feel if they do not say, that it lacks some of that divine evidence it ought to have. It does not commend itself by indisputable testimony to be of God. The understanding will believe, and 'tis a natural belief, that where so great and superior a Cause does truly work as this elevating faith, a real and divine *effect* will appear. The Spirit that borrows the aid of the Almighty Spirit, cannot conceal or disguise the great alliance. A city that is set on an hill cannot be hid.[5] It cannot be the victim as other men are of ungovernable grief or joy on very small occasions. It cannot live on as other men do from month to month, from year to year, very little changed,—with very little improvement of purpose, and very little enlargement of its action.—Set it down, my brethren, in your hearts that if there is no improvement there is no religion.

Neither of these views of religion, neither that which makes it only occasional at sickness or death; nor that which limits it to the use of good observances, finds any support in reason, or in the doctrine of the Revelation itself. The revelation proceeds on the assumption that man is sinful, and may become good. And in all the blessed doctrines of our Saviour, the faith he teaches is one of endless effort, a striving after all good, and no indolence of faith, no torpid

4. Matthew 5:46.
5. Matthew 5:14.

piety of good wishes and good prayers,—nor Sabbath virtues, nor deathbed penitence,—but beneficence, and humility, and chastity, and resignation, and diligence, and watchfulness.

Therefore, I cannot but think that Christianity is yet but in its infancy in the world. Only a few minds are *religious*. Only upon a few minds has the light of truth dawned so clearly that they live in obedience to it, and live in the effort to carry up every faculty to its highest pitch. "A Christian," said Young, "is the highest style of man."[6] Whenever Christianity shall have produced its full effect upon human character, to say that a man is a Christian will produce a truer admiration and love in the common mind, than to say he is a hero, or he is a philosopher. Indeed the name of a Christian will comprehend the praise of heroism and philosophy.

When our Saviour was in the earth and was discoursing with his disciples he told them in a parable of the faithful stewards who doubled the treasure entrusted to them, and they were rewarded; and of a slothful servant who hid his lord's money in a napkin and buried it in the earth; and when a long time was past and the day of reckoning came; he said to his Lord, Lo there thou hast what is thine—and his lord was angry with that servant, and commanded that the one talent should be taken from him and given to him that had ten; *for, to whomsoever hath shall be given, and he shall have abundance; but whosoever hath not, from him shall be taken even that which he hath.*[7] My friends, the great and solemn moral of this parable, is the truth I am urging upon you. It is not unconfirmed to any breast. It is written in every chapter of your own experience. It is written in your observation of every one of your acquaintance. It is the biography of every member of your own family. You are yourself but an example of the truth of that ancient allegory.

And what is the inference at which we aim? It is this—that no man should think that he *standeth*. In the words of the apostle in our text—Let him that thinketh he standeth, take heed lest he fall. Let us understand that Religion consists in doing, and never in having done, that the life, the essence of religion consists in *progress*, in *effort*. Let us understand that the hour is lost which has not made us better—that Religion hath the most minute application to every part of life; that it must chasten the levities of conversation; take away not only its malice but also its exaggeration and folly; make it true to the man and the occasion. If this were done it were a great help to the peace and the instruction of the world, and this can be done without taking from conversation any of its wit or brilliancy. All that virtue demands is the intention of truth and it may choose what forms of fiction or gaiety it will. Then it will dictate the most exact economy of time and the most zealous pursuit of knowledge. The religious man, in the highest sense of that term, who looks upon all the Creation animate and inanimate as the book which God opens for him to read, and who sees that

6. Edward Young, *Night Thoughts,* "Night IV," line 789.
7. Matthew 25:14-30.

in all, God seems first and ever to consult the advantage of *Mind*—the religious man will burn to profit by that care—to let slip no opportunity of enlarging his understanding, and quickening his perceptions, and storing his memory;—and above all it will dictate a government of all action, a restraint of the appetites and a direction of the affections, that resting of the soul on God which includes all obedience, all faith, all trust.

My friends, in presenting the claims of Christianity upon you under this particular aspect as addressed to man as an *improvable* being, commanding him not to stand still but to advance—I believe I do not choose an impertinent topic. The main mischief we have to contend with is the apathy of men to their duty; their indifference to the great things that are before them. Men do not commit atrocious crimes, but will not seek great virtues. The world is full of moral sluggards who lift their heavy heads to see the greatness of others and never realize that they also might be great. Only make a rigid self-application of the commandment. Only feel that you yourself are capable of improvement, and that not uncertain or far off, but in this very hour and in every hour; that you will do wrong and have been false to the trust the Almighty Father has committed to you, if you go forth from this house with no better purpose than you brought into it,—if you go forth no more humble, no more resigned, no more grateful, no more just. The moment never comes when good may not be done, or evil be forborne—when knowledge may not be gathered,—or good counsel suggested, or a deed of mercy done, or a temptation resisted, or a secret thanksgiving sent up to God. Cultivate this state of feeling, this confidence in your powers and opportunities, and be assured they shall not fail you. Is it not a cheerful and ennobling faith that leads you forth into a spiritual world and shows you an interminable life stretching out before you, made up of opportunities of doing and being good; an eternity, each of whose countless hours, you shall mark with a new triumph, in your spiritual progress that points you to all the great souls whose knowledge and virtue made them lights of their times and teaches you to carry up your individual attainments to the level of theirs, that making effort the natural state of the mind, makes trial pleasant and danger hopeful, whilst the example of our Master and of all good men, and the approbation of God and the certainty of his blessing encourage every exertion? Let not the sense of present deficiency or the memory of past failure operate to discourage you. Let them be warning sounds to leave the dangerous ground of old temptations. And, oh! put not your trust in the poor pittance of merit you have already accumulated. It is good for nothing but as step to more. See the path of the just is like the rising sun shining more and more unto that perfect day.[8]

8. Cf. Proverbs 4:18.

L

This do in remembrance of me.

LUKE 22:19

God has given to us as to each generation in succession the dominion of the world,[1] the care of supporting and carrying forward the frame and institutions of society. We stand on the same ground, breathe the same air, are warmed by the same sun and have the same moral constitution as our fathers. We live in the influences of the same institutions—of Society, of property, of government, of marriage, of the Sabbath.

And therefore are we in all respects in the same condition as they? No. The character of Society is every moment undergoing a change. We stand on the same shores, but in different dress, with different laws, different customs, and new occupations. We read the same books but they speak to us a different sense.

That which bears the same name and stands in the same place is not always the same thing. There has been a large town in Italy called Rome for now near 2500 years but it could only be a child that think and speak alike of the Etrurian Village and the city of the consuls and the city of the emperors and the city of the barbarians and the city of the Popes and the city of artists. No, it is the blessed law of heaven which makes the cheerfulness of this life and the hope of another that our nature should be progressive. The political economist has found out that the average term of human life is longer now than it was some ages since. Great truths which ages toiled to prove, they did prove, and we begin where they ended. The results of an old philosopher are the elements of his pupil. Their harvest is our seed. God has made the acorn such that it will grow to an oak and he has made his moral institutions capable of a far mightier growth. The governments, the laws, the customs into which we are born—they are like the shell or outer skin of many animals—If it do not admit of growth the animal will cast it.

So is it with the institutions of religion. Christianity which at first seemed only calculated to break down the cumbrous ceremonies of the Jewish Law was

---

Manuscript dated September 26, 1829, at Chardon Street. This sermon, which explores the nature of the Lord's Supper, was preached once, on September 27, 1829, at the Second Church, Boston. The Second Church differed from the usual practice in holding its Communion service on the last, rather than the first, Sunday in the month.
1. Genesis 1:26.

presently found to have set up a most forcible appeal against the systems of paganism. It was found fit to be the religion of nations as the law it displaced was not. It is now found in the vast advancement of national intelligence to have made a cotemporaneous advancement. As men think more and demand more, Christianity is found to mean more, has more excitement and more consolation and to be a nobler moral rule with more flexible application to life than a wise man who should have heard it expounded in the dark ages could have dreamed. And here it stands, brethren, in the veneration of our minds shining on with its immortal and cheerful light, outliving a hundred schools of skeptics and now bringing in all the virtue and all the highest minds of this generation into its holy fold. Neither are we to imagine that we have seen all or comprehended all; but let us believe as our forefathers did that God has yet much more light to impart.

So with the striking rite which its founder established, and which this day we celebrate. The time has been, and that very early in the history of the Church, when gross superstition was combined with that ordinance; it was mixed, confounded by the new converts, with the licentious feasts of the pagan worship which they had newly forsaken and turned to a scene of riot—which gave occasion to that word of St. Paul that he that eateth and drinketh unworthily, eateth and drinketh damnation to himself, not discerning the Lord's body.[2] And when the doctrine of the divinity of Jesus at length grew up in the Church, then arose the famous doctrine of transubstantiation or belief of the real presence of God in the bread and wine. The very statement of this notion seems enormous to us and incredible, a proof how much we have truer notions than our ancestors.

Still I think it is very apt to be misunderstood and misused by us and it is important that we should occasionally give a formal consideration to the foundation and intent of the institution.

Jesus perceived that the hour was at hand when his ministry on earth should close.[3] In the painful boding interest of that hour, he was consoled by the good consciousness of the past and the prophetic glory of the future.[4] No disappointment, no horrors of trial could wholly deject one who knew himself to be the Resurrection and the Life.[5] Still there was much to sadden and create doubt. He had exhibited in proof of his mission a power that should amaze his nation. In the face of the sun, and in many places and before crowds he had realized the wondrous histories of their fathers: He had checked or changed the usual course of nature. He had healed the sick and calmed the sea and those that had been dead stood before him glowing with awe among the living multitude. In harmony with this stupendous display he had shown a life of moral perfection—as original in his times, as his miracles. Yet with what success? All had

2. I Corinthians 11:29. In the manuscript, Emerson wrote out the passage only to the word "unworthily."
3. Cf. Matthew 26:18.
4. Cf. John 17:1–5.
5. John 11:25.

well nigh failed to attach credit to his revelation. The madness of the Jewish hope could not see their Messiah in the Carpenter's son. The madness of the Roman scorn could not see a Saviour of the soul in the Jew and the Nazarite.

Therefore he groaned in spirit[6] and might well doubt whether, even in those nearest followers who had seen all and had heard all, the passage of time and the terrors of persecution and the temptations of sense might not shake even their convictions or relax their efforts to transmit the great reformation which was the object of his life.

Perhaps it was with this feeling that he desired to give body and certainty to their recollection by appointing a feast of remembrance.[7] He could not but foresee what perversions must be expected from the extreme ignorance of the world, to degrade the faith he would teach; but he knew that the devout affections of every time and of every heart that acknowledged him would meet round a table spread by him at so awful a moment of his life—that this feast would be a distinction, a badge, a pledge, a rebuke, a remembrancer.

With his knowledge of men he could not but feel that this institution must have a meaning and an use changed and accommodated to every age to which it should descend and not only so but almost peculiar to the mind of every disciple.

He therefore requested his disciples to eat bread and drink wine in memory of him. He set no time, he fixed no number, he added no mystery. He left his ordinance loose to go down to all churches suitable to the wants of all.

Having these views of the origin of the ordinance, I feel no anxiety, brethren, that all men should think alike of its nature and intent. I am willing that every Christian should see it coloured by the complexion of his own mind. It seems to me that it will always seem to one mind an occasion of warning and alarm, to another of encouragement; to one of hope, to another of remembrance; to one of pleasing sympathy, to another darkened by a deep shade of awful history. And further I think that the institution to all men is assuming, and with progress of men's minds will assume, a more spiritual and useful character.

I said it was not important that men should think alike. Still I think there are certain broad views of the Lord's Supper which are the result of the good sense and liberal thinking of the age and which ought therefore to influence our practice much more than they do. And mainly I think it should embrace all men who believe in the divine authority of Christianity and not as now only a small minority.

I believe the whole end and aim of this ordinance is nothing but this, *to make those who partake of it better.* To join the church is not to say I am good, or I have been, but *I desire to be.* It does not intimate, and this I pray you to observe, that a line runs through the world dividing men into saints and sinners, that you have stood on one side and now stand on the other—but believing that there is no man wholly good or wholly bad, you manifest your wish to use this as you

6. John 11:33.
7. Luke 22:17–19.

would use any and every means of strengthing your virtuous propensities. It is a means of warming your affections toward Jesus, God's highly authorized and highly honoured servant, and under God your most effectual friend, a means of quickening your moral perception and amending your character in personal and social regards. And are not these things desirable and obligatory upon all? Why should not all come? There is no foundation, it seems generally agreed, in the rule or practice of the primitive Church for the division that now exists between church and congregation. All who named the Lord's name partook of his supper. And so should all now.[8]

Therefore I would have no one feel himself unfit to come, because he is no more virtuous; and, least of all, would I see a Christian or a Christian Church put a bar in the way of any. Who is he to whom I shall deny the right to sit at the supper of the Lord? I cannot by strait covenants exclude any man, nor can take it upon myself to say that any man's sin shall exclude him. If any man transgress, to him is the more need of Christ's aid; to him the closer application of Christ's address. He came not, he said, to call the righteous, but sinners.[9] I would bring our use of his institutions into an unity with himself. Now all that he said and did is marked by the freest grace. I admire the character of the Saviour not because I was taught to revere it but because as I have grown up and my mind opened I saw in the history of the world none nobler or of softer humanity, and I should feel myself to offend grievously against all I understand of the spirit of his gospel, against all I love of the boundless generosity of his character if I should lift my hand to hinder any from his fold. I should feel myself rebuked by the reproof which he addressed to his uncharitable disciples when they called for fire on his enemies.[10]

No, brethren, it seems to me far more reasonable than that any should be shut out, that we should go to the prisons and bid the culprits come. As a matter of common expediency what harm could result? There are no temptations to any to join the church among us except from good motives. And if the church had unworthy members every man's sin lieth at his own door.[11]

My friends, I think this view of the ordinance that it is simply a means of improvement just as attendance on public worship or the conversation of a wise man or the study of a good book or any thing else that has a tendency to excite the affections or impart light—I think this view not only the true one but the one likely to be productive of the most benefit. It will most profitably direct our

8. From the earliest days of the New England churches, a strong distinction was drawn between those who were full church members and entitled to partake of the Lord's Supper, and those unconverted persons who merely attended services. The distinction began to break down in the seventeenth century when Solomon Stoddard of Northampton chose to regard the Supper as a converting ordinance. Emerson's belated Stoddardeanism was hardly radical for a Unitarian minister in 1829.

9. Matthew 9:13, Mark 2:17, and Luke 5:32.

10. See Luke 9:54-56; "For the Son of man is not come to destroy men's lives, but to save them" (Luke 9:56).

11. Cf. Genesis 4:7.

meditations around the table in the channel fittest for each. It will fill one mind with sorrow for sin and one with the fragrance of holy affections, one with contentment in his lot and one with ardent aspirations for union with the spiritual world. It will teach us to use this privilege with humility and prayer that we may not dishonour it. It will teach us to walk in the world as having received the light of another, as the zealous yet unassuming followers of the meek and lowly son of the Almighty Father who, coming out from Him and from the spiritual world, brought to the human soul the hope of immortal life; the sanction of duty; and the joyful doctrine that man may do the will of God and grow to perfection in his love.

Blessed are the pure in heart
for they shall see God.

MATTHEW 5:8

From these words of our Lord I propose, my friends, to invite your attention to some general remarks upon the soul's perception of God—or connexion with him, which is the substance of religion—to remark upon the infinite advantage of faith over the want of faith and upon the excellence of this connexion as the only rule of action and measure of good. It can never be impertinent in this place to consider our relations to our maker and to strive to give steadiness and distinctness and elevation to our idea of his character—to carry up our idea towards the truth—the truth—which outruns our most rapid conceptions and exceeds our vastest thought and seems to admonish the highest mind of its feebleness. It is higher than heaven—what can we know? It is deeper than the abyss—what can we do? We talk familiarly of God. We apply to his action the analogy of human organs and of human passions. We converse with him in prayer. In private and in public—in whispered words and in solitary action—we do all at some times recognize his being and act in one or another manner because God sees us.—But in all this let us remember that it is not God himself we speak of and think of, but each man's idea of God, which is more pure in one mind than in another but is most inadequate and elementary in all. We feel that our highest theology, i.e., our description of God, must be the gropings of infant weakness, when compared to God himself. It must be thus, because every man is conscious of an increase of purity and truth in his views of the Divine Character, as his own knowledge and especially as his own goodness increases; and that improvement has no limits. And every one's observation may show him that different individuals in the same age, in the same town, even in the same family, pay their homage to very different Gods, that is, to very different conceptions of God. The true God exists unchangeably to all, and they exist by him, but the window of the *mind,* the glass, through which they see him, is clouded and gives an imperfect and distorted image.

The language of prayer is each man's description of his idea of God. The

---

Preached once, on October 11, 1829, at the Second Church, Boston.

prayer of an exalted mind is little else than "Father thy will be done!"[1] but the prayer of wilful men is apt to prescribe indecently both the end and the means. In their prayers, men sometimes insist much on the importance of a blessing which they ask, and give reasons why it should be granted, as if the petitioner spoke to an earthly monarch. Every serious man can trace an improvement in his own practice in this respect.

Brethren, Religion seems to me to consist in the having just views of God and living by them. I think very few minds have right views of him. And yet it is the great business and design of each human soul in the world to purify and educate the idea of God within him. I am sure that as this central thought is improved and made more and more true, the whole man will be improved. As his idea of God loses its superstition if he be superstitious, or its uncertainty, if he be skeptical, as it enlarges to the perfection of an Infinite Father, he will become a person of more talents, he will become a person of better feelings and so a person of more excellent action. Now this is the view of religion which the pulpit needs most to enforce. In past times of the world so much falsehood had mixed and debased it, that it seemed really a condescension on the part of the kings and leaders of society whether raised by rank or genius, whenever touched by the necessities of man they gave their whole support to the cause of religion. Then grew up too that language which will hereafter be felt to be a monstrous perversion—when it needed to caution the young and the aspiring against *being ashamed of religion.* To be ashamed of religion! With as much reason might a man be ashamed of the circulation of his blood, be ashamed of breathing, or of using his memory. To be ashamed of religion! It is to be ashamed of the constitution of the world, of the moral order of heaven and earth, of the immortality of the soul, and of the existence of God—a mind whose being includes his own.—Now no man could think of being ashamed of these things and it is therefore plain that very unjust views of religion must have been held, to have brought such a feeling, and then such language, into use. The right feeling is that religion dignifies the man whose breast it rules—and the more correct his religious feeling, the nobler creature is he.

It is the unspeakable privilege of the soul to see God. All other privileges it can obtain are frivolous compared with this. We will not say with the apostle, We are of all men most miserable,[2] but we must say that all men are miserable, if God did not exist and exist in connexion with us. If God did not exist it is a plain fact—we despair. Eat, drink, act, sin, and suffer; love and hate; do good or do evil in your tiny moment of life—what is your life—but a vapour quickly swallowed up in the immensity of nature?[3] If we were the heads of creation, if man in the earth sickening and dying—was the top of being—and the disputed dominion of the beasts was his best distinction—the nearer he descended to

1. Matthew 6:9-10.
2. I Corinthians 15:19.
3. James 4:14.

them, the less he thought, the happier he would be; for when men came wisely to consider their condition, I fear the earth would smell with suicide.

It may be remarked that if God did not exist the vices of men must stand as an essential part of their character to degrade our views of our nature. If God exist, the vices of men are accidental and curable; man's nature is not to be judged by them, for it is infinitely improvable.

But blessed be God the soul cannot help seeing the seal of the workman on his work. By its native force the soul springs upward from these low doubts to the high ground of Faith. It feels the gladness of doing right, it feels the pain of doing wrong, and so perceiving the law, looks round for the Lawgiver. It becomes conscious of affections that nothing but virtue can satisfy. It is filled with desires of everlasting duration and of an Infinite Mind.

God has sent his holy word into the world to meet these wants, to fix these convictions—to remove the veil from death and set the soul forward on its search after truth and goodness.

But there are unbelievers in the world, who say there is no God[4]—and who dislike these truths in which we put confidence.

Now does any man take another view of it and say that the lover of religion insists upon the dignity of religion but that the atheist insists as reasonably upon his advantage in being emancipated from the dominion of this prejudice—that he is wiser than to be deluded by its hopes or frightened by its fears? We answer that the religious man perceives his own superiority of sight, perceives that the difference of opinion is defect in the other mind, with a perfect conviction. For we are all masters of each other's ways of thinking to a very great degree, by reason of our common nature. Every man knows every other man by himself. And the religious man sees the obstructed state of the atheist's mind as the seeing man beholds the film on the diseased eye. He is himself not what he was but enriched by his new perceptions. He sees that the atheist is in his own state of mind before his heart opened to these convictions. He walks in the light and converses in the society of the spiritual world. He feels that he walks before the face of God and with his approbation. And he knows that the atheist is yet a man as he is and therefore that he also is capable of having his spiritual eye opened to receive the same truth. He perceives also that the atheist is not better but worse for the want of it.

Brethren, we know that God exists and we ought habitually to exalt each other's views of the value of our faith and of the sacred importance of God's revelation of himself. We know that the connexion of the mind with God is the measure of all its solid good. And to every well ordered mind things will appear good or bad in proportion as the presence of God is manifest in them. In Society there is a great deal of frivolity, a great deal of sensuality, a great deal of slander, and all these are disgusting to a serious person because they indicate the

4. Psalms 14:1.

absence of God. The idea of God which is given in the Christian religion is the only explanation that has ever been offered of our own existence and condition. But it teaches us that we have no life in ourselves, that in our sins we are dead, that we only truly live in connexion with God.[5] He is the vine, we are the branches, and if we be sundered from him we die.[6]

Now brethren, it is possible for each of us to abandon our sins and each in the station that now we occupy to enter into this intimate and still growing union with our Father. The experience of holy men has shown it possible, the life of Jesus has shown it possible, and his words have taught us the way. Our own hearts have suggested it. It is possible to keep God's commands faithfully, to converse continually with him in our cheerful and in our graver hours, to avoid every degrading association and so to keep ever an affectionate though humble eye upon God and draw inspiration from his counsels into our life. Is it not possible for each of us in our several places to dethrone our darling sins and set up the spirit of God in their room as the rule and motive of action?

There is a view of it derived from common experience that may recommend it. The mind of man is a chaos till it have some ruling passion. Every man needs some strong influence pushing his efforts in a single direction to give effect to his action. A man who has no profession, no particular calling, is apt to be a man of little efficiency. Our effect upon society depends far more upon the *arrangement* than upon the number or quality of our ideas. What an immeasurable heap of facts can lie obscure in one man's mind—geographical, economical, historical, mechanical and so on—the collection of sixty years of study and observation but an indigested and unprofitable mass. Now introduce some strong and absorbing passion into his soul, some ardent attachment, or fierce resentment, or the desire to deliver his country from a foreign yoke, or to convert his country on any great question to his own opinion, or specially any religious feeling and see how swiftly those disjointed ideas fly into form and order—how his knowledge becomes practical; how he brings the abundance of reasons and events of centuries into logic of tremendous cogency and application to the present hour, and the passing event.

Now the greater this motive which takes possession of the soul the more intense does his power become and the more full and perfect is the development of the faculties and affections of the man.

Now brethren, if instead of an attachment to an imperfect mortal or a sinful hatred or the desire of a low and partial good the love of God be that motive—if the soul be inflamed with a generous affection to its Supreme Friend and sends up its thoughts in a rich stream in that one direction, if it doth all the actions which that love prescribes and abandons all the courses which that love condemns, if it seek his objects and live in his love, and adopt his will—can any thing be imagined more pure and majestic than the life of such a man? Would

5. Cf. Ephesians 2:1, 2:5, and Colossians 2:13.
6. John 15:5-6.

not this bring out every faculty and feeling in its just place and proportion? Would not this love quench the fires of sinful passion, raise the soul above anger, raise it above the frivolity of society, above the devotion to sordid interest and make it scorn slander? Would it not heighten our pure pleasures? Would it not give us temper to bear pain and solace and in the hour of bereavement and calm triumph in the hour of death?

Yet this love is that for which our minds were made. Each of our souls is a mirror formed to reflect the face of God forever, though now perhaps we are turned from the light. The way of duty is but one. The pure in heart shall see him. Let us do his commandments that we may abide in his love.[7]

7. John 15:10.

LII

*If any man offend not in word
the same is a perfect man.*

JAMES 3:2

It is good that we explore the value of common blessings and ponder the obligation of common duties. In our settled order of social life not many are called to
martyrdoms or to opportunities of benefitting states. Our life runs on a beaten
track and the only opportunity of greatness that is vouchsafed to us is that
which is given to all, is not that of great place or events, but that of infusing great
principles into plain and vulgar actions, the power of giving interest and
respectability to the meanest offices—if heaven ordains our lot amidst such—
by our way of doing them, the power of introducing the sacred relation of man
to God into our use of every faculty.

One of our chief powers is that of speech. An old and familiar subject—but
to what observer has it lost its interest? What we do so much we surely ought to
do well. And I wish to invite your attention, my friends, to some reflexions on
the use and enjoyment of this faculty and upon the duties that belong to conversation.

I do not wish to dwell upon the detail of the wonderful contrivances by which
this faculty is produced. It is the noble result that claims all my admiration, the
power of articulate and rational speech—which is the foundation of society and
the delight and the instruction of human life. This great bond of connexion
between the seen and the unseen world, whereby the impenetrable darkness
that covers the soul of man from man is taken away and I am made acquainted
with the inaccessible soul of my brother. Speak that I may know thee was an
ancient proverb.[1] We can only feel its worth by bringing to our imagination the
state of man if this power had been denied. Suppose God had chosen to educate
a race of moral agents apart or together in the solitude of the dumb. We have all
seen some of those sufferers under this grievous infirmity—those poor outcasts
from the sweet society of speaking men. And yet we see them under circumstances of great alleviation; by their intercourse with those who speak as well as

---

Preached twice: October 18, 1829, at the Second Church, Boston, and April 2, 1837, in East Lexington.
   1. Cf. Ben Jonson, *The Discoveries,* in *Ben Jonson,* ed. C. H. Herford, Percy and Evelyn Simp-
son (Oxford, 1925-1951), 2:451: "Language most shewes a man: speake that I may see thee."

by particular instruction the calamity is lessened. In our institutions for the deaf and dumb, the instructors, let it be remembered, are those who speak and are enabled to be of infinite service to those unfortunate persons by teaching them modes of communication that nothing but speech could have enabled them to invent. And yet after all is done what a little it is—what slow and struggling conceptions they form, what a crippled mind is the mind of the dumb. Compare their existence and intercourse with the intercourse of witty, learned and wise among speaking men—and it seems as if Providence in denying them speech had withheld half the good of being.

Yet these, though almost shut out from the active world of men, have some imperfect communication, have their own inarticulate speech. To get the full conception of the value of the power we should try to contemplate the frightful solitude of those who should have none. What were the state of minds that God had enclosed in unsocial bodies, with no language even of signs? You may place them side by side if you will in their appointed place and appointed duties, but they are separated more effectually than if Oceans sundered them; the thought of one cannot penetrate to the thought of the other. They cannot cooperate—they cannot have affections—and the heart is oppressed by its pity for so forlorn a being.

Now compare this unformed sufferer with the finished man. He speaks—and is understood. The cheerful daylight of a sympathy and common intelligence is let in upon the dark firmament in which his thoughts roll. Society is produced—not only hand joins with hand in physical aid and support but the soul finds fellowship—discovers that in other souls the thoughts, the affections, the powers are formed and ordered upon the same springs, turn on the same poles, as its own. Minds that confer together, heat and quicken each other to greater intensity of affection to that which both love. They modify and alter each other's opinion and purpose. The light that is in one mind is speedily imparted to the other without loss to the first. If one mind be superiour, the other is benefitted in exact proportion to that superiority by the intercourse. And not only is there this mutual benefit by the exchange of knowledge by which in almost every case each man is a gainer, but a separate and remarkable advantage arises to each, that his own knowledge is increased by his efforts to impart it. Under the stimulus of conversation a man musters his thoughts more vigorously, and brings them out from their obscurity into air and light,—observes their relation to other truth more narrowly than before; corrects them; and carries them to yet farther conclusions; and so feels himself to be wiser in conversation than he was in silence. Bacon said—"t'were better that a man should relate his thoughts to a statue than let them pass in smother."[2]

It were a very interesting inquiry though leading too far for the limits of this discourse to trace the Uses of Conversation. It has one general use to which I

2. Francis Bacon, "Of Friendship," in *The Works of Francis Bacon,* ed. James Spedding et al. (London, 1857-1874), 6:440-41. Cf. *JMN* 5:295.

will advert a moment. It is the natural institution for the Diffusion of Knowledge. The profound wisdom of one man, and the rare opportunities of another, are, by this easy process, brought into the common treasury of mankind, with advantage and pleasure to both the public and the individual. Any one may be satisfied of this benefit who will consider how much practical wisdom passes current in the world in the shape of vulgar proverbs. These little maxims of worldly prudence are a part of the inheritance that have come down to this age from all the past generations of men. They have given us their institutions, their inventions, their books,—and, by means of conversation, have transmitted their commentary upon all the parts of life in these proverbs. They were originally doubtless the happy thoughts of sagacious men in very distant times and countries, in every employment and of every character. No single individual, with whatever penetration, could have attained, by himself, to that accurate knowledge of human life, which now floats through the conversation of all society, by means of these pithy sentences. We are all of us the wiser for them. They govern us in all our traffic;—in all our judgements of men;—in all our gravest actions.

It is impossible not to notice the enjoyment as well as the advantage which our Heavenly Father has provided for us in this noble endowment of speech, not to feel how it diminishes the burden of life, and augments its pleasure; not to remember the happiness that is in the voice of a friend; not to remember how much stronger is truth when 'tis recommended by eloquence. There is a pleasure, a luxury which is one of the most refined delights permitted to man, which results from listening to the conversation of exalted minds when they possess to any high degree this talent of communicating their thoughts. Fine conversation is very rare. It is the fruit of talents and situation in society which are granted to but few—and the best eulogy of this art is in the convictions of them who have heard it. It is exhilarating to the soul beyond all other stimulus. It moves upon the mind with creative force. It gives heart and life to the listener and to a religious mind suggests the feeling of its immortality—with a conviction sometimes beyond that of argument or evidence.

But whilst I look with admiration and pleasure at this rare and costly fruit I am far from being insensible to the goodness of the Creator in that sweetness which all of us, down to the least favoured of mankind, derive from this faculty. It is the breath of social life. Solitary confinement is limited by our penal laws to a very short period as, if protracted, it is found to be a privation intolerable for human nature.[3] How does this free expression of ourselves lighten labour and lessen pain. There is a consolation, which the poor village gossip in the midst of her infirmities derives from treasuring up and relating her little anecdotes and feelings, which will not pass unnoticed by any observer of God's beneficence.

3. Massachusetts penologists were strongly opposed to the "solitary system" adopted at the Eastern Pennsylvania Penitentiary in Philadelphia, which took in its first prisoner on October 25, 1829, just a week after Emerson's sermon. In 1828, the Boston Prison Discipline Society reprinted Lafayette's attack on the plan, calling it a "revival of the system of the Bastille." See *Reports of the Prison Discipline Society of Boston* (rpt., Montclair, N.J., 1972), p. 191.

Having spoken of the excellence of the power of speech in regard to its use and of its pleasure, I come now to speak a little of the duties that respect Conversation.

With all the glory of this gift there is also a sadly sore side to Conversation. The tongue instructs, consoles, pleases, rebukes, encourages, but also it rails, flatters, lies, and blasphemes. The virtues of man have made it their organ and his passions also may make it theirs. Our conversation is a very large part of life, and by our words therefore we shall be justified or condemned. It has every degree of merit. It may be wholly sinful or it may be so rich and pure as is the discourse of angels. It is important therefore to keep it to its right office and to find rules for its government.

It is one of the secrets which conversation discloses to us that our minds are made after one model. If it were not so, if every mind had different principles of right and wrong; different tastes; if that which was true to me, was false to my neighbour; and what one conscience condemned as mean, another extolled as heroic;—the faculty of speech would only be the organ of hopeless contradiction and perplexity. But we find there is a certain *standard idea of man* which we all have in our thoughts in our conversation. In every dispute, we have tacit reference to it all along. If we talk on any question of speculation with a man who seems to us to be in great error, we always believe that at last, perhaps not in this life, but somewhere, sometime, he will come to the truth; he will see as we see; will come nearer to this standard—man, which we believe exists for both. This feeling amounts to so strong a confidence, when a man is very wrong-headed, that we don't feel it to be of great importance to set him right, sure that he will come right hereafter if left to himself.

Now in that very standard, we have a rule, a guide for the regulation of our discourse. Let us not come below that standard. Let us not offend against it. Let us not offend the man within the breast.[4] Let it be remembered that in all our talk, truth is the end and aim. When therefore in argument you convince your opponent, remember that it is truth and not you that wins, and so be not elate, but grateful that the attainment of it is given to you. But when you are overcome by fair argument and find your reasonings false and vain, then if you keep your good humour it is you that win. There is a high, a Christian nobleness in that victory over egotism when a man in the zeal of debate doth frankly and joyfully yield himself to the manifest truth of his adversary. It is brave and Christian to do so but not many men can. It was said of a celebrated American statesman that he was content to stand by and let truth and reason argue for him.[5]

My brethren, the check upon conversation that will supersede all others is the religious feeling, the sense that we are God's children. It will elevate its tone above its frivolity or a criminal degradation. It will take away its personality in

4. Adam Smith, *The Theory of the Moral Sentiments* (London, 1853), 185. Used in *L* 1:174, *JMN* 2:263, and "Heroism" (*CW* 2:146); used also in Sermons I, II, IV, XXI, and XXXVIII.

5. William Lowndes (1782–1822), Republican representative from South Carolina. See *JMN* 4:38; used in Sermon CLXIV.

which it is so prone to fall and supply all the courtesy to the persons and reverence to the topics that is due to them.

We can all of us form high ideas of the value and pleasure of social intercourse. But how poor is our practice. He that should go from house to house should find what low, unprofitable and quarrelsome talking is degrading and embittering society. How ignorant! I would that men would consider that every injurious word we utter recoils on the head of him that utters it. In hot contention we are apt to forget ourselves. You were rudely assailed by him with whom you talk and you retaliate as sharply. But it is strange how entirely five minutes will sometimes change the complexion of a word. It appeared just now a fair retort, a frolicsome sally;—but now it appears a wanton and unfeeling taunt which you would give an estate to recall. I know there are sometimes outrages in conversation where indignation seems justifiable. Your feelings are wounded by unprovoked insult. But now, whilst your just anger trembles on your lips— Consider. Revenge is mine—I will repay, saith the lord[6]—Fear not then that the cause of justice shall suffer by your forbearance and the transgressor go free. If in that moment you will be firm and silent he cannot go unpunished. The laws of God's justice in the Universe will assert themselves. If you meekly abstain from taking your own vengeance when the opportunity offers, he will inflict it on himself. The recollection of his angry word will return to him by night, it will follow him by day. You shall see it in his altered, apologising demeanor whenever you meet him for months, for years. He feels the superiority, the divinity of forgiveness and bends with all external advantages, despite of himself, before your meek magnanimity. Thus you shall reform him but never by angry words.

The apostle in our text saith, If any man offend not in word the same is a perfect man. A great deal of good may be done in the world by good conversation, a great deal of harm by any other. We are all going to our homes to renew the conversation interrupted for a short space by the meditations of the sanctuary. Let us take heed to our words. God may have given to few or to none among us the power of wit or of eloquence but he has given to all the power to know the pure, the benevolent and the true from the impure, the selfish and the false. Let us think before we speak and speak as unto God as well as unto men.

6. Romans 12:19.

LIII

So then every one of us shall give
account of himself to God.

ROMANS 14:12

It is one of the great questions which the human intellect has proved incompetent to solve—to reconcile the free agency of man with our dependence on God. I suppose it must always puzzle the keenest perception, for the difficulties are of that nature that time can offer nothing new towards a solution of them. This is not to be wondered at, for as our minds are finite, there must somewhere be a boundary to our knowledge. And it is the wise remark of Paley that "true fortitude of understanding consists in not letting what we know to be disturbed by what we do not know."[1] Now, we know that we are free to all the purposes of moral accountability. The most intrepid teacher of the doctrine of necessity knows that man is in some sort free, and he cannot look upon the housebreaker or the pirate with the same feeling with which he regards a maniac who in his delirium has committed some act of violence. When we say that we are free we rest on a conviction that is too mighty for reason and must stand whether reason can sanction it or no. We feel in every action that we may forbear, that we are unquestioned masters of our own purposes.

Yet though God has indisputably given us liberty and doth in the arrangements of his Providence most carefully protect it, we ourselves can part with it. Our freedom is not like an entailed estate—a possession we cannot alienate. It is a very delicate and evanescent property—It will not belong to you without you go and take it—will not stay with you without you use it. At the same time our whole worth depends upon our freedom. A man is respectable only as far as his actions are his own.

If a man from fear or from the compulsion of the law gives up to you an estate, do you feel any gratitude to him as if he had bestowed it at his own instance? There have been actions that command applause of multitudes and

---

Manuscript dated October 24, 1829, at Chardon Street. Preached three times: October 25, 1829, at the Second Church, Boston; January 9, 1831, at the Second Church, Boston; October 29, 1837, in East Lexington.
1. See William Paley, *Natural Theology: or, Evidences of the Existence and Attributes of the Deity, Collected from the Appearances of Nature* (London, 1802), 6: "The consciousness of knowing little need not beget a distrust of that which he does know." Cf. *JMN* 6:37.

others that move indignation of men that when we come to look nearer and see the situation of the doer we find he was no more entitled to the praise or the blame than the actor on the stage is to be commended for the skill of his drama, or the strings of a viol for the harmony that is drawn from them.

All religion of course implies the doctrine of human liberty. All the commandments are addressed to free agents, or they would be but hollow brass and tinkling cymbal.[2] And so the Scriptures in many places preach this doctrine of a separate personal accountability with great solemnity. One of these passages is the text of our discourse. So then every one of us shall give account of himself to God. Each of us shall render account for himself. None can by any means redeem his brother,[3] nor will any intercession that is not founded upon and seconded by our own exertion, be of any avail. Let us spend a few moments upon this consideration, so agreeable to reason, as well as Scripture. Let us distinguish the virtue which is our own, from that which is a mere accommodation to the expectations of others. Let us consider the evil, that, if we are not watchful, may redound to our souls, out of some of heaven's choicest blessings.

In the course of events here a great deal takes place to endanger our freedom. Motives of great strength come in often on the side of good life which increase as the general influence of Christianity increases, and tend to produce a certain decent sluggish servant of God's commandments, but with the absence of all enthusiasm and all the highest graces of character. Every outward influence that acted upon a man must be taken into the account and goes so far to diminish the praise of his virtue or the condemnation of his vice, in the eye of God.

This tends to the peace of mankind as it is one barrier against the vast force of sin which threatens sometimes the being of society.

I know, there remains evil enough at the best. There is no situation in human life to which temptations do not swarm. Wherever God bestows the gift of intelligence and the power of becoming happy the evil angels come in with allurements to lead him astray. "As soon as there is life there is danger."[4] Yet it cannot be doubted that some circumstances are very much more favourable than others to a good life, by the barriers they raise against the common vices, barriers independent of the moral principle of the man. There is the greatest difference between the degree of exposure of the young person born of good parents in frugal competence and receiving a good education—and the young person who grows up a neglected orphan in the midst of vicious associates.

And the merit of their goodness is proportionate. If the last withstand successfully the disadvantages of his fortune and practise the rules of rigid virtue, he will be contemplated with a respect the other will not obtain, for his virtue has been tried, is proved to be of a robust constitution, is felt to be his own—free—underived. The same difference of peril to conscience may be remarked in different callings and different habitations. One profession is safer than

2. I Corinthians 13:1.
3. Psalms 49:7.
4. Madame de Staël, Germany (New York, 1814), 2:315; cf. JMN 6:37.

another—one town than another or the country than the city life. One guards a man from great crimes much more than another—does not shut out temptation, that is impossible—but confines the soul to another kind of trial.—Now the danger is that the goodness in any of us, which is practised out of compliance with circumstances, should be regarded with complacency as superseding the necessity of exertion by entitling us already to God's regard. Whereas the fact is that it only raises the standard of virtue by which we must be tried, increases the claim on us.

Our social life in its very constitution, by the very blessings it bestows, is unfavourable to this independence of character. It makes the men and women of imitation. A man praises what he is expected to praise and does what he is expected to do. It needs great energy which must be bottomed on very strong perceptions of truth and falsehood, to run against the direct stream of every body's sympathies. We subscribe to popular charities. We praise popular men. We assent to prevalent political opinions and adopt the public modes of thinking of right and wrong out of servile compliment to the judgment of others without reflecting that the appeal always lies from this decree to the sovereign tribunal of conscience—without remembering that the public is not to render up an account, but the individual must; not society but each man is forming the character of heaven or of hell.

When we analyze the actions we see, we can't but feel that a great part of the moral rectitude that keeps society sweet, springs from mere propriety. Young men and young women do or forbear many things in a virtuous way, not with direct reference to conscience but to opinion. *Not to give offence* is the ruling motive. And it happens that the only way to give offence to nobody, is to do right.[5] And so from lower motives, a respect for virtue prevails.

Now virtuous conduct is so infinitely important to us that we feel it to be matter of devout gratitude when it can be strengthened by whatever means. It is God's mercy not to be slighted when he puts us in circumstances favorable to it, when the force of habit can be brought to its aid, or any succour is given to the actions essential to the well being of man. Such is our constitution that virtuous practice from whatever motive will probably lead to its practice from good motive. Yet compared with the original virtue that shines by its own light this borrowed, reflected goodness is but a dim and waning ray. God has appointed our birth in New England and so we have not the licentiousness of London or Paris.

If this is all, do we not bury our ten talents in the ground?[6] The merit of all action is measured by the principle. And that life is defective that is governed by any less than the highest. It is well surely that our hands are not red with blood—that we are innocent of gross offence, but we ought to be virtuous, we ought to be aware that we are not tried by the same law as those of lower

5. "the only . . . right": used in Sermon LV; see n. 6.
6. Cf. Matthew 25:14–30.

advantages, that we are not enough to be innocent; that each of us, in our several professions and families, should be fountains of good principle to all around,—and not that we should carry our little urn to others to be filled, and to be filled according to their own contents whether sweet or bitter waters. If our virtue is wholly derived, it is plain that we are liable to failure in the failure of others. It is good that for all the tendency of our social institutions to virtue, yet we feel how poor and worthless is the interested, tributary, obsequious virtue of the mere partisan who is good because his sect are so, or of the fashionist who goes to church because well bred people do, compared with the athletic virtue that grows up nursed by temptation, self existent, self-consulting, a tower of strength equal to the shock of great emergences. This is indeed its peculiar property—only virtue is free, absolute, selfexistent.

When I consider the additional life and force that comes to a human soul by every virtuous action; by every new conquest it makes over itself; when I consider the strong sense of union with God, and, flowing therefrom the clear perception of their own immortality which the most virtuous men from age to age have expressed,—it seems to me that immortal life consists in the acquisition of virtue; that God is not alone self existent, but that every mind that he has made which feels the dignity of a free being and on the ground of its own convictions adopts this law of God's action, thereby becomes a sharer of his own eternal nature and thus hath the principles of its own life within itself. It is surely a grand view of human nature which has been more distinctly understood in our own time that in proportion as a man becomes good he becomes conscious of his own eternity, and needs no revelation to complete his assurance.

This is the sense of the language of our Lord, that he would give living water of which if a man would drink he should never thirst but it should be in him a well of water springing up unto eternal life,[7] this the sense in which he said, If thou wilt enter into life keep the commandment and when he declared to Mary at the tomb of Lazarus, I am the resurrection and the *life*.[8] Immortal life does not consist in a more enduring frame, in a heart that beats unceasingly and freedom from disease but in fulfilling as Jesus did in his place the whole will of God in ours; in the transferring of the whole being from self to God, and to the whole creation, which is God's, and so making the eternity of truth and justice and love, our own.

Brethren, through the blessing of God we live at a time when all classes of men seem more affected than heretofore with the spirit of Christianity. True interpretations of the Scripture have currency. Good institutions flourish. The children come to the Sunday School. The mature have found out the value of Libraries. Scientific institutions are opened—Men go to and fro and knowledge is increased[9]—Public charities are multiplied and a portion of aid is

7. John 4:14.
8. Matthew 19:17 and John 11:25.
9. Cf. Daniel 12:4 and *JMN* 6:61.

expected from every man to the cause of goodness and truth. Now let not this good be an occasion to us of evil. Let us not because the world is good feel that we may trust public principle to be the guide or the measure of our own. This degree of general goodness is the achievement of numberless efforts and sacrifices and prayers of Christians now departed to God. But it is only a *degree,* and it calls upon you for incessant diligence, to stop every retrograde motion and to urge it onward. First and chiefly among your obligations God has committed to you the care of your own soul, a stake of immense worth, and exposed to innumerable dangers. Be not satisfied to have your little bark towed by the great fleet of the state as you sail in sunshine because the waters are smooth and all are going the same way. But imitate the wise pilot who takes his helm into his own hand and sets his own sail and studies the variation of the needle, and the revolutions of the stars to guide his course, that he may be equal to his duty, when the convoy is parted, and the storm arises, when he is left alone amid the rocks and currents of the pathless sea. In the frivolous idleness in which time is apt to be spent let us remember that a solemn judgment shall number our hours.

Let us not be content with this precious endowment of faculties to eat and drink, to go out and come in year after year till the smooth cheek is seamed with age without ever putting the most of them to any sort of use, not marking your existence by a single original trace—the tame creature of society making a compliment when others look for it, and committing a sin when others look for it, altogether unmindful of God's care and God's provisions for you in this life and in the future, unmindful of the hosts of examples that beckon you onward, forgetful of the love of Christ, and his doctrine and his Cross.

Let us feel that it is high time that we awake out of sleep.[10] That we be not mere spectators of the play of Providence but fellow workers in it. Let us conduct life on a system. No man knows till he has tried how much knowledge or how much action he can crowd into an hour or to what heavenly heights he can carry this low interrupted and uncertain being. The paths of virtue and opportunity are many and infinite. To each is his own course. Go forth with new resolution on your way and the awful bar of judgment that rises before you shall become bright with beams of everlasting glory.

10. Romans 13:11.

LIV

Can the Ethiopian change his skin, or the leopard his spots? Then may ye also do good, that are accustomed to do evil.

JEREMIAH 13:23

I propose to invite your attention to some reflexions upon the force of Habit. It is so prominent a law of human nature, and the passage of every day furnishes us with so many striking illustrations of it, that it is familiar to all. But the triteness of such topics is no reason why they should be excluded from their turn in our meditations. We come to church that we may live better at home, and the homeliest facts are therefore best entitled to our attention.

In that which we call Habit, our identity and our power of improvement seem to reside. To describe our habits, is to describe ourselves. "A man" has been called "a bundle of habits."[1] Suppose we were otherwise constituted. If every morrow we should wake up without any increased facility to our duty from today's efforts; if we should find it as hard to fix the attention on what we have been doing all day, as if we had never attempted it before; if we recognized the face of a man, or a new fact no better the tenth time, than the second time it was presented—we should have sad cause enough to deplore our refractory nature, and must desist fatigued and unsuccessful from every experiment to increase our knowledge or our usefulness. We must give up in disgust all business, all study, all hope of strengthening affections, or reconciling aversions. All improvement, it is plain, would be at a stand, and man would lose his worth.

The powers of inanimate nature remain unchanged; the ice is no colder, and the fire no hotter, the magnet draws with the same force, the stone has no more tendency to fall, nor the vapour to ascend, than when Adam was sent into the Garden. But man is subject to another law. It is the well known property of

---

An earlier and later manuscript of this sermon were marked "Princeps" and "Palimpsest" respectively by Emerson. The earlier manuscript is dated November 6, 1829, but was apparently never delivered; the second manuscript carries the notation "Preached at Second Church Nov. 8, 1829"; the additional inscribed date of July 10, 1831, refers to its second delivery at the Second Church. The sermon was delivered in its revised form a total of five times, having also been given December 20, 1829, in Cambridge; September 19, 1830, in Concord, N. H.; and July 3, 1836, in East Lexington. The earlier version is given in the Textual and Manuscript Notes.

1. Not located.

intelligent being to repeat any action with less difficulty than to begin it; further, to do with ease the thousandth time that which was done with great pains the first; further, to do it with such steadily increasing torrent of will and power, as to require the greatest efforts to resist and change a course of action.

And herein resides the force of human beings. The world is full of illustrations of the advantage accruing from it. Go into the shop of the cunning artificer. See how dextrously he works; how swiftly he takes advantage of every little chance occurring in his task; how fast, and with what precision, the work goes on; and how finished and faultless is the result! We who look on could not have done it in years. Yet he has only the same limbs, and no more muscular activity, or power of mind than another. His apprentice can perform each single motion of the hand or foot, each impulse of the saw and the plane, as well as he. But the secret of his skill is in *Habit*. The incessant practice of the same movements, every day for twenty years, has given his hand a steadiness and speed which nothing else than the same use can bestow.

Take another example in the eminent scholar. Here are some of God's choicest gifts. Here is a quick and powerful attention, a strong memory, a wise judgment. This mind, if its circumstances and education had been different, would perhaps have taken delight in the marshalling of a battle or in the more complex combinations of a campaign. But to a more humane and noble life has God appointed it. From its earliest days it has been dedicated to a discipline of continuous thinking; to the examination and use of intellectual images to the labelling and ticketing (if I may borrow the expression) of thoughts; and the orderly distribution of them in the cells and warehouses of the Memory. And with what effect?

That solitary and reserved man hath a rich and peopled soul. Though he lives apart and hath acquaintance but with few men, the dwellers on all the face of the earth are familiar to him; he knows the fathers of every race. In the overgrown splendour of their empires, he can tell the mean original from which they sprang; the virtues and fortunes, the religion, the arts, laws, revolutions of each, he sees them all from where they lurk in their dark causes, to where they come in to take their place in the procession of events. Better than all this long chronology the peace and war of nations—to him is known the genesis of science, what have been in departed ages the beautiful entertainments of the human spirit; how it imagined; how it reasoned; how it concluded; how it soared to the idea of God, and what explanations it devised of human life. To this teeming soul of his, no fact is worthless—as it is to most men—every one hath an hundred sides and is related to facts he already possesses. Leave him alone, and he is society to himself. He cannot take part in the song of the musician, nor in the festivities of the men of pleasure; he cannot dig; he cannot bargain; he is fit for nothing else, but he is admirable in that one thing which he professeth.

This is but one instance of the power derived from Habit to the fine endowments of the human intellect. For this man perhaps was gifted by nature no more liberally than another—the companion of his childhood—who surpassed him at school but has all his days been so immersed in the details of a minute business that he finds himself unable to retain in his mind with any accuracy the political changes of his own state from year to year.

These are but two individuals selected out of a host of instances as large as the population of the globe. For every man is what he is, not by original creation, but by his way of living, that is, by his habits. We are in general very insensible to the infinite assistance life derives from this principle, it is so omnipresent. Thus in order to read a sentence in a book, it is necessary that the eye should successively see all the individual letters of every word. Yet, by use, the eye traverses them so rapidly, that a man becomes incredulous of this fact until it is recalled by seeing a child who has not this *use,* attempting the same thing.

The great doctrine of the Division of labor,—so well known as a law of Political Economy, rests wholly upon this principle, is an attempt to avail ourselves to the fullest amount of the power of habit. A nation is classed out into professions, and trades and subdivisions of trades, that all the skill and power which can result to all, from each hand doing incessantly but one thing, may be gained. Thus a thousand hands go to the manufacture of a lump of sugar.[2] And the advancement of every art seems to depend upon the carrying out yet farther, this distribution of its processes.

We may carry this analysis into all parts of life, and we shall find every where abundant proof of the great and continually increased accession of strength which we derive from simple repetition of the same acts. The first step was a vigorous effort; a later step is made without any effort. A still later step it is easier to make than to withhold. So the surgeon who could not see blood without fainting comes to perform the most critical (and, to the spectator, most hideous) operations of his art, with composed face and unerring hand. The seasick boy that a few months ago loathed his life in his first adventures on the ocean is now heedless of its awful dangers, and sings cheerily in the shrouds amid the bellowings of the storm. The veteran soldier of twenty campaigns thinks of his ration or some trifling mistake of discipline at the moment when the new recruit at his side turns pale at the spectacle of two hostile lines in the act of engaging,—or at the explosion of the Ordnance.

If there be in our constitution a principle of such strength, it behoves us to attend to it, to see if it touches our *moral* nature. We know that it does. All our experience shows us that it does enter into our moral nature with the same force as into the bodily or the intellectual action. It is no idle alarm, believe me, which we perceive in our breasts when now and then we hear a warning voice against the power of habit. This power *is* tremendous, and when it is corrupt, it is the strength of our nature arrayed against our good. The great God who made us, and gave us this proclivity or readiness to take and keep one direction with increasing momentum of action, has not seen fit in his wisdom, to guard it from abuse. He has left the door of abuse wide open.

2. *JMN* 6:18.

He gave us the principle, but left us the application of it. He gave us the power, like a blind giant to be our servant, to work with all his might for our comfort; to do our errands of benevolence in the earth; and to bring aid to our side in every fainting hour of conflict; but he left us free to make him our master, if we chuse, and to surrender the heaven born reason to lie in bondage to his brute force. Here he is, with his vigorous hands, equally ready for any work,—to traverse land and sea for knowledge, or to save and hoard and multiply wealth, or to go like an angel of mercy round the globe, scattering health, and truth, and comfort, or to fight with temptations at home, and uplift the standard of Heaven in the very tents of sensuality and selfishness;—or, to make life a curse to ourselves and others, by all the arts of wickedness. He will make or unmake, he will do good or destroy,—but some way he must work. He is of an industrious nature. Here he is in your house, and the harm he may do, is your own proper peril.

My friends, I speak in figure, (yet scarcely in figure) but the danger I speak of is real, and language can hardly represent its extent. I do not wish to affright you with the shadow of rare and uncertain evils. I will not even afflict you with the history of those two madmen of habit, the *miser* and the *drunkard;* let them pass now—though it is too bold to hope that there is nothing of that insanity among us. But I desire to warn you against risks that hourly besiege each one of us, and risks, that, as far as we can lift the veil of the future, threaten to affect us, from month to month, from year to year, yea, from age to age in our endless being. In the faith of Christ, in the faith of immortal life, I desire to warn you against the smallest taint of evil existing in you, *because, there are such things as habits*. I beseech you to consider that every action you do is either the beginning of a habit, or is part of a habit already existing. And the terror of this consideration lies in this fact, that we are not one thing, and our habits another, but that we are formed by them, and changed by them.

Men talk sometimes as if their nature was some solid and settled frame over which thoughts and feelings passed and repassed like pictures before the eye, without penetrating its substance, or disturbing its repose; as if the habits of years might be assumed or got rid of as indifferently, as the garments we wear. Is the nature of each of us so solid and stable? On the contrary nothing is more fluctuating. It changes from hour to hour. All our actions react on ourselves. Our power of action is the helm of our boat, and the least turn of the rudder turns the whole boat. We must beware of this mysterious nature of the human soul. It has this dangerous power of self-change, self accommodation to whatsoever we do. As in the fable of one of the heathen poets, the nymph who wept became a fountain, and the nymph who pined became an echo,—so, in the stern law of moral nature, we are always changing from what we are to what we wish to be, from what we are to what we do.[3]

Be not deceived. In this stream of life we are not immoveably moored to any bottom, and if we do wrong and don't succeed, we cannot come back to where

3. The stories of Arethusa and Echo are told in Books III and V of Ovid's *Metamorphoses*.

we were. That *where* is gone.4 For as all our powers grow by their own exercise, so they perish by disuse. As you follow new desires you are changed from what you were, and those powers that once you had, are *dead*. They do not exist; and what can you hope from them?

You own, your temper is apt to master you. Do you think because you are sure you was gentle in your youth, that you therefore have a warrant that you shall never reach that malignity that tempts a man to murder? You put your trust in perished affections. As well might the mariner sail for islands which the sea has long ago swallowed because he says they are put down in ancient charts.

They who do good become good, they who do evil become evil. You cannot recall the feelings of childhood and make them permanent now. No more can the bad man do right when he has vitiated all the springs of feeling and action. He has no eye to see the right, no fingers to feel it. The disease is universal in his frame, and he loves the vices which he practiseth.

Perhaps thus a good man may become a bad man by insensible departures, and (I shudder as I make the application) whilst yet society is sounding the praises of one of our acquaintance for the amiableness of his character, he has already ceased to deserve the praise and is rapidly declining on the road to malignity and lowest sensuality.5

Far be it from me, brethren, to exaggerate a danger that is great enough at the least. I do not forget that the goodness of God leads us to repentance,6 that the return from these dreadful descents is possible. O yes it is possible and therefore we preach the peril of habit and the duty of penitence. But the light which now streams upon you in the cheerful world of men, the voice of God's word, the misgivings of your mind in the prosecution of an evil course, the affectionate advice of your parent, the upbraiding eye of your friend, of your sister, of your brother,—these are the very strivings of the Spirit of God with you, which, in the melancholy words of the Scripture, "shall not always strive."7 The light is always becoming dimmer as you wander from it—the chance of your return is every day becoming less. We talk much of repentance but we seldom repent. Ten persist in a vice for one that quits it.

The main mischief as you must see that makes the dreadful interest of this inquiry is that Habit sears the Conscience itself—the danger lest the Conscience should cease to make a true report, so that our very compass becoming useless we should not know the way to right. But God has so far protected this his minister in the soul, that though, as we sin, it points to lower and lower degrees of right,—yet its divine instinct is never wholly subdued. It always points *from* Hell. It always points to a better than the worst course, and, if we will only follow its direction, it will continually acquire greater steadiness and greater truth.

4. "It has . . . gone": cf. *JMN* 3:167.
5. Compare the two preceding paragraphs with *JMN* 3:167-68.
6. Romans 2:4.
7. Genesis 6:3.

Brethren, the inference that flows from this survey of our nature is single and clear. *Beware of your habits.* In the conviction that they make us what we are, all our observation upon the subtlety of their inroads upon us, should make us vigilant and suspicious of ourselves. If we find ourselves skeptical of what we desire to believe,—perhaps that skepticism is a measure of our departure from truth. If we can tell a falsehood without shame—if we can please ourselves with taking an unjust advantage of our neighbor, if we can live useless or worse than useless in sloth and wantonness,—these things are fatal symptoms of our downward tendencies, and tomorrow we shall be worse than today. Or if yet good motives have not lost their power and you are restrained from gross vices—yet if you find yourself negligent of your connexion with your heavenly Father—and far removed in virtue from the virtue of the best men, from the men of God that have lived in the earth;—O mark that distance well, for every day and every moment by the laws of your nature is making it wider, and your chances of happiness and of safety less.

LV

*But thou, when thou prayest, enter into thy
closet, and when thou hast shut the door,
pray to thy Father, which is in secret,
and thy Father which seeth in secret,
shall reward thee openly.*

MATTHEW 6:6

The duties upon which the teachers of Christianity are most tempted to enlarge
are those which belong to the perfection of individual character. Our religion
takes the individual out of the mass and reminds him of the burden he must
bear alone.[1] It recommends the duties of self-command, of the connexion of the
soul with God;—it teaches that to each soul is its own destiny which is stript of
all connexions and friendships—the soul hath neither father nor mother nor
wife nor sister. Its relation to God, itself alone knoweth and no stranger of all
the vast family of intelligent being shall presume to intermeddle therein. All the
day of its goodness it seeth him. All the night of its vice it mourneth and tosseth
and lacketh his presence. We naturally dwell upon the dangers of society, upon
the contagion of evil example and of corrupt conversation.

But let it not be thought that the religion we strive earnestly but always
imperfectly to teach, is of so partial and oblique a vision as to overlook or to
disparage man's social nature. No religion could prove its claim to a divine
origin, which did not acknowledge the existence and provide for the good of
society which is surely of divine origin. And these relations are never forgotten
by our Lord and his apostles.

Nothing can be more shallow and shortsighted than unqualified declamations against society. It will not do for the poet even to pretend to live in
communion with nature only—for she is dumb and lifeless except as she
receives language from man. It is the voice of active intellectual society which
the recluse hears. It is only to obtain its purer enjoyments that he has removed
himself from its press. It is society, which he pretends to spurn, that has opened

---

Manuscript dated November 14, 1829, at Chardon Street. Preached twice: November 15, 1829, at
the Second Church, Boston, and April 9, 1837, at East Lexington.

1. Cf. Galatians 6:5.

his eyes to the charms of the woods and the hills. Take him at his word, cut off his intercourse and leave him alone for months and years—not in a preparation to return to the world,—but always to dwell by himself, and you reduce him to the condition and the complaints of a prisoner.

A very little consideration will satisfy us that all that to the common eye magnifies our idea of the power and dignity of the individual man depends on his state of union with his race. The power of each of us is increased or diminished with the power civil and intellectual of the nation to which we belong. If each of us lived in the world emperor of himself and his acre of ground without any social responsibility or league, the opinion of Solomon would be worth no more for its efficacy or its repute than the opinion of the fool.

But now by means of the social system, I am better for the wisdom of every one of my contemporaries. I partake of the increased well being of the community, which is promoted by every ray of genius and every spark of virtue which the obscurest individual contributes. So the distinctions of merit assert themselves with a wholesome and life-giving effect. Though not accurately or uniformly, yet there is throughout a general tendency to send the highest intellectual power to the highest civil place. And where genius does not nominally sway the sceptre of the state it very often does practically.

A man of uncommon endowments is thus taken from a narrow unprofitable position and made to mould the destinies of thousands and millions that wear another colour on the skin and live under another Zone. A striking illustration of the general advantage of which I speak may be seen in such a government as the British empire now extended over different parts of the globe. If a private person, the inhabitant of an obscure village, perhaps poor and wholly helpless himself is injured, by means of the institutions of society he can avail himself of moral and physical enginery that shall hunt the offender through the world, that shall search under the line or in the forests of Labrador or in the jungles of Bengal and bring him to justice wherever he lurks within the limits of the civilized world.[2]

Another eminent advantage which we owe to society is the facility with which by means of the press the thoughts of every man of genius are sent to all Christendom, as the lightning shineth out of one part of heaven even to another part of heaven.[3] Now this immense circulation that is thus given to individual powers of whatever kind, whether of learning, of art, of virtue, of practical improvement, is not only good as it brings *benefit* to each man's door, but also as it is an inducement to each man, to do the most and the best he can. Not to the great and ambitious alone, not to those who desire to write their names on the forehead of the age,[4] to make their private thought the preponderant opinion of their country, not to such alone is the perception of the vast power one man may wield, (through these arrangements of Providence,) an encourage-

2. Compare the two preceding paragraphs with *JMN* 3:168.
3. Luke 17:24.
4. Cf. *JMN* 6:20.

ment to strain their efforts more, to tax yet farther the resources of the fath-
omless mind, or to recommend themselves by yet higher unquestionable merits
to the greatest number of men,—not to these only, the sons of fame—does the
cheerful voice of society sound as an inducement to exertion, but to every son
and daughter in its ample fold do the domestic relations come home as a most
powerful spring of action. No man can bear the execrations of other men; nor
can any contemplate the sincere approbation of other men without desire.

> "Praise is the salt that seasons right in man
> And whets the appetite for moral good."[5]

Then the surest way to give cause of offence to nobody is to do right,[6] and 'tis
plain as the sun in heaven that this is the strongest foreign aid which God has
provided in the world to the cause of virtue.

This is but a sketch or rather allusion to the good of society which I must not
now enlarge.

Yet whilst we are thus knit together,[7] whilst we are thus obviously designed
to receive pleasure and excitement from our social ties—he would take a very
imperfect and injurious view of our nature who in his regard to the social
should overlook the personal duties, who should forget the great preeminent
unpartaken relation in which man stands to his Maker.

It seems to me a fact of much importance that whilst the mind explores and
acknowledges these blessings of social life that religion does yet command us to
remember that before God we are solitary unrelated men. When it has established the social law it confirms and defines it by an individual law. It said, 'It is
not good for man to be alone.'[8] It says also, 'Go into thy closet and shut thy
door.' These are not two laws but one. In order that thou mayest go into the
world, go into thy closet and sit with God. It seems true that no man is fit for
society who is not fit to stand alone. It seems that just in proportion to the
perfection of each man considered as an individual will be the excellence of the
society of which he is a part. But those who won't pass examination alone,
grow worse and not better for being overlooked in a host. For imperfections are
hid in a crowd, and the less can lean on the larger and there are many shadows
under which they lurk unobserved—and the wholesome fear of scrutiny and of
insecurity is taken away. Society is injurious to us if we are not sufficient to
ourselves; it becomes a pillow to our indolence; a mantle to cover our sins from
us.

It cannot be too strongly felt by us that every man whilst he ministers influence to all others, and receives in his turn influence from all,—is at the same
time absolutely imperially free. All other things are for him, and he is by the
necessity of his nature under God at the head of the creation. When I look at the

5. Edward Young, *Night Thoughts,* "Night VII," lines 419-20; see *JMN* 2:137 and 6:87.
6. See Sermon LIII, n. 5.
7. Colossians 2:2, 2:19.
8. Genesis 2:18.

rainbow, I find myself the centre of its arch. But so are you, and so is the man that beholds it a mile from both of us, and so is every beholder though they be hundreds of thousands. So also the globe is round, and every man stands at the top, and when he looks up at the firmament is himself under the centre of its azure dome, the king on his throne, and the menial in his stables no less.[9] It seems to me he should read there the solemn moral that by himself and alone he is accountable for all the good which the world has shown him. We should learn not to judge ourselves by the flattering comparison of our own with neighboring merits, and so make God's gift of society an apology for sin; but to measure our virtue by the unerring standard writ by his finger within, and confirmed by his word by Jesus Christ. In fine the sentiment I wish to urge is only this, Let a man make himself perfect without reference to the judgments of society, and then he is fit for society as a benefactor and an ornament.

Therefore let a man try his own spirit in retirement and solitude, that he may adjust his purposes by his own judgments, that he may give opportunity to his soul to think and express itself. Almost every man when he sits alone in his chamber with his book, hath sometimes had those searching glances at life that penetrated beneath the outward shows of things and gave him for a moment the truest estimate of wealth and fame and sensual pleasure, that for the moment he regarded them from that height from which angels and God regard them, and saw precisely how far they were objects of legitimate desire. By much sitting alone and the custom of thinking, these views will become habitual.

It would be of great service to us in the discharge of our social duties if we would be much alone, if we would make it not an accidental and irregular effort but an object of serious pursuit to increase our knowledge and to train in ourselves habits of continuous thought,—habits of religious meditation, that so we shall make our mind so rich that all things shall take somewhat of its nature. It shall colour all it looketh upon. This makes the peculiar dignity of the mind, that when it is elevated it makes its own place, it draws from society all its good and suffers from none of its evil. Let me offer a very obvious illustration of this remark. We go to church and suffer ourselves to depend for the profit we get there upon the accident whether the services shall be administered with ability or not. The taste of the times is grown fastidious, and if the preacher does not gratify the imagination or enlarge our conceptions of God, we go away unedified, unsatisfied, and possibly chagrined. My brethren, if the preacher was in fault so is the hearer. The mind that is in a religious frame, in a highly excited state—welcomes with delight every new truth which the reason or learning of the pulpit can bring to the cause of religion but it does not depend on them for its devotion. It hath fire on its own altar. It brings to church such cogent arguments of God's providence, such warm love to Him that it fills the house with fragrant piety, it gives fervor to prayer, enthusiasm to praise and sense to sermons.

And so it shall be with our minds in all the opportunities of life, in all our use

9. "whilst he ministers . . . less": cf. *JMN* 3:168.

of society. "A wise man," said Milton, "will make more use of an idle pamphlet, than a fool will do of sacred scripture."[10] And what improvement would come to society if every member were a finished man or a finished woman who had learned to obey God rather than men,[11]—I leave to your imagination.

Brethren, it is the confirmation of our faith that we see in this world the moral laws of God asserting themselves. And as in other things so in this. By the natural working of things a man's acquaintance becomes a measure of his merit. Every thing draws to its kind, wisdom to wisdom, and folly to idleness. And so I think there is a deep truth in the vulgar observation that "a man may be known by the company he keeps." If you permit yourself to be the slave of passion, and to suffer the bad example and lowest prejudices of society to make you easy in your sin and keep you down; you shall find they will confine you to the intimacy of such as you; of the frivolous, the worldly, perhaps the fraudulent, the debauchee, and the hypocrite. And just in proportion as by consulting yourself in solitary thought and worshipping with no veil to intercept between you and the Father of Spirits—you shall find your enlarging mind shall introduce you to those of similar condition—you shall find yourself surrounded by the pure in heart, and the wise, and the ardent laborers in the cause of charity and presently you shall pass in peace, as by natural progress, to the exalted society of the spiritual world.

10. Milton, *Areopagitica,* in *The Works of John Milton,* ed. F. A. Patterson (New York, 1931–1938), 4:315. See *JMN* 6:70.
11. Acts 5:29.

LVI

If our gospel be hid it is hid to them that are lost, in whom the God of this world hath blinded the eyes of them that believe not, lest the light of the glorious gospel of Christ who is the image of God should shine unto them.

II Corinthians 4:3–4

It cannot be disguised that there is a great deal of practical skepticism in the world. The warning voice of preachers has ever dwelled upon the small number of the saved. And ask any man of high principle how many persons of his acquaintance in whose integrity he implicitly confides as beyond suspicion, and he will not count far without hesitation. What does this amount to? It amounts to this: that the majority of men have not a faith sufficiently lively in the truths of religion to overcome the clamorous importunity of present interests. It is not that a man does not believe that it would be better in his own eye and that of others to lose his own property than to possess himself unfairly of his neighbor's, but the evil consequences of a fraud are so obscure and contingent, and the advantages are near and plain, and so he runs the risk and enjoys the certainty on penalty of an uncertainty. Now no man acts against his sense of duty without being desirous of a good excuse, and so every such man catches at whatever suggestion affords any colour to conduct which himself condemns. Most men learn to favour atheism as they cease to do right, both because it makes the best apology for their own way of living, and because it insults and wounds that system of action, and those persons whose principles are a standing reproach to their own.

I know most men do not trouble themselves to give any systematic account to themselves why they should act as they do; but go on to gratify their passions because they distinctly conceive certain advantages in so doing and do not distinctly conceive any equal advantage of being upright. But I apprehend there

Manuscript dated November 21, 1829, at Chardon Street. Preached three times: November 22, 1829, at the Second Church, Boston; March 6, 1831, at the Second Church; and February 12, 1837, in East Lexington.

are always some who are forced to throw some sop to the craving reason and as far as I can make it out from the lives and conversation of these persons, it is in this wise.

The occupation I pursue, the enjoyments I seek, are suited to this world in which I live; ample gratifications are here, for the passions I indulge, and so the life I lead, seems every way a life very suitable to the world I inhabit. I see no other world. I am assured of no other. If my maker, of whom you pretend to know a great deal, shall transfer me to another world, the same desire to suit myself to my condition, will there induce me to accommodate my action to the customs and tendencies and interests thereof. You say that the soul is immortal. Grant it be so. Why is it not reasonable to suppose that by the life I lead I am performing one part of the discipline of my powers, and when I come to another state, will do what is there to be done?

Now the answer that is to be made to this plea is twofold.

First; whilst the world around is suited to these evil courses of yours,—you do have assurance of another world which is not suited to them. Your soul is another world. That wonderful inmate of this body is full of desires and of powers that are strangers in the impure and crooked ways wherein you compel them to walk.

As long as you keep any reverence for the laws that are within—so long you cannot help walking in the light of a better world than society around you presents and feeling your sin rebuked by the whisper of thoughts from that inner kingdom.

In the second place the advantage which Religion procures is, when compared to the advantage of the man of this world, as is the whole to a small part. Every thing else than the way of life enjoined by Religion is an imperfect and partial exercise of the human powers. A Religion is a theory of human life. Every religion true or false professes to give an account of the origin, the duty, and the destiny of the human soul. And now I entreat you to consider attentively what it is at which true religion aims. It is not to guide you directly to happiness. In a general sense it does, but the distinction between religion and worldliness is that the latter aims directly at pleasure, and procures it too,—that is, the kind which it seeks, and religion teaches to contemn it. It candidly professes to walk in a narrow and difficult road. It does not promise you honours. It often receives them on its way, and always makes you worthiest of them, but this is accidental to it, and not the main design; and sometimes it covers you with present obloquy.

The precise object of a Religion I take to be this—*by exhibiting a true account of the soul and its relations to induce it to act in a manner agreeable to its whole nature.* It proposes to educate the soul, to bring out into full growth, part by part, every power and every capacity. The tendency of worldly life is to nourish and bring out only a part, only one branch, or one side. It is the effect of one exercise of the body to strengthen an arm, the lungs, or the feet. It is the object of one trade to supply one want. The smith gives his whole industry and ingenuity to the forging of anchors, the navigator to making the shortest voyage, the merchant to the securest bargain, the painter to the perfection of his forms, &c.

And in the soul, the tendency of common life is to exercise the active, or the persuasive, or the contemplative, or the social power alone, and so the event of death finds the soul qualified to be a very good *part* of the social system in which it has been dwelling, i.e., in the shop, in the town where it acted,—but a very bad *whole,* not at all qualified to an unit, to stand by itself. One power is pampered to monstrous disproportion, and all the rest are withered by neglect. This person was an excellent sailor, or merchant, or public officer, but a very imperfect man. Take this soul from the place and society of life and it will fall flat; its supporters are withdrawn. Now instead of this poor time-serving huckstering way of life, Religion proposes a more noble. It would give a generous care to the *whole.* It sees in man a nature too costly to be tampered with and it aims to rear the youthful citizen of the universe with a wise regard not to the particular places and pursuits where it chances to find it, but to the indications of a godlike strength and temper it observes. The dark risks that are to be met in the moment succeeding the event of death it prepares to encounter, not by the stock of merit acquired in the past, but, *by the actual condition of health, and power of self-preservation, into which its habits have brought the soul itself.*

Every body observes the fact that the same event affects different persons with the widest difference of force. A man is but a grown child, yet the petty disaster of a wound or a slight denial that vexes the child's heart all day does not disturb him when he is a man two minutes. Well now, Religion applies this illustration to the whole course of things here, in its effect upon the soul. The reason why the events of life are disagreeable to any is not a poison in the events themselves but is a childhood or want of strength in the soul. The tides of the world roll and the winds of fortune blow different and contrary ways in endless agitation, and the soul has not yet acquired the art of balancing itself and so is their sport. Like the young seabird unskilful to withstand the blast, it is driven before it, but by and by it will not only have the art to suit itself to the veering forces of sea and sky, but it will have a poise and a motion of its own. There are successive revelations which Religion makes to the Soul to inform it of its own wondrous nature which must be received by it before it is fully ready for its duty.

It is to learn that when the soul is true to itself, itself is by its relation to God *the greatest thing in the universe,*—and so never to stoop to a false shame, to feel that health, birth, gold, popularity, fashion, beauty are coins, are counters, whose varying value is always that which itself chuses to assign them. No more, no less. It may wither them to straws; it may swell them to worlds.

Another of these facts—I call them revelations from their importance, which perhaps it shall learn—is *that its own virtue is life,* and so to teach it to expel the fear of death. If the soul can die, it is only by contracting deadly sin;—the seed of death is sin. Virtue is immortal, unchangeable,—is of the very nature and substance of God Himself; and so that which is wholly virtuous lives as by God's life.

Another of these great lessons is that its happiness is wholly independent of what is outward, and is the proper fruit of its inward constitution and resources and so teaches it to cut off all its dependences, and to set up for itself—a solitary and eternal and independent agent. Without God we are nothing but with him we are all things.

It does indeed admit with awe and adoration a strict dependence upon God—but that relation shall hereafter become by virtue one of absorbing affection so that it is rather cooperation—fellow-working, as Paul says—than subjection.[1]

I do not know where this union of the soul with the Deity is expressed with more grandeur than in an enthusiastic expression of an ancient philosopher, "that the good man differs from God only in his duration."[2] Christianity has removed that difference in teaching the immortality of the soul; and Jesus accordingly teaches his disciples to *be one with him in the Father, and to be perfect as he is perfect.*[3]

Thus Religion provides for the good by the culture of the soul acting on the belief that this child of God will be seen as its powers are brought out to inherit the self-existence of its Sire.

I hope it will be seen that in this manner Religion has the advantage over every form of skepticism in the world. For if the darkest imagination of the atheist were true, if we came hither by chance, and should pass hence we know not whither—certainly in any event and with the most tremendous risks—it were best we should go most informed, most armed, most powerful into the dark of our fate.

Such is the claim of any form of religion to greater reasonableness than that Skepticism which, because there is no certainty of the future, snaps the chain of probabilities and lets all go.

I wish now to add a few words upon the excellence of Christianity when tried by this test. If the preparation of the soul be the design of a religion, and setting aside all but their internal claims, none can vie with the doctrines of Jesus, the very objections that have been urged against them being evidences of their fitness.

The humility and the charity that are taught in the New Testament, it is frequently urged, are too overstrained to be practicable. Sell all that thou hast, saith the Saviour, and give to the poor.[4] And who so smites the one cheek, turn to him the other also.[5] But if this religion is designed not simply as a police for the world in which we live, but for the culture of the soul—it is right it should not be pinned down to the limits of social prudence—but should go on to the reach of these prospective directions.

1. Emerson may have had in mind either II Corinthians 6:1 or Colossians 4:11.
2. "Bonus vir tempore tantum a Deo differt" [Emerson's note]. Seneca, "De Providentia," *Moral Essays,* trans. John W. Besore (London and New York, 1928), 1:6; used in Sermons CIV and CLXV, "Ethical Writers" (*EL* 1:359), and "Plutarch" (*W* 10:312).
3. Cf. John 17:21–23 and Matthew 5:48.
4. Luke 18:22; cf. Matthew 19:21 and Mark 10:21.
5. Cf. Luke 6:29 and Matthew 5:39.

Perhaps we condemn the sternness of these rules because we are not yet far enough Christians to see their divine truth. It does appear to the modern mind that a patience in bearing injuries that should literally fulfil this precept would be weakness and not virtue. Yet the life of many a martyr in the history of the Church will show us the sublimity of patience, "the unresistable might of weakness."[6] Wherever it flows from principle, wherever it is coupled with the scorn of death, the patience of injuries will never provoke contempt.

And he holds his goods in the spirit of Christian charity. He complies with the command "Sell all that thou hast" who holds his substance for the good of the human race; who so holds God's gifts as that if they go from him he shall not feel himself impoverished; and if they be multiplied he shall not grow idle and proud.

Brethren, I have attempted to exhibit the superior reasonableness of faith or a religious life over an irreligious life, in an aspect that seems to me very important, because it makes it the solemn duty of every man to lead this life, whether he has had opportunity to examine the evidences of revealed Religion or not. In a few years or days or hours each of us in his turn will be called to give up the ghost. A life of sensual enjoyment will give us no advantage in the grave. The possession of great wealth will give no more. Great bodily strength and infant weakness must share the same fate. There is only Virtue, only the acknowledgement of God and so the unceasing cultivation of the divine strength of the soul which can give one soul any advantage over another in that hour, or can at all create in it that calm and enlightened confidence which can meet that event with firmness and hope.

6. Milton, "Of Reformation in England," in *The Works of John Milton,* ed. F. A. Patterson, (New York, 1931–1938), 3:5. Used in "John Milton" (*EL* 1:156) and in *JMN* 5:505.

LVII

Bless the Lord o my soul and forget not all his benefits.

PSALMS 103:2

I congratulate you, my friends, on the return of this ancient anniversary. I am glad it is our privilege to celebrate a festival at once so natural and so singular. The civil authority of the country calls upon us to quit our business, to suspend the routine of common duties, and come together today with the deliberate purpose of considering our enjoyments, and referring them to their author. It is the pleasant duty of this day to throw the griefs we use to brood over, into the shade; to survey the sunny side of life; to look at the *beauty* of things we are accustomed to value only for their *use;* to own what God perceived, when he rested from the creation,—that the work was good.[1]

To this end, friends are assembled; families are called together; the father sees his children once more resume their place at his board; the brothers, whom years and engrossing affairs have long divorced from that inseparable union in which childhood bound them side by side, in school, and at play, and in their morning and evening prayer,—return for a season into that old familiar bond: sisters greet each other again and rejoice that the formation of new connexions has not weakened the dear tie of blood. The mystic chain of consanguinity which joins each individual to so many more in society, is explored again, each link is counted and brightened, and the strength of the whole increased in the strength of the parts.

This day the forsaken are visited, the forgotten are remembered. On such an occasion no face comes without interest to the domestic circle, but brings with it the memory of all its years, the recollection of all its blessings. Who is there, when men recount their enjoyments, who has not some success to relate, some past satisfaction, some secret joy, to add to the heap?

In this pure holiday, the coarse conflicts of interest for a moment are forgot; the all pervading voice of political animosity is felt to be unseasonable; a worthier feeling in man subdues for the time his malice, his avarice, and his ambition,

---

Manuscript dated November 25, 1829, at Chardon Street. Preached once, at the Thanksgiving Day services at the Second Church, Boston, November 26, 1829.

1. Genesis 1:31.

and an hour of good humor and charity and gratitude, is the last hour of the dying autumn.

Such is the feeling awakened by the light of this day through the hundreds of thousands of the people of New England. In this frame of mind, they go up to the house of God. The rational happiness of his children is pleasing to the Father of all men. The just enjoyment of his bounty is itself an act of praise.

Let us give ourselves up to the sweetness of this satisfaction. Let us collect in our memory the cheerful images of agreeable events. Let us indulge the eye with the pictures of hope. Let us not be shamed by the experience of past defeat out of our trust and exultation in the magnificent endowments of our nature. Let us not despair of the Commonwealth of man. Let us give the glory of our blessings where it is due. Let us justify our joy by our praise.

I apprehend, brethren, that a very superficial survey of our condition would satisfy us that he whose lot is least favoured amongst us, has cause enough to be grateful. Men are ungrateful, I believe, always from their ignorance. In most of our trials, the fault is not in the event but in man, that he is unhappy. The contrivances for happiness will amaze us if we will look for them.

Take only those advantages, to which, if he desire them, every member of civilized society has access. Consider the good of civilization, the good that no man reckons because it belongs to all. You live in the bosom of refinement, and forget that you enjoy it. Look out at the condition of near one half of your fellow men at this moment, and see where the scale of good inclines. Modern Science has been incredulous of the fabled patriarchal life of savage man, and has sent its missionaries across either ocean to visit those distant islands where the barbarous rudiments of society are still seen,—where still no knowledge is accumulated, or desired; no metals wrought; no institutions framed; no future explored; no revelation known. And what was the result? Did the sailor who circumnavigated the globe, who passed by all the abodes in which humanity is found, from the isles that spot the Southern Pacific to the cold latitudes of either pole,—did Byron, or Cook, or Mackenzie, or Humboldt fall in with any Elysian Fields, or any Fortunate Isles?[2] In the barren coasts of New Zealand, or Van Diemen's Land,[3] did the visitor find the solitary inhabitants respecters of mutual rights, hospitably introducing the stranger to the paternal tent of their chief; yielding to a pure and spiritual religion, the homage they denied to priestcraft; and was civilization really a contamination to the pure manners of the children of the isles?

Or was not all the terrible strength of civilization in request to defend its children from fraud or ferocity? Man had grown no wiser in the solitudes of the

2. Admiral John Byron (1723-1786), English explorer of Patagonia; Captain James Cook (1728-1779), English explorer of Hawaii and the Pacific; Sir Alexander Mackenzie (1764-1820), Scottish explorer of the Pacific Northwest; Baron Alexander von Humboldt (1769-1859), German scientist and explorer of South America and the Caribbean.

3. Former name of Tasmania.

Pacific. Mercy, and peace, and righteousness, and chastity were the strangers of another zone. The common brotherhood of the same race that keeps even beasts from devouring each other, was outraged by the cannibal.

These travellers went on a munificent message of knowledge and charity. They bore to the poor savage the arts and implements that were the overflowings of cultivation; they came back with a sad contradiction of the poetic visions of the golden age. They found that with the strong was violence, with the timid was deceit. They found that depravity was not the fruit of refinement, but was planted where ever the seed of man was sown.[4]

The result fell in with that noble doctrine of modern Politics that the moral character of a community is mended or relaxed with the greater or less security of property, and, that on the same security of property, civilization depends.[5]

Now consider a little in detail what vast advantages each of us owes to our social condition. Let any one truly consider it, he shall see. All the men in the civilized world are the manufacturers of my happiness. How little could I do of myself, and lo! how much I enjoy. I could not have builded a house, they have builded me towns. I could not in years have cleared a square mile of the ground around my dwelling, and they have felled the forests for me, and crossed the land with good roads, withersoever I would go; arched every river with a bridge; and lined the coast of the sea with floating castles spreading their impatient wings toward every region on earth.

I could not have found entertainment to please the hours of one month's solitude; they have made society for me, how various in its excellence! the wise, the beautiful, the witty, the inventive, the amusing, the singer, the orator, the artist.

How little could I have found out by myself of what was done out of my immediate neighborhood, and specially out of my own time, and so the wisdom of the dead and the purposes of the distant are expressed for me in books, or in newsprints, or in letters.

It is not much that each man wants for his particular share, yet a very little examination will show at what a cost of means and toil that little is procured. The labour of thousands on thousands is employed to provide the common household stuffs which every one of us finds at home. For the oil of my lamp they harpoon the whale in the cold seas of Greenland and Labrador. To procure me the convenience of a table a gang of woodmen are penetrating the unexplored forests of Yucatan and Honduras. A ship must sail a year to bring me a cup of tea, and the elephant is slain in Siam and the brooks of Brazil strained through a sieve, for the ivory and the gold, that adorn the common trinkets and instruments of daily use.—To furnish a single apartment, what lands have not been ransacked! The islands, the desart, the mountains,—the bowels of the earth, and the bottom of the sea, the edge of the precipice, every place of toil

4. "Modern Science . . . sown": cf. *JMN* 2:287–88.
5. *JMN* 2:288. Used in Sermon XII; see n. 14.

and danger has been searched for the utensils and food and ornaments which all can command.

For all these advantages of social life, for admission to this great theatre in which all nations play a part and all individuals contribute their mite,—what is the ticket of admission?—Why, no more labour, and in a great portion of instances not so much labour, as the Indian in our western wilderness pays for the few and wretched comforts which he can obtain. Every man pays his own labour at whatever rate it is valued, whether a dollar, ten, or a hundred dollars a day.

But all this power is the gift of God. Every art is the effect of the natural progress of the human mind in the way of truth. In exact proportion as the human mind attains knowledge, in the same proportion does its dominion over the material world advance. And every improvement reacts upon man the inventor to refine refinement, and add to power.

Every day brings report of new facilities in the intercourse of men, whereby the difficulties that have encumbered centuries are removed, the distant is brought near, and the same effect is produced upon a nation as if all its powers were reduced into one half or one third the space of ground it occupies. It will be as if a square foot of ground would produce as much bread as an acre produced before.

But, my friends, these advantages which civilization gives us are but a part and a very small part of our genuine causes of gratitude. They are but the outside portal of the temple in which the soul worships. To these gorgeous shows of the world we are to be related but a little time. We shall sometime be superior to the need of them. They are great, but the soul is greater. And the time may come in its progress when all the arts on which the splendid structure of modern civilization rests shall seem in your soul's eye as the toy by which infant faculties were amused and exercised. The more intense the excitement that all the social arts can bestow on the mind, the wider does its prospect become of its own power and of the works it can achieve. "Truth," it has been said, "becomes power by domestication,"[6] and so every ingenuous mind will dwell with more delight on the increase of its knowledge than upon any other possession.

Is it not a cause of thanksgiving—the prosperity of the Sunday School; of the primary school; of the Lecture room; of the library; and the multiplication of these institutions whereby our city is becoming one wide Lyceum for the diffusion of useful knowledge?[7] Would you find cause of praise, then look within

6. Samuel Taylor Coleridge, *Biographia Literaria,* ed. W. J. Bate and J. Engell (Princeton, 1983), 1:85: "In energetic minds, truth soon changes by domestication into power." See *JMN* 6:35 and 191.

7. The American Sunday School Union was established in 1824. The beginnings of the lyceum in America are usually placed in late 1826, with the appearance of Josiah Holbrook's article proposing "associations for mutual instruction in the sciences" in the *American Journal of Education*. The first organized lyceum was established soon thereafter by Holbrook in Millbury, Mass.; the idea took hold in Boston, where, by late 1828, organizational meetings were being held under the chairmanship of Daniel Webster.

you at the powers of mind that seek this food. Go analyze the *imagination* compared with whose speed the lightning loitereth on his way[8]—Go study the secret of the *Memory,* and detect, if you can, its way of storing truth. Observe how life is a game of question and answer, of which all material objects suggest the first, and the soul is occupied in framing the replies. Go rejoice in the *affections* of the heart, which this day, as we have already noticed, find peculiar gratification, and which make the gratification of every day and of all being.

Then there are the blessings of which this holy place whither we are come up reminds us—the great confirmation of the conclusions and hopes of the human soul in regard to the future by the gospel of Christ. This is the supplement to all.

There are those to whom the boasted advances of Art are of little account. There are those who lie racked with pain, to whom external conveniences can give little pleasure. There are some who in the downfall of cherished hopes, in the bereavement of dear friends, have no relish for their good. It seems to them all vanity. There are some who are pinched with poverty—some frightened by impending dangers,—mortified by shame, torn with remorse, threatened with death. To all these, and who are they that are not included? the precious faith in an overruling Providence, and the vision of everlasting life which Jesus has opened to the soul, are reason of gratitude compared with which all other things are insignificant.

Come then, my friends, let us praise God that we are alive; that we are thus elevated in the scale of being; that he has enabled us to attain such a sovereignty by Art over the world where he has set us. Let us praise him yet more, for the great endowments of the Understanding. Let us praise him for the affections which bless us. Let us praise him for the revelation of his Son, for the example of Jesus. Let us praise him for the resurrection from the dead, and for the eternal life we have already begun. Let us thus praise him with our lips and in our hearts,—by giving as we have opportunity to the poor—by all the acts of a holy life.

8. *JMN* 6:48.

LVIII

*For where your treasure is
there will your heart be also.*

MATTHEW 6:21

The sermon on the mount is as remarkable for its simplicity as for its moral excellence. None can complain that its sense is abstruse. No disciple can regret that his master speaks in parables. It speaks to the most familiar relations and duties of human life in language of unquestionable authority and directness. Jesus seems to have sat on the mountain in Galilee, and to have availed himself, according to his usual practice, of the objects present to the eye, and the passing events; and to have drawn from them the moral he would teach his disciples. All the imagery is rural, and full of life. He beheld perhaps in the wide landscape the distant mountain towns, and he said a city that is set on a hill cannot be hid.[1] He saw the lilies whitening the meadows, and the birds flying over his head,—the trees loaded with different fruit and the husbandmen ploughing in the fields below, and he directed the attention of his audience naturally to these objects.[2] By our ignorance of these circumstances which guided his discourse we doubtless lose much of its eloquence. Perhaps the multitude heard from below the blast of a proclaiming trumpet, when he said, "When thou doest thine alms do not sound a trumpet as the hypocrites do in the streets."[3] For these transitions are very abrupt and so were likely to have been occasioned by accident. Such an one is the lesson in the text, "Lay not up for yourselves treasures upon earth."[4] Perhaps he alluded to recent events known to all, or perhaps to some occurrence at the moment. But whatever was the occasion, the sentiment is beautiful and true, and its own solemn interest may recommend it to our attention.

Where your treasure is there shall your heart be also. But what is the treasure concerning which this direction is given? The rich have flocks, and herds, houses, and land, and ships and money. The statesman hath his patronage and

---

Preached twice: November 29, 1829, at the Second Church, Boston, and again at the Second Church, May 1, 1831.
1. Matthew 5:14.
2. Matthew 6:28, 6:26, and 7:16.
3. Matthew 6:2.
4. Matthew 6:19. Emerson wrote: "Lay not up for yourselves &c."

his office. The renowned man has his fame. The artist his profession, the scholar his books. But all are not powerful, or rich, or renowned, or wise. A great many persons in every community are deprived by misfortune or disease, of all means of subsistence, and are pensioners on the bounty of the rest. A great many more only earn by their daily labor their daily subsistence and a few days' sickness in the year would make a serious subtraction from their comforts. Next to these, is the great bulk of every community, the mechanic, the merchant, the farmer, the professional man, the office holder, whose labour affords them from year to year an income which economy makes sufficient to meet their household cost, and the expense of the education of their children. But they have no fund beyond this, and every one is obliged to deny himself a great many more expenses than he indulges, in order to be at all beforehand with the year against any unlooked-for emergency.

The great part of mankind have no padlocked vault; no casket of gems or gold or silver have they to hide from thieves and preserve from rust.[5] What then is the treasure which man has in all circumstances, which he may dispose as he will, and so dispose as of his heart also?

The treasure to which the lesson of our Lord applies, the treasure which belongs to every man is—that object on which he bestows all his *labour,* in its widest sense, that is, all the use of his faculties. It is sometimes what was given, and sometimes what was acquired. It is the use of all the gifts with which God has endowed him of whatsoever description—whether genius, wit, birth, vigor of bone, goodnature, friends, courage or skill.

The wealth of the rich is not more his treasure than the learning of the scholar is his; the strength of the strong, the project of the sanguine, the beloved object of the lover, the praise of the poet, the wine of the drunkard, the children of the mother; the power of a king.

Truly then spake our Saviour that where was the treasure, should be the heart. It is a law of our nature which may be observed every where *that where we give our attention long and steadily we cannot help giving our affections too.* The power of Habit comes in here as everywhere to the aid of Reason, making what was difficult not only easy but pleasant, and the heart is imperceptibly lodged in the field of our exertion. If our labour, if the use of all our faculties is given to any matter, we feel as if therein we had wrapped up so much of our selves, and learn to rate it with a new value.

This is that excellent provision of God's Providence so often noticed that not what is of greatest intrinsic worth but what is most dearly bought is most highly prized. The attachment to home owes a great part of its strength to this fact. It is commonly observed that the Swiss and the Scotch are of all the nations of Europe most attached to their homes. And the lands of which they are thus overfond are the poorest and barrenest in Europe. The Swiss peasant has carried up the very soil of his little garden patch by basketsfull, and laid it down on

5. Matthew 6:20.

the bleak grey granite floor which was all Nature gave him. So the poor Lap-landers who were brought to the splendid cities of London and Paris grew homesick on being deprived of the nauseous food to which the frozen famine of their native shores has driven man, in those ends of the earth, and which the pains they are at to procure it has endeared to them. The fact is one in them all. They love what is little worth; and the reason is the same in all and is more extensive still. Things are valued by us as they represent to us our own exer-tions. Wherein men put their labor they put their love.

The final cause in this particular fact is obvious. It is a noble and observable part of that economy which is kept in God's works that not in rich soil or beautiful landscape alone, should the eye find delight, where temperate suns shine, and fertile soils extend;—then men would occupy only a scanty belt of the globe, and lose certain tendencies toward the development of lofty virtues that exist in rugged and difficult circumstances, but he has made man's affec-tions the pliant companions of every thing which offers any scope to his indus-try. Nothing so rude, so unclean, so untractable, but love can convert it into a source of pleasure.[6]

It is thus that the mother in her anxious watching, month after month, year by year, the wants of a diseased or crippled child,—comes to have the strongest attachment to that one of her offspring who most needs her care, and who seemed at first the least likely to obtain it.

Any one may see the importance of this principle as it becomes a motive to exertion—a mainspring of human enterprize. But it is obviously liable to abuse. It will give value to deformity as well as to symmetry. It may give value to vice as well as to virtue. And therefore the Divine Teacher declares the rule, Lay not up treasure on earth but lay up treasure in heaven.

But where is heaven? and how shall we lay up our labors there? Heaven is the spiritual world of the good. Heaven is not a place but the state of a holy mind. Heaven is purity of heart, for saith Jesus, "blessed are the pure in heart for they shall see God."[7] It is humility; for he said also, Blessed are the poor in spirit for theirs is the kingdom of heaven.[8] It is not even a registry of actions and events. It is merely the state of heart which they have induced. Therefore to lay up your treasure in heaven it needs not that you should go out of this world, or forbear the society, and quit the people or the works, or the interests thereof. Oh no; but in the midst of it, in the shock of all its interests in the tumult of events, amidst the allurements of pleasure, the temptations of trade, amidst all the delusions that mislead men and the hurry of affairs that confounds them—here in the capacities of your own soul is the kingdom of heaven to be found.[9]

It consists in making the right choice in all the alternatives that every day offers you. Your soul is one colony of that Holy Empire. The kingdom of

6. Compare the two preceding paragraphs with *JMN* 3:53.
7. Matthew 5:8.
8. Matthew 5:3.
9. Cf. Luke 17:21.

heaven is to be established in your soul by suppressing the rebellion of the passions, and by introducing therein the Law of the King of Heaven and Earth.

No, you need not go out of the earth. You are to lay up your treasure in the love of all that is truly lovely; in the veneration of all that is good; in the conversation of the wise; in the domestication within your own breast of all truth, in the dedication of your soul, as a chapel, whence prayer shall always rise to the King of Heaven; in the severities of self-command; in the benevolence of your feeling; in the good sense of your discourse; in the vigor of your services to your friends, and to all men. For, these things are incorruptible. From the mixed mass of this world's objects you are carefully to pluck out that which is eternal, and give your attention to making it yours. The reason that Christ gives for not laying up treasure here, is that moth, and rust, and thieves will deprive you of them. You are therefore to aim at getting things that are indestructible and unremoveable, and then you set time and chance, moth, and rust, and robber, at defiance. If a man accustomed to seek entertainment for his leisure hours in frivolous talk, having been made sensible of the robbery thus committed on himself, retires to his chamber, and, by perseverance, acquires the habit of being happy alone, by useful reading and patient reflexion,—he has done himself an eternal good, he has made a step towards heaven—because he has provided himself with an incorruptible pleasure, a pleasure whose means he can always command and a pleasure that refines and augments itself.

If any man has injured you and you by a strong effort not only abstain from retorting the ill office but succeed in keeping your temper so perfectly that you are occupied with pleasant thoughts and virtuous designs at the moment he imagines you rankling with spite—you have made a great step towards the kingdom of heaven. You have missed indeed revenge but you have made a great advance towards a perfect superiority to all injury. You have gone a great way towards securing your happiness forever. For if you do again as you have done in this instance, (and what can hinder?) of course you have extracted the venom from human malice. To become superior to these harms, what is it but to take so much evil out of the Universe? In losing your susceptibility to it, evil ceases to be evil to you.

Further, if a man accustomed to self-indulgence and self-seeking disposition, to a living to this world and a negligence of another, comes to perceive clearly the being of God, and his own relation to Him, and so as a dependent and disobedient child sets himself in earnest to the study of God—a study which is the most practical and of the strongest effect of any in the world,— that man is laying up a vast treasure in heaven, for he is supplying himself with motives and measures of action that can neither die nor change. He is opening to his spirit contemplations of inexhaustible richness and providing for his affections a Friend that shall fill their infinite desire.

Brethren, the conviction that this eternal treasury in which we are to deposit our good is not on high, or below, or afar, but here within our breasts,—that we carry within us these depths of enjoyment and of course the opposite capacities of woe, should startle us with fear and curiosity at the great practical secrets of happiness and power that sleep in our bosom. If the kingdom of heaven is there, so is the prison of Hell. Yet which of us has accustomed himself in his daily work to consider what a stake depends on his action? Let us fulfil the grace of God in our behalf. Let us explore all the happiness we can. And as long as we find the great law of the moral universe hold that every good deed is a step upward, let us mount day by day, hour by hour, deed by deed, and thought by thought to his presence. Our master whose precept we have been considering, confirmed the gracious words that proceeded out of his mouth by his sufferings and sacrifice. He poured out his costly blood, he laid up the treasure of his life in heaven. Let us go then to his spiritual feast; and whilst, at his command, and, as we believe, with his sympathy, and intercession, and presence, we eat the bread and drink the wine of his table, let us wisely consider the days that remain to us in life and lay them up for heaven.

LIX

Let us not be weary in well doing, for,
in due season we shall reap, if we faint not.

GALATIANS 6:9

It is a reflexion continually forced on the notice of thoughtful men how inadequate are the effects which we produce to the powers that are expended upon them. A man is a collection of faculties so wonderful and which are harmonized to each other and to the world with such divine art that we cannot enough praise the wisdom and goodness that formed him. But the life of man is a series of useless exertions, of disappointments, of pains.

There is a want of continuity in the labors of a man which makes them fail of any great effect. All the truths of Christianity fail of their use when only they are used as casual and temporary rules.

The Apostle therefore subjoins to his solemn instructions, And brethren, Let us not be weary in well doing for in due season we shall reap. In accordance with this sentiment I propose to offer a few remarks upon the value and obligation of Perseverance.

Many happy things are found or done by good fortune. I should rather say by the kindness of God. Such things are a gratuitous unpromised mercy if they are rightly used, but because they are not, they often prove real evils. But the earth and all that is therein are the assured rightful property of perseverance. They are promised to it by the written law and by the unwritten law of nature, the uniform experience of men.

By the energy that resides in the human Will all difficulty has been overcome. The face of the earth has been changed; her secret powers have been extorted from nature. I read with pleasure the following passage in the English moralist in speaking of works of art, "If a man were to compare the effect produced by a

---

Two manuscripts of Sermon LIX exist, the earlier one marked "Princeps Ed." and a revision marked "Palimpsest." It is likely that the undated earlier version was delivered on December 13, 1829, at the Second Church, Boston, since the first page carries hymn and scripture citations. The revision was most probably done for the second delivery, June 27, 1830, at the Harvard College Chapel. Subsequent deliveries occurred September 12 at the Purchase Street Church; September 19 in Concord, N.H.; April 3, 1831, at the Second Church; and July 3, 1836, in East Lexington. For the last delivery, Emerson wrote a new introduction. In all, Emerson delivered the sermon six times. The earlier version is given in the Textual and Manuscript Notes. The sermon elaborates a journal entry for December 7, 1829 (*JMN* 3:169).

102

single stroke of the pickaxe, or one impression of the spade, in construction, with the general design and the last result, he would be overwhelmed with a sense of their disproportion. But these petty operations incessantly repeated in time surmount the greatest obstacles, and mountains are levelled, and oceans bounded, by the slender force of human beings."[1]

But this is but a faint type of the changes produced by the same power upon the *mind*. It is led forth from ignorance and fear and sin to the heights of wisdom and power and virtue. By the changes within it, it produces corresponding changes on all without. It changes the face of all events, and the relations of all other minds to itself. It learns to draw good out of seeming evil; to convert the darkest adversity into the richest prosperity; and from being the slave of all things, to command all things by commanding itself.

In proportion to the value of peserverance is the difficulty that impedes it. It is easy to begin. There is no good object which men will not undertake with alacrity. The imagination always decorates what is new with agreeable colours. The child is not more absorbed in undoubting delight at his new toy or dress or book or playfellow than the man in his new project of business or the community in the last public enterprize. If it is an illusion, it seems to come from the benevolence of the Deity, the charm in which we can always invest from earliest childhood down to tottering age, whatsoever is untried. And thus enterprize and labour are forever reanimated. But to a man who has no fixedness of purpose this provision has a baneful influence.

The world is always soliciting us with the attractions of every novelty. Whatever we are doing is condemned in an undisciplined imagination in comparision with what we might be doing in stead.

The lavish waste of life, from this cause, the utter shipwreck that is made of the richest powers God has given the conscience to keep, and the miserable insignificance to which the whole life of great numbers of men seems to end, give this subject an importance that cannot be overstated. I am not dealing, brethren, with imaginary cases. The life of the great majority of men is a heap of beginnings.[2] Cast your eyes around you and you shall remember too many instances where the confidence that powers exist is attended with the acknowledged inability to command their prosecution of any useful end. We are not masters of our faculties. We coax our powers instead of commanding their service. In common conversation we admit almost without shame because the disgrace is shared by so many, that we are one and our faculties another. We are cautious of pledging them to any good work within their competence, lest they should recoil from it. We say I am afraid to promise thus and so, lest I should not feel disposed to such exertions. And so we are content to pass along from one stage of mediocrity to another in a perpetual childhood of the morals and the intellect not so much endowed as coupled with powers which we can only

1. Samuel Johnson, *The Rambler*, ed. W. J. Bate and Albrecht B. Strauss (New Haven, 1969), No. 43, 1:235. Used in "Ethical Writers" (*EL* 1:369).
2. Used in "Old Age" (*W* 7:328).

occasionally use, ignorant amidst the riches of all experience; slothful and unhappy where the world that is present, and the world to come, are the prize of action. (He that will not command himself must serve another. And what is more common than to see a mind of fine native endowments unable to disguise or shake off the tyranny of an inferior mind who possesses the single advantage over it of acting with the unity of an absolute will.)

Especially is this pusillanimity apparent in the religious history of men. What makes the interest which every one feels in religious truth, however inconsistent with his occasional gross acts of vice and with his daily life of unbelief? What but this, that there is not one of us who has not felt the sacred fire of the love of God—oh many a time kindling up within him, prompting him to all good practice and to a great many specific resolutions. Whilst the hour of good influences lasted, he resolved henceforth to lead a new life, to husband his time, to enter on new studies, to devote a portion of his exertions and means to the good of others. He resolved to abstain, to put a guard upon his tongue, to discipline his thoughts, to serve God, to honour and imitate Jesus. These designs were projected in a glow of piety, were celebrated in his soul with a solemn service of hopes and prayers. The spirit hath her thanksgivings and Sabbaths as well as the state and through all her faculties it kept holy day and conceived a deep joy in the perception of its own change and goodness. But after all this preparation what feeble effects! Something he did toward realizing his purpose, but it was a most unlucky time, some very unseasonable circumstances occurred; unusual temptation; strange interruption; unlooked for obstacles; and the good purpose was postponed and by and by forgotten.

Who is there among us that does not remember his defeats? Who that must not own himself the cause? Men of immoveable purpose are very rare. The world is full of effeminate, undetermined, inconstant persons who carry a cowardice in their bosoms that invites opposition. Here and there is a man of another temper, born for victory, because he persists in his purposes, who counts dangers the companions and allies of illustrious minds, who is strengthened by difficulty and obtains his ends.

My brethren, to all of us whom experience has made distrustful of our strength the Apostle says, Let us not be weary of well doing. And all the hope that remains for us in the future is in the heed we give to the admonition. The encouragements to Perseverance lie deep in our nature. They have connexion with all that is grand in our being.

Who knows the power of the human will? Only the term of life can limit its effects.

Suppose the life of a single man of practical mind to have been prolonged through the 6000 years of human history—is there any reason to doubt that he alone might have invented all the arts which now enrich the world? You do not know what any man, your neighbor, your brother, with whose thoughts you have been familiar for years, can perform. You do not know what yourself can do.

No man knows till he has tried how much he can accomplish—nor then—how much more, if he had not ceased from trying. (Never to give over is the whole secret of success.) No man can say—"Thus far, no farther!" to the will of man.[3] And God doth not say it. We say no man can do what is impossible,—but who can see the limits of the possible, which hath no limits? The best facts in human history, those which the mind contemplates with the most intense pleasure, are the instances of the resistless force of the resolute mind when directed to just ends. To illustrate this force I might call your attention to the exploits of perseverance in the past, or to the far greater effects that yet lie wrapped up in the powers of men. I might satisfy the cautious of the advantage of perseverance because it harvests all its least gains, and the prudent know well that life and happiness are made up of little parts.[4]

I might win the greedy by showing them that there is scarce any thing in life so insignificant but it contains the seed of greatest results; that "most poor matters point to rich ends,"[5] but that the chief advantages do not show themselves at the beginning, and those only who persist can ever know what is most worth seeking after.

I might gain the philosopher by reminding him that in God's Providence every thing has its price, that small advantages are easily procured but the treasures of nature are hid in the mountain ribs of difficulty, in the secrecy of time, and months and years and counsel and labor must dig for them. Thus if a man is oppressed with adversity,—a jest, a cup of wine, a scene of public amusement are cheap means of momentary relief; but a habit of patience founded on religious principle, which is the perfect medicine, he cannot procure in an hour or a day. It will cost thought and strife and mortification and prayer.

But there is one view of this subject so commanding that I think no one can apply it to his own condition and prospects without emotion. It is the view of the power simply existing in the mind.

God has imparted that power—let me rather say that portion of Himself—to the virtuous man, that whilst he perseveres he cannot be subdued. But it is not only to endure that we have force but also to act. Every thing which it conceives possible the upright mind can do. I do not forget, brethren, the endless obstacles, the small means a single human being can command, or his precarious health or his short and uncertain life. If from all or any of these he fail and grow faint-hearted, the fault is in himself and not in events. But in due season we shall reap, if we faint not. Small obstacles will bend and conform to great purposes. I say that to any really great and virtuous end the human will is invincible, not to man's eye which sees a little but to the eye of God, which sees all. For, if it be rightly considered, it is evident, that every great action is done first in the mind, before it is done to the eye. Action is only the realizing of the thought. The

3. Cf. Job 38:11.
4. Used in "Introductory" (Human Culture Series, *EL* 2:221).
5. Shakespeare, *The Tempest*, III, i, 3–4. See *JMN* 2:268; 3:75, n. 47; 6:26; and 6:80.

invention of a new machine was perfect in the mind of the inventor before it was realized in his model of wood or brass. The poem was in the soul of the poet before it was written on paper. The battle of the American Revolution was won in the hearts of our patriots long before the tardy march of events had closed the war.[6] Shall I ascend to a high moral instance, the highest the history of the earth can furnish? The Crucifixion was met and endured and triumphed over in the garden, and the morning of the Resurrection had dawned on the spirit of the Saviour, before yet the traitor Judas had betrayed him to his murderers.

Whensoever a virtuous mind hath fixed its eye steadfastly upon a great object and hath thoroughly understood the difficulties and hath laid its means even with them and hath warmed its own energies to that degree that in itself it hath bridged over the gulf between it and the object and has fully satisfied itself that the object is practicable to it—then and there the victory is won, though it should please God to interrupt the execution by paralyzing its energies and striking that mind out of being.

It is more important that these victories should be won by the mind than that the events should turn up as we desire. It was a just illustration by which the ancient philosophers represented life as a game of skill played for a trifling stake. No matter whether you lose or gain the stake the whole merit lies in playing well. God has placed the soul in the world in the midst of many opportunities of usefulness. By all its right action it generates a certain amount of power which it applies to the objects with which here it is conversant. These objects perish but the power in the soul survives and will soon be called forth to new and nobler uses in heaven.

It remains to state the limit and the exception to the force of Perseverance which have been already intimated in the foregoing remarks.

This prowess which God has given or permitted us to attain, is not promised to all action, but only to virtuous action. The command in our text is Be not weary of *well* doing, for in due season we shall reap if we faint not.

It should be considered that there are two conditions required to make the perfection of an intelligent being, one that all its powers should be subject to the one executive will; the other that the will itself should own the sovereignty of moral principles. Unless the Will is the servant of God, it were better that the powers of the man were not servants of his Will. There are in society what are called self willed men, headstrong persons that are always bent on impracticable objects, who always stand in their own light and whose whole career is a series of defeats. And so all vicious desires are baulked of their expected gratifications. All error, all vice is unnatural and things fight against it; the interests of other men fight against every man's Vice. It has the seeds of strife and defeat within itself. But all virtue is natural; it is in harmony with all things. All men are by nature its well-wishers and helpers; things seen and unseen work with it,

6. See John Adams, letter of February 13, 1818, to Hezekiah Niles, in *The Works of John Adams,* ed. Charles Francis Adams (Boston, 1856), 10:282. Cf. *JMN* 3:168.

and so besides its own might, it hath the might of earth and heaven to reinforce it. It was the perception of this truth which prompted the exulting sentiment of Paul—I can do all things through Christ which strengtheneth me.[7]

My friends, the days and months and years of our life are fast melting away from us and if we would save those that yet remain from being as unprofitable as so many of the past, let us learn this great and costly secret of spiritual strength. Let us put on that manly self command which shall conquer indolence and conquer pleasure and aim at nothing less than the highest good it can acquire. It is the summit of all greatness and it is within the conception and so within the reach of every mind down to the humblest of God's children. It is not the brilliant geniuses nor the men visited with occasional enthusiasm in religion who accomplish the greatest results, but it is the patient, advancing, indefatigable spirit that will not give an inch of ground, that repeats his trial to seven times and to seventy times seven that wins the highest place in God's kingdom.[8] Whatsoever thy hand findeth to do, do it with thy might[9]—And this immoveable purpose is thy might. Is it the search of truth, the discipline of your intellectual powers in which you are engaged? Teach your mind then to retain the subject of its examination in thorough disregard of the attractions of all other thoughts no matter how hopeless seems the search of truth, how long it eludes you, with a tenacity that relinquishes its being rather than its purpose. He that would conquer, must have the heart to fail a thousand times of success rather than once of his endeavour.

Has God set before you any opportunity of usefulness? Has he made any dependent on you for the comforts of life? Has he put it in your power to feed the soul, to fill it with knowledge, to train it up to virtue? Do you meet with discouragements? Are you called to make serious sacrifices? Be not weary in well doing. O do not decline the struggle which in his high providence he offers you.

It is your apprenticeship to great vocations of trust and power in God's moral universe. Choose well your objects and when you have chosen, persevere in their accomplishment. In due season you shall reap. Habit is the succour God sends in aid of Perseverance, that is he decrees that what you have done laboriously you shall do easily. And if the aid shall be long postponed, if success is deferred, yet abate not your efforts remembering that though God sees fit to honour goodness generally with signal success, yet the main advantage which he proposes from your exertions is in yourself; thereby you are educating immortal energies, an invincible soul that shall presently be admitted to the invisible world like an angel armed with all virtues and powers for eternal actions.

7. Philippians 4:13.
8. Cf. Matthew 18:22.
9. Ecclesiastes 9:10.

LX

But when the fulness of time was come,
God sent forth his son, made of a woman.

Galatians 4:4

The return of the venerable festival of Christmas recalls the mind to the special consideration of the event which this season commemorates. It doubtless owes much of the cheerful interest men feel in it to sympathy, and much to long usage and tradition. No warm heart but gains new fervor from the thought, that it mixes its own pleasure with the joy of Christendom, or that does not rejoice to remember that in the best part of the world the love of man has decorated this day for ages with all agreeable superstitions and all affectionate customs.

But independent of sympathy and time-honoured use, the occasion hath a moral interest of its own, and a good man would grieve if that were abated. We will not quarrel with the different regard which different men shall bestow on it. Every solemnity has a different import to almost every observer. Let it be so with this. Let it be reverenced with all sensual pomp in Rome; with all national pride and love in England and here with only a moral observance. That were indeed a joy to the lover of God. But see that ye do it. Do not carry your protestantism beyond the form. If you bereave religion of types, leave the things signified. If you take down the green boughs, do not forget the hope.[1] If you dispense with the feast, do not despise the joy. If you do not outwardly keep the Christmas, revere the Christ.

I press the claim of this occasion on your gratitude and joy because it is a permanent and perpetual reason for those feelings. The Christmas I would keep, is not peculiar to this season, or to one Church, but will be celebrated in every sober mind inasmuch as no man can think on the Nativity of Christ without referring to that event by the most natural association, all the blessings of which Jesus was the author or the means of communicating to men.

Manuscript dated December 26, 1829, at Chardon Street. Preached three times: December 27, 1829, at the Second Church, Boston; again at the Second Church, revised, on June 17, 1832; and finally, with a new introduction drawn from Sermon XIII, on December 25, 1836, in East Lexington. Since Emerson dated the second-delivery revisions and alluded to the third-delivery introduction in the Preaching Record, it has been possible to restore the text to its first-delivery form. All revisions are given in the Textual and Manuscript Notes.
   1. Decorating the church interior with evergreen boughs at Christmas was a common practice of Anglican churches in America.

In the multitude of topics which have equal pertinence to this subject I will select two, which refer to the *kind,* and to the *extent* of the advantage which accrues to the world from the manner of Christ's coming.

When the Word was made Flesh,[2] when the mind which was to contain and unfold by miracle and by doctrine the revelation of God was cloathed with a human form, was born of a Jewish woman, and sent out into the light of worldly life to have the sympathy and influence, the love and the hatred, the tears, infirmities, fear, and death of man, then, the inestimable advantage of a *personal* interest was imparted to the truth which he taught. The more this is considered, the more important will it appear. The relation of Christ to the Revelation, as its actor, and representative, and proof, is, as the relation of a fact to a theory. It is only a fact that puts skepticism at rest. The Indian prince scoffed at the traveller's story that in his country, water became solid in winter, until ice, produced by artificial means, was shown him. Men treated with contempt the idea of Columbus of crossing the unknown western waters in a common ship with common men, until he crossed it.

Not otherwise is it with the virtues of the soul. How vague and cold is our regard for patriotism, courage, purity, honesty, compared with our attachment to those qualities in the person of a friend. They are dead possibilities till they live in a soul. Who would care for an empty ship foundering in a tempest? It is the presence of breathing loving men therein that tortures us with interest in their danger. And they say in the arts that a landscape is imperfect without animals and men; so the infinite field of moral truth is a wearisome and barren immensity till it is peopled with examples.

Thus only can truth and virtue come to have the solidity of fact and thus only can it become the object of the affections.

Who knows how much is visionary and how much is practical in moral excellence until an example has been set? As the East Indian made himself merry at the thought of solid water and the contemporaries of Columbus with his project—not much otherwise do men in licentious times and licentious men in all times scoff at great virtues and believe there is no such thing as love of virtue for its own sake. What can convince them? Nothing but a living example. A man as they are, not enslaved, as they are, to vice.

Well now, apply these views to the goodness of God when he sent his gospel to men. He did not write it on the sky but he sent it by that man whom he had ordained. The lesson we were to learn was not taught by unaffecting and disputable aphorisms which came none knew whence, and were confirmed none knew by whose experience, but was to be read in the warm lines of present visible action, in a life where every deed was level with every word. The superiority of spiritual good to worldly pleasure was urged to poor men and rich men, by a man who *acted* with an utter indifference to pleasure. A Jewish peasant, the poor man's and the children's friend, who had not only no external dignity,

2. John 1:14.

but no house,[3] set his hand upon society, and changed the face of the world,—
for he lived as he taught. He said, he came from God, and there, before the eyes
of multitudes, he made blind men see, and the dead arise. He said, that, man
should never die,—and after he was dead he showed himself to his friends and
said Peace be with you.[4] And thus he made his powers sensible, and his divine
light a matter of biography.

And what has been the consequence? Why, what must necessarily result from
this power of God invested with the interest that belongs to a person? All that is
good in man has leaped with joy at his name. The ardent affections of good men
in all ages have clustered around him. On him human hope has clung. On Him
has its honor rested. Indeed that tendency of the affections to call what we love the
best,—to proceed from good will to love, from love to idolatry, has manifested
itself here, and the welcome which the human race gave to their moral Saviour,
has added to him titles of esteem and veneration till succeeding generations have
been led, in the extravagance of love, and in disregard of his own caution, to
confound the dignity of him that was sent, with that of him who sent him.[5]

This indeed is to be lamented, as the natural reaction has been, when the
falsehood of these ascriptions was perceived, that skeptical men have questioned the essential truth of the religion into which so much falsehood had
entered. Wisdom here as everywhere shuns the two extremes of skepticism and
bigotry, and yields an enlightened and hearty homage to the best Friend of
Mankind, and not eager to give more honor than is demanded, will not be
constrained to give less than is due. I will not leave this interest which we have
been considering in the character of the Saviour without remarking that there is
a practical good in cultivating it as far as we can. It is extremely favourable to
our own progress in virtue to carry always before us the reverend Image of his
mild but inflexible virtue, his spirit of trust and of prayer and of learning, to feel
in him that attachment we owe to a virtuous friend.

The second topic which I mention is that the advantages brought to men by
Jesus Christ are universal in their extent. The song of the angels proclaimed
good tidings of great joy to *all people*.[6] These things were done after the sublime way of Him that sendeth rain upon the just and upon the unjust.[7] It was
sent to the circumcised and to the uncircumcised, to the learned Greek and the
proud Roman, to the soft Asiatic, and the unlettered barbarian.[8] It was sent to
those who would receive it and to bless those who received it not. Look around
you, my brethren, and see how many in the world, in the multitude of affairs
and the provocations of appetite are absorbed in what is seen and temporal and
do not know to any practical purpose that a Son of God was ever born to press
the awful truth of the unseen and eternal upon mankind. They stop their ears to

3. See Isaiah 53:3 and Matthew 8:20.
4. John 20:21.
5. For "his own caution," see Mark 10:17–18.
6. Luke 2:10.
7. Matthew 5:45.
8. See Galatians 2:7–8 and Romans 1:14–15.

the music of his speech.[9] Yet to them, I say, it speaks peace. They catch something of the melody of those accents that echo now through the whole world. Who is there whom the faith of Christ hath not somehow benefitted? It is like God's good after the nature of God unconfined. It is like the light of the sun, and the balm of the air. It is by the light which the humanizing, civilizing, invigorating influences of Christianity have poured around every place where the human mind works, that the philosopher has found out the errors that deface Christianity and he has sought to turn its own arm against itself. The infidel who dwells in a Christian land owes to Christ that security and comfort and kindness of which he makes so bad an use. The unjust man, the bad neighbor, the faithless friend, the persecuting bigot, are sheltered from injury and retaliation by the precept of Jesus, "I say unto you, forgive your enemies. Pray for them that despitefully use you."[10] Thus has God comprehended within his mercy the Evil and unthankful, and all the institutions and all the effects of the gospel do plead as with a thousand tongues to their hearts and seek to reconcile them to God. It does not stop—it advances and shall advance by the same divine impulse from which first it came from nation to nation until the gracious promise is utterly fulfilled.

The memory of the just is blessed.[11] There is so much that is frivolous in our daily life, and so many temptations to spend our time and powers amiss that, it seems to me, a good mind will welcome every noble recollection as a relief and a stimulus to virtue. The character of any virtuous man who was faithful unto death,[12] is a missionary of hope and consolation to all the living. Much more efficacious to human nature is the life and death of its great Benefactor. When sometimes on a view of the majesty of nature, we are oppressed with a sense of our own insignificance, when the individual feels how small is his part of being, how short his term; when we consider all the cares and efforts which the decent support of life demands, all the crosses, and interruptions, and disasters, and sickness and sleep, which cut yet shorter the action of this span of existence;— when we think how little we accomplish that will give us any pleasure to remember hereafter, it may yet restore serenity to the soul, to reflect that the perfection of virtue and wisdom have dwelt in clay as short-lived and as suffering as our own, and that the outward circumstances of Jesus Christ were cast in a fashion at least as low and comfortless as ours. Yet the steps by which he surmounted his trials are such as we can take. God has put no obstacle between us, and his exaltation, which he has not given us power to remove. And above all, he that was born in Bethlehem, was born to announce to the soul that sinneth not, that when heaven and earth should pass away, it should endure whilst God endures, and pass from one degree of truth and virtue to another forever and forevermore.[13]

9. Cf. Acts 7:57.
10. Luke 6:27–28.
11. Proverbs 10:7.
12. Revelation 2:10.
13. Cf. Matthew 24:35, Mark 13:31, and Luke 21:33.

LXI

The night is far spent, the day is at hand,
let us therefore cast off the works of darkness
and let us put on the armor of light.

ROMANS 13:12

This night brings the year to a close. The planet on whose surface the Creator has placed us, is now finishing one more of its revolutions round the sun. One act more in the great labour of external Nature is concluded. The earth has fulfilled the round of its four seasons, has fed its population of animals from the worm up through fish, insect, bird, and beast, to man with another harvest, and cooled its zones with the breath of a new winter; and now the signs in heaven admonish us that the journey is ended and the goal is reached—that the vast orbit we traverse has been measured to its last etherial miles, that one verse more of the eternal song of the stars is sung, and that another year is added to the life of its inhabitants.

Be it so. What is there in this time to cause anxiety? God is great. Time is nothing to Him. Each moment his power is to his works a new creation. And so if the year is done a new year shall begin; the Earth is not weary and the sun is not dim. There is no need that this ship of the heavens which has floated us so far, should now stop after its mighty voyage to refit or refresh itself, but without cessation, without rest, away it shall go as a bird on its solitary and grand flight through 1500,000 miles in a day, bearing its precious freight through the deeps of space forever and ever.

True it is, that God is great, and his work shall not fail; but man is feeble and must die, and his life is measured by a few years. What is our life but a vapor?[1] Each of these revolutions of the earth shall thin this assembly now so full of life and thought. How many of us shall sleep forgotten before the next is completed! A still larger number of us shall have paid the common debt before the second. In ten years a fourth part of us will have died and in fifty or sixty years not one individual that breathes in this house shall breathe in the earth. The freshest cheek and the firmest frame must sink alike.

Manuscript dated December 31, 1829, at Chardon Street. Preached once, as the Evening Lecture, December 31, 1829, at the Second Church.
   1. James 4:14.

> "How loved how honoured once avails thee not
> To whom related, or by whom begot,
> A heap of dust is all remains of thee,
> 'Tis all thou art, and all the proud shall be."[2]

Oh then whatever duration belongs to the world we inhabit, if our term is so short it becomes us to mark its boundaries well, to gather up the fragments that nothing be lost,[3] and to pause on the limits of its periods and consider ourselves.

And now when individuals and towns and states are making up their audits, and calling their servants to account, it is well that the soul should make up her audit, and call her servants to account; should summon her faculties before her, and ask them rigorously what they have done; see how the performance tallies with the promise, the amount of effect with the amount of the means. It is fit we should come up to the house of God, and invoke all that is great in the greatness of the feeling. In breaking the silence so full of sense, I desire, brethren, only to convey to each heart the moral of the time. It is not to speak my own words that I have come, but to be, as nearly as I can, the tongue of the occasion and the Hour.

It is an Hour without flattery or fraud. It is that hour which to all men is honest and free spoken, and all the wit and guile and mirth that is in the world, cannot keep down the expression of its irresistible sense.

It hath truth and it will speak. Good humour cannot smooth it over, nor occupation divert, nor fashion fritter it away. He is more or less than man that is not made thoughtful by the last hour of the year. Sometimes a man will be perforce true to himself, and this is one of those times. The last hour of the year will show to every mind a different aspect. For it is, if I may call it so, the monumental hour. It looks backward to the past and collects its ashes. It shows to each mind the epitaph of its own departed year, writ with a pen of unerring truth, and we have come up to this house bearing in our breasts that solemn inscription. We labour with the feeling. The responsibility of time is too weighty for us.

It is meet then that we yield to this impulse and consider before God what we have done in the past year, and what it has done for us. A great deal it has done independent of our agency. The corn has grown when we have slept,[4] and the arts and institutions and perhaps the feelings of men have made a progress which we have not had power to hinder or promote. The dominion of man over matter is increased from day to day in which we all have an interest.[5] The great amount of knowledge that is already accumulated bears fruit daily in new disclosures of truth. Light has come into the world.[6] The sin or the ignorance of

2. Alexander Pope, "Elegy to the Memory of an Unfortunate Lady," lines 71–74. Cf. *JMN* 2:134.
3. John 6:12.
4. Cf. Mark 4:26–29.
5. Cf. Genesis 1:26.
6. John 3:19.

man has been visited with a great series of disasters in the commercial interests and many of us have suffered sorely from the blow without having to accuse ourselves as the cause.[7]

And so a thousand events, good and evil, have transpired. Friends have been taken from our side. The godly man ceaseth and the faithful fail from among the children of men.[8] He who was wont to stand where I stand, has been withdrawn from his duties and now sees the sun of this year of his trials set in a land far distant from the home of his fathers.[9] New connexions have been formed around us; or old connexions, from which we reaped affection and advantage, have been snapped asunder, or our own pleasant dwelling has been the house of pain; the children, the friends, that made the sinews of our strength, have gone down to the narrow house; or "the life that made our own life pleasant, is at an end." Or a yet darker, darker providence has filled our eyes with tears, and our hearts with desolation, when vice has crept into the hearts which we trusted; when the good principles of those on whom our souls staid themselves, have been poisoned; and a father has declined from his integrity; or a brother has been false to our bosom; or we have learned "how sharper than a serpent's tooth it is, to have a thankless child."[10]

These events came not from the dust, but were dispensations of that high providence that doth as it will in human affairs. And what belonged to us was to use them rightly. In success, not to impute it to our own right hand and be proud; nor to fortune and grow giddy; but to God and be thankful. In the general distribution of good and evil worldly gifts, to receive them with a reverent eye, that saw beyond them the Almighty Giver, with a boundless resignation to his Will.

But the year is gone to bear record in heaven not only of what it has done for you, but what you have accomplished. There are some whose souls spotted with sins who have abused this departing period to the devising and ripening and practice of schemes of fraud,—others, who have sinned against the law of Truth; have injured the reputation of good men; have spoken falsely to gain safety, or favour, or money; others, who have drunk deeply of the cup of sensual excess, who have sinned, and lie in wait to sin again; innocence their prey and virtue their bye word; and others who have listened to their malignant passions, have tyrannized over their families, have hated and cursed their neighbour and cannot thank themselves if their hands are not yet red with blood. Are there any

7. After the Erie Canal opened in 1825, New England experienced continual cycles of surge and decline in commercial activity. Land values fell as commodities from the West became cheaper and more abundantly available; westward migration increased; and the rise of manufacturing towns was accompanied by periods of overproduction. According to Walter B. Smith and Arthur H. Cole (*Fluctuations in American Business, 1790–1860* [Cambridge, Mass., 1935], 66), 1829 showed a distinct drop in commodity prices.

8. Psalms 12:1.

9. Henry Ware, Jr., had been in poor health since he collapsed in the summer of 1828. The following spring he embarked on a trip to Europe that was to last for nearly a year and a half.

10. Shakespeare, *King Lear*, I, iv, 310–11.

such amongst us, brethren? Does any part of this guilt sit heavy on the souls of any of us? To such I say, Beware of yourselves; there is terror in your nature if Revelation will not reach you. It has been the opinion of wisest men on a survey of the human mind that God had lodged a Judgment Seat therein, when he formed the Memory. It may be doubted whether the actions we think forgotten, are lost, or only latent. It may be questioned whether any thing that has once been in the soul is ever lost, that when the grossness of the body is gone every fact shall be found to live in the mind with its original distinctness, and so no shroud of time be suffered to come between us and our faults. And so though now you sleep undisturbed on a sinner's pillow and are already forgetting your own crimes, this year which is closing shall have its own resurrection. You shall see it return day after day, day after day and still new months of crime, new periods of wo settling down on your spirit.

But gross offenders are not often found: there is law and public justice for them. Children of this world! Children of sloth and luxury, what shall it say of you? Man of ease and pleasure who have made its moments soft! Have you had peaceful nights and prosperous days? Have you been richly clothed and have you dined delicately? Has every month brought you an increase of taste and skill in points of fashion and new accuracy in judging of the relish of meats and the flavor of wines? The better the worse. There are some things a good man would wish to be ignorant of. And have you indeed that sense of well-being which proceeds from feeding sweetly and fully? That is to say, is the part of God in your nature really become the servant to the part of beast in you? It was an ancient observation that the Belly hath no hearing,[11] and so it were vain when so short a part of a year is left to spend counsel upon you.

I know very well that the great number of those whom I address cannot reproach themselves with an idle year. You say you cannot charge your conscience with intemperate indulgence or with indolence. You have been diligent in your business. You have been up early, and late to bed. You have added something to your gains every week, something every day. Sunday is your only time of rest and hardly then for your thoughts. He that does not provide for his family, you hold worse than an infidel. The post office may tell of the extent of your correspondence. Your accounts shall speak for you, you have squandered nothing; have omitted no opportunity of lawful gain; and you have defrauded no man; it is all the fruit of fair industry—the watching of your eyes; the toiling of your brains; and the sweat of your brow.[12]

The mechanic points with confidence to the success of his labour; to the number of his works; and who can surpass their contrivances and finish? The merchant, to the extent of his speculations, to his loaded warehouses and his journeying ships. Another to the unknown difficulties of his professional duty,

11. Emerson may have found this in Seneca's "On the Renown Which My Writings Will Bring You." See *Seneca ad Lucilium Epistulae Morales*, trans. Richard M. Gummere (London, 1934), 1:148.

12. Cf. Genesis 3:19.

to the crowd of his clients, what heaps of facts has he not collected, what hidden
conclusions has he not brought to light? Another has travelled and sailed thousands of miles on the public business. Another has toiled at home. Another
points to the silent but indispensable advantages of her female exertions, the
exemplary order of domestic arrangements, or the decent livelihood how
hardly earned by activity and economy that have no cessation.

And this is the account that each of us shall render of his year—that we have
eaten bread of carefulness and earned and enjoyed our sleep[13]—that our
worldly substance has been increased, that we have pushed ourselves forward in
the world and drawn the eyes of men on us by our fame or success in earthly
affairs! And is this all?

Take heed to yourself my brother, my friend, it may be there is one in this
house who has lived more in an hour than you in this vast year of cares and
actions and pleasures. What is it in the eye of the great Father of all spirits, who
has lit this wretched clay with a spark of his own deity, that you have cared for
the ornament and comfort of this clay alone, and neglected *himself,* his spirit
within you?

He gave you the wondrous powers of the intellect, and he asks for their fruit.
He gave you the strong affections of the heart, and he asks for their exercise. He
gave you the powers of active benevolence and he looks to see your charities. He
gave you the strong perception of duty. He gave you the knowledge of himself
and the life of his Son and he looks to see your sacrifices, your piety, and your
prayers. O say not you are poor and low.

I take it for granted that there is not one who hears me, however high or low,
however limited in his advantages or faithful in their use, that might not be
better than he is—and that he can make no one good exertion in vain.

O consider, I beseech, how much you have lost, how deeply you have failed. I
do not appeal less to your reason, than to your feelings. Consider gravely and
sternly the energies that run to waste in your constitution. Consider the power
of the mind over time, that the great God has imparted to every soul that will
worship him somewhat of his own almightiness; that every ignorant and, much
more, every sinful human soul is an untilled soil that by cultivation would be
loaded with fruits of everlasting goodness, that every waking moment is an
empty urn which you can fill with treasures of love and wisdom.

Consider that you are capable of knowing the laws of the universe, of filling
by your own exertions that neglected thirsty soul with infinite draughts of
truth, that you are capable of doing as angels do, that here, in this low and
sinful world where you pass among your fellows either insignificant or disliked
by the most of them, you may go on your way crowned, through the Energy of
your own benevolence, with the dear love of all who know you, blessed by the
inmost wishes, those effectual prayers that are heard in heaven, that so you shall
make your moments live with all the holy delight of intellectual and religious

13. Cf. Ezekiel 12:19.

being, and so that virtue of God shall pass into you as a child of God that one day shall be to you as a thousand years.[14]

Brethren, Jesus Christ the Lord hath come out of the spiritual world to reveal to us the Eternity of the Soul. To the soul is no bounded time; to the soul which has accepted the light of the gospel with gratitude and united itself unto God is pardon promised, and life Everlasting. Something I trust this year has done to commend that truth to our hearts. Something to reconcile us to God.

And now, brethren, it rests with us to finish the year with its just conclusion. To many of us it is certainly the last; the lamp of our life is burning already in the socket. And so I hope we shall not separate without such sober attempts to make ourselves better as seem proper to the hour and which only the soul can do for itself. Now that so much time has gone, now, my friend, that God so long has sustained your life and fed you with bread, and lighted you with the cheerful sun and the stars, comforted you with social ties, instructed you with the voice of parents and friends and so much wisdom as is in the world—yea and saved you, if you will, by Jesus Christ,—now that one great period of your probation is drawn to an end—if tomorrow he shall send up the sun into the firmament to light you into a new period of his goodness and long-suffering,—will you go forth without one tribute laid upon his altar, without a resolution, without a prayer, without a blessing on his holy name?

This night is far spent, the day is at hand. The clock must strike the knell of a few more hours and the only redemption that it is yet in our power to make of a year not so well used as it should have been is to hallow its last moments by a pious vow, that shall hold us when it is gone; that shall save to virtue the time which yet it may please God to grant us, to save the Year whose air we have not yet breathed, whose inviolate hours as now they are spread all bright before you, it lies with you, to pollute or to bless.

14. II Peter 3:8.

LXII

Henceforth I call you not servants, for the
servant knoweth not what his Lord doeth;
but I have called you friends, for all
things that I have heard of my Father,
I have made known unto you.

JOHN 15:15

I believe, my Christian brethren, that no good man can read or hear these words without sincere satisfaction. For this language is not confined to the twelve disciples to whom it was first addressed, since Jesus has himself in the context extended its signification to all his church by declaring the conditions of his friendship. "Ye are my friends, if ye do whatsoever I command you."[1]

On the encouragement afforded me by these words, I am now going to speak of the reciprocal regard which they authorize us to feel and to express towards, I will not say the *memory,* but the character and the living spirit of the great Founder of the Christian Religion. I know that many minds are offended when expressions are made use of with any degree of confidence importing our love to Christ. It is Christ who loved us, they say, but any profession of warm regard on our part is reckoned by them not only unbecoming but the veriest presumption.

But is no such regard entertained by us or any of us? I would fain hope that after all those are set aside whom custom or frivolous reasons usually bring to Church there are many who engage in the exercises of Christian worship with an enlightened and sincere pleasure; that they have brought with them here and do habitually carry in their minds a lively affection like that borne to a venerated friend, yet exalted and peculiar in its strain, to Jesus. And if so, it seems to

---

Two manuscripts of Sermon LXII exist, an earlier, undated one, and a revised version dated January 16, 1830, at Chardon Street. The earlier version (given in the Textual and Manuscript Notes) was evidently delivered January 10, 1830, at the Second Church, Boston, and the revised version was prepared for the second delivery, January 17, at Beverly, Mass. This version was given again February 7, as an Evening Lecture at the South Congregational Church; September 24, as a Friday Lecture at the Second Church; and February 5, 1837, in East Lexington. In all, Emerson delivered the sermon five times.
    1. John 15:14.

me just and becoming not to shut it up in the breast, like a burdensome or sinful secret, but to give it the freest utterance. I judge it not proper to apologize for any language implying that feeling out of any unwillingness to disturb mistaken scruples, much less out of any fear of sneers at hypocrisy.

I wish rather to justify this boldness of access from his own lips, and not only so but to show that this confident affection flows necessarily from the natural feelings of every good mind when false religion has not put obstructions in the way. I think that we cannot help (if any goodness is in us) loving our religion and as we love it imbibing a sacred attachment to its author.

I am led to make these remarks because I am persuaded that not only do men generally rather respect than love religion, but it seems to me that very good men incline to a certain diffidence and a separation of their religious views from common feelings and the cheerful common speech of men, which is alien to the spirit of trust and deep and equal love which the character and professions of Jesus ought to inspire. As in the relations of earthly friendship civility will never be received as a return for love, so in heavenly things respect is a bad substitute for devotion. I am not now speaking to that hollow respect which is a mask for indifference or contempt, I speak of the feelings of truly religious minds when they worship with this averted countenance, which is dictated by a spirit of fear. Why is it so—whence this darkness? The relation of Christ to the soul of a good man is in itself sufficiently near and distinct; may be as clearly ascertained as that of any other friend absent from the flesh, and would awaken the same emotions had not those views which should most readily have grown up in the hearts of his followers, been chilled and repressed by the errors of the understanding. We hear his voice but it is harsh and stern. We hear it as a voice of judgment, of an Accuser, of a Denouncer,—not of the moral Redeemer, the mild Intercessor, the soul's personal Friend.

This is a great evil. It seems to me very important that the prejudice which has blended Christianity with the dark forms of Paganism, which has made it terrible, and built the Church by the grave yard should be removed, because the enemies of religion take advantage of this timid relucting, aweful reverence paid to our faith, and with a bad kindness come to deliver us from what we seem to fear. Far more reasonable would it be, like Paul, to *glory* in the Cross of Christ.[2] Far better, to let our eager acceptance correspond with the frankness of his welcome. He says, *I have called you friends.* Far better to hold the faith in that spirit of preference and joy, as counts all dross but that, and to be true to that one friendship, though all the world go away.[3]

It will be my aim then in the few remarks that follow, to fix your attention on the fact that precisely in proportion to our elevation of character, will be the love we bear to Christ and his doctrines, and then to remove some objections that seem to lie against this glorying in the Christian faith.

2. Galatians 6:14.
3. Cf. Philippians 3:7–8.

I. It is a very important truth, sustained both by reason and experience, that the feeling of friendship to Christ and of honor to his precepts, does continually grow warmer, as the character becomes purer. In a bad man, such a feeling cannot abide. For, likeness of nature is necessary to all sympathy, and the more likeness, the more perfect the sympathy. It was the saying of a truly great statesman, that "he never knew a man that was bad, fit for an action that was good."[4] Quite as true is it, that a bad man and a good man can never be true friends. Goodness loses its nature in the eye of a thoroughly depraved being, (if we can conceive such an one,) and appears the extreme of weakness and delusion. A perfect understanding is indispensable to a perfect sympathy. And we cannot comprehend that quality in another to which there is nothing resembling in ourselves. Nor is it an exception to this rule, when we say that by such and such rare instances of virtue, envy was overcome, and a momentary admiration extorted from the corrupt. We only mean that the effect of blazing merit upon partially depraved minds, was such as to startle the conscience within them, to rouse itself to an unwonted exertion, and to reassert, for a moment, its sovereignty in the soul.

But if it is the habit of vice to be insensible to the charm of virtue, is it to be wondered at, that sinful men should not only have no love, but should nourish in their hearts a hostility to Christ, since having incapacitated themselves by their own evil habits from understanding his moral perfections, they perceive every act of his to stand in contrast, and every rule of his, to be a condemnation, of themselves? It was to be expected, from their characters, that Judas should sell him, and Caiaphas crucify him, and, not the less, that voluptuous and selfish and malignant men of every generation should deny and blaspheme him. It is a terrible but natural manifestation of the free agency of man, that the great company of wicked men should thus be able, age after age, one after the other, to take into their own hands the spear, and thrust it into his side.[5]

And is it not also most reasonable, that they who, by the practice of his commandments, by much meditation on the noble beauty and utility of his doctrines, by prayer and determination, and by action also, have made themselves more and more like him, and so continually more capable of estimating him, should be continually drawn closer to him in affection; that obedience should be raised into reverence, and reverence should ripen into love, that in the progress of a virtuous mind, as by reflexion it should put on the manly robe, it should perceive the power of indefinite expansion to which God had appointed it by making it in his image,[6] should perceive that God had confined it to no low bounds, but had urged it in the spirit of a solemn confidence to feel for its moral Saviour, the kindness not of a servant but of a friend. And many there are, who know this by experience, though oftener, I believe this is true of those whose

4. Edmund Burke, *Speeches in the Impeachment of Warren Hastings, Esquire,* Third Day, in *The Works of the Right Honorable Edmund Burke* (Boston, 1867), 10:59. See *JMN* 6:38.
    5. See John 19:34.
    6. Genesis 1:26.

manner of life has been solitary, than of those who are bred in contact with the world. I believe there is many a poor heart, overlooked by the bustling multitude, and *happily,* (I may say,) shielded by the obscurity and obstructions of its lot from the common influences of society, without other education or instructor save the bible only, that sits alone, engrossed with the study of its own thoughts, where all wisdom is, and the image of Jesus comes into its solitude, as he should come, a friend to a friend. Such an one marks with tranquillity his own increasing power over his propensities; knows his increasing worthiness in the eye of his divine Instructor; speaks to him with an unblamed familiarity, that is just in the eye of God, though the knowledge of human opinions might check it to silence.

II. I proceed to notice one or two objections that may be thought to reprove such expression of attachment as I have supposed.

I shall be told that there is always danger of dwelling with complacency upon our small progress in virtue, and, on the ground of it, laying claim to the praise of being of Christ's party, and identifying our imperfections with the interests of God's cause. I do not think there is danger. A man may wish to impose on others the belief that he is a good man, but he cannot impose on himself. For there is always this simple test of any true advancement in religious life, namely, that every step increases the extent of our prospect, so that with every acquisition, we more clearly perceive our own deficiencies. So that such a thing was never heard of in the world, as a good man trumpeting his own triumphs, but the well known and universal habit of goodness is, to be reaching forward to farther attainments. Or to answer this objection in a few words, if we have made progress in goodness, we shall want more, and if we have not, we shall not be able to persuade ourselves, that we love him in whom the goodness of heaven dwelt.

Again; it may be alleged as a reason for forbidding this forward attachment, and, on any occasions, avowal of attachment to Christ and his law, that the revelation speaks to man not in a friendly but a commanding tone; that it uses a monitory, a menacing, sometimes a denouncing language, that it was a voice crying Repent!, that it lifted the veil in part from the tremendous retributions of the future state and announced the wrath of God upon every soul of man that doeth evil. This seems to me a false objection.

Far be it from me, brethren, to remove any of the terrors of the law from the evil doer, but this I say, that to the well doer it hath no terror. It is a law denouncing judgments—terrible beyond imagination to a sinful soul, but the same law breathes peace and inmost joy to the good. It is a sufficient reason to account for the hostility of the infidel, that whenever he turns, or is turned towards the gospel, he sees its face full of danger to himself, but in proportion as a man becomes good, he leaves those terrors beneath him, and although he knows full well that they exist in all their force to others, and would so exist to him if he were in the degraded circumstances of others—yet now they affect him no more. He acts by the force of more generous motives than fear: he is the servant of love; and perfect love casteth out fear.7 The laws of the gospel are in this respect precisely like human laws. The laws affixing fatal penalties to the commission of piracy and murder exist for the best citizen as well as the worst. And a man really guilty of those crimes, skulks ignominiously from street to street, and from town to town, for months and years, under the liveliest terror, looking every moment when the vengeance of the violated law shall consign him to the gibbet. But what man of reputable standing amongst us would not feel himself insulted if it were supposed that these laws had the slightest influence over his actions or purposes? Is it not so with the true Christian? As the true religion hath its rise and progress in the soul, as his mind becomes more and more united to God, does he not cease to fear, and become superior to the thunders of the law?

Is it not then to be desired, that the disciples of Christ might put on a manly front and frankly express the joy of believing and the uplifting peace and hope that springs from an affection set upon a heart so large, a dignity so pure and unrivalled as his? It should not be thought strange if we who by God's direct revelation walk in the light of an everlasting hope, and are now come out of the painful ignorance, which perplexed the understandings and sat heavy on the hearts of best and wisest men in the elder world—we, to whom is explained the mystery of our life; and who are taught the lesson of serenity and trust, by the knowledge that the government of the Universe is in the hands of One Wise and Just,—it should not be thought strange if we value infinitely this gospel and him who brought it in his hand and in his heart from God; if our trust and joy in him should sometimes overgo the limits of a cold respect and rise to exultation. Wheresoever we go we are in the treasuries of truth with which God means we should enrich ourselves. Wheresoever we go we are watched over by an anxious, an affectionate Providence. All events, all connexions, all conversations into which we are thrown are significant of its will, and virtue is to be got there. We live in an omnipresent hope. The good we seek we already taste, and know that it has not limit nor end. We are heirs of God, and joint heirs with Christ.8 And he, the chosen minister of God who was sanctified and sent to men, with this communication, and who taught us by his own life, how we should live to secure these advantages, hath declared that if we do his commandments, we shall abide in his love, and if in his, then in God's.9

Brethren, I should labour most carefully to guard the remarks I have been making from misconstruction, but that the errors into which, if mistaken, they would lead, are so obvious I have only been anxious that it should be felt by us that Christianity is not something to be defended and respected, but something to be panted after and gloried in, that we should make it known that we look on our part in it as a majestic privilege, and that each of us should feel that we may

7. I John 4:18.
8. Romans 8:17.
9. John 15:10.

seek such worthiness as to have a fellowship, a brotherhood with that glorified person who brought it from God.

Finally; as Christ loved us, we ought also to love one another.[10] It has been often the subject of complaint that the bands of Christian friendship are no more strictly drawn. A little consideration would show us that when Christianity shall have wrought a farther effect on mankind, a stronger union, a more useful intercourse will be the natural consequence. For in the pursuits that now absorb the strength and talents of men every man is the rival of his brother. Men seek for wealth and fame and office. But since of these things there is only a certain amount, what one gets another must want. But when in the progress of wisdom out of the spiritual world into this world, instead of money men shall pursue virtue and instead of fame pursue truth, they must cease to envy and oppose each other, for these are infinite things and all true lovers of them are lovers of one another, and aiding in each other's mutual advancement. Meantime it is in the power of every Christian to promote this great social cause by his own devotion to it; to unite with his Master and his Friend in fulfilling in his own life the eternal commandments of his Father and our Father.

10. I John 4:11.

LXIII

Be not conformed to this world, but be ye transformed by the renewing of your mind, that ye may prove what is that good and acceptable and perfect will of God.

ROMANS 12:2

We are come up again to the house of God to praise him, and to pray unto him, and to inquire of our duty from his holy word. "Be not conformed to this world"—is the lesson which we read. The admonitions of the Scripture speak as loudly and reproachfully to us as they did to the men of the sinful age in which they were first uttered. But a reproach is only such when it is deserved. The commandment, Thou shalt not kill,[1] awakes no lively emotion in the soul that is innocent of blood; it is heard with a calm assent; but to another soul it sounds like a harsh accusation.

Would a man then know himself and how he stands with God? Let him read over carefully each of the old commandments, and the new commandment of Christ,[2] and see whether any of these ancient laws sounds harshly in his ear. If any does, that is the commandment which he has not kept.

But the tables of stone and the books of the New Testament are not all the commandments we have. God has many more monitors than these. It is strange how his Providence gives a tongue to every event and condition and place and hour. All our acquaintances are made the voices of accusation or praise. Let a man run over in his mind the names of the persons with whom he converses in the world, if he find he bears to any an unfriendly feeling, that person is one whom he has injured, or before whom he has offended.

Sad it is to consider how the lessons which all time has taught the world have failed of effect. One generation calls to another, and saith, Look at our history and beware. One dying man acknowledges in his condition the effect of his character and beseeches his children and his fellows to lay it to heart, and they bury him and as if they were mad walk in his evil ways. There is not a sceptic on

---

Preached twice: January 24, 1830, at the Second Church, Boston, and again at the Second Church, September 4, 1831.

1. Exodus 20:13 and Deuteronomy 5:17.
2. Exodus 20:1-17, Deuteronomy 5:7-21, and John 13:34. Cf. Romans 13:9.

earth of intelligence enough to make his opinions worth attention, who does not admit the good tendency of virtue and the evil tendency of guilt. All the history of man is moral. The vices of every nation have been visited with ruin; the vices of every man with unhappiness. Yet nations repeat the one sort and individuals repeat the other sort. The present is always too strong for the future. There are many men to whom the next fifteen minutes are more than a counterpoise for all the coming years of life, and almost every man promises himself old age; i.e., who will snatch a present pleasure at the risk of years of harm, whilst their calculations leave the future life out of the account. Next above this class, there are a great many who look at life, as it were, with the eye of an animal not of a man, so that though they postpone the enjoyment of this hour or day to the enjoyment of the whole year or of ten years, yet they apply this more generous calculation to the *same objects* as the least elevated class.

Thus the most degraded sort of men—whether the savage, or he that is made savage by vice, when he holds his cup in his hand, knows perfectly well the consequences of his indulgence and that the advantage and respectability of all his future life is the bribe offered him for forbearing this insignificant pleasure. Yet is this little present so large in his eye as to shut out all that great alternative.

Well how do the wiser sort? Why the great multitude of men, who disdain this brutish shortsightedness, and who behold the future years, with so clear an eye, as to give up every day with the greatest ease, such indulgences, because they see how fearfully uneven is the bargain, yet they have little superiority to boast. For what is their aim? It is only a longer and truer enjoyment of the same things. It is only to eat their meat and drink their wine for many years and in pleasant circumstances safe from the contempt of their fellows or the fear of the morrow. It is only a little purification and elevation of the same pursuit. This is what I meant by saying they look at human life with the eye of a brute. It is true the great number of prudent men do sometimes consider the chances of the whole future. They desire to combine a degree of safety for that future with this paramount regard to the enjoyments of animal life. They see indeed how the name of virtue dignifies and recommends and flavours these common gratifications, and they make some sacrifices of time and some of inclination to the claims of religion. They see so much of the usefulness of good principles that they abstain from venting their ill humor when provoked. They distinguish themselves by their modesty and moderation and justice. They manifest some regard for sacred things. They attend at least a part of the Sunday at Church. They carry this seriousness further and sometimes direct their own thoughts to the doctrines of religion and satisfy themselves that there is some evidence for its laws. Still they value it most as it keeps society in order and allows them to sow and reap their harvest of worldly good with none to molest or make them afraid. And then, brethren, of those to whom what is true and holy has really come home, to those who are engaged in the improvement of their characters, who study with interest the life and discourses of the Saviour of men—to such, to you who I hope are such, is there no interruption, no backsliding—no neglect of prayer, no sin of omission or commission? Let me read you a passage from an ancient English poet which, though quaint in the expression, is full of truth:

> Lord with what care hast thou begirt us round!
> Parents first season us; then schoolmasters
> Deliver us to laws; they send us bound
> To rules of reason   holy messengers
> Pulpits and Sundays; sorrow dogging sin
> Affections sorted   anguish of all sizes
> Fine nets and stratagems to catch us in
> Bibles laid open millions of surprizes
>
> Blessings beforehand; ties of gratefulness
> The sound of glory ringing in our ears
> Without our shame, within our consciences
> Angels and grace; eternal hopes and fears
> Yet all these fences and their whole array
> One cunning bosom sin blows quite away.[3]

And is this the history of the world?

This would be disheartening indeed to all lovers of virtue, to all who hope well for man; this gloomy experience casts a shade over all the future and is only to be resisted by the consoling fact of a few glorious exceptions and by that strong hope that dwells in the bottom of the Soul (that spark that lives among the ashes of the past) that amendment is never late, (that with God all things are possible),[4] the conviction that power is never wanting to us when we will be true to ourselves.

But clearly does it show how much the human race want of Reflection, how little they use that godlike power of thought which is their best power. They rejoice in the tongue which sets them above the brute; in the hand, and with reason, as the little engine surpassing in its usefulness all mechanical means, which clears forests and which builds cities,[5] but the power of Reflection which is common to them only with Angels and God, the power of classifying all things into knowledge—illuminating the Universe by the discovery of purposes and then regulating a life—presiding over future hours, years, aye, and ages by the determinations of the will, establishing a law that shall extort good out of events yet unborn, and shaping out beforehand the unhewn quarry of all the soul's future existence into the city of the living God[6]—this great attribute is lightly esteemed and seldom used.

---

3. George Herbert's "Sinne," which Emerson read in December 1829 in Samuel Taylor Coleridge, *Aids to Reflection,* ed. James Marsh (Burlington, Vt., 1829), 255–56. Emerson later included the poem in *Parnassus* (Boston, 1875).

4. Matthew 19:26 and Mark 10:27.

5. Cf. "Doctrine of Hands" (*EL* 2:230): "A man in the view of political economy is a pair of hands, a useful engine quite able to subdue the earth, to plant and build it over."

6. Hebrews 12:22.

Men are good by fits and starts, exhibit occasional and irregular virtues, but the carrying on of a good life, the laying out of a scheme of consistent action that nowhere violates the laws of God, and suits the whole of our being, is seldom studied. It is strange that they do not apply the analogy of their common affairs to the conduct of this great affair and so become wise. They do not set out upon a voyage without anxious and long preparation, without the most careful provision against every wind and every probable or possible contingency—without much forethought and calculation.

But how many more dangers beset the soul on her voyage over the waves of this world! how many indolent calms, when no progress is made; how many mists hide the face of heaven from the eye; how ignorant is the pilot; how weak and easily drawn into mutiny are the faculties, by which her course is to be helped; and how vast is the price of the cargo, and the need of guiding it to its destined home!

Yet each new adventurer spreads his little sail as hastily and improvidently as if all was daylight and calm weather and the port was one every eye could find! And hence it is that all along the sea of human life we meet those hideous wrecks—that alarm us with the remembrance that they set forth with hopes and advantages as fair as ours.

Were it not a noble ambition, brethren, to make this voyage well, to study the science of life, to think less of other skill, and learning, and enterprize, and more of this main Art of Life to which all gifts are but private and subordinate, and to separate ourselves with a portion of that industry we cheerfully give to the getting the means of living and studying the method of life?

I do not affect to represent it as a light task, this duty of steady Reflection upon the principles by which we should live. If it had been easy it would not thus have been neglected. The world would not have been compelled in its weary list of great men to point only to a few spotless characters, and to blush for all the rest. It is not easy. On the contrary, there is nothing in the way of hardship men will not submit to sooner than to the intolerable labour of thought.

Is not this true? Is there any man who supposes that it is not in his power to retire within himself and to accustom himself to determine in his own mind whether the things that are said are really so, and arrive at truth by his own conclusion? Every man believes he has this power. Yet how many use it?

I suppose most of us have yet to learn practically that truth which all the wise of all ages have agreed, that through the use of our own soul only can we ever come to true knowledge, to independence and tranquillity. You may be very rich, you may be politically great and come no nearer to independence or peace. For these consist in fearing no change and no enemy; and that freedom must arise from having no enemy and being incapable of change. This being admitted brings it at once to the state of the soul, and not of the circumstances. He whose good consists in his wealth, or in his bodily vigor, or in a momentary popularity, can never be free from fear, for he is always exposed to change. But he who lives only for the *improvement of his character,* only to acquire more knowledge, and to become more useful, who acknowledges God's sovereign right in him and would gladly be transformed from temporal desires and renewed in the image of eternal good—he who thus lives has no enemy and fears no change for every event contributes to his good, and the loss of wealth, or of health, or of human favor, or the death of friends, or his own death—none of these things move him, for, none can rob him of what is his precious property, his entire trust in God and his unceasing endeavours to make himself better or, in the language of the apostle, transform himself into his glorious likeness.[7] Of course he is calm; of course, he is independent and happy.

But I return to the question. Were it not almost a novel, certainly a noble ambition worthy of the pursuit of each of us first to settle in the mind the principles, and then to carry out in action the practice of a good life? It is, I venture to say; the character of a good man is something which the coldest judgment cannot contemplate without enthusiasm. We have theories of virtue, oh many a one, but they can be questioned and attacked and denied. But a good man, who has nothing to be explained and no apologizing circumstances to be considered, is an argument of God not to be got over.

Say not that such men when they appear are not valued, that the world does not trust them, that vulgar minds put mean motives on good actions. Commanding virtue will always have its full effect. In the basest mind, in the bottom of life, there is apprehension enough of virtue. The worst man is a child of God and retains something of the sentiments of our common Father, and gives homage to real goodness. A truly virtuous man is the bulwark to the virtue of a thousand. It is the richest gift a man can make to the world, let me say to the Universe, the exhibition of a perfect life, and there is not one of us who is not capable of it.

Hitherto men have laboured to be great instead of to be good. And that experiment has failed. They have found the good they sought for rotten. They have been disappointed and sour. In our country does the history of administrations lead you to believe that success in that career was unmixed happiness? Is it better in other countries? It has been remarked that in the chief country of the world in our age several of the eminent statesmen to whom her power has been confided have found life so insupportable that they have died by their own hand.[8] It was said by one of the most able statesmen of the last century, a man of great talents and great success, when in no ill humor, "The best of life is but just tolerable; 'tis the most we can make of it."[9] No virtuous man would consent to this deplorable confession. Cheerfulness is the natural fruit of virtue. The good

7. The allusion seems to conflate Romans 12:2, the text of the present sermon, with Romans 6:5.

8. Robert Stewart Castlereagh (British Secretary of War, 1805, 1807-1809) committed suicide at the age of 53 in 1822.

9. Jonathan Swift, as quoted in Joseph Spence, *Anecdotes, Observations, and Characters of Books and Men* . . . (London, 1820), 74. See *JMN* 3:176; used in *EL* 2:219.

man sees this glory and sees its miserable end. He follows it to the grave and sees the poor cheat on human opinions that is covered with all this idle parade. It is a bitter satire on human folly.

And for this, he says, you have lived? And all your labors and results and wealth and renown are only so many steps from the road of human happiness. Better sleep in infancy than reach such a maturity. Better far is the portion of that little child cut down innocent in the morning, than yours who have lived on to the grey shadows of evening. The soul of the child hath no sin, and yours is spotted with manifold offence.

> Beneath this stone an infant lies
>   To earth whose body lent
> Hereafter shall more glorious rise
>   But not more innocent
>
> When the archangels trump shall blow
>   And souls to bodies join
> Thousands shall wish their lives below
>   Had been as short as thine.[10]

Brethren, I could wish and pray that to us it belonged to set forth this model of a perfect life, that we might leave the idols of the world—the gratifications which men have sought and seek, and worship the true God.

Be not conformed to this world but be ye transformed by the renewing of your mind to the likeness of another world.

He who truly engages in the science of living well will not be long unacquainted with the example and teaching of Jesus. For this was the truth which he came to declare. He came with no flatteries in his mouth to the pride or the appetites of men. He set up neither fame nor wealth nor pleasure nor even knowledge as the high mark of human effort. He taught the hard lesson of Self-denial. He said, If any man will come after me, let him deny himself, and take up his cross, and follow me.[11] This then was the theory of a good life, which came out from heaven and was confirmed by miracles. What is self-denial? Self denial is only one form of expression for perfection of the moral character. It means the denial of self-indulgence. It means the subordination of all the lower parts of man's nature, to the higher, so that the individual doth nothing contrary to reason.

Now if a man will so deny himself, he will raise himself above a man; he can do no wrong. He is that pure one, to whom all things are pure.[12] There is an absolute independence about such a soul which it is elevating to contemplate.

It is sometimes asked—must not the Christian do thus and so for the sake of example?

10. Not located.
11. Matthew 16:24 and Mark 8:34.
12. Titus 1:15.

I think it may be answered that if he is a denier of himself he need never consult the consequences of his actions, but may leave them with God. His example will never be quoted with sincerity, as giving sanction to any thing evil. His actions cannot be misinterpreted. One part of his example interprets another part of his example. He may safely trust his virtue to bear itself out in the world. Our Saviour sat with sinners, yet none ever thought of quoting him as sanctioning sin.[13]

I know the word Self-denial sounds repulsive as a principle of action, but let it be remembered that the self-denial of the gospel is a denial only of the low and is a gratification of the noble parts of our self. Its great proof to the serious mind is that it doth now in this world enter on the heaven, which it promises. It already redeems you from all servitude to fear. It makes you master of yourself. It brings you nearer alway to God, and every step of your progress makes you stronger and more peaceful and more hopeful, takes away something of mortal infirmity and puts something of immortal enjoyment in its stead.

13. "Self denial is only . . . sin": cf. *JMN* 3:175–76.

NOTE ON SERMON LXIV _____

No manuscript of Sermon LXIV is known to survive. The Preaching Record indicates that it was delivered fourteen times: January 31, 1830, at the Second Church; February 18 as a Thursday Lecture (presumably at the Second Church); March 14 at Hartford; March 21 at Philadelphia; April 4 at the Brattle Street Church; April 18 at Concord, Mass.; April 25 as an evening lecture at the South Congregational Church; June 6 at Waltham; July 18 at the New North Church; February 13, 1831, at the Second Church; April 10 at the First Church; April 17 at the North Church, Salem, Mass.; June 5 at Burlington, Vt.; and September 18 at East Lexington.

LXV

*And as ye would that men should do to you
do ye also to them likewise.*

LUKE 6:31

True success in life consists in striking the mean between the love of self and of our neighbor. Neither the gospel nor any other law denies that a man has a good deal to do in the world for himself before others. He has to supply his animal wants; he has to store his mind; to see for himself; to hear for himself; and to think for himself; all which he must do, as these are things which nobody will do for him: and which, if he refuses to do for himself, he will not be able to do for any body else.

Moreover; it is also true that these claims of Self upon us have no natural limit or end. A cup may be filled; the dry ground may be flooded with rain; or the frosty ground may be warmed to fertility or may be scorched to sand by the midsummer sun, but to self there is no satisfaction, for by its nature each new gratification does not so much gratify as multiply its wants. If man is made acquainted with a new luxury, that straightway becomes necessary to his comfort; if he obtain the knowledge after which for months he has been aiming, it only whets his appetite for more; if he reach the virtue of whose sweetness he is enamoured, it has the effect to remove the scales from his eyes and show the soul how far it is from perfect goodness.[1] So that it is plainly impossible for man to say—'I will do what I ought for my self, and *afterward* set about my social duties; go away, my neighbors, and come tomorrow, or by and by, when I have got my education, or my office, or my property, or filled up my experience, or made my peace with God,—and then I will succour, or feed, or teach you.' Thou hypocrite! this year thou shalt die. Thy own dust and thy neighbour's shall lie side by side, and he who made you both, and set you together in the earth to owe and pay a mutual debt shall call you into judgment.

It is plain, brethren, that whilst the demands of insatiable because infinite self

---

Manuscript dated February 6, 1830, at Chardon Street. Preached seven times: in the morning of February 7, 1830, at the First Church, Boston, and in the afternoon of the same day at the Second Church; February 14 in East Cambridge; February 21 at the New South Church, Boston; March 28 in Philadelphia; February 5, 1832, at the Second Church; and November 5, 1837, in East Lexington.

1. Cf. Acts 9:18.

are receiving attention, so *at the same time* must the demands of our fellow man upon us. And this necessity is met by the arrangements of Providence. God has so intwisted our life into that of those who are next us, that our own good is promoted by the good of others; our own education carried forward by our attempts to instruct others; our virtue quickened by all endeavours to stimulate others; and, in fine, our whole power increased by its communication to them.

I ask your attention, 1. To those circumstances which plainly show the intention that we should serve each other. 2. That benevolence as well as beneficence is required of us.

1. It cannot be unnoticed how inseparably the individual's good is linked to that of others, so that whensoever and whatsoever innocent efforts are made for the most confined personal betterment, the same effort, to its whole extent, ameliorates the condition of mankind. So fast are the cords of social being drawn, that its good and its evil are never insulated, but every little rill of personal advantage penetrates through unseen channels to places where the agent never meant or imagined his influence would be felt. The wealthy wretch who shuts his door on the beggar in the winter night, and grudges the pittance of his contribution to the necessities of the state, and denies to his own frame, almost the comforts of life, is nevertheless compelled to benefit his fellow men, at a greater distance than his narrow soul ever comprehended.[2]

His house, his clothes, his food, his medicine, are products whose price he must pay to the encouragement of honest industry. The order of the elements does not consent to selfishness. If you make a fire to warm your corner, you must warm all those who are in the room. If you daintily feed, and delicately dress your own body, you will liberally pay the wages of labour, and the more diligently you procure your own convenience, the more effectually you contribute to that of others. It was an early discovery of political Economy that in no form could labor be exerted to less advantage, than in an attempt to confine its fruits to the laborer. The man who should set himself to build his own house, weave his own clothes, make his own shoes, teach his own children, and so prevent the price of these conveniences from enriching his neighbors, would presently find himself the poorest of them all. Whilst, on the contrary, that laborer who seems to throw himself generously on society by giving up his life to a single branch of mechanical industry, as the nail, paper, cotton manufacture, neither of which can in itself produce a morsel of bread,—finds himself able to benefit in the highest degree himself and his household.

And in like manner all the right exertions which any man makes for his good is so much good got for all. Every furrow on the brow of toiling ambition is an index of some new acquisition bought by the genius and industry of one to the country in which he lives. In all classes of all communities, thousands of minds are intensely occupied each in his place and profession, the merchant in his compting house, the mechanist at his model, the statesman at his map and

2. Cf. Luke 16:19-31.

tariff, the scholar at his ancient text, the lawyer at his code, each stung with an emulation to raise himself above his equals—each almost absorbed in the prospect of good that shall accrue to himself,—but each no less contributing to the utmost of his means to fix and adorn human civilization. He that grows rich by his own enterprize, has smoothed and not obstructed the way he has trodden. He that makes himself illustrious by his inventions, has by those same inventions, added facilities to art,—solaces to life. He that loves splendor, and adorns his house, adorns his city. He that prints a good book, to immortalize his name, creates an immortal influence in the minds of his countrymen.

And the same is true of every right exertion from the highest to the humblest of intellect.[3] I believe in the next place that the converse of this proposition is demonstrably true, that when we aim at others' good we are really obtaining our own. But far be it from me to offer this fact in the light of a motive to Benevolence. It can only be presented as a motive to those hardened self-seekers who are incapable as yet of being reached by any higher one. The only way in which this fact like the last becomes interesting to the lovers of God, is as an evidence of the perfect harmony of the laws of their Father's kingdom. Thus are the intentions of God plainly shown that his creatures should serve one another.[4]

2. But all this is mere beneficence; it is good for nothing without it is accompanied by benevolence or the will to do good.

A man may say, if thus the common and the individual good are yoked in one,—in pursuing my own interest, I shall sufficiently consult the interest of the whole. I have no separate duty. Oh no, there is abundance of pain which it is your appointed duty to remove. What! shall we be satisfied with this general advantage derived to others from our selfish action? Shall we be content to throw to our fellow men the offal of inevitable benefit; make a virtue of necessity, and say, *Take this which I cannot keep?* They take it, but not from you. It is not yours to give. It is the overflowings of his bounty, which the common Father made theirs, by the constitution of things. He decrees that you shall spare them this, and he commands you to give them something of yourself. He commands you to make sacrifices for them. He commands you to measure their claim by no cheap estimate, but by the dear standard of your own desires. The last message that came out of heaven was, Do as you would be done by, sealed by the blood of God's holy Son. Yet who knows not, brethren, what mass of selfishness is in the world! I am not going to describe the atrocious extremes of self-love which finds matter of joy in the misfortune of another and hugs itself in the fraud or the cruelty which has made another's wealth our own.

But there is a great deal of selfishness among us hardly blamed as sin; a great deal of civil, assuming, polished selfishness, that overlooks the interest of the *world* in seeking its own; that would burn down its neighbor's house, to bake its

3. "It cannot be . . . intellect": See *JMN* 2:304–6
4. Galatians 5:13.

own loaf. You shall find selfish men in elegant society. You shall find them among cultivated minds. Sometimes you may find a man who bears in his manners and his conversation marks of good breeding and good sense, who betrays in his judgments a delicate perception of the beautiful in art and nature, one who has learning, and pleasantry, and language at command, and even a relish for refined friendships, and yet with all this hath the frost of selfishness about his heart, who never willingly postponed the smallest advantage of his own to the greatest of another man, when he dared to refuse.

You have seen such an one perhaps, a man who talked of sacrifices and censured illiberality. But you found that when he freely gave, it had been better to give less, for, they were those little pieces of ostentation which one cannot withhold and be called a gentleman. But if the good were to be defended against the many, he was dumb; if the nameless were to be succoured or instructed, he had no means or time; if the company into which he was thrown were not of his degree, he kept surly silence. In the circle of his own friends no pains taken to give him pleasure met with any suitable return; like other offenders he had his apology, he complained that he was not in good spirits, or excused his moroseness upon the score of diffidence. But there is as much difference between the silence of modesty, and the silence of pride, as between whiteness of complexion and the whiteness of death.

I think this sort of selfishness the more dangerous because it passes by us in such good company, that it passes unreprehended, and the young who see it, and the old who feel something like it in themselves are not put upon their guard against so reputable a vice, as they are when it appears unmixed as in the miser or the sensualist and is hooted at by all.

It is bad enough every where but it is frightful in the young. It seems to me so black a sore that it ought never to pass unnoticed in a child. And yet you may sometimes see a parent praise the smartness of a child who shows a premature shrewdness in his childish dealing, in looking out for himself; or utters the sentiment of triumph at another's fall. That parent is by his applause planting the seed of the second death in the bosom of his child.[5]

If any lesson should be the aim of education it should be the rule of Christian benevolence. The child is in no danger of not learning that he is to take care of himself; Nature will teach him that from day to day. But it should be impressed on him by all means, by example and precept and the repetition of both, that it is base to forget the comfort of others in seeking his own. A child of two or three years, is old enough to understand in practice the lesson of the Lord Jesus that it is more blessed to give than to receive.[6] Put a guard on your own lips before him. Teach him God's lesson of love. Let him not hear you deny your aid to what is good or your strength to what is feeble. Let him not hear you insult over distress or slight the calamity which prostrates a stranger.

5. Cf. Revelation 21:8.
6. Acts 20:35.

I know not, my friends, what is more comfortless than the condition of the man who loves nothing but himself. His influence, his good or evil deeds, are an atom in the whole,—but see then its effect on him. It imprisons him in the darkest and coldest corner of God's glorious universe, the sealed chamber of a selfish bosom. Look what is lost! Others may say, Look at the resources of the eye and ear; see how infinite is outward nature! The benevolent man saith, Yea, but see how infinite is this *world of men*! see how much there is to love! see how much to benefit! But he whose thoughts never travelled beyond himself, knows no form of being beyond the snug precincts of his own flesh; he to whom his own unopened mind is the type of man, whose own heart, spotted with sin, and as small as the mustard seed, is the human heart, and is all his measure for the wide circumference of human affection,—that man will get a very false and a very base account of men, and acting, as he must, on that most injurious presumption, all men will naturally be provoked to show him their worst temper and will resist his approaches as invasions and insults. Every man knows that the presence of a proud man provokes in men a reserved and haughty air, and the dealings of a selfish man call up a show of interest on the defensive. To the selfish men show themselves selfish, to the froward they show themselves froward.[7] This fact of the state of mind of the beholder should always be kept in mind to qualify his report.

The tradesmen hurrying to their business look at the crowd that pass as so many hungry consumers of Bread, engaging in a fierce competition for it with themselves. They see each other in the act of trade with the sharp eyes of interest lying in wait for every advantage, and disputing for every cent. What can be more fretting and dispiriting? It seems to such an one, in a moment of ill humor, not much better than tearing the morsel from each other's mouths.

But stop, and take off this film from the eye. Look again. Each of those persons is a son, brother, husband, friend. Each of those persons—take the most disagreeable of all—is somewhere tenderly loved, is somewhere regarded as a benefactor or a companion, the treasurer of bosom secrets.

Each sustains relations,—oh remember it well,—to God in heaven, and perchance owned them this morning on his knees. Each is a child on which God's Eye is fixed,—and what a futurity opens before him! is capable, as all spirits are, of such a mighty generosity as now you would shrink to contemplate, and would make you ashamed of your poor orts and ends of goodness and glory. This is the picture which the man of benevolence sees,— (how much truer than the first!) and many an apology can he find in his soul for the blackest sin of his offending brother.

My friends, I wish the comparison of that selfishness we may daily observe all around us, (and how often within us)—with the golden rule of our Master, might set this subject before us in its importance. It was not only a doctrine, it is the history of his life, the glory of his death. Love is a name for almost all virtue,

7. Psalms 18:26.

and Selfishness for almost all vice. It seems to me this virtue is one of that sovereign character that it should command from us a most vigilant regard. At all times, it should govern us, but it seems to me, brethren, that these cold winter winds plead earnestly with us for its remembrance now. There is not one of us, I suppose, who might not find within a stone's cast of his own house, some child of pain and want who suffers severely from want of comforts which it is in our power to bestow, or to obtain. Let the Lord's maxim carry us to those cheerless rooms as messengers of consolation. As ye would that men should do to you do ye unto them likewise.

LXVI

Are not five sparrows sold for two farthings
and not one of them is forgotten before God?
But even the hairs of your head are all numbered.
LUKE 12:6–7

Every one who searches with a sound judgement into the foundation of the argument of Natural Religion is made sensible sooner or later that the belief in God arises from a necessity in the mind. The history that is in each of our memories of our own life and our observation of our acquaintance, the history of families and the history of large portions of the human race, will all confirm this remark—that the human mind shows in all circumstances a natural want of something stronger and wiser than itself, that it is itself a thing imperfect, and in its very structure shows that it is a part, and demands more,—as much as the eye implies the being of light, or an infant the being of some who can feed and protect it.

And so every man, wherever born, however insulated from men, hath his own religion, or vestiges of it, and some who deny it differ less in their sentiments than in their language. One worships the person of God, and one the attributes. This man bows to Baal and that believes in what he calls his genius, or honours one day above another.[1] It all springs from the same wants of the soul, whether the individual honour Jove, or Brahma or the Holy Virgin or a Saint. If puffed up by vanity they affect to doubt, or, disordered by the corruptions of the religion believed around them, they do doubt the faith of their country, they are yet found to believe in lucky and unlucky days, in signs and omens, which are the fragments of a belief in God.

Having this idea of superintendence,—of God,—in some way settled and conformed to their stock of knowledge, they are at ease—they are capable of much more efficient and self-satisfactory exertion—they are stronger than before. In the conviction that this superior power is on their side they can do wonders.

If this idea is disturbed—by vice, or by reason, or by sophistry, they are at

---

Manuscript erroneously dated February 15, 1830, at Chardon Street. Preached twice: February 14, 1830, at the Second Church, Boston, and again at the Second Church, March 18, 1832.
    1. Cf. Romans 14:5 and Galatians 4:8–10.

once made uneasy,—sometimes furious, sometimes depraved, sometimes dejected. This is true, for I am only turning well-known facts into general propositions. I only wish to call your attention to the fact, that this idea of God, is got not by accident, or by research, but results from the structure of the creature, man.

Now the discoveries of science—not the instructions of revealed religion but the discoveries of science,—have compelled men to believe, that nothing is made without a purpose; no limb, no bone, no antennæ, no hair, no feather, without a distinct purpose that is disclosed as our knowledge is increased. In a world then where every thing has some reason why it is so, is then this leaning of the human soul—this feeling round for a support,—without purpose? this inevitable, natural prayer of all intelligent nature—convulsing sometimes the system in the utterance, and when denied utterance, depraving it—without purpose? Is it not a finger pointing upward to the great Spirit?

The belief in God being thus gotten, the doctrine of Providence is the application of that belief to the government of the world. Just as great or as little as is the idea of God, just such is the opinion men form of Providence. The pagan, whose religion is very gross, believes in a low, jealous, selfish patronage that reaches him and his family or his tribe, and hates every body else. His god knows a little more and does a little better than a man. One god thwarts another, as man contends with man. A great many popular superstitions held in different countries, some admitting, some rejecting any higher power than their local deities, are only forms of polytheism. The vulgar superstition of the fairies, is the idea of a petty Providence. As man's knowledge enlarges, that is, as his mind applies itself to a larger piece of the universe, he sees the unbroken prevalence of laws; the grass grows in Egypt by the same natural order as in Ohio; the man of one district fears death like the man of the other, and knows as well what it is to love, and to have, and to want. All languages are alike in their structure,—can be translated into each other, and all customs look to similar and intelligible ends. The same course of conduct every where leads to analogous results, and the sentiments of mankind are substantially the same in all countries.

By these observations the inquirer is led to the fact that the kingdom of nature is not a government of partial and manifold provinces, but hath one constitution through all its parts; and whatsoever intelligence superintends it, must be one, as far as his own observation reaches,—and not knowing where to stop, he calls this government universal and infinite.[2]

I conceive it to be of very great importance that we should thus extend our ideas from the relations of the individual soul to God, and obtain a view of God's relation to all that happens out of ourselves, to other minds and to the whole course of things,—which is the idea of Providence. These two views of God must essentially assist and throw light on each other.

2. Compare the six preceding paragraphs with *JMN* 3:179–80.

I desire to offer you by way of defining my idea of Providence, two or three illustrations of design not made apparent in a few days or years but showing this superintendence extending over centuries and nations.

Every science daily discloses more and more proofs of this kind. And after astronomy none has brought more wonderful proof of the wisdom and power of God than the examination of the globe we inhabit.

The science of geology, which treats of the structure of the Earth, has ascertained that prior to the period when God created man upon the Earth, very considerable changes have taken place in the planet. It is made probable the various rocks that are now found broken upon it covered it as so many crusts one without another. But the soils are formed by the decomposition of these stones and so in this position that mixture of them which is essential to the production of vegetable life could never have been effected. By internal volcanoes, or other means, these strata have been broken and raised and are now found lying as may be seen in mountain countries in oblique and perpendicular instead of horizontal layers, so as to yield their various treasures to man and to the soil.

This is yet more striking in the case of coal, so important to old countries and recently to this.

It is well known how vastly the great development of the commerce of Great Britain and thence of the great civilization of that country is indebted to the boundless abundance of its mineral treasures. In consequence of the abundance and accessibility of this mineral in that island, and its opportune association with beds of iron ore, they are enabled to surpass all other nations in the extent of their manufactures. But the discoveries of geologists have shown that the coal, which is undoubtedly a vegetable formation, is the relic of forests that existed at an unknown antiquity before the era of the creation of mankind, by the overflowing of the sea and other changes of the surface, and had been buried below the surface at too great a depth to be reached by man. But before the creation of our race, certain great Earthquakes or other convulsions have lifted up these mineral beds into ledges so that they are found extending from 1000 feet above the level of the ocean to unknown depths below it. And so it happens that these vast beds of fuel so essential to man's comfort and civilization, which would have been covered by the crust of the globe forever from his use or knowledge, are thus brought up within reach of his little hands; and a great work of nature in an antiquity that hath no record, is made to contribute to our pleasure and prosperity at this hour.[3]

Now when I see this event, I cannot help regarding it as a work done by God, for some such design as I find it answers. If it stood alone, I might say it was an accident; but since my mind is familiar with instances of benevolent design,

3. The four preceding paragraphs are used in "The Uses of Natural History" and "The Relation of Man to the Globe" (*EL* 1:15-16 and 33-34, respectively).

when I meet a coincidence so strange and beautiful, I cannot help referring it to his hand.

If a mariner wrecked on our coast should find refuge in one of the huts erected on the rocks by the Humane Society, for the use of such sufferers, would he doubt whether this shelter had been built by design? And when we, in this late age, see this magnificent charity yielded after the manner of its Author, to the enterprize and diligence of man, shall we call it an accident?

The lesson it teaches me is that what men call the disorders of nature, as earthquakes and floods, are yet contained in a high Order and are ministering to good, remote yet certain—and that all the changes are guided by a Providence.

This is from nature. Let me call your attention to another instance from the arts. God is the author of those faculties of man and those capabilities in outward things by whose union the arts are invented, and when I am struck by any happy exhibition of these powers I am led to grateful remembrance of his goodness. When turning over one of the best arguments from nature of the Being of God that has ever been drawn, that namely which is contained in a dialogue in Xenophon's Memoirs of Socrates,4 I cannot help admiring the immortality thus given to the fugitive thoughts of a conversation and which come to strengthen my faith from so far a spot and through so long a time. There was a child who wished he could hear all the things that were said in the world. He did not consider that his wish defeated itself, inasmuch as if the air were elastic, and all sounds came to every ear, the ear would be paralyzed with the thunder of the promiscuous report. But how much better is this provision, I say to myself as I read this book by which the feeble voice of one man is heard by me across the din of so many ages, the tumult and the fall of so many cities, the convulsion of so many empires as have been since Socrates uttered the sentiment which this day reaches my eye. The connexion is but this moment completed between the soul of the great Teacher and mine.

Although this is an instance familiar to any thoughtful man who opens a book—and more forcible in the case of a text read from the conversations of Jesus or the books of Moses—Yet I have purposely named a profane author because the instances belong to an Evidence entirely independent of revelation.

When I see this wonderful effect so important for the instruction of the race, for the preservation and transmission of truth, can I doubt that it was foreseen, can I doubt that it was intended by the Almighty in his gifts to mankind? Yet is this but one of many. The lesson it teaches me, is that God interests himself in the education of the race of man, in their progressive improvements;—and so I get a nearer view of his Providence.

If then I extend my observation into the daily life of men as it passes under my eye, and see how invariably *moral* are its results; what retributions take place, or begin to take place, in the world; how the selfish are disliked; and they who

4. Xenophon, *Memorabilia,* trans. E. C. Marchant (London, 1923), 57.

love others, are loved again; how sure are the rewards of diligence, and the punishments of sloth; how faithfully a regard to the laws of the universe is attended with safety and success, and a neglect of them with ill health of body, and disquiet of soul; how certainly men obtain those things which with a single eye they pursue—A miser, if he live long enough, must grow rich; a man that seeks God, and God only, must grow good, and so of the pursuit of knowledge, of friends, of distinction, &c &c.

When I consider the wonderful laws which are discovered to prevail by the political Economist; and which as strikingly indicate a moral design as any other,—If all these be considered, I am compelled to own that a spirit of matchless intelligence frames and keeps the constitution of society, that there is no escape to the state or the family or the individual from its all pervading energy. And I come yet nearer to the perception of the Almighty Providence. I had intended to offer a few very striking examples, coincidences from history that appear to me to imprint the same doctrine, but I must postpone them.

I know that it may be said that it is useless to go about for examples of a Providence since if the doctrine is admitted, the Creation is full of them, and if it is denied, the same explanation can be given of these as of any other, as the formation of the eye and ear. I will not ask what is that *other* explanation? for there is none. But there is such exquisite pleasure always derived from the perception of any design, that to a religious mind such allusion is never unwelcome.

There is yet a nearer view of God's Providence in which the soul hath a deeper interest, its dispensations of private lot, the apportionment of sorrow and success in life, as trial, as discipline, as reward, or as prophecy. None but a man's self knows how happy or unhappy he is (The heart knoweth its own bitterness, and the stranger doth not intermeddle with his joy),[5] for it is not the outward but inward condition which makes his weal or wo. But this is a subject by itself.

All I see and hear and feel teaches me to believe in a Providence general and particular, and *particular* because it is *general*. I believe that nothing is uncertain in its infinite plan; that every thing is grooved into its place; that the blessings of our life are as much procured under his will as the Tishbite when fed by the ravens,[6] that the seeming exceptions and violations of the general Order, are made to contribute to ultimate good; that madness hath its uses, and sin is not fruitless to the whole. I believe that God hath that interest in every event that it is impossible to separate his part from man's part in any; for our souls grow in him as the oak grows in the globe, or rather as the animal body in the earth, made of it, supported by it, yet having an independent will. But whilst reason points to these conclusions and all that we know confirms them, I am

5. Proverbs 14:10.
6. I Kings 17:4-6.

well aware how much the vastness of the subject seems to forbid the confidence of our understandings.

Therefore we welcome the clear light of revelation to supply these dim glimpses of pious experience. We welcome with joyful gratitude the declaration from God by his son that he is our Father, and that all things are subject to him and that all things work together for good to those that love him.[7]

Let us deserve that care. Let us remember that it is only virtue which can secure the safety that springs from the Divine favor.

7. Romans 8:28.

LXVII

*There is a spirit in man and the inspiration
of the Almighty giveth them understanding.*
Job 32:8

The fact that we have a twofold nature of body and of mind which though now existing in an intimate and mysterious union are wholly unlike in their qualities is acknowledged by all men and recognized in all the languages on earth. This fact is at the foundation of religion which addresses only one part of our nature and promises no permanence to the other. It declares to man that his body is of the dust and must return thither,[1] but that his mind is of God, like God, and is to be raised unto him, that if it be not contaminated by a subjection to that body which should be in subjection to it, it shall live with God. "There are given to you," say the Scriptures, "exceeding great and precious promises that ye might be partakers of the divine nature, having escaped the corruption that is in the world through sin."[2]

This fact, the community of nature between the mind and its maker, is declared continually in the scriptures, that the spirit of God is in us;[3] that it beareth witness that we are his children, that all good comes to us from an union with him, and all evil from a separation from him.[4]

I wish to speak of some of the attributes of our spiritual nature. And naturally it is an object of great interest. Man is slandered when he is represented as incurious about spiritual things. He has been baulked of knowledge where he expected to find it, and so listens with apathy at last; or, it may be, because they who teach the things of heaven are seekers with only the same advantages for discovery with those who hear, and so their report is often barren, but any fact carrying conviction with it, that respected the structure of the mind, or powers that yet slumbered there, or the future condition of the soul, is generally listened to with intense curiosity. Who ever has joined in the conversation of a large company or has attended a lecture to a mixed audience where any striking

---

Manuscript dated February 27, 1830, at Chardon Street. Preached three times: in the morning of February 28, 1830, at the Second Church, Boston, and in the afternoon of the same day at the Purchase Street Church; and again at the Second Church, December 11, 1831.
  1. Genesis 3:19.
  2. Cf. II Peter 1:4.
  3. Cf. I Corinthians 3:16.
  4. Cf. Matthew 5:9, Luke 20:36, John 11:52, Romans 8:16 and 9:26, Galatians 3:26, and I John 5:2.

fact or suggestion was thrown out with regard to the mind, such as might arrest the attention of a philosopher—will have noticed how instantly the silence deepened, marking that this was a sentiment which had equal interest for every person who understood the language. Who knows not the terror, suspending the powers of speech and motion, with which men have believed in the appearance of departed spirits? Any strong assertion of the soul's immortality or any fervent sentiment involving that fact goes to the heart of all men.

The extreme interest with which every man regards the signs of uncommon intelligence in animals, which seems to be a representation in shadow or a prophecy of the human mind, may show the curiosity we have concerning this nature. If an act of reason could be shown in a brute would it not attract universal attention and doubt?

This seems to me a high and cheering fact, this sharpness of the spiritual ear, to catch the grateful sounds of its native land.

Ye are the temples of the holy Ghost.[5] Nor let it be said, I pray you, that religion is a luxury and a greatness; that the best portion of society enjoy it, in different degrees, and come up happily to its elevating ordinances,—but that there is a vast number of men and women who live to their senses, and neglect their souls; who indulge themselves in every vice with an utter contempt of this alleged relation to a spiritual perfection; or who put no other restraint on their grossness than that evil prudence which moderates the crimes of today that it may wallow in tomorrow's crimes. Say not that this wretched part of every community which embraces many of this world's favoured children (I mean those who possess external advantages) have no knowledge of this spiritual greatness whereof they are heirs. I say they all confess it. In the lowest depths that man sinks himself to; in the worst slough of selfishness and unrestrained excess,—there is some intimation of his high descent, some spark of redemption the floods of sin have not quenched. The corrupt and corrupting sensualist in his degradation acknowledges his spiritual nature, that nothing is graceful or commends itself to the whole man without it, and feels that his pleasures are nauseous without its radiance. He tries to throw the charm of poetry and sentiment about his sins. He talks of Bacchus and Venus. He is aware that a sentiment must be forced in to keep sin from putrefaction and smelling in our nostril. Nobody ever came to an innocent person and talked barefacedly of a crime but always put some gloss upon it that implied the existence of moral sentiments. Murder was never advised as murder but as revenge, which is wild justice, or with ulterior ends which could be varnished over. And so with Avarice, Lust, Intemperance. No crime walks the earth but in the dress or with the name of some spiritual grace, and the great labor of the moralist every where is only to strip off the disguise and show the pretender as he is.

I propose to ask your attention to some of the attributes of our spiritual constitution.

1. Consider first the manifest superiority of the spirit over our bodies and

5. I Corinthians 3:16.

over all things; that life in us by which we are the interpreters and ministers of the Universe. As fire converts all things to its own form, so doth the mind feed indifferently on all nature. Who hath understood the way of the soul in man? Unseen it came, uncomprehended it acts, alone and unbeheld it departs. Observe the familiar fact how entirely the subtle spirit of man, unknown itself, to any other, is able to impart its own colour and nature to all that it knows; to all that it beholds. The mind plays its own tune on every thing: the mourner spreads the infection of his sadness over the countenance of all his friends; of all the bystanders; the melodies of youth and pleasure sound in his ear like painful dirges; the glorious roof of heaven seems to him but a pall; and the sun like a lamp in a sepulchre. The whole world is changed. Such strange power hath the soul in its emotion to infuse itself into the world.

And so when in some instance you have met with unexpected good fortune—how has it changed to you the whole aspect of things. And the faces of men that had seemed selfish and hostile, whether strangers or friends, now seemed to wear congratulation, and the earth shines with good, and echoes with happiness; there is beauty which we overlooked in the meanest weeds; resounding joy in the cities; silent praise in the fields. Mountains and hills break forth into singing and all the floods clap their hands.[6] Such is this dominion of the spirit that the outward world seems only a mirror to reflect the thoughts of the soul. Every animal in nature is to our eye a symbol of some moral quality in ourselves; the fox is cunning, the ape is folly, the viper is ingratitude, the ant is industry, the light is our emblem of knowledge, and darkness of ignorance; warmth is our emblem of charity and cold for selfishness, and so the mind goes up and down the world writing its own name on every phenomenon.[7]

On the eye of an ideot the whole world is nothing but a parcel of lines and colours. It is the spirit that opens the door into the beauty and order of the world. Then who can tell the powers of the mind, the *memory* which makes the past present; and *hope* which makes the future present; and so the mind triumphs over the world and embalms and immortalizes in itself the fading impressions of changing matter.

2. Consider in the next place the independence of spiritual distinctions on outward things.

The greatest powers of mind and the rarest virtues have been exhibited alike by poor men and rich men; in freedom and in servitude; in cold climates and in hot climates; by men and by women. When God raises up for the instruction of the human race any uncommonly gifted intellect it is as likely to be found in the laboring man's cradle as in the family of the rich. And in one profession what is the history of genius but a history of struggles between unfavorable circumstances and inward energy? And take all the biographies of all the great minds that have ever acted in the world and there are not two who have had similar

6. Cf. Psalms 98:8 and Isaiah 55:12.
7. Emerson uses a similar idea and some of the same illustrations in *Nature*, (CW 1:18).

education; so that there is no outward mark by which the wise child can be known from the fool; and no rules can be given by which genius can be disclosed in the brain of man.

The distinction of sex does not belong to the spiritual world. Our Saviour says that in heaven they neither marry nor are given in marriage,[8] that is to say there is no sex to thought or virtue, and the kingdom of heaven is the world of thought and virtue.

And as poverty, sickness, ill company, business have not prevented the intellect from acting with effect, much less have they hindered the moral perfections in the soul. Outward evils were the food and the occasion of virtue. By sorrow it learned repentance, by disappointment it learned steadiness and resignation, by hatred of men trust in God. By death it came to Life.[9]

And as it triumphs over circumstances so it does over events. As the mind improves, things that once vexed and afflicted us pester and afflict us no more. We get upward, though slowly.

3. A third attribute of the spirit is its infinite nature. Our bodies grow to the height of but a few feet; we can walk but a step at a time; we can lift but a small weight. But our intellectual and moral powers are a very striking contrast to this pinched ability. Who ever knew so much that he could learn no more? In knowledge and in goodness every step you make is only more preparation; all that you have known or done is only a point of support where you get a better purchase to make a new exertion. To know much is always to desire to know more. And every additional fact the mind acquires is an aid to its enlarging purposes. Every thought is a lamp which casts light into the darkness of the future to guide the mind as it explores its way into the dark of things. How ignorant we are. After years of constant learning the first questions yet remain to be asked. Yet did no one ever feel this ignorance to be a prohibition or natural obstacle to inquiry but only a motive to it, a persuasive invitation, and the more generous the mind the more sensibly it has felt the call. And herein, in this inborn and ever growing appetite for knowledge, have wise men found an evidence of the immortality of the soul. For, said they, if we should live to seventy years and the eyes not grow dim, nor the ears deaf, which are the porches of knowledge,[10] should we be able to learn all we wish to know? No, not in seven hundred years, or at the end of seven thousand, we should only be young scholars in the endless stores of truth. And therefore if God did not mean to mock us in giving us this craving curiosity after the angels' food, he by it declares to us the future life.[11]

And if the argument be a good one as it applies to the intellectual powers, is it any the less good as it applies to the moral powers? Did ever a man come to the end of Virtue, grow so good that he could not be better?

8. Matthew 22:30, Mark 12:25, and Luke 20:35.
9. Cf. John 5:24 and I John 3:14.
10. Cf. Shakespeare, *Hamlet,* I, v, 63, and Sermon XLI, n. 1.
11. Psalms 78:25.

Or does he not rather by every step only discover his deficiencies and learn better how to act, and when he dies he is more fit to live than ever before?

4. Another great attribute of spiritual nature is the immutability and perfection of its laws. I speak not now of a property of our minds but of a property of that element in which they belong; of the law by which they live.

Our spiritual nature is apt to receive so little of our attention, we are so much engrossed in the care of the body, that we neglect the fact of the stern uniformity of spiritual laws and act in violation of them. There is no imperfection or irregularity or liability of being deceived. Whosoever shall fall upon them will be ground to powder.[12] As in matter it takes an ounce to balance an ounce, so a spiritual advantage cannot be gained by any thing not proper to produce such an advantage. It is in vain that men try to take the spiritual world by an arm of flesh.[13] That which is born of the flesh is flesh and that which is born of the spirit is spirit.[14] And these distinctions are eternal. Men live as if the body might stand instead of the mind; as if reading the bible might serve for living by it; as if giving money was charity; or sitting in a pew was a compliance with the command, Thou shalt love the Lord thy God with all thy heart.[15]

But an age of ceremonies can never win the least advantage in the spiritual world. It is wholly real. Hypocrisy cannot exist in it. It is only the act of the mind that can affect the mind and hypocrisy is the substitution of the body for the mind.

Every religious rite may be the occasion or the channel through which pious sentiments may flow, but they have no sacredness of their own. The church walls are holy but only so to holy minds. The aisles of the church may be the council chamber of sin.[16] (When the Antinomians broke open churches and washed sheep in the baptismal font, those sheep were not baptized.) We come up to the temple to pray. A petition is offered in behalf of the assembly, but it is not the words in which it is conveyed, nor the house whose walls echo it, nor the standing congregation, that can give any virtue to our supplication: the blessing which attends it, is not promiscuous, nor equal: it singles out with omniscient perception each solitary heart that prays, and according to its offering, so is the blessing which rests upon it. As it is with prayer, so is it with baptism and the supper of the Lord. Just so far as those forms or any forms are vehicles of the feelings of those who take part in them, so far are they accepted in heaven and productive of good on earth and no farther.

Your souls are holy by the inhabitation of God's holy spirit, who dwells in them; your bodies are holy by the inhabitation of those sanctified souls.[17] The uniformity of these laws extends to all you do. There is nothing done for

12. Cf. Matthew 21:44 and Luke 20:18.
13. Cf. II Chronicles 32:8.
14. John 3:6.
15. Matthew 22:37, Mark 12:30, and Luke 10:27.
16. *JMN* 6:75.
17. Cf. I Corinthians 3:16.

nothing. You cannot have honor without being honorable. You cannot be pure without giving up your impurity.[18] You cannot be loved without becoming lovely. You cannot receive without asking; nor seek without finding; nor be happy without deserving.[19] And in this sufficiency and perfection of spiritual nature consists the power of the mind. This is the way in which God says to it, 'All things are yours.'[20] For he has shown it how to get all things; to clothe itself with his power; to be united to him by love and to live with him forever.

This highly endowed spirit is promised life forever more. It is offered in its very nature and in the circumstances in which it is placed, an eternity good and evil. But why is it thus endowed? Is there no return, no price to be paid? Much has been received only that much may be rendered.[21]

Why need I enumerate the powers of the soul? Each one whom I address carries within him a copy of the divine nature; and every one who hath ever addressed himself to God in prayer, who is engaged in striving to conform his life to the will of God, hath a more sublime revelation of the glory and promise of his nature than any words can express.

I beseech you, brethren, that you will not consider these great attributes as subjects of agreeable speculation and no more. If the remembrance and the obligation of them are not carried into the street and the closet and the bosom, they are worthless. If they are so carried as reasons of action and pledges of our connexion with God, they are an antidote in the end, against the sharpest calamity, they place the soul on a ground so high, that the inconveniences, the disappointments and fears of daily life cannot reach its tranquillity. A hasty word, an affront, a petty disaster; or, what are esteemed the great evils of life,— the loss of property, disease, bereavement, will not easily shake the soul that perceives itself to be the residence of that *mind,* whose will is Providence, which ordains all events, which can restore whatever it removes with increase of a hundred and a thousand fold;—and whose will is regarded by the soul as its own. And I hope it will not be said, that, however in the church, or in our silent retirements, we can reach these lofty views of the connexion of God with the soul, yet is it impossible to bring them home to the soul, to realize their presence, in the press of company and temptation, in the harassing anxieties of commerce, or mechanical labor, or, even in the less agitating round of household affairs. I know, brethren, the condition and temptations of different men are very unequal, and I do not wish to underrate real difficulty, but I believe that what seems so difficult, is yet far from impossible. If we will be greedy of small spiritual acquisitions,—and not believe that that can *never* be attained, which is not attained at the first, nor the second, nor the tenth trial,—we may accom-

18. The statement derives from a comment by Edward Stabler (1769–1831), a Quaker preacher from Alexandria, Virginia: see *JMN* 3:266. A version of the sentence is used in "The Divinity School Address" (*CW* 1:78).

19. Cf. Matthew 7:7–8 and Luke 11:9–10.

20. I Corinthians 3:21.

21. Cf. Luke 12:48.

plish more than the irresolute can conceive. By the continual effort to domesti-
cate our highest sentiments in our lowest affairs, we shall find them no
hindrance but that they give sweetness and dignity to all that we do. It is the
triumph of this part of our nature—its independence on circumstances. The
man of disciplined soul, i.e., the Christian, is always in heaven. The city or the
fields are alike to him. In a shop, in a crowd, in a prison, he can separate himself
from impure contact, and embosom his soul in the sublime society of his recollections, his hopes and his affections. In every place there is a duty, in every
event there is occasion of prayer. It is a maxim of state, that an ambassador
carries his country with him. So do our minds.[22] Every place and society
affords temptations to selfishness, to one man; opportunities of benevolence
and devotion to another. In every place, in every moment, we may renew our
communion with God, and offer our sacrifice, and delight in his love. For he is
in us, if we will seek him. Every moral agent is a temple which he hath built for
himself, and his spirit dwelleth therein, forever and ever.

22. "independence on circumstances . . . minds": cf. *JMN* 3:261. The passage in Emerson's
Blotting Book Psi occurs below another entry on the same page dated June 25, 1831. If the passage
was written after that date, it was either adapted from the sermon or the sermon version belongs
only to the third and last delivery.

LXVIII

Thou hast been faithful over a few things:
I will make thee ruler over many things.
Enter thou into the joy of thy Lord.

MATTHEW 25:23

We are sensible of very great degrees of difference in the virtues of different men. But to what height religion can carry our moral powers, we are wholly ignorant. God has hid the attainments of angels from us in his own heaven. Of course, we measure the exaltation of our moral heroes upward from the depths of human sin, and we say, Lo! what elevation, what perfection of character!

But probably when we escape from this pinfold of our life, when we are able to contemplate God more nearly—we shall have done extolling the mixed drossy grains of human virtue and make a higher and more difficult standard. What we know is but a point to what we do not know,[1] and what we do is a trifle to what can be done.

We can hardly quote too often the beautiful saying of that man who knew so much more than his fellow-men, Sir Isaac Newton, "I don't know," he said, "what I may seem to the world, but to myself, I seem to have been only like a boy playing on the seashore, and diverting myself in now and then finding a smoother pebble or a prettier shell than ordinary, whilst the great ocean of truth lay all undiscovered before me."[2] When we cast our eyes upward to the possible action of the heavenly world, to the vaster comprehension and higher relations of spirits, do we never suspect that what we call great virtue here may be mean and frivolous compared with what the good shall be?

But though this is probably true and will hereafter so appear to us, yet we must not therefore despair when we see the very imperfect goodness which mankind attain and we find our virtues are mixed, uncertain, feeble. We see men surrounded with temptation, and finding an apology for yielding to it, in

---

Preached three times: March 7, 1830, at the Second Church, Boston; February 24, 1832, as the Friday Evening Lecture at the Second Church; and November 5, 1837, in East Lexington.

1. Joseph Butler, quoted from Robert Plummer Ward, *Tremaine* (Philadelphia, 1825), 3:125–26. See *JMN* 6:64; used in Sermon XXXVI, "General Views" (*EL* 2:358), *Nature* (*CW* 1:25), and "Immortality" (*W* 8:341).
2. Joseph Spence, *Anecdotes, Observations, and Characters of Books and Men* (London, 1820), 54. See *JMN* 3:177.

the example of the major part of society. If you measure their conduct by what we know of duty, by the commandments of Religion, we find such alarming delinquency in it, that we are apt to be discouraged, and say with David, there is none that doeth good, no not one.[3] It would be better to remember that something is to be laid to the account of our constitution; to consider that God has here set us down to be tempted and tried; that it has come within the scope of his counsels, that man should be acquainted with vice, and earn the crown of virtue in overcoming it. Instead of desponding or taking an evil example from the vices of bad men we ought to consider the vast inequality of the condition of different men in their advantages for knowing and practising the duties of religion. Consider here among us in the most enlightened and moral part of Christendom the contrast of circumstances. One child is born of pious parents and the force of temptation is all along counteracted by good lessons and good company, by every outward bias the mind of man can receive.

Another child is born in a prison at the foot of the gallows of abandoned parents and turned out early into the street to be educated by bad boys and to feel the pinches of extreme want. If from these two persons the same obedience is expected, and they are to be judged by the same law, what squadrons of angels must not descend to protect, to influence, to save the last! What shield must not God's justice interpose between him and the else inevitable destruction to which he is exposed! No, brethren, the divine justice considers the *ability* to do right, as well as the *Commandment*. It receives the widow's mite,[4] as well as the benefaction of the rich; the first penitence of the poor outcast, on whom human laws had no mercy, as well as the easy offering of the time and the talents of the disciple who obeys from love and not from fear.

It is to be feared that when men, in view of the overmastering temptations of the world, say the demands of the gospel are too high for human infirmity to reach unto, it is said by those who would not comply with them if they were less. And surely it is true that the law of God is fixed and uncompromising, and will not truck and huckster with men for a partial obedience when they please to refuse a perfect obedience. But the law is yet merciful. And when men's ability is little, that little receives the reward of much. Jesus says to him that had wisely husbanded two talents, 'Well done! thou hast been faithful over a few things.' Let us carry home the moral to our own life. If men say that the temptations of the world are a fearful overmatch to the motives of duty, and intimate that as we cannot do all we may as well do no part, let us remember that a little virtue will not be despised, that the least sacrifice to principle is in the sight of God of great price. A cup of cold water God will accept.[5] Christianity puts its claim within your means. It takes you at your own word. You say splendid virtues may issue from here and there a solitary soul but they are so rare that they can never become the subject of calculation. The gospel will do after the

3. Psalms 14:3 and 53:3.
4. See Mark 12:42 and Luke 21:2.
5. Matthew 10:42. For the "pearl of great price," see Matthew 13:46.

manner of those who wish to compass an end and care not so that is compassed for the greatness of the particulars. As, to further our public charities, we can't get great donations and should make the donors bankrupt if we did,—men are content to get the same amount slower by fairs and children's contributions, so Christianity despises nothing because it is small, provided only that it is according to your ability. It says, Be not discouraged if you find more difficulties in your path to heaven, than in the first ardour of youthful resolution, you anticipated. You have aimed at great conquests with too much confidence in yourself, and are dispirited now by apparent failure. Hope on. Be thankful with growing better by small and almost imperceptible acquisitions, only see to it that you husband them well.

Herein the divine wisdom practises on the known principles of human nature. Though these small accumulations are slower, yet are they safer—though the society of the good become one of moderate merits and the results are more remote, yet vast numbers can belong to it, who would be excluded from one of prouder aims. And as all who have a stake though ever so little will look after it, this secures the sympathy of such a vast assembly as could not otherwise be brought to see their own interest in the interests of religion.

My friends, I wish the words of Jesus might prevail with us to direct a new attention and a greater respect to the improvement of our characters by small degrees. What is biggest is made up of minute parts. "Drops make the Ocean; sands compose its shores;"[6] and every advantage gained by us, however partial, over our bosom sin, is a fragment added to us from the Divine Nature.

Besides there is no such thing as a small virtue. Virtue is always great, and, to the least action which it inspires, it imparts something of grandeur. Whatever else of power or splendour there is on earth, can be shown to be trifling by a comparison with something better, but a virtuous sentiment is absolute greatness. And this magnitude may often be seen in their consequences. In morals you can never measure the consequence by the cause. A petty act of injustice or a trifling act of beneficence done in a corner often grows in its issues to an influence of uncontrollable strength.

No, virtue is not little in itself, or in its consequence. Littleness consists in the purpose not in the act. And the more consideration is given the more it will be felt that nothing of virtue is too small to be desired.

If therefore there is any one who hears me who is conscious that he is not very good, who has ever felt or made any apology for his faults in the unmeasured demands of duty, I beseech him to consider if he cannot lay some foundation for a virtuous character by aiming at a little instead of so much. A few good actions,—one good action, is something done. Let him feel that it is his object to get a small capital of virtues. It matters not how few coals kindled the fire. This done, this beginning made, this modest stock of goodness acquired, all things will work well. Every thing in the Universe draws to its kind. We get a taste for

6. See *JMN* 6:40 and 6:225.

Virtue as we advance in virtue. He will presently feel that the only way to keep one's virtue in repair, is to refresh old merits with new ones.

Be suspicious of yourself. Use a careful discretion in the formation of your virtuous character. Do not sound a trumpet before you and set out with loud protestations to your kindred and friends that now you are going to lead a holy life[7]—'Come all and see my spotless example.' It is a bad omen for the depth and permanence of your reformation that it begins in talking. But go alone and deal faithfully with yourself, and find out what is that particular fault which you commit every day, which you can hardly help committing, nay concerning which twenty times you have tried to persuade yourself very good persons have done the same thing and so perhaps after all, it is no such heinous matter. Select that one fault, and not underrating and yet not overrating the temptation, seriously consider how it may be encountered, whether peradventure you cannot avoid the occasions of it today, and tomorrow prevent their return; and on the third day return to the same contest. Live to the purpose of stopping that mischief. No pains are too great for so great a good. Our ruling sin is the inlet of more sin and more danger than the eye that only sees to the doors of the tomb.

What then are your infirmities? Are you master of your appetite?

Let him who would make small gains in virtue great, observe the rules of a strict discretion. If you have only a little time for reading you would be careful to take up the book where you left off, and keep the thread of the discourse unbroken in your mind. If you skip from page to page, your advantage will be less. Let us do the same in our search after virtue. Do not aim today to be careful in speaking the truth, and tomorrow, neglect that and seek something new, and the third day, to be industrious in increasing your knowledge. But make your efforts on a system. If today you can forbear every expression of peevishness by forbearing to speak; try, tomorrow, to forbear it,—which is a far harder task,—in conversation.

Positive abstinence is always easier than an exact moderation in all our gratifications.

Temperance in eating and drinking, and early hours, which is temperance in sleep, are of those virtues which keep the doors of the temple.

The rigid government of the body will produce a clear head, and give us a command over many hours that the habit of indulgence has in some way made useless before. If this self-restraint is accomplished from any motive it will produce a clear head. If it is accomplished from the desire of pleasing God— then it becomes virtue, and it will produce a light heart, that pure and affectionate spirit which prophesies to us of good and leads on to more.

Or perhaps your ruling sin is inordinate selfishness. You cannot part with any portion of your earnings to relieve the wants of your destitute friend. If you suspect that here is your strongest temptation, combat this hard heart with

7. Cf. Matthew 6:2.

specific resolutions. Speak kindly to him. Give him a little. For that trifle, you shall find you love him better, and can give him more, so carefully has God armed virtue with unexpected helps in the structure of society.

Or if you chiefly offend against the law of *truth;* if in the course of your daily trade you overpraise your commodities; if in social circles, you tell the lie of vanity, or of calumny, or of flattery,—then direct your whole strength to that one point. Aim to speak truth. Correct and qualify your too general assertion. This also shall bring its speedy reward. "I judge," said a man of great worldly wisdom, "by every man's truth of his degree of understanding."[8] And so does every man. And the habit of measuring one's assertion before it is uttered, increases the acumen of thought and begets in other men unfailing confidence in what you affirm.

Indeed, my friends, the first thing we shall be struck with in our attempts to make any accessions to our virtuous character is that any degree of persistency in such an attempt is rewarded by a growing facility in the practice; a facility which becomes pleasure; a pleasure which becomes delight; and ever leading on to a far more rapid and more exalted progress. The whole difficulty lies in the early steps. The great strides which the soul makes afterwards are not of greater exertion. It takes a million no longer to become two million than it takes one cent to become two cents.

I trust, my brethren, I shall not be misapprehended as aiming to lower the lofty standard of a religious life. I believe there is no quackery in morals. A man to be happy must be good. A man to be happy must enter in connexion with God. But there are first steps to be taken. There is a time *to begin.*

But I fear many men pass through life without any efforts, as such, towards the education of the soul. Now I cannot think but we do a most useful service if we remove only the rubbish from the doors of his spirit which is the temple of God. And perhaps there is no one of us who have come up hither but if he will diligently explore his recent experience may find reason to think that by concentrating his efforts upon one point he may gain a peace which he has never possessed. He may prepare himself with greater hope for the hour of death and the day of judgment. He may anticipate the declaration, Well done good and faithful servant, thou has been faithful over a few things. Enter into joy.

---

8. See *The Letters of Philip Dormer Stanhope, Lord Chesterfield,* ed. J. Bradshaw (London, 1892), 1:59. Quoted in *JMN* 4:73 and 6:63; used in "The Superlative" (*W* 10:168).

LXIX

We then as workers together with him
beseech you that ye receive not
the grace of God in vain.

II CORINTHIANS 6:1

During my recent absence from this place, Christian friends, the year has been completed from the day of my ordination to the Christian ministry.[1] I am unwilling to let the occasion pass without notice. Our life is hurrying to an end. And as we pass from stage to stage, we find a sad but wholesome admonition in the notice we take of these measures of time. Especially do these seasons demand attention when like this, they mark out periods of duty; when conscience, the truth teller, looks down on the poor performance of our imperfections and sternly points at the high requisition—all unfulfilled; when the hope and the vow of the first day of a year of time is put side by side with the remembrance of the last; when we come to see what a train of inconveniences, infirmities, private disappointments and sins come in to hinder and postpone the execution of our designs. In view of this contrast between what was purposed with what has been done, man eats the bitter herbs of regret and becomes acutely sensible of the sore side of his condition.[2]

Suffer me then to offer you some remarks suggested by the occasion on some of the obligations that arise to you and to me out of the pastoral relation. I have said that the first feeling on considering the sanguine hopes of a past year in close connexion with their defeat is the deepest regret at failure.

And I, brethren, when I only look back on this span of time, which I had hoped would be rich with life and thought and action, when I see how the facts shrink from the promise—how little I have done and how little I have learned, even with the best hope I can dare to form of good derived from the connexion thus far established between you and me—I confess I am oppressed with doubt and sorrow, and if I stopped with this view, I should despond.

This sermon, Emerson's retrospect of his first year as minister of the Second Church, was preached once: April 4, 1830, at the Second Church, Boston.

1. Emerson was ordained on March 11, 1829. On March 9, 1830, he took his wife to Philadelphia, hoping the change of climate would alleviate her tubercular symptoms. During this absence of nearly a month, Emerson preached in Hartford and Philadelphia.

2. Cf. Exodus 12:8 and Numbers 9:11.

156

But this is not right. This is too limited a view. Why art thou cast down, oh my soul, and why art thou disquieted within me? Hope thou in God.[3] That we should deeply mourn and truly repent of our own negligence is most suitable to our condition and nature. But it is also suitable to our nature, and to the faith we hold fast as the children of God, and the disciples of Christ, that we should bate no jot of heart or hope.[4] It would argue a self-sufficiency from which I pray to be preserved, to suppose because we have done little, that little has been done. What am I, that I should let my private contrition cloud my views of God and the doings of his providence among men? What? that I should lament over the inefficacy of any one or more means of good as if the purposes of God's benevolence were obstructed thereby. It is true, God enables us to be of use to our fellow-men,—each according to his several gifts,—and rewards our goodness by making us see often the fruits of our exertions. But all the time, we are in a strong sense, instruments in his hand, and 'tis reasonable to suppose he would have procured the same good for his children, whether we had acted or had forborne to act. Preaching, what St. Paul calls "the foolishness of Preaching,"[5] is but one voice in the choir of the world. The doctrines of the gospel, the Spirit of Christ is preached to men not only by the tongues of ministers; and the written Scriptures; but by the events that daily occur; by all the lives of those who live; by the remembrance of all those who are dead; by the connexions with society which trade, or curiosity, or pleasure, or want, or consanguinity, or love make us form; by the development of the affections; in short, by all the parts of each man's personal experience. I take this to be an indisputable truth. For all men are at all times drawing insensibly a moral from what they see doing around them; and with this moral (as it appears to those who have deduced it most clearly) the precepts of Jesus strictly coincide. Now if the pulpit is silent these thousand teachers do not cease to speak. If the pulpit is false, if it is afraid, if it speaks smoothly, or superstitiously,—this ceaseless instruction of God's Providence *goes on,* and is never false or superstitious or afraid. It contradicts them and accuses them. Nor can these events, nor can Religion, ever want articulate voice. We may extol the individual merits of one man as much as we will, but the truth which he teaches perishes with no man. He was only a spectator with more or less advantages for seeing the ways of God, but the same advantages exist and will commend themselves to other eyes who will also declare them. O do not think

> "Tho' men were none, that Heaven
> Would want spectators, God want praise."[6]

So then neither is he that planteth any thing nor he that watereth but God that

---

3. Psalms 42:5, 42:11, and 43:5.
4. John Milton, "To Mr. Cyriack Skinner upon His Blindness," lines 7–8.
5. I Corinthians 1:21.
6. John Milton, *Paradise Lost,* IV, 675–76.

giveth the increase.7 This is the reason why our consciousness of imperfection and sin should not discourage us in our work.

Think not, my friends, that I find in this way of thinking any apology for remissness in a pastor or other teacher in the discharge of his duty. I say it only as the just consolation of that comparison between what is required with what has been performed, a comparison which without this relief would lay on our shoulders a responsibility overwhelming. I make no apology for remissness. If I have neglected my duties, I shall leave it in silence. I shall not add the guilt of excusing it. The minister of Christ will find motive and sermon in his name against all indolence. He must be instant in season and out of season.8 He must so serve the altar that he is never from it. He is to carry the light of God's presence with him always, not to wear a grave face or to talk from the Scriptures but to wear a pure heart out of which a good conversation, good manners, good actions, shall proceed as naturally as clean water from a pure spring. This leads me to another point.

But the activity which is the duty of a Christian minister in the discharge of his office, is of two kinds, preacher and pastor, and often in some measure incompatible.

He attempts with no better spiritual light than his brethren enjoy, to study the scriptures and to explain God's laws and exhort them to comply therewith. A man who is presumed to have inclination and ability for the study of religious principles, is set apart for their discussion, because no man can discuss them without study, and all men are benefitted by having them discussed. But he must deserve the attention of those who come to him to be moved to the love of God by speaking wisely. He is the last who may be indulged in talking inconsiderately. He should not bring to the service of God what he would be ashamed to offer in the service of man. But every one at all accustomed to attend to what passes in his own mind may know that for the most part the thoughts which are greatest and truest, do not flash upon the soul in a moment in all their fulness, but are, first, remote possibilities, then, opinions, then, truth, as our knowledge increases; that different minds require different culture to bring them into action; that though the light of duty is always present to all, the reason of duty, is not; that sometimes silence and solitude, sometimes conversation, sometimes action, sometimes books, are necessary to repair the flagging powers of the soul, and enable it to carry on its inquiry. And just in proportion to a man's respect for the soul's good of his brethren will be his anxiety to prove all things—to hold fast that which is good9 and thence his care to do whatsoever he can to quicken and help the often uncontrollable faculties of his mind.

But the laws of thought are not accommodated to the divisions of time. The services of the church are periodical, but the development of truth within the

7. I Corinthians 3:7.
8. II Timothy 4:2.
9. I Thessalonians 5:21.

mind is not. Obviously then the minister who makes it an important aim to convey instruction must often stay at home in the search of it when his parishioners may think he would be more usefully employed in cultivating an acquaintance with them. You will therefore have the charity to think, when you do not see your pastor as often or at the times when you could wish it, and he desire it, that he may be employed with earnest endeavours to speak to you usefully in this place.

Another subject of which I am naturally led to speak is the character of the exhortations of the pulpit. I believe none who hears me can be more sensible of their faults than I am. But I have spoken to you of our faith and duty as well as I could. We come often to church and our time is spent here in the same way. I certainly do not hope with each new day to engage your minds with new thoughts on the topics here treated—which are of immemorial meditation. The man who speaks to his fellows on the duties they owe and on the relations they sustain to God, must ever insist on those commandments which he thinks they have broken, whether those laws have been read to them one time, or a thousand. I do not think it necessary to say to you, Do not worship idols; for Christianity has shamed the idolater, and broken the image. I do not think it necessary to say to you, Do not kill; Do not steal; Do not commit adultery; because they who do thus are not often in this house, but I do think it important to say, Love the Lord thy God, with all thy heart: Love thy neighbor as thyself. Do not bear false witness; Be temperate; pray; give; because we are at all times liable to offend in some one of these points. Moreover some of these commandments touch those parts of action which never reach their limit, but admit of infinite improvement; and the spirits of just men in heaven may add fervor to each other's love and devotion, by exhorting each other to a celestial benevolence, to a seraphic prayer.[10]

All spiritual truth is open to the investigation of all. But, as in our country, we all have our several and beloved home; among men, our select friends; among things indifferent,—our own caprice; among innumerable books, our chosen pages; so is it here. Every mind hath its favourite resorts in the spacious domain of truth, its church of virtuous thoughts, whither it repairs morning and evening;—its own heaven where it takes calm but glorious surveys of God's Providence; where it finds solemn motives to do justly, love mercy, and walk humbly,[11] where it best learns the lesson of serenity and trust.

I shall count it no reproach if I am reminded that my subjects have little variety. I count it the great object of my life to explore the nature of God. For this I would read and think and converse and act and suffer, and if I shall

10. Emerson here defines his ministry as less concerned with the Old Testament Law embodied in the ten commandments of Exodus 20:1-17 than the new commandments announced by Christ and recorded in Matthew 22:37-40, Mark 12:30-31, and Luke 10:27. With "the spirits of just men in heaven" cf. Hebrews 12:23.
11. Micah 6:8.

succeed in enlarging in any degree, your conceptions of the divine nature and government or confirming your convictions, I shall praise him that he has permitted me to be so honoured an instrument in his hand.

To another point I must say a few words, namely upon what is your duty in the observation of public worship. The difference in the attendance on church in the two parts of the same day you are aware is often very great. It cannot be that any very extensive changes have taken place in the situation of families. I fear we are doing ourselves great harm when we begin to relax, in any point, the fidelity of our religious observances,—and mainly the keeping of the Sabbath. The duty of religious improvement is plain enough. It is every man's first and peculiar business. You have chosen me to aid in its public functions. I conceive it then becomes yours to make me as useful to you as possible by bringing hither a devout temper and hearing with what candor you can.

Of course I do not speak with any the least reference to personal feeling. I have no right and certainly no disposition to call upon you here for personal attention. But I do beseech you to give attention to your own spiritual habits and not permit any negligence of a devout custom to grow into a habit with you. Believe me, it will grow fast to an alarming laxity and libertinism. Religion is a plant of that delicacy that will not bear the least tampering as the costliest fruits are soonest spoiled. In the hour of youth and joy and self-confidence you may esteem these things as decorous customs, and neglect them in your own heart;—but, o, the hour will come, and probably many before you go out of this world, when in sorrow, in danger, in anxiety, in solitude, the deep and eternal value of a religious faith shall make itself felt in your heart—when you shall weep at the long neglect that has estranged you from it and darkened your moral perception and thrown an immoveable shade over the evening of your days; or shall rejoice over every humble act of worship, every public offering, every closet prayer as the means that have brought the Spirit of God into your mind and fixed it an eternal inhabitant.

The year is gone and we remain. It has carried many of our brethren and sisters to the world of spirits, who were wont to keep holy day with us and come up to the house of God in company—the old man is gone, full of days,[12] and the infant whose eye had not yet grown familiar with the sun. It has multiplied our days and advantages. And what have we done my friends? Have we multiplied our connexions with heaven? have we studied in the school of Christ? What proficiency have we made in our imitation of his example? Have we complied with his ordinances? Have we eaten of his bread and drunk of his cup? or have we done the same in a spiritual sense? I fear, brethren, the best of us would tremble if we should be called to a strict account, if it should be numbered against us how many duties we had neglected, how frivolous, how sensual, how selfish, how unjust we have been. Let us pray and let us strive that the year which has begun should be brightened by the proofs of our repentance and our

12. Psalms 55:14 and Genesis 35:29.

piety. Let us consecrate anew these old walls that have heard the prayers of faithful men for three generations,—by coming duly under their holy shelter with the love of God in our hearts, that we may be able to contemplate the future with calm delight and may go away when God calls us from the means and exercises of his grace here to the boundless joy and glory of the spiritual world.

Happy is that people whose God is the Lord.

PSALMS 144:15

We are summoned on this occasion to consider in a peculiar manner the general offences of the people and to pray for the community in which we live. And when we consider the advantages derived to us in our passage through this world from living under a good form of government, the great influence which it may exert upon our characters, and our happiness; his civil relations become an object of serious attention to a Christian.

A bad government may check the progress of knowledge and indefinitely multiply the ordinary amount of temptation; it may have that degree of corruption that no man can act with it unless at a sacrifice of principle. And all the experience of man is, with few exceptions, a tragic tale of the pernicious connexion between the ruler and the ruled.

In a well constituted state, the government itself will be out of sight, will not be the prominent and exclusive object of attention whenever the country is considered.[1] But all the past history of man is little more than a story of governments. The people, their occupations, their habits, their thoughts, their intellectual and religious condition are thrust aside, or only appear as they acted in relation to their ruler.

It becomes then, at all times to every thoughtful Christian a question of interest, what is the extent of his means of affecting the public mind; and a subject of devout gratitude, whenever Providence has ordered his lot in mercy in a country where the rights of men are recognized by the laws.

It has pleased God eminently to distinguish us with these civil advantages. We eat a harvest which we have not sowed. We are born to an inheritance which was paid for partly by the toil and suffering of the last generation, and in part by

---

Like Sermons XVII, CXIII, and CL, this was written for Fast Day, a day of penance decreed by the civil government of Massachusetts annually since 1694 for the first or second Thursday in April. Sermon LXX was delivered three times: twice on Thursday, April 8, 1830, at the New North Church in the morning and at the Second Church, Boston, in the afternoon; and, with a revised introduction referring to the election season, on November 13, 1836, in East Lexington (see Textual and Manuscript Notes).

1. In the lecture "Politics," Emerson wrote, "the less government we have, the better" (*EL* 3:242; repeated in the essay "Politics," [*CW* 3:126]). In Emerson's day and since, the idea has been associated with Thomas Jefferson; see his *Memoir, Correspondence, and Miscellanies* (Boston, 1830), 2:85.

earlier labourers, by the exertion of many an ardent soul in this country and in England for two or three centuries past.

But however procured, (and it was not procured by us) it exists to us the most perfect government—most perfectly answering to a Christian man the purposes of a state of any one on human record. The advantages of a government, it is agreed, must always be negative. It cannot do any good to the intellectual or religious character of the citizen. Such benefit must arise to him from himself; if it occasions him no harm,—if it leaves him in entire freedom, as long as he injures no body—I call it a perfect government.

And this good condition of safety is certainly secured by our social system to every citizen. Unseen itself it envelopes him like the air. A man of retired habits may live ten years in the unmolested pursuit of his own calling and excepting the payment of his tax, and his service on a jury, never have his notice called to the fact that there is a government, and a code of laws. But if his property or his rights are invaded either where he stands, or in another town, or another land,—he finds that this sleeping Law whose existence he had forgotten, hath an arm of Power that can reach from sea to sea, from nation to nation, and demand redress for him all over the earth.

This good government we have. It is not yet to be procured. It is now possessed. All that rests with us is to preserve it. These institutions are far too excellent, and far too rare in the history of the world to be exposed to the slightest risk.

Yet all men are impressed among us with a sense of their danger, of the uncertainty of their tenure. Thus far the evil operation, if there be any, has not reached the privileges of the citizen. If it is felt at all, it is not felt beyond the offices of the state, beyond the machinery of the government itself.

But as the number of the offices of the government is many thousands, if any great evil should operate therein, its influence must needs be extensive, and must command the vigilance of all.

Then all men are sensible of the mischief of a licentious press as it is used for party purposes. All men are hurt and alarmed by the flood of slander that is every week and every day poured over the land by the madness of party spirit, destroying the peace and fame of good men, corrupting the ear of the people, and familiarizing the public mind with profligacy and avarice under the name and pretensions of patriotism.

There is yet another evil sign to our country in the strong tendency to disunion that blazes out in the discussion of every political question. All things are seen with partial eye. The strong voice of Self interest seems to be thought an overmatch for every other plea, and the abominable maxim of little calculators—"The world will last our day"—is almost avowed as the rule of political action. These evils all good men lament; and most have an impression that they are growing worse. Yet no one seems to imagine that he himself or his friends or his party are concerned in the guilt.

But how should it happen that in this virtuous nation such evil things should be done? It cannot be that a colony of bad men should have settled in the bosom of the land. There must be a traitor in the camp of Israel.[2] It must be that the good are not good enough; it must be that the bad derive a countenance from the good. It must be that the standard of private virtue is nowhere very high, that God's commandments are disobeyed by his children, that those who are called Christians have not the spirit of Christ. Consider whilst we so readily repeat and deplore the fact of the increasing profligacy in the public morals, if we ought not rather to lay our hands on our own breasts, and say, *we are the men.*

Let it be considered by us that a small amount of evil in those who are reckoned the good sort of people, becomes pretty coarse depravity when imitated on their authority in another class,—in a class where the restraints of opinion and of standing are less. The Newspaper which is a scourge to the country is only the common and tolerated degree of vice exhibited—like the insensible motion of the hand of a watch made sensible by being lengthened on the dial of a clock. People say as bad things of each other in good society as are printed in the worst papers. Then if people would not read bad papers, they would not be printed. But they are received by persons whom all would say are incapable of abetting a corrupt cause.

As it is with this ferocious calumny, so is it with the selfishness that appears in public measures. It is only the selfishness of private life magnified by being put on a great scale, and under the searching scrutiny of a nation's eyes. They who act after this manner are not acting in any new and original way. They are following their habits. They are practising the lessons which they have learned in the common usages of trade, which men well-reputed in the world for virtue permit themselves to sanction. Indeed they are acting as they have always acted in their families and with their neighbours, and have not found that it injured them with any other persons than those whom it injured, or that it forfeited their place in society. They have had the instinct, it is true, not to show this fang to those whom it was important to conciliate, but only to such as might be overreached or oppressed. Moreover, whatever acts or attempts of a political character you most loudly condemn as sordid, did not by any means belong exclusively to those who were the agents, but had or expected the countenance of multitudes, or certainly they would not have been done.

It is thus that the political measures of this nation and of every nation may be regarded as an index whereon the average degree of private virtue is made known to the world.

It may be stated as a general law that the rulers of a country are a fair representation of the virtue of a country. In a virtuous community men of sense and of principle will always be placed at the head of affairs. In a declining state of public morals men will be so blinded to their true interests as to put the incapable and unworthy at the helm. It is therefore vain to complain of the

2. Perhaps an allusion to the perfidy of Achan, described in Exodus 7.

follies or crimes of a government. We must lay our hands on our own hearts and say, here is the sin that makes the public sin.

And it should be felt by us also that this average public virtue is never a fixed amount but always fluctuating; that it depends not on masses, but on individuals; and that each of us every day does somewhat to raise or to depress it. Let no man shelter himself under a false modesty, as if what he did or said could be of insignificant consequence in the vast aggregate of action. Every one knows that when men come in their business to consider how far they may honourably go in this or that transaction, a few opinions, the names of half a dozen men who would approve or condemn the course, are quoted as authority and commonly decide the question in each man's mind.

Nothing in this world ends in itself. High virtue will surely be attended with deep respect. It is of God and cannot be overlooked. It will prove a stimulus and encouragement to goodness where ever it goes. It will confirm the wavering purpose and rebuke the newborn sin. Virtue tends to create virtue as surely as vice to beget vice.

Let it be deeply felt by you that however you may despair—a solitary individual—to do any thing of importance to stay the public degeneracy, yet when it is directed to your own character not a single exertion is without effect. This is the true way to reform states. You compel people to be better by being better yourself. For you do something to raise the standard of virtue in the world, which is always the average of the virtue of the individuals. What said the Saviour? Let your light so shine before men, that others seeing your good works may glorify your Father which is in Heaven.[3]

Whilst thus you fulfil the duty of Patriotism let it never be forgotten by us that our duties are appointed to us here only for a little time. We are citizens of the heavenly country.[4] Are you unable to controul your sorrow at witnessing the corruptions of the state? Rejoice that the hour cometh when God will release you from your service here and join you to a purer society—a peculiar people.[5] But do not therefore relax your zeal to improve the character of your fellow men. The privileges, the high places of that state are given to those who have most efficiently laboured in their place and duty on earth—according to God's commandments. Thus hath Godliness the promise of the life that now is and of that which is to come.[6] It should give us pleasure to reflect that the piety which we owe to one country enjoins the patriotism which we owe to the other and that God has so harmoniously joined together the good of this temporal and of that eternal world, that every effort which we make with a pure heart to deserve his favor, every struggle with temptation, is so much done to purify and so to perpetuate the civil institutions of our land.

3. Matthew 5:14.
4. Cf. Hebrews 11:16.
5. Cf. Deuteronomy 14:2 and Titus 2:14.
6. I Timothy 4:8.

LXXI

*Keep thy heart with all diligence,
for out of it are the issues of life.*

PROVERBS 4:23

The wise king of Israel saith to his Son, Take care lest thy heart be corrupted, for from thence come the causes of a long and happy life.[1] The passage has been understood to refer, as that of our Saviour in Matthew, does,[2] in terms, to the extreme solicitude with which the Jews abstained from putting certain meats into the mouth. Take no thought, said Jesus, and here would Solomon say, what goes into the mouth, but what comes out of the heart. I propose to offer at this time, some remarks in illustration of a rule from such venerable authority, and so highly sanctioned.

In the lowest sense of this language, and a sense to which the imperfect faith of Solomon often leads him to limit his instructions, a long and happy life in the earth is promised to the diligent cultivation of virtuous feeling.

And the testimony of experience concurs with this declaration inasmuch as nothing more powerfully contributes to prolong and sweeten life than that cheerful habit of mind which comes from innocent and regular affections.

The larger sense, however, is the obvious and undeniable one which declares a good heart to be the best good—a sentiment than which none is more grateful or more true.

This truth does not belong to books and Scriptures. It is not the slow deduction of reason, nor confined to prophets or learned men. It is God's truth, known to all human nature, perceived in all action, heard in all speech, written in the expression of every countenance. A child will find out as quickly as the profoundest philosopher if those who are in the room with him have good feelings or not, and makes up his mind as decidedly as the sage, upon the superiority of a good heart to all other merits. "Oppression," it has been said, "will be felt where it is not seen,"[3] and the greatest part of the bitterness of life is

---

Preached three times: April 11, 1830, at the Second Church, Boston; November 27, 1831, again at the Second Church; and February 12, 1837, in East Lexington.

   1. Emerson paraphrases the advice of Solomon to his son in Proverbs 4:23.

   2. Matthew 15:11–20.

   3. Harrington [Emerson's note]. The reference is apparently to Aphorism V ("The people cannot see, but they can feel") in James Harrington, *Aphorisms Political,* 2d ed. (London, 1659). See *The Political Works of James Harrington,* ed. J. G. A. Pocock (Cambridge, 1977), 762.

occasioned, by our neglect or our contempt of the feelings of others, that is to say, by a thousand petty pieces of selfishness; a thousand slight assumptions, in word or manners; numberless instances in which we have lent our help in some degree to the propagation of a slander; and the daily returning occasions when we make a headache or the east wind an apology for venting our bad humour upon all to whom our situation gives us leave to be tyrannical. At the bottom of all the fraud and cruelty that is in the earth is *the bad heart,*—the capital oppressor of mankind.

The good heart is in like manner the benefactor, the cheerer, the light of the world.[4] From the heart go out all the affections that bind us dearly to our parents and friends, that make us feel an injury to our natural protectors to be more criminal than the same offence to a stranger, that bind us to show kindness and deference to all our household—to all our neighbors—and especially to the unfortunate—in fine, that press upon us the claims of country and mankind, that show us a certain amiableness and perfectness in good actions done to others beyond the accurate amount of benefit conferred, that makes indeed that part of well doing, that cannot be calculated, often the most in our esteem, that makes a kind intention or a kind wish outvalue a costly gift.

Every man is well enough acquainted with human nature to say who among his acquaintance have good hearts and who not. In the hours of ease and in the business of life, we are more indifferent to the distinction between characters. Interest and civility will serve our turn, and we put up with them. But when misfortune changes our affairs, when we are sick, when the life or the reason of a dear friend, is taken away or he has forfeited his virtue—then when the distressed mind turns about on every side for sympathy and consolation, then it knows the inestimable worth of a true heart to which it can apply itself in all its length and breadth and turns away with aversion from the fluent civilities and ostentatious kindness of the great, to the support that perhaps in a more prosperous hour it had slighted.

That heart which feels its duty to God will always most strongly sympathize with man.

Solomon annexes to his charge, the declaration, "for out of it are the issues of life." And this is true because in the heart are contained first the direction of the intellectual life and secondly the promise of eternal life.

I. The good heart gives a good direction to the opinions. In the uncertainty of our knowledge we are very often called to act on dim probabilities; the man who has the habitual desire to give all men their due will always incline the scale toward the general good and the man who prefers himself—toward his own. It was remarked of an eminent philanthropist that though he had not great talents, he had a *certain natural propensity to be in the right.* And it is truly so, that the good man often does things which he feels to be good, without being able to assign the grounds of his belief. It has been finely said, "The heart hath its

4. John 8:12.

arguments, with which reason is not acquainted."[5] We are judges of right and wrong by a divine instinct, but we explain our practical conclusions of it by a slow comparison of manifold and contradictory considerations.

Yet when so explained they are found to justify the choice and to verify the maxim that there never was jar or discord betwixt just sentiment and sound policy.[6] But the hard heart; may God who delivers us from temptation, deliver us from that. It deforms all the action; it corrupts all opinion; it poisons even our very goodness; for the just or the bountiful act that is done on selfish calculation hath the soul of justice and of bounty taken out. It is dead works without faith. It neutralizes even the effect of God's precious gift of a great understanding by making it an object of suspicion and fear. And plainly will not he who loves men be more likely to act wisely and efficiently in any good undertaking for them than he who loves only himself?

Thus out of the heart come the issues of intellectual life.

II. In the second place, out of the heart are the promises of everlasting life. Religion springs up spontaneously in the virtuous soul. If you look round you through the circle of your acquaintaince, you shall find that those whose benevolence is the greatest, whose life is purest, are always those who have the strongest faith in the Providence of God and the future state. Indeed this brings a mighty internal evidence to our faith that just as men do good the religious faith is confirmed. It is receiving the very reward promised to obedience.[7] But the bad heart shuts out the light and influences of God's spirit from itself, for it doubts and argues and reasons downward till it doubts of God. It punishes itself with the gloom of despondency. It finds out that the Father of the Universe is a delusion of men; that there is no life in us; that there is no hope for us; that the human soul hath been lying to itself all these past ages; that the great promise of the human understanding is false; the glorious perception of a Providence which, as we grow wise, we just begin to discern, and all our years disclose more and more traits of the infinite perfection—is a dream. Alas! Is there no reason to think, that it is the mind perverted because the heart is hard? It is the evil heart of unbelief.[8]

Keep then thy heart with all diligence, for out of it are the issues of life, the perception and promise of life everlasting.

But is it asked whether there be not great difference in natural endowment and whether one person does not receive a warm and sympathizing and another a cold and phlegmatic temper? Undoubtedly there is great original difference in this respect among men. But what then? Do we continue such as we are born? Or does not a warm heart grow cold and a selfish man grow generous by indulging one or another habit? Is it not true that a bad man can become worse

5. See *Pascal's Pensées,* trans. Martin Turnell (New York, 1962), 163; and *JMN* 6:39 and 6:367.
6. Edmund Burke, *Letters on a Regicide Peace,* Letter III, in *The Works of the Right Honorable Edmund Burke* (Boston, 1866), 5:407. See *JMN* 6:24.
7. Cf. Exodus 19:5 and 23:22.
8. Hebrews 3:12.

and a good man better? Have you never heard of a change of heart? The doctrine of Christ is Repent.[9] Then is the difference of original endowment a fact altogether *from* the purpose. Take that heart you have; and keep it well; let no unclean thought,—let no low and miserable contrivance of selfishness,—enter it. Let in the light of God's word thereon. Let the affectionate remembrance of Jesus dwell there. Keep it with diligence—for it is the centre and spring that gives its own colour and savour to all the periods of being which have just begun to roll over you. All that Omnipotence can do for you, all the riches of the Universe are lodged therein. Keep it with diligence and you shall find no cause to complain of what God has withheld.

The way to keep the heart, is to do the commandments, to do justly, love mercy, and walk humbly.[10]

Here indeed is all that makes the importance of the command,—here in the fact that these affections may be trained up by our exertion. Is there any that is young among us, let him ponder the precept in his heart. The libertine, when reminded of the ruin his sensuality shall cause, ascribes his crimes to his natural kindness of heart; but all the time, his indulgences are making his heart cold and impenetrable to the claims of his fellow beings.—O shun as the gates of death the first temptations of sensual pleasure. And is there here a single soul that earnestly desires to comply with the precept of the text, let me counsel, let me beseech him to cherish in his bosom as a mean to that end a veneration for what is holy, to beware of the habit of foolish jesting; of that soul-destroying folly that casts its jest at great and small alike; that turns into mockery all that is sweet and solemn in human affection and sneers at all that is grand in human hope. It has been the calamity of the age we live in that men of great powers of mind and wofully depraved hearts, have done what they could to ridicule whatever is respectable and great. Let their work perish with them. No man reads the Bible without being conscious of more elevated sentiments and better purposes. But I desire no better rebuke to this madness than that any intelligent person should express the feeling with which he rises from one of these books of derision. I ask if he is not oppressed with a forlorn emotion as if he stood on the wreck of all that was desirable in being. He feels the truth of the language of Solomon, I said of laughter—it is mad.[11] He has lost the energy of his benevolence; he has lost the delight he took in whatever was good or beautiful and has he got any compensation?

The most disagreeable expression of the human face is a sneer. It is the expression of a devil.[12] It never sat on the lips of those men who are ornaments of our race. It is recorded of Jesus that he wept, never that he smiled, much less that he gave way to merriment.[13] I was walking early one morning in the coun-

9. See, for example, Matthew 4:17.
10. Micah 6:8.
11. Ecclesiastes 2:2.
12. Cf. Byron, "The Corsair," I, ix, 31; and *JMN* 1:324.
13. John 11:35.

try, before sunrise, and hearing repeated peals of loud laughter, I looked up and found it was within a jail.

To our condition, always liable to sin and pain and death, a serious collected demeanour, is far more becoming. Far better is the exhortation of Paul, "Be ye therefore sober and watch unto prayer."[14]

Finally, brethren, none of us liveth to himself, and none of us dieth to himself.[15] When the heart is diligently kept, its aspirations will naturally ascend to Him who formed it and who claims it for himself. We seek for a perfection which we cannot find. We seek for something which is stable and infinite—we seek for a peace which passeth not away. Jesus Christ who is the Way and the Truth and the Life shall lead us unto the Father[16]—our wills shall be lost in his—our faculties shall be absorbed in the study of his perfections.

14. The exhortation is Peter's (I Peter 4:7).
15. Romans 14:7.
16. John 14:6.

_____

Suffer little children and forbid them
not to come unto me for, of such is
the kingdom of heaven.

MARK 10:14

The instructions of every teacher betray the peculiar character of his own mind. Indeed every man's conversation, whenever he speaks sincerely, lays the most stress on those merits which he most strongly desires to obtain himself. The scholar will urge the value of learning; the man of business extols the advantage of practical knowledge; the sanguine man thinks that all great men are distinguished by their enterprize, the retired man praises the contemplative life.

We are interested therefore when we hear that a peculiarly gifted teacher of the Divine character and will has come into the world. We are curious to learn what is that temper or habit of mind which he shall inculcate.

Jesus took little children in his arms, and prayed God to bless them, and said to his disciples that the spirits in heaven were such as these.[1] This gracious word has been the comfort of parents in every age of the church. It might be chosen too as one of the distinguishing features of the gospel, not found in other systems of religious belief. But it has a higher interest: when we consider the character and authority of him who said it, it has the highest practical importance. We ought to know what this means because Christ has declared to his disciples—Unless ye be converted, and become as little children, ye shall in no wise enter into the kingdom of heaven.[2]

Let us therefore ascertain as clearly as we can the sense of this commandment.

Unless ye become as little children—Certainly at first it is an unlooked for precept. What! are these little children the models of imitation to the fullgrown and finished man? These children, whom we take all the pains in the world to change into men and women, and outrunning in our impatience the progress of nature we put forward in dress, in language, in manners, in arts; striving to

---

Manuscript dated April 24, 1830, at Chardon Street. Preached three times: April 25, 1830, at the Second Church, Boston; May 8, 1831, again at the Second Church; and December 25, 1836, in East Lexington.

1. Perhaps a conflation of the sermon text with Mark 10:16 and Matthew 18:10.
2. Cf. Matthew 18:3 and Luke 18:17.

make them outgrow, as fast as possible, the habits of infancy, and assume the habits of mature life! Is it possible that this helpless, weeping child, ignorant of all things,—and so in danger from all—untried by temptation, and therefore, though innocent, not virtuous,—is it the last excellence and happiest state of man to resemble this?

Why, what perversity, then, is all this laborious system of education; these schools, this unremitted parental discipline, undoing this state and carrying the new man farther and farther every day from the perfection of his nature?

My friends, Jesus was not in the habit of teaching anything absurd. As far as men have practised in his school they have found his rules of life to be in strictest coincidence with the laws of our highest nature. And so it will be found, I believe, in this, that this rule is in harmony with our own observation.

Of course it cannot be the ignorance and imbecility of the child, which the Saviour meant to recommend; for ignorance and imbecility can never be respectable. But is there not any thing in the character of childhood, which a good education would leave there? which time and chance are apt to hurt? Is there not any thing therein that is not inconsistent with knowledge and strength, that might remain with great advantage in the trials of life, in the press of action, in the hour of death and in the world to come?

I believe we shall all answer, There is. If it be rightly considered, it will appear that a good education does not aim to take out of us the characteristics of infancy but only adds to them what is defective. There is something, there is much in the child, which it is painful to miss in the man. There is something there, which the world makes worse; something which the passions of mature years are prone to weaken, or alter, or destroy,—and which is worth more than all they give instead.

This quality or collection of qualitites that mark the new being just dismissed from the hand of its heavenly Father is called *Simplicity of character,* and is well known to us as the grace and excellence of childhood.

I wish to inquire what are the true qualities that make the character which our Saviour recommends; *next;* to consider the unfavorable influences in common life, which are apt to destroy it; and *lastly;* to consider in what manner we ought to attempt to regain this character.

I. Whoever considers the character of children with any degree of attention is struck with a certain directness of thought and feeling in them which does not commonly continue into middle life. They have acquired but a very little knowledge, but their intellectual operations upon that little, are quick and exact. They are not wise; their judgment is very defective; but not from incorrectness of reasoning but from the poverty of their information.

In the next place, they have no dissimulation, or indirect dealing; but the most perfect frankness in the expression of their sentiments. Their yea is yea, their nay is nay.[3] They speak the truth. When they are pleased, they express it;

3. James 5:12.

when they are displeased, they express it. They don't know how to flatter, nor, when you are sick, do they say 'You look well'; nor say 'You have done right,' when they think you have done wrong.

Their moral perception is as delicate as their judgment is rude. They are slow to understand a jest, but they are quick to feel injustice. The Conscience in them hath the fineness of its first edge; and they feel a sharper compunction for a petty lie or disobedience, than a bad man for burglary or enormous fraud.

Joined with this innocence, is the unrestrained indulgence of the natural affections of the heart,—believing in the goodness of all whom they meet, and expressing their simple love without hesitation to all.

So the attributes of faith and of trust are conspicuous beauties in the character of children. The child believes what you say; and it has a confidence in your good meaning.

Whatever being acts in a manner that is true to its nature, is always respectable. In all affectation, there is meanness. And any one may recall instances in his own observation when wit and fraud are baffled and put down by the plain dealing of children. And such is the pleasure of innocence, and the unchecked exercise of the affections, and of truth, that the recollection of their early days is pleasant to all men: and this fact has acquired for childhood the fame of being happy. And doubtless it was in the love of this purity, this benevolence, this truth, so like his own, that Jesus gave it his memorable benediction.

II. But how does this simplicity which belongs to infancy differ from the character of later life? Jesus says, "*Unless ye be converted* and become as children."[4] What becomes of this grace so highly prized, that he should speak to his disciples as if they had lost it, and must now aim to recover it? It came to them without effort. Can it not be kept without effort, or if lost, recovered?

No, it cannot. By God's permission we are exposed to numberless influences unfavorable to it. As the young advance into life, they find that men are selfish; and in pursuing those advantages which gratify their self love, they overlook the weightier matters of justice, kindness, humility, devotion. They are checked in the expression of their own sentiments from want of sympathy, and yield to the influence of example, and go in the way of their fathers.

The passions grow up to strength, and become our tempters. Necessary in its just exercise to our wellbeing, every one tends to mislead and blind and ruin us in its excess. Our love of pleasure, our love of gain, our love of power, our love of praise,—every one in turn or together acts to draw us out of the straight path. We grow sour, we grow cunning; we grow covetous. Worst of all we grow hypocritical. As we sin we become cowards, and shrink away from the decision of the natural sense of mankind upon our true conduct and try to make them think we do something else. We depart, we depart, and wo for us that we do, from the simplicity of infancy, and learn the duplicity of the world. Look around you, my friends, and you shall see its effects: they are written in broad

4. Matthew 18:3.

characters all about us. A great deal of life is in masquerade. We are hardly aware how much insincerity is in ourselves, or those around us, until we are startled now and then by meeting a person of great simplicity, or by noticing the contrast between the character of Jesus, and the character of very respectable men among us. Then we find how far we are from the pure standard of truth and nature. Men contract a habit of insincere talking; of adopting almost unconsciously the opinions of other people because they are theirs; of using a great many expressions and forms of unmeaning civility, which sometimes cover real ill will. But—Except ye become as children—Except ye leave falsehood and love truth ye cannot be fit for the kingdom of God.

Then the simplicity of the gospel is as much opposed to *desires of false good,* as to false words and pretensions. We seek temporal pleasure at the risk of that which is eternal. We seek our own advantage at the cost of our neighbor, not seeing that his and ours are one. We seek to gratify our anger, forgetting that it is a greater satisfaction to overcome it. We seek ease and indulgence, ignorant that they can only be truly enjoyed after privation and labor. But Christ calls our eyes from earth to heaven; from the riches of care, to the riches of knowledge; from pride to humility; from lust to the happiness of affection; from the love of self to the love of God and of all his creatures. I understand then the passage to read thus. 'Except ye be converted and become as children in the simplicity of your thoughts, ye shall not come into that state of mind which constitutes heaven.'

III. But how shall we be converted, and regain this simplicity? It seems to me, my friends, that this is the lesson which God teaches us by all the discipline of this life. He clothed us in a divine simplicity at the entrance of our being to show us what was our happiness. But the simplicity of childhood was one of accident; a gift, not an acquisition; liable to pass away with the situation of ignorance and quiet to which it belonged. He then has made it our business to replace that white robe of nature by one of our own weaving, that native simplicity by an acquired simplicity, got by effort, approved by reason, secured by use, and so not liable to pass away. We were born—it seems—speakers of truth, with moderate appetites, lovers of others, and without sin. We were early exposed to temptations whereby our taste and desires were depraved. God commands us to return by *our own exertions* to the same habits of action. But it will not be innocence, it will be something far more glorious, it will be virtue. It will not be an accident nor dependent on the will or actions of any other, it will be our own and inalienable. It will not be weak, it will be strong; it will not be ignorant and foolish, it will be wise. And is it not the natural effect of all the picture of life which he exhibits before us to show us the value of this grace, and to help us to gain it? Experience comes in with his sharp but wholesome teaching. The good that for years you have painfully sought, having at last obtained, you find now was not worth seeking. Late in life you find your power, your wealth, or your fame, have cost you too much; have been paid for by your peace of mind, which was the very good you aimed to procure by them. The passion and the courtesy which once you affected you find it wise to drop, and to let your social feeling be the rule of your civilities as it was in childhood.

Every day has added some commentary upon the inconvenience and mischief that springs from slander, from flattery, from exaggeration, from all kinds of untruth, and you learn to speak truth as you did in childhood.

In fine, all our experience and all the word of God and all the example of Christ concur in enforcing this one great lesson upon us. Every conquest we make over our besetting sin, every improvement we feel we have gained, we perceive is one step more to simplicity of character,—to that unity of purpose and word and action, that is in God, and in the children of God.

Let us, therefore, brethren and friends, consider whether we are of the kingdom of heaven by the simple truth and goodness that is in us, or whether we are far from it in the doublings and labyrinth of worldly allurement. Let us be wise in season. Let us imitate the divine simplicity that shone in all the life of Christ. Let us get it by aiming steadily at it in all we do, by speaking the truth, by acting always from great motives and no more from mean ones, by recognizing the presence of God the Father of the Universe in every action.

LXXIII

*Now we see through a glass darkly, but then
face to face; now I know in part but then
shall I know even as also I am known.*

I CORINTHIANS 13:12

It is remarkable that the Christian Revelation, whose greatest value must always be reckoned the assurance it gives of the immortality of the human soul, should be so little explicit upon this very point, should give so little distinct information upon the nature of that happiness which it teaches us God has provided for them that love him.[1]

We attempt to mitigate the grief of one whose earthly hopes have just been buried in the grave of a son, a husband, or a father, by directing the mind to those spiritual advantages which may naturally arise from a separation from the body. But the afflicted soul is often skeptical. It says, for faith give me sight. It says, Yes, I own these views would go far to remove my grief if I could only have the same evidence for them that I have for the existence of present objects.

Now the consolations that spring from a belief in a future state are or will be needed by every individual soul, and therefore this is a question which has a deep interest for every mind that is capable of thought.

The question is—Why is no clearer light thrown upon the nature of the future state? Now to pretend to be master of such a question as this would obviously be presumptuous. Yet I shall attempt to show that we have some reason to think that it would not be useful but injurious to have more light, if more were possible, and if it would not be useful but injurious, it would not surely become the all wise and good Being to give it.

I. A greater knowledge of the next life would probably unfit us for the duties of this. It is matter of common experience that the expectation of any event in which we feel a strong interest occupies the imagination to that degree as to exclude all the objects of ordinary importance. Not only the anticipation of a

---

Preached four times: May 2, 1830, at the Second Church, Boston, in the morning, and at the First Church, Cambridge, in the afternoon; Friday, March 25, 1831, as the Monthly Lecture at the Second Church; and October 23, 1836, in East Lexington.

1. Cf. Romans 8:28.

176

political event, an approaching invasion, a peace, an election, but much less imposing occurrences, and the nearer the more affecting—the approach of a popular disturbance, a holiday, a quarrel—or some threat, or some hope of speedy pleasure to one's self or one's friends, will make us in a great measure incompetent to the care of our business, incapable of a steady attention to any thing else than the peculiar occasion of our hopes or fears.

Thus the wisdom of men has always acquiesced in the wisdom of Providence in concealing from us the time and the mode of our death. Fifteen or sixteen persons die in this parish every year.[2] In all probability therefore there are several of us who are now in this house who will never see the leaves fall, and the winter return. But if a visible hand should now point out the victims among us, does any one doubt that it would cause a great amount of misery? What unprofitable dejections! neglect of affairs! what dismay in families! what confusion of thought! what ceaseless terror!

Does any one doubt that it would be a great evil, the acquisition of that knowledge not guarded by the addition of any more?

Well now as the expectation of death would make life in a great measure useless and wretched, so the expectation of the great life that follows, if a strong illumination were thrown upon the objects of that world, would distract yet more powerfully our attention from its just objects.

It would seem from the great care and contrivance manifested in man's position here in the material world, that some important ends were to be answered thereby.

But if there be any purpose to our life, it will be plain to us on a moment's reflexion that purpose would be frustrated by the supposed foresight. God designed doubtless that we should obtain here in the earth an accurate acquaintance with the properties of matter; a knowledge of moral distinctions; and of the human character. This knowledge all do acquire in some degree. I do not mean knowledge got by book learning or rules of art, to which comparatively few have access. I mean that knowledge that is got by sight, by touch, by taste, by smelling, by hearing,—by action, by passion, by speech, by want, by trade, by injury, by love, by aversion. The amount of knowledge that is acquired involuntarily in twenty or forty or sixty years is very great. Who could count or measure all the various information of an old man? And yet what deductions are to be made from the stock if you reckon all the hours and weeks and months when pleasant or painful accidents withdrew his attention from passing objects and fixed it on some one. Yet even this time is not wholly lost since he gains a minute acquaintance with that individual object.

However unable we may be to explain in detail the advantages of these acquisitions, yet when we consider what a costly equipment we have of faculties and helps, manifestly suited to this purpose, it becomes evident that it was a

2. Emerson's holograph list of the deceased, with the dates of the funerals, survives in the papers of the Second Church, deposited at the Massachusetts Historical Society.

main purpose of our Creator, to give us knowledge, and we cannot doubt it is essential to our welfare.

But suppose from the spot where we stand we looked down on the vast eternity we presently shall enter, when a fever or consumption shall dismiss us from the body. Is it not probable that we should be afraid or bewildered or delighted with what was before us to that degree that we should cease to see the ground where we stand? that we should neglect our relations, our offices, our studies, our health, thinking all things mean in comparison with objects so mighty—whilst at the same time this neglect would disqualify us for a connexion with those vaster relations, on which our attention fastened, if this is, as it appears, a state of necessary discipline to prepare us for *them*?

II. The second reason which I have to offer seems to me yet more plain and conclusive. It is, that if a greater knowledge of the future state were given us, it would destroy our freedom, and so make us incapable of virtue. If you command a drunkard to put down his glass untasted, and hold a pistol at his head to prevent him from refusing you, is there any merit in his abstinence? If you promise your child a great reward if he will go into the street and feed a beggar, is there any virtue in his obedience or in his alms? And would there be any more merit in your spiritual mind, in your temperance, in your charity, in your honesty, in your diligence, if you saw as clear as the sun at noon, the literally *everlasting* consequences of two courses of conduct?—if you saw a soul in torment,—the gratifications of the earth removed, and so itself torn by its wild desires, without hope and without rest; if you saw a soul in bliss,—its majestic powers deriving enjoyment from all the minds, and all the orders of being throughout the illimitable Creation, and imparting enjoyment as much and as far?

If the mist of our ignorance should roll away and reveal all this—is it possible that we should any more be liars or misers, or fraudulent, or unchaste? We should be bribed to goodness. We should be frighted from crime. We should have no choice in our action; no liberty; no virtue.

But now it is the pleasure of Providence so far to obscure the consequences of actions that we can choose the right for its own sake, that we *can run some risk,* when we deny ourselves for the sake of our principles. If you forego for conscience' sake indulgences which you can easily procure and securely enjoy, and undergo, instead, privation and hard labor, you now are supported in that struggle by a sublime satisfaction,—a feeling that you have kept the commandment for God's sake and not for the sake of a reward in sight. You have had, and you have used an opportunity of developing within you a noble principle of disinterested love,—and have chosen the good part,[3] come what may. Now this is a principle confessedly the very highest of which we can conceive; the very best preparation for an immortal life; and which, it is clearly impossible, could

3. Luke 10:42.

have had any existence on the supposition that the Future State had been more fully disclosed.

III. These considerations weigh with me to show the folly of this common objection that the Revelation is imperfect. Our restless and unthinking passions make us demand to see our friends in the other world, to know their enjoyments, their hopes, their fears, whilst a little reflection would satisfy us, that this wish could not be gratified without frustrating the purposes of Eternal Wisdom in the education of man. But there is one farther consideration which may serve to mark yet more clearly the absurdity of this demand. It is, that we have already enough knowledge, and that we have as much knowledge of the nature of the future state as in the nature of things we can have. We have in our own minds intimations sufficiently clear for the direction of our conduct. If this life is a preparation for the next, we have every reason to believe that the next is not a new being, but a continuation of this, and the degree of happiness we enjoy hereafter will spring from sources familiar to us now. But it is plain that to some of those sources death puts a final end. Thus here we enjoy eating and drinking and the accumulation of external goods. But as we brought nothing into this world, we can carry nothing out.4 But here also we enjoy the happiness of others in proportion, and the greater is the gratification, as we ourselves have been instrumental in producing it. We enjoy the discovery of new truth. We enjoy the feeling of power—over our faculties and over our passions. We enjoy wonderfully the notice of our own improvement in virtue. We enjoy a belief of God's approbation when we attain to it above all joys.

And all these sources of pleasure are entirely independent of our bodily organization, and will doubtless only be refined by our separation from the body. Thus much we know and on these facts we can act. But these intimations are from within not from without.

It is perhaps impossible that we should know by any external communication more than we know already concerning the kingdom of heaven. It is admitted by our Saviour that there are some truths which the mind would not receive though one rose from the dead to unfold them.5 Truth must not only come, but it must come to the prepared mind. Our enjoyments are not alike. One man is made happy by the opportunity of going to Church. Another man is made unhappy by being induced to go to the same place. It is probable that the enjoyments of heaven could not be revealed—could not be made intelligible to any but good men, to any but minds already formed for them, any more than you can explain to a blind man the glory of the sun. It is only in proportion to our knowledge that we conceive the pleasures knowledge can give, and in proportion to our goodness, that we desire more goodness. Here then is the only Revelation of the Future State to our minds, that it shall be more and more

4. I Timothy 6:7.
5. Luke 16:31.

distinctly perceived by us what is its nature, precisely as we more and more faithfully perform the conditions on which its happiness is promised. The pure in heart, says our Saviour, shall see God. The poor in spirit have the kingdom of heaven.[6]

And this is the sense of Paul. The natural man receiveth not the things of the Spirit of God; for they are foolishness unto him; neither can he know them, for they are spiritually discerned.[7]

We arrive then, brethren and friends, at this plain practical conclusion, that we should not repine at the defects of our knowledge since we possess in our own hands the only means in the universe, by which that defect can be supplied. Keep the commandments and you shall reap their fruit. Do God's will, you shall enter into his rest.[8]

And not by the hearing of the ear or by the speculations of the inquisitive understanding can its nature be declared; but only by the seeing of the eye,[9] only by the actual presence of the heart itself with all its love and the obedience of all its powers can the nature of heaven be opened to the mind. Whilst it is future you can not know it. It must be present within you.

6. Matthew 5:8 and 5:3.
7. I Corinthians 2:14.
8. Cf. Hebrews 4:1.
9. Job 42:5.

LXXIV

The last enemy that shall be destroyed is death.

I Corinthians 15:26

That is a good manner of life that is ready for all emergences. So live as to be ready to die. Our fathers in their turn have all tasted of death. Now our turn is nearly come. We have had our day. We have eaten and drunken, bought and sold, we have conversed and rejoiced and wept, we have seen the face of father and mother and friends, we have beheld the wonders of the world, we have been in towns, and in the fields, and on the sea, we have read the Bible and other books and conversed with men and had desires and affronts and pleasure and pain. We have heard of heaven and hell. We have seen proof of the being of God, and learned what was told and what was disputed of the offices of Christ. We have had our share of the sweet and bitter cup of being. Now let us be willing to take leave; for, others wait for our places. Let us

> Walk thoughtful on the silent solemn shore
> Of that vast Ocean we must sail so soon.[1]

This is the language which experience always addresses to us and to which always we turn a deaf ear. We do not desert our pleasures, our occupations, nor our hopes, and projects. We go on—the feeble darling of one year and the ruined frame of eighty, as long as it can resist by vital energy the laws of matter, as long as it can lift an arm, or speak, or see,—we go on forming schemes having reference to this world, and rarely do our afflictions gall us so sharply and still more seldom do our spirits reach that height of heavenly desire that we say, "Lord now let thy servant depart in peace."[2] We pray for life when there is nothing else left us.

Nor do I, brethren, feel any disposition or any commission to rebuke this strong instinct. To him who looks with a rational and ardent curiosity at every fact which bears on the evidence of the future state, this tenacious love of life

---

Manuscript dated May 8, 1830, at Chardon Street. Preached three times: May 9, 1830, at the Second Church, Boston, in the morning, and at the Hollis Street Church in the afternoon; and January 15, 1832, again at the Second Church.

1. Edward Young, *Night Thoughts*, "Night V," lines 669–70. See *JMN* 6:72 and 123.
2. Luke 2:29.

must be deeply and fairly considered. No advantage is gained to faith by denying or concealing it. We must have all the facts. Truth first, and then expediency.[3]

It is said that religious people commonly take as much pains to live as others;
that in common conversation among Christians, death is always regarded with
fear, and recovery from sickness or escape from any peril of life is considered by
them an object of congratulation, as much as by men entirely without habits of
religious thought. And it seems to me, I should think death was as studiously
avoided by them, and it is spoken of generally in reference to this life, that is, the
death of the young and the good deplored as a disappointment, the death of the
old with a mixed regret, and the death of bad men without sorrow. This much is
true, but that good men and bad men regard death with the same sort of fear, is
not true. Or that our religious faith and character has no effect in qualifying our
natural apprehensions of death is not true.

There are many considerations which induce us to believe that God intended
that we should watch our life with great solicitude. God has wisely appointed
Fear to guard the gates of Death so that neither we should depart from life
without permission nor that we should neglect the duties of our station. And I
shall attempt to show that not only is death in the order of God's Providence
made an object of fear to all men, but further, there is some ground for thinking
that a religious man would have a greater love for life than an irreligious man.
And, finally, the revelation of a future state whilst it is imperfect can only relieve
and not wholly remove the natural fear of death.

I. The fear of death is in the first place a strong instinct as much as the
knowledge how to breathe or how to eat is instinctive. As no time and no reason
wears out the appetites, so long as the body remains in health, so neither does
the *sovereign* appetite *for living,* ever yield to decay, in a healthy condition.
Every man defends himself from a blow, or a wild beast, or a fall, not by a
process of reasoning but by the impulse of this instinct. And let his mind go
through what process it may, with respect to the desirableness of being, the
moment he is surprised by danger, he will resist or avoid an injury that threatens
him. Now this instinct will belong to good men and to bad men alike, and will
operate just as far with one, as with the other.

II. In the second place, the fear of death will be proportioned, of course, to
the value of life. I see no reason to doubt that life has a good deal of enjoyment
for a bad man. Positive pleasure springs to him from health, from food, from
company, as to others. God bids the sun rise and the rain descend upon the
good and upon the wicked.[4] But his enjoyments are of a low kind, and when he
swims in a sea of prosperity, they are not increased in the proportion of his
seeming success. For every enjoyment of the higher sort which another man
would derive from his advantages he fails to find. You see each particular good,
with an accurate eye, but you do not see each particular evil which neutralizes

3. *JMN* 6:37.
4. Cf. Matthew 5:45.

it. You see the crowd of friends, but you do not see the secret enemies. And one enemy will cause a man more pain than twenty friends can remove. You see the pride but not the mortification. You see the pleasures that tempted him but he hides in his bosom the fear of detection.

I suppose the maxim that every vice produces its own misery has coincided with human experience long enough to be believed.[5] You know this man has done and doth wrong. You must trust the laws of the Universe, that they are rendering him his reward. He has not the good he seems to have. He has the happiness of cattle, but it is disguised by pains which the cattle have not. And often it may be those pains are so intense that he looks towards the grave with a gloomy wish that there might be no resurrection from its clods. These things go to weaken the value which a man over whom religious considerations have no influence may be supposed to have for his life.

But a good man's life is far more valuable to him. He really lives in a better world than his neighbor. His virtues have made life dear to him. Wherever he goes, into whatever houses, into whatever company, he finds himself surrounded with remembrancers of his own merit. He is reminded by happy faces, by benefits done to him, of the recollection in which his pure intentions, his charity, and his honesty, are held. Respectful attentions, confidence, requests, and the dear love of noble minds, show him how much good he has done and may do, and strew his way of life with purest satisfactions. To him then existence has a worth that springs from his own worth and enhances by so much the very moderate estimation which life has in the eye of his bad neighbor. The memory of a day to the virtuous man is a medal given for a meritorious exploit, and which is prized not for the ounce of silver, but for the honor.

But there is yet another and still nobler association that comes in aid of the love of life. This world not only presents itself to the good man as the scene of past virtuous pleasure, but as the field of all his future exertions. Here are the objects of his benevolence; the evils which he has seen and determined to remove; the friendships he will form; the duties he will discharge; the virtues he has resolved to acquire. This great hope, this animating purpose belongs indeed to all rational nature,—and it warms the heart to think of it. There is not one of us (I trust in God there is not one) but contemplates the next year, the next month, as a season of improvement, and feeling the secret dissatisfaction of sin, promises himself to break its fetters. I know this feeling gives a glory—alas! too often deceitful,—to every man's view of tomorrow. Much more doth it shine in the vigorous purposes of him who all his life has given battle to temptation, and who reckons the day lost that has not made him better.

Once more; his life is valuable, because it was given by another being, and is witnessed and governed by him. Religion makes life respectable, makes life venerable as it represents man dwelling under the eye of God, and the tender mercies of the Father of the Universe, resting upon his weakest child.

Now can any one doubt that the present life (for we are not yet considering

5. See Samuel Taylor Coleridge, *The Friend,* ed. Barbara E. Rooke (Princeton, 1969), 1:103.

the effect which the belief of another will produce) will be to such a man a far higher and nobler thing than it can appear to a vicious person, and that on the supposition that there was no other life he would be more loth to resign it? We are supposed to love our friends in proportion to the good offices we have done them. Of course to a benevolent man the world must be dear with more affection, since he has shown kind offices to as many as he has known. And every name in his household, every true heart in his kindred, in his community, or on the face of the earth with which he has communed is one more bright object, is one more tie by which he is bound to its place. In short, if the solemn pretension of all the wise since the world began that goodness is the way to felicity have any truth, then it is plain the good man has manifold reason to cling to life on the supposition that there was no other—beyond the profligate and the fool.

III. Now let us consider the very important effect which is made by the doctrine of the Future State. It is not to be doubted that the solemn weight of evidence which God has given to our minds in behalf of this Faith does remove a burden from the soul of painful doubt. It is to all religious minds an unspeakable consolation. But there yet remains much darkness upon it. There is a great difference between the relief we demand and the relief we have obtained. There is an immense difference between the faith we have in our present existence in this house and the faith we can have in the relations or the being of a future state. For this darkness wise reasons unquestionably answer. On a former occasion I attempted to show that we can assign some reasons with great probability why this veil should be drawn over heaven and hell.[6] But the veil is there.

Had it pleased God to make it just as certain that life and a far more elevated social enjoyment into which our dear friends should come and rejoin us should continue the moment succeeding death—had it pleased him that this fact should appear as certain as is the perception to each of us at this moment of the presence of one another, does any man imagine that death would have any terror? But these mighty affections men bear to one another are traitors to them; these affections by which our Father has joined the members of the human family together; and the moment one asks himself, if he be ready to die, the thought of children, or parent or lover or friend dismays him, the thought of those whom he would not leave, and who cannot bear to be left by him. It may console those who distrust themselves because they cannot vanquish this apprehension that the Son of God when he was in the world did not reprove the tears of the mourner and showed forth his father's might in restoring the dead to the prayers of weeping affection.[7]

Moreover, it should be considered how much this love of life appears to have been intended by Providence, since the more faithfully we undertake and perform our private and public duties, the more strong are our ties to life—binding us up in that cause which we promote. But on the other hand let it be considered

6. See Sermon LXXIII.
7. John 11:33–44.

the beneficent operation of the same affections is not less sure on the other side the grave. They whom we have followed to the doors of the other life and have seen them go in still draw us to them. We have a property in the other world, and a strange sweetness is mingled with the expectation of our own departure.

These reflexions are offered to show that there may be better feelings than an unworthy cowardice which should lead to the general language of all men, good as well as bad, in speaking of death. I have spoken on the supposition that all do regard death with a feeling of terror when it is plain to all experience that there are many who, on the support of a Christian hope, meet it without a fear, and many whose bosoms beat with a pious curiosity to know what it shall reveal to them. Almost every man sometimes feels a thrill of awe. There are some who are habitually eager to depart, on whom the hope of a better life has wrought so far, as to beget an impatience of the best enjoyments of this.

But our times are in God's hand. Whilst it does not become us to express any intemperate contempt or aversion of life, it is yet very plainly an imperfection of faith to dread its end. What has been said may show that we are not to desire its end. Neither are we to dread it. The more virtuous we grow, the more, we are taught, shall we perceive the independence of virtue on time and place; the more diligently we worship God by prayer and by obedience, the more clearly we shall feel that his presence and his love make all places alike; and that every object we justly value, is secure in his keeping. Nor let it be forgotten that faith is one of the rewards of virtue, and that as we grow better, we shall dismiss, one after another, our doubts, until we see God as we are seen by him, and know as we are known,[8] when we shall obtain the victory over death, the last enemy, through our Lord Jesus Christ.

---

8. Cf. I Corinthians 13:12.

LXXV

*Let every man prove his own work and then
shall he have rejoicing in himself alone
and not in another, for every man
shall bear his own burden.*

GALATIANS 6:4–5

The times in which we live are much agitated by the discussion of religious questions, and the community is, for the most part, distributed into two great parties, by a line which runs between sect and sect, or divides the same sect into two parts. One of these may be called the *rigid* and one the *liberal* party. (I avoid for obvious reasons the use of the word *orthodox,* which is always used arrogantly when applied to a man's self and ironically when applied to another.) This is by no means a casual or temporary division; he is much mistaken who thinks this warfare is transient or is confined to this country or this age. Its seeds are as old as the human mind. Both parties are founded on principles inherent in our nature, and both build their system upon unquestionable facts. Indeed the same division of opinion may be traced beyond theology into the discussion of every question, upon which men take sides with any degree of zeal. There is a rigid and a liberal party on ethical and metaphysical questions, on questions of education, on the questions of free trade and of civil government.

I propose to consider what are the great principles that lie at the foundation of the two prominent parties of the Christian World. This consideration will lead us to see what dangers and what duties arise out of this controversy.

There is in the nature of man a distinct and strong feeling of approbation at the sight of a good action in himself or in another.

There is also in his nature a distinct and strong feeling of disapprobation at the sight of a bad action.

On these two principles, which are not at variance, but both true, the two

---

This sermon on the distinction between the "liberal" and "rigid" parties in religion (that is to say, the Unitarian and Calvinist-Trinitarian sects) reflects the earlier controversy between William Ellery Channing and Samuel Worcester, as well as the so-called "Wood 'n' Ware debate" between Henry Ware, Sr., and Leonard Woods. Emerson's formulation reappears in the lecture "Society" (*EL* 2:108) and in such later essays as "The Transcendentalist" and "Historic Notes of Life and Letters in New England." The sermon was preached three times: May 16, 1830, at the Second Church, Boston; on the evening of September 19, 1830, in Concord, N.H.; and June 30, 1831, as a Thursday Lecture, presumably at the Second Church.

186

parties severally stand. The *liberal* party take the principle of *man's capacity for virtue* and from that ground survey the Creation. The *rigid* party take the principle of *man's liability to sin,* and from that ground survey the Creation. From these two fountains flow their feelings towards God and man. The rigid party in the church, alarmed with the contrast between the grievous guilt that is in man, and the perfections of God, look up to him with dread, and conceive him as the Judge of action, and the Punisher of sin. The virtues on which they most insist are penitence, renouncement of worldly pleasure, and prayer.

The liberal class of Christians, touched with the benevolence that appears in the Universe, and with the great powers and desires of man, and with the signs of a moral Providence which appear—delight in conceiving God under the Parental relation, as holding out encouragements to human virtue and as being Himself an object worthy of endless study and love, whom to know aright is life eternal.[1] And they commend naturally the virtues of gratitude, of resignation, and of diligence.

If we consider it still more particularly we shall easily perceive how naturally each of these systems can flow from one of these partial views and how close a mutual relation the different doctrines of each system have within itself.

Thus if any one of us should be led to an exclusive or only a disproportionate attention to the single feeling of remorse for sin,—(that feeling which is peculiar to rational nature,) it is not difficult to analyze the process by which he is led to adopt the popular doctrines of the stricter church. First, he feels that an indefinable evil hangs over him. He has offended God, a being of unknown power and unknown purposes. There may be no bounds to his displeasure and to the bad consequences to himself. Of course his soul is oppressed with *fear.* Its active powers are paralyzed, its affections cramped, and all its energy directed to an anxious exploring of ways of escape, a way of atonement. Great sacredness attaches to all opinions concerning it. Fear makes the spirit passive. It only asks what it must do.[2] It makes no conditions. It questions nothing. This is the state of mind most apt for unlimited credulity. And this may account for the remarkable fact that this stricter class of Christians have always set so high a value upon Faith—because a strong faith indicated a strong sense of sin. The spirit bowed by a consciousness of its guilt and of God's anger counts it presumptuous to cavil at the statements of the Scriptures concerning his nature and laws. The conditions of any law are better, it says, than it deserves, and whatever it receives from him, it will reverence.

I do not conceive that all the doctrines usually held by this class of Christians have a necessary connexion with their first principles. Thus the doctrine of the Trinity is I think *accidentally* a part of their creed. An Arian might be a member of the rigid party for all his views of the inferiority of Christ to the Father.[3] Yet

1. John 17:3.
2. Cf. Acts 16:30.
3. Arianism takes its name from Arius, a Greek Christian theologian who died in 336 A.D. Arians questioned the relation of the persons of the Trinity, some holding that the Son was a God yet inferior to the Father, others that He was the most perfect of men. Unitarians, from the eigh-

with this foremost feeling of the sinfulness of the heart, they appear to have read the Scriptures with a devout if with an erring eye, and to have made a systematic but partial application of its language to the support of their opinions.

It is just as easy to follow the steps taken by another mind which setting out from a consideration of the pleasure we take in the right use of our powers, arrives at conclusions very far remote from the former. A mind of generous nature is early taught to contemplate with delight and reverence its own faculties;—to reverence them for their use; to believe, that, as God gave them, they are imperfect copies of his own perfections; and that he is well pleased in the good they produce; that the purposes of God are best deduced from his works; that, as the world is full of contrivances for use and pleasure, and not one for pain, (pain only resulting from some ignorance or abuse of nature) it is reasonable to think that he designed always the happiness of his children, that as we possess freedom and as all those powers are extremely susceptible of cultivation that nothing can be more manifest than that we should become more wise, more true, more just, more temperate, more kind, and so more happy, every day; that a day is full of duties; life a term of education. What blessings, opportunities, hopes, and truth, exist in this world, to those who will seek them! Then what unspeakable cheerfulness and dignity has the gospel of eternal life poured over the future! And if the good, the exaltation, the felicity of man is the object of God's arrangements concerning him, and none so noble, so divine, can be imagined by us, then a sufficient reason is given for the existence of all pain, because it is all of use; and a sufficient reason is given for the interference of the special economy of the Christian Revelation, because we cannot conceive a richer gift from God than the announcement of the future life on such conditions as it is offered.

From these views they are naturally led to give all their views of God a degree of trust and love becoming more perfect as they are sure their actions please him; they are also induced to put their whole reliance, in order to obtain his favor, upon their Works, including all voluntary action. Believing the end he had in view was their happiness, and knowing that only in one way can that be secured, by doing right, they come to value states of mind only as they are marked by that surest index, the deeds.

These views also claim in their behalf the strong testimony of the Scriptures. But as the human mind must always be the interpreter of Scripture, they explain the Scripture in conformity with the laws of the mind; they appeal from the letter to the spirit and find one meaning in the word and the works of God.[4]

These two great systems of religious opinion being once established, the well known disposition of the human mind to magnify its own, ensures to each the total force of its espousers. Each advocate labours in his own cause with all his means. He strengthens its argument, adorns it with his genius, and rejoices by

teenth century onward, were often referred to as "Arians." See James Hastings, *The Encyclopaedia of Religion and Ethics* (New York, 1910), 1:775–86.

4. Cf. II Corinthians 3:6.

his goodness to show its good effect. Each will have in course of time its fair proportion of powerful thinkers. Many men have dedicated their entire life to the cause of a religious creed. Men of great minds and best dispositions

> Who, born for the Universe, narrowed their mind
> And to *party* gave up what was meant for mankind.[5]

In this way, each cause in the course of one or two centuries, does its best; shows all that influence it can exert; what height of virtue it can sustain in its followers; what scope it gives to action; what life they lead, and what martyrdom they can bear. Thus a chapter of man's history is unrolled before us, from which valuable instruction may be drawn. (If we have eyes, let us see it. If we have ears, let us hear what the Spirit saith unto the Churches.)[6]

Now the first great objection to the state of the Church is that it is the effect of a party spirit and all party is exclusive. Each of these opinions, we have seen, is based in a great truth; and, of course, the Christian character must embrace the foundations of both. But, by the operation of this jealous warfare, by adopting one opinion, you are understood by the multitude, and are in the greatest danger to be understood by yourself, as branding the other opinion, and excluding yourself from the peculiar good fruits of it. The majority of men do not make nice distinctions, and the moment a line is drawn between sects they show their zeal by pushing as far from it as they can into the unsafe extreme of the part they have chosen. This makes the objection which good men have to the use of names whenever they can be avoided. It is an objection to the denomination Unitarian that it tends to make those who do not hold their general sentiments, Trinitarians. For it is but too true a maxim that people generally end with being, what they are accused of being.[7] And who is there in our times who has had opportunity of extensive observation, but can name, not individuals but families, and communities, with every opportunity of being enlightened, who have actually been kept out of the progress to which they had every right and hope by the deep trenches that have been digged and the stakes that have been set in the fields of thought that have made it a party consideration to think thus and so? The question is not—What did God intend?—What saith the human heart? But, How do the Unitarians believe? And what must I as a Calvinist say?

Now, my friends, an active and honest mind that loves God and is truly anxious to do his Will, will take its place in the middle ground, and borrow something of eternal truth from both of these opinions. Whilst one usurps the Christian name to consecrate the rancour of bigotry, and another turns the liberty wherewith the gospel has made him free into a cloak of licentiousness,

5. Oliver Goldsmith, "Retaliation: A Poem," lines 31–32; see *JMN* 2:207.
6. Cf. Mark 8:18.
7. *JMN* 3:132.

this humble disciple rejoices with trembling.[8] He feels deeply the weight of his sins; he deplores the power of temptation; with prayer, with tears, with terror he watches over himself and his occasional backslidings. He dares not think lightly of a crime or presume on the mercy of God.

But though he is cast down, he is not destroyed—a more perfect love casteth out the fear.[9] He is buoyed up with an infinite satisfaction when he considers that the arm of omnipotence is enlisted on the side of Virtue. When he sees the munificence with which his Father hath endowed the race, in their intellectual, moral, and social gifts, the gentleness with which he leads them upward, and lastly in the great hope he hath disclosed, abolishing death. Life to him is far too dear, too solemn a preparation to be soured by hatred, or dishonoured by folly, or wasted in speculation, which was given for virtue.

The next great mischief that comes of the controversy is not only losing the portion of truth which is contended for by that party you oppose, but it begets in you a disposition of all others the most adverse to true religion. The very front of the Christian religion hath this maxim, *Love the Lord your God with all your heart and thy neighbor as thyself.*[10] But the banding ourselves in religious parties hath a strong tendency to make us dislike and denounce our neighbor, if he does not think as we do. And so out of your devotion to a Christian denomination you forfeit the blessings of the Christian religion. To some men it is almost impossible to speak with kind feelings of the other religious party. There is the greatest difference I know in this respect in constitutional self command. And it becomes an important duty to govern ourselves by our knowledge of this circumstance. If you are always in perfect good humour when you talk of your opponents, if you can reckon with perfect confidence on your principles and prudence that you will utter no expression which a cooler reflexion might condemn—why then you may venture on that question with as little scruple as on any other. But if you cannot—don't touch it—turn from it and pass away. The principle God implanted in us to use to others, was *love,* and to use toward ourselves, *Jealousy.* But this evil habit makes us reverse them, and be jealous of others, and indulge ourselves.

Brethren, these things ought to be considered by us, that in the warm discussions of the day, we may not miss the substance whilst we grasp the shadow. Every man ought carefully to ponder the evils of party spirit, that he may be a partisan, when he must be, without them. I do not think it is possible entirely to keep aloof from these communities of opinion. When a persecution arises against an opinion which you hold, you must avow your sentiment, and join the weaker party in their defence. We are to use all our means to spread the knowledge of true religion, and we must unite with others to make our efforts of any avail.

But let us cleave, in the midst of parties, to an independence of party. If your

8. Galatians 5:1 and Psalms 2:11.
9. II Corinthians 4:9 and I John 4:18.
10. See Matthew 22:37-39, Mark 12:30-31, and Luke 10:27.

education and temper dispose you to some austerity in your religious views—if you incline to revere God with awe rather than to love him—let that fear of him and the fear of sin make you abhor to judge your brother for his trust and his gratitude. And if you fear most the extremes of the rigid Christians and their propensity to a faith without knowledge yet be careful that you frankly own the good that adorns them, our brethren of other belief. Let us love and copy their seriousness, their bounty, their fear of sin; and join to it an affectionate trust in God, an ardent progress from virtue to virtue, an undaunted resolution to seek and maintain the truth and a hope of good hereafter which no evil nor disappointment nor failure can take away.

LXXVI

*He taught them as one having authority
and not as the scribes.*

MATTHEW 7:29

These words are not only remarkable as they express the feeling produced by the instructions of Jesus in the promiscuous assembly of his countrymen but also as they are descriptive of the impression made by him as a moral teacher on all succeeding times. I shall attempt to show the nature of this distinction, and, as in all respects he was an example for us, to show how far we may hope by imitating his virtues to share in his power.

Jesus taught as one having authority. How was he able to give this dignity to his instructions?

He was not like Paul learned. For all that we know the carpenter's shop and his mother's humble house were his only academy. And never in his discourses does he refer to any other books than those of the Jewish Scriptures.

He was not a subtile reasoner. It is the fame of a few men that they have analyzed every action and every thought of man into its first elements; that they have received nothing until it was proved, and have shaken the evidence of the best authenticated facts and have introduced doubt under the foundations of every opinion. Others there are who have applied the same ingenuity to better purpose, and have done what they could, to fortify with impregnable reason every useful custom, every important truth. Neither of these sorts of skill was the merit of Jesus of whose instructions it is one of the most remarkable features, that he does not reason at all. He proves nothing by argument. He simply asserts, and appeals to his divine commission. Christianity could not be defended if it looked to its author for a systematic account of its pretensions arranged by the rules of logic.

Nor was it by powerful declamation nor insinuating arts of address that he attained this end. Nothing can be more simple than the style of his discourses.

For a preliminary sketch for this sermon, see the journal entry for May 12, 1830 (*JMN* 3:185–86). The sermon was delivered on May 30, 1830, at the Second Church, Boston. It was extensively revised on March 31, 1832, and delivered the next day, April 1, at the Second Church. Subsequent deliveries occurred March 23, 1834, in New Bedford; March 8, 1835, at the Second Church, Waltham; April 12 in Watertown; June 28 in Framingham; January 24, 1836, in East Lexington; and August 21 in Concord, Mass. In all, Emerson delivered the sermon eight times. The revised version and an early draft are given in the Textual and Manuscript Notes.

It is the style of conversation. Nor by the charm of a great name nor the state-liness of manners of a sage; the story of his life shows us how free were his habits of intercourse with men. Many passages seem to show the wonderful deference with which he was approached, yet so entirely did this spring from other causes than physical accomplishments, that no pen has transmitted one syllable respecting the personal appearance, or the manners, or the voice of so remarkable a personage.

How then was it, if he was not learned, or subtile, or dogmatical, or eloquent, like many of his later disciples, that he spoke with an authority which they have never obtained?

I conceive it was because he taught truth and the supreme kind of truth, that which relates to morals, to a greater extent than any other, because he taught what man recognized as true the moment it was declared, because speaking on his own convictions he expressed with unexampled force the great moral laws to which the human understanding must always bow, whilst it retains its own Constitution; for the great laws of the gospel, my brethren, are they which after all our doubts, after running the round of skepticism, we return to acknowl-edge with new conviction. He spoke of God in a new tongue. He spoke of him not as the philosophers had done, as an intellectual principle, but in terms of earnest affection, as the grand object of all human thought; that a connexion with him was the home and beatitude of the soul.

He spoke of sin as the disease of man, as an evil of unknown consequence, full of danger and leading to death.

He opened the great doctrine of benevolence to the human race, showing them that glory did not exist in selfish seeking, but in bearing one another's burdens, in meekness, in returning good for evil, in doing good to all men.

He spoke of heaven, as the natural felicity of a good mind resulting to it from the harmony of its affections with truth and God. He spoke of it, of the *spiritual* good, as the only good worth seeking for.

He spoke of the immortality of the soul as the law of moral nature, as the effectual consideration to bind us to virtue and warn us of vice.

He was a preacher of righteousness, temperance and judgment to come.

There are many faculties in the mind but the highest faculty is the conscience. And there are many parts of truth but moral truth is the greatest. It was his full understanding of this superiority that distinguished Jesus as a teacher. It was the value of this truth that gave him his spiritual empire. Do not think that he owed to the curiosity and reverence that followed one possessed of miraculous power the weight of his lesson. The same truth will have the same effect from whatever lips. Doubtless a mind so pure and so great as his will succeed in giving to all its utterance the expression of its own grandeur. His character was consistent, part with part, and the mighty work of his hand was justified by the mighty word of his mouth. His miraculous powers were not separate but harmonized into his character. But believe rather that the hand was strong because the soul was filled with heavenly knowledge.

It is not the power to make surprising changes in matter, to heal the sick, to wake the dead, that can act on the soul of man with most effect; it is that command of truth which can pour light as a flood through the soul that best can touch the soul. He that can reveal to me the great secrets of my own nature, which I see to be true the moment they are disclosed, will have a deeper influence on me than he who chains my limbs. And these truths will have their full effect every where provided it be really truth in the mind of him that utters it. I know there is great difference between teachers; there is a vast difference between the power of two teachers ordinarily classed under the same name and understood to teach the same faith. The reason is that in one, his doctrine is to himself *living* truth, and he speaks it as he sees it; and in the other, it is *dead* truth,—it is passively taken and taught at second hand; it lies like a lump of foreign matter in his intellectual system, separate and inoperative.

It is, compared with the same truth quickened in another mind, like a fact in a child's lesson in geography, as it lies unconnected and useless in his memory, compared with the same fact, as it enters into the knowledge of the surveyor or the traveller. This is a distinction which I apprehend every one, at all attentive to his own thoughts, will readily understand. Every one will remember how often he heard in youth without heeding it, any one of the common proverbs that pass from mouth to mouth, and the lively satisfaction he derived from the perception of its truth, the first time that his own experience led him to express the same fact in similar language. Hence too the common remark of the new force which a man gives to any common place fact, when it is the fresh result of his own observation. Truth is always new from the mind that perceives it.

Then, moral truth hath that exalted dignity that it commands reverence. Every thing else is subsidiary to it. It is remarkable how this mastery that belongs to it shows itself in the *tone* that is taken by its teacher, as much as in the facts that are presented. A tone of authority cannot be taken without truths of authority. It is impossible to mimick it. It proceeds directly from the perception of great principles. It is powerful because truth always convinces. And people always know whether they have been convinced or not. There is therefore no artifice possible in the dealing of truth. He that hath it in himself, will move you. He will speak with authority. He that hath it not, will labor with his rhetoric and his learning in vain. Jesus hath it, but he has not monopolized it. His mission was to communicate it, and precisely in the same measure with it, he communicates his power over men. And thus, many a disciple in different ages of the church, hath learned of Christ so much of his truth,—hath had infused into his own being, so much of his master's spirit, that he hath spoken with a corresponding portion of his master's authority.

But does so much force and value belong to the possession of moral truth? What becomes of the distinction between speculative and practical knowledge? Is it not daily said that it is far easier to preach than to practise? O yes, it is easier to repeat from remembrance the good doctrines that are sounded through the world. It is easier and implies no high attainments in virtue; but to announce to others from your own mind the great rules of your own life; to tell what you aspire after with a selfjustifying hope; "what you fear; and what you love; the secret memoirs of the soul in relation to the Deity;"[1]—this is to give your own character or your own theory of character, and such teaching comes with authority and implies a virtuous life.

But if this natural force belongs to truth how happened it that he of whom we speak was despised and rejected of men?[2] How happens it that truth should yet make such slow progress in the world? It is the distinction of truth that it should be admitted at once. It has been said, "We seem to recognize a truth the first time we hear it."[3] O yes; but human passions and narrow views of self-interest fight against it. A man is pledged by education and connexion and faith to a system of false doctrine. You place before him a great truth which he had not felt and cannot gainsay or resist. He does not deny it. Nobody denies a truth, but he labours to believe that it is not inconsistent with his own system. If he is a good man, it enters with its full force into his soul, despite of his prejudice, and modifies his former belief. If he is not a good man, if he is attached to his opinions not for their own sake but only because they are means to gratify his interest, his power, his hatred or his pride, then he will not welcome you, nor your truth. He too will feel the force of your doctrine, but he will hate you and speak evil of you because you have wounded the cause to which he is joined, and he has not greatness enough to see that the cause of truth is far more his own, than that of any perishing sect.

Brethren, does Jesus speak to us with authority? Do we receive his doctrine with joy? Or as each sentiment falls from his lips do we feel that it condemns us and so feel towards him as an enemy? Let us beware of being found fighting against the truth. We cannot contend against spiritual truth and be innocent, for our own consciences bear witness to him within us. Let us not be slower than the multitude who first heard him, but let us pluck out from ourselves the only enemies his words can find in the human heart, our own sins, our false estimates of earthly good, our sensual, our selfish, our uncharitable thoughts, and we shall find that as we do this the voice of our Saviour becomes the voice of a friend, sounds to us full of consolation, of promise, of praise. At last, when truth has had its whole effect on our minds, it will gain its fulness of authority by becoming to us simply the echo of our own thought. We shall find we think as Christ thought. Thus we shall be one with him and with him one in the Father.[4]

1. Madame de Staël, *Germany* (New York, 1814), 3:333; see *JMN* 6:176–77.
2. Isaiah 53:3.
3. Bernard le Bovier de Fontenelle, quoted in Madame de Staël, *Germany* (New York, 1814), 2:270; see *JMN* 3:55. Used in "The Uses of Natural History" and "Society" (*EL* 1:25 and 2:99).
4. Cf. John 17:21.

LXXVII

Let no man seek his own,
but every man another's wealth.

I Corinthians 10:24

It is a distinguishing feature of Christianity, and so has been a great commendation of it, that it enforced the social duties with a stronger emphasis than any moral code had done before. Peace and good will were the first words it uttered,[1] and alms giving and charitable institutions have attended the establishment of Christianity in every country. But it is an exaggeration to say that Christianity first taught the law of benevolence. God taught it to the first man, and to every man in the Constitution of his own mind, and in the Constitution of society. The law of love, the duty of seeking the good of others and postponing our own to it, is no obscure or local doctrine. It hath gone out into the ends of the earth. It hath teachers and examples in every savage tribe. To die for friendship, for love, for the protection of the innocent or for our country was always accounted noble. It is an universal sentiment.

To shrink from these generous impulses and prefer the present good of self was always reckoned cowardly and infamous.

And so the duty of charity in its peculiar sense, i.e., assistance to the indigent, is very plain. And no man denies the obligation. It would argue a mind of ferocious temper, to deny it broadly. But how little is the duty felt, how little understood, how imperfectly discharged! Men do not deny the obligation to be charitable but they cavil at every particular occasion of charity that brings an appeal home to themselves.

In performing my duty on this occasion I shall not confine myself simply to asking your contribution for the unhappy sufferers in our community who receive the aid of this Lecture but I shall endeavour to do my duty as a Christian minister by showing first, the considerations from Natural Religion in favour of the duty of Charity, secondly, the sanction which this virtue has from the Christian religion, and lastly, to consider some of the objections made against eleemosynary institutions.

Preached twice: June 6, 1830, as the evening Charity Lecture at the Old South Church, Boston, and in revised form, including a report on the Evangelical Treasury, July 3, 1831, at the Second Church, Boston. The revised version is given in the Textual and Manuscript Notes.

1. See Luke 2:14.

196

A great deal is said about the importance of charity but it usually comes from those who plead for its gifts and they naturally urge the claims of the particular object they wish to recommend. But men do not feel as they ought the intrinsic excellence of Charity itself. They do not feel how much it is necessary to their own happiness, how indispensable a part it is of a finished character to comply with this duty. They do not perceive that he who withholds his aid from his fellowmen is more a loser than his fellowman from whom he withholds it, that the soul of man was made to act for others as much as his body was made to breathe the air, that it is the natural action of man to impart his knowledge, his virtue, his possessions, his goodwill, the way in which he moves towards the perfection of his being, the way in which he grows great.

For when it is truly considered I suppose it will be acknowledged that judging truly and not after custom he is the greatest man who lives to produce the greatest good.[2] He is the greatest man in the world, that is, most nearly arrived at the perfection of his nature, who would be the greatest loss to the world and that is the best mind in existence whose loss to the Universe would be most injuriously felt.

There is no character that does not produce its fair impression on society and so the amount of practical power is always precisely measured by the amount of effect.

A king whose moral or intellectual effect on a nation is insignificant may be sick and die, and his place shall be speedily filled by as good a successor and his departure shall not cause one pang in any community or in any family, scarcely in one individual.

But if there should be within the dominions of that king a mind which is not more its own property than it is the property of the country or the age in which it acts, a mind which is nearly allied to God by the love of him, and which by the inevitable effect of that love, exercises the deepest and most salutary influence on all surrounding minds and through them on society, being everywhere quoted and everywhere admitted to be the best argument and witness of the effect of divine truth, and further if this mind should apply itself in all its length and breadth to the public good, should be the instructor of his country, the central spring of all the great beneficent enterprizes of the times, and if such an one die, if this amount of good influence be withdrawn from the community, now and not before is greatness perished, though the forms of mourning and panegyric would be less, a severe loss has been experienced, it will be far more truly mourned, a torch has been extinguished that rayed out knowledge far and wide and made the earth light with its beams.

The loss is great but it will speedily be repaired. It is only the loss of future influence, for all the past continues to have effect. Good works have an afterlife and remain in the world to bless and to stimulate others to the like. But it is not

2. Cf. Francis Hutcheson, *An Inquiry into the Original of Our Ideas of Beauty and Virtue; In Two Treatises*, 2d ed. (London, 1726), 177.

the world that has been the gainer from the action of such men, but themselves, far more. The world has had their services but could easily have had others. The world would have been a loser indeed, if there had been no more, but God's moral and intellectual treasury is never exhausted. If one man refuses his mite to his service, God will use and honour another. But consider the man himself; how has he been exalted, ennobled! All his powers have been called into use and all have been invigorated by their use.

He has been accustomed to live and move to great principles, he disdains to act by mean ones. The beauty and the glory of humanity is in him. His moral powers have been exercised and have got their supremacy, and so he has acquired a confidence in the prospects of human nature, he has dealt with its best and noblest features, he has the great feeling of brotherly love and with it the reciprocal trust of all men. And so he was not made in vain. No particle of God's energy in him is lost. He exists for the good of the creation. He exists for boundless joy.

And then he stands on an immeasurably higher level than ever external distinction could secure for a man.

Man's natural greatness is to do good.[3] His nature is wonderfully plastic and his Creator has formed him capable of an accommodation to his objects of pursuit. He seeks the good of the Universe and enlarges himself to the vast objects he contemplates. Or he prefers a solitary, selfish enjoyment and so shuts up one door of his soul after another, seals every avenue, and is buried in himself a living tomb.

All the seeds of weakness in his frame are those tendencies which draw him from the good of others to his own. His appetites war against his greatness. How? because they seduce him to seek a good that begins and ends in self. His passions are injurious to him only when, like Avarice, Envy, Ambition, Pride, Revenge, they tempt him to contract his out-stretching branches, and tie them inward to himself, instead of letting them send forth their vigorous limbs into the firmament.

God has made all things double one against another.[4] If you have the love of your neighbor in you, you will be loved in that proportion.

I seem to myself like one who should say the sun is bright and the fire burns, whilst I urge so manifest a truth as the excellence of the great principle of Charity. For that we were made to communicate and to do good as we have opportunity is set down in God's handwriting on all parts of life.[5] What is speech for? what is genius for? what is your grace, your learning, your industry, your wealth, power, eloquence, if once they are put out of use? Try to separate them to your own exclusive benefit. It is impossible. Do it as far as you can and

3. Cf. *JMN* 3:174: "Man's natural goodness is to do good to others." See also Sermon LXXIX, n. 6.
4. Ecclesiasticus 42:24; see *JMN* 2:340 and 6:143. Used in Sermon IV, "Ethics" (*EL* 2:153), and "Compensation" (*CW* 2:64).
5. Galatians 6:10

you become a burden to the earth and hateful to yourself. Every power in man is disgraced by being applied to inordinate selfseeking.

Yet is the plea of Charity but half complete. God has not left this duty to win its way into the use of men by the simple view of its advantage, but has given it the authority of religion also. He has made it a prominent feature of his revealed will. He says, Do good to all. Love your enemies. Bless them that curse you. And have a charity beyond the giving your goods to the poor or your body to be burned.[6] And when you have done all, say, We have done only our duty.[7]

He has lodged us here on the earth for a few fleeting years and commanded us to look on all men as our brethren, to labour affectionately and unceasingly to promote their good, to think and speak and act kindly to immortal man, though in rags or in guilt.

He has promised to judge us as we judge, to be merciful unto the merciful, to remember and repay the cup of cold water with heavenly blessings.[8] And so the hopes and the character of the soul and its relations to God are connected with our fidelity to this virtue by God's special act as well as by the operation of ordinary laws.

Thus is it our duty by our natural constitution, and still further by direct command, to practise the whole duty of charity.

To these views thus generally stated every mind will respond for they are founded in nature and in scripture. But men are, I think, very prone to escape from the performance of the duties they enforce by various ingenious objections which they urge on plausible pretences of the public good against each specific proposal. In the first place, they say promiscuous charity is very pernicious and so we recommend to them the wants of some well managed institution. But no. Eleemosynary societies are pernicious too. They create the evil they would cure and so selfishness ties up its purse and hardens its heart with the worst of all pretensions that 'tis for the public good, and charity is made the plea against charity. These are words but not reason. God who made the reason never authorized them. He made the heart. The plea against charitable actions founded on the abuse of charity is entitled to all attention when it is made against one appropriation in favor of another, but not when it is made against all. Not when it is made against fretful hunger and pinching cold. Stop your ears against it. Don't be reasoned out of your charity. Don't be reasoned out of your bowels of compassion.[9] That throbbing heart within you which shrinks and shudders at a brother's woe is a truer teacher than the selfish statesman. 'Tis all wrong. Suppose it is not the most judicious of charities. It is better to do good in a less efficacious way than not at all.

If you will do good by Charity do not have too delicate a perception of the possible evil. The abuses of charity are not the worst evils on earth, nor those of

6. Cf. Matthew 5:44 and Luke 6:27-28, and 6:35; I Corinthians 13:3.
7. Luke 17:10.
8. See Matthew 7:1-2, 5:7, and 10:42.
9. Cf. I John 3:17.

most extensive mischief. The selfishness of Man, which refuses to give, is a greater evil than pauperism, and might give the statesman as genuine alarm. If two charities are proposed to you, chuse between them. But do not fear that out of your aid to either any gross mischief will come to the community. When I see the wise and good men that are the trustees and dispensers of public bounty, I cannot think any wasteful or absurd use will be made of my contribution. When I see how sharp an oversight the public eye keeps on public funds, I do not fear but a conspicuous bad effect will be counteracted by a new check. Every day modifies and improves our great charities. Their injurious operation is continually guarded, and they continually are brought to act with more and more directness upon the evil they design to remove. That they all do some good cannot be denied. Regard each of them and all of them only as experiments. In view of the great mass of evil something must be done. But which of a thousand expedients to adopt? We do not know. Then make some one, and if it is not the best one, it will still be one experiment, one step, not to be gone over. Every charitable institution, the least useful of all, will produce good by direct and by indirect consequence. Because, let it be remembered, one of the greatest evils of poverty is the privation of many of the best aspects of human nature. It sees the selfish and sore side. Show it the strenuous exertions of society to remove its woes. Every sufferer who has been relieved by it will be the better and will think more kindly of the world. If it do no other good it will do this. It will be a great sentiment of brotherly love embodied, and the hearts of men will warm to each other when they behold it. A great institution to alleviate want is a noble spectacle. What more beautiful can the world show me than a city ramparted around with great charities, doing God's office as God's steward to its lame and blind and sick folk, educating its young by free schools and sending its domestic missionaries into the chambers of poverty and vice?

It is a grateful sight to the eyes of God and men and so is every spirit into which the grace of love has fully descended and which is therefore itself an asylum in which wo may always find relief.

Therefore, brethren, if we value the proper training of our own affections, and our faithfulness to God's commands, let us be clothed with beauty of this eldest grace. Beware of turning a deaf ear to the calls of Misfortune and Want upon us. Let us consider every such call a beckoning of God's Providence to us, an opportunity to do good and become good. Let us regard the beggar as the Lord's messenger taking account of our stewardship. If you think his plea a bad one and withhold your help, be careful that you bestow it somewhere else. Do not avail yourself of that excuse and omit the gift altogether.

We hold out to you, brethren, this evening, the hands of the poor, and ask of you for their wants what your heart will bestow. If God has prospered you, if the disasters of broken credit, of baffled exertion, of hopeless indigence and weary and painful disease have been spared you, let your just and religious hands do what they can to help them on whom these trials have sorely fallen. And the blessing of the poor man which is heard in heaven, and the blessing of God and the blessing of your own expanded heart shall be your reward.

LXXVIII

Now is the accepted time, now is the day of Salvation.

II Corinthians 6:2

The Scriptures represent God as offering to the children of men in his Word and in his Providence all those blessings that are expressed in the word Salvation, that is to say, a deliverance from all the misery and ignorance that is caused by sin; an exaltation from a state of moral slavery to a state of liberty; from a state of increasing weakness, danger, and depravity, to a state of growing health and power and beneficence; in short, from a condition in which we are a growing pest to the world and to ourselves to a condition in which we become continually more useful and more blessed, and that, forever.

This is the Salvation which Jesus Christ brought from God, which is, (as I read the bible,) offered to all, conferred upon none; not lavished upon any soul, but proposed to every soul, to be obtained by its exertions, and cannot be obtained in any other way.

But what grace is given? how long do the doors stand open? Not a day, not an hour is indulged in the divine commandment for deliberation. Choose this day whom you will serve.[1] Now is the accepted time. Now is the day of Salvation.

It will be my endeavour in the following remarks, to show the reasonableness and the importance of this declaration.

I. Now is the accepted time, because now is the time when the offer is made.

One of the great sources of illusion by which men suffer themselves to be deceived is the reference of our existence to the past. We are accustomed to speak of the past as having had some real existence to us; to speak as if we were not new men and women, but as if we took up the story of the world where our fathers left it; as if one individual were a part, and not a whole; as if we wrought

---

Manuscript dated June 12, 1830, at Brookline. Preached nine times: June 13, 1830, at the Second Church, Boston, in the morning, and at the South Congregational Church in the afternoon; July 11 in New Bedford; August 22 in Brookline; June 24, 1831, as a Friday Lecture at the Second Church; June 12, 1836, in East Lexington; June 30 as a Thursday Lecture in Concord; October 9 at the Second Church, Waltham; and March 26, 1837, in Lowell. The pencil inscription "Salem" on the first page of the manuscript suggests that Emerson may also have delivered the sermon in that town, though there is no reference to it in the Preaching Record. Certain portions of the sermon anticipate the opening of *Nature* (1836).

1. Joshua 24:15.

201

a few threads into the web of a common destiny; as if the truth which was trite on earth, was trite to us. It is the pernicious habit of men to group themselves together and conceive because the gospel has been proclaimed a great while it has been proclaimed to them a great while. And so we slight the lesson we have never learned, though it come from God; we say, why this has been heard before; these warnings are old; this maxim is old;—Well what if it is? is that any reason why it should not commend itself to you and to me if it be the word of eternal life? So you may say the world is old; the air is old. The sun has shone a very long time. Men have always eaten bread and always used hands and eyes and feet. Yet is the use any the less needful now to any individual?

No; neither is the natural nor the moral world old, but altogether new. In a very clear and important sense, Old things are passed away, all things are become new.[2] The air that we inhale this moment is but just now exhaled from the great reservoirs of nature. The whole vegetation of the earth is now renewing it. Every mineral, every animal substance is carrying forward the great chemistry from which we obtain the atmosphere that shall sustain our bodily life for another hour. So for the food you eat; the winds are now blowing, the sun is now shining, the water is now flowing, the stones and plants and animal remains are now undergoing decomposition in earth's great laboratory that are to enliven, warm, moisten, and nourish the green herb that Providence has set apart to sustain you, in the form of corn or of flesh.

So is it the will of Him who existeth forever and ever continually to replenish his *moral* universe,[3] and as it were to create a new world to every new mind. The virtue and the vice, the knowledge and the power of our fathers, of our Country, of our kind, are of no more use or harm to us, than as they have entered into our bosoms, and become our own virtue and vice, knowledge, and power. What if there is truth in the world? That only is true in *my* world which I perceive. All other, until I perceive it, is as much incapable of helping me as if it were false.

What matters it that we walk on the same orb, amidst the same forms of outward nature? Every man stands exposed to his proper influences; exists in a combination of circumstances, that is new and unexampled. Men walk side by side through life in the same land, in the same town, and street, whose education has been wholly different, whose modes of life are wholly unlike, whose habits of thought are widely remote, who are, as if they were reared on opposite sides of the globe.

And not only is the discipline to which one man is subjected, different from the discipline of any other, but it is suited to his moral wants, it is part of a series of lessons. If we believe that God is preparing us here for another state of being we must believe that every part of our discipline is important and one part as much as another.

It is this present hour, and its breathing event, it is the disaster you now suffer,

2. Cf. Revelation 21:4-5.
3. Cf. Revelation 4:9.

it is the temptation you now contend with, the work you do, it is the book you read, the fear that works in you, the love that glows in you, the compliment that flatters you—the hope that cheers, the pain that rends you; these things are the tongues through which the voice of God is now speaking to your soul. It is each of these events, the least no less than the largest, which the Christian receives as the recent messengers of God to him, prompting him, each one, to more diligent cultivation of the graces of the spirit. These are his trials; this is his life; these are the facts upon which God shall try his soul, whether it hath kept or whether it hath transgressed the commandment.

But all these events pass unheeded, days, months, and years together, over the unawakened mind. Men have the habit of slighting whatever is *usual.* If the power and wisdom that is displayed unceasingly in the government of the Universe should cease, if it were displayed only at intervals, it would command their speechless reverence, but now, it is familiar, and cannot; they speak or they act as if it would be superstitious to interpret it as having any peculiar significance. Because it is *usual;* because it never fails.

And does it cost less power and goodness to furnish forth the great Universe for ages and for eternal time than it would for the exhibition of an hour? Does it cost less to weave around you that vast and complex and delicate system of relations to so many men, and so many events, by which now your powers and affections are developed, than it would to send you a special miracle or a periodical revelation for your instruction?

It is strictly reasonable to believe, as the Scriptures teach us to believe, the present moment contains instruction directly addressed by the Deity to the mind. Each moment brings to you in its peculiar trial or lesson the pointed offer of salvation from God. Yes, my friends, this and no other is the accepted time. For do you think this moment or any moment is sent to you without its use? Do you think God trifles with you in his solemn gifts? Does he load you with his munificence of powers and opportunities or any part of it to no purpose?

I say then that the apostle utters a truth which all the understanding within us confirms and all the analogy of external nature, when he says, Now is the accepted time, now is the day of salvation. Now is the time, because now is the offer made; now is the danger pressing; and now must the deliverance be procured—or probably never. I say probably never because another day will bring another danger, and you cannot then contend with the present enemy, and its own. If then you shall succeed in obtaining victory over strengthened bad habits, shall get Salvation from that hour's sin, yet the evil effect of this day's sin will yet remain to retard your progress.

For what is the salvation we seek? What is it we are pleading for? What is it 'the day,' what is it life, and reason and revelation were given to us for? Is this salvation a certain specific good which once gotten by us is got forever; some act to be done by us, which then becomes extinct, and no more shall be heard of? Something which has its beginning and its end? Many men use this word familiarly without apprehending its meaning.

This salvation is not definite partial good, but vast as intelligent being and without end. It begins with the first dawn of moral perception in the soul, and it is to be sought in every action and every step of progress as long as God shall endure. So long and so far, therefore, must the soul's efforts to obtain it, be made. In every hour, in every moment, as long as you exist, salvation must be got from the sins of that hour and moment. And the present time, therefore, it is manifest, is the only time that the laws of God's universe allow to obtain the salvation from present temptations.

II. Once more; Now is the accepted time, and not the Future. I have said that men have a pernicious custom of considering themselves in reference to the past, as carrying on a great drama, and so getting rid of the individual responsi-bility which every man's conscience lays upon him in a crowd. But neither may men fly to the *future,* for refuge. I have already anticipated in part this division of my subject in speaking of the nature of Salvation. But to consider it by itself. *Now* is the bosom of the future. O consider, you who will compound by stern-est self-denial in time to come for this one indulgence that is near your heart, and involves no great transgression,—o consider, how truly this moment is the child of the last, and how closely it resembles its parent.

Consider how many tomorrows have failed to keep their promise. How much the same person you are today that you were yesterday, and this month as the last month, despite all the flattering expectations, the glowing purposes you can remember to have formed, aye, and perhaps also the earnest prayers you have uttered. O, let not this experience plead in vain. This experience is another tongue by which God speaks to you. Be not twice betrayed by the same snare. But consider that the day you anticipate and will thus mortgage to God may never come to you on earth; and, if it should, that you have no firmer hold of days to come than of the past; that they will speed on swifter wings and age and care and regret will make them as slippery foundations for reformation as the worst of the past has been.

Therefore, brethren, let us be as wise men and do as those who know that now is the accepted time—the day of salvation. Let us feel that tomorrow and the next day and all the days that remain to us in life, if more remain, will bring their several claims on our powers of body and mind, and ought not to be embarrassed with the wretched incumbrance of today's neglected work. Let us feel that eternity which presses upon us, will bring, in its vast duration, duties as vast, and will bring besides, as God liveth, a sure retribution for the evil done in the body. Let us therefore make haste to live whilst it is called today. Let your conscience open God's book of remembrance within your own breast. Read therein, my brother, whether you have yet learned in your own proper experi-ence the great law which Jesus declared was the end of all Revelation, to love God with your whole mind, and your neighbor as yourself. "If you love me, keep my commandments."4 This is the measure of our love to him.

See then how many of his laws you have violated. If you find that the first

4. Luke 10:27; John 14:15.

commandment has not yet become a living law to your soul, then read the Scriptures with a careful eye, then watch with diligence the Providences of God that come to you; they are full of meaning, and the watchful eye shall find it out. They come to warn, to arouse, to console, to advise you, to wean you from the world, to lead you to heaven. They all say to you, now is the accepted time, now is the day of salvation.

LXXIX

To do good, and to communicate forget not.
HEBREWS 13:16

It is my duty to bring before you this day the claims of the ancient association for charitable purposes in this society, upon your bounty. In a Christian Church a plea for charity is always seasonable. A Christian Church should have a heart as large as the family of man. A hand always open whilst any wants and any ability to relieve them remain.

But as God rather seeks in us the development of our own affections than the amount of aid which we can render when he sends us the opportunities of doing good, so it becomes me to press from reason and revelation the general duty of Charity, than to urge the claims of the particular institution whose wants are to be presented to you.

Charity is written on the front of Christianity, of which it is the beginning and the end, but as all the laws of the New Testament were not new when it was preached, and were only then illustrated and sanctioned and exemplified, but had existed as long as the human mind, and from time to time had wrought their blessed fruits in a great and good man;—so this virtue is taught to men by all the appearances of the outward world, by all the course of human affairs. When we inspect the works of God, we find that every thing is made to answer some purpose beyond the continuance of its own being. To select a single instance; a tree of the forest, when it is closely examined, is found to have an organization of consummate art capable of performing within itself from year to year, all the delicate and varied processes that belong to its perfection, and though every part is most tender and delicate in its origin, yet it arrives at that robust condition, that it can resist the cold, and the wind, and repair the injuries it receives, and outlast many of man's generations. But how soon would the eye of man weary of the microscope, if his examination only detected means of

Manuscript dated June 26, 1830, at Brookline. Preached five times: on the occasion of the annual report of the Evangelical Treasury, June 27, 1830, at the Second Church, Boston; June 3, 1832, as the Charity Lecture at the Old South Church, Boston; March 9, 1834, in New Bedford; March 8, 1835, at the Second Church, Waltham; and November 8 in East Lexington. A second manuscript, lacking sermon number and dates but giving the same information about the Evangelical Treasury, is apparently an undelivered draft of the present sermon. This draft version is given in the Textual and Manuscript Notes. The first half of the sermon bears comparison with the "Commodity" chapter of *Nature* (1836).

promoting the good of the vegetable itself; if nothing was in a tree, but the means of enlarging, continuing, and propagating a tree. It is the usefulness of this being and mainly its usefulness to man that gives it so much of his regard.

It is the ornament of the earth. It gives hospitable shade to man and beast. It yields its fruit after its kind for food.[1] It is timber for towns and for navies.

These are its direct services to man. Are these all its uses?

It hath abundantly more to accomplish by its existence. Its roots grasp the earth, and prevent the inroads of sand upon the soil. Under its shade, plants arise that could not grow without its protection from the sun. Every leaf hath its functions to perform to the atmosphere. Its evaporation cools the air. It exhales new and healthful elements for animals to breathe. When its leaves fall, they supply rich nourishment to the new plants.

Yet here is but a portion of its uses. As the observer more nearly examines it, he finds it a world by itself, peopled with a vast mass of life. It is the residence of countless animals of various forms and habits, both social and solitary species; some that fly, and some that creep,[2]—to which it affords habitation and food. The bird builds its nest and sings in the branches; the squirrel lays up in its cavities his winter store; the caterpillar weaves his web with his community, and then spins his own shroud and waits his resurrection in a summer morn; and on every bough the worm and the fly find their mansion, and administer their little commonwealths of every kind, down to the minute herds of insects who take their colour from the leaf which is the pasture over which they roam.

These are some of the purposes which are answered by one of the countless forms of matter around us, all of which have their uses more or less important and various. It is not their uses, but our knowledge of their uses, which is limited. The progress of science every day discovers more fully the part which every vegetable, every mineral, and every animal hath assigned to it in the general economy.

The animal creation are the laborers for man and nature. The bee carries the fertilizing dust from flower to flower. Not only those serve us who bear our burdens, the camel, the reindeer, and the horse, but the birds and beasts of prey and the little cities of insects are not less indispensable to us which devour the vast excess of corrupting animal and vegetable matter that else would taint the atmosphere.

So is it with all. God has made nothing for itself alone. Every element to its whole extent of being is useful. The waters work for us. They do not limit their beneficence to bearing our frail ships. The broad basin of the sea cools the world by its evaporation; and forms the clouds that the moisture may journey from land to land; and it conceals another kingdom of life within its bosom.

In the economy of Providence there is neither prodigality nor parsimony. Nothing is hoarded for one. Nothing is permitted to be separated from the

1. Genesis 1:11.
2. Genesis 1:20 and 1:24.

general good. Every thing is made to minister to the widest beneficence. There is no graveyard in nature, no tomb for useless decay. The mouldering forms from which life is departed, are immediately converted into new forms of strength and beauty,—they live again, again they minister to power and happiness.

Nor do the sun and moon and the stars move and burn for their own pleasure, nor does the earth roll in unprofitable light through space. For use they shine, for the good of intelligent beings they revolve, for times, and for seasons, for months, and years, for health and life, for mind, for moral nature, for virtue, for truth.

But all these great agents of mercy are involuntary benefactors. It is conscience in man that gives them a tongue. It is we, who, by our nature, read the moral, and not they who intelligently say it. The bee bears you no good will, whilst he separates the honey and kneads the wax which you shall use. The world-enkindling sun in his cloudy tabernacle, is inert and brute as the dust we tread upon. It is not they who bless us, it is the beneficence of God working through them that we feel; it is the goodness of him who makes the winds his wings,[3] and the clouds his servants, and the sun his minister. He breathes the life of his love through their silent frame. He impresses his purpose on the clod and it teems with life,[4] and through the Universe as through the mouth of a prophet he speaks to the heart of his children.

It is God whom we perceive in the happiness we derive from outward nature and not the means he uses. The powers of nature have no purpose of kindness. All their beneficence, as far as they are concerned, is a blind mechanism. But what they fail to show us it is given to man, the likeness of God,[5] to unfold. He is made capable of a better beneficence. It is the glory of man to do good and know that he does it,[6] to confer benefits on others with the intent to produce good as an end. God has made men to be voluntary benefactors, and to this capacity He has added the richest powers of producing happiness.

But there are two classes of voluntary benefactors. I. Those who do good at no cost to themselves, II. Those who do good at a sacrifice. Not all men who do good with equal success do it with like motive or like merit. God has made good the natural fruit of all innocent exertions; it springs from every right exercise of our powers as heat springs from motion in bodies. So that if merely you walk in the path which nature has marked out for you; if guided by a wise selfinterest you seek to develope all your powers of body and mind in the best way, you will become a benefactor of society. The honest merchant whose leading motive is the acquisition of an estate for himself is a public benefactor by the wide human intercourse which he mediates. The physician, the jurist, the historian, the man of science, the teacher are still more directly useful. So is every mechanic and labourer. So is every man and woman down to the very

3. Cf. II Samuel 22:11 and Psalms 18:10, 104:3.
4. See Genesis 2:7.
5. Genesis 1:26.
6. Cf. *JMN* 3:174: "Man's natural goodness is to do good to others." See also Sermon LXXVII, n. 3.

humblest, so long as without infringing on the rights of others they seek law-fully their own ends.

Although such incidental good done to men has obviously no pretensions to high virtue, yet it mixes insensibly with the pure principle of benevolence. For men cannot see that the good of others, which, after their own, will naturally be dear to them, is daily promoted by their exertions, without taking a pleasure in promoting it, and so it becomes a part of their purpose to produce it.

No man can live long in the world with a steady endeavour to improve himself without discovering that the good will of others is essential to his hap-piness and that the only way to procure kindness is by showing kindness. The golden rule, "Do as you would be done by,"[7] is not more a precept of Chris-tianity, than it is the clearest deduction of worldly prudence. Thus all that superficial benevolence which is called politeness, an useful system of mutual concession which keeps even the selfish and sour-tempered from being bad neighbors—all this, though doubtless it is heightened and refined by the holy Christian law of love, yet may not proceed from any higher origin than this of self interest.

Nor can it be denied that the motive of a much more splendid class of actions is often of the same kind.

The statesman who, moved with the hunger of fame, renders his country the most important service; the soldier whose ambition prompts him to most dar-ing adventures in behalf of humanity; the man of genius, that, in aiming at the gratification of his own tastes, instructs his own age and all posterity; all these, though in proportion to the greatness of their powers, I believe more generosity mixes with their views, may yet be referred to the first description of good agents, and do not attain to the praise of Charity.

II. But the Second Class is those who do good *at a sacrifice*. And this it seems to me is the condition of Charity; the will to do good for itself, whatever it may cost. And the Charity is commensurate with the sacrifice. There are those who feel it to be their daily vocation, their indispensable duty to do good, not as a flourish and commendation to their own bye ends, but as itself the highest end; who cannot eat their bread in peace unless they have earned it by removing a portion of evil; who count that they have lost a day, if they have not done man a good office; who espouse the cause which others forsake; who see the hand which others cannot see, beckoning them here to the hungry, and there to the ignorant; who submit to privation, that others may abound; who prefer the useful to the honoured place; who are ministering angels sent forth to multiply those who shall be heirs of salvation.[8] These are not the inert laborers, the *unconscious* distributors of God's bounty, we considered before; these are *of God;* his spirit is in them; they act on principles of an infinite grandeur. And not only the blessing of them that were ready to perish rests upon them,[9] but as our

7. Cf. Matthew 7:12 and Luke 6:31.
8. Hebrews 1:14.
9. Job 29:13.

happiness arises chiefly from the benevolent or malevolent character of our own feelings, they dwell in a heaven from which the selfish are shut out by living in the exercise of the noblest emotions.

My friends, I have endeavoured to set before you the fact that the lesson of Charity is taught us in the strongest possible manner in the material works of God, and in the moral economy of man. I know not how God could more distinctly teach us that we should be kind to our fellow creatures than he does by the ordinary operation of his laws. For precisely as a man separates his good from the common good, he becomes hateful; as he finds his own within the general well being he becomes beloved. To a man kind to his family, seeking exclusively the comfort of his wife and children, we feel a low degree of regard. The man who manifests a strong desire to promote the happiness of his friends, of useful institutions of the town in which he lives, with a love which seems to be quickened by his hostile prejudices to other institutions and other communities, has made a higher advancement. But by his exclusiveness he makes all who are out of the circle he has chalked, his natural enemies. He that loves his country, will be loved by that country. But he that makes the whole world his country, and beholds a brother in the face of every man, will naturally be loved and reverenced by all the good. The archbishop of Cambray said, "I am more a Frenchman than a Fenelon, and more a man than a Frenchman."[10] And must not his happiness be seated highest and surest who has that interest in all men as to feel that whatever profits any man profits himself, that every event benefits some whom he loves, every wind blows a blessing to him, and his good feelings are reflected to him by every object in the Universe?

But God has not left this lesson to its own effect. He has added to this instruction of nature the explicit instruction of his word. It is with reason that a religion coming from God insists chiefly on love to man. It is what we might expect that the bearer of that message should have been one who counted not poverty or reproach or death an evil, so that by any means he might redeem his brethren from the greatest evil.

Therefore, brethren, let us take heed that these loud lessons are not lost upon us. Let not us alone of all the creation be backward to pay our debt of service in our place and station to the wants of others.

Do not faint because little effect comes from your exertion. Give your efforts a new direction. The success of a Charity is a measure of the wisdom that directed it but by no means of its moral merit.

And God does not want our aid to remove evils, but he wishes that we should have the disposition to do well to all, which is itself a removal of the greatest evil in the world.

It remains to state to you the uses on which our humble fund has been expended in the last year and to solicit your aid to it.

It is known to most of you that the Evangelical Treasury is a charitable

---

10. François de Selignac de la Mothe-Fénelon, quoted in Joseph Spence, *Anecdotes, Observations, and Characters of Books and Men* . . . (London, 1820), 27. See *JMN* 3:173.

association of members of this religious Society, who become members of the Treasury by the payment of one dollar a year. There is a committee recently appointed to solicit subscriptions. It is the custom of the Standing Committee of the Society to grant permission to have an annual contribution taken in the Church. These are the two sources from which the means of the Treasury are drawn. The present number of subscribers is ninety five. The contribution taken the last year was $87.

The management of the society is confided to fifteen Directors annually chosen. During the past year $139.00 have been expended. The annual appropriation of $35.00 to the parish Library, which has no other aid except a trifling sum from the Church, and is an object of such manifest utility that it needs no commendation of words.

To the Hancock Sunday School more immediately under the care of this Church $40.00 have been given.

In aid of the sick and indigent persons within the parish who have always received the particular attention of the Directors only $14.00 have this year been expended by the Treasury, as an additional sum was assigned for this purpose by the Church.

To the Evangelical Missionary Society, the object of which is to aid feeble societies in the support of public worship, and which has been accustomed to look to our treasury for a part of its means, fifty dollars have been given.

These, brethren, are the objects which our Treasury desires should prosper, and this the aid, small but it is hoped effectual, it has afforded them. You see plainly that from the limits of its subscription list, it relies much upon the annual public contribution. If you think these objects important, if you desire that these and such as these should prosper; if there is so much light in your understanding and so much love in your heart that you can feel the solemnity of the simple petition which in such a claim as this the Providence of God brings to your ears;—if you will that the sorrows of indigence and sickness should be alleviated; that the Sunday School should not go down; that good books should be circulated and that the poor should have the Gospel preached to them;[11] then, out of your abundance give freely, or out of your savings, give a part; that the cause of mercy may not decline in our care.

But, oh my brother, be assured that the greatest want in the case is not the necessities we plead for, but your own. God can provide an offering for himself. God can instruct the ignorant, and comfort the poor, and heal the sick, by others than by you. But no otherwise than by your own mercy, can he render unto you mercy.[12] Only by the love that is in your own heart to others, can the love of the Father be shed abroad in you. Therefore, if you think this charity has no call upon you, I beseech you, do not neglect that which has, as surely there is one, wherever it may be.

11. Cf. Matthew 11:5.
12. Cf. Matthew 5:7.

LXXX

We have heard with our ears, O God,
our fathers have told us what work thou didst
in their days in the times of old.

PSALMS 44:1

The return of this anniversary cannot fail to awaken in our minds the recollection of God's peculiar favors to our country and to quicken our religious feeling. No feeling is more natural to a pious mind than the love of country. The good heart sees God in all events and in none more than in those that call out the loftiest sentiments in our nature.

And though perhaps it needs no more power in God's Providence to stir the thoughts of thousands than to arrest the attention of one mind, yet always we feel a deeper admiration at events which by one effect cause millions to rejoice together, than when the pleasure comes only to our door. It is in our eye more godlike in its origin and in its effect, and what mysterious grandeur in the consciousness of sympathizing with vast numbers of men, in acting on the feeling that is shared by a nation in the same hour.

We feel that in some sense we are brothers. We own a consanguinity whose bonds of endearment distance, inequality of fortune, dissimilarity of colour, of opinion, of habits, of interests, do not dissolve. Sympathy with vast numbers in any innocent sentiment is always elevating and useful. It gives a shock to selfishness, to all mean pitiful feelings. For a host cannot act together to any mean end. They sublime the petty purposes of individuals immediately into great principles, bad or good.

But to conspire with a state or nation in the indulgence of virtuous emotions; in the commemoration of illustrious dead; in the defence or assertion of truths and rights, does dignify in a peculiar manner the individual. It searches and cleanses the chambers of his soul with a mighty energy and gives him a prospect of his own place and duties from a commanding eminence.

Let us not then turn aside from the natural topics of thought which the light

---

Manuscript dated July 3, 1830, at Brookline. Preached once, on July 4, 1830, at the Second Church, Boston. Emerson's reading in Thomas Jefferson's recently published *Memoir* in late March and early April (see *L* 1:297-300) may have been prompted by his need for a new Fourth of July sermon. This, after Sermon XLII, is his second.

of this day should suggest to an American bosom. Let us remember our obligations to our race, to our countrymen, to our fathers. Let us take account of our blessings in a spirit of devout gratitude and consider what duties are imposed on us.

We cannot help observing in these days of commemoration that one of the most pleasing objects of human thought is the power of a great and good name, the influence that survives a patriot. There are certain historical names of almost every nation, which have become proverbial expressions for the love of liberty. The names of the martyrs of freedom, whether in Greece or Rome or England or America, have become the property of mankind. They cannot be pronounced without causing in every mind a passing tribute of homage; a thought of generosity and self-devotion, however momentary. The patriot has no longer life than the tyrant; perhaps it is much shorter and infinitely more laborious and unsuccessful. It ends prematurely perhaps by poison or the gibbet. His body moulders in the dust—but his power is not destroyed in the earth. Then first it begins to live. That name, that poor name a mere sound, a representative of the dead, contains in it a power which is stronger than armies or batteries or princes. It sounds in the ears of great emperors and they turn pale. No physical force, no array or confederation of military or naval power is anywise a match for a naked name. It arrives at last at that degree of might that it silences the flaming line of cannon, and overcomes the greatest armies, and changes powerful kingdoms. And this for the most simple and obvious reasons; for every trustee of power is a man, every general and every soldier is a man, and the name of the patriot is an allusion to a principle that is in the breast of every man, in the handwriting of God, which a child understands and desires, which all men pant after in proportion as their nature is unfolded.[1] Now let it be remembered that this useful and growing influence belongs to these names, not for a short time or in a little corner, but diffuses itself through every land, and from age to age, bringing discredit upon oppression and new strength continually to the cause of human rights. Thus the names of the leaders of the American Revolution are current far beyond the broad domain to which under God they secured a constitution; they are repeated with reverence and emulation on both sides of the Andes, in France, in Greece, and throughout Europe, they encourage the hearts that are ready to fail, they persuade them not to despair of the cause of mankind, and so contribute day by day to accelerate the final victory of right over wrong. Does it not, this influence, amount to such puissant force that the heroes who thus served men, and who perhaps in their own day grieved over their failure, would willingly have encountered all their suffering to purchase it and count their defeats most glorious success?

But our patriots did not fail. This day commemorates not only their trial but also their complete success. They have made our duties not difficult and hopeless but plain and easy to be rendered. Let us consider what they are.

1. Emerson's argument closely parallels that of William Ellery Channing's celebrated "Likeness to God" sermon (1828); see *The Works of William E. Channing*, 8th ed. (Boston, 1848), 3:245–47.

What is this principle of Patriotism? It seems to me, brethren, that it hath a different form in every breast. It is every man's view of the love that he owes his country. And it is obvious that every man's idea of his country is different.[2] For in each, it is a collective idea, made up of a general consideration of many particulars. Take a foreigner in our streets, a man of miserable condition who is begging his bread among us, as once he did at home, and gather from his conversation his idea of his country. After the general and vague idea of a large territory surrounded by certain lands and waters, his thoughts concentrate themselves upon certain familiar places and persons, a small town, a few fields, and some thirty, fifty or a hundred persons not much wiser or better than himself. These particulars make up all the idea of country about which he can reason.

Take another native of the same land, a man of consideration on account of his birth, his wealth, and his connexions, but not of more generous sentiments, and analyze in like manner his notion of his public duty.

You find his country far more refined in its external signs. He knows many of the prosperous and the gay in his own land, he has sat at many tables, he has had part in many important interests, and he enriches his picture with far more accurate particulars of worldly good, of civil refinement, of manners, of arts, than the last.

Take yet another man of great moral and intellectual excellence and speak to him of his country. The word carries him back not to the earth alone, but to all that is beautiful in its history, to the image of the conversation and virtues of all the best men now dwelling in it, to all their works, to the common purposes and hopes which bind them together, and there is in his soul an army of brave spirits, a strong confidence in great blessings intended by God for men and to be procured by the labors of himself and his compatriots; whatever is best and holiest in the human imagination enters into his idea of country.

Is it not plain that the love which he bears to his country must be a far more worthy and noble principle, than that of the others? He feels the tie of fellow countryman strongest that binds him to the best citizen, and the strain of patriotism the most when it draws him to the purest action.

Herein we may learn as in a mirror our own duty. Let us realize that we constitute the state; that the present generation, (and each of us is one of its members) determine for themselves the character of their country. Let us consider that each of us carries in his own mind an idea of his country which is made up of his own habits and opportunities and associations and wishes; the America of the selfish and ambitious man is no more fair or noble abode than the means of gratifying his turbulent vanity; that the America which the sensualist loves, is a sty of gross gratifications with which he has defiled the land that gave him birth, and any cave which concealed his vices from the execration of his fellowmen would be as precious in his eyes as the land of the Pilgrims. The patriotism of the lover covetous of money, prizes the soil of his fathers only for its market. He has no reverence for its Constitution or its laws but as they affect

2. Cf. *JMN* 3:201.

his own traffic and his eye sees no greatness in its ample regions, no beauty in its splendid cities, no honor in its citizens, each free as a state but as they help or hinder the transactions of his warehouse.

Not thus did God mean we should love our country, not for convenience, not by calculation, when he implanted in us that wondrous sentiment that makes the heart leap at every appeal—that inexplicable feeling that hath its source in the depths of the soul that makes us love the grass that grows in our own sod more than all the spices of another soil; that makes us love the grim rocks that guard our country, and the cold wind that roams over it, and the grey waters that wash it beyond all the softness of other climes, and all the verdure of other fields.

O, my friends, not this low, corrupt, unhonoured America be the image in our hearts. It was not such an one that fifty four years ago was declared free. It was not such an one that the Puritans sought to build the cities of their Zion in its untrampled snows. It was not such an one that our Fathers spent their lives and fortunes to save.[3] On this holy morning, uniting in its light the infinite hopes of religion, with the thrilling assurances of civil liberty, let us unite in supplication to the great Father of our spirits, who calls us to be children and not slaves, that he would please to exalt our minds with just affections to our country, that the unexampled advantages of our native soil may not be lost on us. Let the America we love be that hallowed asylum of religious liberty which heroic men, persecuted in their own country, sought and found.

Let it be the country consecrated by the unaffected piety of our fathers, by their anxious desire of the spiritual good of their posterity. It is the place where the sceptre of hereditary rank was broken by those who might have secured it to themselves.[4] It is the field of a thousand sacrifices of ease and fear to freedom. It is the world of hope. It is the School of our children. It is the Holy Ground where the Temple of God rises after such forms and opinions as his children desire, as freely as the trees of the forest grow. Think of it as the home of every good institution, of every hopeful effort, of intelligent, industrious, virtuous men. Let us think of it as a land enlightened by the Sun of Righteousness,[5] where every useful and merciful act shall be done, where we shall resist temptation and take *hold* on life, where the race of glory shall be run, and Jesus confessed and God owned by the general mind of men and his will done. Let such an America dwell in your mind as the object of your patriotism and it can never be too ardent. It can never be exclusive. If we will fill our breasts with the love of such a country we shall do all to make ours such an one; we shall do all to remove the evils that already are eating into its prosperity; and finally we shall carry our country with us into whatever land or whatever world the Providence of God shall call us now and forevermore.

3. Emerson echoes the conclusion of the Declaration of Independence, which he may have read recently in Jefferson's *Memoir, Correspondence, and Miscellanies* (Boston, 1830), 1:21.

4. Jefferson reports in his *Memoir* (4:470) that Washington had told him in conversation (October 1, 1792) that "as to the idea of transforming this government into a monarchy, he did not believe there were ten men in the United States whose opinions were worth attention, who entertained such a thought." Jefferson replied that "there were many more than he imagined."

5. Cf. Malachi 4:2 and Matthew 13:43.

LXXXI

By their fruits, ye shall know them.

MATTHEW 7:20

This is a very important truth, but its force is very partially felt, and the clear apprehension of it in the whole extent of its application would work a great change in the characters of men. I shall attempt to explain in the following remarks the import which I understand our Saviour to convey by this word.

I. First, that as every tree bears in its fruits a mark by which its class and species may be indisputably known and distinguished from all other plants, so every mind hath his mark of character which cannot be concealed, by which he may be known for that which he is, whatever pains are taken to disguise it. Now this great truth, which, after a man has considered it a little, appears manifest as the sun, certainly is not perceived to be a truth by great numbers of men, else there would not be the abundance of affectation, direct falsehood, and indirect pretension that is now in the world. Indeed a man must attain to a high measure

---

Preached ten times: July 4, 1830, at the Second Church, Boston; November 7 in Dedham; December 19 in Charlestown; August 14, 1831, at the Second Church; August 28 at the Friend Street Chapel; November 13 in Waltham (for Samuel Ripley); April 29, 1832, at the First Church, Boston; December 1, 1833, in New Bedford; February 14, 1836, in East Lexington; and August 7 in Concord, Mass. Sermon LXXXI exists in two manuscripts, each mutilated and incomplete: an earlier one, containing the opening, and a later one, much revised, which contains the conclusion. The revision was done no earlier than August, 1831. The last delivery was heard and recorded by George Moore, of Concord, who indicates in his diary that Emerson used a text from Proverbs 10:9: "He that walketh uprightly walketh surely: but he that perverteth his ways shall be known." Moore's summary of the sermon follows: "Deception is so common a thing that we are all apt to fall into it without being conscious of it. The every-day dealings of men, their common intercourse all shew that men try to appear what they are not. But whatever may be the appearances put on, a discerning, a discriminating man will surely detect the counterfeit. If at the commission of every evil act, the word fraud, theft &c. were written upon the forehead of the deceiver, his character would be more suddenly, but not more surely known than it is under present circumstances. A man's reputation is the shadow of his character, and it is as true as our shadows to our bodies. A man may succeed in deceiving a few with whom he is but little acquainted for a short time—but his character will be known. And it is generally, almost universally true, that a man receives all he deserves, that a just estimate is made of his life and character. The upright, the good man sees truth by the light of his own virtue—but the wicked stumbles upon the ignorance caused by his vices" (quoted in Kenneth Walter Cameron, *The Transcendentalists and Minerva* [Hartford, Conn., 1958], 2:465).

The text of the two manuscripts is given here seriatim, the second beginning with the paragraph marked "2." Lacunae are indicated by ellipses.

of wisdom in order to see this truth so clearly as to keep his practice from being tainted by any the least duplicity. The wisest and best persons are very apt occasionally to lose their hold of this truth and act as the unwise.

In proof of this, see how much deception is attempted among men. Scarcely any man but labours to be thought somewhat better than he is. Not, I believe, for the most part because men take any pleasure in being esteemed more honest, more temperate, or more intelligent than they are, but because without the pains . . .

There are certain effects proper to virtue which nothing but virtue can produce,—a certain height and regularity of good action: To counterfeit that, would need a simulation of virtue so assiduous that it would become virtue itself.

What is all this talk about obscurity? There is no obscurity to moral nature. God is ever present, ever felt, and He is the Universe.

Now, brethren, how much useless repining, how much injurious pretension would the clear perception of these truths prevent. If we would ponder these truths it would produce a wonderful alteration in the conduct of society; if men would be content to be wholly real; if they would be content to be what God made them, and feel that not in coveting some other manners, or other place in society, or other powers, but in unfolding and using that capacity and opportunity which God gave them, their true greatness and honour lies, therein alone was solid satisfaction, and therein their great power.

It would supply us with a better principle of action than the fear of censure or the love of praise. Instead of these, the certainty that every past act and every past thought is represented by the actual condition at which now we are arrived, will make the desire of perfection which God made us to seek the law of our life. Then the friendship, the counsels, the example of Jesus will be welcome to us; then the desire of God's favor will continually increase within us.

The consideration of these facts should lead us not only to avoid the impracticable attempt to show as ours the fruits of another stock, but it should quicken us to bring to perfection in ourselves the best fruits that can grow in the soil of man. O consider whether our idea of what man can be and can do, comes from the prayer and insurmountable purpose of our own bosoms or whether we are gazing idly abroad on others' action instead of working hard at home. It is a bad fruit by which a corrupt stock may be known, if you make the vice of the times the palliation of your own. I know the times are evil and the world bad but the times are our life and we are the world.

I see a great deal of crime and a low state of moral and intellectual order, which makes the reading of the New Testament sound like a reproof instead of being, as it ought, a narrative of what passes amongst us. I see in the land a few cultivated minds, a few souls raised by their accomplishments and their toil to be eminent Christians, but what multitudes of men are all uncultivated, are, I might almost say, spiritually lame, and deaf, and blind. They do not judge for themselves, and how can they act in their own right? They lean on others' opinions. They can hardly be said to act voluntarily but by chance. The great soul ordained to be God's image,[1] yea, and fellow worker in this low world, there he lies, inert, unbalanced, chained.

II. The second sense in which our Saviour's words are to be understood is no less important, that every man has his fruits inasmuch as every man has the full effect on Society to which his talents and virtues entitle him. I have laboured to show that there are no counterfeit reputations; that every man passes for what he is worth in the opinions of men;[2] but I believe that much more is true than this, namely, that every man's power is exactly proportioned to his merits, because the effects of action are inevitable and are to the eye of God and of enlarged minds as plain and closely connected as physical causes and effects. Every seed puts forth its leaves and every quality of the mind puts forth its effects. If you are good all your good will tell in the impression it makes on the world. If you are bad all your evil will work mischief to its whole extent. That is to say, in all the world no action is lost, but every one from the most imposing to the most insignificant hath its entire effect because every thing you know and every thing you do contributes its part to your present state of mind and to your future actions. I do not say that every effort you make will be attended with the success you hope for it, but I say that every effort has effect; has a degree of success; every act of perseverance profits you, for though you think it fails, it makes your next exertion better directed, and more effectual.

Only wisdom and goodness can really raise your happiness, your self esteem, and every man always secures from others that respect which his true estimate of himself entitles him to. . . .

passes through this world in a cloud and passes out of it before half its faculties are yet opened. Some one inferior faculty is much used for inferior purposes, the affections are engaged in unnatural alliances, an appetite or a faculty given for some low function is brought to a diseased strength and the rest of the man lies waste.

Yes, all this is true, and why? Why so many imperfect characters? this man amiable but dishonest, that a good father or husband or son, but indolent and sensual, this one having fine genius, a good writer, but a loose liver, and that man temperate and upright but jealous.

Is this God's fault or man's? Does God send the soul into the world in this shabby incapable condition?

We are but fragments of ourselves. For whilst we believe ourselves capable of an unbounded progress in every sort of knowledge and in every virtue, we do make very small progress in some one or some few. . . .

2. We know what is in each other by what is in ourselves. We have a common

---

1. Genesis 1:26.
2. Used in "Religion" (*EL* 2:95) and "Spiritual Laws" (*CW* 2:91, 2:92)

nature. As in a glass face answereth to face, so the heart of man to man.[3] We know very well what temptations have force over us, and how they have force, and we know what considerations have had power to neutralize them. We are well acquainted in our own experience with the affinities that exist between virtues and between vices. We know that integrity and independence are coupled; that servility is apt to be accompanied by backbiting; that sloth and sensuality dwell together, and the love of money with a hard heart. When we see slight but certain intimations of one quality we expect the other as naturally, as when we see smoke, we conclude there is fire.

Indeed we know that none of our actions are solitary,—but all, flowing from a permanent will, will be like to each other. If we have felt the hardness of our neighbor's heart we know that all others will feel it who come as near to it as we have. There will be a uniformity in all the habits of every mind. As every animal seeks its proper nourishment amidst many other animals; as a sheep and a bird and a bee and a snake feed under the same tree, but each knows its own food, and does not mess with another,—so does every mind, by an instinct as inevitable, seek in whatever place, or event, or society, that food which is proper to its own present life, whether that be good or evil. So two men shall read the same book, and to one it shall be balsam, and to the other it shall be poison, because one is pure and one is corrupt. From the same page, from the same conversation, from the same discourse, each of them will be struck with different passages, and carry them away in his memory. Whilst Paul was esteemed by Timothy as the friend of God, and the apostle of Christ, the barbarians of Melita thought him Jupiter, and by Felix he was kept as a valuable captive whose ransom would be large.[4] Paul meantime was the same person, and an acquaintance with him would have made their views of him alike. Each of these views of him were only reflections of their own minds back on themselves. And every mind as it skims over the world of man and nature only draws to itself whatever substance is like itself.—I conclude this topic by remarking that we know a great deal of the workings of our nature which we never have expressed in words, and often do we form very just opinions of what a man will do in particular circumstances, without being able to state to ourselves the grounds of our belief.

3. I might name in the third place the fruit of men's labors as one mark by which they are known to us, because there is always a reason for every success and for every miscarriage. How far it belongs to a man's own self and how far to events which he could not control, will be felt by those who know him. But time will not permit me to push any farther these considerations.

I use these considerations to show that the soul that is in man doth always

---

3. Cf. Proverbs 27:19.

4. Timothy's regard for Paul may be inferred from Paul's epistles to him, though in fact no one but Abraham is called "the friend of God" (James 2:23). Emerson's recollection of the episode at Melita seems to conflate Acts 14:12 with Acts 28:1-6. The expectation of a ransom by Felix, procurator of Judea, for the imprisoned Paul, is recorded in Acts 24:26.

publish its nature.⁵ I beg the attention of every reasonable mind to the fact to which our Saviour calls your attention, that you can do nothing in secret;⁶ that every act and every thought,—the most solitary, private,—does contribute its part to make you what you are, what you appear, that every attempt to palm off upon men as yours, a character or a quality of character which is not yours is baffled, and loads you not merely with the discredit of a deception, but with the moral iniquity of a deception. If I fail to show it, it is not the less true, and your own consideration shall . . .

Every action has its expression as much as every countenance, and a man can no more hide all his actions than he can always hide his face. In general a man's reputation is the shadow of his character and is as true to his character as the shadow to the body. If for every crime that a man should commit there should instantly appear on his forehead the name of his offence, as *fraud,* or *slander,* or *homicide,* and for every virtue, it should there be writ, *humility, fortitude, charity, patriotism,* there would be a more gross and sudden means of publishing character, but hardly more certain, than does now exist. A man's real character is the consequence of his actions and his reputation is the enumeration of his actions, and it is not possible that whilst these are bad that can by any art be made to appear good.

I say a man's reputation is true to his character. Certainly it cannot be pretended that every individual's character is unerringly known to every individual with whom he has intercourse. Else the word hypocrisy would not be in use. We know that we are continually correcting our opinions concerning other men, which would not be if we judged rightly of their qualities at first sight. But though the impression which a man makes upon one person may be false yet the impression which he makes upon all the persons with whom he has dealt must, taken together, be true to his character. And as there is a continual intercourse among men, the overestimate which is made of him by those who witness one part of his actions is corrected by the underestimate that is made of him by those who witness another part. And if his goodness or his wickedness be extraordinary, the more excited is the curiosity of his fellowmen.

Thus, brethren, we may see by the simple observation which all of us are able to make within the walls of our own houses, and in the little company with whom we have intercourse of business or friendship in the world, the simplicity yet the perfection of the means by which God has provided that we shall be known and rewarded for what we are and what we do. It may teach us, as all youth is a prophecy of manhood and all this world seems to be a prophecy of another, it may teach us the nature and mode of that judgment which is carried on in the world of spirits. But whatever else it may suggest, let it at least teach us distinctly this one lesson, that, take our life through, we pass here exactly for

5. Used in "Ethics" (*EL* 2:149).
6. Cf. Mark 4:22.

our true value, and that however favorable may be the dispositions of our friends, they cannot rate us higher than we deserve, nor our enemies lower. Let every one carry this feeling in all his action: I am thoroughly known and weighed whatever I have imagined; I may hide my act of guilt but I cannot hide its effect or make it produce the effect of goodness.

Every past act and every past thought is represented by the actual condition at which now I am arrived. We shall see the folly of deception. And thus we shall be led to a better principle of action than the fear of censure or the love of praise,—we shall follow the *truth* and the truth shall make us free.[7] Having learned this lower truth, we may then ascend to the higher, that, if we are thus laid open to the observation of our fellowmen and of ourselves, much more are we seen and known by him who made us. As we do his commandments we shall feel that light from him shines into every soul that he hath made, and that the stillest secret that is buried in our minds is as clear to his eye as the Heaven of Heavens; that we must always live in his sight; and, as we grow virtuous, this conviction, instead of filling us with alarm, will more and more constitute our felicity.

7. John 8:32.

LXXXII

Whosoever shall exalt himself shall be abased;
and he that humbleth himself shall be exalted.

MATTHEW 23:12

It can hardly have failed to attract our notice what great commendation is bestowed in the Scriptures upon the grace of humility. The wise Solomon delights in speaking its praise. "Pride goeth before destruction and a haughty spirit before a fall. Better it is to be of a humble spirit with the lowly than to divide the spoil with the proud." "With the lowly is wisdom."[1] And especially in the New Testament is it the characteristic of Christ in his birth, in his fortunes, in his associates, in his carriage, in his doctrine, that he was lowly of heart.[2] He declared to his disciples that the poor in spirit were blessed, for they shall see God.[3]

Yet this quality thus highly extolled is not surely in itself a virtue of any high merit. It cannot compare in its importance, as measured by effects, with industry or justice or temperance or charity. And these virtues have their current value in the world; but lowliness, as it is not an object of specific exertion, that is, as no man feels the same strain of his conscience to be humble that he does to be honest, so it is disesteemed.

Preached three times: July 18, 1830, at the Second Church, Boston; October 28, 1831, as a Friday Evening Lecture, presumably at the Second Church; and January 8, 1837, in East Lexington. This sermon on humility draws on a journal entry for July 15, 1830 (*JMN* 3:190). Emerson outlined the sermon in pencil on a blank page at the end:

> Humility praised in SS [scriptures]
> Yet Humility not ⟨itself⟩ a virtue like Industry or Charity
> But a *sign*
> Sign of moral health
>   of knowledge
>   of hope
>   of seeing God
> Knowledge of God then is the cause of true Humility
>   also—the measure of it
> Popular mistake yᵗ pride is good—Byron
> All pride is false
> Exhortation to be humble

1. Proverbs 16:18–19 and Proverbs 11:2.
2. Matthew 11:29.
3. Matthew 5:8.

Those who are not diligent or brave or useful, think well of those who are, but those who are not humble do not wish to be. Why is it then the mark of so much praise in the New Testament? The reason why it has received so much honour from Christianity, is not, that, it is itself a virtue of great cost, but because it is *a sign of a certain character which is of great worth.*

We do not want men of single virtues. The world is full of fragments of Christians. This man is amiable, but he is dishonest; and that man is called upright, but he is intemperate; and a third is correct in all his habits and observances, but he is a bigot. But the gospel does not aim to train one faculty or virtue but to educate and raise the whole soul. He that is guilty in one point is guilty in all.[4] That is, all are the worse for the imperfection of any and so it selects humility as being a sign of the moral health. It is a descriptive and infallible mark of particular dispositions from which it proceeds as naturally as an acorn from an oak.

What then is it the sign of? A truly humble deportment, not assumed with an awkward and disgusting hypocrisy for some low end, but habitually and naturally shown, is a sure token that the man does not regard himself as the top of the creation, and all other beings and interests as of inferior value; but that he has some notion of his true place; that he has discovered that he has a great many wants; that he has failed of a great many attainments; that he knows his faults, and that he is engaged in endeavors to improve himself. The proud man is one who, practically ignorant that there is any thing or any being above him, looks habitually down upon all below himself. The humble man is one who, having discovered how much there is above him, looks habitually up to those objects. Humility is not a possession but an attitude of the spirit, taken by a good mind.

The wise man is humble because he knows little, and he sees that much is to be known. The man of a generous comprehensive ambition is humble, because he compares his greatest actions with the far greater that might be done.

But chiefly he is humble who sees God in all things and hath such a living belief in him that it affects all his thoughts. He then perceives himself to be his dependant child, a minute part of his works. A haughty look is not for him. It will not do for him to despise. God who is infinite, and hath all existent within himself, cannot be humble, neither is he proud. But man who receives all, must be. It is proper to the nature of creatures.

It is in this faith that the grace finds its true source and home. What can I offer God but my humility, when most clearly I explore my relation to him? I have nothing, I am nothing that is not his gift. All this world of sense and thoughts that have formed my history, are his teaching. I float on the tide of his beneficence. Even virtue, carefully as he guards our freedom, in some sort God must originate. Its motives, its hopes, the being that perceives it, and the objects and relations in which it is perceived are constituted by Him. I would be jealous of

4. James 2:10.

human freedom, yet even that has its limits. It is *we* do wrong or right and not God. Yet let a man consider the fairest action of his life and say, "it is mine," and glory in it,—and he is rebuked by the irresistible perception that all his aids, his knowledge, his motives, by which he overcame, were given him by God. God only is great, all in all.

And I, deformed with error, spotted with sin, not master of my will or my being for one moment beyond the present, and loaded all the time with a bounty whose worth I do not yet know—shall I contend with Him for my merits? shall I bring this shrinking soul to make a boastful sum of its deserts? If all the gifts he has bestowed on all had been accumulated on me, if he had enabled me to acquire degrees of virtue unknown among the children of men, yet I were still but an atom in the light of his love, and the more I am, only the more dependant, and what would remain to me to offer him but my lowly thanks?

An acknowledgment of God is the foundation then of Humility. Indeed it does not follow but accompanies this faith. For if any one will think what these words mean—to say—*a man believes in God,* is to say at the same time, that he is very humble.

This belief in God is thus the natural source of this disposition of the mind; and the more exalted is this faith, the more profound will this feeling be. But it is not only the source of it, but also its measure. The humility in which we are to be clothed, is not always to make us compliant. It is to make us the servant of all our brethren, but never to permit us to bend our independence to pay the least grain of incense to any external advantages. No man on earth is so far from servility as the truly humble man. We are to hold all vice, all meanness, in a sovereign scorn. Always we are to speak the truth. Always to defend the right. It must sometimes happen that we shall be embarrassed when the claim of other duty interferes with the practice of humility, that is, when an outward act of humility would be cowardly or dishonest. Here then God has provided us with an unerring measure of duty. If our humility grows on the true stock, grows out of a habitual reference to him, it will never lead us astray. And this is the only scale upon which the degree of it can safely be measured. Let a man not try by an effort to be humble as he would try to conquer a temptation, to work with diligence, or to reason, but let him fix his thoughts steadily on God, and read as plainly as his conscience will let him what God thinks of his present circumstances and there will be no danger but he shall exhibit in his carriage precisely that humility which belongs to the occasion.

And here I shall be pardoned if I introduce an incidental remark which is strongly forced upon my mind. It is that this fact, that the faith in God will thus supply us with an infallible measure of humility, and any candid skeptic must admit that it will, is certainly a very pleasing and unexpected presumption in favor of his being, and the natural suitableness of that idea of God to the human mind.

It is with reason then, brethren, that this grace is highly commended in the Scriptures, if it be the sign of the soul's health as the bloom in the cheek is the sign of bodily health. It is well to commend it, moreover, if it be the natural fruit of faith in God and if that faith be its measure. And yet, my friends, it does not find much favor in the world. Humility is reckoned mean and ungentlemanlike. The poems and novels that are read by half the world are filled with descriptions of the opposite character—men of forbidding, diabolical pride. These writings are popular because this is an exaggerated image of popular feeling. Men affect pride. The word pride is equivocal and is continually applied in a good sense as a commendation. We speak of an 'honest pride.'[5] Young men especially are apt to be misled by this reading, the good company and good repute in which this vice is found, and when once they have lost the satisfactions of a pure conscience they go for refuge to this stubborn pride and find a sort of support in the selfreliance and misanthropy of this fictitious superiority.

Now this is gross delusion. The word pride is used to denote no good or desirable quality, but it rightly belongs to humility.

What is it that draws so much interest to the fictitious or real hero of the poet and the world? It is his freedom from all fear, his perfect self command, his contempt of trifles and of meanness. It is these qualities and not his haughty hatred of others which engage our respect. For if a true hero, equally possessed of all these high and rare qualities, and, at the same time, full of gentleness, and a highminded love of mankind, should be placed side by side with these imposing ruffians, they would lose all their honor. For mere affectation of superiority, when no true superiority exists, sinks into sulkiness and becomes ridiculous. But courage and self command and contempt of trifles belong to true humility and not to pride.

So it is with all pride in ourselves or in others. It is all false. It is all mean. That man alone is truly honourable who cannot be made ashamed. But when I see a proud man, I feel that here is one who can be shamed. For all his demeanour declares that there is a world within him that he never rightly saw, that there is something he doth not see that if he could see would sorely mortify him. But a humble man cannot be shamed. For he sees what is true, and the acquisition of more truth will not show this to be false.

Let us then, brethren, apply habitually to our selves this valuable test. Let us observe if we ourselves are lowly in order to know if we are far from the kingdom of heaven. If wherever we can with impunity we indulge ourselves in the habit of contradiction and of an angry maintaining of our opinion instead of simple pursuit of truth, if we find we dwell much on what we have done, and the good opinion men have manifested towards us, let it be a sign to us that 'we have faculties that we have never used';[6] let it be a sign to us that we are not answering the ends of life, that the thought of God which contains the happiness of heaven is not unfolded within us; that the peculiar feeling essential to the vigor of religious life, the fear and hatred of sin, has not strength enough in our minds to be depended on for a defence.

True humility will make us strict in dealing with ourselves and tolerant in

5. Edward Young, *Night Thoughts,* "Night VI," line 127.
6. The quotation occurs, without attribution, in *JMN* 3:167.

construing the motives of others, for it well knows what different measure of light and opportunity God has given to men.

It will teach us contentment with our lot by teaching us that important lesson that there is no degradation but sin; that the highest created spirit may have its duties assigned it in the lowest places, as high and low are measured in worldly esteem. It will make us a great deal less jealous than we are of what we are pleased to call our dignity, by which we mean for the most part the fashionable estimation of those with whom we converse in life.

It will correct all these errors by the feeling that they ought not be careful to stint their love and bounty to whom God has been so good, and that he cannot fear a humiliation who by lowliness dwells with God.

LXXXIII

Add to your faith, virtue,
and to virtue knowledge.

II PETER 1:5

We have come up again to the sanctuary to worship God. The sight of this place and its holy symbols will be a joy to us or an accusation according to our own frame of mind, since last we met. Whatever joyful hope it may communicate to our thoughts, I am afraid it will have something of accusation to all of us. The best are not good. Our views of religion are not high enough. We are too easily satisfied. In every human heart, conscience, if we listen, is heard to say, that never we have done enough. Is there any disposition to appeal from this charge? Certainly not, if we compare with our best notions of what we ought to be, the real characters of men. Consider the character of any one of your acquaintance apart, study minutely his actions and capacities, his feelings, his faults, his conversation, and you will hardly escape from the conviction that here are means for the formation of a perfect character however far the individual may now be wandering from the intentions of his Creator.[1] And so you would say of every individual whilst you considered him alone, and the more critical the inquiry, with the more confidence you would rest in your conclusion. For it is slight and remote views of man that dishonour him, not searching and just ones. Yet now behold the community that are composed of these highly endowed individuals! behold their action! learn their reputation! see what half-wise unfinished men they are! what habits of herding together out of weakness to get aid and countenance; how few are there among them who act from any better motive than custom; how few find in themselves the sources of their conduct! Is not the reflection forced upon you that in almost every instance the character has received only a partial developement, that particular faculties such as the accidents of our circumstances had demanded had been cultivated whilst others were totally neglected and because of their defect the man in a degree depraved? Here is a man who has an excellent capacity for business but he has no heart. And here is a man of tender sensibility but he is entirely destitute of any perserverance. We know a man of a most bountiful disposition who is

---

Preached once, on July 25, 1830, at the Second Church, Boston.
   1. Cf. *JMN* 3:190.

peevish and tyrannical in his family; and another who is kind to his family and friends, but gluttonous and unchaste. And not only so, that particular merits are balanced by signal defects, but from the gross neglect of his powers the whole character suffers, and that redeeming quality with the rest. For if one member suffers all the members suffer with it.[2]

Moreover, not only will men compared in their particular characters one with another show great incompleteness but also in classes and communities. You must bring the idea of what man can hope to become from your most retired and exalted meditations else society will act as a covert to its own crimes. The same circumstances act as a common temptation to vast numbers of men, and each finding himself no worse than others, they all keep each other's sin in countenance and each one is worse than he would have been in a purer community. Thus every man makes what he calls experience the measure of the height of virtue he may be expected to attain. He tells you in vain, would you tax his principles at such an exorbitant rate, the bible demands a great deal; it is true, but what of that? Human nature is no better now than heretofore, and it has never been equal to such incessant and ethereal toil. He will live as well as his neighbours and his ancestors, and he doubts not God will consider him. This is an excuse that may propagate itself for ages and keep nations down at a base level. The only answer to it is in an appeal to the undiminishing standard that every where exists in the human breast, which never in one mind was known to rank itself even with the practice but always somewhat higher, and the more it is observed the higher it rises.

Now these are matters that concern every one of us in the nearest degree. Against this vast experience of human lowness and vice the great assurance of Conscience stands good, that God has made us capable of an indefinite improvement, which shall depend on ourselves. He has here given us access to boundless knowledge on one condition, that we labour ourselves to gain it. He has prepared for us the felicities of virtue on one condition, that we forsake all to acquire it. There is an immeasurable difference between what we are and what we are capable of being. And out of this view, the practical duty becomes full of weight that every man should explore his soul and consider what it means to cooperate with God, in his own education. Another cannot put it to us but each man can put it to himself.[3] There is no question like this which will be felt to be great in proportion to the greatness of the soul, which will overawe the wise and shake the brave, whether we ourselves are engaged heart and soul in the work of self-improvement, whether we are systematically aiming to answer the ends of our being.

In what does spiritual improvement consist? It has two conditions, knowledge and virtue. I shall speak of both.

I. The first condition of improvement is the acquisition of knowledge. Apart

2. I Corinthians 12:26.
3. Cf. Samuel Taylor Coleridge, *Aids to Reflection,* ed. James Marsh (Burlington, Vt., 1829), 88.

from the first motive to acquire knowledge, that is, for its own sake, some degree of it is essential to virtue, and to all high virtue a great deal of knowledge is necessary. In proportion to our efforts to become better, and in proportion also to the gifts we have received from God, the importance of cultivating the intellect will be felt by us.

This is very imperfectly considered. Men distrust the connexion of knowledge with religious character. There are a great many persons who think a good deal of their religious character and who would be shocked at the idea of having made great mistakes concerning it, who speak with a degree of contempt of intellectual acquisitions, as objects of pursuit to a religious mind. It seems to me there cannot be a surer sign of false views of God. Fanatics always warn us against intellectual religion. A great portion of the religious books that are current in the world contain this doctrine and it is because their writers were the victims of this error that these books are for the most part proverbially disagreeable reading.

But what is the great cause in an honest mind of the growth of infidelity? What is it that next to vice shakes in any mind the empire of religion but the idea that it is the offspring of unenquiring custom, that it sanctions ignorance, that it looks askance on free thinking? And the moment when, drawn by a new and false lustre, the intellect begins to act with vigor—agitated by great doubts—the moment that new pleasure is tasted, who can wonder at the conviction that this is the natural habit of the soul, and the self-respect and feeling of new power which accompany it are hailed as pledges of the truth of the new opinion?

There can scarcely be an error more pernicious to the interest of an immortal being. It has grown out of the aversion men have felt at seeing the gifts of genius prostituted to vice. The true distinction is that the moral powers must be supreme in the soul and then let the intellectual powers store as much truth and attain the highest skill in adorning and using it, their nature will admit.

But to sneer at a faith of the intellect is mad enough. Who made that power and what is it and who has it? God imparted it to you. It is his own nature. It is inseparably connected in him with his moral attributes and so in you with your moral action. It is the eye of your soul, the counsellor of the hands. It is one half of your heaven. It is the kingdom in which you reign over the Universe of matter.

And who has it? Every man who has been a just object of admiration, Socrates, Plato, Paul, Newton, Milton, Fenelon, and the rest. Nor these alone have it. Each of us hath it, but where are its effects? There it lies sleeping in your breast. Ye know not what spirit ye are of.[4] That which should be to you the interpreter of all the kingdoms of truth lies there a slave to the lowest wants. It is a hewer of wood and a drawer of water to the body.[5] Its best use perhaps is to increase wealth, power, or fame. But it should be the auxiliary and guide of

4. Luke 9:55.
5. See Joshua 9:23–27.

virtue. It delivers us from a crowd of low and gross temptations. In our times especially it seems to me the very Redemption that has been provided, I trust, to counteract the force of the love of gain. The love of the natural sciences is beginning to spread among us the study of plants, of minerals, the history of beasts, birds, and insects, and as the interest which is felt in them goes wider and deeper, it may have the effect to supplant in some degree the absorbing passion for wealth by supplying new measures of happiness and simpler and more spiritual pleasures.

But I hear at once the old exclamations. How can the man of laborious life who only earns by unremitted toil the means of living with comfort, stop his busy hand, shut his workshop, or his warehouse, and leave providing for his family that he may cultivate his mind? I answer, in the first place, that his sense of the duty of cultivating his intellect is to modify his ideas of what constitutes the wellbeing of his family, and in the second place, he is to make the exercise of his trade the school for the increase of his knowledge. It is a great mistake to think that knowledge is only to be gained by the reading of books. The Universe is full of knowledge. Every place, every event, every man, every conversation, every action are stores of truth.

There only needs the perception of this fact that God has surrounded us with a world of knowledge but gives it to us only on one condition, that we make on our own part an unceasing effort to acquire it, that a man carry to his work a strong sense of the duty of cultivating his mind, it only needs this to make every scene and every labor instructive to him, to make the sky and the waters and the stones speak to him of himself and of God.

Then men would submit to that rarest labor—to think. Then they would task their faculties which now remain untasked to any higher purposes than the good of the body. Then the soul would see God's being and perfections and Providence confirmed to it by the abundant light that every object in the Universe would shed upon it.

I must leave for the present this great topic which deserves the most intense consideration of every one of us.

I have left myself only time to mention the second part.

II. The second element of self-improvement is virtue, and to this God has subjoined the same condition as the last, that we must cooperate with him to bring it out in us, that we must work for it or we shall not receive it. Do not imagine that salvation from spiritual death can fall into your hands. Do not imagine that Christ has bought it for you; that these symbols of his suffering have any vicarious force; that Christ can, or that God can, *without your own self-originated action,* add to your virtue. No, you must go and fetch it. You must search and find it. You must contend and win it. And do not say this truth is trite. If you will seriously put it home to yourself whether you are making progress in the conquest of appetite, in the love of God, and how near you have brought yourself to that calm and holy region where the face of God is always beholden night and day and the Lamb is the light thereof,[6] you shall find the inquiry is full of interest.

Therefore, brethren, let us be exhorted by the Apostle to add to our faith in the Divine Revelation, knowledge; and to our knowledge, virtue. By an enlargement of the restricted sense in which the apostle used the terms these will comprise all that follows—all the law of duty. For if these things be in you and abound, they shall make you that ye be not barren nor unfruitful in the knowledge of our Lord Jesus Christ.[7] Then ye shall be indeed his disciples and heirs with him of God's infinite love.

6. Cf. Revelation 21:23.
7. II Peter 1:8.

LXXXIV

He that getteth wisdom, loveth his own soul.
PROVERBS 19:8

On a former occasion I called your attention to the duty of self-improvement as it divides itself into its two departments of wisdom and virtue. I propose to pursue at present the first of these topics and to offer some considerations upon our capacity for acquiring knowledge, the true modes and limits of those acquisitions. Mere knowledge is not wisdom, and it becomes us to consider in what manner it must be sought in order that we shall really be the better for all that we know.

I. The first point to which I wish to ask your attention is to our capability of acquiring knowledge. For all its interest as a practical doctrine depends upon this. Are we capable of it? Are all men capable of attaining much higher degrees of intellectual cultivation than they now attain? The experience of mankind, it is commonly said, is nearly uniform, that in all cultivated nations knowledge is the property of the few and the multitude never accustom themselves to any exercise of the mind beyond what necessity demands. And so those who have never made any exertions for their own improvement and therefore do not know what power there is in the will of man, condemn every effort to produce great changes by the diffusion of knowledge throughout society, as visionary.

And so it would be, if we hoped by any action of others to accomplish the end. But it is proposed to be done by making them workers themselves. It is proposed to present such motives to all men as that every man shall cultivate himself that little patch of ground which his Creator enclosed in the beginning for his use, ordaining him to reap as he had sown.[1]

Now, 'tis a very unfair and deceptive way of looking at human interests to group men together, and say the multitude cannot acquire knowledge. The multitude consists of a great many individuals and those individuals are not by any means all possessed of an equal amount of knowledge. No two are alike. There is every degree of intelligence in the collection, from that which touches wisdom down to an approach to savage life. Then no one is altogether high and

---

Preached once, on August 1, 1830, at the Second Church, Boston. The manuscript is incomplete, lacking the conclusion. As the opening sentence indicates, the present sermon is a sequel to Sermon LXXXIII.

1. Cf. Galatians 6:7.

no one altogether low on the scale. If every one has his fault, so each has some excellence, some motive, some peculiarity of condition, some attachment which binds him to some exertions for the attainment of valuable knowledge.

To say that great degrees of improvement cannot be attained by the multitude, is to say that it cannot be done by all these individuals. But pick out any individual from the Whole and no man will say it cannot be done by him, that he is incapable of any improvement. No man that ever lived, who was reputed of a sound mind, would use such language and least of all those who had done most to improve themselves.

The fact is that every mind needs only to have its attention thoroughly aroused to be made conscious that worlds of knowledge are open to it on every hand. We are separated by thin partitions from a thousand discoveries. Any one may be made sensible of this who reflects how few steps there were in the process of thought which led to any of the greatest inventions that adorn the history of man, as the finding of the press, the circulation of the blood. Thus the discovery of this country rested on a few simple but decisive data: the shape of the globe; the general improbability of so much water; and the record that a human body had drifted from the westward of an unknown cast of features. These facts, known to many, when presented at last to an active mind, fond of great adventure, determined him to search for America.[2]

So the discovery of the great law of gravitation. Whence came it? An apple fell from a tree and Newton seeing it said, why should it not fall up as well as down or sideways? How far does this power of the earth to attract bodies extend? Why not infinitely far? Perhaps the moon falls to the earth and the earth to the sun. These casual thoughts ended in this great and beneficent result. They had probably occurred in a similar connexion to many others but the probability which they possessed in these great minds required certain habits of mind which are very rare and not easily acquired, the habit of meditation—of patient thinking—of seeking for truth. Now these habits are voluntarily formed, they are susceptible of great cultivation, and every man may acquire them in some degree and in great degrees. And yet thousands of men go out of this world without ever having formed them.

It seems probable that we are at all times only a few steps removed from discoveries as wonderful and as valuable. The thoughts which shall guide to them glance through our minds but without fruit from our want of these self-originated habits of using them.

There are discoveries of more moment to us than of new arts or countries. We are always near to an understanding of ourselves and our duties and that testimony to God's Providence with which the whole world is refulgent, and it needs only this discipline of ourselves to make it worth a kind of knowledge not

---

2. Emerson's source is Washington Irving, *A History of the Life and Voyages of Christopher Columbus* (New York, 1828), ch. 5. See also *JMN* 3:176.

only accessible to all but the manifest duty of all, and yet how few are they who search it out.

It is this voluntary act of patient thinking which distinguishes man from man. True Wisdom consists in a simple comparison of our thoughts with a desire to know what is true. And all men are capable of attaining to some degrees of this power if they will seek it; and all do seek it who labour in earnest to please God.

And it may easily be seen that this does not depend for its existence on any external circumstances, upon wealth or rank or friends or the nature of our common employments. Wisdom may be gathered with equal success in the cornfield as in kings' houses. Many of the wisest men have been of low external condition. Every calling, every work of man, contains the materials out of which the conclusions of Wisdom are drawn. There are infinite ranges for the mind in the very narrowest spheres of observation. Only observe how a strong passion, when it would express itself, turns every thing, like fire, to its own nature.

Fill a mind with the love of God and the affectionate pursuit of truth, and it will speedily find out the great secret that the whole Universe is full of harmonies; that every thing is significant; that every trade hath its moral; that the material world is only a language by which moral truth is uttered; so that a man's daily business will be to him only a new version of his bible; reminding him, at every turn, of its words, and not only so, but illustrating and proving them.

II. Another consideration of great practical importance is that as we are all capable of seeking truth, so we must seek it for ourselves. The knowledge that has been accumulated by others is of no use until it has been verified by us. In providing for us the abundance of his bounty God has not imparted one encouragement to indolence. For all the learning and sound judgment and ample experience that has been in the world, no man is wiser by one poor thought who is not wise in himself. These, like all other of God's gifts, are means of helping those who help themselves. It is the law of his Empire which was stated by Jesus, "To him that hath shall be given."[3] It is of no use that the sun shines and the world is full of light if your eye is blind. The improvements in the useful arts, the refinements of Civilization, have indeed made life more luxurious to us than to our ancestors, but the treasures of their collective wisdom cannot become ours except by our raising our minds to the same level as theirs.

The path of the Earth through the space has long been accurately described, yet not one man of a thousand of those who now walk on the earth knows any thing about it. So in moral nature, the whole nature and duty and happiness of man have been a thousand times described. Every temptation has been pointed out, rules of action prescribed to suit every conceivable exigency, yet is the whole theory to be learned again by every one of us in his own proper experi-

3. Cf. Matthew 13:12, Mark 4:25, and Luke 8:18.

ence. We are continually coming up in our own career with the progress of human wisdom, that is, confirming old proverbs by our own experience. And so we always shall be. It is thought that in heaven we shall have vast accession of new knowledge. I believe the laws that hold here belong to the mind and not to the place and so will hold there. We shall know as we are known because we shall make new efforts in a freer state.[4]

III. We are led to a third practical consideration, which relates to a selection in our search of truth. All truth is valuable to all. "All truth," it has been said, "is practical,"[5] but one star differeth from another star in glory and not less does moral truth from all other.[6] The knowledge of moral nature is the highest species of knowledge. It is of the nature of God and of man's relation to him and of all our duty.

IV. The last consideration which I have to offer is one of paramount importance, that all Wisdom is of the *heart.* In order to have wisdom we must have right feelings. It has been very justly said that "Folly proceeds as often from want of proper sentiments as from want of talents."[7] And we can discern abundant reason for this rule. For in the heart is the infinitude of man.[8] The affections give depth to our nature. The knowledge of a heartless man is superficial and unlovely and without use.

When we say *all Wisdom is of the heart,* what do we mean by 'heart'? We mean by heart in this emphatic sense, a sympathy with men and a devotion to God. And this definition will furnish a full account of the benefit derived by it to the intellect.

For in the first place our feelings will furnish us a far more certain clue to what is in man than ever reason could, and so make us at home in every place and prepare us for just observation, it rights us, brings all things to their level and proper places. And probably we have all sometimes met with a person of no ostensible advantages of education and secluded from common means of information, but who has a benevolent heart that finds so ready acquaintance with every other heart that thoughts and views pass easily into it from every one, and he sees things in such a steady light that you cannot help feeling a great deference for his opinion.

And in the second place, if the dispositions are right toward God, if man feels deeply and reverently towards the great Source of all Being, feels his own existence as dependent upon Him, as a ray from the Sun, he will not fail to find his reward in every moment. He will be delivered from all false estimations. Viewing all things in their dependence upon God he will begin in the right place and

4. Cf. I Corinthians 13:12.

5. Sampson Reed, *Observations on the Growth of the Mind* (Boston, 1826); rpt. in Kenneth W. Cameron, *Emerson the Essayist* (Raleigh, N.C., 1945), 2:16. See *JMN* 6:191; paraphrased in *Nature* (*CW* 1:8).

6. I Corinthians 15:41.

7. See *JMN* 6:70, where the quotation is attributed by Emerson to William Hazlitt.

8. In "George Fox" (*EL* 1:180–81), Emerson attributes "the doctrine of the infinitude of Man" to Fox and the Quakers. Cf. *JMN* 7:342.

will give them theirs. Viewing things from the centre he will see them all roll in order. It has been maintained by some Christians, that, as the soul became united to God, it would learn all the sciences, not by the tedious analysis now in use but by consciousness, because God is the source of all; all exist in him, and as the mind became participant of his nature, it would read them by its knowledge of him. These speculations are too sublime for the reach of our knowledge. But though they ought to be carefully limited, they have a foundation in truth. We know the *style* of God, by loving him. When the soul joins itself to God, it is at a point of rest. It is no longer a victim to endless agitations. The passions, the appetites no longer warp its judgments. It sees things as they are. It acts with unity and effect. It gives system and use to all its knowledge.

See what little effect the great progress of knowledge has had upon men. The beautiful order of the heavens has been disclosed to us; the economy of animal life, the circulation of the blood, the power of steam, the compass, the laws of political economy, the Representative system of government, and a host of wonderful truths have been brought to light. Well, are people any the less foolish or less worldly . . .

LXXXV

*It is not a vain thing for you
because it is your life.*

DEUTERONOMY 32:47

We are come up again to God's house to worship him. My friends, I wish this may not be to us an unmeaning act. However true it may be, that, to a great part of every community religion is either unknown or is disagreeable or is a matter of form, it is quite as true that the consideration of it is, and always will be, the most important concern of every one of us. And however ignorant we may be of the nature of religious feeling, we all have some degree of acknowledgment of this fact. If a man is brought into the company of a man learned in the languages, he may value highly this accomplishment, he may wish he possessed it, but he feels no necessary shame at his own ignorance. Nor if one is known to be a skilful chemist is his science felt to be any rebuke upon those who do not know the laws of chemistry; nor if a man can build a house, or forge an anchor, does he, by his knowledge, cast any shame upon those who cannot; because we know that life is insufficient to enable one man to acquire more than a very limited acquaintance with more than one or two departments of knowledge, and if his acquaintance does not lie in one, we presume it does in another. But if a man is thrown into the company of a person distinguished for his attainments in a religious life, and he himself be deficient in that respect, he feels this deficiency to be culpable. Every virtue in the good man reflects dishonour on the vices of the bad man. This is a knowledge of which all are capable and to which all are bound. Religion does not take any inferior or even any equal place among the objects of human pursuit. It is the head and ruler of them all.

And what is Religion? It is the knowledge of God. It is to every mind the knowledge of God in his connexion with itself. Not surely a system of doctrines asserting incomprehensible facts which it cannot explain and whose truth or falsehood it really does not concern me to know, but, when presented to my

Preached eight times: August 15, 1830, at the Second Church, Boston; August 22 in Brookline; October 31 at the Purchase Street Church, Boston; January 9, 1831, at the South Congregational Church, Boston; July 31 at the Second Church; January 1, 1837, in East Lexington; January 22 in Concord, Mass.; and August 20 in Waltham (for Samuel Ripley). There are two manuscripts, one marked "Princeps Edit." and the other "Palimpsest." It is not known at what point the revision was made, though both versions seem to have been delivered; the later version, given in the Textual and Manuscript Notes, is incomplete, lacking the conclusion.

237

mind, something which I feel instantly to be true, and not true after the common order of truths; something which comes secretly into me but has a rightful dominion over me; truth of which the soul is not the parent, but the child, by which I find that all my being is affected, and all the wants of my nature are supplied.

The Scripture says, It is not a vain thing but it is your life. And this expresses very nearly the sentiment which I apprehend every Christian entertains respecting our faith. When this knowledge of God enters into the mind it is not only felt to be valuable but it is itself the best witness of its truth. By this I mean to express the belief that the applicability of our idea of God to the real wants of human nature, is the very strongest evidence of its truth. It solves every speculative difficulty, and it meets every practical difficulty with a perfect remedy, as nothing else can, and therefore I believe it to be true.

I conceive that our belief in God stands in this respect on the same foundation of evidence as our belief in the Copernican System does.

The Copernican System asserts that the sun is stationary and that the earth moves around it, a fact which though confirmed by our reason is contradicted by our senses, for the earth seems to stand still, and the sun to go round it every day. Now the ground on which this theory stands is that it furnishes a complete solution of all the movements which we observe in the planets as no other theory does, and nothing has ever been observed which is inconsistent with the supposition of its truth, and therefore all men have acquiesced in its truth.

Is it not so with religion? The unbeliever says, My senses do not teach me so. I see the world of matter but I see no God; I behold no miracle; I believe neither angel nor spirit. But the Christian says,—some account there must be of all I behold and feel. This professes to be so. I have tried this faith in my own experience; I see that it gives a satisfactory explanation of every doubt and I accept it.

Thus is it an explanation of every speculative difficulty. It gives us a rational and consistent account of the origin and destination of our race, of the inequalities of condition and the existence of pain and death. Let me offer another illustration to suggest its practical value.

If a savage is shown a watch and told that it will measure the passage of time, probably he will not believe you. It is of no use, to convince him of the fact, that you show him the elegance and exquisite contrivance of the machine, it is only an object of ignorant wonder to him. But make him acquainted with your artifical division of time and then make him understand how this is adapted to it, so that he himself finds the time of day, and he not only believes you but he becomes perfectly convinced that this was made for that very purpose.[1] So you may tell a man of God, of his nature, his perfections, and his relation to the

---

1. See Sampson Reed, "On Animals," *New Jerusalem Magazine* 2 (1829): 26; rpt. in Kenneth Walter Cameron, *Emerson the Essayist,* (Raleigh, N.C., 1945), 2:36. This was also a favorite illustration of William Paley's; see his *Natural Theology, Or Evidence of the Existence and Attributes of the Deity,* 12th ed. (London, 1809), esp. 1-17.

human soul. He thinks you are an enthusiast; he does not believe you because he does not understand you. But once let him apply his own heart to the seeking of God, let the sentiment of devotion get possession of his breast, and the idea of God explains and vindicates itself. It is not any longer an idea, a theory, a sentiment; it is itself a living soul; it is a life within life. It is, as it has been truly called, the life of God in the soul of man.[2] He perceives how naturally this belief harmonizes with all that he knows, and not only so, but is the best explanation of all. It is the light of the world,[3] and this perfect congruity of the idea of God to man and human life convinces him of the being of God. The spirit beareth witness with our spirit that we are the children of God.[4]

Consider this a little. If I could bring myself to doubt the being of God, I should be left in a state of absolute perplexity as to the origin of man, and of the world, and as to every event that occurred within and without me; and I should be left in a state of miserable apprehension as to all the future. And though I might perceive the general good consequences of virtuous conduct, I should feel that it had been bereft of its great sanction, i.e., its agreement with the nature of him who is the Maker and the Soul of the Universe. Man is affrighted at the solitude in which he is left, and left wholly without consolation for the evils of his present condition. I am left without support against the human injustice or neglect. In my prosperity who shall secure me from a downfall? In my extreme sorrow who shall hear my moanings? In my fear who shall avert the danger that menaces me?

But restore to me my faith in God. Teach me that there is a Creator and Governor of the world who made man to know and love and resemble him, and you put a soul into nature that was dead before. You give a source and a government and an object to human life.

And not only so but you give a rule of life, an unerring standard by which to measure the value of every object and the claim of every duty upon us. This is a fact that deserves all consideration. Would a man know how meek he ought to be and where humility becomes servility? Let him keep his eye upon God and he will not fail. Would he know how careful he should be of his bodily wants, and when that care becomes excessive? Here also is his rule. Would he know what is the measure of his charity and what it means to give all his goods to the poor?[5] Here also he will learn to hold all he has in trust for others, to live for others. And so of every question that can be proposed. Now this fact, that the notion of God is a perfect regulator of duty, seems to me a strong proof of the adaptation of our minds to that notion, i.e., testifies to its truth.

In the next place it suits the changes of life as well as the habits of action.

Look at the strange inequality of human condition. See, with all this indwell-

2. The reference is to Henry Scougal's *The Life of God in the Soul of Man* (London, 1677), which Emerson read in the Boston edition of 1823.
3. Cf. John 8:12.
4. Romans 8:16.
5. Cf. Matthew 19:21, Mark 10:21, and Luke 18:22.

ing consciousness that they were made for all that is great and good, into what base extremities they fall. See the soiled and swollen hands of the poor. Think of the wretched pittance of bread for which so much labor is performed and all their time taken up and all the delights of thought and conversation forgone. All refinement, all the elevation which comes from consulting and administering great interests is denied to them. But this faith more than compensates for every want. It reveals to that fainting wretch a Being before whom the differences of condition all disappear. No high, no low, no great, no small with him. These distinctions were of the *body*. This speaks to his *moral nature*. He is not the equal of rich and powerful men. He is the equal of angels, of seraphim, formed of the same spiritual body, subject to the same laws, capable of their knowledge and their pleasures, comprehending what they comprehend, a spark of the same fire, a ray of the same source of light from which they came, mean as he may be, not too low for the power and the love of God to stoop, nor too far from him to inhale the breath of an immortal life. These great views are not more grand than true. They do not sound like a fable to him. He understands what you mean. He feels their fitness to him. He feels that his miseries, his poverty, his disadvantages, do not exclude him, but qualify him rather for this spiritual kingdom, that he is capable of acting on principles which glorify his rags and straw into the discipline of a moral agent, and the means and occasions of heavenly virtue. What change has not this produced in his mind? He felt before that he was wretched and that he was wronged;—wronged by being shut out from enjoyments to which others were admitted and of which he was as capable as they. Now he feels that he may walk in his lowly place with the meekness yet with the dignity of an angel. He reads in his Bible that the chosen Son of God was born in a manger, was despised by men, and died on the cross with thieves.[6]

I have said that religion shows its applicability to man in equalizing the differences of condition, in showing what height of excellence is within reach of the lowest of mankind. But, brethren, we are all poor and low enough in our external nature.

What shall guard the most robust frame a year, an hour, from the inroads of decay? Time every moment is undermining our health and our life. Not virtue, not youth can save you, though they may make the blow more exquisitely felt. Not only time but sickness assails us, cuts down our brightest hopes in a moment, defeats instantly every purpose, paralyzes your strength, and embitters the languid hours with advertisements of your mortality. What balm has Gilead for this calamity?[7] I believe there are no considerations but this we speak of that can render any adequate comfort to the bed of sickness and the fear of death. But the firm persuasion that God is with us,[8] that our friend has done this, and that by our place in his love it is made a matter of indifference whether

6. Luke 2:7, Isaiah 53:3, and Matthew 27:38.
7. Cf. Jeremiah 8:22.
8. Cf. Matthew 1:23 and 28:20.

our days on earth are few or many, and whether they are passed in action or in confinement, will gild the gloom of the darkest sorrow.

Finally, brethren, it will save us from sin, the capital evil of our nature, which depraves and destroys us. The conviction of God's presence and action upon me in every moment is the perfect antidote to sin, which is spiritual death.[9] In this sense also, It is not a vain thing. It is our life.

Therefore, brethren, if the idea of God, which is the foundation of religion, has all this evidence to our understandings and all this accumulated and irresistible evidence to the heart that has sought it out, I pray you let us not neglect it. Let us keep the commandments. Let us awake our minds to what is real and great, to the privilege of walking with Him who made us, one in will with Him, removing his displeasure that now rests on our evil actions, calling down new measures of his love upon us, that we may hope when life which is fast passing away is ended, to enter into his rest.[10]

9. Cf. Romans 6:23.
10. Cf. Hebrews 4:3-11.

LXXXVI

And he spake a parable unto them, to this end,
that men ought always to pray and not to faint.
Luke 18:1

It is the first obvious objection that is made to representations of the duty of prayer that it is not becoming to beings of finite nature to dictate to an infinite Being what blessings they require, but in a spirit of profoundest deference to leave all to his Wisdom and thankfully accept not only his gifts but own the wisdom that selects them and suits them to us. This sentiment is certainly a just one and, so far from being inconsistent with religion, will present itself with the most force to the most pious mind. But it will not appear an objection to prayer, but as an indispensable condition to our supplications. It supplies the first postulate, the previous consideration without which prayer should not be offered. Before we begin to pray the mind settles this in forming its notion of God. He knows all my wants. The Spirit says, Grant these things that I ask if consistent with thy will, that is, with what thou knowest to be my wants. The very first want in the eye of God may be our want of knowledge of our real condition. But after this consideration has been fully and fairly weighed it may still be contended on good grounds that there is the deepest necessity of prayer; that it springs directly from our relation to God by natural consequence not less than from positive precept; that it has an influence so salutary upon us, as to furnish a forcible evidence of its propriety.

I propose to offer to your attention a few practical considerations, first upon the general utility of prayer, second upon its proper objects, and thirdly upon its efficacy.

Prayer is the expression of human wishes addressed to God. But who is the God that I address? Behold, I go forward, and he is not there, and backwards, but I cannot perceive him; on the left hand where he doth work, but I cannot behold him; he hideth himself on the right hand that I cannot see him.[1] It is

---

Manuscript dated August 28, 1830, at Brookline. Preached three times: August 29, 1830, at the Second Church, Boston; December 23, 1831, in the evening at the Second Church; and December 18, 1836, in East Lexington. The second delivery is referred to in the Preaching Record as a Friday Evening Lecture, and in the manuscript as a Monthly Lecture: both refer to the usual pre-Communion service held on the Friday before the celebration of the Lord's Supper on the last Sunday of each month.

1. Job 23:8–9.

most true that whilst the evidence without is irresistible and is confirmed by the heart within, our faculties are yet unable to comprehend him. But we worship him by forming the most pure and elevated conception of which the mind is capable. When we consider what is our thought of God we find that it is our own soul stripped of all inferiority and carried out to perfection,[2] aided by all the images of power which the sight of His works can give. But it is attended by the faith that we have made some approach to him and that he supplies the defects of the worship. He is infinite as I am finite; He is sinless as I am sinful. He is all wise as I am all ignorant. He is strong as I am weak, and self subsistent as I am wholly dependent.

Well now, prayer is the effort of the soul to apply itself in all its length and breadth to this sovereign object, that is, it is the attempt to carry up our mind to a greater mind and converse with it as we converse with men. Let us consider what will be the natural effect of this habit.

What can be more salutary to the mind than this habitual contemplation of perfect purity and wisdom? this continually returning consciousness that it is overlooked by a perfect being, the habit of voluntarily bringing itself to undergo this divine investigation?

What is the effect produced on our minds by association with men? Is there not always, (especially where there is any desire to obtain help of them,) a voluntary accommodation of our state of mind to theirs? In urging your views upon your fellowman, you take something of the tone of his feelings, that you may give him something of yours. You are conscious that in order to give any efficiency to his exertions in your behalf, you must bring your feelings and his as much to an accord as you can, that you may both see as with the same eye and hear with the same ear. If his views are narrower than yours, you must enlarge his mind. If he is higher and better than you, you must adopt and act upon his greater principles. It was said by a wise man, "He who borrows the aid of an equal understanding, doubles his own; of a higher, raises his own to the stature of that which he contemplates."[3]

What then must be the effect, judging from this plain analogy, of conversing with one who is wholly pure and benevolent, and whom, we know, cannot be deceived?[4] What must be the effect of continually applying to Him who is Truth and Love for the gratification of those desires which are nearest to the heart? Must we not also strive to sympathize with him? Will not our faces shine as we steadily look at his light?[5] Shall we not become like that which we behold? Or to use the language of the apostle to the Corinthians, "Beholding as in a glass, the

2. Cf. William Ellery Channing, "Likeness to God," *The Works of William E. Channing,* 8th ed. (Boston, 1848), 3:233: "The idea of God, sublime and awful as it is, is the idea of our own spiritual nature, purified and enlarged to infinity."

3. Edmund Burke, "Substance of the Speech in the Debate on the Army Estimates in the House of Commons, on Tuesday, February 9, 1790," in *The Works of the Right Honorable Edmund Burke* (Boston, 1866), 3:219. See *JMN* 3:183.

4. Compare this and the four preceding paragraphs with *JMN* 3:182–83.

5. Possibly an allusion to the Transfiguration; cf. Matthew 17:2.

glory of the Lord, we shall be changed into the same image from glory to glory."[6] And is not this in fact agreeable to all experience? Does not sincere praying always make good men? Does it not give a heavenly elevation and completeness to the character which mere talent however vigorous never did bestow?

No one ever saw one of those pious men who use prayer without respect. I have seen a man who prayed without ceasing.[7]

II. Let me now say a few words respecting the objects of prayer. The strict meaning of prayer is petition, and it is sometimes said we should ask for nothing but that God's will be done.[8] But this seems to be too close restriction. It seems to me to strain too hard on the weakness of nature. If truly I believe that all things are disposed by a Providence which amidst the grandeur of its counsels yet nourishes a tender interest in me, that I cannot be so insignificant but a personal tie connects me to God, then truly I cannot help when I am in danger asking his aid to deliver me, and when I am delivered pouring out my acknowledgments. The more strictly I reason upon the mode of his operation in the world, I shall only the more sensibly realize his presence, his participation in every action of life, in every shade of thought, and therefore, in every thing that interests me, I shall speak to Him.

I conceive that the proper objects of prayer are whatever are a man's justifiable desires. Every man dwells in a world of his own. There are a life, a health, a condition, friends, events, thoughts, knowledge, pardons, blessings for him to pray for, that are personal to him. And for these, both external and internal, so far as his happiness is engaged in them, he is bound to pray. Is it said that the Christian faith puts that contempt on outward things as to make it unworthy and even sinful to ask God for this world's good? I answer—It teaches us not to despise the world, but to walk with moderation and purity in it; to use it as not abusing it; whatsoever we do, to do as in the presence of God.[9] It calls my attention to the glory of this city of God and teaches us how to sanctify all the changes of life.[10]

If a man find this world pleasant and not loathsome; if his virtues have made it cheerful; if he feels that his friends deserve his love; if life seems to him desirable and full of noble objects that deserve the whole stress of his thought and his action; if, with all his convictions of the superiority of those objects which are not to be seen or touched, but are of the world of spirits, he is filled with earnest desires to have his present life prolonged,—let him frankly express those desires to their full extent. Surely before God let him not affect to underrate the present good for which daily he expresses his gratitude. But also let him respect those his convictions that there is a better kingdom, an unmixed good.

6. II Cor. 3. 18 [Emerson's note].
7. I Thessalonians 5:17.
8. From the Lord's Prayer; see Matthew 6:10 and Luke 11:2.
9. Cf. I Corinthians 10:31 and Colossians 3:17.
10. Compare this paragraph with *JMN* 3:183.

And if he suspect himself of low contentment with sensual good, let him recollect himself, and pray earnestly for better light and higher love. With equal propriety as one man prays for the first, another man asks for the last alone. One man, by reason of greater spiritual progress, sets a very different value on life than another. One rightly will pray for it. Another does not desire it and so rightly does not pray for it. Both pray sincerely and so are made better continually—more heavenly by their petition and so continually make prayers more spiritual and more acceptable[11]—until finally Prayer becomes simple submission to God's will and the expression of joy at perceiving that its own desires are right with God and so that whatsoever it desires is performed.

III. Having spoken of the use and of the objects of prayer I wish to add one remark upon the question whether it is reasonable to expect that our prayers can ever affect the course of things, that is to say, whether they have any other effect than upon ourselves, as certainly St. James would intimate when he says the prayer of faith shall save the sick, and "The effectual fervent prayer of the righteous man availeth much."[12] And as our Lord declared when he said, Ask and ye shall receive.[13] This will appear reasonable from two considerations.

Unless the freedom of man be an empty name, unless all future events are tied in bands so strait that even the will of God cannot alter them, prayer may affect them as much as action and for the very reason that it becomes action. What truly we pray for we shall spend all our powers to obtain and God will help them that help themselves.

In the second place, if we conceive of God as in every moment of duration operating not upon an antiquated system of government but upon a view of the immediate needs of the Universe, we shall then feel that it is necessary that all the facts should have some share in determining his operation and the soul's earnest desires are one of the facts.[14]

Therefore, brethren, since prayer is thus in reason and in experience adapted to make us better; since our own wants speak loud what are the true topics of prayer; and since the efficacy of prayer is assured to us both by the reason of the thing and by the word of God, let us not neglect this first Christian duty. Let us use prayer as the key to unlock the morning and to lock up the night. Let us hallow every moment with it. Let us use this great power to dignify our life and to connect every action on earth with the world of spirits. It will make us leave off sinning and it will go far to make us leave off suffering, because evil changes its nature to the good and becomes means of good. Finally, it will make us meet for the inheritance of the saints in light.[15]

---

11. "One man . . . acceptable": cf. *JMN* 3:183.
12. James 5:15–16.
13. Matthew 7:7–8 and Luke 11:9–10.
14. Cf. *JMN* 3:167 and 183.
15. Colossians 1:12.

LXXXVII

I beseech you therefore brethren by the mercies of God that ye present your bodies a living sacrifice, holy, acceptable unto God, which is your reasonable service.

ROMANS 12:1

The shortness of life and the importance of improving it are old topics, but as they get a new and increased interest from every hour they are the more seasonable, the oftener we have heard them. The great art which religion teaches is the art of conducting life well, not only in a view to future well-being, but in the very best manner, if there were no future state. Every serious man looks to religion for the supply of wants which he deeply feels. We want such views of life and duty as shall harmonize all we do and suffer;—as shall present us with motives worthy of our nature, and objects sufficient for our powers of action. We want principles which shall give the greatest strength to our social union, and the greatest efficacy to social action. We want principles which shall guide us in every transaction of life; that shall attend us into the shop, and the factory; that shall make contracts, and project enterprizes, and give gifts, and receive favours. We want principles that shall direct our education when we are young, and select our profession and control its exercise when we are mature; that shall assist us in forming our friendships and connexions in life. We want principles that will bear the scrutiny of solitude, of doubt, of experience; that will fortify us against disaster; that will enable us to overcome every temptation, and every fear; and make us respectable and happy in ourselves when we have nothing and hope nothing on earth.

The Revelation of Jesus Christ discovers in us such principles and appeals to them. It withdraws man from looking for his motives to the world, outward, and directs him to look within. It shows him a Divine Eye that cannot be

Preached nine times: September 5, 1830, at the Second Church, Boston; August 26, 1831, as a Friday Evening Lecture at the Second Church; June 10, 1832, at the Second Church; September 4, 1836, in East Lexington; March 25, 1838, again in East Lexington; April 8 in New York; April 29 in Waltham (for Samuel Ripley); August 15 in Watertown; and January 13, 1839, in Concord, Mass. For the last five deliveries, the sermon was, according to the Preaching Record, "enlarged by [the] Lect[ure] on Religion" (see *EL* 2:83–97).

deceived, that fixed within his soul, commands a perfect prospect of his whole being,—all he does, and all he wills,—and passes judgment upon all. It teaches him to conform all his actions to this superior will; for, this is God working in him, both to will and to do. It teaches him that some things perish, and that other things never die. It shows him that truth and right are of God, everlasting, and impart their own eternity to the soul that embraces them with its affections. It is in the power of man, so far as, obeying this voice, he puts aside the force of vulgar motives, and, refusing the service of his senses, subjects himself to the law of his mind,—puts off, so to speak, his human nature, and puts on the divine nature;[1] it is in his power to obtain a degree of participation (I speak it with reverence) in the attributes of God;[2] to enter into that peace and joy, that unmixed delight in goodness, and that universal love which are in Him; and, so entirely to apply his own spirit to the Divine Mind, that he shall be, as it has been expressed, a drop in that ocean, moving with him, acting with him, partaking of his felicity.

Blessed among men be the name of Jesus of Nazareth! illustrious and beautiful his history! This immense elevation of Man from his capricious, low, and too often descending course of action to this interest in and cooperation with the Providence of God, is suggested directly to our minds from his gospel. He gave his doctrine the authority of his life. In a degenerate age, in a degraded country, himself of low birth and suffering a malefactor's death, he spent his few years in conformity with these principles in such manner as to exemplify to all time their infinite superiority.

It is in the Spirit of that master whose principles of life he is expounding that the apostle Paul enjoins us to present ourselves living sacrifices.

The duty to which we are called is nothing less than an unceasing effort at self culture, or, in the words of the apostle, a patient continuance in well doing.[3] We are endowed with the power of voluntary action and taught to turn our freedom to this end. Our present condition, is one extreme from which we are to depart, and this height of a divine nature the other extreme towards which we are to aspire.

We are to present ourselves living sacrifices. This is our work, and it admits of no delay. It is our first and present business. I shall offer, my brethren, a few of the more urgent reasons which speak to every mind, of whatever power, or condition, in behalf of the life to come,—in behalf of an immediate unceasing labour to become better.

I. Let it be considered by us that there is a retribution in every hour for past action and therefore no time must be lost. Already our good and our evil actions are gone before into judgment, and their rewards are visited on our heads. We

1. Cf. Ephesians 4:22–24.
2. Channing, in the "Likeness to God" sermon, speaks several times of human "participation" in the attributes or nature of God. See *The Works of William E. Channing,* 8th ed. (Boston, 1848), 3:229, 3:239.
3. Romans 2:7, the original, canceled text for this sermon.

interpret the Scriptures when they speak of judgment as always referring to God's award upon character after this life, and so are apt to forget that the laws of God are eternal, and, as they have no end, *so they have no beginning*. When do you think they will begin? after a thousand years or a hundred or ten? Or when you enter? Wherever there is moral action, these laws take place. Wherever there is character, there is judgment. It will be admitted by all who have thought much upon life, that, in a great degree a compensation takes place in our condition for all the qualities of the man. Go where you will, you shall work out with great fidelity your own effect, make the same impression and eat the same fruits. Every hand shall hold a whip to your vices, and a laurel for your virtues. Such is the force of spiritual nature that every thing takes the hue of our thought. The peevish man finds his way full of crosses; the benevolent man full of charities. The world is but a mirror in which every mind sees its own image reflected. Every thing speaks wisdom to the wise, and sensuality to the sensual, and worldly hope to the ambitious, folly to the frivolous, and God to the good. As a man thinketh so he is and so he receives.[4] This seems to hold through all our intellectual and moral properties. It is so with our possession of truth. Let a man have a strong grasp of truth, and every where he shall find confirmation.

If a man have clear and pious perceptions of the Unity of God, of the tender love of the Universal Father, and have learned to live with him in prayer and in action as his child, if in these views his heart delights—let him go where he will, he shall not find strange Gods. In the churches of his brethren of other persuasions, Catholic or Calvinistic brethren, in the temple of heathen, the Unity of God and his parental love shall be preached to him, and new and unexpected conviction of the truth will dawn upon his mind out of arguments offered against it. And as truth finds light so error finds its own darkness in all the creation. And if he surrender his understanding and receive error, his errors shall seem to him to be confirmed by the world. So is this the law of all action. All things are double one against another.[5] Love and you shall be loved. Hate and you shall be hated. Judge not and ye shall not be judged, saith our Saviour, for whatsoever measure ye mete, it shall be measured to you again.[6]

A retribution, however imperfect it may be, does thus run into every moment of life, so that prosperity cannot give peace to the bad man, nor adversity take it away from the good man. It will not therefore do to neglect your soul a moment, lest you reap a harvest of thistles for a harvest of wheat.[7] Brethren, if these things are so, if even very imperfect justice takes place, it is plainly no world for careless and improvident persons. It will not do to live by accident, we must live by design. We must do nothing without intention. Every thing admonishes us never to slacken our heed, but always Watch. We must have

4. Cf. Proverbs 23:7.
5. Ecclesiasticus 42:24. See *JMN* 2:340 and 6:143; used in Sermons IV and LXXVII, "Ethics" (*EL* 2:153), and "Compensation" (*CW* 2:64).
6. Cf. Luke 6:37–38.
7. Cf. Job 31:40.

intention in manners, we must watch our conversation, watch pleasure, watch in the street, watch in the closet, in all things to make the voluntary offer of ourselves to our maker.

II. But a second reason why we ought to hasten to make our sacrifice is our constant liability to changes and care, to disease and death. Look back, brethren, at any of your deliberate purposes of improvement and recollect the sad interruptions that intervened between the design and the performance. A thousand cares beseige the most favored condition. There are always mistakes to be corrected, there are difficulties to be encountered, a livelihood to be earned, relations to be assisted, there are losses to be repaired and public as well as private duties to tax your time.

Then sickness comes and cuts down in a moment the vast projects of hope, and suspends the labours of benevolence. He lays his grievous hand, it may be, on the best years of our life and turns to nothing the most manly and prudent schemes, puts a stop to labor, and to study, and bids you wait, whilst he loosens the sinews of strength, and drains the blood, and puts pain and weariness into the bones, and makes the heart sick with hope deferred.[8]

And what is sickness, but the forerunner of death? We are of that feeble frame that every accident threatens our being, the wound of a pin will let out our life; a fever, a humour, a draft of cold air will destroy it, and put a final period to all our intercourse with men, all our repentance, our perseverance, our enthusiasm, our faith, our hope on earth. Tomorrow, today, the next moment, it may be the turn of any of us, the strongest, the youngest. It will not do then for such manner of persons as we are, brethren, to postpone for an hour any serious purpose, much less the main purpose for which we live.

There are other considerations that speak loudly to us but these two will suffice to the wise, that every moment is already reaping the consequences of action, and the fact that we have not a warrant on our being for another hour. These facts should prevail with us to give our utmost heed to use what ease and health and talents and means we have in a present obedience to the commandments, a pressing toward the mark of perfection,[9] the surrender of ourselves to God.

Every one of us should give that he has. The way is plain—the work is simple—we are to give ourselves in every moment living sacrifices. We are to give *ourselves,* that is, all that we have. We are to give *ourselves,* that is, the whole of our being, the present as well as the future. We must give not what we would, but what we can. Some of us have the trial of sickness; that need not prevent; we are to give our sickness. There is perhaps no more costly and acceptable offering than the obedience of a holy life on a sick bed. It is easy to be resigned to God's will when that will gives us prosperity and usefulness, but in the loitering months and years of sickness, to bring the reluctant spirit to feel a cheerful

8. Proverbs 13:12.
9. Cf. Philippians 3:14.

submission, to be left out of the race, to send up thanksgivings to him that has stricken us, to feel glad that he doth not need our service, to feel that thousands at his bidding speed and that they also serve who only stand and wait,[10]—that is a severe and difficult duty, but that also is to present ourselves living sacrifices, holy, and acceptable to God. It may please him to reward such virtue upon earth. It may please him to restore us to new and wider usefulness in his service, but surely he will reward us in our character and eternal condition.

Finally, brethren, in whatever condition we are, in fear, in misfortune, in ease, in youth, in age, let us present ourselves to God, let us not be conformed to this world, but be transformed into the likeness of the eternal world.[11] Here on earth let us keep the laws and observe the customs and think the thoughts, and speak the language of Heaven, and God shall administer every aid, and shall make us pass with joy from this present world to the world of spirits.

10. John Milton, Sonnet XIX ("When I Consider . . ."), lines 12 and 14.
11. Romans 12:2.

LXXXVIII

*What! know ye not that your body is the temple
of the Holy Ghost, which is in you, which ye
have of God, and ye are not your own? For ye
are bought with a price, therefore glorify God
in your body, and in your spirit which are God's.*

I CORINTHIANS 6:19–20

We are obliged to the gospel not for reasonings or for particular rules but for principles. All the facts recorded in it are of inestimable value as they elucidate or establish these principles but otherwise neither these nor any facts can have any other than a momentary and unconnected value.

It is a maxim of science that a method of discovering truths is of more value than the truths it has discovered, because the number of these must be finite, but the store of truth it can yet elicit is inexhaustible. So it is a far more important event in the life of any man, the establishment in his mind of a true principle of action, than is the occurrence of any outward act, as any change in his life, his recovery from sickness, his removal to a new country, his obtaining an education, his success in trade, his living under a good government, a happy marriage, his long life, the merit of his children.

These are good to him as far they are consequences of good actions, but the acquisition of a principle is far more real good than any number of actions which it has taught him to perform. Because these are limited, these are only single fruits of the tree and perish in the using, but the acquisition of a sound principle is a change for the better in the tree itself.[1]

It is a revolution in the character of the man, which looks not only to his few years on earth, but far down through all the future ages of his being.

It seems to be so plain as hardly to be worth adding, that as is the principle, such will be the measure of the actions. And yet this is not a truth so universally accepted among men but that a man who is acting from a low selflove and

---

Manuscript dated September 11, 1830, at Brookline. Preached three times: September 12, 1830, at the Second Church, Boston; November 6, 1831, at the Second Church; and March 5, 1837, in East Lexington.

1. Cf. Matthew 12:33.

augmenting his own power or riches from no higher motive, imagines that he looks down upon a servant or a labourer in his household who serves him as unto the Lord and not unto man, imagines that because his house and his means are larger, his own views are liberal compared with theirs, whilst in truth he is an object of their pity.

And because of this truth that the principle regulates the action, a great action costs no more exertion than a mean one, that is to say, a mind under the habitual influence of great motives, will perform its wonders of magnanimity and wisdom, as easily, as a selfish man his contemptible things.

Now, brethren, I wish to invite your attention to a great principle of action which the gospel supplies. Know you not, says Paul, that your body is the temple of the Holy Ghost which is in you, which ye have of God and ye are not your own? For ye are bought with a price, therefore glorify God in your body and in your spirit which is God's. It seems to me there is matter for much consideration in these words, and in the kindred passage in the third chapter of the epistle.[2] They teach us a doctrine that should fill us either with consternation or a joyful peace. They teach with great distinctness by far the most affecting and fruitful truth that can be announced to us, that God dwelleth with us, the Spirit of God is the spirit of man, that we are bought with a price which is not less than all his mercy in our creation and education by his Providence and his word. If we are doing his will here is matter of joy; if we are grieving and offending him we are not wronging a being of great power remote from us and who may overlook us in the immensity of his works.

I am aware that the allusion in the third chapter is not to individuals but to the whole church. Ye, as a church of Christ, are a temple of God and he dwelleth in you. But this is in substance the same assertion, for it is only as made up of spiritual natures that a church can be the temple of God, and it is only as God is present to the individual members that he can be present to the church. But in the present passage, the sense is yet more clear and striking. St. Paul exhorts them to shun every uncleanness, because they are God's temple.

Now the doctrine of this and similar passages is that, there is in every human mind, however obscured or partially developed, a power greater than that mind; that we perceive that we are not our own; that we have no right to do whatsoever we please, but ought to obey this higher power, that the spiritual nature in us is of God, in his own likeness;[3] and that when we exhibit great measures of goodness or wisdom it is not from ourselves that we are drawing, but from something deeper and vaster than man, that we are but cisterns and God is the fountain. Our spiritual nature is not something different from God's but is communicated from him, is a part of him, and a life of holiness consists in a continual effort at a separation from the flesh and its works, and the consummation of a more perfect union of our spirit with God. This idea is suggested in

2. I Corinthians 3:16.
3. Genesis 1:26.

different forms throughout the Scriptures. Good men are called men of God, or men in whom the Spirit of God dwelt. God is said to dwell in the heart of the humble, and the Son of God was raised above his brethren only by a fuller measure of the same gift. And Jesus saith of himself, the Father dwelleth in me, He doeth the works.[4] So also he saith, "If a man love me, he will keep my words and my Father will love him and we will come unto him and make our abode with him."[5] And John saith, If we love one another God dwelleth in us.[6]

Now, brethren, are these sounding words or are they the statement of a fact? I take them to be a fact. They seem to me to be wonderfully coincident with all the views which wisest men have always taken of our nature and with all that we feel within ourselves. No man ever did wrong without feeling that he offended against a principle greater than himself,—without feeling that he was acting on a principle less than the highest. What is right but a conformity with God in action? What is truth but a conformity with him in thought?

Let me ask your attention to some applications of this great principle.

1. Herein is the reason of that mighty energy with which good men have acted when they have suffered every evil rather than offend their conscience, when they lost their means of living, and their friends were taken away, and they were imprisoned, and tortured, and put to death. What supported them, asked their oppressors, against such evils? It was not manhood, for all the blessings that man asks on earth, they might have had by an opposite course of conduct. It was not man, it was God; they leaned directly upon their divine nature, and God was all sufficient for sorer trials. The height of the tower must depend on the breadth of the base, and they rested on a Rock broader than the world.[7]

2. Herein is the difference between a good cause and a bad cause. A bad cause must be propped by continual shifts and frauds and force, and the moment they are withdrawn it falls; it has no depth of earth, no foundation in God who is everywhere present in man's nature. A good cause needs no external helps. It is grounded in God and so approved by all within us, and all men are its natural allies, and it stands forever and ever.

3. Here too is the difference between truth and error. Truth is one, because God is one. Who ever doubted, as he reasoned with his fellow man in an earnest desire for truth, that the hour would come when both would think alike? That we think so differently, is in great part because we sin so much. It is because we are indolent and will not think; because we have a sordid interest to defend an opinion, and shut up our eyes, or because we are proud or angry, and so are afraid to think, that is—it is because we cling to the flesh in us, and not to the spirit,—to the human and not to the divine nature, that the world is so shaken with sects and quarrels. But if in a humble attitude of inquiry, stripping yourself

4. John 14:10.
5. John 14:23.
6. I John 4:12.
7. "The height . . . base": used in *JMN* 4:38 and "Ethics" (*EL* 2:148). For Christ typified as the Rock, see I Corinthians 10:4.

of every passion, seeking no selfish end, you will let the oracle within you be heard, you shall find there is a wonderful tendency to unanimity in human opinions.

4. It is here that the faith we teach finds its sanction or nowhere. I say to a thoroughly good man, if such an one there were, *It is only so far as you find Christianity within your own soul that I recommend it*. If in any commandment that it utters there is a voice of conscience within you saith, Son of man, forbear! then my tongue shall not urge it upon you. But if there you find an echo to the great command, Love the Lord your God with all your heart, keep that law. If there is a voice bidding you love your neighbor, keep that also,[8] and whilst wholly you surrender yourself to him, I know that God in your heart will approve every law which he hath made.

My friends, let us faithfully consider this great principle of action which the gospel gives us. Let us carry it home to our own bosom. Let each one of us, of what sex, or age, or condition soever, consider that God is with us and in us, and ponder well what those words mean. The authority of conscience and the love of truth in us is the manifestation of Him; and therefore let each man, seeing how unbefitting to us is any negligence of ourselves, any heedless following of others, *hold his own nature in a reverential awe*. Let every man so account of himself.[9] Let him attempt with all his heart and in perfect simplicity to receive this idea, that to build up his own being on this eternal foundation is his work in the world, consisting in a continual selection and separation of that which is sinful from that which is divine, that he himself is a holy thing and that nothing profane, nothing unchaste, nothing selfish, nothing false, should defile him, that the Spirit of the Almighty is living within him.

If ever you have found in yourself any approbation of what is good, any love of what is true, however mixed with imperfection or interrupted by vices, o, honour this spark, this ray of God within you, showing that its source is close at hand, and hasten to break down every barrier, to open every door and chamber of your soul, that this spirit of God from its hiding place in your inward parts may come forth as a flood, may circulate through every part of you that the union may become perfect.

Will it not help us, my friends, when we go from the safety of this house and of the Sabbath into the midst of the various temptations of business, of the table, of solitude, and of company, will it not help us to keep unspotted,[10] to reflect that of all business our first business is to build up such a character as shall be a fitting temple of God; that every where, we are to carry ourselves worthily of this celestial inmate and that by so doing there is no place or condition or occurrence from which something of strength, some addition of truth or of virtue will not be gained?

It is one of the safest maxims as it is of highest authority to judge men by their

8. See Matthew 22:37–39, Mark 12:30–31, and Luke 12:27.
9. Romans 14:12.
10. Cf. James 1:27.

fruits and principles by their consequences.[11] Let this be brought to that test. Will the acknowledgment of a divine nature within your soul hurt you? Will it hurt your neighbor? Will it excuse your malignity? Will it steal or kill or commit adultery? Will it be wrapped up in self, and forget to heal the sick and feed the hungry? Will it let you treat a brother or sister with neglect because they are obscure, or rather will it not erect a tribunal in our bosoms such that purity shall almost seem impure, such that our righteousness shall tremble before it? Or will it suffer us to be proud, or say by our own hand or our own strength we have done this,[12] when it acknowledges that only its sins are its own and all its goodness and all its power is the manifestation of God?

Finally, let this doctrine explain to us the place and the nature of the good which Christ has brought us. If his sacred words shall be kept by us; if he shall persuade us to be meek, pure in heart, lovers of our brethren, and hungry after all righteousness that so God shall fully dwell and reign in us,[13] then in truth he will have filled to us the office which prophets foretold, and his own miracles attested; then indeed Jesus will have redeemed us, will have saved us by leading us to God; then we shall be one with him, and with him one in God.[14] Let us bless God, for his goodness to us; let us go forth with joy, and with hope. We have that principle which shall serve us for instruction, and for happiness, not only in all the scenes of human life, but when the shadows of the present things are passed off from our spirit, we have a guide for our course through the wonders of heaven, the never-ending growth of an immortal soul. Know ye not that your body is the temple of the holy ghost which is in you, that ye are not your own, for ye are bought with a price, therefore glorify God in your body and your spirit which are God's.

11. Cf. Matthew 7:20.
12. Cf. Isaiah 10:13.
13. Matthew 5:3–6.
14. Cf. John 17:21–22.

*In a little wrath I hid my face from thee
for a moment, but in everlasting kindness
will I have mercy on thee.*

Isaiah 54:8

The long prevalence of Christianity in the world has produced in the minds of men a gradual but decided improvement in the views that are entertained of God. Though there is abundance of ignorance in men's minds concerning him, though he is in the world and the world was made by him and yet the world perceives him not[1]—yet it is undeniable that a far greater number of men search for God in the true heaven that he inhabits—in the soul and not in the body. They understand that they were made in his moral image not in his natural.[2] The truth is dawning on the world that Jesus Christ was the express image of his person only inasmuch as he was a better man than any other.

Men perceive that God is not honoured but dishonoured by ascribing to him the passions of men. There were always in the world a few men who perceived this; now, the popular language respecting God recognizes it.

One proof of this is the abundance of flippant objection and ridicule that is aimed at the unphilosophical language applied to God in the Old Testament. That his hands and feet, his footstool and throne, his laughter and his repenting are spoken of is thought a proof that there was no inspiration, nothing divine in the ten commandments, in the history of the Israelites, or in the prophecy.[3]

Now that this language is really faulty there is no doubt; that it is injurious to the character of God on the supposition that it ever meant all it said, if really it was understood by the Jews as similar language would be understood by the Americans, I suppose it was not; for all their speech is a bold allegory and it is not to be supposed they imagined God had eyelids, nostrils, shield, and sword,

---

Manuscript dated September 25, 1830, at Brookline. Preached six times: September 26, 1830, at the Second Church, Boston; October 23, 1831, again at the Second Church; October 2, 1836, in East Lexington; October 9 at the Second Church, Waltham; October 30 in Wayland; and December 4 in Concord, Mass.

1. Cf. John 1:10.
2. Cf. Genesis 1:26.
3. E.g., for hands: Genesis 49:24 and Psalms 95:4-5; for feet: II Samuel 22:10 and Nahum 1:3; for footstool: I Chronicles 28:2 and Psalms 99:5; for laughter: Psalms 2:4 and 37:3; for repenting: Jeremiah 18:8 and Jonah 3:9.

any more than that Wisdom had spread a feast or stood at gates, or that the trees clapped their hands.[4]

One remark as to this cavilling at the Old Testament; those who used in a barbarous age to barbarous men a barbarous imagery, did convey truth by its means. The sentiments which they uttered in this coarse allegory, were true and sublime, and would constantly tend to purify and exalt the human soul, and to enable it to throw off these husks as fast as was good, and save the precious truth that was inside. On the contrary, the evil disposition which leads men nowadays to sneer at every thing connected with the spiritual world is false in heart whilst it is true in words. These men have been taught by Christianity and first by the ancient Jews, though they own it not, how to speak of God, and whilst they pretend to honour him with their lips,[5] the disposition which despises or opposes any sincere religious sentiment is really hostile to God and contains the seed of all idolatry. They are relapsing fast to that idolatry out of which these Jews were emerging when thus they spoke of the most high God.

One of these hyperbolical expressions the most frequent in the Old Testament is that in the text, the wrath of God.

But is not God angry with sin? Are not the judgments that afflict nations rightly ascribed to God's disapprobation? To his will, certainly, to his wisdom, to his love, not to his anger.

The Wrath of God is not just language. Christ has taught us better. Take the words in their fulness of meaning and the human mind would be confounded. The Hebrew poets, following out the analogy of human passions when they speak of God as angry, magnify the anger of a man and arm it with the powers over nature with which God is armed. Thunder, and hail, and cold, and darkness, and fire, the swiftness of flight, myriads of armies, pestilence and famine, plagues of reptiles and mildew, drought and inundations are the ready weapons with which they represent God as doing his will on these occasions. If it were possible for the God of nature to burn with human indignation and desire the destruction of the beings he has formed in such beautiful order, these means or means more simple and fatal are easily conceived by which the purpose might be accomplished. Let him loosen one moment the invisible link which binds atom to atom which we call *cohesion*—what makes one particle of granite adhere without cement to another particle of granite, and all would fall readily enough in flat ruin; the eternal hills of rock and iron would float in waves like water or be diffused in fluid like air.

Or let snap the old chain by which his creation holds, the law of gravitation, (for whose existence no cause but God's will can be assigned,) the unwearied force that holds fast these bright worlds at enormous distances to the sun at the centre, and from century to century brings them safe round to the last inch of their faithful revolution. Loose the ethereal cord and how would each orb start

4. E.g., for eyelids: Psalms 11:4; for nostrils: Exodus 15:8; for wisdom: Proverbs 9:1-5 and 8:3; for trees: Isaiah 55:12.

5. Isaiah 29:13.

from its path into a lawless track, speeding away into unknown depths far from the friendly lamp of the system into pure destruction of all life.

But why prescribe any means to him who makes all means? The will that made may unmake. It is as easy to say *Let there be not* as to say *Let be.*[6]

I wish to say that the whole notion of God's anger and its outward manifestation is unsuitable. Wrath is unreasonable. It is in application to man a temporary want of wisdom. Anger is called madness,[7] and can never be applied therefore to God the all Wise who is Wisdom and Love and who dwells passionless and pure in all his works and not so much dwells in them as ever makes them. He is that by which they are. Soul of our souls and safe guard of the world.

Thus in the first place God is never angry.

But as the wrath of God is an application to him of the character of man, so the judgments which we call his wrath are only the reflection of our timorous and sinful selves. God's wrath is man's sin.

Thus among the Jews or among us, if a mildew or a drought or a frost affect the harvest, if over the region we inhabit, the heavens are as brass and under the earth is sand,[8] if an epidemic disease waste a nation, instead of recognizing the wise hand of an universal governor who is operating good even by these means, forgetting the numberless instances in our own experience where nature by one deviation corrects another and always vindicates God's wisdom in the end, the moment an evil comes, our faint hearts, fearful by reason of sin, call it a judgment and cry out God is angry, because we know that we deserve punishment.

The guilt of man paints the clouds with angry faces as the murderer reads an accusation in every countenance.

In the next place, the guilt of man does actually turn all good into evil to himself.

Thus we have considered the meaning of the word *wrath*. It means, the sufferings of man. It would be easy to show more at large how the evil in us brings outward evil, that as we are not to say God tempts no man,[9] so we ought not to say that God is angry with any, but in both cases we are the tempters, and we are the occasions immediately or remotely of our suffering. It might be shown that the Providence of God does not neglect the particulars in its general administration.

But I pass to a more pleasing topic suggested directly by the words of the text.

Let us now consider the word *mercy,* or, the relief of those sufferings. (Under the explanation we have given, it will appear that man's happiness must come from his character, not from his condition.) 'In a little wrath I hid my face from thee for a moment, but in everlasting kindness, will I have mercy on thee.' This is the measure of God's love. This is the proportion of his mercy to his terror.

6. Cf. Genesis 1:3.
7. Horace, *Epistles,* I, ii, 62.
8. Cf. Deuteronomy 28:23.
9. James 1:13.

The sense I draw from it, is, that all our sufferings are small and momentary compared with the enjoyments to which we have access.

Let me open this truth in a few particulars.

I. In the first place, let it be considered that the *sources of happiness are always at hand*. The moral philosophers who have enumerated the important conditions of well being have considered them as being the discipline of the temper; of the imagination; of the opinions, and of the habits;—all of them within the reach of every one. If to these you add *bodily health,* why that is also in a great measure attainable by us, and not many of us can say that our unhappiness has the want of that for its cause. I say then that the sources of happiness are always at hand. Suffering is occasional, local, limited. The source of happiness—why here they are, and every where. Life is a source of happiness; the light of day; the faces of men; the aspect of nature; the power of speech; the bodily functions; the memory; the imagination; the reason; the affections.

There is not a corner of God's earth so sullen and dark, there is not an hour of the threescore and ten years,[10] but if a man will exert himself to find them he can find within his reach abundant materials of pleasure. They spring up everywhere as beautiful and unregarded as the grass at our feet. Am I told that if I look more narrowly, I shall also find that the world is full of suffering also, I believe so—and every one of these joys is a suffering if wrongly received, but there is no person, let his straits and sorrows be what they may, who has put to the best use every power that was left him and has failed to make life comfortable.

Consider a single example to show how cheap and accessible is happiness. It is the law of our nature that every exercise of kindness is attended with positive pleasure to the doer. The feeling of benevolence when indulged towards any individual or to an institution or to our country or to the world is always grateful to us, and the feeling of ill will, on the other hand, is disagreeable. Now it is always in the power of every human being at all times to seek or at least to desire the advantage of others, to occupy his thoughts with wishes and purposes for the welfare of those with whom he converses, carefully to extinguish every rising wish unfriendly to them, to enjoin on himself to pray for their prosperity and to seek always the fair side of every character and the bright side of every event. It will not be denied that all may do this, and this is to draw from a never failing fountain of enjoyment.

What is to hinder the poor and the sick and the bereaved and the ignorant from unlocking to themselves this door of heaven? Take one whom God has seen fit to visit with almost all privations and disadvantages, low born, sick, unfortunate, dependent on others for his daily bread, take such an one and let him from God's word have only learned this law, to love his neighbor as he loves himself,[11] and in spite of the inferiority of his condition, to learn to rejoice in every new success that comes to the young and the great—and I say this man has

10. Psalms 90:10.
11. Matthew 19:19 and Mark 12:31.

learned a secret of happiness which is converting his obscurity into glory. He shall be richer and greater and more beautiful than those favoured ones whose advantages he delights in as his own. His poverty, his sickness, his losses, his ignorance, are temporal and will pass away as clouds, but this conquering love is eternal. In the oriental metaphor, God has hid his face for a moment, but in everlasting kindness he will have mercy on him.

II. In the Providence of God our sufferings are light and brief compared with our sources of enjoyment because our happiness is never dependent upon accident but is dependent on ourselves. It is the most obstinate error that ever afflicted mankind, the belief that happiness resides in the possession of certain outward advantages. Whilst every one who takes the trouble to look at all into the nature of man sees that happiness can never be conferred on him but must be got by him—at least by his cooperation with the arrangements of his Heavenly Father. The advantages of a good country, good parentage, intelligent and virtuous friends, health, good sense, beauty, riches, are excellent gifts when they are well used, but every observing man has seen instances in which each one of these, and, very probably, instances in which all of them together, were possessed, and yet the possessor was unhappy. All external things are unable of themselves to make us happy. Merit is an indispensable element of a mind at ease. Nobody was ever happy without merit, let their powers or circumstances be what they might. All the language of the Scriptures has one tendency as it applies itself to human duty. Do thus and thus thou shalt receive. Thou hast been faithful to thy work, therefore enter into joy.[12]

It is a remarkable confirmation of this great doctrine of religion that all men give as if unconsciously in the universal desire manifested by men to *appear happy*. It is an old observation, that men in general will rather suffer real pain, than be thought to be unhappy.[13] This would not be, if they considered their enjoyments as depending simply upon the appointments of Providence, but plainly shows their opinion that want of happiness argues want of merit. We have all of us noticed in others, perhaps sometimes in ourselves, the willingness to exhibit the advantages of our condition, though well we know they have lost their power to gratify us, and we relish the admiration they excite in others, as at least evincing their opinion that our labours and wishes have been wisely directed.

As this view seems to me an important one, I proceed to notice an objection that may be urged against it. It is sometimes observed that men surrounded with great external advantages are of a querulous temper, and are continually ready to expose to their friends the inability of all these means to content them. They are miserable, they own it, in spite of all that is done and all that is given

12. Cf. Matthew 25:21.

13. Emerson is developing an idea of Dugald Stewart's; see *The Philosophy of the Active and Moral Powers of Man*, in *The Works of Dugald Stewart* (Cambridge, Mass., 1829), 5:533n; and *JMN* 3:193.

because of some single gift withheld, some eyesore, some Mordecai that sits in the king's gate.[14]

This apparent exception certainly deserves consideration but I think it will not be found to contradict in any degree the general observation. Let the man who thus opens his mortifications to the eye of his friends encounter the eye of a stranger and he will hide them. He will be found eager for the admiration which just now he disclaimed; and let the stranger tell him that he is a poor wretch in the midst of all his splendour, and he will be offended to the quick. The reason why he takes off the mask from his wretchedness to his friend, is that he not only desires to appear happy, but also he desires to be happy, and in obeying the impulses of this principle, he unbosoms himself to his fellow man, to obtain the gratification of that hearty sympathy which can only be given when they stand in true relations to each other, and have a thorough understanding of each other's feelings. This surely is not inconsistent with the truth of the general position.[15]

Indeed, I think we may be convinced that all men have an obscure perception that virtue is the source of happiness, by simply putting to our own hearts the question—*Am I happy?* I apprehend, every one will find precisely the same scruple to affirm it, that he would feel if he were asked, "*Am I without sin?*"[16]

Here then is God's everlasting kindness manifest to his children, that he has made men capable of securing their own well being and not dependent for it upon time and chance, that he has chained to every act of goodness its own reward, and since he has endowed us with a free Will, he has therefore given us at all times access to the Heaven that consists in doing right.

It is very important, however, to guard this statement. Though we feel that all before us is in our own power, that we may choose virtue if we will and so be happy, yet we feel that all our past attainments in virtue and so in happiness are not our own. The greater the conquest we have gained the more deeply we feel our dependance, that God is the origin of that virtue that is most our own, and to say not of our own strength or wisdom but by God's help we have done this.[17]

III. But there is yet remaining a consideration of the more literal meaning of the text which has been the foundation of our remarks. There are the blessings that belong to piety, to living with God, which Revelation discloses and which in an especial manner are offered to those from whom, in the Jewish phrase, God has hid his face in present wrath. Are there those who suffer deeply, far more than friends, even the nearest, imagine, under some overwhelming calamity, from whom God seems really to have hidden his face, for they cannot understand the kindness of his Providence? Let them rejoice in this spiritual

14. Mordecai was an irritant to the ambitious Haman in the Book of Esther; see Esther 5:13.
15. Compare this paragraph with *JMN* 3:196.
16. Cf. *JMN* 3:195 and John 8:7.
17. Cf. Isaiah 10:14.

encouragement; for if all their life shall be darkened by these judgments, yet is it but a moment. And what is any mortal grief when measured with the hope of the Gospel? What is sickness, but a finite number of unpleasing sensations? What is fear or sorrow or undeserved reproach to a soul—a child of the Divinity living in him and with him, the friend of Christ, and on its way to heaven? But commonly and more properly God is said to hide his face from sinners. Indeed, God's wrath means man's sin, for it is only he who is conscious of crime who feels that he has changed thus fearfully the complexion of God's will towards him. And to us in our sins, to every evil habit of each of us, this offer of pardon is sent. We find in our own breasts that his face is hid from us by reason of these offences. And what is his Everlasting kindness with which he has mercy on us? What is it but the everlasting gospel whose truths and warnings and hopes sound always in our ears? The innumerable precepts of our own experience, the admonitions and graces of good men, the motives that plead with us to correct our selfishness and luxury and indolence; the Sabbath day; the doctrines of Christ, and his supper, and his death—all these are the everlasting kindness which has no limit or hindrance but what we ourselves create by entering into new defilements which hide God's face yet farther from us.

Therefore, brethren, let this divine word sink deep into our hearts, and fill them with worthy contemplations of the character of God, of his dealings toward us. If we find that we are strangers to his everlasting kindness, let us hasten to awake and explore the world within us, and see if we have not made some great oversight and mistake in our search after happiness. Be persuaded it is not God, it is we ourselves that always are wanting to ourselves. Let us hear the gracious words of our teacher, God's holy Son, "Come unto me all ye that labor and are heavy laden and I will give you rest."[18] Let us seek the fountains of spiritual nature and we shall never thirst.[19] Let us keep the commandments in the hope of the gospel and we shall find that though God may have hid his face from us for a moment, yet in Everlasting kindness he will have mercy upon us.

18. Matthew 11:28.
19. John 4:14.

XC

*For what is a man profited, if he gain
the whole world and lose his own soul?*

Matthew 16:26

All the instructions which religion addresses to man imply a supposition of the utmost importance, which is, that every human mind is capable of receiving and acting upon these sublime principles. That which is made for an immortal life must be of an infinite nature. That which is taught that its daily duty lies in overcoming the pleasures of sense, and in being superior to all the shows and powers of this world, must indeed have something real and noble in its own possessions. And that which can sustain such relations to God as will justify the uniform language of the Scripture in speaking of good men must have costly and venerable attributes. It is no small trust to have the keeping of a soul. And compared with their capacity men are not such as they ought to be.

It is the effect of religion to produce a higher self-respect, a greater confidence in what God has done for each of our minds than is commonly felt among men. It seems to me, brethren, that a great calamity with which men are contending after all the preaching of Christianity is their distrust of themselves. They do not know, because they have not tried, the spiritual force that belongs to them. If a man has a soul, he has an infinite spiritual estate, he has a responsibility that is tremendous, simply in the view of the duration of its being; but far more so in the view of its nature and connexions.

If God has made us with such intention as revelation discloses, then it must be that there are in each of us all the elements of moral and intellectual excellence, that is to say, if you act out yourself, you will attain and exhibit a perfect character. Our Saviour, in the confidence of all the worth which his instructions supposed in human nature, says to his disciples, What is a man profited though he gain the whole world, and lose his own soul? The lesson that may be gathered from this scripture, is, to value our own souls, to have them in such estimation as never to offend them, and this is the theme of the present dis-

Preached four times: October 3, 1830, at the Second Church, Boston; February 3, 1831, as a Thursday Lecture, presumably at the Second Church; April 2, 1837, in East Lexington; and November 12 at the Second Church, Waltham. This sermon on self-reliance may have been suggested by Samuel Johnson's *Rambler*, No. 135 (see *JMN* 6:101), and may also have been influenced by William Ellery Channing's sermon "Likeness to God."

course. I wish to enforce the doctrine that a man should trust himself; should have a perfect confidence that there is no defect or inferiority in his nature; that when he discovers in himself different powers, or opinions, or manners, from others whom he loves and respects, he should not think himself in that degree inferior, but only different; and that for every defect there is probably some compensation provided in his system,[1] and that wherever there is manifest imperfection in his character, it springs from his own neglect to cultivate some part of his mind. I am afraid of this great tendency to uniformity of action and conversation among men. I am afraid of the great evil done to so sacred a property as a man's own soul by an imitation arising out of an unthinking admiration of others. I believe God gave to every man the germ of a peculiar character.[2]

The ends of action are the same, but the means and the manner are infinitely various. As every man occupies a position in some respects singular, every man has probably thoughts that never entered the mind of any other man. Cast your thoughts round upon your different acquaintances, and see if any two present the same character to your imagination.[3] And the more finished the character the more striking is its individuality. And the better is the state of the world, the more unlike will be men's characters, and the more similar their purposes. If you name over men that have the most decided greatness you will find that they present very dissimilar ideas to your thought. Abraham, Moses, Socrates, Milton, Fenelon, these are all eminently good men yet how wholly unlike.[4]

But instead of society's exhibiting this striking variety of mind there may be noticed everywhere a tame resemblance of one man's thoughts and conversation to another's. The gardeners say that the reason why vines were thought to fail in this country, was that they tried to get out of one soil the flavor that belonged to another soil, would raise Madeira grape in America when often the fruit is very different that grows on either side of the same fence, and much more in different latitudes and continents. But cultivate in every soil the grape of that soil. In like manner, men fail in neglecting the intimations of their own inborn intelligence out of an unlimited deference to other characters. Let them on the contrary have greater confidence in the plan yet to them unknown which the moral Architect has traced for them. If he has appointed to it some present defect or less measure than he has given another, as will doubtless be true, he has also given it its own excellences. Explore the mine and make it yield such ores as are in it.[5] Be sure that nothing therein was made in vain.[6] It is not uncommon to hear a man express with great interest his regret that he possesses some particular manner of intellectual superiority or some quickness of feeling

1. Cf. *JMN* 2:341: "Every defect in one manner is made up in another."
2. Cf. *JMN* 3:190.
3. "As every . . . imagination": cf. *JMN* 3:187.
4. "And the better . . . unlike": cf. *JMN* 3:190.
5. "The gardeners . . . it": cf. *JMN* 3:190–91.
6. Cf. *JMN* 3:10 and Sermon IV, n. 17.

which, though reckoned advantages, he thinks rather stand in the way of greatness. It seems to me this self-condemnation is ungrateful and injurious. He
thinks this quality is not good, because others who are great do not have it. Let
him rather trust the wisdom of God and extort from these faculties all their
treasury of good. When I look at the vegetable world, I admire a tree, a flower,
and see that each oak and each lily is perfect in its kind though different in its
proportions and number and arrangement of branches and leaves from every
other oak and lily in the field.[7] And shall I not believe as much of every mind;
that it has its own beauty and character and was never meant to resemble any
other one, and that God pronounced it good after its own kind?[8] Every man has
his own voice, manner, eloquence, and, just as much, his own sort of love, and
grief, and imagination, and action. He has some power over other men that
arises to him from his peculiar education and the cast of his circumstances and
the complexion of his mind, and it were the extreme of folly if he forbears to use
it, because he has never seen it used by anybody else. Let him scorn to *imitate*
any being. Let him scorn to be a secondary man. Let him fully trust his own
share of God's goodness, that if used to the uttermost, it will lead him on to a
perfection which has no type yet in the Universe save only in the Divine Mind.[9]

One measure of a man's character is his effect upon his fellow-men. And any
one who will steadily observe his own experience will I think become convinced, that every false word he has uttered, that is to say, every departure from
his own convictions, out of deference to others has been a sacrifice of a certain
amount of his power over other men. For every man knows whether he has been
accustomed to receive truth or falsehood,—valuable opinions or foolish talking,—from his brother, and this knowledge must inevitably determine his
respect.

Now what is it to speak from one's own convictions, to trust yourself,—what
is it but to keep one's mind ever awake, to use the senses and the reason, to rely
on your birthright of powers which God bestowed? But how little of this virtue
enters into conversation. Men speak not from themselves but from the floating
parlance of the time;[10] they think—what is expected to be said?—What have
others said?—what is safest to be said?—instead of what they hold to be true. Is
it not wonderful that they do not see the infinite advantage that he must possess
who always listens only to himself? I think this cannot be illustrated better than
by comparing the looseness of men's discourse upon those questions most
deeply interesting to our nature with the cogency of their talk in common
affairs. How clear and strong is the language of a man speaking the truth in
things concerning his ordinary business, that a commodity sold for so much,
that a stage runs on such a road, the wind blows from such a quarter, or such
were the numbers of a contested vote. No ingenuity, no sophism that the learn-

7. Cf. Matthew 6:28 and Luke 12:27.
8. Genesis 1:11–12.
9. "When I look . . . Mind": cf. *JMN* 3:198–99.
10. "But how . . . time": cf. *JMN* 3:187.

ing or eloquence of a man would intrude in such a conversation could be any
match to the force of their speech. It would be ridiculous weakness. For when
men converse on their pressing affairs *they* do not so much seem to speak as to
become mere organs through which facts themselves speak.

Now that is precisely the way in which God seems to justify those who
withdraw their eyes from every thing else, and fix them on their own thoughts
only. They become, as it were, passive, and are merely the voice of things. If a
man would always as exclusively consult his own thoughts as men do in these
things, he would always speak with the same force, a force which would be felt
to be far greater than belonged to him or to any mortal, but was proper to
immortal truth.[11]

It is important to observe that this self-reliance which grows out of the Scripture doctrine of the value of the soul is not inconsistent either with our duties to
our fellow men or to God. Some will say, to press on a man the necessity of
guiding himself only by the unaided light of his own understanding, and to
shun as dangerous the imitation of other men seems inconsistent with the Scripture commandments that enjoin self abasement and unlimited love to others,
and also with our natural relations to other men who are older and wiser and
better than we are. Certainly it is our duty to prefer another's good always to
our own, and gratefully to borrow all the light of his understanding as far as it
agrees with ours, but the duty is quite as plain, the moment our own convictions of duty contradict another's, we ought to forsake his leading, let him be of
what wisdom or condition he will, and without fear to follow our own.
Brethren, I beg each of you to remember, whether, when you have in any
instance forsaken your first impressions of a book, or a character, or a question
of duty, and adopted new ones from complaisance, you have not by and by been
compelled to receive your own again, with the mortification of being overcome
by your own weapons.[12] Certainly other men, especially good men, are entitled
from a good man to all respect. I honour the modesty and benevolence which is
respectful to men of worth and thinks there is soundness in all their opinions.
But I honour more this image of God in human nature which has placed a
standard of character in every human breast which is above the highest copy of
living excellence. Every man has an idea of a greatness that was never realized.
Take the history of a great and good man, of Newton, or Franklin, or Washington, and explain all its details to the most obscure and ignorant wretch that
wears the human form, and you shall find that whilst he understands all its
elevation he will be able to put his finger upon imperfections in that life. Which
shows that in his heart there is a greater man than any that has lived in the
world.[13]

Nor, on the other hand, let it be thought that there is in this self-reliance any
thing of presumption, anything inconsistent with a spirit of dependence and

11. With the last two paragraphs, cf. *JMN* 3:199.
12. "forsaken your . . . weapons": cf. *JMN* 3:199.
13. "Take the . . . world": cf. *JMN* 3:200.

piety toward God. In listening more intently to our own soul we are not becoming in the ordinary sense more selfish, but are departing farther from what is low and falling back upon truth and upon God.[14] For the whole value of the soul depends on the fact that it contains a divine principle, that it is a house of God, and the voice of the eternal inhabitant may always be heard within it.

A good man, says Solomon, is satisfied from himself.[15] An original mind is not an eccentric mind. To be wholly independent of other men's judgments does not mean to come under their censure by any extravagance of action. But it is only those who are so that can bear the severest scrutiny of other men's judgments. It is by following other men's opinions that we are misled and depraved. It is those who have steadily listened to their own who have found out the great truths of religion which are the salvation of the human soul.[16] My friends, let me beseech you to remember that it is only by looking inward that the outward means of knowledge can be made of any avail. The soul, the soul is full of truth. The bible is a sealed book to him who has not first heard its laws from his soul.[17] The drunkard and the voluptuary might as well read it in an unknown language as in their mother tongue. And it is this fact that gives such immense meaning to the precept Know Thyself.[18] To him who has reached this wisdom how ridiculous is Caesar and Bonaparte wandering from one extreme of civilization to the other to conquer men,—himself, the while, unconquered, unexplored, almost wholly unsuspected to himself. Yet Europe and Asia are not so broad and deep, have nothing so splendid, so durable, as the possessions of this empire.[19] What shall it profit a man though he gain the whole world and lose his own soul?

My friends, the deep religious interest of this question is apparent to you. The body we inhabit shall shortly be laid in the dust, but the soul assures us, with the voice of God to confirm it, that it will not die. Let this strange and awful being that we possess have that reverence that is due from us. Let us leave this immoderate regard to meats and drinks, to dress and pleasure and to unfounded praise, and let us go alone and converse with ourselves, and the word of God in us. What that bids us do, let us do with unshaken firmness, and what it bids us forbear, let us forbear. Let us love and respect each other as those who can assist us in understanding ourselves. And let us hear the distinct voice of Scripture which has taught us to forsake the world and its vanities and deceptions, and seek God who is to be worshipped in our hearts.

14. Cf. *JMN* 3:199.
15. Proverbs 14:14.
16. "It is by . . . soul": cf. *JMN* 3:199.
17. Cf. Isaiah 29:11.
18. See Sermon XXVII, n. 2, and Sermon XLVII, n. 4.
19. "And it is . . . empire": cf. *JMN* 3:192.

Appendix: Sermon XLVII[A]

This sermon fragment, headed "XLVII" but without a biblical text, was written and abandoned shortly after Emerson's attendance at the Harvard Commencement activities of August 25, 1829 (see *L* 1:280).

Manuscript: Four sheets folded to make four pages each; folios nested and sewn with white thread through the center fold. MS p. 3 and pp. 5–16 are blank; pages measure 25 x 20.3 cm.

Began Aug ↑30↓ 1829

The past week has called the attention of the community to the literary institutions of the country. This anniversary has a very deep interest to a large portion of the community who have received their education at the College to a still larger portion through their interest in sons or brothers or friends & to all men who love their country & the cause of knowledge & virtue in it. The occasion has past ⟨its⟩ with its pleasures & its pains. After the fable comes the moral. It is the office of the pulpit in all things that are seen to suggest the unseen part, to speak for the future in all the engrossing scenes of the present and there is so much more to be seen & heard in this occasion than meets the e⟨ar⟩ye or ear of careless observers there is so much instruction to the religious eye of man in this week that I cannot forbear ⟨craving⟩ asking your attention to such reflexions as this peculiar anniversary awakens.

Eighteen years after the landing of our forefathers at Plymouth they founded the College & dedicated it to Christ & the Church. Since that time the institution has flourished in the good will and honour of the country, has been the principal centre ⟨of⟩ whence the rays of science & useful learning have penetrated to every town & village in the country it has furnished many generations with ministers for the altar & teachers for the young & counsellors in the laws and skilful physicians & able statesmen & good citizens.

But what I wanted to do was to describe to you the feeling which the sight of that house excites in sober men. We go up to the Commencement as it is called and we get a just picture of life. There sits a great throng of learned & prosperous & fair ⟨&⟩ men and women willing to hear with applause the first public efforts of the graduates There sits the beautiful an object of much admiration and unconscious how dangerous it is and there many a young heart is beating with the desire of distinction before the fathers of the state is looking

impatiently forward into active life with unmeasured hopes of the high & honoured part he shall take therein. To the eye of the stranger all appears a show of
↑reason &↓ pleasure & hope a good ambition appears to be excited by the
display of the premiums of a good ambition, it is a meeting of families & old
friends, a day of innocent & elevated entertainment. But there is a vein of
sadness in this festival that does not belong to any other if you could uncover the
hearts of the old & of the young men that come up to the celebration. Each
scholar

Textual and Manuscript Notes

In these notes, a physical description of the sermon manuscript is followed by a record, keyed to the text by page and line number, of all of Emerson's insertions, cancellations, variant passages, and transpositions, as well as all editorial changes not covered in the categories of silent emendation outlined in the Textual Introduction. The text given here is a literal genetic transcription of the manuscript and therefore differs in some respects from the edited version above. Editorial matter is enclosed in square brackets, while Emerson's brackets are represented as curved. All inscription is in ink unless otherwise noted.

The symbols used in these notes are explained in the list below. Matter that immediately follows a cancellation without space or symbol of insertion, as in "⟨i⟩It" or "⟨we⟩you," should be understood as having been written directly over the canceled matter.

Symbols

⟨ ⟩	Cancellation
↑ ↓	Insertion
/ / /	Variant
[ ]	Editorial insertion
{ }	Emerson's square brackets
¶	Paragraph

Sermon XLIII

Manuscript: Four sheets folded to make four pages each; folios nested and sewn with brown thread; pages measure 25 x 20.5 cm.

Lines	Page 19
4	↑it is said↓
5–6	the⟨se persons⟩ ↑lovers . . . pleasure↓
8–11	try ⟨to think they⟩ ↑to↓ . . . not ⟨strowed⟩ ↑sown↓, [addition in ink over pencil] . . . a⟨n⟩ ↑very↓
13	Calvinists ⟨we f⟩ no
18	y⟨e⟩ou
22–23	back ⟨not only⟩ to {what ⟨C⟩ modern . . . to} the dark ⟨impossibilities⟩ ↑faith of Athanasius &↓ of Calvin [The editors feel that if this were an early emendation, Emerson would, in the course of so many deliveries, have canceled "what . . . to" rather than continue it in brackets; the original version is therefore retained as probably belonging to the first delivery.]

271

Page 20

6–7   who ↑⟨which⟩with . . . disciples,↓
14–16   Gods /one/simple/ . . . & ⟨revivals⟩ ↑conversion↓,
20–21   Calvin ⟨& Priestley⟩ &
22–26   churches. [end of page] [The following paragraph of notations occurs
        in pencil:] ¶ Wish men wdnt appeal ever from their soul to their
        memories from observation to words of rote. then wd. they see that
        remove they have in themselves the barrier to keep out the waters of
        infidelity for suppose the revelation removed the terrors of the future
        the soul wd assert them for the terrors of guilt are in itself & not in
        Gods arbitrary will Difficulties may beseige some points but not this
        The soul that sinneth shall suffer.
         ↑⟨It is with this view I have chosen this subject ⟨↑in the hope↓⟩ that
        we may led to⟩ ⟨↑It is well then we shd keep in mind those views of
        Xty↓⟩↑It . . . gospel↓ ["It . . . gospel" written in ink over "It . . .
        Xty" in pencil] ↑which make us↓ . . . & ⟨torment⟩ to shake the
        sinner, ⟨rather if we will ponder it well we shall sin no more & suffer
        no more⟩ or rather it has ⟨that⟩ ↑such↓ . . . more.↓
28   marked—⟨is⟩ common
34–35   ↑Many . . . lodestone.↓ {If [bracket in pencil; there is no companion]
37–(21)1   place /assumes/is found to have/ . . . regular ⟨lines⟩ ↑curves↓ about
        the ⟨main⟩ magnet.

Page 21

4   ↑as . . . dust↓
5   this ⟨order⟩ ↑familiar fact↓ . . . God⟨.⟩'s ↑moral action.↓
6–8   one /unlively/dull/ . . . until ⟨the windows of the soul are opened &
        God is revealed⟩ ↑its . . . forth ⟨by the presence of the idea of⟩ when
        God is revealed↓
10–13   own ⟨perception⟩ belief, ↑all . . . powers ⟨arrange⟩ ↑throw↓ them-
        selves ⟨anew⟩ ↑irresistible arrangement↓↓ . . . solit⟨ude⟩↑ary inde-
        pendent↓ ⟨of⟩ value . . . agency—⟨as⟩ Nothing
22–23   ↑from your own experience↓ to your ⟨own⟩ conscience than I could
        ⟨pourtray.⟩ ↑hope to unfold.↓
24–25   is ⟨ma⟩ shown . . . is ⟨wearied down⟩ ↑wakened at every step↓
28–30   distance. ⟨There is a sublime view of God's Providence in this regard
        which I cannot help alluding to though I know the mind often revolts
        at it as too violent theory. It is as it was stated by its advocate the pious
        Bishop Berkeley that the *material world exists only as it is perceived.* I
        ⟨behold⟩ ↑admire↓ the sun in the firmament, but how know I that the
        sun is there? Because my eyes attest it. But how can I learn if my eyes
        give me a true report? When I observe the things immediately around
        me, ⟨my⟩ one sense confirms another, my hands feel the book which
        my eyes see. But that is all the evidence I have; the senses agree, but if
        they are wrong I have no means of learning what is right. I cannot ⟨go
        on⟩ learn any thing outward but by their means & cannot find out
        whether they tell me truth. Of course it is very clear that my evidence
        of the real being of the sun is very different from my evidence of my

own love or hatred, my own purposes, &c. which do themselves appear to me without the intervention of any organs. ⟩

⟨Reasoning in this way, it is plainly possible, that God sets the human mind alone & himself directly by his agency gives it these impressions of earth & sea & sun & stars & man & beast, that all that we behold is not an ancient primeval Creation covered with the moss of many an age but Gods immediate act upon each of our minds at this moment of time. And thus in a most wonderful & exalted sense *in him we live & move & have our being.* ⟩

↑But↓ [added in pencil] Men . . . God ⟨at a distance⟩ ↑from afar↓, . . . period ⟨for⟩ ↑put . . . at↓

34	fall ⟨to pieces.⟩ ↑asunder↓
35–36	↑by nature . . . God↓
38–39	himself—⟨His Prov- [end of page] The same power is needed this moment as was needed the first moment to produce the same effect. ↑To him↓ It is the same to uphold as to establish. It is a creation of each /moment/instant/. [variant in pencil] I look then at my present being as now received, as now sustained by the Omnipresent father. ²{I receive ¹{therefore when I look abroad} directly from him these impressions of earth & sea & sun & stars & man & beast All that we behold is not an ancient primeval work covered with the moss of many an age, but fresh with life—Gods immediate act upon each of our minds, at this instant of time. And thus in a most emphatic sense *In him we* live & move & have our being. ⟩ ¶ The

Page 22

12	consideration ⟨of a part⟩ of
14	¶ ↑III.↓ ⟨But⟩ I
15	↑God . . . experience↓
17–20	faith ⟨should⟩ ↑can↓ . . . Religion. ⟨I desire great latitude in attempting to develope this idea.⟩ ↑Living . . . *perfection*↓
21–28	believe ⟨it⟩ ↑desires & glimpses of this beatitude↓ /ha⟨s⟩ve been the ⟨motive⟩ ⟨↑law↓⟩ /are constantly attained [end of line] degrees of it are the law/ of millions ↑whose names are not known in↓ in the . . . animating ⟨good deeds⟩ difficult exertions↑,↓ [comma in pencil] . . . from ⟨pits of darkness⟩ ↑depths of sorrow↓ & hopeless defeats. ↑I . . . history↓ [addition in ink over pencil]
29–31	God. ¶ ⟨↑{This line one of yᵉ finest passages in History.}↓⟩ ¶ ⟨The Christian⟩ ↑My . . . th⟨is⟩ese . . . of ⟨reli⟩ piety. . . . here;↓ Let
33–34	↑unintelligent↓ . . . creation⟨s⟩

Page 23

2	own ⟨connexion⟩ ↑likeness↓ /with/to/
4–6	↑the filth of sin↓ . . . gives, ⟨& the filth of sin⟩ that . . . ↑giving visions of↓
8	urgent ⟨distress⟩ ↑danger↓
11	of th⟨e⟩is

16–18   the ⟨thot which⟩ ↑assurance whose exultations↓ . . . ↑step he makes in↓

23   ↑through all the / prosperity / advantages / of his condition↓

33   & ⟨br⟩ embodied . . . for ⟨the Universe,⟩ ↑all souls,↓ [emendation in ink over pencil]

35–39   ¶ ⟨Oh⟩ ↑My brethren↓ . . . prosperity ⟨when the heart is cheered⟩ when . . . eye ⟨dwells⟩ is . . . ↑& . . . enthusiasm↓

39–(24)3   ways ⟨of hope⟩ ↑in wh. we walked↓ . . . fortune ⟨it is⟩ to . . . ↑aspirations of↓

Page 24

7   ↑they lived↓

11–12   ↑as he languishes alone↓ . . . disease. ⟨B⟩ Peace he saith ⟨to his⟩ ↑my↓ . . . ↑sorrow of↓

19–20   ↑Forsaken . . . counsels↓

23–33   ↑remand my dust to dust↓ . . . it ⟨pants⟩ aspires. ¶ ⟨My brethren, can we gain any better preparation for life or death than this lofty relation to the Most High. ↑This is the feeling proper to each of us. ⟨W⟩ This is to live & move & have our being in God. ²{Will it excuse our sins, ¹{Is this lax?↓⟩ ↑My . . . sins?↓ {He . . . ↑so↓ . . . right} [last set of brackets in ink over pencil]

37   & ⟨ardour.⟩ zeal.

Sermon XLIV

Manuscript: Four sheets folded to make four pages each; folios nested and sewn with white thread along left margin; pages measure 25 x 20.6 cm.

[Above Bible text:]   juvenis 4 [in pencil]

Lines   *Page 25*
Bible Text   ⟨Are ye unworthy to judge the smallest matters? I Cor. VI., 2.⟩ ↑— Martha . . . 42↓

2   finding ⟨eminent genius⟩ ↑great talents↓ & ⟨eminent goodness⟩ ↑virtues↓.

5   ↑production of the↓

11–12   little / remembered / regarded /

12–16   ↑He . . . ↑confined means the↓ Ease of procuring information↓ {There is / no country / hardly . . . globe/ . . . ↑private↓ . . . ↑or . . . door↓ . . . curiosity}

19   in ⟨perfect⟩ solitude,

23   farmer ⟨r⟩looks

24   ↑much↓

25   as ⟨civilization advances⟩ ⟨↑refinements↓⟩ ↑you approach cities↓,

Page 26

1–2   microscopic; ⟨it devotes the same attention to pebbles it once did to mountains⟩ Dress . . . to ⟨public⟩ opinion

4	& ⟨rusticity⟩ ↑vulgarity↓,
6	mind its
9–14	atmosphere ⟨for⟩ ↑& . . . mountain↓ a⟨↑n↓⟩ hundred miles ↑distant↓ & examines the ⟨form⟩ ↑anatomy↓ . . . {And this . . . ↑to a remarkable degree↓. . . . Prussia, ⟨who⟩ ↑that . . . he↓ . . . Europe, ⟨that⟩ he . . . cellar.} ⟨There are men of a capacity for great & generous views who will sit & calculate long on the means of getting their chair nearer to the fire than his who sits next them.⟩ This range ↑of↓
17	a ⟨most ambitious circuit⟩ ↑⟨vast⟩ ↑great↓ extent↓.
18	that ⟨same⟩ Power
21	danger very
23–24	the ⟨intellectual⟩ eye ↑of the mind↓ . . . great ⟨specu⟩ ↑contemp↓lation
29	ones'
32	gravest ⟨importance⟩ ↑consequence↓.
33–35	↑soiled or↓ . . . ↑stupidity or↓ gross ignorance ⟨or stupidity⟩ and . . . ↑a↓ well bred ⟨people⟩ ↑acquaintance↓
40	in ⟨seals & pencils ↑& watch↓⟩ ↑trinkets,↓

Page 27

1	so ²insignificant or ¹absurd,
2–3	↑You . . . selfishness↓
3–4	a ⟨man⟩ ↑person↓ . . . sit & ⟨calculate⟩ ↑meditate↓
5–6	a ⟨worthy⟩ ↑generous↓
7–8	in ⟨h⟩ our houses;—a ⟨most⟩ low-lived ["most" canceled in pencil]
9–10	↑way of↓ . . . attainment⟨s⟩↑s↓ ⟨& regards.⟩ They . . . clothes ⟨is⟩ are
14–16	toys. ↑of petty comforts.↓ ¶ To feel ⟨how insignificant⟩ ↑what nothings↓ . . . they ⟨shrink away to their own nothingness⟩ ↑appear,↓
18–19	presence of ⟨Newton⟩ ↑⟨such⟩ a man ⟨as⟩ of ⟨immense⟩ /intellectual power/great powers of mind/↓ . . . that ⟨great man⟩ ↑person↓, that ⟨he shd. be splendidly clothed.⟩ ↑this . . . rich?↓
21	↑or mean↓
22–23	graceful ⟨↑in↓⟩ when
25	over ⟨the pretension⟩ ostentation
26–27	a ⟨large⟩ company ↑of strangers↓. . . . the ⟨splendour of⟩ ↑fine personal↓ appearance & ⟨decoration⟩ ↑tasteful dress↓
28–30	& ⟨a man⟩ ↑let one of the company↓ discover⟨s⟩ a surpassing wit & ⟨wide⟩ ↑/extensive/rich/↓ . . . ↑& weighty↓ . . . shows ⟨dwindle ↑away↓⟩ ↑are forgotten↓.
31	these ⟨accomplishments⟩ ↑appearances↓ ↑of others↓ ["accomplishments" canceled and "appearances" added in pencil]
32	↑Can . . . contempt?↓
33–38	of ⟨strong effort⟩ ↑great diligence↓ or ⟨of absorbed devotion⟩ ↑concentrated . . . piety↓ . . . reign. for . . . esteemed, . . . ↑or . . . it↓,

39–41 receive. ¶ ⟨Well now my friends I think it becomes a Christian to despise trifles⟩ ↑The . . . overestimate ⟨arises⟩ will be felt when ⟨we⟩ ↑tis↓ consider↑ed↓ that ⟨if⟩ you must degrade them ⟨in⟩ ↑from their↓ importance or they will↓

42–44 their ⟨importance⟩ ↑value↓ of supposing ⟨them⟩ ↑certain indiff. things↓ . . . you. ⟨⟨Hence the evil of what we call bugbears.⟩⟩ Nothing

Page 28

3 till ⟨a⟩ ↑the↓
6–7 ↑on comfort↓
12 of ⟨trifles⟩ ↑them↓. ⟨I knew of ⟨g⟩ a good man who always prayed⟩ ↑It . . . prayer↓ that ⟨he⟩ ↑we↓
14–15 ↑or a feast or a frolic↓ . . . or ↑an affront↓ a headache.
16–18 —his ⟨universal energy⟩ ↑works↓, . . . for ⟨the exercise of ⟨soaring⟩ ↑great↓ affections upon noblest objects⟩ ↑continual . . . minds↓,
20–23 ↑furious↓ . . . between ⟨two or three⟩ stragglers ↑on the lines,↓ . . . an ⟨immeasureable territory⟩ ↑immense inheritance↓ . . . ↑of joy or grief↓
24 too ⟨h⟩ anxious
31–33 this ⟨neglect⟩ ↑small esteem↓ . . . magnanimity. ⟨But this⟩ ↑It↓
34–36 trifles. ¶ ²{And . . . simplicity.} ¹{Our . . . deportment.}
38–39 individual.— ⟨I do not bid you cease to do little things for you cannot help it Your duty lies among them. But don't carry them out of their own sphere dont exalt them above the moon.⟩ ¶ Especially ⟨does⟩ ↑shd.↓
40–41 them. ⟨The first rule⟩ ↑A great principle↓ . . . ↑early↓ . . . is ⟨this,⟩ ↑to↓

Page 29

1 example. ⟨If your⟩ ⟨Do not⟩ ↑Do not↓
5–8 be ⟨des⟩ opened . . . conflict ⟨that may cover him with glory⟩ ↑on . . . depending↓ as ⟨c⟩presenting . . . the ⟨severest⟩ ↑laborious↓ . . . not ⟨let him talk⟩ teach
10–13 ↑with . . . almost↓ . . . is ⟨romantic with⟩ ↑made venerable by↓ . . . ↑show him its science↓ . . . measured ⟨by⟩ ↑in↓
15 come. ⟨have bored its surface & by examination revealed its history for ages past of deluges of convulsions & slow change⟩ Show
17 ↑with glowing reverence↓
20 Resurrection⟨—⟩&
22 ↑& Alfred↓
24–25 energies ⟨on such mean things ⟨D⟩as children generally pursue.⟩ ↑with such casual or ⟨poor⟩ ↑wretched↓ . . . upon.↓
26 ↑of mean occupation↓
29 the ⟨frigid degrading⟩ ↑meanspirited↓
31 the ⟨importance of⟩ ↑value↓
33 are ⟨great⟩ ↑important↓.
34 difficult, ↑to . . . views,↓
38 reference ⟨of⟩ ↑in↓

| 39 | ack [end of line] knowledgment |
| 39–41 | In . . . yr. ⟨might⟩ ↑/heart/strength/↓ . . . yrself.↓ |

Sermon XLV

Manuscript: Two sheets folded to make four pages each, nested, in the center of which is a loosely inserted folio bearing Inserts "A" and "B," inscribed continuously on the first two pages (last two pages blank); this gathering is followed by three stacked folios, from the second of which the first leaf, bearing evidence of writing on both sides, was cut before the fascicle was assembled (the text is continuous). Folios sewn through left margin with white thread; pages measure 25 x 20.3 cm. A slip of paper, 5.8 x 18.4 cm, affixed with red sealing wax to the right and left margins at the bottom of MS p. 9, contains an unlabeled revision of the canceled passage it covers. Another slip of paper, 10.4 x 9.6 cm, affixed with red sealing wax to the right margin of MS p. 17, contains another unlabeled revision.

Lines	*Page 30*
Bible Text	⟨Blessed are the pure in heart for they shall see God. Matt. V. 8⟩ ↑The . . . right rejoicing . . . Ps. XIX. 8.↓
2	body. ⟨To find⟩ ↑The observation that↓ the mind los⟨ing⟩↑es↓
6–7	produce ⟨in⟩ mental . . . with ⟨sad⟩ ↑gloomy↓ & distressing ⟨thoughts⟩ ↑images↓,
9–10	a ⟨result⟩ finer . . . refined ⟨speculation⟩ ↑notion↓ . . . re⟨s⟩lation
14	should ⟨again⟩ ↑re↓produce
15	that ⟨soon⟩ ↑presently↓ [addition in ink over pencil]
18	↑the observer is mind↓ [addition written as if to go after "matter; that"; a caret after "*mind*," indicates placement]
20	for ⟨every mind⟩ ↑all men↓,
24–(31)1	man. ⟨↑In yᵉ morng. I offered you some remarks upon yᵉ common consent of all men ⟨with⟩ yᵗ ⟨yˢ⟩ yᵉ obedience to this part of our ⟨nature⟩ ↑constitution↓ makes yᵉ substance of religion & now to some farther ⟨remarks⟩ ↑considerations↓ on its nature.↓⟩ [This passage, now canceled, was probably added for the afternoon delivery, September 13, 1829, at Springfield, when Sermon XXXI was given in the morning.] ¶ There can be no ⟨darkness⟩ ↑ignorance↓ . . . mind ⟨I⟩ ↑as to↓ what ⟨I⟩ ↑is↓ mean↑↑t↓

	Page 31
2–3	being ⟨admitted⟩ ↑affirmed↓
4–5	↑in secret↓ . . . do ⟨&⟩ whilst
7–10	have ⟨de⟩ borne . . . ↑criminally↓ . . . duty ⟨neglected &⟩ ⟨/defied/dishonoured/⟩ ↑violated.↓
12	perception ⟨it is ⟨↑these are↓⟩ the stamina, the nucleus of man⟩. You
14–15	you. ⟨⟨It is vain to attempt to define it⟩ ↑I am perfectly aware of the difficulty of defining so simple a tho't & it is only with the view of uniting the meaning of these expressions p. of d. & f. of duty yᵗ I have enlarged↓⟩ ↑It . . . all↓ but . . . what ⟨I am talking about⟩ [cancellation in pencil] ↑amount . . . terms↓, ["amount of meaning I affix" in ink over pencil]

18–20   *itself.* ⟨I wish to assert my convictions⟩ ↑It shd. be felt↓ . . . feel
            ⟨the⟩ ↑a↓ degradation ⟨of⟩ ↑in admitting↓
23–33   ↑own↓ fame ↑or profit↓, . . . we ⟨will⟩ ↑desire to↓ [emendation in ink
            over pencil] be ⟨true⟩ ↑just,↓ . . . holy. ¶ ⟨This doctrine ⟨is as⟩ that all
            virtue springs from self-love, looks to the advantages of virtue, is as
            shallow as it is libellous.⟩ [cancellation in pencil] ↑Insert A A {It . . .
            vice.}↓ [Inserts "A" and "B" (see below) are written continuously on the
            first two pages of a four-page insert. "A" is marked off with brackets
            and labeled "A"; the beginning of "B" is marked off with a bracket, but
            lacks a closing bracket and is not labeled.]
34   that ⟨with⟩ ↑holding↓
38–(32)13   virtue. ⟨But there is no elevated mind which does not perceive a
            certain meanness unworthiness in this love of goodness, does not feel
            that Virtue is⟩ [canceled in pencil] [end of page] ⟨its own reward in a
            far higher sense than that it secures splendid advantages in the long
            run to its votary⟩
                ⟨↑{Insert B}⟩ ⟨⟨But yᵉ⟩ ↑The↓ defender of yᵉ selfish system says yᵗ
            we love virtue & practise it simply because we think it will be our inter-
            est to do so.↓⟩ [in the left margin, circled, the phrase "prudent piety"]
                ⟨Now the only objection which the defender of the selfish system
            can urge with any plausibility whilst he views the⟩ ↑⟨Now⟩ ↑But↓
            here are↓ ⟨multitudes of people who in the past & the present time
            have bravely sacrificed their interest, their pleasure, their health, or
            their life, to the feeling of duty. ⟨Now⟩ ⟨↑But↓⟩ the ⟨only⟩ answer
            ↑made by the objector↓ to this practical argument,⟩ ↑{Insert B} {To
            be . . . all ⟨hope⟩ unworthiness . . . argument is↓ is, inheritance.
            ¶ ⟨⟨⟨I shall be permitted as the question is a very important one to
            repeat, that one set of men say that we love virtue & ⟨do its
            commandment⟩⟩ practise it simply because we think it will be our
            interest to do so & another set of men say that we love virtue for its
            own sake apart from our knowledge of its rewards & that we can
            conceive of its being practised where there was no hope of obtaining
            its rewards. ↑and that we maintain yᵉ latter opinion.—↓}⟩ ↑We
            ⟨answer⟩ ↑reply↓ . . . rewards.—↓ [addition on a slip of paper
            affixed to the right and left margins with red sealing wax, obscuring
            the canceled passage "{I shall . . . opinion.—}"] [end of page] ¶ ⟨{Yet
            that we are capable of perceiving the sovereign & selfexistent excel-
            lence of duty apart from any consideration of consequences, must be
            evident to any who will consider our strong sympathy in any difficult
            act of virtue.}⟩ The heart

                                    Page 32
15–19   ↑You . . . tho 1000 y. ago . . . blood↓ ⟨T⟩What . . . from ⟨the old-
            world stories that fill our books⟩ the heroism . . . Socrates, ⟨from⟩
            the . . . independance
19–20   Yet ⟨they⟩ ↑these old-world stories↓ . . . ↑the passage of↓ centuries
            ⟨have passed⟩ & in these ↑remote↓ ends of the earth. ↑Now . . .
            beautiful?↓ ["of their effect . . . beautiful?" in ink over pencil]

24–27 ↑because . . . exertions,↓ . . . prevailed. ↑and yet . . . practised.↓

27–(33)1 presents ↑to↓ . . . beautiful. {⟨Among . . . commanded him⟩ ↑There . . . who ⟨have⟩ without . . . opinion↓ . . . truth.} [The cancellation of "Among . . . commanded him" (occurring at the bottom of the MS page and ending in mid-sentence) is evidently an error.]

33–34 by ⟨a falsehood⟩ ↑denying . . . him↓. . . . ↑make↓ inquir⟨e⟩y of him ⟨if he had seen him.⟩ & threatened

36 ↑communed with himself &↓

39–40 of /a/the/ sublim⟨e⟩est↓ [emendations in ink over pencil] . . . agent /who ⟨gives⟩/the giving/ [cancellation and variant in pencil]

40–(33)1 all. ⟨⟨It will be observed that the truth or falsehood of the story makes no difference⟩ The assertion is that we⟩ ↑Now, . . . read this idle tale↓ approve↑s↓ this ↑supposed↓ . . . truth.}

Page 33

2 we ⟨approve it?⟩ not condemn ⟨the⟩ ↑an↓ integrity ↑or a patriotism↓ ⟨as⟩so

5 ↑moving↓ [The entire paragraph, "But . . . removed?", is in ink over erased pencil.]

7–9 removed? [end of page] ⟨virtue only for its loaves & fishes shd we applaud this.⟩ What . . . virtue. ⟨If you tell a tale⟩ ↑↑And . . . depravity↓ Repeat any anecdote↓

11–27 {Samuel . . . ↑forever↓ . . . an ⟨absurdity⟩ a contradiction, . . . this.} ¶ ⟨↑We cannot appeal, it is true, to the heroic story of all that we have known in the Christian Church to be done & suffered without any hope of earthly reward & with the certainty of poverty & reproach & death—we can't appeal to these because, as was just now said, the hope of immortality may be said to have sustained these exertions. But there are stories true & false of the adherence to this pure principle among nations where no hope of immortality prevailed⟩ ↑Insert X X {I ⟨urge⟩ ↑present↓ . . . ↑reference to↓ this world⟨s⟩ . . . us.}↓

28–29 us, ⟨my brethren,⟩ to . . . to ⟨these⟩ ↑any↓

30–(34)7 contemplations. ⟨Let us⟩ ↑I . . . might↓ . . . nor ⟨gains any⟩ ↑augments our↓ . . . ↑struggling↓ . . . ↑of life,↓ . . . itself⟨,⟩ obscure or defeated⟨,⟩ may . . . those ⟨whose⟩ whom . . . partake.— ¶ ⟨If⟩ ↑Whilst . . . if↓ . . . fear of ⟨hells⟩ ↑the↓ torments ↑of hell,↓ . . . judgement⟨, dwelling strongly⟩ ↑on . . . often↓

Page 34

9–11 sot & the ⟨epicure⟩ ⟨or the bankrupt⟩ ↑prodigal↓ . . . of ⟨our Lord⟩ ⟨↑the apostle↓⟩ ↑our Lord↓ be true that ⟨with the *heart* man believeth is un[illegible]⟩ ↑Thou . . . heart↓ . . . publican ⟨goeth down⟩ ↑shall go up↓

17–18 life. ⟨Evil⟩ An . . . world ⟨sa⟩ diseases

20–21 or ⟨it is⟩ ↑exists↓ . . . him. ⟨But this is not so.⟩ ↑But . . . antidote↓

23–25 ↑virtue & every↓ . . . our ⟨action⟩ ↑conduct↓

32–33   the ⟨eternity⟩ eternal . . . duty. ⟨It has no decaying smell⟩ The
                 ⟨circumstances⟩ ↑actor & the actions↓
35–37   Our ⟨opinions⟩ ↑habits↓ . . . grow /up/old/
38–(35)3   Seraph. ⟨What is there of materialism in that feeling? When you
                 calmly contemplate that one perception which has animated every
                 man since the creation of the world do you think you shall die? die out
                 of the Universe? die out of that perception? & die forever & ever?
                     It seems to me it is our hold on the eternal world It seems to me to
                 extend its own eternity to every mind it governs. In the immensity of
                 the future here is our anchor. But I am afraid ↑now↓ to touch this
                 topic for I cannot do justice to my own conceptions of its grandeur.—⟩
                 ↑Your . . . mind ⟨reverts⟩ ↑comes back↓ . . . precisely ⟨as⟩ ↑in yᵉ
                 measure yᵗ↓ . . . comforted↓ [This addition is on a slip of paper
                 secured to the right margin with red sealing wax; on the verso appears
                 the following:] ⟨I forbear⟩ I believe ⟨in the⟩ the duty of man to seek
                 always truth My opinions have continually been varied or modified in
                 my past life & I have every reason to believe they will contin[MS torn]
                 to alter.

                                        Page 35
4   there ⟨of mortality⟩ in

                                    Sermon XLVI

Manuscript: Four sheets folded to make four pages each; folios nested and sewn through
the center fold with black thread; pages measure 25 x 20.3 cm.

Lines   *Page 36*
Bible Text   hold ⟨of⟩ ↑upon↓
2   that ⟨from whats⟩ its ⟨doors⟩ ↑gates↓
7–9   ↑The individuals . . . survives ⟨& the procession of the faithful fills
                 the street⟩ & the church. ↑is filled↓↓ [The emendations within the
                 addition are in pencil.]

                                        Page 37
4   by ⟨their⟩ ↑your↓
7   a ⟨serene⟩ ↑pure↓
12   ↑or your . . . arms↓. [in pencil]
12–14   to a ↑undeceiving↓ love [addition in pencil] . . . multitude ⟨Come⟩of
                 the
20–21   place of ⟨sweet memories⟩ ↑pleasing recollections↓ & ⟨hallowed⟩
                 ↑unspotted↓
22   gratifications; ⟨that⟩ ↑who↓
32   you ⟨whet⟩ be
37–38   unbelieving [end of page] it . . . which ⟨offuscate⟩ ↑wrap↓
39   your ⟨rugged will⟩ ↑hard heart↓;

                                        Page 38
1   of ⟨the⟩ ↑obscure↓

4	↑now pretend to↓
6–7	↑always↓ . . . to ⟨congratulate one another⟩ ↑rejoice together↓
8–9	↑I . . . God,↓
14	mark, ⟨of⟩ ↑whereon↓ . . . act. ⟨T⟩ In
15–16	↑No . . . other⟨s⟩ beings . . . condition.↓
18–20	The ²elephant & the ¹horse . . . the ⟨nest⟩ ↑web↓ of the ⟨bird⟩ ↑spider,↓ or the ↑wild beast's arts of↓ hunting ⟨of the wild beast⟩ ↑his prey↓
21–22	the ⟨mark⟩ ↑boundary↓ . . . man ⟨*hopes* & *advances*⟩ improves
25	set,⟨"⟩
31–34	education, every ⟨new interpretation of⟩ ↑new . . . of na↓ nature, ↑every new art,↓ . . . ↑church & its↓. . . with ⟨mighty⟩ ↑incalculable↓ benefit to ⟨the race⟩ mankind.
35–38	we ⟨discover⟩ ↑find out↓ . . . pretension. ⟨The law of progress, the on-look of human nature, is its distinguishing & beautiful law⟩ And . . . ↑with . . . observation,↓ with all ⟨our⟩ ↑the↓ distrust ↑we have acquired↓ . . . novelties, / or ⟨of⟩ / and all/ romanc⟨es⟩ing

Page 39

3	he / stands ready to be/ is capable of being/
4–5	↑yᵗ yᵉ impediments . . . him;↓
8–13	¶ ↑I can speak for myself.↓ I, ⟨for one,⟩ ⟨↑myself↓⟩ believe . . . now ⟨amongst us⟩ ↑in the earth↓ . . . ↑in me↓ the hope ↑I have seen↓ . . . with ⟨that⟩ ↑such↓ . . . it↑s↓ . . . ↑the fervour of↓
13–17	ever ⟨bribed⟩ ↑warped↓ . . . satisfy ⟨our⟩ ↑the↓ craving ↑human↓ . . . ↑little↓
18	soul⟨s⟩ that inhabit↑s↓
19–20	has ⟨measured⟩ ↑computed↓ . . . guaged
21	↑the↓
25	↑Socrates &↓
26–27	the ⟨mountains⟩ ↑cornfields & vineyards↓ . . . insanity ⟨rages in⟩ ↑disturbs↓
34	↑England of↓ Asia o⟨r⟩f America
41–42	he ⟨p⟩has

Page 40

1–2	circuit. ⟨↑Ask him again⟩ Remind . . . intentions↓ And . . . he ⟨p⟩has
8	¶ For ⟨this is⟩ ↑these . . . are↓
10–11	↑fame . . . yᵉ↓ [addition in pencil] earth has nothing ↑in . . . is↓
12	it ⟨bears⟩ inherits
15–18	↑which prudence rebukes↓ in tha⟨e⟩at ⟨credulity⟩ ↑simplicity o↓ of ⟨all society⟩ ↑the public↓ . . . expect ⟨in⟩ an
20–22	Sabbath. ↑{Insert A} A {I . . . mysterious ⟨trust⟩ ↑feeling↓ . . . solemn ⟨expectation⟩ ↑confidence↓ . . . shroud.}↓ ["expectation" canceled and "confidence" added in pencil]

Sermon XLVII

Manuscript: Four sheets folded to make four pages each; folios nested and sewn along the left margin with white thread; pages measure 24.7 x 20 cm.

Lines	Page 41

Bible Text ↑He that hath no rule over his own spirit is like a city broken down and without walls Prov. 25 28↓ [rejected as a late addition as evidenced by its being written around a secondary set of hymn citations inscribed in pencil]

1-2 the ⟨full &⟩ faithful ⟨performance⟩ obedience . . . ↑of observance↓

3-6 ↑those . . . public↓ [addition in pencil] . . . ↑the importance of↓ each ⟨point of obedience⟩ ↑virtue↓ . . . appear /every/all/ other commandment↑s↓ ⟨was unnecessary⟩ ↑were superfluous↓,

17-(42)4 ↑mainly↓ . . . of ⟨our⟩ the man. ↑{Insert A} A {So ↑among↓ the ancient↑s, the↓ . . . which ⟨they⟩ ↑he↓ . . . ⟨P⟩Chilo—⟨r⟩Regard . . . Watch ⟨the opportunity⟩ ↑occasions↓. . . things. ⟨↑Another— ↓Love conquers all things.⟩ ↑Another . . . to↓ Bear & forbear. ⟨All which are true each⟩ ↑Now . . . considered↓ They . . . rest.}↓

Page 42

4-5 desireable . . . succession ⟨view⟩ consider

7 ancient ⟨philosophers⟩ ↑wisdom↓

11 city. ⟨This ↑is but↓ another form of expression of duty⟨,⟩—the ruling the spirit, the govt of yᵉ soul.⟩ Let

14 narrow & ⟨single⟩ ↑⟨unique⟩ single;↓ ⟨yᵉ direction of a single agent⟩ yᵉ

18-19 helm. ↑& as . . . by ⟨a⟩its ⟨single intelligence⟩ ↑own pilot↓↓ In

21-22 of /one/self/, for when ⟨the question⟩ you . . . this ⟨entire⟩ sole

24-26 to /protect/clear/ . . . says ⟨Does not every man ⟨who⟩ in every action whether you call it right or wrong do what he chuses but t⟩ The good . . . last & ⟨highest⟩ ↑strongest↓

28 conduct ⟨more than⟩ ↑over↓ another ⟨as⟩ ↑& call it↓ self-controul⟨ed⟩?

31-32 follow⟨,⟩ ↑one as another,↓ If . . . much ⟨⟨p⟩natural⟩ parts of my ↑natural↓

36-(43)8 ↑with it↓ . . . perception↑,↓ ⟨in every mind⟩ a . . . other ⟨feelings⟩ principles . . . *subjection of* [end of page] *of . . . its* ⟨least⟩ *feeblest . . . transgressed.* ¶ ⟨{When it is perfect as now & then once in a century comes a ruler of himself it not only governs the life but reaches every muscle of yᵉ face & appears in yᵉ physiognomy.}⟩ ¶ This . . . nature this . . . world ¶ ⟨It is a singularly safe & honorable property ↑There are numberless illustrations of it↑s value↓ in yᵉ ordinary life cases where degrees of it are attained under yᵉ influence of ordinary motives↓ Put⟩ ↑It . . . in ⟨yᵉ⟩ ordinary . . . ↑of it↓ . . . motives↓ ↑Put↓

Page 43

12-18 threw ⟨him⟩ ↑it↓ . . . he shall ⟨do well⟩ ↑escape danger;↓ . . . himself.⟩ ⟨In the⟩ ↑There are↓ common risks ⟨that men run particularly at sea⟩ ↑continually . . . seas↓ . . . that ⟨would⟩ appear . . . that ⟨could⟩ see↑s↓ . . . time ⟨Yet we see the survivors of fifty battles die in their beds⟩ and yᵗ . . . themselves wh. ⟨necessity⟩ has . . . ↑men↓ in many a↑n↓ ⟨stormy⟩ hour

20–22   way ⟨is seen⟩ of . . . hope ⟨yᵗ⟩ in . . . ↑in . . . Providence↓

23–25   account. ↑& . . . of a ⟨hundred⟩ twice . . . bed.↓

28–32   in ⟨dissimulation⟩ ↑manners↓ . . . portray ⟨it⟩ ↑namely yᵉ highbred fashionist↓ what . . . in ⟨that character⟩ ↑a person↓ . . . idle⟨—the high bred fashionist⟩. ⟨He⟩ ↑The fashionist↓

33–35   those ²fleeting & ¹local . . . & ⟨sometimes the conscience.⟩ ↑the rigour of principle.↓ . . . . of ⟨society⟩ ↑fashion↓

40   feelings ⟨&⟩ ↑or↓ expressions

Page 44

4–6   young ⟨men⟩ ↑& upon yᵉ mature & upon ⟨yᵉ⟩ grey hairs↓ . . . world. ↑simply . . . command.↓

7–9   ↑& fashion↓ ²have ¹all . . . command, ⟨as⟩ in

13   life, ⟨have⟩ the

20–21   the ⟨mind⟩ ↑soul↓ . . . gratifications; ⟨a st⟩ a war,

24–25   reason. ⟨My brethren you are surrounded with temptations oh abstain abstain abstain.⟩ ¶ ⟨It⟩ ↑Religion↓

26–27   good. And ⟨surely there is something⟩ ↑points . . . is↓ . . . ↑over . . . dominion,↓

34–40   were ⟨true⟩ ↑probable↓ . . . ↑our↓ . . . th⟨is⟩e . . . ↑self-collected↓ . . . a /foolish hazard of ourselves/licentious want of preparation & anarchy & disagreement among the principles./ [Second variant inscribed in pencil on the facing blank page:] /disagreement among the principles of action in our own bosom/ ¶ ⟨It is⟩ We

Page 45

2–3   ↑much . . . life↓

4–6   indulgence. ⟨If y⟩You ⟨are tempted to fretfulness to⟩ ↑perhaps . . . of a↓ a sulky & selfish humour. ⟨Upon th⟨at⟩e occasion↑s↓ when that is tried you must learn this grace.⟩ ↑Some . . . trial↓

8   or ⟨as⟩ if

13–14   man. ↑who . . . mastery.↓

14–15   is ⟨fretted⟩ ↑provoked↓ . . . ↑sometimes↓

19   keep /an iron/ceaseless/

25   oil yᵗ ⟨has⟩ is

27   left ⟨no ti⟩ myself

29–30   conscience ⟨is enthroned in your bosom⟩ ↑by . . . actions↓

32   your ⟨stern & blessed⟩ ↑immortal↓

33–34   ↑You ⟨have⟩ are . . . theirs.↓ [in pencil]

34–35   protected ⟨he has made thee strong in thyself.⟩ ↑His . . . thyself.—↓

38   philosophy. ⟨Oh no⟩ I

40   ↑O no↓

42   the ⟨monitory⟩ kind monition of the /Lords supper/ordinances of religion/, ["ordinances of religion" in pencil; probably a late variant, after 1832]

Sermon XLVIII

Manuscript: Five sheets folded to make four pages each; first three folios nested, followed by two stacked folios; first leaf of the second folio has been cut out, the stubs bearing evidence of writing on both sides (the text, however, is continuous). Sewn through the center fold of the nested folios and along the left margin to attach the stacked folios, all with white thread; pages measure 25 x 20.3 cm.

Lines	*Page 46*
Bible Text	↑Who shall ascend into yᵉ hill of yᵉ Lord or who shall stand in his holy place. He yᵗ hath clean hands & a pure heart—He shall receive yᵉ blessing from yᵉ Lord— Ps 24. 3.4.5.↓ [written in ink over a hymn number ("89") in pencil; rejected as a late addition]
2–3	Works. ↑to . . . soul.↓ ⟨Wh⟩ It
5–6	Thus ⟨in⟩ the . . . ↑(↓which . . . Christians↑)↓ [additions in pencil]
10–11	radical ⟨difficulty⟩ doubt
11–15	circumstances. ⟨{As the human understanding is finite it must somewhere find limits it cannot pass difficulties it cannot explain uncertainties it cannot remove.}⟩ ¶ When . . . a ⟨[illegible]⟩ ↑particular↓ . . . when ⟨in all⟩ on . . . to ⟨point in⟩ ↑take one &↓ . . . concluded ⟨not⟩ that ⟨there⟩ this is not ⟨a partial⟩ ↑an accidental↓
16–19	the ⟨concl⟩ speculations . . . perhaps ⟨very⟩ inadequate.
21	Works.) ⟨I am not so vain as to⟩ ↑In . . . not↓
23–26	Still ⟨the pulpit is the proper organ of common sense on this topic⟩ ↑I . . . me,↓ . . . inquiry upon [end of page] [At this point one leaf has been removed; both recto and verso of the remaining stub show evidence of writing, though no words have been recovered.] upon . . . lost. ¶ ⟨He ⟨thu⟩ reads his history of privation & abasement & insult & disappointment & pain all borne with a steady self devotion for the sake of mankind
	⟨His⟩ He reads the precepts the rules of life which he taught & his heart responds to their truth & /acknowledges/owns/ that he taught as one having authority
	⟨He finds that certain simple observances were authorized by him as excitements of religious feeling & he complies with them.⟩⟩ ↑upon . . . lost.↓ [end of page]
	⟨Well now if he asks himself what does God require of him ⟨H⟩he answers a simple obedience in his whole life to the laws of natural religion. And if he is asked what additional obligations has Xty imposed? He answers, nothing is my duty now that was not my duty before but I see it plainer & therefore do it with more cheerfulness & surer conviction.⟩ ¶ I believe
	Page 47
1–2	¶ ↑The question . . . ↑to our salvation↓ than ↑simple↓ obedience ↑to the moral laws.↓↓ ["to our salvation" and "simple" added in ink over pencil; "to the moral laws" written in ink over "to yᵉ ⟨Divine laws⟩ moral laws." in pencil]

7–10   safe. ↑all . . . course.↓ [addition in pencil] ¶ ⟨The⟩ ↑This . . . into↓
        two great classes ⟨of⟩ ↑as↓ Xns, among us, ⟨divide upon this more
        than upon any point &⟩ ↑The defender of↓ [addition in pencil]
        ↑Each party↓ take↑s↓ ⟨their⟩ ↑its↓ departure ⟨each⟩ from o⟨f⟩ne of
12   own ⟨point of⟩ view
15   is ⟨meant⟩ ↑contended for↓
16–18   certain ⟨expressed⟩ ↑statements of↓ doctrine⟨s⟩ . . . ↑merely↓
20   works↑,↓ [addition in pencil]
23–26   ¶ ↑I believe . . . a very partial {Insert A} {A} {a very partial . . .
        consideration.}↓ Still ↑if . . . commended↓
35–36   end [end of page] the . . . well ⟨of⟩ as of the useful. ⟨g⟩Good
38–40   ↑or profane or complaining↓ . . . even ⟨of the will⟩ to . . . *Every*
        ⟨exertion⟩ *act*

Page 48

2–3   them. ¶ ⟨And why then it is asked does Christ & his apostles lay so
        much stress on faith? Jesus [end of page] Believe on me, & the
        apostles say Believe. ⟨By⟩ ↑The↓ faith that Paul & the apostles teach
        is simply the belief in the great truths of Christianity an *operative*
        faith, and a faith that bears fruit in works is ye only good & true one.
            I too am ye advocate of faith. The doctrine of works that we are
        urging implies a faith without which they could not exist and all that I
        wish to condemn is any separation any exalting of faith apart from
        action.⟩ ¶ No
4–6   no ⟨plea⟩ ↑claim↓ . . . distinction. ¶ ⟨Another Christian thinks this a
        cold & imperfect statement of duty. He thinks Christianity a great
        deal more than a declaration of the immortality of the soul & of
        human accountableness. He thinks there is a certain *faith* beside a
        disposition to do its works. He feels he says the need of something
        more. And he finds that the Saviour & his apostles insist on some-
        thing more.
            I believe this difference of opinion grows from ye observation y^t
        good actions may be done from bad motives. It is the same evil which
        we indicate when we treat of the importance of principles as dis-
        tinguished from actions. But whether apart from virtue—apart from
        virtue practised for virtues sake there be any requisition of the gospel
        may be questioned.⟩ ¶ ↑But↓ Every
8–11   point. ⟨The doctrine of the virtue of⟩ ↑There . . . in↓ . . . ↑& this
        doctrine↓ . . . when ⟨its brother errors⟩ ↑the other . . . Error↓
11–12   Luther ⟨indeed⟩ ↑even↓ . . . epistle ⟨maintains⟩ ↑sets forth↓
16   ↑These . . . comment.↓
18–21   so, ⟨blinded⟩ ⟨↑callous↓⟩ ↑insensible↓ . . . that ⟨has any⟩ speaks
        . . . find any ⟨confidence⟩ respect.
22   ↑for↓ . . . & ⟨effectual⟩ ↑humble↓
25   hell.) ⟨All the theology in the world⟩ Intervals
27–28   ↑And if↓ In ⟨some⟩ ↑any↓ . . . ↑we . . . here↓.
37   the ⟨models & monuments⟩ ↑body↓
37–(49)1 presence they . . . the ⟨giver⟩ ↑doer,↓

Page 49

3   ↑shd.↓

7   virtue ⟨by our best hours & in general⟩ by . . . our ⟨works⟩
            ↑performance↓.

8   ↑a↓ momentary

13-15   ↑Then . . . hours & what . . . merit.↓

17   up ⟨its shells⟩ a month ago↑;↓ ⟨in some unusual inundation⟩ but

20   your ⟨m⟩ Master

22   Christianity ⟨that it⟩ &

24   sai⟨th⟩d

27-28   ↑tongue of↓ . . . of ⟨might⟩ power.

34-35   ↑Faith adds . . . God↓ Faith ⟨is the⟩ teaches ⟨of the duty of Prayer⟩
            ↑us to *pray*↓

35-36   Affection ⟨The⟩ reason dictates ⟨duty⟩ ↑works:↓ . . . reason ⟨dic-
            tates⟩ ↑prescribes↓

37   pleasant. ↑Works are the clean hands Faith is the pure heart.↓ Works
            [rejected as a late addition, corresponding to the inserted sermon text
            from Psalms 24; see the first note above]

38   ↑&, as I believe,↓

40-(50)6   God. ⟨For the highest & ⟨finest⟩ ↑best↓ aspect in which man can be
            contemplated, is in his connexion with God, aiming at a conformity
            with his Will.⟩ ¶ ⟨I conceive that works m⟩ ↑Let . . . that↓ . . . live
            ⟨together⟩ ↑blended in one character↓ . . . man. ⟨I believe that the
            light of⟩ ↑Therefore↓ . . . exhibits ⟨a better effect⟩ a better . . .
            man↑'s nature . . . him↓ . . . religion. ↑(B) B {the effect . . . circum-
            stances ⟨is⟩ ↑can↓ . . . considered.}↓

Page 50

8-11   ↑where . . . together↓ . . . ↑Hume &↓ Voltaire ⟨& Montesquieu⟩
            left

13-14   which ⟨hope⟩ ↑interest↓ . . . nor ⟨falsehood⟩ ↑sophistry↓

25-26   trust, ⟨the⟩ when . . . in ⟨our⟩ the

27   effort ⟨to do his Will.—⟩ of

Sermon XLIX

Manuscript: One sheet folded to make four pages, followed by four sheets folded to
make four pages each, folios nested; first leaf of the first nested folio has been cut out,
with the loss of a portion of the canceled text that continues onto MS pp. 5-6. Sewn with
white thread along the left margin; pages measure 25 x 20.3 cm.

Lines   *Page 51*
Bible Text   ↑forgetting those things wh. are behind & reaching forth to those wh.
                are before I press toward yᵉ mark for yᵉ prize of yᵉ high calling of God
                in Xt. Jesus↓ [This second sermon text, from Philippians 3:13, is
                rejected as a late addition.]

4   our ⟨psalms⟩ ↑psalms↓?

7-8   ↑See . . . time. Eph V. 15.↓ [set off by a large bracket to the left]

10   by ⟨b⟩which

12   die? of [end of page] of
13   are / pushed forward / disciplined /
16   & ⟨common end.⟩ ↑plain purpose↓
17–18   ↑like . . . body↓ . . . made ⟨for growth⟩ ↑itself to use all↓

Page 52

4   acted↑;↓ & ↑for this↓
9   eternal ⟨orbit⟩ ↑round↓,—
23–25   ↑the level of↓ . . . lower. [end of MS p. 4] ⟨we are afflicted; for this we
            are ⟨prospered⟩ ↑rejoiced; It is designed↓ to show us practically &
            every moment that we are not creatures of necessity but creatures of
            free will, improvable beings not moving like the silent orb⟨s of
            heaven⟩ ↑we tread upon↓ in an inextricable circle but going back-
            ward or going forward in ⟨the spiritual world which is our home⟩
            ↑our moral career↓ at our own free choice, & just as far & as fast as
            we will.
                ⟨The vegetable is formed of the ⟨same⟩ particles of a decaying
            vegetable & grows up & decays & its particles are ↑only↓
            reproduced in a new form.⟩
                For this we are introduced to all this variety of character taught the
            elements of so many arts & the idioms of so many languages for this
            we are introduced to all this variety of character
                Yet who remembers this when he rises in the morning & when he
            lies down at night ⟨when h⟩ Who carries this thought with him as his
            motive, as the companion of his soul, his one dear & eternal solace
            when he begins his work, when he goes to his store, when he enters
            his family, when he retires to his chamber; when he is excited, ⟨when
            he is⟩ ↑and↓ tempted, ⟨when he is⟩ ↑and↓ bereaved, ⟨when he is⟩
            ↑and↓ prospered. ↑I do not deny that↓ there are such men, but they
            are few ↑{That he is made to be improved by every hour of his life}↓⟩
            ¶ ↑But↓ In . . . practi⟨s⟩ce
26   indeed ⟨assent⟩ ↑yield a heedless approbation↓ to ⟨these⟩ ↑pure↓
28–31   not to ⟨the⟩ ↑our↓ limited but to ⟨the⟩ ↑our↓ . . . not ⟨merely⟩
            verbal
33   ↑probably↓
35   the / popular account / account yᵗ ⟨passes⟩ ↑goes↓ current in our
            common speculations /.
37   occasional ⟨m⟩ rule
40   But ⟨no,⟩ see
40–(53)9   a ⟨mortal⟩ ↑severe↓ . . . house; ⟨when we lie down without hope in
            our bed⟩ when . . . then ⟨for the first⟩ men . . . ↑now . . . end,↓ . . .
            by ⟨me⟩ ↑us↓? ⟨That mans religion is vain.⟩ ↑It . . . at ⟨atonement,
            or remorse.⟩ ↑penitence, . . . remorse↓↓ ¶ ⟨It is of ⟨vast⟩ ↑great
            practical↓ importance that our views of ↑what↓ Religion ↑means↓
            shd. be ⟨right⟩ ↑sound↓. For it is ↑our opinion of what is↓ the
            health↑y state↓ of the faculties. ↑Tho' our practice may be faulty we
            must yet regard↓ The⟨ir⟩ religious life ⟨i⟩as the perfection of man
            ⟨which always we seek⟩ ⟨& never fully attain a point yᵗ always

outruns us⟩ ⟨↑and always flies before us↓⟩ ↑I speak not now of any
sect of Xns but of every sect ↑And↓ It will not do to have a low
standard, for the actions will always be lower. ↑I speak of that which
is independent of speculative opinions & above all speculation↓↓⟩ ¶
But

Page 53

14–18	↑the sum of↓ . . . religion—⟨its⟩ the . . . principle ⟨of⟩ ↑that makes↓ such lofty pretensions. ↑as religion certainly does.↓
19–22	h⟨u⟩igher . . . country, ⟨than⟩ ↑as↓
25–26	indisputable ⟨evidence⟩ ↑testimony↓
29–30	{A . . . hid.}
31–33	from ⟨day⟩ month . . . ↑its↓
36–38	↑neither that . . . observances↓ find any support ⟨in the teaching of Christ or⟩ in ⟨the general fact that God sent a revelation of his will⟩ ↑reason, . . . itself↓ ⟨It⟩ The
41–⟨54⟩2	faith, ⟨a⟩ ↑no↓ . . . but ⟨watchfulness⟩ ⟨↑denial↓⟩ ↑beneficence↓,

Page 54

8–9	When↑ever↓ Christianity ↑shall have↓ produce⟨s⟩d . . . upon ⟨the⟩ ↑human↓
11	comprehend ⟨whatever is best in these names⟩ the
13–18	¶ {When [bracket in pencil] . . . of ⟨a⟩ ↑yᵉ faithful . . . & ⟨of yʳ⟩they were rewarded; ⟨but yᵉ⟩ & of a↓ slothful servant ⟨who⟩ ↑who↓ . . . when ⟨the⟩ ↑a↓ . . . he sa⟨ys⟩id to . . . hast ⟨that⟩ ↑what↓ . . . was ⟨wroth⟩ ↑angry↓
23	unconfirmed ⟨in your own experience.⟩ ↑to any breast.↓
23–24	own ⟨life⟩ ↑experience↓
26	allegory.} [bracket in pencil]
27–28	["We shd redeem" is written in pencil in the space between the lines "And . . . aim?" and "It . . . *standeth*."]
31–34	↑that . . . better—↓ . . . its /slander⟨ous⟩/malice/ [variant in pencil] but also its ⟨romancing &⟩ exaggeration ↑& folly↓; [emendations in pencil]
35–38	{If . . . that ⟨truth⟩ ↑virtue↓ . . . will.}
39	most ⟨craving appetite for⟩ ↑zealous pursuit of↓

Page 55

1	all, ⟨his⟩ [end of page] God
4–6	↑all action, a restraint of↓ . . . includes ⟨all virtue⟩ all
9–10	impertinent ⟨or inapplicable⟩ topic.
11	duty⟨,⟩; [The original comma is not canceled but lost in the interlined addition that follows as the next sentence. Not seeing it, Emerson inserted a semicolon.]
11–12	↑Men . . . But ⟨splendid virtues are still more rare⟩ will . . . virtues↓
14–15	↑Only make a ⟨set⟩ rigid . . . commandment.↓
19	you ⟨entered⟩ bro't

23–31   ↑Cultivate . . . you.↓ . . . cheerful & ⟨excellent⟩ ennobling . . .
         world ⟨& gives you opportunity for a never ending succession of
         these triumphs⟩ ↑& shows . . . progress↓ . . . the ⟨means of surpass-
         ing intellect that [one word illegible]⟩ ⟨↑great souls↓⟩ ↑great↓ ↑souls
         . . . them↓ . . . to ⟨put your⟩ carry up your ↑individual↓ . . . trial
         ⟨cheerful⟩ ↑pleasant↓

35–36   ↑to leave . . . temptations↓

37–39   more. ⟨Let him that thinketh he standeth take heed lest he fall.⟩
         ↑↑See↓ The . . . day↓ [cancellation and additions in pencil]

Sermon L

Manuscript: Four sheets folded to make four pages each; folios nested and sewn with
white thread through the center fold; pages measure 25 x 20.3 cm.

Lines   *Page 56*

3   air ⟨see⟩ are

5–7   of ⟨government⟩ ↑of society,↓ . . . Sabbath, ¶ And

21   begin ⟨with⟩ where

25   animals—If ⟨they⟩ ↑it↓

                                 Page 57

6–7   with ⟨an⟩ ↑more flexible↓ application to life ⟨which⟩ ↑than↓ . . .
         could ⟨not⟩ have

10   ↑all the virtue &↓ [in pencil]

11   fold. ⟨Nor⟩ ⟨then⟩ ↑Neither↓ . . . comprehended all↑;↓ [emenda-
         tions in pencil]

12   as [end of page] forefathers

13   striking /ceremony/rite/

14–19   ↑The↓ Time ⟨w⟩has ⟨when⟩ ↑been↓ . . . when ⟨very⟩ ↑gross↓ . . .
         ordinance; ↑{Insert A.} A {It . . . unworthily.}↓ And [Emerson's
         clipped reference to I Corinthians 11:29 is here supplemented from
         the Bible to make a grammatically complete sentence; no doubt
         Emerson supplied the missing portion of the verse from memory
         during his delivery.]

33   exhibited ⟨amaz⟩ in

36–37   & /stilled/calmed/ . . . ↑glowing with awe↓

39   ²original ↑in his times↓, ⟨as ¹rare,⟩ as his miracles. ↑Yet with what
         success?↓—⟨Yet⟩ all

                                 Page 58

5–6   who⟨se⟩ had . . . not ⟨obliterate th⟩ shake

10–17   remembrance. ⟨Whilst he foresaw⟩ ↑He . . . foresee↓ . . . expected
         ⟨fr to⟩ from . . . ↑he↓ would teach; ↑but↓ . . . ↑that acknowledged
         him↓ . . . a ⟨board⟩ table . . . pledge ⟨a remembrancer⟩ a rebuke, a
         remembrancer. ¶ /He must have felt/With . . . feel/ [variant in
         pencil] . . . to ⟨the⟩ ↑every↓

24–30   It . . . history. [sentence lacks internal punctuation in the MS] ↑And
     . . . assuming ⟨a more spiritual⟩ & . . . character.↓ ["in conformity
     with all true and natural" inscribed in pencil above the addition] ¶ ↑I
     . . . alike↓ [addition in pencil]

34   authority of [end of page] of Xty & not as ⟨at⟩ now

37   better↑.↓ ⟨not to⟩ To

38   It ⟨argues⟩ does

Page 59

3–4   ↑under God↓ . . . in ⟨even its⟩ personal

5   desireable

10–12   come; because . . . see a⟨ny⟩ Christian ⟨put⟩ ↑or a Christian Church
     put↓ a⟨ny⟩ bar

16   sinners↑.↓ ⟨to repentance.⟩ I

19–21   up ⟨I⟩ & my . . . ↑in . . . world↓ . . . nobler or of of . . . I ⟨know⟩
     ↑understand↓

27–31   come. ↑⟨In a⟩ As . . . door.↓ ¶ ⟨I think this view of the ordinance that
     it is simply a means of improvement just as coming to church—is not
     only the truest view but the view likely to produce the most advan-
     tage. ↑It will most pro⟨b⟩fitably direct our meditation ⟨at the⟩
     around the table↓ It will teach us to use this privelege with humility &
     prayer that we may not dishonour it. ⟨It will most profitably direct
     our meditations at the supper⟩ to walk in the world as having received
     the light of another—as the zealous yet unassuming followers of the
     meek & lowly son of the Almighty Father, who coming out from him
     & the spiritual world bro't to the human soul the hope of ⟨immortal⟩
     immortal life the sanction of duty, & the joyful doctrine that man
     may do the will of God.⟩ ¶ My

32   as ⟨com⟩ attendance

Page 60

4   privelege

Sermon LI

Manuscript: One loose leaf followed by three sheets folded to make four pages each;
folios nested and sewn with white thread through the center fold; pages measure 25 x
20.3 cm. Between the first and second leaves is a loose sheet, 20.8 x 17 cm, inscribed on
one side, which does not appear to belong with this sermon. For further description, see
textual note to p. 62, line 10, below.

Lines   *Page 61*

7   idea⟨s⟩ of

13–14   action, we . . . recognize his [end of page] his being

18   theology↑, i.e. our description of God↓

20   purity ⟨& streng⟩truth

22   every ⟨mans⟩ ↑one's↓

Page 62

1	else⟨,⟩ than
4	↑which↓
7–8	↑& living by them↓.
8	And ⟨it seems to me I may say⟩ ↑yet it is↓
10	him. ↑{Insert X}↓ [No insert marked "X" occurs with this sermon, although laid in at this point is a loose sheet with marginal traces of red sealing wax; this sheet, however, was never attached to any page of the present manuscript. It also lacks the central vertical fold present on all other leaves of the fascicle, which suggests that it must have been laid in some time after the delivery of the sermon.] ↑↑They form a burden of evidence wh. I cannot withstand↓ Yet true it is that in the face of all the adoring universe of conspiring facts the fool hath said in his heart there is no God. In the powerful language of yᵉ modern poet

> Forth from his dark & lonely hiding place
> The owlet Atheism sailing athwart the noon
> Drops his blue fringed lids & holds them close
> And hooting at the glorious s[word obscured by sealing wax] he
> Cries out, ⟨w⟩Where is it?

It is the madness of the mind but I believe God never gave up any to it whose heart was not first depraved. I
I had rather said the great Lord Bacon. And therefore God never wrot a miracle to convince Atheism for his ordinary works convince it↓ I am sure

11	As ⟨this idea⟩ his
13–15	a ⟨man⟩ ↑person↓ . . . a ⟨man⟩ ↑person↓ . . . a ⟨man⟩ ↑person↓
21–22	perversion—⟨the⟩ ↑⟨when⟩ ↑when . . . caution↓ the young and aspiring ⟨were cautioned⟩ against↓
23–24	ashamed of ⟨his blood⟩ ⟨breathing⟩ ↑the . . . blood,↓ be ashamed ↑of breathing, or↓ of using his memory. ↑To be ashamed of religion!↓
32–33	privelege . . . priveleges . . . frivolous ⟨to⟩compared
39	earth ⟨was⟩ sickening

Page 63

1–6	when ⟨he⟩ ↑men came↓ wisely ↑to↓ consider⟨ed⟩ th⟨is⟩eir condi-tion, ↑I fear↓ the ⟨world⟩ ↑earth↓ would ⟨be offensive⟩ ↑smell↓ with ⟨the smell of⟩ suicide.— ¶ ↑{It . . . curable ⟨& th⟩ man's . . . improvable.}↓
23	↑mind,↓
28–29	↑He sees . . . convictions↓
29–30	light ⟨of the spiritual⟩ & converses
32–33	man ⟨with like capacities to himself,⟩ ↑as he is↓ . . . recieve
35–36	¶ Brethren ⟨I desire⟩ ↑we . . . ought↓ habitually to exalt ⟨your⟩ ↑each other's↓ views ⟨ & my own⟩ of
37–(64)1	himself. ↑{Insert A} A ⟨Brethren⟩ {↑We know yᵗ th↓ [addition in pencil] The connex. of yᵉ ⟨soul⟩ ↑mind↓ . . . propor. . . . ↑in them↓. . . . God.—}↓

Page 64

3–4   ↑in our sins↓ we are dead ⟨in our⟩ sins that [emendations in pencil]

5–6   ↑if↓ . . . die. ¶ ⟨Our connexion with God. ¶ The connexion of the
mind with God is the measure of all its solid good, and to every well
ordered spirit things will seem well or ill in proportion as the presence
of God is manifest. In society, there is a great deal of frivolity. A great
many men & women spend a large part of life in the debate and the
performance of insignificant things. They look grave & deliberate at
questions whether they shall go out, or come in,—what they shall
eat—how they shall dress—when it is of no importance how they
decide & disgusts every serious person. It disgusts because it indicates
the absence of God.

In society there is a great deal of sensuality. The moment the
satisfaction of the natural appetites passes the boundary of necessity,
intemperance & sensuality begin. ⟨The moment they begin⟩ And we
pamper the body to the slaying of the soul. Every one may remember
how inconsistent with the fervours of piety are the fumes of wine &
the oppression of a feast.⟩ ¶ Now

7–8   growing ⟨connexion⟩ ↑union↓ with ⟨God⟩ ↑our Father↓.

16   it ⟨in yr⟩ ↑derived from↓

21–24   immeasureable . . . study & ⟨action⟩ ↑observation↓

28–30   those ⟨loose⟩ disjointed . . . of ⟨mighty⟩ ↑tremendous↓

Page 65

3   the ⟨p⟩ devotion

5   solace & ⟨hope⟩ in ⟨extreme⟩ ↑the↓ . . . & ↑⟨sober⟩ calm↓

9–10   light—↑The way . . . him↓

Sermon LII

Manuscript: Four sheets folded to make four pages each; folios nested and sewn through
the center fold with white thread; pages measure 25 x 20.3 cm.

Lines   *Page 66*

2–3   duties ⟨Few of us⟩ ↑In . . . many↓ . . . mar↑t↓yrdoms . . . benefitting ⟨countries⟩ ↑states↓.

4–9   ↑opportunity of↓ . . . ↑to . . . given↓ . . . of ↑great↓ . . . our
⟨performance⟩ use

11–12   much ⟨it⟩ we . . . attention ⟨brethren⟩ my [The entire paragraph is
in ink over pencil; the pencil version is as follows:] One of the chief of
our powers is that of speech. An old & familiar subject—but its
interest can never be exhausted. What we do so much we ought to do
well. And I wish to invite your attention to some considerations on the
use & enjoyment of conversation & ⟨the⟩ upon the duties that belong
to it.

15   ↑detail of↓ wonderful

17–18   speech—⟨the⟩ which . . . the ⟨power⟩ instruction

19–21   ↑impenetrable↓ . . . inaccessible ⟨secrets of the⟩ soul

24-(67)1   ↑We . . . men. ↑& yet we see . . . lessened.↓↓ ["& yet we s" in ink over pencil]

Page 67

3   persons ⟨that⟩ by
10-13   tho' ⟨imperfect⟩ ↑almost . . . the ⟨general⟩ ↑active↓ world of men↓ . . . speech. ⟨I was thinking of those that shd have none to illustrate the value of the accomplishment,⟩ ↑To . . . state↓
14-15   signs. ⟨They stand⟩ ↑You may place them↓ side by side ⟨it may be⟩ ↑if you will↓
18   the ⟨mind⟩ ↑heart↓
20   this ⟨infancy⟩ ↑unformed sufferer↓ with the ⟨gifted⟩ ↑finished↓
22   roll⟨ed⟩. Society
27   They ²alter and ¹modify
34-37   ↑Under↓ The . . . musters & his thot's ↑more vigorously,↓ . . . before; ⟨& so⟩ corrects . . . conclusions; ⟨thus "waxing wiser than himself"⟩ & so
38-39   {Bacon . . . smother."}
40-41   of ⟨pulpit⟩ ↑this↓ dis⟨cussion⟩↑course↓
41-(68)2   has ⟨a⟩one . . . ↑natural↓ . . . The ⟨great gifts⟩ ↑profound wisdom↓

Page 68

5-8   ↑practical↓ . . . proverbs. ⟨They are in⟩ These . . . are ⟨an⟩ ↑a part of the↓ . . . this ⟨generation⟩ ↑age↓ from all the past ⟨ages⟩ ↑generations↓
11-12   distant ⟨&⟩times & ⟨lands. No⟩ ↑countries↓
12-13   ↑single↓ . . . ↑by himself,↓
15   the ⟨better⟩ ↑wiser↓
16-20   ↑all↓ our traffic;— . . . actions. ¶ ⟨It becomes us⟩ ¶ It . . . ↑not↓ to feel how it ⟨lightens⟩ ↑diminishes↓ the ⟨load⟩ ↑burden↓ . . . remember ⟨how reason & truth come recommended⟩ ↑how↓
21-24   is a [end of line] a pleasure ↑a luxury↓ . . . from ⟨fine⟩ ↑listening to the↓ conversation. ↑of . . . they ⟨are⟩ possess ⟨this⟩ ↑to any high degree↓ talent of communicating th⟨is⟩eir tho'ts.↓
26   of ⟨conversation⟩ ↑this art↓
28-30   the ⟨hearer⟩ ↑listener↓ . . . immortality—⟨beyond the virtue⟩ ↑with . . . that of↓ of
33-34   ↑all of us down to↓ . . . ↑It . . . life.↓
34-36   ↑penal↓ . . . ↑found to be↓ . . . privation ⟨too⟩ intolerable for human⟨ity⟩ ↑nature↓.
37-39   gossip ⟨finds⟩ ⟨↑derives↓⟩ ⟨↑or the tenant of the almshouse⟩ ↑in . . . infirmities↓ derives↓ . . . feelings ⟨to attentive ears⟩ which [last cancellation in pencil]

Page 69

2   its ⟨enjoyme⟩ pleasure
3-10   Conversation. ¶ ⟨In⟩ ↑With↓ . . . ↑is↓ . . . ↑sadly↓ sore side to ⟨the⟩

Conversation. ⟨It⟩ ↑The tongue↓ ⟨is the organ of instruction solace
joy rebuke⟨s⟩ encouragement⟩ ↑instructs . . . encourages,↓ . . .
rails, ⟨lies⟩ flatters, . . . theirs. ↑⟨It is what we do every day.⟩ Our
. . . angels. ⟨And each of us brethren are every day taking a part in
it⟩↓ It [cancellations in pencil]

17	which ⟨we find⟩ we
23–24	↑when . . . wrong-headed↓
27	it. ↑Let . . . breast.↓
30	↑& not you↓ that wins, ⟨& not you⟩ &
31–32	you. ⟨&⟩ ↑But↓ . . . by ⟨truth⟩ ⟨in the ardour of dispute⟩ ↑fair argument↓
33–35	↑high a Xn↓ . . . the ⟨ardour⟩ ↑zeal↓ . . . ⟨cheer⟩↑joy↓fully . . . ↑of his adversary.↓ It is brave & ⟨magnanimous⟩ ↑Christian↓
36–37	↑It was . . . him↓ [addition in pencil]
40	will f take

Page 70

2–5	them. ¶ ⟨Theres a good deal of poor quarrelsome controversy⟩ ↑We . . . what ⟨bald⟩ ↑low↓ . . . talking degrading &↓
6–7	How ignorant ↑I wd yᵗ men wd consider yᵗ↓ Every . . . utter ⟨is injurious to⟩ ↑recoils . . . of↓
9	as ⟨briskly as you can⟩ ↑sharply↓. But ⟨stop⟩ It
12	↑I know↓ There
16	↑by your forbearance↓
17–18	↑The . . . yᵐselves↓ [in pencil]
24–25	but ⟨not⟩ ↑never↓ by ⟨vituperation.⟩ ↑angry words↓
28	other. ⟨God has given to few of us the ability⟩ We
31	power to of wit

Sermon LIII

Manuscript: Four sheets folded to make four pages each; folios nested and sewn through the center fold with white thread. Leaf containing Insert "A" (verso blank) attached by red sealing wax to upper and lower right margin of MS p. 2 (now loose). Pages, including insert, measure 25 x 20.3 cm.

Lines   *Page 71*

4	new. towards
5	finite↑,↓ [addition in pencil]
9–12	necessity ⟨must⟩ knows . . . the ⟨robber⟩ ↑housebreaker↓ or the pirate ⟨as⟩ with . . . violence ⟨We⟩ When
15	own ⟨action⟩ ↑purposes↓
16	do⟨e⟩th
18	is ⟨a ve⟩ not
19	not ⟨come⟩ ↑belong↓
21–22	far as ⟨he is free⟩ ⟨↑far as↓⟩ his
25–(72)3	There ⟨are⟩ ↑have been↓ . . . ↑of men↓ . . . the ⟨actor⟩ ↑doer↓ . . . stage ⟨to the wit of Shakespeare⟩ ↑is . . . of ⟨the tragedy⟩ his drama↓,

Page 72

4-17   them. ¶ ⟨⟨All⟩Each of us ⟨are⟩is to render up an account of our
          ⟨actions⟩ ↑for himself↓. None of us can by any means redeem his
          brother nor will any intercession that is not founded & seconded
          upon our own exertion be of any avail It is very important [stray letter
          "a" above "important"] that we shd not mistake a ↑forced &↓ passive
          virtue for an active virtue—an unresisting assent in our words &
          actions to the strong current of society when it sets in towards moral
          observances for the difficult & honourable merit of a ⟨religious life⟩
          Christian character.⟩

          ⟨A monk who should freely submit himself to the religious aus-
          terities of the order of La Trappe would excite more admiration than
          the same conduct in brother of that order⟩

          ⟨This is a familiar fact which has great importance in determining
          our estimates of virtue. ⟨↑A↓⟩ {Every outward influence that acted
          upon a man must be taken into the account & goes so far to diminish
          the praise of virtue or our condemnation of his vice.}⟩

          ↑{Insert A} A {All . . . And so ⟨even⟩ the . . . blessings↓ ¶ ⟨Yet⟩
          ⟨i⟩In the course of ⟨Gods Providence⟩ ↑events↓

19-23   [stray phrase "yᵉ character" above "produce a"] . . . highest ⟨gifts⟩
          graces of character ⟨↑Insert A↓⟩ ↑Every . . . or ⟨our⟩ ↑the↓ . . .
          God.↓

26   ¶ ↑I . . . best↓

29   astray. ⟨And⟩ "⟨a⟩As

30-32   that ⟨the⟩ some ⟨s⟩ circumstances . . . to ⟨virtue⟩ a good . . .
          vices↑, barriers↓

33-35   ↑degree of↓ exposure⟨s⟩ of . . . in /middle life/frugal competence/
          . . . young ⟨man⟩ ↑person↓ . . . an ⟨orphan⟩ neglected orphan in
          ⟨vicious society.⟩ the

40-41   underived. ⟨So it is with⟩ ↑The . . . in↓

Page 73

1-2   life. ⟨o⟩One . . . another—⟨but⟩ does

4   practised⟨,⟩ out

9   life ⟨it is which⟩ in

11   A⟨s⟩ man

14-20   ↑popular↓ charities. We ⟨admire⟩ ↑praise↓ popular men. We ⟨give in⟩
          ↑assent to↓ to prevalent ↑political↓ . . . without ⟨thinking⟩ ↑re-
          flecting↓ . . . the ⟨original &⟩ sovereign . . . that ⟨not⟩ the public ↑is
          . . . account,↓ . . . must↑;↓ ⟨render up his account;⟩ not society but
          each ⟨member is to go to⟩ ↑man . . . of↓ heaven or ⟨t⟩o↑f↓ hell.

24-26   ↑Not . . . prevails—↓ [in ink over pencil; pencil version lacks punc-
          tuation and underscoring]

27   virtuous ⟨habits are⟩ ↑conduct is↓

29-31   ²favorable ¹circumstances ↑to it↓, . . . the ⟨practices⟩ ↑actions↓

31   that ⟨the⟩ ↑virtuous↓

33-34   the ⟨natural⟩ original . . . ↑that . . . light↓ . . . reflected ⟨light gives⟩
          ↑goodness is but a↓ dim & waning ⟨beams⟩ ↑ray↓.

36–37   Paris. ¶ ⟨It is a pale & sickly growth But⟩ ↑If . . . ground?↓ [addition
                in ink over pencil] ⟨t⟩The merit
39   any ⟨th⟩ less
40–(74)4   blood— ⟨Yet I need not say how much better it would be that we shd
                be *virtuous* than innocent that each of⟩ ↑that . . . not ⟨required⟩
                ↑enough↓ [Emerson may perhaps have intended to cancel "to be"
                also.] . . . of us↓ us, in . . . around, ⟨than⟩ ↑—& not↓ . . . according
                ⟨as their waters were⟩ ↑to their own contents↓ . . . ↑waters↓.

                              Page 74
6–10   others. ⟨ / Yes we / We ought indeed to / feel grateful to Heaven⟩ ↑It is
                good that↓ [cancellation and addition in pencil] for all the ⟨consent⟩
                ↑tendency↓ . . . ↑interested↓ . . . ↑↑who . . . so↓ [in ink over pencil]
                or . . . do↓ compared with the ⟨glorious⟩ athletic
11–12   ↑This . . . selfexistent↓ [addition in pencil]
17–23   expressed,—⟨It⟩ ↑it↓ . . . the ⟨obedience to this law of God⟩
                ↑acquisition of virtue;↓ [emendation in ink over pencil; pencil version
                reads: "acquisition of this virtue"] . . . that ⟨whoso⟩ ↑every . . .
                being & [end of line] & on . . . convictions↓ adopts this law ⟨of⟩
                [cancellation in pencil] ⟨his being partakes of his etern⟨ity⟩al⟩ ↑of
                Gods action, [ink over pencil] thereby . . . nature↓ & thus hath the
                ⟨seeds⟩ ↑principles↓ of ⟨his⟩ ↑its↓ own life within ⟨him⟩itself. It is
                surely a grand ⟨precept⟩ view . . . been / frequently suggested / more
                distinctly understood in our own time /
26   the ⟨e⟩language
31–35   frame in ⟨heaving lungs⟩ ↑heart that beats unceasingly↓ . . . the
                ⟨devotion⟩ ↑transferring↓ . . . God↑, & . . . ↑which is God's↓
                [additions in ink over pencil] & ↑so↓ . . . own.↓
37–38   ↑True . . . currency.↓

                              Page 75
3   ↑we may trust↓ public principle ⟨may⟩ ↑to↓
9–15   {Be . . . great ⟨vessel⟩ ↑fleet↓ . . . sea.}
18–21   in ⟨for⟩ year . . . use ⟨content with being a part of the machine of
                society⟩ not . . . ↑the tame creature of society↓ making a ⟨bow⟩
                ↑compliment↓
24   forgetful of [end of line] of
26   ↑of yᵉ play of Providence↓ . . . in ⟨the plan of Providence⟩ ↑it↓.
30   ↑course↓.

                              Sermon LIV

Manuscript (earlier version): Five sheets folded to make four pages each; first four folios
nested and sewn through the center fold to the remaining folio with white thread; pages
measure 25 x 20.3 cm. A slip of paper, 7.5 x 17.9 cm, is affixed with red sealing wax to the
left margin of MS p. 15, covering the bracketed material it is to replace (verso blank).

[The text of the earlier version follows:]

LIV.   Princeps

Can the Ethiopian change his skin, or the
leopard his spots? then may ye also do good,
that are accustomed to do evil. Jeremiah. 13-23.
(Vide II Peter 2. 19.—)

I propose to invite your attention to some reflexions upon the force of habit. It is so prominent a law of human nature & the passage of every day furnishes ⟨every one⟩ ↑us↓ with so many striking illustrations of it, that it is familiar to every breast. But the triteness of such topic⟨is⟩s is ⟨f⟩ no reason why they should be excluded from their turn in our meditations. We come to church, that we may live better at home, & the homeliest facts are therefore best entitled to our attention {Is it impertinent to discuss the best mode of doing what I have done a thousand times if I am going to do it again tomorrow.}

In that which we call Habit our identity & our power of improvement seem⟨s⟩ to reside. To describe our habits is to describe ourselves. "A man is a bundle of habits." Suppose we were otherwise constituted. If ↑every↓ ⟨to⟩morrow we should wake up without any increased facility to our duty, from todays efforts; if ⟨the power of attention⟩ we shd. find it as hard to fix the ⟨power of⟩ attention on what we have been doing all day, as if we had never attempted it before; if we recognized the face of a man, or a new fact no better the tenth time than the second time it was presented—we should have sad cause enough to deplore our refractory nature & must desist fatigued & unsuccessful from every experiment to increase our knowledge or our usefulness. We must give up ↑in disgust↓ all business all study all hope of strengthening affections or reconciling aversions ⟨in disgust.⟩. All improvement it is plain would be at ⟨an end⟩ ↑a stand↓ & man would be like seaweed drifting on the waves.

The powers of inanimate nature remain unchanged the ice is no colder & the fire no hotter the magnet draws with the same force the stone has no more tendency to fall nor the vapour to ascend than when ⟨Noah came forth from the ark or⟩ Adam walked in the garden. But man is subject to another law. It is the well known property of intelligent being to repeat any action with ⟨more⟩ less difficulty than to begin it; ↑further,↓ to do with ease the thousandth time, that which was done with incredible struggles the first; ↑further,↓ to do it with ⟨that⟩ ↑such a↓ steadily increasing torrent of will & power as to require ⟨incredible⟩ ↑the greatest↓ efforts to resist & change a course of action.

And herein resides the force of human beings. The world is full of illustrations of the ⟨principle⟩ ↑advantage accruing from it.↓ Go into the shop of the cunning artificer. See how dextrously he works; how swiftly he takes advantage of every little chance that occurs in his task; how fast, & with what precision his work goes on, & how finished & faultless is the result! We who look on, could not have done it in years. Yet he has only the same limbs & no more ⟨natural⟩ muscular activity or power of mind than another. His apprentice can perform each single motion of the hand or foot, each impulse of the saw & the plane as well as he. But the secret of his skill is in Habit, the incessant practice of the same movements every day for twenty years, has given his hand a steadiness & speed which nothing else than the same use can bestow.

⟨What else is⟩ ↑Take another example in↓ the Scholar⟨?⟩. ↑Here are some of Gods choicest gifts.↓ Here is a quick & powerful ⟨mind⟩ ↑attention↓, a strong memory, a wise judgment; ↑This mind↓ if its circumstances & education had been different ⟨it⟩ would perhaps have taken delight in the marshalling of a battle, or in the more complex combinations of a campaign. But to a more humane & noble life has God appointed it. From its earliest day it has been dedicated to a discipline of continuous thinking; to the examination & ⟨measure⟩ ⟨application⟩ use of intellectual images; to the labelling & ticketing (if I may borrow the expression) of thoughts; & the orderly distribution of them in the cells ⟨chambers⟩ & warehouses of the Memory. And with what effect?

That solitary & /reserved/retiring/ man hath a rich & peopled soul. Though he lives apart, & hath acquaintance but with few men, the dwellers on all the face of the earth are familiar to him; he knows the fathers of every race. In the overgrown splendour of their empires, he can tell the mean original ⟨w⟩from which they sprang; the virtues, & fortunes, the religion, the arts, laws, revolutions of each, he sees them all ↑from ⟨their first nativity⟩ where they lurk ⟨encased⟩↓ in their dark ⟨nativity⟩ ↑causes,↓ to where they come in to take their place in the procession ↑of events.↓.—Better than all this ↑long chronology of↓ peace & war of flesh & blood—to him is known the genesis of science; what have been in ↑departed↓ ages the beautiful entertainments of the human spirit— how it imagined; how it reasoned; how it concluded; how it soared to the idea of God; & what explanations it devised of human life. To this teeming soul of his, no fact is worthless; every one hath a hundred sides & is related to facts he already possesses. Leave him alone & he is society to himself. He cannot take part in the song of the musician, nor in the festivities of the men of pleasure, he cannot dig, he cannot bargain, he is fit for nothing else, but he is admirable in that one thing which he professeth.

This is but a happy ⟨illustration⟩ ↑instance↓ of the power derived from Habit to the ⟨subtle powers⟩ ⟨regal⟩ fine endowments of the human intellect. For this man ⟨h⟩perhaps was gifted by nature no more liberally than another ⟨who went before⟩ ↑the companion of his childhood, who surpassed↓ him at school but has all his days been so immersed in the details of a minute business—that he finds himself unable to retain in his mind with any accuracy the political changes of his own state from year to year.

These are but two individuals selected out ↑of↓ a host of instances as large as the population of the globe. For every man is what he is not by original creation but by his way of living, that is, by his habits. We are in general ⟨altogether⟩ ↑very↓ insensible to the infinite assistance life derives from this principle, it is so omnipresent. Thus ⟨we cannot⟩ in order to read a sentence in a book it is necessary that the eye shd successively see all or almost all the individual letters of every word. Yet by use the eye traverses them so rapidly that ⟨it⟩ ↑a man↓ becomes incredulous of this fact until it is recalled by seeing a ⟨a⟩child who has not this *use* attempting the same thing.

It is to avail ourselves ⟨in its⟩ ↑to the↓ fullest amount of this principle that we use the division of labour A nation is classed out into professions & trades ⟨each having endless subdivisions⟩ ↑and subdivisions of trades↓ that all the skill & power which can result to all from each hand doing incessantly but one thing, may be gained. A thousand hands go to the ⟨mak⟩ manufacture of a lump of sugar. And the advancement of ⟨th⟩ every art seems to depend upon the ⟨farther⟩ carrying out yet farther this distribution of its processes.

↑It is upon the experience of this law that the great doctrine of political economy of yᵉ divison↓ [addition in pencil]

↑The great doctrine of the Division of labor so well known as a principle of political economy is only designed to avail ourselves as to the fullest amount of the power of habit.↓

We may carry this analysis into all parts of life & we shall find every where abundant proof of the great & continually increased accession of strength which we derive from simple repetition of the same acts. {"Il n'y a que le premier pas qui Conte."} The first step was a vigorous effort. ⟨What has been done once can be done again.⟩ A later step is made without any effort. A still later step it is easier to make than to withhold. So the surgeon who could not see blood without fainting comes to perform the most critical & ↑& to yᵉ spectator↓ hideous operations of his art, with composed face, & unerring hand.

The seasick boy that a few months ago loathed his life in ⟨the new terrors of⟩ ↑his first venturing on↓ the ocean, is now heedless of its awful dangers & sings cheerily in the shrouds amidst the bellowings of the storm. {The veteran soldier of twenty campaigns is thinking of his ration or some trifling mistake of discipline at the moment when his new comrade turns pale at the spectacle of [end of page] two hostile lines in the act of engaging, the explosion of the ordnance, & the sallies of the Cavalry.}

Brethren, if there be in our constitution a principle of such strength it behoves us to attend to it, to see if it touches our moral nature. ↑{Insert A} A {We know that it does enter into our moral nature with the same force as into the bodily or the intellectual action.}↓ It is no idle alarm↑, believe me,↓ which we perceive in our breasts, when now & then we hear a warning against the power of habit. This power is tremendous, &, when it is corrupt, it is the strength of our nature arrayed against our good. The great God who made us, & gave us this proclivity or readiness to take & keep one direction with increasing momentum of action, has not ↑seen fit↓ in his wisdom ↑to↓ guard⟨ed⟩ it from abuse. He has left the door of abuse wide open. No; ⟨h⟩He gave us the principle but left us the application of it. He gave us the power, like a blind giant to be our servant, to work with all his might for our comfort; to do our errands of benevolence in the earth; & to bring aid to our side in every ↑fainting↓ hour of conflict; but he left us free to make him our master↑,↓ &↑, if we chuse,↓ to surrender ⟨bring down⟩ the heaven-born reason to lie in galling bondage to his brute force. Here he is with his vigorous hands, equally ready for any work, to traverse land & sea for knowledge, or to save, & hoard, & multiply wealth, or to go like an angel of Mercy around the globe scattering health & truth & comfort or to fight with temptations & uplift the standard of Heaven in the very tents of sensuality & selfishness—↑or to make life a curse to ourselves & others by all the arts of wickedness.↓ He will make or unmake he will do good or destroy but ↑some way he↓ must work↑.↓ ⟨some way.⟩ ↑He is of an industrious nature.↓ Here he is in your house, & the harm he may do, is your own proper peril.—

My friends, I speak in figure but the danger I speak of is real & language can hardly represent its extent. I do not wish to affright you with ↑the shadow of↓ rare & uncertain evils. I will not even now afflict you with the history of those two madmen of habit, the miser & the drunkard; ↑Let them pass now,↓ though it is too bold to hope that there is nothing of that insanity among us; but I desire to warn you against risks that hourly beseige each one of us, & ↑risks that↓ as far as we can lift the veil of the future, threaten to affect us from ⟨age to age⟩ ↑month to month, from year to year, yea, from age to age, in our endless being.↓

In the faith of Christ in the faith of immortal life I desire to warn you against the smallest taint of evil existing in you, *because, there are such things as habits*. I beseech you to consider that every action you do, is either the beginning of a habit, or is part of a habit already existing. And the terror of this consideration ⟨rests⟩ ↑lies↓ in this fact, that, *we* are not one thing, & our habits another, but ⟨w⟩that we ⟨do, that is it which we⟩ are ↑formed by them, & changed by them.↓

Men talk ⟨as if⟩ sometimes as if their nature was a certain solid & settled frame, over which thoughts & feelings passed & repassed like pictures before the eye, without penetrating its substance, or disturbing its repose; as if the habits of years might be assumed or got rid of ⟨as the dress we wear⟩ as indifferently as the garments we wear. Is the nature of each of us solid & stable? On the contrary, nothing is more volatile & fluctuating. It changes from hour to hour. All our actions react on ourselves. ⟨Every action⟩ Our power of action is the helm of our boat & ⟨with every⟩ ↑the least↓ turn ⟨affects the direction of⟩ ↑of the rudder turns ⟨her⟩↓ the whole ↑boat↓. We must beware of th⟨e⟩is mysterious nature of the human soul. It has this dangerous power of self-change, self-accommodation to whatsoever we do. As, in the heathen fable, the nymph who wept became a fountain, & the nymph who pined became an echo, so, in the stern law of moral nature, we are always changing from what we are to what we wish to be, from what we are to what we do.

Be not deceived We are not immoveably moored to any bottom—and if we do wrong & don't succeed we cannot come back to ⟨the⟩ where we were. That *where* is gone. For ↑as↓ all our powers ⟨live by⟩ grow by their own exercise, so they die by disuse. As you follow new desires you are changed from what you were & those powers that once you had are *dead*. They do not exist. And what can you hope from them? ⟨{As well might the mariner relying on ancient ⟨map⟩ ↑charts↓ sail for islands which the sea hath swallowed⟨.⟩, ↑as you hope the malignant man will abstain from malice because once he was gentle.↓

You cannot live over your childhood. No more can the bad man do right when he has vitiated all the springs of feeling & action. He has no eye to see the right no fingers to feel it. ⟨His diseased⟩ The disease is universal in his frame & for healthy members he hath foul excrescences & he loves the vices he practiseth.}⟩ [The bracketed passage is canceled by a covering slip of paper (verso blank), affixed with red sealing wax to the left margin, which contains the following revision:]

↑You own your temper is apt to master you. Do you think, because you are sure you was ⟨once⟩ gentle ↑in your youth,↓ that you have a warrant that you shall never reach that malignity that tempts a man to murder? ⟨As well might the mariner sail for islands⟩ You put your trust in perished affections. As well mt. the mariner sail for islands, which the sea has long ago swallowed, because ↑he says↓ they are put down on ancient charts. (Insert B) [Insert "B" is relocated from the preceding page, where it originally followed the sentence ending ". . . what we do."] B↓ {They who do good become /good/ angels/. They who do evil become /evil/ fiends/. We are alway progressing one way or the other. You who stand there are on the way to the nature of an angel or a devil.}

↑We are alway exposed to the attacks of temptation No man is safe.↓ Perhaps thus a good man may become a bad man by insensible departures, and (I shudder as I make the application) whilst yet society is sounding the praises of one of our acquaintance for the amiableness of his character—he has already ceased to deserve the praise & is rapidly declining on the road to malignity & lowest sensuality.

Far be it from me, brethren, to exaggerate a danger that is great enough at the least. I do not forget that the goodness of God leads us to repentance that the return from these dreadful descents is possible. O yes, it is possible & therefore we preach the peril of habit & the duty of penitence. But the light which now streams upon you in the cheerful world of men, the voice of Gods word, the misgivings of your mind in the prosecution of an evil course, the affectionate advice of your parent, the upbraiding eye of your friend, of your sister, of your brother,—these are the very strivings of the Spirit of God with you, which, in the melancholy words of the Scripture "shall not always strive" The light is always becoming dimmer as you wander from it—the chance of your return is every day becoming less. We talk much of repentance but it is very rare. Ten persist in vice for one that turns back.

⟨Brethren, the inference that flows from this survey of our nature is single & clear. Beware of your habits. This observation that we make of the subtlety of their inroads upon us should make us vigilant & suspicious of ourselves. The sea gains imperceptibly upon the sands, but in time ⟨it drowns the Continent⟩ the victorious waves roll over the Continent⟩

The main mischief, as you must see, that makes the ⟨fatal⟩ ↑dreadful↓ interest of this inquiry, is, that Habit sears the Conscience itself—⟨so that it⟩ ↑the danger yᵗ ⟨it shd.⟩ the Conscience shd.↓ ceases to make a true report—so that our very compass is in a measure useless, & we do not know the way to right. But God has ↑so far↓ protected this, his minister in the soul, ⟨in such measure⟩ that though, as we sin, it points to lower & lower degrees of right, yet its divine instinct is never wholly subdued. It always points *from* hell. It always points to a better than the worst course, & if we will only follow its direction it will continually acquire greater steadiness & greater truth.

Brethren, the inference that flows from this survey of our nature is single & clear. Beware of your habits. In the ⟨s⟩ conviction that they make us what we are, all our observation upon the subtlety of their inroads upon us should make us vigilant & suspicious of ourselves. If we find ourselves skeptical of what we desire to believe, perhaps that skepticism is a measure of our ⟨distance⟩ ↑departure↓ from truth. If we can tell a falsehood without shame,—if we can please ourselves in taking an unjust advantage,—if we can live useless,—or worse than useless, in sloth & wantonness,— these things are fatal symptoms of our downward tendencies, & tomorrow you will be worse than now. Or if yet good motives have not lost their power, & you are restrained from gross vices, yet if you find yourself far removed ↑in virtue from the virtue of the best men↓ from the men of God that have lived in the earth, if you ⟨are⟩ ↑grow↓ negligent of your connexion with your Heavenly ⟨f⟩Father,—O mark that distance well—for, every day & every moment, by the laws of your nature, is making it wider, & your chances of happiness & of safety less.—

Manuscript (revised version): Eight sheets folded to make four pages each; folios nested and sewn through the center fold with white thread (the first and last leaves have separated); pages measure 25 x 20.3 cm.

Lines	Page 76
18–19	would ⟨be scarcely more⟩ ↑lose his↓ worth↑.↓ ⟨than the idle seaweed drifting on the waves.⟩ ¶ The

	Page 77
9	faultless ⟨are⟩ ↑is↓ the result⟨s⟩!
42	but ⟨a happy⟩ ↑one↓ [emendation in pencil]

	Page 78
9	all or ⟨almost all⟩ the
30–34	{The veteran . . . engaging↑,↓—↑or at↓ . . . Ordnance↑. {↓& the sallies of the Cavalry.} [additions in pencil; added period and brackets suggest an intention to delete the final phrase] ¶ ⟨Brethren,⟩ if [cancellation in pencil]
37–38	beleive . . . a- [end of page] against

Page 79

5	in ⟨galling⟩ bondage
17	even ⟨now⟩ afflict
20	bes⟨ei⟩iege [emendation in pencil]
26	or ↑is↓ part
29	was ⟨a⟩ some
38–40	the ⟨heathen⟩ fable . . . of ⟨our⟩ moral

Page 81

10	restra↑i↓ned

[The following fragment, on both sides of a separate leaf, has been catalogued by the Houghton Library as Sermon No. 54C, though a note with the manuscript indicates that it was found with Sermon CLXIV]:

It was the saying of a wise man, 'Remember that tomorrow is a new day.' the sense of this advice I understand to be this, not to live tomorrow as we have lived today; not to live tomorrow as we are accustomed to live; but to revise our habits every day by the light of reason. The importance of this ⟨advice⟩ rule will be felt by any one who considers the strength of habit. In the experience of each one of us, are probably facts that almost justify the language of the text, and which demand of us a serious ⟨consideration⟩ ↑reflexion↓. ⟨No man⟩ ↑There is none among us who↓ believes himself so old that he may not live another day or year, & most of us are either beginning life with every hope, or at least flatter ourselves that ⟨the⟩ many years of life on earth are appointed to us. Let us see to it, then, if our habits are yet to form, that we ⟨set them right⟩ form good ones & if ⟨not⟩ ↑they are formed↓, let us ⟨see if they have not enslaved us.⟩ ↑be aware of their strength & see if they are not too strong for our safety.↓

Sermon LV

Manuscript: Five sheets folded to make four pages each; folios nested and sewn with white thread through the center fold; pages measure 25 x 20.3 cm.

[The following variant opening, inscribed on MS p. 2, was presumably written for the second and last delivery of the sermon, April 9, 1837, at East Lexington; it replaced the original sermon text on MS p. 1 and the original first paragraph ("The duties . . . conversation"), which is struck through with two lines on MS p. 3:]

↑Now ye are the body of Christ, & members in particular. I Cor. 12. 27.

↑These words of Paul which he applied to the Xn Church I would extend by an allowable application to ⟨society in yᵉ Xn world⟩ the whole society of the Christian world.↓

I propose to invite your attention at this time to some reflexions upon a subject to which ⟨I⟩ ↑we↓ have already repeatedly directed ⟨y⟩our meditations. [emendations in this sentence in ink over pencil] I mean our connexion with society. The ⟨present dis⟩course ↑of my remarks↓ will go to reconcile the two ways of viewing our duty which are commonly presented & which I am apprehensive ↑sometimes↓ appear inconsistent. [emendations in this sentence in ink over pencil] I wish to ⟨praise⟩ ↑commend↓ society, & to ⟨praise⟩ ↑commend↓ solitude, & show the relation of one to ↑the↓ ⟨an⟩other.↓

Lines   *Page 82*
Bible Text   closet, & ⟨shut the door⟩ when
1–5   which ⟨we⟩ ↑the teachers of Christianity↓ . . . character. ⟨We⟩
             ↑⟨Th⟩Our religion↓ take↑s↓ . . . remind↑s↓ . . . alone. ⟨We⟩ ↑It↓
             recommend↑s↓ the duties of se⟨f⟩lf-command, . . . ↑It teaches↓
7–8   of ⟨the Universe⟩ ↑all . . . to↓ intermeddle⟨th⟩ therein.
10   lacketh hi⟨m.⟩s ↑presence.↓
11–12   conversation ¶ ⟨But⟩ let [cancellation rejected as a late emendation]
13–14   to ⟨contravene⟩ ↑disparage↓
14   No⟨thing⟩ ↑religion↓
18–(83)4   ¶ {Nothing can . . . ↑unqualified↓ declamations ⟨in praise of soli-
             tude &⟩ against . . . voice of ⟨social⟩ ↑active↓ . . . ↑It is . . . press.↓
             It is society ↑wh. he pretends to spurn, that↓ . . . hills ⟨& the rocks.
             Yet he pretends to spurn it.⟩. Take . . . ↑cut off his intercourse↓ . . .
             preparation ⟨for society⟩ ↑to return to the world,↓ . . . himself⟨.⟩,
             ⟨A very⟩ & you . . . prisoner.}

                                          Page 83
5–6   ↑to the common eye↓ . . . ↑the individual↓
11   ↑for . . . repute↓
12   by ⟨dint⟩ ↑means↓
18–20   genius /is/does/ not nominally ⟨↑wield↓⟩ ↑sway↓ the ⟨governor⟩
             ↑sceptre↓ . . . often ⟨is⟩ ↑does↓ practically. ¶ ↑The power possessed
             by the novelist who writes to all Europe from his closet.↓ [notation in
             pencil; end of page] ¶ A man of ⟨fine parts⟩ ↑uncommon endow-
             ments↓
24   the ⟨world⟩ ↑globe↓.
25–29   ↑the . . . village↓ . . . himself is ⟨robbed or insulted⟩ injured, . . .
             shall ⟨search⟩ hunt . . . justice /if he skulk/wherever he lurks/
31–34   ¶ ↑Another . . . heaven↓
36–37   good ↑knowledge imag projects↓ [notations in pencil at bottom of
             page, centered below the last line of the continuous text] [end of page]
             as it brings ⟨a⟩ *benefit* . . . do ⟨himself⟩ the
39–(84)4   preponderant ⟨will⟩ ↑opinion↓ of ⟨America⟩ ↑their country↓ . . .
             ↑to . . . more↓ . . . ↑the resources of↓ . . . society ⟨act⟩ ↑sound↓

                                          Page 84
7   the ⟨genuine⟩ ↑sincere↓
10–11   the ⟨only⟩ ↑surest↓ . . . ↑in heaven↓ . . . ↑foreign↓
14–15   enlarge—⟨I will only hint its fourfold value to us as the place of /
             speech/intercourse/, the place of affection, the place of example &
             the place of joint action.—⟩ ¶ Yet
16   ties—⟨yet⟩ he
19–20   Maker. ¶ ⟨Why because in a moral view it is not enough to know that
             a man is in society but what is his condition in society. Society is a
             palace to one man & a dungeon to another man, an education to one
             & condemnation to another.⟩

⟨Now to beings so knit together, so obviously designed to receive pleasure & excitement from social being why should they not be addressed as social—Why speak of society always merely as a picture before the eye of the living man—or as an instrument in his hand—or as a dangerous influence & why lay such stress upon the unsocial duties—upon self command, upon exertions aimed at the improvement of self in knowledge, in endurance, in disregard of opinion?⟩ ¶ It

21–26   religion ⟨should yet teach us to act as⟩ ↑does . . . are↓ solitary unrelated men. ↑{Insert X} X {When . . . law. ↑It said, 'It is not . . . alone.'↓ It says ↑also↓ . . . God.}↓

29   pass ⟨muster⟩ ↑examination↓

33   is [end of page] is taken

34–35   a ⟨shroud⟩ ↑mantle↓ . . . from ⟨ourselves.⟩ ↑us.↓

39   ↑under God↓

Page 85

2–3   ↑& so . . . thousands.—↓

5   azure ⟨wall⟩ ↑dome↓, . . . menial ⟨at his footstool⟩ ↑in his stables↓

9   ⟨g⟩Gods gift

11   ↑In fine↓ The

14   man ⟨cultivate much⟩ ↑try his own spirit in↓

16–17   itself. ⟨Every⟩ Almost . . . book, ⟨he⟩ hath

23–27   ↑in . . . duties↓ . . . that ⟨a man⟩ ↑so we↓ shall make ⟨his⟩ ↑our↓

28–29   ↑peculiar↓ . . . mind ⟨above all splendour⟩, that . . . draws ⟨all its benefit⟩ from society ↑all its good↓

34   gratify ⟨our⟩ ↑the↓

37–38   which ⟨genius⟩ ↑the reason↓ . . . it ⟨is⟩does

Page 86

3   woman ⟨↑after the perfect stature of Christ↓⟩ who [addition in ink over pencil; pencil inscription reads: "by yᵉ perfect stature of Xᵗ"]

5   in ⟨society⟩ ↑this world↓

6   things go in [Emerson meant to write "so" presumably.]

7   mans ⟨society⟩ ↑acquaintance↓

8–9   idleness. ⟨Hence⟩ ↑And . . . in↓ the vulgar ⟨proverb⟩ ↑observation↓

18–19   wise, & [end of page] & . . . ↑in peace,↓

Sermon LVI

Manuscript: Five sheets folded to make four pages each; folios nested and sewn with white thread through the center fold; pages measure 25 x 20.3 cm. A slip of paper 17.4 x 12.3 cm, containing Insert "A," was affixed with red sealing wax to the right margin of MS p. 6 (now loose).

Lines   *Page 87*

1–2   ¶ ⟨There⟩ It . . . world. ⟨It has ever been t⟩The . . . ↑has ever dwelled upon↓

4	↑in whose integrity↓ he implicitly confides ⟨in⟩ as beyond ⟨tempta-tion⟩ ↑suspicion↓,
14	↑what↓ever⟨y⟩ suggestion ⟨which⟩ affords
15	to ⟨love⟩ ↑favour↓
19–(88)1	¶ ↑I know↓ Most . . . to ⟨be rich⟩ ↑gratify their passions↓ . . . in ⟨being rich⟩ ↑so doing↓ . . . conceive /yᵉ/ any equal/ advantage of being upright. ⟨Some⟩ ↑But↓ I apprehend ↑there . . . who↓

Page 88

10	thereof. ⟨Why is it not reasonable to suppose on the supposition⟩ You
11	th⟨e⟩at
22–23	of ⟨angels⟩ ↑tho'ts↓ . . . inner ⟨heaven.⟩ kingdom.
24–25	is ⟨that⟩ ↑when . . . advantage↓
29	I ⟨beg⟩ ↑entreat↓ you⟨r⟩ ↑to↓ consider⟨ation to the fact⟩ ↑at-tentively↓
31–32	a ⟨loose⟩ ↑general↓ . . . religion & ⟨pleasure⟩ worldliness
33–34	↑It . . . road.↓
34–36	you ⟨the⟩ honours ⟨of this world.⟩. It often ⟨picks the purest gems⟩ ↑receives . . . way↓, . . . is ⟨not its object⟩ accidental
38	¶ The ⟨true &⟩ precise
43	arm ⟨or the chest.⟩ ↑the lungs or the feet.↓
44	to ⟨do one⟩ supply
45–(89)1	↑making↓ . . . the ⟨best⟩ ↑securest↓

Page 89

6	↑i.e. in the /family circle,/shop,/ . . . acted,—↓
9–10	↑This . . . very ⟨ill⟩ ↑imperfect↓ man.↓ [emendation within the sentence in pencil] Take /it then/this soul/ [variant in pencil]
11–16	withdrawn. ↑Insert A A {Now . . . not ⟨to its obscure native spot, nor⟩ to . . . temper, it observes.}↓ ↑And as all things warn it of death.↓ [written on a slip of paper attached by red sealing wax to the right margin of MS p. 6; on the verso is "place" three times and two sketches of heads, all in pencil] The ⟨mighty⟩ ↑dark↓
21–22	the ⟨misfortune⟩ ↑petty . . . denial↓
26	↑childhood or↓
27	↑of fortune↓
30–31	have ⟨skill⟩ ↑the art↓ to suit itself to the⟨ir⟩ veering forces ↑of sea & sky,↓
31–33	The↑re are↓ . . . nature must be ⟨witnessed⟩ ↑received↓
34–37	when ⟨the influence of God dwells upon ⟨the⟩ it⟩ ↑is true to itself↓, ↑itself is by its relation to God↓ . . . *universe*↑,↓ ⟨is an intelligent soul⟩—& so . . . ↑health,↓ birth, ⟨fame⟩ gold . . . ↑coins, are↓ counters, whose ⟨whole⟩ ↑varying↓ value is ↑always↓ that which ⟨our imagination⟩ ↑itself↓
38	may ⟨value⟩ ↑wither↓ them ⟨as⟩ ↑to↓ straws; it may ⟨value⟩ ↑swell↓ them ⟨as⟩ ↑to↓ worlds.
39–40	revelations—from their importance ↑which . . . learn↓ is ⟨the grand one⟩ *that*

43   lives ↑as↓ by
45–(90)3   these /revelations/great lessons/ ["great lessons" in pencil; "great"
                written over in ink] . . . independant . . . a ⟨free⟩ ⟨sovereign⟩
                ↑solitary & eternal↓ & independent ⟨Being⟩ agent.

Page 90

6–7   relation ⟨becomes⟩ ↑shall hereafter become↓ [emendation in pencil]
                . . . ↑as Paul says↓
11–12   has ⟨brought⟩ removed
14–17   *perfect.* ¶ ⟨I hope it will be seen that the advantage of religion consists
                in the ⟨elevat⟩ culture of the soul The more its powers are bro't out,
                the more self existent does it become⟩ ¶ ↑Thus . . . God ⟨shall⟩
                ↑will↓ . . . Sire.↓
18   that ⟨this⟩ ↑in . . . the↓ advantage ⟨belongs to religion⟩ over
22–25   were ⟨obviously⟩ best . . . into ⟨our⟩ the dark of our fate. ¶ ⟨This
                being⟩ ↑Such is↓ . . . ↑form of↓ . . . than ⟨al⟩ ⟨univers⟩ that ⟨form
                of⟩ Skepticism
27   to ⟨speak a little⟩ ↑add a few words↓ upon the ⟨perfect solution
                which Xty affords⟩ ↑excellence of Christianity↓
28–30   ↑If↓ The . . . be⟨ing⟩ the . . . ↑& setting aside ⟨their⟩ all . . .
                claims↓ [addition in pencil; "their" canceled in ink] . . . Jesus The
                very . . . of ⟨its⟩ ↑their↓
33   too /severely taught/overstrained/
35–38   ↑simply as a police↓ . . . not ⟨have⟩ be . . . the ⟨height⟩ ↑reach↓

Page 91

4–5   the ⟨history⟩ ↑life↓ of ⟨George Fox the Quaker⟩ [emendations in
                pencil] ↑many a martyr in the hist of yᵉ Ch.↓
7–8   will /not/never/ [variant in pencil] provoke contempt ¶ ⟨And for the
                charity of the New Testament we do not desire in opinion or in
                practice to adhere too literally to a noble doctrine. You are responsi-
                ble for the care of your goods to God who gave them. The spirit of
                Christian charity enjoins you to hold them as an accountable steward
                not in ostentation, not to hoard them in love of them, not in luxurious
                expense for the sense nor in frivolous expense for vanity but to hold
                them as having a reasonable soul to hold them as being above them &
                not their servant to hold them with that liberal hand which knows that
                all their value is in their use & that they belong to the whole human
                race as well as yourself in such manner as that if they go from you you
                shall not feel yourself impoverished & if they be multiplied you shall
                not grow ↑idle or↓ proud.⟩ ¶ And
10   so ⟨administers⟩ holds ⟨its⟩ ↑Gods gifts↓
15   life, whether [end of page] whether
21–24   soul ⟨that can train it up to that calm Confidence which shall meet
                that event with firmness & hope.⟩ ↑which . . . hope.↓ [emendation in
                pencil and ink; pencil layer reads: "which can give one soul any
                advantage over another in that hour, or can at all ⟨create⟩ create in it
                a calm & enlightened confidence which shall meet that event with
                firmness & hope."]

Sermon LVII

Manuscript: Five sheets folded to make four pages each; folios nested and sewn with white thread through the center fold; pages measure 25 x 20.3 cm.

Lines	Page 92
Bible Text	Lord ⟨all his⟩ o my
2	privelege
6	pleasant ⟨office⟩ duty
10–11	↑the father . . . board;↓
15–16	rejoice ⟨to find⟩ that the for⟨ce⟩↑mation↓ . . . not /weakened/⟨destroyed⟩/ the /dear tie/⟨sympathy⟩/ of
16–20	chain of /kindred ⟨blood⟩/consanguinity/ which . . . ↑counted &↓ brightened⟨.⟩, ↑& the . . . parts.↓ ¶ ⟨The father sees his children once more resume their place at his board;⟩ ↑This day↓ . . . the ⟨remember⟩ forgotten
21–22	↑no↓ . . . all ⟨his⟩ ↑its↓

	Page 93
1	↑& gratitude,↓
6	↑The just . . . praise.↓ [in ink over pencil]
9	defeat⟨s⟩ out
19–20	↑the good that . . . because ⟨all⟩ it belongs to all.↓
21–22	↑one↓ . . . the /advantage lies/scale of good inclines/. [variant in pencil]
28	curcumnavigated
38	from ⟨subtle⟩ fraud or ⟨untameable⟩ ferocity?

	Page 94
10–12	¶ ↑The result . . . that ⟨fine⟩ ↑noble↓ doctrine of ⟨the⟩ ↑modern↓ Politic⟨al⟩s ⟨Economist⟩ that . . . depends.↓
13	consider ⟨yet more⟩ ↑a little↓ . . . advantages ⟨we⟩ ↑each of us↓ owe↑s↓
14	↑Let . . . see↓ [in pencil]
17–21	the ⟨forest⟩ ↑ground around my dwelling,↓ . . . ↑impatient↓
23	excellence↑!↓; the
27	& ⟨e⟩specially
31	of ⟨labour &⟩ means ↑& toil↓ [emendation in pencil and ink]
34–35	& ⟨New Britain⟩ ↑Labrador↓—⟨For my⟩ ↑To . . . a↓ table ⟨the⟩ ↑a gang of↓ [After the addition of "Labrador" the emendations are in pencil and ink.]
37–39	tea, ⟨& the cup usually comes as far as the liquor.⟩ ↑& the . . . the ⟨rivers of⟩ brooks . . . adorn ⟨our least instruments⟩ ↑the common . . . use.—↓↓ [additions in ink over pencil]

	Page 95
3	↑of social life↓ [ink over pencil; pencil inscription has a terminal comma]

5–6   in ⟨far the⟩ ↑a↓ great⟨er pro⟩portion . . . western ⟨forests⟩ wilder-
       ness
8   ↑ten, or↓ a hundred ⟨or a thousand⟨s⟩⟩ dollars
21   of ⟨joy.⟩ gratitude.
25–27 ↑arts on wh. the↓ . . . ↑rests↓ . . . which ⟨its feeble⟩ infan⟨cy⟩t
       ⟨was⟩ ↑faculties were↓
27–28 ↑the↓ excitement . . . wider ⟨is⟩ ↑does↓
29–(96)1 achieve. ¶ ⟨Let who will be thankful with good reason look within
       him & study the secret of the Memory⟩
           ⟨Let him analyze the imagination compared with whose speed
       lightning loitereth⟩
           ⟨Let him study the secret of the memory & detect if he can its way
       of storing truth. Let him observe how life is a game of question and
       answer of which all material objects suggest the first & the soul is
       occupied in framing replies. ↑Go rejoice in the affections of the heart,
       which this day as we have already noticed find peculiar gratification
       & which make the gratification of every day & of all being.↓⟩
           ↑"Truth," . . . possession ⟨Is it not⟩↓ ⟨↑{Insert X}↓⟩
           ⟨X {}Is it not . . . the ⟨multiplication⟩ prosperity . . . this
       food.⟨}⟩

Page 96

14   are ⟨those⟩ ↑some↓
16   are ⟨those⟩ ↑some↓ . . . ↑some↓
18   included⟨,⟩↑?↓
20   gratitude ⟨to⟩ ↑⟨before⟩ compared with↓
25   of ⟨Reason⟩ the Understanding.
27   ↑Let us praise him↓
28   him ⟨in⟩ ↑with↓

[The following notation appears in erased pencil at the end of the sermon:]

               for the health of the people
               the ⟨f⟩abundance of harvest
               whatever success of interests
               the civil liberty
               the means of knowledge
                   schools & colleges &c
               [illegible word] of affection
               for the holy light of truth
               for the life of Jesus
               for the hope beyond death

Sermon LVIII

Manuscript: Five sheets folded to make four pages each; folios nested and sewn with
white thread through the center fold; pages measure 25 x 20.3 cm. A slip of paper, 12.3 x
16 cm, containing Insert "B," is affixed with red sealing wax to the right margin of MS
p. 4.

Lines	
	Page 97
Bible Text	Matt. /7/6/21– [variant in pencil]
1	¶ ⟨Jesus on the mountain in Galilee warns his followers not to lay up their treasure in the earth.⟩ The sermon
2	can ⟨complain⟩ ↑regret↓
4	↑& directness↓.
8–9	beheld ⟨the⟩ ↑perhaps↓ . . . distant ⟨cities⟩ ↑mountain towns↓ ⟨of Ramah ⟨&⟩or Tabor⟩, and
11–12	↑the trees . . . fruit↓ . . . his ⟨he⟩ audience
14	of ⟨their⟩ ↑its↓ eloquence. Perhaps the⟨y⟩ multitude
18–19	yrselves &c Perhaps ["treasures upon earth" supplied from Matthew 6:19]
21	& ⟨has⟩ its
23	¶ ↑Where . . . also↓
25–(98)1	The ⟨renowned man⟩ statesman hath his ²office & his ¹patronage.

	Page 98
5–7	daily ⟨support⟩ ↑subsistence↓ & ⟨to whom⟩ a . . . their ⟨income⟩ ↑comforts↓.
8	↑the professional man,↓
10	household ⟨expenses⟩ ↑cost↓,
14–15	¶ ↑The great . . . have↓ No padlocked vault; no ⟨glittering⟩ casket . . . ↑to hide . . . rust.↓
18–24	which ⟨is p⟩ belongs to every ⟨hu⟩man ⟨soul⟩ is—⟨all that he brings to pass⟩—⟨is⟩ ↑that . . . bestows↓ all his *labour,* ⟨all his fruit,⟩ in . . . ↑all↓ . . . faculties↑.↓ ⟨& the direction of his affections. It is more than this⟩ ↑It is sometimes . . . acquired↓ . . . ↑the use of↓ . . . ↑of whatsoever description↓—⟨beauty⟩ ⟨↑genius↓⟩ ↑whether genius,↓ wit, ⟨high⟩ birth, . . . or ⟨cunning⟩ ↑skill↓. ¶ The wealth . . . than [end of page] ¶ The wealth . . . than
25–35	↑is his↓; . . . drunkard↑, the . . . mother; ↑the↓ . . . king↓ ¶ ⟨⟨{that is a man's treasure that he will scream if you touch that is a mans treasure which is the main object of his life which is never long out of his thots to which all other objects however ardently sought are only reckoned as means for promoting this}⟩⟩ ¶ ↑Insert B [written on a slip with blank verso attached with red sealing wax to the right margin of the preceeding page] B Truly . . . treasure, ⟨was⟩ ↑shd. be↓ . . . *affections too.* ⟨Into⟩ (Insert A) [written on MS p. 5 below the canceled passage above] A ↑The power . . . exertion.↓ If . . . learn to ⟨va⟩rate it with a new value.↓
36–37	Providence ⟨that⟩ ↑so . . . worth↓ what
38	↑The attachment to home ⟨is⟩owes great . . . fact.↓

	Page 99
1–5	him. ⟨The Scot's case is less hard but he labors much to reap little.⟩ So the ↑poor↓ . . . ↑frozen↓ . . . driven ⟨them⟩ ↑man, . . . earth. ↑&↓ which the ⟨toil⟩ pains . . . them.↓↓
7–8	↑Things . . . exertions.↓

8–15   love. The ¶ The final . . . ↑particular↓ . . . is ⟨I conceive⟩ a noble . . .
          not in ⟨wealth⟩ ↑rich soil↓ or beaut⟨y⟩iful ⟨↑landscape↓⟩
          ↑landscape↓ . . . ex⟨pand⟩↑tend↓;— . . . development . . . scope to
          ⟨hardy⟩ ↑this↓

18–20   watch↑ing,↓ . . . offspring, who

21–27   it. ¶ ⟨Such is the plain meaning of our Saviour that where our treasure
          is there will our heart be also. It is the motive to all exertion the
          mainspring of all enterprize that our /⟨interest⟩ in/affection
          toward/ every thing keeps even pace with our exertion⟩ ¶ ⟨But Jesus
          tells us not to lay up our treasure on earth but to lay it up in heaven.⟩
          ¶ ↑Any . . . the ⟨value⟩ ↑importance↓ . . . ↑it ⟨gives⟩ becomes↓ . . .
          Teacher ⟨guards it with⟩ ↑declares↓ . . . heaven. ¶ ⟨Our treasure
          then is⟩↓ ¶ But

28   {not a place but}

31   heaven. ⟨Therefore⟩ It is not

32   state of ⟨mind⟩ ↑heart↓

35–38   the ⟨s⟩tumult of events, ⟨affairs⟩ amidst . . . ↑in . . . soul↓

39–40   right ⟨alternativ⟩ choice . . . you. ⟨Where? In yourself⟩ ↑Your . . .
          Empire.↓

Page 100

2–3   Earth ⟨Your soul is one Colony of that holy Empire⟩ ¶ ↑No . . .
          earth.↓

5   in the ⟨acquisition⟩ domestication ⟨of⟩ within

9   incorruptible. ⟨In⟩From the

15–32   defiance. ⟨Therefore get spiritual gifts.⟩ (Turn to A) A {If . . . seek
          ⟨his⟩ entertainment ⟨in⟩ for his leisure hours in ⟨the⟩ frivolous . . .
          refines & ⟨ever⟩ augments itself} ¶ ↑Insert B B {If . . . have ⟨not⟩
          ↑missed↓ indeed ⟨tasted the sweetness of⟩ revenge . . . great ⟨step⟩
          ↑advance↓ [emendation in ink over pencil] . . . ↑(& what can
          hinder)↓ . . . malice. ⟨To bereave⟩ To become . . . you.}↓

35–36   so ⟨diligently⟩ ↑as↓ ↑as . . . child↓ sets himself ↑in earnest↓ to the
          study ⟨ & cultivation of that relation;⟩ ↑of God↓—

Page 101

1–2   ↑of woe↓, . . . that ⟨are⟩ ↑sleep↓

3–4   ↑Yet . . . action.↓

6–7   ↑moral↓ . . . us /ascend/mount/

8   {Our

10   out ⟨the⟩ his

Sermon LIX

Manuscript (earlier version): Five sheets folded to make four pages each; folios nested
and sewn with white thread through the center fold; pages measure 25 x 20.3 cm.

[The text of the earlier version follows:]

↑Let us not↓ Be ⟨not⟩ weary ⟨of⟩ ↑in↓ well doing, for in due season we shall reap, if we faint not. Gal. 6.9.

On a former occasion I offered to your consideration some reflexions on the ⟨power⟩ ↑principle↓ of Habit. From several examples we attempted to get some measure of its ⟨mighty⟩ force & to inform ourselves of its ⟨way⟩ ↑mode↓ of operation The object of those views was only this, that by being aware ⟨what an⟩ ↑how great &↓ active a force ⟨was⟩ ↑existed↓ in us, & how impossible it was to keep ⟨him still⟩ ↑it [end of line] it ⟨inactive⟩ at rest↓, &, at the same time, it being true, that we could make the whole of its strength serviceable to our Will,—a daylaborer for our real profit—we might be excited to an unceasing watchfulness over this dangerous ⟨power⟩ inmate to keep it from ⟨bursting the boiler & scalding us⟩ turning its activity from our aid to our ruin.—

↑{Insert A} A {But before a good habit can be formed much effort is required— ⟨before that aid can be obtained to virtue.}⟩

{There are two conditions required to make the perfection of an intelligent being; *one,* that all its powers should be subject to the one executive ⟨w⟩Will; & this one condition commands the honour of all others to Cromwell & such like. the *other,* that the will itself should own the sovereignty of moral principles.}

What we despise ourselves for is the pusillanimity that fails to take command of our own powers & lets them flaunt in the wind.↓

I wish to invite your attention at this time to thoughts upon the formation of those habits, upon what is necessary for us to do for the old, for the middle aged, but especially for the young ↑to do↓ in order to secure this great natural engine on the side of conscience. In short I desire to recommend the duty of Perseverance in good works.

Many happy things are found or done by good-fortune, I should rather say, by the kindness of God. Such things are a gratuitous unpromised mercy. But the earth & all that is therein are the ⟨just⟩ assured ↑rightful↓ property of perseverance. They are promised to it by the written law; & by ↑the↓ unwritten law of nature; & by all the history of the past.

By this energy that resides in the human Will ⟨the⟩ all difficulty has been overcome the face of the earth has been changed—her secret powers have been extorted from Nature & truth dragged forth from her latent place in the human soul. ↑{Insert C} C {↑It is remarked by the great English Moralist—in considering ⟨the⟩ a pyramid or a canal—↓

⟨"All the performances of human art at which we look with praise or wonder are instances of the ↑resistless↓ force of Perseverance. By this the quarry becomes a pyramid & distant countries are united by canals⟩ If a man were to compare the effect produced by ⟨one⟩ a single stroke of the pickaxe or one impression of the spade with the general design & the last result he wd be overwhelmed with a sense of disproportion But these petty operations incessantly repeated in time surmount the greatest obstacles & mountains are levelled & oceans bounded by the slender force of human beings."— Much more will this hold in moral achievement.↓ To a virtuous man Habit is the succour God sends in aid of Perseverance, that is he decrees that what you have done laboriously you shall do easily. [sentence circled in ink] ⟨Yes it is great to persist ↑make the first↓⟩ ↑Great is the reward of persisting with firm steps in spite of difficulty↓—but those first steps of virtuous endeavour are often hard indeed. Not ⟨↑indeed↓⟩ the very first ↑but those that follow the first. It is always pleasant to begin.↓. There is no good object which men will not undertake with alacrity. The imagination always decorates what is new with agreeable colours. The child is not more absorbed in undoubting delight ⟨with⟩

↑at↓ his new toy or dress or book or playfellow than the man with his new project of business or the community in the last public ⟨scheme⟩ ↑enterprize↓. ⟨And⟩ ⟨i⟩If ⟨these are ↑charms of novelty↓⟩ ↑it is an↓ illusion⟨s, they⟩ ↑it↓ seems to come from the benevolence of God—the charm in which we can invest ↑up from ⟨the beginning of life⟩ earliest childhood,↓ down to tottering age, whatsoever is untried. And thus enterprize & labour ⟨is⟩ ↑are↓ forever reanimated.—O yes, all our plans are well & eagerly begun.

⟨But, having no root they soon wither away.⟩ ↑But↓ Who perseveres? Not one in the thousand. A million seeds perish for one that takes root.

The ↑life of a↓ great majority of men ⟨are bundles⟩ ↑is a heap↓ of beginnings. I am not dealing, brethren, with imaginary cases, but with the history of real men & women as your hearts shall witness. What makes the interest which every one of us feels in religious truth, however inconsistent with his occasional crimes and his daily life of unbelief. What but this, that there is not one of us who has not felt the sacred fire of the love of God—oh! many a time kindling up within him,—prompting him to all good practice,—& to a great many specific resolutions. He resolved to ⟨use⟩ ↑husband↓ his time;—he resolved to read; he resolved to give certain sums of money to charitable objects; he resolved to abstain;—to speak wisely;—to think with method; in some way to devote his powers to the advantage of others—to serve God—to imitate Jesus.

We coax our powers. ⟨We sp⟩ In our common conversation we admit without shame that we are one, & our faculties, another. We are cautious of pledging our powers to what they may recoil from. And so we are content to pass along, married to powers we cannot effectually use, unable to counteract or disguise or shake off the /influence/ tyranny/ of another & inferior mind who possesses this sole advantage of acting with the unity of an absolute Will.

↑{The whole strength of Napoleon founded on two opinions I. that he was master of himself II. that he was the Child of Destiny. The first was a legitimate royal title to him. The second was the spawn of false Religion. Remove them both & where were Napoleon?↓

These designs were projected in a glow of ⟨[illegible]⟩piety; were celebrated in his soul with ⟨holiest⟩ ↑solemn service of↓ hopes & prayers. The spirit hath her thanksgivings & Sabbaths as well as the state, & through all its faculties, it kept holy day, & conceived a deep joy in the perception of its own change & goodness. ↑But after all this preparation what feeble effects!↓ Something he did toward realizing his purpose but it was a most unlucky time,—some very unseasonable circumstances occurred; unusual temptation; strange interruption; unlooked for obstacles;—& the good purpose was postponed, & by & by forgotten.

Who is there among us that does not remember his defeats? Who that must not own himself the cause? ⟨The wa⟩ ⟨Immoveable⟩ Men of immoveable purpose are very rare. The world is full of effeminate undetermined ↑bashful↓ persons who carry a cowardice in their bosoms that invites opposition. Here and there, is a man of another temper, born for victory, because he persists in his purposes,—who, (to adopt the phrase of a man of this habit of mind,) if he encounters a battery, *carries the battery;* who is strengthened by danger, & obtains his ends.

The encouragements to Perseverance lie deep in our nature, they have connexion with all that is grand in our being & grow out of our connexion with ⟨things⟩ ↑the external world↓. Who knows the power of the human Will? Only the term of life can limit its power. Suppose ↑the life of↓ a single man of a practical mind such as Franklin to have been prolonged ⟨from the creation up⟩ through the 6000 years of human history, ↑is there any extravagance in supposing↓ would he not alone have invented all the arts with which that period has enriched the world? *Never to give over* is the whole secret of success. You do not know what any man—your neighbor, your brother, with whose thot's you have been familiar for years, can perform. You do not know what yourself can do. No man knows till he has tried, how much he can accomplish,—nor then—how much more, if he had not ceased from trying. ⟨There's no Thus far no farther⟩ No man can say "Thus far, no farther!" to the Will of man. And God doth not say it. We say, no man can do what is impossible,—but who can see the limits of the possible which hath no limits?

I am embarrassed, brethren, by the greatness of my subject, & I know not how most forcibly to ⟨re⟩present it to your minds. I hesitate whether to call your attention to the exploits of resolution in the past, or to the far greater exploits that lie wrapped up in the *powers* of men. The world is crowded with instances ↑of the resistless force of the resolute mind,↓ but all that is past, is as nothing to what might be.

I might satisfy the cautious of the advantage of perseverance—because it harvests all its least gains, & life & happiness are made up of little parts. I might win the greedy, by showing them that there is scarce any thing in life so insignificant but it contains the seed of greatest results; that ⟨in the⟩ "most poor matters point to rich ends," but that the great advantages do not show themselves at the beginning, & that those only who persist can ever know what is most worth seeking after. I might gain the philosopher by reminding him that in Gods Providence every thing has its price, that small advantages are easily procured, but the treasures of nature are hid in the ⟨ribs of mountains⟩ ↑mountain ribs of difficulty, in the secrecy of Time,↓ & months & years & counsel & labor must dig for them. Thus if a man is oppressed with care—a jest, a draught of wine, the theatre, are cheap means of momentary relief—but a *habit of patience,* which is the perfect medicine he cannot procure in an hour or a day. It will cost thot & strife & mortification & prayer

But there is one view in which the subject is best presented, because it seems to include all other views. ↑It is when the power is contemplated in the mind alone↓ It is this that God has imparted that power,—let me rather say—that portion of himself to the virtuous man, that whilst he perseveres, he cannot be subdued. ↑{Insert X} X {There is a passage of Dr Johnson in which he speaks of the power of man to bear pain which I believe no man reads without delight. "It may be questioned whether the ²body & the ¹mind are not so proportioned that the one will bear all that can be inflicted on the other; whether virtue will not last as long as life; & a soul well principled will not be separated sooner than subdued"—But it is not only to endure that we have force but also to act.}↓ Every thing which it conceives possible, the mind can do. ↑I know the force of the expressions I use↓ [in pencil] Tell me not of obstacles, of the small means a single human being can command, of his precarious health, of his short & uncertain life. If he fail & grow faint-hearted, ⟨it⟩ ↑the fault↓ is in himself & not in events. Small obstacles will bend & conform to great purposes. I say that to any really great & virtuous end the human will is invincible not to man's eye ↑which sees a little↓ but in the eye of God ↑which sees all↓. For if it is rightly considered it will be found, that every great action is done first in the mind, before it is done to the eye. Action is only the realizing of the thought. The invention of a new machine was perfect in the mind of the inventor before it was realized in his model of wood or brass.

The poem was in the soul of the poet before it was written on paper. {Napoleon was conquered in the mind of Wellington before he was conquere⟨on⟩d on the field of

Waterloo.} The ↑battle of the↓ American Revolution was ⟨f⟩ won in the hearts of ⟨her⟩ our patriots, long before the tardy march of events had closed the war.

Shall I ascend to a high ↑moral instance↓, the highest ⟨moral instance⟩ ↑in the history of the earth?↓ The Crucifixion was met & endured & triumphed over in the Garden, & the morning of the Resurrection had dawned on the spirit of the Saviour, before yet the traitor Judas had betrayed him to his foes.

Whensoever a virtuous mind hath fixed its eye steadfastly upon a great object, & hath /considered/understood/ the difficulties & hath laid its plans & hath warmed its own energies to the degree that, ⟨it⟩ in itself, it hath bridged over the gulf between it⟨self⟩ & the object, & has ⟨coolly⟩ ↑fully↓ satisfied itself that the object is practicable to it—then & there the victory is won, though ⟨God⟩ ↑it↓ should ↑please God to interrupt the execution by↓ paralyz⟨e⟩ing its energies & strik⟨e⟩ing that mind out of being.

↑The mind is a steam shop where power is generated no matter for what uses↓ [in pencil]

↑Let it be remembered by us that tis more important these victories shd. be won in the mind, than that the events shd. turn up as we desire. Life is a game of skill. No matter if we lose the stakes so that we play well↓

Let it be considered that God places the soul in the world in the midst of many good projects to exercise its faculties upon them. By its conversation & works it generates a certain amount of power which it applies here to certain present objects. But these objects are accidental & will soon be removed & the soul will be summoned to apply the same habits to new & far nobler uses in heaven.

⟨I do not define⟩ I am far from wishing to ⟨a⟩ give to these ⟨truths⟩ any appearance of extravagance or paradox. I wish to state the limit & the exception which have been already intimated in the remarks I have made. This prowess which God has given or permitted us to attain ↑tho' belonging in a degree to all action,↓ is not promised to all action, but only to *virtuous action*. The command in our text, is, Be not weary in *well* doing. I know very well there are in society what are called selfwilled men who are ever bent on impracticable objects—who always stand in their own /light./light & whose whole career is a series of defeats./ /All vice/All error/ is unnatural—& things fight against it, the interests of other men fight against it; it has the seeds of ↑strife &↓ defeat ⟨& death⟩ within itself. But all virtue is natural; is in harmony with all things; all men are by nature its well-wishers & helpers; things seen & things unseen work with it; & so besides its own might it hath the might of heaven & earth to reinforce it. It was this ⟨sentiment⟩ which prompted the exulting sentiment of Paul "I can do all things thro' Christ that strengtheneth me." ⟨It⟩ ↑The good man↓ hath Christ, ⟨it⟩ hath God to ⟨its⟩his friend.

My friends let these considerations ⟨have their weight with us⟩ & prevail with us not to be weary in well-doing. Has God set before you any opportunity of usefulness. Has he made any dependent on you for the comforts of life. Has he put it in your power to feed the soul to fill it with knowledge—to train it up to virtue? Do you meet with discouragements? Are you called to make serious sacrifices?—Be not weary in well doing. O do not decline the struggle ↑wh. in his high Providence he offers.↓

It is your apprenticeship to great vocations of trust & power in ⟨his⟩ Gods moral universe. Choose well your objects, & when you have chosen, persevere in their accomplishment. Let no postponement of your success abate your efforts or your ardour remembering that though God sees fit to honour goodness generally with signal success yet the main advantage which he proposes from your exertions is in yourself thereby you are educating immortal energies an invincible soul that shall presently burst into the invisible world like an angel armed with all virtues & powers fitted for Eternal Actions.

Manuscript (revised version): Seven sheets folded to make four pages each; the gathering consists of five nested folios followed by a single folio; these were tucked into the outermost folio and the whole cross-stitched through the left margin with white thread. Pages measure 25 x 20.3 cm.

Lines	Page 102
Bible Text	↑Let us not↓ ⟨B⟩be ⟨not⟩ weary

[The following variant opening, inscribed in pencil on MS p. 2, was written for the afternoon delivery on July 3, 1836, at East Lexington, when Sermon LIV was given in the morning:]

↑In my discourse this morning, I offered to your attention some remarks on the danger we are in from our evil habits. Our experience of the power of this principle ought to impress us us with the importance of making the whole of its strength serviceable to our Conscience; a day laborer for our real good. But the lesson which all experience teaches us is that we more readily run into a bad habit than a good one, that whilst our ⟨d⟩ resolution relaxes our appetites & passions do not relax & so overcome, that there is a want of continuity in the exertions↓

1	¶ ⟨Every thing that is said of the force of habit impresses the mind with the importance of our making the whole of its strength service-able to our Will; a day laborer for our real good.⟩ ¶ It
3	them. ⟨The faculties⟩ A
13–14	Perseverance. ¶ ↑What is essential to the formation of good habits↓ [notation in pencil] ¶ Many . . . fortune ⟨but⟩ I
16	↑because they are not,↓
22–(103)1	nature↑.↓ ⟨& truth dragged forth from her latent place in the human soul. It has been said of the construction of a pyramid that⟩ ↑I read with pleasure [ink over pencil] . . . art↓ "⟨i⟩If . . . ↑in construction↓ [addition in pencil]

Page 103

7–8	of ⟨power &⟩ wisdom
18	is ⟨i⟩an illusion,
21–22	↑But . . . provision ⟨becomes.⟩ has a baneful influence↓
24	in ⟨our⟩ an
31	↑too many↓
33–34	↑We . . . faculties.↓ [ink over pencil]
34	powers⟨, and⟩ instead
37	good ⟨end⟩ ↑work↓
38–39	↑{We . . . exertions.}↓ [ink over pencil; pencil layer reads: "We say I am afraid to promise this, lest I should not feel disposed to such exertion"]
41–(104)1	↑we↓ can only ⟨be said to be⟩ occasionally ⟨ours⟩ ↑use↓

Page 104

3–6   ↑(↓He . . . must ⟨obey⟩ ↑serve↓ . . . will.↑)↓ [parentheses added in
           ink over pencil]
26   {Men . . . rare.} [brackets in pencil]
29   purposes, ⟨who (to adopt the phrase of a man of this habit of mind) if
           he encounter a battery, carries the battery,⟩ who
36–37   being. ⟨I think the bare idea of a mind whose purposes cannot be
           shaken⟩ ¶ Who
39   mind s to have

Page 105

10   m⟨a⟩en.
15   the ⟨great⟩ chief
31–32   subdued. ⟨{It has been well said of the power of man to bear pain, "It
           may be questioned whether the mind & the body are not so propor-
           tioned, that the one will bear all that can be inflicted on the other;
           whether virtue will not last as long as life; & a soul well principled
           will not be separated sooner than subdued."}⟩ But . . . act.} [can-
           cellation and brackets in pencil; for the quotation from Samuel
           Johnson, see Sermon XXVII, n. 4]
33   ↑upright↓
36–37   ↑But . . . not↓
39   to ⟨Gods⟩ ↑the↓

Page 106

10   thoroughly ⟨considered⟩ understood . . . its ⟨own⟩ means
21   its ⟨go⟩ right
22   conversant. ⟨But t⟩These
30   ¶ It ⟨will be⟩ should

Page 107

6   secret. of
11–15   men /of/visited with/ [variant in pencil] . . . ground, that ⟨never
           gives over⟩ that repeats his trial ⟨the seventh⟩ to seven . . . in ⟨the⟩
           ↑God's↓ kingdom ⟨of heaven⟩ Whatsoever
17–20   retain ⟨its thought⟩ the subject of its examination ⟨in spite of being
           baffled⟩ in ⟨spite⟩ ↑thorough disregard↓ . . . eludes you⟨.⟩, ↑with
           . . . being ⟨before its⟩ rather than its purpose↓
34   deferred yet yet

Sermon LX

Manuscript: Four sheets folded to make four pages each; folios nested and sewn along
the left margin with white thread; pages measure 25 x 20.3 cm. A sheet, 20.3 x 14.8,
containing Insert "A," is attached with red sealing wax to the right margin of MS p. 4; a
separate folio (inscribed on the first two pages with the revised conclusion) is attached
with red sealing wax to the upper and lower right margin of MS p. 16.

[This Christmas sermon was revised for delivery on June 17, 1832; a substitute introduction, meant to replace the original first two paragraphs, is inscribed in darker ink on MS p. 3:]

↑And when the fulness of time was come, God sent forth his son made of a woman. Gal. 4.4

The thoughts of God are not as our thoughts saith the prophet [cf. Isaiah 55:8]. In one sense they are not, & yet in another they certainly are. For we are made in his image & when the sensual & sinful part is so subdued that our opinions & feelings flow from our inmost self, that is, from the celestial principle, then we approve what God doth & our own actions are measured on the same scale. Certainly it would not have occurred to men of worldly wisdom, that the way in which God would redeem his ancient promise to the Jewish people & found an everlasting kingdom that should not be cut off would be to send not an angel or glorious visitant but a child born of an obscure peasant woman

But as Xy has wro't its effect the wisdom of this providence has appeared to men. ⟨They⟩ ↑Godly minds↓ have adopted the thought of God Men have been able to see & approve the manifest benefit derived to mankind by sending a man among men by sending a poor man to the poor↓

Lines	
	Page 108
1	¶ ↑The return of↓ ⟨T⟩the . . . mind ⟨from its wide contemplations⟩ to
19	press ⟨this reas⟩ the
20–22	The ⟨Christmas⟩ ↑solemn jubilee↓ I would keep, is not /peculiar/ graced by forms/ to ⟨this season⟩ ↑a day↓, or to ⟨one⟩ ↑a↓ Church, . . . mind ↑whenever the event is remembered↓ inasmuch [The foregoing emendations occur in the same dark ink as the substitute introduction above and are rejected as late revisions.]
	Page 109
2–4	refer ↑the first,↓ to . . . & ↑the second↓ to [rejected as late revisions] . . . the ⟨Advent of⟩ ↑manner↓ Christ⟨.⟩s ↑coming↓ ¶ ↑I. And first the interest ↑created by him↓ is of a *personal* kind.↓ ¶ When [rejected as a late addition]
7	influence ↑of men; to receive↓ the↑ir↓ love & the↑ir↓ hatred, ↑to partake↓ the [rejected as late additions]
9–10	taught. ⟨The more this is considered the more important will it appear.⟩ ↑Insert A [in pencil and ink] A [in pencil] {An interest such as only attaches to *persons,* was created in the truth which he taught The more this is considered, the more important it will appear; & this, in two ways; namely, that, thus only can it become the object of the *affections,* & thus only can truth & virtue come to have the solidity of fact.

How vague & cold is our regard for patriotism, courage, purity, honesty, compared with our attachment to those qualities in the person of a friend. They are dead possibilities till they live in a soul. As no man wd. care for an empty ship foundering in a tempest; but it is the presence of breathing thinking men therein, that tortures us with interest in their danger: and as they say in the arts, yᵗ a landscape is imperfect, without animals & men,—so, the infinite field of moral

truth is but a wearisome & barren immensity till it is peopled with
examples.} [brackets in pencil] ↑—Again, the relation of Xt↓↓ [Insert
"A" written in dark ink on sheet attached by red sealing wax to the
right margin; rejected as a late revision] The relation of ⟨a person⟩
↑Christ↓

12   at ⟨rest⟩ ↑an end↓. [rejected as a late emendation]
15   contempt ⟨the idea of⟩ Columbus↑' idea↓ [rejected as a late emenda-
              tion]
17–27   soul. ⟨{How [bracket in pencil] . . . of ⟨our⟩ ↑a↓ . . . landscape ⟨is⟩
              is imperfect without animals & men so . . . examples.
                 ⟨Who knows how mu⟩ Thus . . . affections.⟩ [cancellation in
              pencil and ink; rejected as a late revision (cf. Insert "A" above)]
                 ⟨Then w⟩Who
32–33   example. ↑Nothing but↓ [rejected as a late addition] A man . . .
              enslaved ⟨to vice⟩, as they are⟨.⟩, ↑to vice.↓
42   ↑not only↓

Page 110

4–5   he ⟨rose &⟩ showed . . . ↑& said Peace be with you.↓
10   him. ⟨To⟩On
13–15   ↑which↓ . . . titles of ⟨love & honour⟩ ↑esteem & veneration↓ . . .
              in⟨to⟩ the extravagance of love, ↑& in . . . caution,↓
17–19   been ⟨the⟩ when . . . questioned ⟨all⟩ ↑the essential truth of↓
21   ↑& hearty↓
23–25   due. ⟨It is not only⟩ ↑I will not leave↓ This ⟨personal⟩ interest . . .
              Saviour ⟨it is well for each of us to remember it is important to⟩
              ↑without remarking that there is a practical good in↓ cultivat⟨e⟩ing
              as
28–29   friend. ¶ ↑II.↓ The [rejected as a late addition]
36–39   many ⟨of us⟩ in . . . the ⟨itching⟩ ↑provocations↓ of ⟨pleasure⟩
              appetite are ⟨but⟩ absorbed . . . of ↑the↓ unseen

Page 111

1   the ⟨angels song⟩ ↑music of his speech↓
1   I say, ⟨it is come⟩ ↑it speaks peace↓. [emendation in pencil]
2   ↑of those accents↓ that echo⟨es⟩ now [emendation in pencil] . . . the
              [end of page] the whole ⟨earth⟩ world.
3–4   ↑is↓ like God's good ↑after . . . God↓
5–8   air. ↑Insert X X {It is . . . and ⟨the⟩ he . . . itself}↓ [insert moved
              from its original position in the paragraph between the sentence
              ending "despitefully use you.'" and the sentence beginning "Thus has
              God"]
17–19   came ⟨unt⟩from . . . fulfilled. ¶ ⟨The same feelings that justify us in
              paying honor to this occasion whilst we consider the auspicious event
              of the birth of Christ ⟨we are about to celebrate his⟩ ↑justify us in
              celebrating the supper of his↓ death⟩ ¶ The memory
21   recollection ⟨every relic ↑of a truly great event yᵗ has transpired in yᵉ
              earth↓ of a precious life⟩ as a relief

22	The ⟨life⟩ ↑character↓
23–24	efficacious ⟨is th⟩ to human
26–28	when ⟨we⟩ the individual . . . is ⟨our⟩ ↑his↓ part of being, how short ⟨our life⟩ ↑his term↓; . . . interruptions, & ⟨feebleness⟩ ↑disasters↓,
35	can ⟨surmount⟩ take.
38–40	should ⟨abide⟩ ↑endure↓ whilst God ⟨abides⟩ ↑endures↓, . . . forever & ⟨ever⟩ forevermore.

[The following addition is inscribed on pp. 1–2 of a four-page insert (pp. 3–4 blank), attached by red sealing wax to the upper and lower right margin of MS p. 16, the last page of the sewn fascicle:]

↑One word to the day & the hour. It has been announced to you that our ancient house of worship is to undergo some important repairs & the circumstance will separate us for several weeks. In a life so uncertain as ours even so trifling an event should not pass unmarked. For which of us is well assured that he shall ever again take his seat in this house where his fathers & brethren & sisters have now for so many generations worshipped the Eternal after the instructions of Jesus Christ. Which of us is better assured of life & earthly happiness than ⟨the young⟩ our townsmen & acquaintances ↑the young, the amiable, the excellent↓ whom the ⟨last week⟩ waters have swallowed in such a fearful moment. Verily in the midst of life we are in death. Is there any way to be rid of the gloom & the fear which such events occasion. Is there any ⟨way⟩ courage which cannot be daunted, any peace which nothing can interrupt any insurance which ↑can↓ protect life & whatever is more than life. There is none but religious principle ⟨and that is enough⟩ ↑in wh. yᵉ man of Bethlehem must be our instructer↓. ⟨Let us⟩ Brethren let me entreat of each of you the effort of thought to bring home to your own mind the question whether you do not think in your inmost self that by ↑receiving↓ the principles of Christ into the heart & life a man is better equipped for all & any events, for all possible contingences for long life for disappointment for persecution for sickness for success ⟨for⟩ in this world, for translation by death into other worlds or other mode of living than by any other principles or any other means that the imagination can suggest. I know what your answer must be. Let this then be our parting thought; let this be our returning tho't if we are permitted to return, & let us recognize this tho't when we are permitted to worship in a spiritual & immortal temple.

June 17, 1832.↓

Sermon LXI

Manuscript: Six sheets folded to make four pages each; folios nested and sewn through the left margin with white thread; pages measure 25 x 20.3 cm. Something was once affixed to the bottom of MS p. 12 with red sealing wax; MS p. 13 was extended at the bottom by the addition of a slip of paper, affixed with red sealing wax, to accommodate the lengthy Insert "A."

[Above Bible text:] *Last Night of the Year 1829.*

Lines	Page 112
Bible Text	↑The night . . . 13 Romans, 12—↓

7–9	↑vast↓ orbit ↑we traverse↓ . . . & that ⟨we who dwell upon hereupon have one year less to live.⟩ ⟨adds⟩ another year ↑is added↓
14	↑of the heavens↓
17	1500,000, miles [There is a slight space after the "5"; Emerson probably read the figure as "fifteen hundred thousand."]
18	ever. ↑everlasting oil↓ [in pencil between paragraphs]
20	↑What . . . vapor?↓

Page 113

5	then ⟨if⟩ whatever
7	↑& to . . . ourselves.↓
10	summon her ⟨servants⟩ faculties
15–16	↑that I have come↓,
22–23	is not made thoughtful [tentatively canceled with thin line] ⟨does not perceive the moral of⟩ ↑by↓
24	those. times.
25	will ⟨be⟩ ↑show↓
31	↑yield to this impulse &↓
34	& ⟨th⟩perhaps
35	The ⟨progre⟩ dominion

Page 114

1–2	been /punished/visited/ . . . interests ⟨of which⟩ ↑&↓ many
4–8	transpired; ↑{Insert X} ⟨Friends have been taken away from our side He who should stand in their place has been withdrawn from his duties & sent out a pilgrim ⟨into a distant land⟩ & ↑sorrowing↓ sees the sun set in a distant land⟩ ¶ ↑X {Friends . . . ⟨his⟩the home of his fathers.}↓↓ new
12–13	↑"↓the life . . . pleasant, ⟨has been taken away⟩ ↑is at an end."↓.
15	those ⟨wh⟩ on
22	& ⟨be⟩ grow
23	general ⟨p⟩ distribution of ⟨pleas⟩ good
27–(115)15	accomplished. ↑{Insert A} ⟨But the grossness of sensual indulgence is rare⟩ A {There are some whose souls are ⟨stained⟩ spotted . . . devising & /completion/ripening/ & practice . . . fraud.—others, . . . ↑safety, or↓ . . . ↑innocence . . . word;↓ . . . ↑if Revelation will not reach you.↓. . . . be /questioned/doubted/ . . . think ⟨are⟩ forgotten, . . . be ⟨doubted⟩ ↑questioned↓ . . . And so though now [At this point, Insert "A" is extended onto a slip of paper attached to the bottom of MS p. 13 with red sealing wax.] . . . for them. Children of the world & c & c}↓ Children of this world!

Page 115

24–25	no /ears/hearing/, . . . ↑when . . . left.↓
31	rest. ↑& hardly then for your tho'ts↓ [addition in pencil]

Page 116

4	female /skill/exertions/,

7–8	year—⟨that our worldly substance has been increased⟩ that we have eaten
11–12	all? ¶ ⟨My brother my⟩ Take
14–15	spirits, ⟨who instructs you by his Providence,⟩ & has
22	his Son & he ⟨looks to see⟩ your [lightly struck through]
23–26	↑O say not you are poor & low ¶ ⟨There is not⟩ I . . . that ⟨w⟩there . . . no ↑one↓ good exertion in vain.↓
29	your ⟨frame⟩ ↑constitution↓.
31	almightiness; ⟨↑{B}↓⟩ that every ⟨human soul⟩ ignorant
33–34	goodness↑. {B}↓ ⟨that "spirits can crowd eternity into an hour, or stretch an hour into eternity."⟩ ↑B↓ {that every . . . wisdom.}
39–40	↑thro . . . benevolence↓

Page 117

4	Soul. ⟨Something I trust has been done in the past year to send the truth of that revelation The night of our life is far spent the day of the resurrection is at hand it becomes us to remember the word of the Lord Jesus when he was in the flesh to his disciples Watch ↑& pray lest ye enter into temptation & what I say unto you I say unto all↓⟩ [addition in pencil] To the soul is no ↑bounded↓
11	as seem⟨s the⟩ proper
13	lighted you⟨r⟩ with
20–21	name? ¶ ⟨An interval of solemn thought yet remains⟩ ↑This . . . hand↓.
23–27	↑by↓ . . . hold ↑us↓ . . . hours ⟨it lies with⟩ ↑↑as . . . spread↓ . . . with↓

Sermon LXII

Manuscript (earlier version): Five sheets folded to make four pages each; folios nested and sewn through the center fold with white thread; pages measure 25 x 20.3 cm.

[The text of the earlier version follows:]

LXII.

⟨Behold⟩ Henceforth I call you not servants, for the servant knoweth not what his ⟨L⟩lord doeth; but I have called you friends, for all things that I have ⟨made⟩ heard of my Father, I have made known unto you.

John XV. 15.

I believe, my Christian brethren, no good man can read or hear these words without sincere satisfaction. For this language is not confined to the twelve disciples to whom it was first addressed, for Jesus has himself in the context extended its signification to all his church by declaring who are his friends. "Ye are my friends, if ye do whatsover I command you."

Many minds are offended if any thing is said with any degree of confidence of our love to Christ It is Christ who loved us but any profession of warm regard on our part is reckoned by them as presumption.

Yet I would fain hope that many of those who are now assembled in Christian worship have come up with an enlightened & sincere ⟨satisfaction⟩ ↑pleasure↓ & that they have brought with them here & do habitually carry in their minds a lively affection such as that borne to a venerated friend, yet exalted & peculiar in its strain, to Jesus. I judge it not proper to apologize for any language implying that feeling out of any fear of sneers at hypocrisy or unwillingness to disturb the peace of scrupulous persons.

I wish rather to justify this boldness of access from his own lips & not only so but to show that this confident affection flows necessarily from the natural feelings of every good mind when false religion has not put obstructions in the way. I think that we cannot help (if any goodness is in us) loving our religion & loving its author.

⟨And it seems to me very important that this prejudice should be removed from our minds because the enemies of religion take advantage of this⟩ [end of page]

I am led to make these remarks because I think that not only do men generally rather respect than love religion but that it seems to me that very good men incline to a certain diffidence & separation from common feelings & /common/cheerful/ language in their religious views which is alien to the spirit of trust & equal love which the character & professions of Jesus ↑which is dictated by a spirit of fear↓ ought to inspire. The relation of Christ to the soul of a good man is in itself sufficiently near & distinct; may be as clearly ascertained as that of any other friend absent from the flesh. but those views which shd most readily have grown up in the hearts of his followers have been chilled & repressed by the errors of the understanding. We come slow & cold at his call.

It seems to me very important that /the prejudice/every thing of this kind/ which has made religion sad & stern, & built the church by the graveyard should be removed from our minds, because the enemies of religion ⟨religion⟩ take advantage of this [end of page] timid relucting aweful reverence borne to religion & with a bad kindness come to deliver us from what we seem to fear. Far more reasonable would it be like Paul to glory in the cross. Far better to let our eager acceptance correspond with the frankness of his welcome. He says, I have called you friends. Far better to hold the faith in that spirit of preference & joy as counts all dross but that & be true to that one friendship though all the world go away.

It is a very clear & important truth that this regard of friendship to Christ & of love to his religion will continually grow warmer as the character becomes purer. ⟨A bad man & a good man can never be true friends⟩. Likeness of nature is necessary to all sympathy, & the more likeness the more perfect the sympathy. It was the saying of a great statesman that "he never knew a man that was bad, fit for an action that was good." ↑Much more true is it that a bad man & a good man can never be true friends.↓

Goodness loses its nature in the eye of a thoroughly depraved being (if we can conceive such an one) & appears the extreme of weakness & delusion. A perfect understanding is indispensable to sympathy.

⟨And⟩ ↑Nor is it an exception to this↓ when we say that by such & such rare instances of virtue envy was overcome & a momentary admiration extorted from the corrupt we only mean that the effect upon partially depraved minds was such as to startle the conscience within them to rouse itself ↑to an unwonted exertion↓ & reassert its sovereignty in the soul.

Is it then to be wondered at, that sinful men should not only have no love but nourish in their hearts a hostility to Christ when having incapacitated themselves by their own evil habits to /approve/understand/ his /character/moral perfections/ they perceive every act of his to stand in contrast & every rule of his to be a condemnation to themselves. It was to be expected from their characters that Judas should sell him & Caiaphas crucify him & not the less that the voluptuary & the selfish & the malignant ↑of every generation↓ should deny & blaspheme him. It is terrible but natural that thus the free agency of man should be manifested that thus /they/the melancholy company of wicked men/ should be able age after age one after the other to take into their own hands the spear & thrust it into his side.

And is it not also most reasonable that they who by the practice of his commandments, by much meditation on the noble beauty & utility of his doctrines, by prayer & determination & by action also have made themselves more & more like him & so continually more capable of estimating him, should be continually drawn closer to him in affection that ⟨reverence⟩ obedience should be elevated into reverence & reverence should ripen into love—that in the progress of his mind as by reflexion it should put on the manly robe it should perceive the privelege of indefinite expansion to which God had appointed it by making it in his image perceive that God had confined it to no low bounds but urged in the spirit of a solemn confidence to feel to its Saviour the kindness not of a servant but of a friend

I believe there has been many a poor heart overlooked by the bustling multitude, & happily I may say shielded by the obscurity & obstructions of its lot from the common influences of society ⟨that sits alone⟩ without other education or instructor save the bible ⟨alone⟩ only, that sits alone engrossed with the study of its own thoughts, where all wisdom is, and the image of Jesus comes into its solitude as he should come, a friend to a friend. Such an one marks with tranquillity his own increasing power over his propensities, & ⟨feels⟩ knows his increasing worthiness in the eye of his divine Instructor; he speaks to him with an unblamed familiarity that is just in the eye of God tho' the knowledge of human opinions might check it to silence.—

Tell me not that there is danger in dwelling ↑with complacency↓ upon our small progress in virtue & on the ground of its laying claim to the praise of being of that party, & identifying ourselves with the interests of religion. I do not think there is danger. A man may wish to impose on others the belief that he is a good man but he cannot impose on himself For there is always this simple test of a↑ny↓ true advancement in religious life, namely that every step increases ⟨our⟩ the extent of our prospect, so that with every acquisition we more clearly perceive our deficiencies. So that such a thing was never heard of in the world as a good man trumpeting his own triumphs, but the wellknown & universal habit of goodness is to be reaching forward to farther attainments

↑Nor let it be alleged as↓ Another reason ⟨may be offered⟩ for forbidding this frank attachment & on ⟨some⟩ ↑any↓ occasions avowal of attachment to Christ & his commandments, namely, that the revelation speaks to man in a warning in a ⟨minatory⟩ menacing sometimes in denouncing language that it was a voice crying Repent; that it lifted the veil in part from the tremendous retributions of the eternal world & announced the wrath of God upon every soul of man that doeth evil.

Far be it from me, brethren, to remove any of the terrors of the law from the evil doer, but to the well doer it hath no terror. It is a law denouncing ⟨all⟩ judgements terrible beyond imagination to a sinful soul but the same law breathes peace & inmost joy to the good. There is sufficient reason for the hostility of the infidel that whenever he turns or is turned towards the gospel he sees its face full of ⟨fear⟩ ↑danger↓ to himself but ⟨the moment⟩ in proportion as a man becomes good he leaves those terrors below him, &

though he knows full well they exist in all their force to others & would so exist to him, if he were ↑the degraded↓ in other circumstances—yet now they affect him no more. He acts by the force of more generous motives than fear: he is the servant of love. And perfect love casteth out fear. The laws of the gospel are in this respect precisely like human laws. The laws affixing fatal penalties to piracy & murder exist for the best citizen as well as the worst. But what man of reputable standing amongst us would not feel himself insulted if ↑it were↓ supposed that those laws had the slightest influence over him. At the same time a man really guilty of those crimes skulks ⟨like a ghost⟩ for months & years ↑from street to street & from town to town↓ under the liveliest terror looking every moment when the vengeance of ⟨the public justice⟩ ↑th⟨ose⟩e violated law⟨s⟩↓ shall ⟨drag⟩ ↑consign↓ him to the gibbet.

I desire that the disciples of Christ might put on a manly front & frankly express the joy of beleiving & the uplifting peace & hope that springs from affections set upon a heart so large a dignity so unrivalled as his—Let it not be thought strange if we who by Gods direct revelation walk in the light of an everlasting hope and are now come out of the painful ignorance which perplexed the understandings & sat heavy on the hearts of best & wisest men in the elder world, we to whom is explained the mystery of our life & who are ⟨shown⟩ taught the lesson of serenity & trust by the knowledge that the government of the Universe is in the hands of One just & wise let it not be thought strange if our trust & joy should sometimes rise to exultation. Wheresoever we go, we are in the treasuries of truth ⟨which God⟩ with which God means we should enrich our selves. Wheresoever we go, we are watched over by an anxious an affectionate Providence. All events all connexions all conversations into which we are thrown are significant of its will & virtue is to be got there. We walk in an omnipresent hope. ⟨We⟩ The good we seek we already taste, & know that it has neither limit or end. We are heirs of God & joint heirs with Christ. And he who was the chosen minister of God who was sanctified & sent to men with this communication & {who was not only by his Word but by his life the Light that lighteth all men that come into the world} who taught us by his own life how we should live to reap these advantages hath declared that if we do his commandments we shall abide in his love—& he said to his disciples Henceforth I call you not servants but I have called you Friends.

Brethren, I should labour most carefully to guard the remarks I have been making from misconstruction, but that the error into which if mistaken they would lead is so obvious. I know very well how

But I wish it shd be felt that Christianity is not something to be defended & respected but something to panted after & gloried in that we look to it as a privelege & that each of us may seek such worthiness as to have a fellowship with that glorified person who brot it from God.

↑Finally↓ And as Christ loved us we ought also to love one another. It has been often the subject of complaint that the bands of Christian friendship are no more strictly drawn. A very little consideration wd. show us that when Christianity shall have wrought a farther effect on mankind a stronger union a more useful intercourse will be the natural consequence. For in the pursuits that now absorb the talents & strength of men every man is ⟨his brothers⟩ ↑the↓ rival ↑of his brother.↓. ⟨The⟩ Men seek for wealth & distinction & office. But ↑since of↓ these things there is only a certain amount, ⟨&⟩ what one gets another must lose. But when in the progress of wisdom from the spiritual world into this world, men instead of money shall pursue virtue & instead of fame pursue truth, they will cease to envy or oppose each other for these are infinite things, ⟨& every man may aid⟩ and all true lovers of them are lovers of one another ↑&

aids in mutual advancement↓. Meantime it is in the power of every Christian to promote this social cause by his own devotion to it, to unite with his Master & his Friend in fulfilling in his own life the eternal Commandments of his Father & our Father

Manuscript (revised version): Eight sheets folded to make four pages each; folios stacked and sewn with white thread along the left margin. Pages measure 25 x 20.3 cm.

Lines	Page 118
15–16	reasons /↑{↓have brought to Church I would fain hope that many of those who are now engaged in the exercises of Christian worship have come up to them↑}↓/usually . . . worship/ [brackets in pencil; variant in pencil on facing page]

Page 119

8	think ⟨we⟩that
9–10	author. ¶ ⟨Is not this very clear? Yet⟩ ↑I . . . because↓ . . . ↑that↓
16	a ⟨hollow⟩ ⟨↑poor↓⟩ ↑bad↓
19	they ⟨have⟩ ↑worship with↓ . . . which ⟨are⟩ ↑is↓
23	up ⟨in⟩ [end of line] in
25	but /are slow & cold to come/it is harsh & stern/.

Page 120

7	↑Quite↓ As
27	of ⟨evil⟩ wicked
30–31	his ⟨life⟩ doctrines,
40	experience, ⟨but⟩ ↑though↓

Page 121

2–3	multi⟨t⟩ [end of line] tude
30–31	man ⟨in⟩ not . . . a ⟨warning⟩ monitory,
34	↑This . . . objection↓ [in pencil]
36	↑this I say, that↓ [in ink over pencil] to the ⟨evil⟩ [canceled in pencil] well
41	& ⟨although⟩ although

Page 122

9–12	↑Is . . . soul as . . . law?↓ [in ink over pencil; second sentence of pencil layer varies: "As the true religion hath its rise & progress in the soul, as his mind becomes united to God, does he not cease to fear, & become superior to the thunders of the law—"]
14–15	beleiving . . . ↑an↓ affection⟨s⟩
31	sent ⟨into the world⟩ to men
40	privelege

Page 123

11	th⟨is⟩e spiritual ⟨in⟩world

Sermon LXIII

Manuscript: Six sheets folded to make four pages each; folios nested and the inner five folios sewn with white thread along the left margin; pages measure 25 x 20.3 cm. The outermost folio, containing the revised introduction and conclusion, is not included in the sewing. The original conclusion is followed by the date "24 Jan. 1830," while the revised conclusion carries the two dates "Jan 24 1830 / Sept 4 1831"—all in the same hand and ink as the revised conclusion itself.

[The following new beginning was added for the second delivery, September 4, 1831. It appears to have substituted for the original text and first three paragraphs, which are set off by brackets:]

Be not conformed to this world, but be ye transformed by the renewing of your mind that ye may prove what is that good & acceptable & perfect will of God. Rom. 12.2.

"The present," said an English moralist, "is always the rival of the future." It is so in our daily experience. We find ourselves still children, still tempted to do what offers a present gratification at the expense of future regret. Let us look around us at our homes, our friends, ↑the dead & the living↓ our place in life, the expectations of others, what we have done yesterday, what we mean to do tomorrow,—and something of reproof and dissatisfaction will come to our mind from every object, admonishing us how often we have failed,—that in all things we have come short of our duty.

↑And many such records there are of our failing virtue↓ [last sentence in ink over pencil]

Lines	Page 124
Bible Text	⟨If any man whosoever will come after me, let him deny himself & take up his cross & follow me. Mark 8.34.⟩ ↑{Be not . . . Rom. 12.2.↓
1–3	¶ ↑We are . . . read.↓ [ink over pencil; pencil layer varies: " . . . come again . . . praise him & to learn our duty & the lesson of his word."]
6–8	↑The commandment↓ . . . ↑lively↓ . . . ↑like a↓ harsh ↑accusation.↓
13–19	¶ ↑But the . . . injured⟨.⟩, ↑or before whom he has offended.}↓↓ ["But the . . . hour." is in ink over pencil; pencil layer varies: " . . . stone are not all the commandments we have. God has more monitors than these. Tis strange . . . to every event & thing & relation & hope."; "or before . . . offended." is in ink over pencil; the pencil inscription ends with a dash instead of a period]
24–(125)2	ways. ⟨↑There is not a sceptic↓⟩ [in pencil, overwritten by "{Insert A}" in ink] ↑A {There is . . . guilt.}↓

	Page 125
3	history ⟨m⟩of
5	is ⟨w⟩always
6–11	future. ⟨With vast numbers of men⟩ ↑There . . . whom↓ . . . ↑coming↓ . . . himself ⟨seventy⟩ old age; ⟨&⟩ ↑i.e. who . . . risk of ⟨future⟩ ↑years of↓ harm, whilst↓ . . ↑life↓ . . . account. ⟨Then⟩ ↑Next above this class,↓ . . . life ⟨so to speak thro a fifteen-minutes ⟨glass⟩ ↑lens↓⟩ ↑as . . . man↓, . . . they [end of page] they ⟨compromise⟩ ↑postpone↓
13–15	class. ¶ ⟨The brute as we know⟩ Thus the ⟨lowest⟩ most . . . ↑the↓. savage⟨s⟩, or ⟨so made⟩ ↑he y^t is made savage↓ . . . his ⟨glass⟩ ↑cup↓
20	↑years,↓ with so ⟨strong⟩ ↑clear↓

23	their ⟨calculation⟩ ↑aim↓?
25	circumstances ⟨unpoisoned by⟩ ↑safe from↓
27	↑at human life↓ with ⟨fifteen-minute⟩- ⟨↑an↓⟩the eye of a ⟨few minutes⟩ ↑brute↓
30–31	the ⟨gravity⟩ ↑name↓
33	religion. ⟨But the main regard is still to this world. They frequent at least a part of the time, the church.⟩ They
41–(126)17	↑And then . . . the world?↓

Page 126

| 18–23 | be dis⟨mal⟩↑heartening↓ . . . man⟨,⟩; ↑this . . . future↓ . . . ↑the ⟨important fact⟩ consoling . . . by↓ . . . (/that God has much better things in store than yet we have seen,/that . . . possible/) |
| 27–35 | ↑in the . . . brute;↓ . . . means ⟨and in the tongue which sets them above the brute⟩ ↑which . . . cities↓ . . . will, ⟨reducing the unborn events of life to system by⟩ irresistible force, [incomplete cancellation] ↑establishing . . . unborn↓ . . . ↑of all . . . existence↓ into the ⟨image⟩ of ↑city of the living↓ God—this [incomplete cancellation] |

Page 127

1–4	by ⟨parts & patches⟩ ↑fits & starts↓, exhibit ⟨[illegible word]⟩ occasional . . . is ⟨never⟩ ↑seldom↓
13	the ⟨importance⟩ ↑need↓
15	& ⟨boldly⟩ ↑improvidently↓
18–19	↑—that alarm . . . hopes as & . . . ours.↓
22	all ⟨private⟩ gifts
27	been ⟨oblig⟩ /confined/compelled/
31–(128)10	thought. ⟨I suppose this will be allowed me when it is re⟨-fle⟩membered that the result of diligent thinking has always been to lead men to one conclusion that tranquillity of mind is to be got only by devotion to higher pursuits than the gratification of the animal wants.⟩ ⟨↑{Insert X at the end}↓⟩ ¶ ↑Is not . . . use it?↓ ↑{X [hand pointing right]}↓ ¶ ↑X [inscribed following the original end of the sermon] {I suppose . . . independance & tranquillity. ⟨We⟩ ↑You↓ may be ↑very↓ rich ⟨beyond the dream of avarice⟩ ⟨We⟩ ↑You↓ may be ↑politically↓ great ⟨beyond the hope of ambition⟩ & come . . . independance . . . ↑freedom↓ . . . ↑being admitted↓ . . . favor, or ⟨of⟩ the . . . independant & happy.↓

Page 128

12	us ⟨to⟩ first
13–14	{It is I venture to say the
21	the /mud/bottom/
27	is ⟨proof & stimulus⟩ ↑the bulwark↓ . . . of it}
29	for ⟨sour.⟩ ↑rotten.↓
30–32	sour. ⟨It was said by one of the most successful of the statesmen of the last century a man of great talents & great success—when in no ill humor "The best of life is but just tolerable; tis the most we can make

of it." No virtuous man ⟨to⟩ would consent to this account. It is remarkable that several of the most eminent statesmen of modern England have died by their own hand.⟩ ↑In our . . . to ⟨be⟩ believe . . countries?↓

36   ↑but↓

38   this ⟨account⟩ ↑deplorable confession↓.

Page 129

5   ↑& renown↓

7   ↑innocent↓

8   {The soul of the child ⟨is innocent⟩ ↑hath no sin↓,

21–22   ↑Be not . . . world.↓

28   him ⟨tak⟩ deny

29–30   was ⟨his⟩ ↑the↓ . . . life. ↑wh. came . . . self-denial?↓

37   independance

Page 130

1   ¶ I⟨f⟩ think

3   quoted ⟨in⟩ ↑with↓

8   ¶ ↑I know↓ The

10   our /nature/self/.

[The following conclusion was added for the second delivery of the sermon:]

A good life must be such a life as unites the claims of the present & the future; that uses this world without neglecting the next; such a life in short, as trains the soul to a knowledge of its resources, to a possession of its powers, & makes it fit to draw the greatest good out of every event. For this the gospel came this was the example of Christ This is the teaching of Paul. Be not conformed to this world, i.e. Do not live in this world as if this was the whole of your being; then, you would be only the first of animals; but be ye transformed by the renewing of your mind,—let the living soul that is within you give direction to your life; that is eternal, & if you obey ⟨them⟩ ↑it↓, will regulate your life by eternal laws, that you may prove what is the good & acceptable & perfect will of God. Instead of living by custom or by the impulses of passion live by reflection—& you shall find favor with God & eternal felicity. A good man once told me that he supposed a virtuous man died before he passed out of this world; that is to say that ⟨su⟩ by the change of his heart day by day from the love of temporal good to the love of truth & righteousness his affections were gradually transferred so entirely to God that he left every thing here without regret & so when he came to leave this world there was no violence in the change his soul was already in the state which heaven requires.

Brethren, let us not any longer be conformed to this world, but transformed by the renewing of our mind. The way is plain Every hour is bringing the oppportunity of working this change. Every hour carries hence its report to the ear of God of our the quickening of spiritual life in each of us or of our spiritual death. Awake to righteousness. Be pure in heart; be humble; be just; be kind; &, amid all the din of this worlds company & temptations, hearken with religious reverence to the voice of God. It sounds within you. It responds to the truths taught in the Scripture Incline your ear & hear & obey & your soul shall live.—

Sermon LXV

Manuscript: Five sheets folded to make four pages each; folios nested and sewn with white thread along the left margin; pages measure 25 x 20.3 cm.

Lines	Page 132
5	↑these are things which↓
7–8	else. ↑¶ Moreover;↓ It [Emerson's paragraph sign added]
9–12	end. ⟨P⟩ A cup . . . the ⟨cold⟩ frosty ground ↑may be . . . or may be↓ . . . ↑so much↓ gratify ⟨but⟩ ↑as↓
12–16	If ⟨it⟩ ↑man↓ . . . becomes ⟨a⟩ necessary to ⟨its⟩his comfort; if ⟨it⟩he . . . months ⟨it⟩he has . . . whets ⟨its⟩his . . . if ⟨it⟩he . . . sweetness ⟨it⟩he . . . from ⟨its⟩his
19	duties; ⟨To those neighbors ⟨t⟩he cannot say⟩ ↑Go away, my neighbors, and↓ Come
24	owe & ⟨perform⟩ ↑pay↓
25–(133)2	plain ⟨then⟩ ↑brethren↓ . . . attention ⟨so⟩ ↑at the same time↓ . ·. . us. ⟨And so⟩ ↑And . . . Providence.↓

	Page 133
5–9	all ⟨attempts⟩ ↑endeavours↓ . . . &↑, in fine,↓ our ↑whole↓ . . . them. ¶ ⟨{I believe it is a demonstrable truth that we always do ourselves good when we do good to others. But this is a low motive for benevolence & can only be presented as a motive to those hardened selfseekers who are incapable as yet of being reached by any higher one. The only way in which this fact becomes interesting to the lovers of God is as an evidence of the perfect harmony of the laws of their Fathers kingdom.}⟩ [brackets in pencil; canceled in pencil and ink] ¶ ↑/Let me then from this lesson of our master invite your attention, ↑1.↓ to yᵉ manner in which God has shown his intention yᵗ we shd serve one another, ↑2.↓ to the duty of benevolence and to the danger⟨s⟩ of becoming selfish into which all of us run./I ask yʳ attention ↑1.↓ to . . . 2. That ⟨voluntary⟩ benevolence . . . us./↓
10–11	¶ ↑1.↓ . . . ↑innocent↓
14–15	every ⟨pe⟩ little . . . to ⟨parts⟩ ↑places↓
16–20	The ⟨hideous selfishness which⟩ ↑wealthy wretch who↓ shuts ⟨its⟩ his . . . grudges ⟨its⟩ ↑the↓ pittance ↑of his↓ . . . to ⟨its⟩his . . . benefit ⟨its⟩his . . . than ⟨its⟩his
31	↑from↓
34–35	nail ⟨pin⟩, ⟨↑furniture,↓⟩ paper, ⟨shoe⟩ ↑cotton↓ manufacture⟨r⟩ ↑neither of↓ which cann⟨ot⟩ in
37–38	↑right↓ . . . ↑so much↓

	Page 134
1–2	↑the lawyer at his code↓ . . . ↑almost↓
11–12	intellect. ⟨⟨↑It mt also be shown that when we aim at others good we are really↓⟩ ↑As thus in seeking our own advantage we are ⟨seeking⟩ ↑promoting↓ the good of others so obtaining our own}↓⟩ I believe . . . is ⟨true⟩ demonstrably

17–22   ↑Thus . . . this is ⟨involuntary⟩ ↑mere↓ beneficence; . . . do good↓ ¶
             ⟨But doth any⟩ ↑A↓ man ↑may↓
24   ↑I have no separate duty.↓
25–26   remove. ⟨But⟩ ↑What!↓ shall . . . our ⟨good deeds⟩ ↑selfish action↓
34–36   ↑sealed . . . Son.↓ [addition in pencil and ink; pencil layer has "was
             sealed"] ⟨Yet there⟩ ↑Yet . . . mass↓ ⟨is⟩of selfishness ↑is↓
37   the ⟨disaster⟩ ↑misfortune↓
39   ¶ ↑But↓ There . . . ↑hardly blamed as sin;↓ ⟨Where is there not?⟩ a
             great

Page 135

5   pleasantry; &
15–17   not ⟨the eminent⟩ ↑of his degree↓ . . . silence ⟨In his own house⟩
             ↑⟨Among⟩ ↑In↓ . . . friends↓ [ink over pencil; pencil layer has
             "Among the"] . . . return; ↑Like . . . apology,↓
24   against ⟨it as⟩ ↑so . . . are↓ when it ⟨is the⟩ appears
26   ↑¶ It is bad enough ⟨in all⟩ ↑every where↓ but it is frightful in
             ⟨children⟩the young.↓ [Emerson's paragraph sign added]
26–27   so ⟨dark & cancerous⟩ ↑black↓
27   ↑And yet↓ You
28   who ⟨utters a⟩ shows a ↑premature↓ [addition in ink over pencil]
30–33   ↑by his applause↓ . . . seed of ⟨war & hatred & death & hell⟩ ↑the
             second death↓ [addition in pencil and ink] . . . child ¶ ⟨It should be
             impressed o⟩If . . . it should be ⟨↑a scorn of↓⟩ th⟨is⟩e ↑rule of
             Christian benevolence↓.
35   precept ⟨th⟩ & the . . . that ⟨th⟩ it
36–38   ↑or three↓ . . . ↑in practice↓ . . . Jesus ⟨when he said⟩ that
41–(136)2   prostrates ⟨your⟩ a stranger. ⟨{If the fire consume a church that is not
             of your communion or name ⟨teach him that your affections⟩ show
             him that your Christian sympathy is commanded by the event.}⟩
             [from "show" to "event" text is in ink over pencil; the pencil layer
             continues: ". . . event & that you feel how low"] ¶ ⟨It has the worst
             effect upon the man himself⟩ ↑I know . . . what ⟨↑picture of
             selfishness is↓⟩ ⟨↑Nothing can be more comfortless than↓⟩ [in
             pencil] is more comfortless than the ↑condition of the↓ man who ⟨is⟩
             loves nothing but himself.↓

Page 136

5–6   say, ⟨l⟩Look . . . nature! the ⟨Christian⟩ ↑benevolent man↓ saith,
8   much ⟨good may here be done⟩ ↑to benefit↓!
9   the ⟨warm⟩ ↑snug↓
14–15   ↑show him↓ . . . ↑& insults↓.
17   dealing↑s↓ . . . call⟨s⟩ up
18   selfish ⟨they⟩ ↑men↓
19–23   ↑This . . . report.↓ [in pencil] ¶ ⟨The laborer⟩ the tradesman ⟨{the
             poor laboring man or woman}⟩ hurrying . . . Bread., . . . competi-
             tion, ⟨that ⟨is⟩ ↑in a moment of ill humor seems to him↓ not much
             better than tearing the morsel from each other's mouths.⟩ ↑for it with
             themselves.↓

23–24	↑with the↓ sharp eye⟨d⟩s ⟨haggling grinding to the last cent⟩ ↑of interest ⟨waylaying⟩ lying . . . cent.↓
25–26	↑It . . . others ⟨eyes⟩ mouths.↓
28	friend ⟨sister wife daughter⟩ Each
30	↑a companion↓
31–32	Each ⟨has⟩ ↑sustains↓ . . . perchance ⟨acknowledged⟩ ↑owned↓
34	↑such↓ . . . generosity ⟨that⟩ ↑as↓
37	bla↑c↓kest
40–42	the ⟨great⟩ ↑golden↓ rule of ⟨Christ⟩ ↑our Master,↓ . . . impor-tan⟨t⟩ce. ⟨strengths.⟩ ↑It . . . death.↓

Page 137

2–9	regard. ⟨{It seems to me to have that claim on us, ↑that I am of opinion,↓ that no Christian ought ever to /refuse/decline/ to per-form a special act of charity ↑that is ⟨presented him⟩ proposed to him↓ without assigning his reason in such manner that it shall be fully understood. It ought to govern our tongues, our hands & our hearts.⟩ {At all . . . its ⟨memory⟩ ↑remembrance↓ . . . find ⟨if he does not know⟩ within . . . of ⟨charity⟩ ↑comforts↓ which it is in ⟨his⟩ ↑our↓ . . . us ⟨there⟩ to . . . likewise.}

[The following new conclusion, as the appended date shows, was added for the sixth delivery of the sermon, February 5, 1832, at the Second Church:] ↑Let us remember that↓ ⟨T⟩the precepts of the gospel are only the history of the spiritual world thrown into the ⟨imperative mode.⟩ form of commandments. If we would enter into the kingdom of heaven, that is, if we would have our own mind become heaven, we must write these laws so deeply there that all our actions shall be expressions of the same; we must cast off the grave clothes of self⟨ish⟩↑-↓love in which our affections sleep, & grow godlike. Our ⟨affections⟩ ↑hearts↓ must expand until like our Fathers love they ⟨contain⟩ ↑embrace↓ the whole family of man; until we learn to measure a good, only by the number of its partakers; & to love ourselves only as instruments of God's beneficence.

Sermon LXVI

Manuscript: Five sheets folded to make four pages each; folios nested and sewn along the left margin with white thread; pages measure 25 x 20.6 cm. A slip of paper, 20.1 x 12.3 cm, is affixed to the lower right corner of MS p. 19 with red sealing wax.

Lines	Page 138
Bible Text	↑Are . . . Luke 12. 6 & 7↓ [in pencil]
6–8	mind /{does demand the being}/shows . . . want/ . . . thing ⟨essen-tially⟩ imperfect, . . . structure ⟨demands more⟩ shows . . . more,— ⟨j⟩as
12–16	it, ⟨in⟩ and . . . differ only [end of line] ⟨in their vocabulary⟩ ↑⟨s⟩less . . . language↓. ⟨One worships Baal one Osiris or Jove or Josh or a Saint or Fate or luck or fairies or an amulet.⟩ ↑{Insert A.} {A {One . . . that ⟨honours⟩ believes . . . same ⟨structure⟩ ↑wants↓ . . . individual ⟨honour⟩ Jove or /Osiris/Brahma/ ⟨or Jos⟩ or ↑the Holy Virgin or↓ a Saint, ⟨or a fairy, or fate, or a charm.⟩}↓ If

19–20   ↑which . . . God↓
22   their ⟨mass⟩ ↑stock↓

Page 139

3   propositions. ⟨It would seem, then⟩ ↑I . . . fact↓,
6–7   science ↑not . . . science,↓ have
9–14   as ⟨we study it.⟩ ↑our . . . is so,↓ Is . . . ↑round↓ . . . support,
               without purpose⟨—⟩? this inevitable, ⟨essential⟩ natural . . . system
               ⟨for⟩ ↑in the↓ . . . depraving it—without purpose⟨—⟩?
15   gotten; the
17   the⟨ir⟩ opinion ↑men form↓
18   jealous ⟨snarling⟩ ↑selfish↓
23   only ⟨other⟩ forms
26   ↑natural↓
29–30   to ⟨like⟩ ↑similar↓
33–34   observations ⟨he⟩ [canceled, then altered to "the"] ⟨↑man↓⟩ ↑in-
               quirer↓ . . . that ⟨no partial & manifold kingdom⟩ the kingdom . . .
               but [end of page] but ⟨is under one⟩ hath
37   infinite.— [Pencil notation in the hand of Mary Moody Emerson:]
               dont *reason* demonstrate it? The idea [illegible word, perhaps "prac-
               tical"] not negated
38–39   thus ⟨elevate⟩ ↑extend↓ our ideas from the ⟨individual⟩ relations of
               the ↑individual↓
42–(140)1   other. ¶ ⟨I believe in a Providence general & particular, and particu-
               lar because it is general. I believe that nothing is uncertain in the
               infinite plan, that every thing is grooved into its place, that the
               seeming exceptions & violations of the general order are made to
               contribute to ultimate good—that madness hath its uses that sin is not
               fruitless to the whole, that God hath that interest in every event that it
               is impossible for us to separate his part from man's part in any for our
               souls grow in him as the oak grows in the globe or rather as the animal
               body in the earth made of it, supported by it, yet having an indepen-
               dent will. Yet whilst Reason points to these conclusions, & all that we
               know confirms them I am well aware how much the vastness of the
               subject seems to forbid the intrusion of our understandings
                   We can only pick up here and there a contrivance & say, see! a God!
               as Newton said.⟩ ¶ I desire to offer you ⟨in illustration of⟩ ↑by way of
               defining↓

Page 140

3–6   nations ¶ ⟨↑And↓⟩ Every . . . kind. ⟨I will draw one from geology.⟩
               [canceled in pencil and ink] ↑And ↑after astronomy↓ . . . inhabit↓
8–9   ↑very . . . planet↓ ↑It is made probable↓
11–13   ↑But↓ The soils are ⟨composed⟩ ↑formed↓ . . . ↑so in this position↓
               . . . could ⟨not⟩ ↑never↓
15–16   ↑as may be seen ⟨in⟩↓ in mountain countries ⟨where they can be seen
               heaved upward⟩ ⟨↑in perpendicular⟩ ↑in oblique & perpendicular↓
               instead of horizontal ⟨ledges⟩ layers,↓
18   ↑case of↓

20–25   development of ⟨British institutions⟩ ↑commerce of G. B . . . coun-
try↓ . . . /the coal in its mines/its mineral treasures/. ⟨"⟩In consequence . . . in ⟨our⟩ ↑that↓ island . . . ore, ⟨& the invariable
contiguity of limestone, employed to flux the iron ore, we⟩ ↑they↓
. . . the ⟨cheapness of ⟨our⟩ ↑their↓ machinery"⟩ ↑extent of their
manufactures.↓

25–31   ge⟨o⟩ologists . . . formation, ⟨was⟩ is . . . ↑by the . . . surface↓ . . .
by ⟨them.⟩ ↑man↓ But ↑before . . . race,↓ . . . these ⟨le⟩ mineral

33–37   to ⟨hu⟩man↑'s↓ comfort & civilization ↑which↓ . . . globe ⟨from
his⟩ forever from his ²knowledge or ¹use, ⟨is⟩are thus brot up within
⟨his⟩ reach ↑of his little hands;↓ & ⟨the⟩ ↑a great↓ . . . ↑pleasure &↓

39   find ⟨in⟩ it ↑answers.↓. If it stood alone, I ⟨should⟩ ↑might↓ say it
⟨was⟩ ⟨↑mt be↓⟩ ↑was↓

Page 141

3–5   ¶ If ⟨an individual⟩ ↑a mariner↓ wrecked ⟨in our bay⟩ ↑on our
coast↓ . . . ↑on the rocks↓ . . . this ⟨house⟩ ↑shelter↓

6   the ⟨way⟩ ↑manner↓

8–12   ¶ ↑The lesson . . . Providence↓ ¶ ⟨The next instance I shall name is
from the arts.⟩ ↑↑This is from nature.↓ Let . . . arts.↓

12   faculties ⟨&⟩ of

15–20   goodness. /{I was}/When/ [brackets and variant in pencil] turning
over {lately} [brackets in pencil] ⟨the⟩ one . . . drawn↑,↓ [addition in
pencil] ⟨I mean⟩ ⟨&⟩ [ampersand canceled in pencil] ↑that namely↓
[addition in pencil] . . . Socrates. I cannot . . . ↑thro'↓ so long a time.
⟨It⟩ ↑There↓

23–27   provision↑, I say . . . book↓ [addition in pencil] . . . since
⟨Xenophon⟩ ↑Socrates↓ . . . my ⟨heart⟩ ↑eye↓

30–32   & ⟨as⟩ ↑more↓ . . . of ⟨the⟩ a text . . . instances ⟨to which I allude⟩
⟨furnish⟩ ↑belong to↓ . . . independant

35–36   ↑Yet . . . many↓ [in pencil]

Page 142

1   diligence; &

7–12   &c &c ¶ ⟨Then⟩ ↑When I consider↓ the ↑wonderful↓ . . . that ⟨an
intelligent⟩ a . . . no escap⟨ing⟩e . . . from ⟨their⟩ ↑its↓

13   the ⟨sight⟩ ↑perception↓

13–15   {I had . . . them.} [brackets in pencil]

19–20   ↑I . . . none.↓

26–27   is ⟨f⟩ {The heart . . . joy} for

28–29   ↑But . . . itself.↓

32–34   ↑that the ⟨course⟩ ↑blessings↓ of our life is as much ↑procured↓
under his ⟨regard⟩ ↑will↓ as the Tishbite when fed by the ravens↓
[addition and emendations in pencil; stray notation "food" also in
pencil]

39   independant

[The following notes occur on a slip of paper, affixed to the last inscribed page of the MS with red sealing wax; the verso, which is otherwise blank, contains the salutation, "Yr obedt. servt. C C Emerson":]

approach the Subj. with the awe of a man

Character of God. The secret of the Universe. Our being in this ch. the harmony of purpose resulting in this harmony of event prove his being. We get at a glimpse by considering that to bring round our domestic individual history he is now heaving the sea he is spreading the Tartar tents over asia⟨tic⟩ he is agitating that mass of human life betwixt yᵉ Mediterranean & yᵉ Arctic Sea yᵗ interests us so much & when our tho't ascends to a distance where Tartary & England & America & the globe of wh. they make a little part dwindle to a speck we see a new effect of yᵉ same power simultaneous with the others by which the ball we inhabit sails thro' space almost with the celerity of light [added above the phrase "with the celerity of light": "It hath no pilot no eye"] & keeps its figure with the accuracy of an intelligent being th along its unmarked road thro the beautiful revolutions of ten thousand worlds. The coal beds.

We grow in the Deity as an oak grows in the globe. It is the law of our being the element without which we have no being.

[Following the end of the sermon are pencil notations in the hand of Mary Moody Emerson:]

In this [illegible word] sermen may be gathered fruits of the pantheist the antinomian the ↑phicicl [physical]↓ nessecarian & the moral will all find tents [tenets?] to his point & wh will support pantheistic views & to the [illegible word] a question Where is the moral duty? In the moral constitution. Aye but that constitution is terrible in the pit of depravity—& it has jails & gallows made on purpose

Sermon LXVII

Manuscript: Eight sheets folded to make four pages each; first four folios nested, and the fifth, consisting of a lighter grade of paper, inserted before the last leaf of the outer folio. These are followed by three stacked folios: the first also consisting of lighter paper; the second, which has the first leaf torn out (evidence of writing on the recto), followed by a single half-sheet loosely inserted before the third and last folio. The gathering is sewn along the left margin with white thread; pages, including the half-sheet, measure 25 x 20.3 cm.

Lines	*Page 144*
Bible Text	Almighty ⟨hath⟩ give⟨n⟩th ⟨him⟩them ⟨life⟩understanding.
3	men & ⟨has modified⟩ ↑recognized in↓
8	subjection ⟨i⟩to
9	promises ⟨whereby⟩ ↑that↓
12–13	maker ⟨is the We do not conceive of any higher nature in the Universe than the mind. It⟩ is declared
15–17	him ¶ ⟨I propose to ask your attention, Christian friends, to some of the attributes of our spiritual constitution. It is important that we should often make this distinction, that we shd. never lose sight of it. For this is our real riches this our door to heaven⟩ ¶ I wish to speak of ⟨the excellence⟩ ↑some of the attributes↓ of our spiritual nature. ⟨It seems to me of that overwhelming greatness, that if I could rightly speak of it I should not have to ask your attention. I feel that there is a

glory in spiritual nature before which all other magnificence is straw, & ⟨to⟩ this sentiment ↑is one↓ with whatever momentary skepticism it may be heard, ↑to which↓ I believe every heart in this assembly, every heart in this world hath sometimes responded.⟩ ↑& naturally . . . interest↓ [in pencil]

19–21   ↑it may be, because↓ . . . but ⟨who does not know, that⟩ any

23–(145)2   soul ⟨would be⟩ ↑is generally↓ listened to with ⟨aweful⟩ ↑intense↓ curiosity. ⟨It is idle to say in answer that Any one knows this⟩ who ever ↑has . . . or↓ . . . any ⟨great⟩ ↑striking↓ . . . noticed ⟨that⟩ how

Page 145

6–12   spirits? ⟨Who knows not how⟩ any strong . . . fact ⟨will make itself felt like an electric chain through the most various assembly that ever met upon earth⟩ ↑goes . . . men↓. ¶ ↑The extreme . . . doubt↓

14–18   land. ¶ ⟨↑All men are formed in the image of God & enriched with this celestial art.↓ Know ye not that⟩ ye are the temples of the holy Ghost? ⟨says the indignant apostle.⟩ [cancellations in pencil] /Say not/Nor let it be said/ [variant in pencil] . . . up ⟨pleasantly⟩ ↑happily↓ . . . ↑that↓ . . . vast /rabble/number/

22   ↑may↓

24   ↑spiritual↓

26   himself ↑to↓;

29–30   acknowledges ⟨that⟩ his spiritual nature ↑that . . . it↓

31   He /throws/tries to throw yᵉ charm/ [variant in pencil] poetry

38–40   dress with . . . is ⟨no⟩ only

41–(146)1   ¶ ↑I . . . constitution↓ ¶ 1. ⟨And⟩ ↑Consider↓ first ⟨let me allude to⟩ the manifest superiority of ⟨our⟩ ↑the↓ spirit⟨s⟩ over our bodies & over all things; that ⟨wonderful virtue⟩ ↑life↓ [last emendation in pencil]

Page 146

2   its⟨elf⟩ own form↑,↓ [comma in pencil]

3–11   ↑Who . . . the ⟨spirit⟩ ↑soul↓ . . . departs↓ [addition and emendation in pencil] ⟨Is it not a⟩ ↑Observe the↓ [emendation in pencil] familiar fact ⟨to each of us,⟩ [cancellation in pencil] how entirely the subtle spirit of man, ⟨unseen,⟩ [cancellation in pencil] unknown . . . beholds. ⟨Have you not known that⟩ ↑The mind . . . thing↓ the . . . bystanders; ⟨that⟩ the . . . like ⟨solemn⟩ ↑painful↓ dirges; ⟨that⟩ the . . . sepulchre? ↑The . . . changed↓ [addition in pencil]

13–14   when ⟨the sinews of the spirit /were/have been/ strung⟩ ↑in . . . met↓ . . . fortune—⟨how did all obstacles dwindle away! the mind overleaped at one bound, difficulties that seemed insurmountable before⟩ ↑how . . . things↓.

18–19   fields. ↑{Insert A} A {Mountains & hills br⟨oke⟩↑eak↓ forth . . . hands.}↓

21   ↑moral↓

22–23   ingratitude; the ant is industry; the

25–28   phenomenon. ¶ ²{It is . . . world ¹{On the eye of an ideot ⟨whose senses are perfect⟩ [cancellation in pencil] . . . colours}. ³{Then . . . mind} [brackets and transposition markers in pencil]

28–29   *memory* . . . present↑;↓ & *hope* . . . present↑;↓ [punctuation and underscoring in pencil]

32   independance

36–38   God ⟨has⟩ raise⟨d⟩s . . . the ⟨wellfed⟩ family

38–40   ↑in one profession↓ . . . unfavorable ⟨condition⟩ ↑circumstances↓

Page 147

1–3   ↑child↓ . . . be ⟨prepared⟩ ↑disclosed↓

5   marriage ⟨but are⟩, that is

8–9   ¶ ↑And as↓ Poverty . . . effect ⟨far⟩ ↑much↓ . . . the ⟨growth of grace⟩ ↑moral perfections↓

11   by ⟨af⟩ disappointment

13–15   ¶ ↑And as . . . the ⟨character⟩ ↑mind↓ . . . slowly↓ [addition and emendation in pencil]

16   third ⟨consideration⟩ attribute

19–21   more? ⟨Or who ever became so good that he could not become better?⟩ In . . . a ⟨landing place⟩ point

23   is ⟨only⟩ an

25   mind ⟨in its adventurous⟩ as

28   a ⟨loud⟩ ↑persuasive↓

40–(148)2   better [Here, after the end of MS p. 18, the following canceled matter clearly belongs to an earlier stage in the composition of the sermon:] ⟨the viper is ingratitude the ant is industry; then light is our emblem of knowledge & darkness of ignorance; ⟨heat is⟩ warmth is our symbol for charity & cold for selfishness; & so the mind goes up & down the natural world, writing its own name on every phenomenon.

The two great attributes of spirit are knowledge & virtue Know ye not brethren by these two possessions or by the capacity for them that ye are the temples of the spirit of God. Know ye not that your minds are the dwelling-place of the spirit that formed them & the world; of that spirit in which resides as one eternal idea the great mass of his works

Consider then the entire independence of spiritual distinctions on outward things ²{In hunger in cold in poverty in pain as well as in the lap of splendour the highest energies of knowledge & virtue may be exercised.} ¹{Man Woman ⟨gentleman⟩ ↑prince↓ menial are distinctions to the carnal eye which the spiritual world doth not acknowledge} They are not known to the soul here they are not known in heaven. [end of MS p. 19]

Consider then the infinite nature of the soul We can grow to ↑the height of↓ a few feet; we can walk but a step at a time; we can lift a limited weight. But the soul in her search of knowledge & virtue hath no bounds that her ⟨own⟩ ↑indolence or↓ [emendation in ink over pencil] sin doth not set. All the past is the seed of the future

And here is the cheerful evidence of her endless being.⟩ ¶ Or does

. . . better ⟨what he shd. seek after⟩ how . . . before [This paragraph is written partly over, and thus cancels, the following passage in pencil:] For in the first respect, ↑that of knowledge,↓ God hath revealed all to us by his spirit, for the spirit searcheth all things, yea the deep things of God [I Corinthians 2:10]. And in virtue what victories are not to be gained, what end is there

Page 148

7	fact ⟨that⟩ of
9	or ⟨power⟩ ↑liability↓
18	a↑n↓ ⟨world⟩ ↑age↓ . . . win ⟨one⟩ the
24–27	may be [The end of MS p. 22 is here followed by two leaves, the first uninscribed and the second torn out, leaving a stub bearing evidence of writing in ink on the recto. The text resumes on the recto of the following leaf (MS p. 27), beginning with uncanceled matter that Emerson had copied above:] [MS torn]nd place may be the occasion ⟨the vehicle⟩ or the channel through which pious sentiments may flow but ⟨hath⟩ ↑they have↓ no sacredness of ⟨its⟩ ↑their↓ own. The church walls are holy, but only so to holy minds. ↑The aisles of the church may be the council chamber of sin.↓ (When . . . baptized.) ⟨You may⟩ ↑We↓ come . . . pray. ⟨Prayers are⟩ ↑A petition is↓
30–31	omniscient ⟨skill⟩ ↑perception↓
32–33	{As . . . Lord.}
33–34	↑or any forms↓ . . . so far they
36–38	¶ Your ⟨bodies⟩ ↑souls↓ . . . souls. ⟨But, ↑in↓ this strange connexion which we form between the visible & the invisible world this wonderous link between the perishing & the Imperishable—we are not passive. We must draw nigh unto God if we wd. have God draw nigh unto us. Just as by virtue our characters approximate the divine, ⟨so the more clearly⟩ ↑by such degrees↓ does he reveal himself in the soul. The perception of Him therein is our pledge of eternal being. I believe it will be found that ⟨none but religious minds⟩ the belief in the immortality of the soul always is proportioned to the ⟨religious⟩ progress of religion in the mind, that none but religious minds have ever professed their belief ↑in this truth,↓ with a↑ny↓ strong degree of confidence, &, that in minds of exalted piety, the faith ⟨was perfect.⟩ ↑freed itself from any mixture of doubt.↓ They saw the light that was not revealed unto the world & were not disobedient unto the heavenly vision. They were filled with awe as they contemplated the stupendous Being to whom they were allied, the vast career that lay before them; the society in which they were to act, & the objects of spiritual action—knowledge & virtue—they were to gain.⟩ The uniformity

Page 149

1	cannot ⟨be⟩ have
4	this ²perfection & ¹sufficiency
9	placed an ⟨eternity⟩ good [lightly struck through]

12–16   ¶ ↑Why . . . express↓ [in pencil]
18–19   If ⟨they⟩ ↑the . . . them↓ [over the following in pencil: "their
            remembrance & yᵉ obligation"]
20–21   ↑so↓ carried ↑as . . . God↓, [over the following in pencil: "as reasons
            of duty & pledges of" followed by three illegible words]
24   dis⟨appointment⟩↑aster↓; [emendation in ink over pencil]
26   ↑whose will is Providence↓
30–32   these ⟨apostolic⟩ ↑lofty↓ . . . impossible to ⟨domesticate⟩ ↑bring
            home↓ them ⟨in⟩ ↑to↓ . . . press of ⟨business⟩ ↑company & tempta-
            tion,↓
35   very ⟨different⟩ ↑unequal, . . . difficulty↓
37   ↑that↓ that can⟨not⟩ ↑never↓

                         Page 150
3–4   ↑that they↓ giv⟨ing⟩e . . . independance
5   soul↑, i.e. the Christian↓
10   his ⟨own⟩ country
11   to ⟨benevolence⟩ selfishness,
15   therein. ↑forever & ⟨f⟩ever.↓

                    Sermon LXVIII

Manuscript: Five sheets folded to make four pages each; folios nested and sewn through
the center fold. A single half-sheet is affixed with red sealing wax at the upper and lower
left margin of MS p. 7. Pages, including the half-sheet, measure 25 x 20.3 cm.

Lines   Page 151
1   of ⟨our⟩ different
4–5   heroes ⟨from⟩ upward . . . ↑Lo! what elevation,↓ [addition in pencil]
9–15   a ⟨point⟩ ↑trifle↓ to what ⟨we might do⟩ ↑can be done↓. ¶ ↑We . . .
            of↓ That . . . Newton, ⟨a little before h⟨e⟩is ⟨died⟩ ↑death↓, said,
            that his knowledge seemed to him a little like a few pebbles picked up
            here & there⟩ "I don't know ↑he said↓ . . . I ↑seem↓ . . . smoother
            ⟨shell⟩ pebble
17–19   the ⟨spiritual⟩ ↑heavenly↓ [emendation in pencil] world ↑to . . .
            spirits↑,↓↓ [comma added in pencil] . . . with what ⟨we⟩ ↑the good↓
            [emendation in pencil]
20–23   ¶ ↑But . . . find↓ [addition in pencil] Our . . . feeble. ⟨We must take
            men as we find them. And⟩ we /find/see/ ⟨them⟩ ↑men↓

                         Page 152
8–9   ↑Instead . . . to↓ Consider
15–17   prison ⟨or⟩ ↑at . . . gallows↓ . . . to ⟨the contagion of corrupt
            associates operated upon by the pressure of extreme ⟨poverty⟩
            ↑want↓.⟩ ↑be . . . want.↓
20   between ⟨them⟩ him

25–39   fear. ¶ ⟨Jesus says to him that had ⟨kept one⟩ ↑used two↓ talent↑s↓
     well; ⟨Thou⟩ Well done! thou hast been faithful over a few things. ¶
     To our own life let us carry home the moral Since men say, that amid
     the temptations of [end of line] of pleasure and gain and mixed
     company, the high rules of Christianity sound too refined, let us
     remember that a little virtue will not be despised. The gospel
     conforms its precepts to this condition. ↑A cup of cold water ⟨God⟩it
     will accept.↓ It puts its claim within your means.⟩ ¶ ↑It is . . . ↑in . . .
     world↓ . . . is ⟨not⟩ true . . . overmatch to ⟨duty⟩ the . . . means↓
     [The addition is inscribed on a half-sheet (verso blank) attached with
     red sealing wax at the upper and lower left margin of MS p. 7.]

40–41   ↑are . . . they↓

Page 153

2–6   ↑greatness of the↓ particulars. ⟨If⟩ ⟨↑As in our public ends⟩ ↑As↓
     . . . charities,↓ we can't get ⟨legacies⟩ ↑great donations↓ & should
     make [th]e [letters obscured by sealing wax] donors . . . —we [end of
     page] ⟨will⟩ ↑men are content to↓ . . . by ⟨cent societies⟩ ↑fairs . . .
     ability.↓

9–11   Be ⟨contented⟩ ↑thankful↓ [addition in ink over pencil] . . . acquisi-
     tions, /&/only/ see ↑to it↓ that you husband them ⟨with ↑more
     than↓ a miser's parsimony.⟩ ↑well↓

14   though ⟨of such society⟩ ↑the society . . . merits↓ the [addition in ink
     over pencil]

17–18   ↑as↓ could not otherwise ⟨honour these objects⟩ be

20–21   the ⟨additi⟩ improvement . . . by ⟨slight graces &⟩ small ⟨virtues⟩
     ↑degrees↓. . . . of ⟨small⟩ ↑minute↓

22–23   partial, ⟨of⟩ ↑over↓

25   which ⟨she⟩ ↑it↓ inspires, ⟨she⟩ ↑it↓ [emendations in pencil]

27   ↑with something better,↓ [in ink over pencil] but a ⟨great⟩ ↑virtuous↓

28   And ⟨so it is⟩ ↑this . . . seen↓

30–32   ↑often↓ . . . uncontrolable strength. ⟨An observant man has cause
     enough to notice how closely rivetted to their actions are all the
     retributions of mercy & falsehood & intemperance. And long long
     after the action itself is buried in the ↑dust of the↓ past, its effects
     spring up fresh in his path. ↑Is↓ The↑re a↓ man whom you have
     obliged↑?↓ whenever he meets you his feelings toward you are
     coloured by the remembrance of a kindness ↑Is↓ The↑re a↓ man
     whom you have wronged⟨,⟩? whenever he meets you, the shade of
     that old unkindness darkens his mind.⟩ [canceled in pencil] ¶ No↑,↓
     . . . itself↑,↓ [additions in pencil]

33–34   ↑And . . . desired.↓ [in pencil]

35–36   that he⟨s⟩ is . . . apology ⟨for⟩ for

40–41   fire. ⟨{He is to give a new direction to the human powers.} Then⟩
     ↑This . . . this mode⟨rate⟩↑st↓ . . . acquired↓

42–(154)18   ↑We . . . virtue.↓ He will ⟨then⟩ ↑presently↓ . . . ones. ¶ ↑modesty↓
     ↑Be suspicious of yourself↓ [The paragraph that follows is written

over the following notation in pencil:] [Emerson's paragraph symbol]
And now, brethren, let us aim to make a little advancement in
goodness by directing our endeavours to definite points.

Page 154

3	↑the formation of↓
6	for ⟨your⟩ the
9	↑concerning↓
13	peradventure ⟨it⟩ ↑you↓
15	of ⟨fighting⟩ ↑stopping↓
16	pains ⟨n⟩are
17–18	↑than . . . tomb↓ [in pencil]
20–21	the ⟨same⟩ ↑rules of a strict↓ discretion ⟨as he who begins with labor to amass property.⟩. If . . . you ⟨should⟩ ↑would↓
23–24	from ⟨place⟩ ↑page↓ to ⟨place⟩ ↑page↓, . . . less. ⟨Do⟩ ↑Let us do↓ the same in ⟨y⟩our search
25–26	tomorrow, ⟨to give more than you can well afford⟩ ↑neglect . . . new↓, . . . ↑to be↓
30–32	exact ⟨temperance⟩ ↑moderation↓ . . . gratifications. ↑[Emerson's paragraph symbol]↓ Temperance
36–39	is ⟨done⟩ ↑accomplished↓. . . . is ⟨done⟩ ↑accomplished↓. . . . prophe⟨c⟩sies
41	↑relieve the wants of↓ your ⟨needy⟩ ↑destitute↓
42	temptation ⟨set⟩ combat this ⟨foe then⟩ ↑hard heart↓

Page 155

4–6	the ⟨business of life⟩ ↑course . . . trade↓ you overpraise your ⟨wares⟩ commodities; . . . strength ⟨at⟩to
8–10	"I judge," sa⟨ys⟩id ⟨Chesterfield⟩ ↑a man . . . wisdom↓, "⟨of⟩by . . . understanding" ↑and . . . man↓
11	and ⟨p⟩ begets ↑in other men↓
18–19	of ⟨equal difficulty⟩ ↑greater exertion↓.
22–24	↑I . . . happy ⟨&⟩⟨ha⟩must enter . . . *to begin.*↓
27–28	of God and let ⟨the man enter there to worship.⟩ And
29	find ⟨how⟩ ↑reason to think that↓

Sermon LXIX

Manuscript: Five sheets folded to make four pages each; folios nested and sewn through
the center fold; pages measure 25 x 20.3 cm.

Lines	*Page 156*
Bible Text	I Cor. VI.1.
1	¶ ⟨Since the last time we met together⟩ ⟨↑In↓⟩ ↑↑During↓ my . . . place,↓
3	to ⟨pass⟩ let
6–12	when ⟨they⟩ like . . . requisition ⟨of Duty⟩—all . . . ↑of a year of time↓ . . . of [end of page] of our

12–18	contrast ⟨with⟩ ↑between↓ what was ⟨designed⟩ ↑purposed↓ . . . & ⟨feels⟩ ↑becomes↓ acutely ⟨the defects of his lot⟩ ↑sensible . . . condition.↓ ¶ ↑Suffer . . . the ⟨experience of the past year that may give you my view of the pastoral relation⟩ ↑occasion ⟨i⟩on . . . relat.↓ . . . the deepe⟨r⟩↑st↓ regret at failure.↓
19	↑only↓
21–23	promise—²{how little I have learned ¹{& how little I have done. ⟨When⟩ ↑even↓ with ⟨my⟩the . . . me—⟨I am chilled with a despondency⟩ ↑I↓

Page 157

1	↑This . . . view.↓
4	nature but [end of page] But
12	fellow-men,—⟨and⟩ each ⟨man⟩ according
14	↑tis reasonable to suppose↓
16	↑Preaching,↓ What
20–22	by ⟨all⟩ the remembrance of ↑all↓ . . . ↑or love↓
23	↑I . . . truth.↓
28–29	or ⟨fals⟩ superstitiously,— . . . Providence—*goes*
29–30	↑It . . . them.↓
33	the ⟨chara⟩ ways
36–(158)1	"⟨If man⟩Tho' men ⟨or Angel were not⟩ ↑were none↓, that Heaven / Would ⟨ever⟩ want . . . praise." / ⟨Let us not therefore imagine⟩ ↑So . . . increase↓

Page 158

3–4	↑in↓ . . . teacher ↑for remissness↓ in
8	↑I shall leave it in silence.↓
11	↑so↓
14–15	proceed. ↑as naturally as ⟨pure⟩ ↑clean↓ . . . point↓
17–23	of ⟨a peculiar⟩ ↑two↓ kind↑s↓ & ⟨I⟩ ⟨calls for some remarks⟩ ↑preacher . . . incompatible↓ ¶ He ⟨is taken one out of his brethren⟩ ↑attempts↓ . . . than ⟨they also⟩ ↑his brethren↓ . . . ↑there↓with ⟨them⟩. A man who ⟨has⟩ ↑is presumed to have↓ . . . by ⟨hearing⟩ ↑having↓
26–27	↑He shd. . . . man.↓
28–34	↑for yᵉ most part↓ the ⟨co⟩ thoughts . . . then, ⟨knowledge⟩ ↑truth,↓ . . . increases. that . . . action⟨,⟩; ↑yᵗ tho'. . . not↓ . . . solitude; sometimes conversation; sometimes action; sometimes books;
35–37	man's ⟨value⟩ respect . . . to ⟨take⟩ ↑hold fast↓

Page 159

3–7	cultivating ⟨their⟩ an acquaintance with them. ⟨Your charity must⟩ You . . . pastor ⟨whe⟩ ↑as often or↓ at ↑the↓ . . . ↑& he desire it↓ . . . you ⟨on the Sabbath⟩ ↑usefully↓
8	¶ Another ⟨point⟩ subject
9	↑I believe↓ None ↑who hears me↓ can ⟨I think⟩ be
12	your ⟨thots⟩ ↑minds↓

18   has ⟨broken yᵉ⟩ shamed
38–(160)2   read ⟨& write⟩ & . . . government ⟨& yo⟩ or

Page 160

4   ¶ To Another
5   of ⟨the Sabbath⟩ ↑public worship↓.
6   ↑you are aware↓
10–13   ↑The duty . . . can.↓
15   ↑& certainly no disposition↓
18   ↑Believe me↓ It
21–28   may ⟨regard⟩ ↑esteem↓ . . . & ⟨neglect⟩ them . . . perception ↑&
                      thrown . . . days,↓; . . . ↑the Spirit of↓
31–32   ↑who . . . company—↓the old man ↑is gone↓
42   be ⟨the⟩ brightened

Sermon LXX

Manuscript: Five sheets folded to make four pages each; folios nested and sewn through
the center fold with white thread; pages measure 25 x 20.3 cm.

[A revised introduction was written after the MS had been sewn, when Emerson folded
the last four (blank) pages forward to the front. This substitute opening was evidently
prepared for the sermon's third delivery (during election season) on November 13, 1836.]

LXX

Happy is the people whose God is the Lord
Ps 144. 15

Religion in its perpetual injunction of the social duties does not omit that important
class of relations which we sustain to our country & to the world. In this country the
existence of universal suffrage, the fact that ⟨the⟩ every ⟨cit⟩ adult man ⟨is a political
actor &⟩ ↑by↓ giv⟨es⟩ing his vote for the laws & the officers exercises a portion of
political power, has made good men feel more strongly the necessity of providing every
young person with some systematic instruction in the history, the laws, & political
institutions of the ⟨country⟩ ↑land↓. It has been thought desireable that textbooks
should be introduced into our schools in which the Constitution of the U.S. should be
explained & the utility of its leading provisions ⟨show⟩ illustrated ⟨a⟩Undoubtedly this
information would be valuable & ought to be provided. ↑It is secured to some extent in
the geographies & histories put into the hands of our children, & in some seminaries by
special instruction↓

But in my judgment a more important aid i⟨s⟩n a sense of ⟨strong⟩ ↑moral↓
responsibility should be awakened in the mind of every individual, that the individual
should see the connexion between private & public duties; should be accustomed to
extend the dominion of his Conscience over these as much as over his secret actions.

⟨It⟩ ↑I am very sensible brethren that it↓ would be a violation of the plainest decorum,
if the pulpit were made the vehicle of proclaiming or of insinuating opinions upon men
& measures. In so doing the Christian preacher ⟨compromises⟩ quits his true &

dignified place & just as surely forfeits the confidence of those to whom he speaks. But it *is* the office of the pulpit to warn men unceasingly of the universality of the law of duty, & to charge them that ⟨what they do they do with open eyes as in the sight of God and of men.⟩ The state can never be in much danger as long as men vote for laws & for lawmakers according to their conscience & introduce into their political action the same regard to rectitude which they feel bound to exercise in dealing with their families & friends. But we are charged in this country with introducing into our political action a certain levity & recklessness, a negligence of the interests of the next generation in our violent grasping after a↑n↓ ⟨pres⟩ advantage of today, in short, a preference in all our parties of the ⟨right⟩ ↑expedient↓ to the ⟨expedient⟩ ↑right↓, which is a dangerous symptom not only for the permanence of our civil institutions but for our own moral health as individual men. In this season of ferment & expectation, I shall ↑not hesitate to↓ ask your attention to the ⟨general consideration of the⟩ source of our social evils, that the heat of our civil & sectional strifes may be tempered by that humility & contrition which arise when we cease to see the mote in anothers eye because we have found the beam in our own.

Lines	Page 162
Bible Text	{Happy
1–7	↑We . . . general ⟨sins⟩ offences . . . And↓} [The brackets presumably indicate what the substitute introduction was meant to replace.] When we ⟨s[illegible]ly⟩ consider . . . our ⟨cou⟩ passage . . . ↑form of↓ government, the ↑great↓ [ink over pencil] influence ↑which it may exert↓ [in ink over "wh. it may exert" in pencil] . . . happiness; ⟨it⟩ ↑his civil relations↓ become⟨s⟩ an object of ↑serious↓ . . . Christian. ↑All govᵗs are mutable, & each man wields a portion of influence in determining their form.↓ ¶ A bad [The added sentence is rejected as probably belonging to the third delivery (1836).]
8–9	temptation↑;↓ ⟨by attaining⟩ ↑it may have↓ . . . unless ⟨he violate⟩ at
10–11	connexion ⟨of⟩ between
12–16	a ⟨good⟩ well . . . But ⟨in⟩ all . . . is ⟨nothing but⟩ ↑little more than↓ . . . ↑their intellectual & relig. condition↓
18–21	↑at all times↓ [ink over pencil] to every ⟨sober⟩ ↑thoughtful↓ . . . when↑ever↓ . . . mercy ⟨a⟩in . . . recognized ⟨in⟩by
24–(163)2	↑partly↓ by the toil ⟨& anxiety⟩ & suffering . . . ↑by earlier labourers↓ . . . centuries. ↑past↓

	Page 163
5	↑human↓ [ink over pencil]
5–9	govt ⟨I apprehend⟩ ↑it is agreed↓ . . . to ⟨my⟩the . . . ↑of . . . himself↓; . . . occasions ⟨me⟩him . . . leaves ⟨me⟩him . . . as ⟨it⟩ ⟨I⟩ ↑he↓ injure↑s↓ no ⟨one⟩ ↑body↓—
10–11	by ⟨the laws⟩ ↑our social system.↓ to . . . ↑Unseen . . . air.↓
15	are ⟨assailed⟩ ↑invaded↓
19	↑yet↓
20–21	too ⟨rare⟩ excellent,

25–26	↑priveleges of the↓ the citizen⟨s⟩↑.↓ ⟨priveleges⟩ ↑If it is felt at all,↓ it is ↑not↓ felt ⟨no farther than ⟨by⟩ ↑in↓⟩ ↑beyond↓ the office⟨rs⟩s of the ⟨govᵗ itself⟩ ↑state↓ ⟨& those connected with them⟩beyond
27–29	↑as↓ . . . operate ⟨upon those who hold them⟩ ↑therein,↓ . . . extensive, ⟨and all are interested spectators of the management of affairs⟩ ↑and must command the ⟨all⟩ vigilance of all.↓
30–31	↑as . . . purposes.↓.
32–34	↑every↓ week⟨ly⟩ & ↑every↓ da⟨ily⟩y . . . the ⟨mind⟩ public . . . ↑& avarice↓
36–37	↑to our country↓ . . . that ⟨sometimes⟩ blazes
40–43	is ⟨foundation of their practice⟩ ↑almost . . . of ⟨daily⟩ political . . . and ⟨all⟩ ↑most↓ . . . guilt.↓

Page 164

1–2	settled ⟨among us⟩ ↑in . . . land↓. ↑There . . . Israel.↓
3	are [end of page] are not
5–8	↑that God's . . . children↓ . . . Christ. ⟨I believe⟩ [cancellation in pencil] ↑Consider↓ [ink over pencil] . . . morals ⟨we may⟩ ↑if we ought not rather to↓
15–16	lengthened / to / on / the
17	not ⟨take⟩ ↑read↓
18–19	by ⟨people⟩ ↑persons↓ . . . a ⟨bad⟩ ↑corrupt↓
21–22	only ⟨private⟩ the . . . searching ⟨eye⟩ ↑scrutiny↓
25	↑for virtue↓
28	↑that it↓
33	↑or expected↓
35–36	political ⟨virtue or vice⟩ ↑measures↓ of ⟨a nat⟩ this . . . ↑degree↓
39	the [end of line] the

Page 165

3	that that this
17–19	that ⟨tho⟩ however . . . to ↑stay↓ the public ⟨weal⟩ ↑degeneracy↓ . . . single ⟨effort⟩ ↑exertion↓ is without ⟨success⟩ effect.
22–23	↑What said the Saviour?↓
25–39	let . . . land. [The following pencil version underlies the ink:] let it never be forgotten by us that our duties are appointed to us here only for a little time. We are citizens of the heavenly country. ↑Are you unable to control yr sorrow at yᵉ corruptions of the state. Rejoice that presently you will presently join a purer people. But do not relax your zeal↓ The priveleges the high places of that state are given to those who have most efficiently laboured in their place & duty on earth according to Gods Commandments It should ["Godliness" inscribed above "It should"] give us pleasure to reflect that the piety which we owe to one country enjoins the patriotism we owe to the other↑,↓ [comma in ink] & that God has so harmoniously joined together the good of this temporal with the good of that eternal world that every effort that we make with a pure heart to deserve Gods favor is ⟨a⟩something done to purify & so to perpetuate the ↑civil↓ institutions of our land

30–31	not ⟨let this⟩ therefore . . . priveleges,
37–38	world↑,↓ ⟨that God so⟩ that . . . ↑every struggle with temptation↓

Sermon LXXI

Manuscript: Five sheets folded to make four pages each; folios nested and sewn through the center fold with white thread; pages measure 25 x 20.3 cm.

Lines	Page 166
3–6	that ⟨of⟩ of our Saviour ⟨does expressly⟩ in . . . mouth; Take . . . mouth, ⟨wh⟩but
7	rule ⟨so⟩ from
9	↑of this language↓,
14–15	from ⟨an⟩ innocent & regular affections. [An added paragraph marked "A" follows, but there is no corresponding "A" in the text; presumably intended for some location after the introduction of the phrase "good heart," it may not have been used:] ¶ ↑A {A good heart is so simple an expression yᵗ ⟨none⟩ ↑I know not yᵗ any↓ can make it plainer. In popular language it stands opposed to selfishness. It is often said of a man full of indiscretion & given to sensual excess—yet he had a good heart ↑i.e.↓ He had just sentiments; he felt & respected yᵉ rights of others tho' he threw away himself But this is an imperfect goodness. The good heart feels the claim of God as well as of man over itself.↓ ¶ The larger
18–19	↑slow↓ . . . ↑prophets or↓
24	↑to all other merits↓.

	Page 167
1	by ⟨the⟩ ↑our↓ neglect or ⟨the⟩ ↑our↓
12–17	↑that . . . mankind,↓ . . . ↑the↓ . . . benefit ⟨received⟩ ↑conferred↓, . . . that ⟨I⟩ cannot
19–20	¶ ↑Every . . . not.↓
21	life, ⟨it⟩ we
22	we ⟨do not quarrel⟩ ↑put up↓
23–29	when ⟨sickness⟩ we . . . reason ⟨or the virtue⟩ of a ⟨near &⟩ dear . . . ↑or . . . virtue↓— . . . ↑on↓ every ⟨way⟩ ↑side↓ . . . ↑to . . . breadth↓ . . . the ⟨hollow⟩ ↑fluent↓ civilities ⟨of⟩ & ⟨splendid⟩ ↑ostentatious↓ . . . a ⟨better⟩ ↑more prosperous↓ hour it had ⟨underrated⟩ slighted.
30–34	¶ ↑That . . . man.↓ [in pencil] ¶ ↑⟨But what is the promise annexed to the command—⟩ ↑Solomon . . . declaration↓ . . . life↓
36	knowledge ⟨it⟩ we
38–40	own. ⟨Hence the⟩ ↑It was↓ remark↑ed↓ ⟨sometimes made ⟨o⟩ concerning a man, that⟩ ↑of . . . ↑though↓ . . . talents, ⟨but⟩↓ he ⟨↑yet↓⟩ had a ↑certain↓
41	↑t↓he ↑good man↓
42	been ⟨nobly⟩ ↑finely↓ [emendation in ink over pencil]

	Page 168
2–22	↑a divine↓ instinct but we ⟨form⟩ ↑explain↓ our ↑practical↓ [ink over pencil] conclusions of ⟨expediency⟩ ↑it↓ . . . considerations. ¶ ⟨But

the hard heart, may God who delivers us from evil save us from that. It deforms all the actions, it corrupts all opinion, it poisons even our very goodness, for the just or the bountiful act that is done on a selfish calculation hath the soul of justice & of bounty taken out. It is dead works without faith. It neutralizes the effect of ⟨genius⟩ ↑Gods precious gift of a great understanding↓ even, by making it an object of suspicion & fear. ↑{Insert X}↓⟩ ¶ ↑Yet [this paragraph written over the following separately canceled ink inscription: ⟨There never was jar or discord betwixt just sentiment & sound policy. But the⟩] . . . ↑And plainly . . . himself. ¶ ⟨Therefor⟩ Thus . . . life↓ [addition in pencil] ¶ ⟨↑X⟩ II. In the . . . But the bad heart↓↓ [end of page] ⟨Then it⟩ ↑But the bad heart↓ shuts

23–24   downward ⟨& denies the faith.⟩ ↑till . . . despondency.↓

24–31   out ²{that there . . . for us ¹{that the Father . . . of men; . . . ↑is false↓; the glorious perception ⟨of goodness & of retribution⟩ of . . . dream. ⟨↑Alas!↓⟩ ↑Alas! Is there no reason to think, that↓ [end of page] ↑It . . . unbelief↓

33–34   life. ↑the . . . everlasting.↓ ¶ ⟨It is the mind perverted because the heart is hard—it is the evil heart of unbelief. Is it not strange how blind men are to this fact & yet every one may see it who will that as men do good their ⟨faith⟩ religious faith grows stronger It is the reception of the very reward promised to obedience. ¶ Keep thy heart then with all diligence for out of it are the issues of life—the perception & promise of life everlasting.⟩ ¶ But

39   ↑indulging one or another↓

Page 169

1–2   ↑Have . . . Repent.↓

5–6   affectionate ⟨image⟩ ↑remembrance↓

6   diligence—⟨and you shall find no cause to complain of what God has withheld⟩ ↑for↓ It

11–12   ¶ ↑The way . . . humbly.↓

14–15   may be /cultivated./trained up by our exertion./ ↑B B Is . . . heart↓

18–19   ↑O . . . pleasure.↓

21–23   ↑as . . . end↓ . . . ↑of the . . . jesting;↓ . . . its ⟨jest⟩ at

26   mind & ⟨thoroughly⟩ ↑wofully↓

27–29   Let ⟨it⟩ ↑their work↓ . . . . ↑No . . . purposes. But↓

31   of ⟨mockery⟩ ↑derision↓.

32–35   desireable ↑in being↓ He ⟨shall⟩ feels . . . ↑He . . . compensation↓

37   It ⟨is⟩ never

38–(170)2 ↑much . . . merriment.↓ {I was walking early [end of page] morning . . . jail.}

Page 170

3–5   ↑always . . . death↓ . . . becoming. ⟨Let us comply rather with⟩↑Far . . . Paul, "⟨b⟩Be . . . prayer."↓

6   live⟨s⟩th

9   We ⟨lack⟩ seek

[Following the end of the sermon is this notation:]

If a man had the unspeakable misfortune to fall into that alienation of the moral feeling as to unsettle his faith in the Being of God let him go ⟨alone⟩ by himself & lament alone. Certainly there is no room for exultation

Sermon LXXII

Manuscript: Five sheets folded to make four pages each; folios nested and sewn through the center fold with white thread; pages measure 25 x 20.3 cm. Between MS pp. 16 and 17 a folio bearing Insert "A" has been loosely inserted; the pages of the insert measure 25.4 x 20.5 cm.

Lines	*Page 171*
Bible Text	↑Suffer little children ↑& forbid them not↓ to come unto ⟨me & forbid them not;⟩ for,↓ Of . . . heaven. ⟨Ma⟨rk⟩tth. 1⟨0⟩9. 14⟩ / Luke 18.16. / Mark 10 14/
7	gift⟨y⟩ed
10	& ⟨ble⟩ prayed
14–16	belief. /But/But it has a higher interest/ [variant in pencil] . . . practical ⟨value⟩ ↑importance↓. [emendation in pencil]
19–20	↑¶ Let . . . commandment.↓
21–22	it ⟨sounds strangely enough⟩. ↑is . . . precept.↓
24–(172)2	women, ⟨whom⟩ ↑and↓ [addition in ink over pencil] . . . we ⟨incessantly aim to⟩ put . . . life⟨?⟩!

	Page 172
9	Jesus ⟨taught⟩ was
12–13	this. ↑that . . . observation.↓ [addition in ink over pencil] ¶ [The next paragraph begins with a sentence set off with brackets as "Insert A" (see below); Emerson has written "Of course" with a line extending downward to the second sentence, beginning "Of course".]
13–15	imbecility ⟨& merely sensual existence⟩ of [cancellation in pencil] . . . be ⟨desireable⟩ respectable.
18–19	↑in the press of action↓
20–22	is. ↑{Insert A} [From the previous page, a sentence marked "A":] {If . . . not /carry us from/ aim to take out of us/ [variant in pencil] . . . only add⟨s⟩ ↑to them↓ [emendation in pencil] what is defective.}↓
30–33	↑¶ I wish to ⟨follow this inquiry into the true⟩ ↑inquire . . . make the↓ character ⟨of what⟩ ↑which↓ our Saviour recommends; ⟨[illegible word] next to /inquire how far/ consider the way in which it is lost/, & in what manner we can hope to ⟨obtain⟩ ↑regain↓ it.⟩ *next;* to . . . we ⟨may hope⟩ ↑ought to attempt↓ . . . character.↓ [following "*next;*" the inscription down to "regain" is in ink over pencil; the pencil version lacks punctuation]
36	commonly ⟨exist⟩ continue
36–40	acquired b⟨y⟩ut . . . exact. ⟨In the next place⟩ They . . . but ⟨all from this slenderness⟩ ↑not from incorrectness of reasoning but ⟨↑from↓ poverty⟩ from the poverty↓ of their information. ⟨But their moral perception is as delicate as their judgment is rude. They are

slow to understand a jest but they are quick to feel injustice.⟩ ¶
⟨Then⟩ ↑In the next place↓

Page 173

1-3   nor, {when . . . '⟨y⟩You look well'; nor} say ⟨they think⟩ '⟨y⟩You
         [brackets in pencil]
6-7   the ⟨sharpness⟩ ↑fineness↓ . . . petty ⟨theft⟩ ↑lie↓ . . . or ⟨murder⟩
         enormous
8-13   ¶ ↑Joined↓ With . . . all. ¶ ⟨It is doubtless the remembrance of this
         innocence ⟨or⟩ & of this unchecked affection that makes the recollec-
         tion of their early days pleasant to all men, & that have given
         childhood the ⟨name⟩ fame of being happy.⟩ ¶ ↑So . . . meaning.↓
         [addition in pencil]
15-16   ↑recall . . . own↓ observ⟨e⟩ation ⟨that often⟩ ↑when↓ . . . baffled
         & ⟨shamed⟩ ↑put down↓
17-19   ↑And↓ Such . . . this ⟨has given⟩ ↑fact has acquired for↓
26   kept without ⟨any⟩ effort,
33   passions ⟨open⟩ grow
36   praise,↑—↓ [addition in pencil] every one ↑in turn or together↓
         [addition in ink over pencil]
38   hypocritical. ⟨We are⟩ ↑As we sin we↓ [emendation in ink over
         pencil; pencil layer reads: "As we sin"]

Page 174

1   all ⟨round⟩ ↑about↓ [emendation in pencil]
8-9   ↑& forms↓ . . . which ⟨often⟩ ↑sometimes↓ . . . will. ⟨This is all at
         war with⟩ ↑But—↓Except
19   God. &
19-20   ↑I . . . thus.↓
26   our /nature/destiny/happiness/ But [variants in pencil]
29-31   one ⟨of acquisition⟩ ↑of . . . acquired simp.↓ . . . to ⟨be⟩ pass
32   appetites, ¹{↑&↓ without sin, ²{⟨&⟩ lovers of others. [Emerson's
         numbering of the phrases to be transposed seems to be in error.]
34   own ⟨voluntary⟩ exertions
36   dependant
37-38   ↑It not be weak . . . wise.↓
40   it? ⟨The⟩ Experience

Page 175

5-6   childhood. ↑{Insert A [The following insert, marked "A" and written
         on the first three pages of a sheet folded to make four pages, was
         loosely inserted after MS p. 16 and added for the third delivery, at
         East Lexington, December 25, 1836:] And let this noble doctrine of
         Jesus not be lost on childhood itself; upon those who though old
         enough to come up to school & to church yet retain unspoiled the
         early feelings of the heart. [addition to this point in pencil]
              I am informed that the ⟨children⟩ exercises of the Sunday School
         close today for the Winter. Let me say to you Children that I hope this

auspicious day, the birthday of Jesus which like a great light among the other Sundays ⟨illuminates⟩ ↑shines over↓ the closing year, brings you much satisfaction

I hope that each of you ⟨sees⟩ remembers with pleasure the Sabbaths of this year; that you have found some benefit in your class; some praise from your teachers lip The youngest of you is old enough to know that no child can be taught faster than it will learn; that all the love & care of your teacher will be vain unless you teach yourself also; and now that you are to leave for a time your teachers, will you not try each Sabbath to be your own teacher—on each Sabbath morn with especial thought to remember your Creator to thank him that you are alive to behold mankind & the earth the sun & moon & to know that by the possession of reason & conscience in ⟨you⟩ one of you is greater & more excellent than the sun & moon. ↑A child to be sure is a small object as you /stand/ run/ in the road ↑on your little errands of duty↓ with a basket on your arm ↑or play among yr mates↓ not so large as any tree. Yet to the mind of that child God has made all things subject the tree the field the rock & all nature. That is, if the child will, he may receive the knowledge which is a sceptre to rule over things. But better than knowledge

But better than knowledge he has provided your hearts beforehand with conscience, like a god sitting in our private chamber; he has made you innocent; lovers of truth; generous, & just. O children, keep these gifts & do not let them go. These are the ornaments of angels in heaven. Do not stain the white soul which God has given you, with ↑a↓ wicked thought. Your ↑voices are↓ musical↑;↓ ⟨voice⟩ do not untune ↑them↓ with a lie. Your hearts are kind,—show each other the beauty of generosity & of self denial; your forms & faces are lovely in the sight of your parents & friends; ⟨↑be temperate⟩ never be a glutton, never deceive, never contradict never be idle↓ ⟨k⟩cultivate virtue & you shall be always beautiful. Ask your parents & they shall tell you: ask the hoary head & it shall tell you; that virtue is forever young & forever beautiful so that the celebrated religious teacher who in his visions saw the heavenly societies declared that in heaven the oldest angel appeared the youngest.↓↓ [last addition ("A child . . . youngest.") in pencil] ¶ In fine

10 God⟨.⟩, ↑& in the children of God.↓ [addition in ink over pencil]
14-17 season ⟨Let us enter into rest⟩ Let . . . Christ ⟨that we may make our part in the future sure.⟩. ↑Let . . . action.↓ [addition in ink over pencil; pencil version omits "in all we do".]

[The following notations appear after the end of the sermon:]

July 1831 The attributes of *faith* & *trust* deserve particular Consideration as they belong to the child, & to the Christian. Remember also the remark of Coleridge that genius is always marked by a preservation of the feelings of childhood. [See Coleridge, *The Friend,* ed. Barbara E. Rooke, 2 vols. (Princeton, 1969), 1:419.] A man of genius is a well informed & wise boy.

July 18 [end of page]

The little child may sing for joy
who shall rob him of his toy
It is an empire to him
By its side kings crowns are dim [end of page]

Open confession is good for the soul.
                                        Fieldings Proverbs

⟨Open rebuke⟩

Sermon LXXIII

Manuscript: Five sheets folded to make four pages each; folios nested and sewn through the center fold with white thread; pages measure 25 x 20.3 cm.

Lines	Page 176
Bible Text	Now . . . darkly [ink over pencil]
2	↑it gives↓
13	consolations ⟨⟨are⟩of which I speak⟩ ↑that . . . state↓
16	is—⟨w⟩Why
19–20	↑if more were possible↓
21–22	it. ⟨Some of these reasons it will be my object to assign.⟩ ¶ I.
24	a /deep/strong/
25	only ⟨a⟩ the

	Page 177
2–5	↑the approach of↓ . . . a ⟨murder⟩ ↑quarrel↓ . . . a⟨ny⟩ steady
8–9	mode of [end of line] of our death. {Fifteen . . . year.} [brackets in pencil]
12	cause an ⟨inconceivable⟩ ↑great↓
13–14	↑neglect of affairs↓ [insertion in pencil] . . . thought! ⟨↑what neglect of business↓⟩ [cancellation in pencil] ↑what ceaseless terror.↓ [insertion in pencil]
18–20	if ⟨that⟩ a . . . our ⟨capricious⟩ attention. from
24–25	¶ ↑↑But↓ If . . . purpose ⟨wh. is sought in this careful placing of man in the material world⟩ ↑to ⟨be⟩our life↓↓ It . . reflexion ⟨that if life has any purpose⟩ that . . . ↑by the supposed foresight↓.
28–31	character. ⟨No It is not⟩ This . . . acquire⟨.⟩ in some degree. ⟨It is not⟩ ↑I . . . by↓ . . . access. ⟨This is⟩ ↑I mean that↓ ⟨s⟩knowledge . . . speech ⟨↑by trade by hunger↓⟩ ↑by want by trade↓
34	measure ⟨the⟩ all
39–(178)1	↑in detail↓ . . . ↑we cannot↓ doubt⟨less⟩ it

	Page 178
7	we s⟨tood⟩tand?
10–11	↑on . . . fastened↓ . . . discipline. ↑to . . . them.↓
13	state ⟨of⟩ were

14–16   you ⟨ask your neighbor *to do* a reasonable ⟨thing⟩ action⟩ ↑com-
           mand . . . untasted↓, and, ⟨at the same time,⟩ hold . . . his
           ⟨compliance⟩ ↑abstinence↓?
17   ↑in↓to the ⟨door⟩ ↑street↓
19–23   mind⟨edness,⟩↑,↓ . . . in [end of page] in your honesty, . . . without
           ⟨food⟩ ↑hope↓
28   be ⟨d⟩ liars ↑or misers,↓
31   to ⟨cloud⟩ obscure
33–34   ↑for conscience' sake↓ . . . enjoy↑,↓ ⟨for conscience' sake⟩ and
40   ↑very↓

                              Page 179

1   had ⟨no⟩ ↑any↓
3–11   ¶ III. ⟨{A third reason why no more information should be given us of
           the Future State is that enough has been already made known
           concerning it.}⟩ ↑{Insert X} X {These . . . ↑that . . . imperfect↓
           . . . . unthinking ⟨grief⟩ ↑passions↓ [last emendation in pencil]
           makes . . . there is ⟨yet⟩ one . . . have.}↓ [A small hand in ink points
           up to the place of insertion on the previous page.]
15   that ⟨de⟩ to
18–19   out. ⟨Then⟩ ↑But here also↓ . . . proportion ↑& the . . . gratifica-
           tion↓ as
21   the ⟨power⟩ feeling
22–23   ↑We enjoy a . . . joys.↓
26   body. ⟨If⟩ Thus
27–28   without. ¶ ⟨Moreover⟩ it
33   the ⟨libert⟩ opportunity
36–37   men. ↑to any . . . sun.↓
38–39   we ⟨acquire a⟨n⟩ love of⟩ ↑conceive the pleasures↓ knowledge ↑can
           give,↓ . . . goodness⟨;⟩, that
39–(180)3 the ⟨true⟩ ↑only↓ Revelation ⟨the⟩ of . . . promised. ⟨Blessed,⟩
           ↑The pure in heart↓ says our Saviour, ⟨are the pure in heart, for they⟩
           shall see God. ⟨Blessed are t⟩The poor in spirit, ⟨for theirs is,⟩
           ↑have↓

                              Page 180

6   God; ⟨neither⟩ for
10   only /mode/means/
12–13   rest. ⟨Not by the hearing of the ear only by the seeing of the eye only
           by the presence of the heart itself can the heaven be opened to your
           mind.⟩ ¶ And

                            Sermon LXXIV

Manuscript: Five sheets folded to make four pages each; folios nested and sewn through
the center fold with white thread; pages measure 25 x 20.3 cm. A separate half-sheet has
"LXXIV" inscribed in pencil on the recto, possibly not in Emerson's hand; the verso is
blank. A slip of paper approximately 15.4 x 19.7 cm, containing inserts "X" and "Y," is

affixed with red sealing wax to the left margin of MS p. 17. If these inserts were prompted by the death of Ellen Tucker Emerson, they would belong to the third delivery.

Lines	Page 181
2	Now ⟨is⟩ our
5–8	↑we . . . world,↓ [in pencil] . . . ↑the Bible & other↓ books & ⟨seen⟩ ↓conversed with↓ [emendation in pencil] men & had desire↑s↓ [addition in pencil] . . . pain. ⟨Now let⟩ We
10	had /time for preparation to depart/our share of the sweet & bitter cup of being/. ["of the . . . being" in pencil]
11–12	us ⟨w⟩Walk
16–20	the ⟨broken⟩ ↑ruined↓ frame of eighty ⟨with new schemes⟩ as . . . our ⟨minds⟩ spirits
27	this ⟨livelong attach⟩ tenacious

	Page 182
1	↑to faith↓ [in pencil]
2	↑We . . . facts.↓
6	↑any↓
8–10	And /as far as I have observed/it seems to me/, I should think ⟨it⟩ ↑death↓ . . . ↑by them↓, & ↑it is↓ . . . ↑& the good↓
11–12	much ⟨I admit⟩ ↑is true↓, [emendation in pencil]
13	in [end of page] in qualifying
16–21	solicitude. ⟨Not only as our usefulness is connected with our health but as this discipline is needful for us it is made agreeable to us. And further⟩ ↑{Insert A} A {God . . . further, &c &c.}↓ there is some ground for ⟨imagining⟩ ↑thinking↓ that a religious man ⟨will⟩ would, ⟨(apart from the knowledge of a future state,)⟩ have ⟨g⟩a
23–24	death. ⟨And I shall request your attention to these latter points in their order.⟩ ¶ I. . . . a⟨n⟩ strong
25–26	↑& no reason↓ . . . appetites; so
28	wild- [end of line] beast
30–32	desireablesness . . . is ⟨off his guard⟩ ↑surprised by danger↓, . . . ↑or avoid↓ . . . threatens. him.
36	↑a↓ bad m⟨e⟩an.
42	with a ⟨sharp⟩ ↑accurate↓

	Page 183
1–2	↑And . . . ↑a man↓ . . . remove↓
5	¶ I ⟨believe⟩ ↑suppose↓
8	him ⟨pain.⟩ ↑his reward.↓ [emendation in pencil and ink] ↑He . . . have.↓ [addition in pencil]
9	is dis⟨q⟩gui⟨et⟩sed
12	a ⟨ba⟩ man
17	remembrancers [end of page] ↑of his↓ own ⟨virtue⟩ ↑merit↓.
18	by /good deeds/benefits/ . . . of ⟨his⟩ the
21	strew ⟨this mysterious⟩ ↑this way of↓
22–23	& ⟨is added to⟩ ↑enhances by so much↓ . . . estimation ⟨in⟩ which

23–26   ↑The memory of↓ ⟨A⟩a day . . . a ⟨glorious⟩ ↑meritorious↓ [emen-
             dation in pencil] exploit, & ↑which↓ [in pencil] is prized ⟨in like⟩
             ⟨accordingly,⟩ [second cancellation in pencil] not . . . the ⟨praise⟩
             ↑honor↓. [emendation in pencil] ⟨Then religion makes life respect-
             able makes life venerable as it represents man living under the eye of
             God and the tender mercies of the Father of the Universe resting upon
             his weakest child.⟩ ¶ But
36–38   often ⟨a⟩ deceitful,— . . . who ⟨t⟩reckons
39   by ⟨God⟩ ↑another being,↓
40–41   li⟨v⟩fe venerable . . . man ⟨tw⟩ dwelling

                                    Page 184
5–6   ↑with more affection↓, [addition in pencil]
8–9   object↑,↓ [addition in pencil] . . . to ⟨this world⟩ ↑its place↓.
13   important /change/effect/
15–16   a ⟨vast⟩ burden
16–17   ↑It . . . consolation↓
17   remains ⟨an inscrutable⟩ ↑much↓
18   we ⟨asked for⟩ ↑demand↓ . . . ↑obtained↓.
21–22   ↑{↓On . . . that↑}↓ [brackets in pencil]
23–27   there. ⟨Though we are acting on great probabilities, they are yet *only*
             probabilities and cannot be expected to influence us as certainties
             when there is a contest between them & certainties. For this reason I
             do not believe that the hopes of heaven ↑& fears of hell↓ if ⟨yet⟩
             ↑much↓ more definitely shown than they are, ⟨& the fears of hell⟩
             would be able to deter a man from sin, if sin were not itself felt to be
             an evil—⟨if it were not conde⟩ if this hope & this fear were not
             seconded by the strong condemnation of *conscience,* which puts a
             present certainty in one scale ↑viz. remorse,↓ against the other
             certainty, ⟨the⟩ viz. the criminal pleasure,—and so society is kept in
             peace & law.⟩ ¶ Had . . . ↑had . . . certain↓
29–39   ↑men . . . another↓ are traitors to ⟨us;⟩ ↑them;↓ . . . joined ⟨us⟩
             ↑⟨the⟩ ↑the members of yᵉ human↓ famil⟨ies⟩y↓ together & the
             moment ⟨a man⟩ ↑one↓ . . . of ⟨his⟩ children, . . . friend ⟨st⟩
             dismays him, ↑the tho't of those↓ . . . him. ¶ ↑{Insert X} [on a slip of
             paper, verso blank, affixed to MS p. 17 with red sealing wax, the
             following passage marked "X":] {It . . . that ⟨ou⟩ ⟨Jes⟩ the . . .
             world ⟨joined his⟩ ↑did not reprove the↓ tears ⟨with those⟩ of the
             mourner & ⟨wrot his⟩ showed . . . in ⟨raising⟩ ↑restoring↓ . . .
             Providence}↓ [The insert clearly overlaps and replaces the first few
             words of the original inscription:] And this seems to have been
             intended by Providence
39–(185)5   since the ↑less we shrink from the labors ⟨of⟩ & action↓ [incomplete
             addition] more . . . strong ⟨will those attachments⟩ ↑are our ties↓ to
             life ⟨become⟩—binding . . . promote. ↑Y [On the same slip of paper
             containing insert "X," the following passage in pencil, marked "Y":]
             But . . . departure.↓ ¶ ⟨I⟩These ⟨say this in order⟩ ↑These reflexions
             are offered↓ to ⟨justify⟩ show

Page 185

7–9   have ⟨taken⟩ ↑spoken on↓ . . . ↑on . . . hope↓

11   them. ↑⟨There⟩ ⟨a⟩Almost . . . feels [The addition, in pencil, continues in ink:] ⟨yᵉ⟩a thrill of awe↓

12   are / anxious/ habitually eager/ [variant in pencil]

14–16   any ⟨c⟩intemperate . . . end. ⟨I⟩ What

24   ↑the last enemy↓ [in pencil]

[The following passage occurs after the end of the sermon:] ¶ The true effect I believe which a good life produces is to satisfy the mind that there is a part of it which is permanent that there are objects which are permanent & that the temper in which death is to be regarded is that of absolute resignation. That we should be "careful of health, careless of life," knowing that as we did not receive life from ourselves so we shall not receive death from ourselves but from a Wisdom abundantly competent to direct the order of things in which we are placed. [For "careful . . . life," see "Essay on the Cure of Gout," *The Works of Sir William Temple* (London, 1770), 3:244, quoted by Samuel Johnson in *The Rambler,* ed. W. J. Bate and Albrecht B. Strauss (New Haven, 1969), 1:322 (No. 60); see also *JMN* 6:18 and 156.]

Sermon LXXV

Manuscript: Five sheets folded to make four pages each; folios nested and sewn through the center fold with white thread; pages measure 25 x 20.3 cm.

Lines   *Page 186*

Bible Text   man bear prove

9   It↑s↓ ⟨is⟩ ↑seeds are↓

10   ↑both↓

11   ↑beyond theology↓

15–17   ¶ I . . . controversy. [Written below a draft version in pencil:] I propose to consider those great truths which are the foundation of the leading sects. This consideration may help us to see more clearly our duty and what are the facts & what are the duties that arise out of this controversy.

21–22   action. ⟨On these two⟩ ¶ On

Page 187

2   Creation. ⟨From these two fountains flow their feelings towards God & man.⟩ The

5   church / struck/ alarmed/

6   concieve

21   nature,) ⟨he will⟩ it

28   it. ⟨Of co⟩ Fear

30   unlimited ⟨faith⟩ ↑credulity↓.

31–32   ↑stricter↓ . . . value ⟨o⟩ upon Faith—⟨which others⟩ ⟨as if⟩ ↑because↓

35   ↑The conditions of↓ Any law ⟨is⟩ ↑are↓ better ↑⟨he⟩it says↓ than ⟨he⟩ ↑it↓

37–(188)3   ¶ I . . . sinfulness of [end of line] of the . . . devout ⟨but⟩ ↑if with↓
. . . opinions. [In ink over pencil; pencil version follows:] I do not
conceive that all the doctrines usually held by this class of Christians
have a necessary connexion with their ↑first↓ principles—Thus the
doctrine of the Trinity, is, I think, *accidentally* a part of their creed.
An Arian might be a member of the rigid party, for all his views of the
inferiority of Christ. Yet with this foremost feeling of the sinfulness of
the heart, they appear to have read the Scriptures with a devout but an
erring eye & to have ⟨↑taken↓⟩ ↑made↓ a systematic but partial
application of its language to the support of their opinions

Page 188

5   pleasure⟨,⟩ we
13–16   of his [end of page] of his . . . more ⟨evident⟩ manifest . . . ↑should↓
. . . more ⟨honest⟩ kind,
21   him ⟨then⟩ & none
26–30   offered. ¶ ⟨If⟩ From . . . to ⟨ra⟩give . . . a ⟨portion⟩ ↑degree↓ . . .
their ⟨chief⟩ whole reliance in . . . favor upon their Works ↑including
all voluntary action↓. [addition in pencil]
34–37   ¶ These . . . they ⟨appeal from the letter to the spirit from the Word
to the works of God as a guide in the interpretation.⟩ explain . . .
God. [In ink over pencil; pencil version follows:] These views also
claim in their behalf the strong testimony of the Scriptures. But as the
mind is the interpreter of Scripture they appeal from the letter to the
Spirit, and explain the Word by the Works of God.

Page 189

1–2   ↑Each . . . thinkers.↓
2   entire ⟨attention⟩ ↑life↓
10–11   ↑(↓If . . . Churches.↑)↓ [additions in pencil]
12   ↑first↓ . . . Church that it is ↑the effect of↓
13   opinions↑, we have seen↓
18   The ⟨multitude⟩ ↑majority↓
20   ↑as far . . . can↓
22–24   avoided. ⟨↑It is an objection to the denomination Unitarian↓⟩ ↑It . . .
it ⟨makes⟩ ↑tends to make↓ . . . Trinitarians↓
24   ↑generally↓
26–30   observation, ⟨who does not know⟩ ↑but can name↓, . . . ↑that . . .
tho't↓
32–33   what ⟨do the⟩ ↑must I as a↓ Calvinist⟨s⟩ say?
34   friends, ⟨a great & good⟩ ↑an active & honest↓
37   and ⟨the⟩ another

Page 190

2–3   sins; ⟨the⟩ ↑the↓ . . . occasional ⟨declensions⟩ ↑backslidings.↓
8   the ⟨intellectual⟩ race,
11–15   or ⟨was⟩ ↑dishonoured↓ . . . virtue. ¶ ⟨In t⟩ The next ⟨place⟩ ↑great
⟨objection⟩ mischief . . . controversy↓ it is . . . ↑portion of↓ truth

which is ⟨in⟩ ↑contended for by↓ . . . it is ⟨generally to adopt⟩
↑begets in you↓

19–20   ↑and so . . . religion↓ [copied in ink from the canceled pencil version
at the end of the paragraph; see next note]

31–32   ourselves. ⟨↑And so out of yʳ devotion to a Xn denomination you
forfeit the blessing of the Xn religion↓⟩ ¶ Brethren [sentence added
and canceled in pencil]

41–⟨191⟩7   party. ⟨Let us frankly own the good that adorns⟩ ⟨↑If we fear the
extremes of the rigid Xn↓⟩ ↑{Insert X} X {If . . . ↑with awe↓ . . .
them}↓ our . . . belief. Let . . . their ⟨charity⟩ bounty,

Sermon LXXVI

Manuscripts: Sermon LXXVI is represented by three separate manuscripts, designated
A, B, and C by the Houghton Library staff. The short, undated Manuscript C is an
incomplete early draft that trails off at the end into detached notes. Manuscript A, based
on it, closely follows the early portions of the C text. The sermon as represented in
Manuscript A was delivered May 30, 1830, at the Second Church, and is therefore
adopted as the present copy-text. Emerson was clearly dissatisfied with the organization
of the sermon, which was in fact delivered only once in this form. On March 31, 1832, he
revised it, producing Manuscript B, the source of seven deliveries. Evidence of this
revision survives in Manuscript A in the form of a brief outline inscribed at the end of the
text, keyed by the letters *a* through *k* (omitting *i* and *j*) to several marked sections of the
text (see figure below). Since these marginal letters make no sense apart from the outline,
information regarding their appearance in the manuscript is provided along with the
outline itself at the end of the notes to Manuscript A below. These notations are followed
by complete transcriptions of Manuscripts C and B.

Manuscript A: Four sheets folded to make four pages each; folios stacked and sewn
along the left margin with white thread; pages measure 25 x 20.3 cm.

Lines	Page 192
Bible Text	He ⟨spake⟩ ↑taught them↓
4–6	distinction. ↑and . . . power.↓
16	opinion. ⟨This was not the⟩ Others
18–19	truth. ⟨This⟩ ↑Neither . . . skill↓ was ⟨not⟩ the
20–21	↑He simply . . . commission↓
24	by ⟨pomp of⟩ ↑powerful↓

	Page 193
1–3	conversation. ⟨And⟩ ↑Nor . . . sage↓ the . . . men. ⟨Although every⟩ ↑Many↓ passage↑s↓ seem⟨s⟩ to
12	to a⟨n⟩ greater
14	moral ⟨facts⟩ ↑laws↓
16	↑for↓ the great laws, ↑of . . . they↓
19–20	↑not . . . an ↑nec↓ intellectual principle↓ in . . . ↑human↓ thought; that ⟨in⟩a [additions in pencil]
25	exist ⟨where it⟩ in

32–33   come. ⟨And it came to pass when they heard these things the
         multitude were astonished at his doctrine⟩ [cf. Matthew 7:28] ¶ There
34–35   his ⟨knowledge⟩ ↑full understanding↓ of this ⟨sphere⟩ ↑superiority↓
40   the /fulness/expression/
42–43   ↑His . . . character↓
44–(194)3 knowledge ¶ ⟨The same truth will have its full effect every where,
         provided, that it really be truth in the mind of him that utters it.⟩ It
         . . . man ⟨like that⟩ with . . . that ⟨mastery⟩ ↑command↓

Page 194

4–6   to ⟨you⟩ ↑me↓ . . . of ⟨your⟩ ↑my↓ own nature, which ⟨you⟩ ↑I↓
         . . . on ⟨you⟩ ↑me↓ than he who ⟨controls your bodily motions⟩
         ↑chains my limbs↓.
7–9   it. ⟨But⟩ ↑I . . . teachers↓ there . . . ↑two↓
11–13   himself ⟨a⟩ *living* . . . system ⟨un⟩ separate
19   ↑any↓
22   remark o⟨n⟩f
30–31   ↑It is powerful . . . not.↓
39   corresponding ⟨measure⟩ portion
44   to ⟨deal out⟩ announce

Page 195

11   it. ⟨I am⟩A ↑man is↓
12–13   before ⟨me⟩him . . . which ⟨I⟩he had not ⟨known⟩ felt . . . resist
         ⟨I⟩He do↑es↓
14   but ⟨I⟩he labour↑s↓ . . . with ⟨my⟩his own system. ⟨And i⟩If
22   sect. ↑{Insert X} X {These are they who see the truth & shun it who
         say like Pilate 'I find no fault in him' [cf. Luke 23:4] & yet give him up
         to be crucified, & make friendship with Herod over their common
         treachery to him.}↓ [This insert, in the same light brown ink as the
         outline and the key letters, was undoubtedly written in 1832 and is
         therefore not adopted into the present text.]
26–27   innocent For
33   its ⟨full⟩ ↑whole↓ [emendation in pencil]
34–35   ↑We . . . thot.↓ [in pencil]

[Following the end of the sermon is an outline (see MS reproduction below) written in
conjunction with Emerson's 1832 revision:]

↑a↓   Jesus announced moral truth
↑b↓   It was *living* truth
             ↑d↓ ²{Dignity & ↑c↓ ¹{advantage of moral truth
⟨↑c↓⟩ ↑e↓   1. a clue to the world
↑k↓   ↑2. Vital connexion between moral truth & right action↓
⟨↑d↓⟩ ↑f↓   ⟨2⟩3. its necessary accompaniment is a tone of authority

    Two Considerations
↑g↓   1. The office of Jesus not distinct from this but
             this was his Messiahship

↑h.↓   2. The truth & the authority accompanying it
       not monopolized by him but attainable
       by all his disciples.

[The key letters from the outline designate portions of the sermon text as follows:]
a. "I conceive . . . his lesson." (p. 193, lines 11–38)
b. "I know . . . perceives it." (p. 194, lines 7–24)
c. "It is not . . . my limbs." (p. 194, lines 1–6)
   "Then, moral . . . to it. (p. 194, lines 25–26)
d. [No passages marked.]
e. [No passages marked.]
f. "It is . . . in vain." (p. 194, lines 26–34)
g. [On an otherwise blank page opposite the passage marked "k" is the following
   notation:] g There is no acceptance of persons with God
h. "The same . . . whatever lips." (p. 193, lines 38–39)
   "Jesus hath . . . master's authority." (p. 194, lines 34–39)
k. "Doubtless a . . . heavenly knowledge." (p. 193, lines 39–44)

Manuscript of outline, courtesy of Houghton Library, Harvard.

Manuscript C: Five sheets folded to make four pages each; folios nested and sewn
through the center fold with white thread; pages measure 25 x 20.3 cm. At the top of the
first page is the notation "Some autobiographical passages here.— JEC" in the hand of
James Elliot Cabot.

Imperfect,
He spake as one having authority, and not as the scribes.
76 [in pencil]

These words are not only remarkable as they express the feeling produced by the instructions of Jesus in the promiscuous assembly of his countrymen, but, as they are descriptive of the impression made by him as a moral teacher on all succeeding times. I shall attempt in the following remarks to show the reason of this distinction

Jesus taught as one having authority. How was he able to give this dignity to his instructions? He was not like Paul learned. For all that we know, the carpenter's shop & his mothers humble house were his only academy. And never in his discourses does he refer to any other books than those of the Jewish Scriptures.

He was not a subtile reasoner. It is the fame of a few men that they have analyzed every action and every thought of man into its first elements that they have received nothing until it was proved & have shaken the evidence of the best anthenticated facts & introduced doubt under the foundations of every opinion. This was not the merit of Jesus, of whose instructions it is one of the most remarkable features that he does not reason at all. He proves nothing by argument. Christianity could not be defended if it looked to its author for a systematic account of its pretensions arranged by the rules of logic.

Nor was it by pomp of declamation nor insinuating address that he attained this end. Nothing can be more simple than the style of his discourses. It is the style of conversation. And the story of his life shows us that nothing could be more free than his habits of intercourse with men. Although every anecdote seems to show the wonderful deference ⟨in⟩ with which he was approached yet so entirely did this spring from other ↑causes↓ than physical accomplishments that no pen has transmitted one syllable respecting the personal appearance, or the manners or the voice of so remarkable a personage.

How then was it if ⟨not⟩ he was not learned or subtile or dogmatical or eloquent like many of his later disciples that he spoke with an authority which they have never obtained?

I conceive it was because he taught truth, to an extent that none other has done. He taught what the human mind recognized as true the moment it was declared, because he uttered from his own convictions the great moral facts to which the human understanding must always bow whilst it retains its own constitution the great facts ⟨which⟩ to which we return after running the round of skepticism, with new conviction He spoke of God in a new tongue He spoke of Him in terms of earnest affection as the high object of all thought

⟨But it will be said is Truth so new or so rare that our Saviour alone had it & none after him has had it How should truth which is the natural element & food of all minds have had such peculiar power in his.⟩ It was by truth he was so distinguished as a teacher Truth is always commanding for it is always valuable to man for its own sake. ⟨But why is not the truth which is repeated by the Christian minister now as powerful as the same truth from the lips of Christ?⟩ Of course, the curiosity & reverence would be more strongly excited at listening to any lesson from one known to be possessed of miraculous power but truth will have the same effect as truth from whatever lips. I suppose that a mind so pure & so great as his, will succeed in giving to all its utterance the fulness of its own measure. His character was consistent, part with part; and the mighty work of his hand was justified by the mighty word of his mouth. But ⟨who p⟩ the truth hath its full effect everywhere, ⟨so⟩ ↑provided↓ that it really ⟨is⟩ be truth to him that utters it. The reason of the ⟨mighty⟩ difference between teachers ⟨of th⟩ ordinarily classed under the same name & understood to teach the same ⟨truth⟩ ↑faith↓ is that ⟨to⟩ ↑in↓ one his doctrine is to his own self a living truth, and, in the other, it is passively taken & taught at second hand, it is a ⟨foreign⟩ lump of foreign matter in his system not understood not operative. ↑a childs lesson of geography.↓

This is a distinction which I apprehend every one at all attentive to his own thoughts will readily understand. Every one will remember how often he heard in youth ↑without heed↓ the common proverbs that pass from mouth to mouth, and the lively satisfaction he derived from the perception of their truth the first time that his own experience led him to express the same fact in similar language. Hence the common ⟨distinction⟩ ↑remark↓ which is made upon the force which a man gives to any old remark if it is ⟨now⟩ the fresh result of his own observation. Truth is always young from the mind that perceives it. A teacher of it in every age commands reverence. {Learning & logic & eloquence in aid of it are beautiful & powerful Without this end they are mean. ⟨The⟩ In themselves they have no other merit than a merely mechanical one. He is a fool who underrates learning in a wise man, but every person of common sense despises it in a pedant.}

There is then ⟨no trick⟩ no artifice possible in the trade of Truth. He that hath it ↑in himself↓ will move you, will speak with authority. He that hath it not, will labor with his sentences, & his learning, in vain. Jesus hath not monopolized it; he came to communicate it; and precisely in the same measure with it, he communicates his power over men. And so, many a disciple in different ages hath learned of Christ so much of his truth hath had infused into his own being so much of his master's spirit that he hath spoken with a corresponding portion of his master's authority.

But ⟨is⟩does so much force & value belong to truth. What becomes of that distinction between speculative & practical? Have we not heard that it is far easier to preach than to practise.

I have another tho't on this subject. When I heard Dr C[hanning] I felt that a development had been given to the best parts of my being as I listened. When I heard [James] Walker he exercised my reason my indignation & so on but ⟨not⟩ did not stretch all the muscles The very best part of me was not touched.—This is not to speak with authority.—True of Walker however only on that narrowing topic Sectarianism.

{If an impostor undertakes to describe to me actions & conversations of one of my friends whom in truth he has never seen, shall I not immediately detect his falsehoods And if a false teacher undertake to describe falsely the movements of the soul which he has not witnessed shall I not feel it to be false?

↑This is my nearest friend.↓

A man cannot carry his conduct higher than the principles from which he acts, any more than a fountain can rise higher than the reservoir.

A man cannot describe as his own, feelings he has never felt

I am disposed to think with Coleridge about the Miracle. [See Coleridge, *The Friend*, ed. Barbara E. Rooke, 2 vols. (Princeton, 1969), 1:518; cf. *JMN* 3:178.]

Manuscript B: Six sheets folded to make four pages each; the first four folios stacked (the third having had the first leaf cut out and showing evidence of writing on the verso, MS p. 10), followed by a single half-sheet and two nested folios; the gathering is sewn along the left margin with white thread; pages measure 24.1 x 20.3 cm. A half-sheet is affixed with brown sealing wax to the upper left margin of MS p. 5. A slip of paper, 12.3 x 18.1 cm, containing Insert "X" is affixed with red sealing wax to the left margin of MS p. 13.

76 [in pencil] lxxvi.

He taught them as one having authority & not as the scribes. Matt 7. 29.

These words are not only remarkable as they express the feeling produced by the instructions of Jesus in the promiscuous assembly of his countrymen, but also, ⟨because⟩ as they are descriptive of the impression made by him as a moral teacher on all succeeding times. In the present discourse, I shall attempt to show the nature of this distinction, &, {as in all respects he was an example for us,} [brackets in pencil] to show how far we may hope by imitating his virtues, to share in his power.

Let us inquire into the means by which he gave dignity to his instructions.

He was not learned. He does not appear to have received any better education than a Jewish peasant. And there is no display of science or ↑various↓ reading in his discourses, nor does he ever refer to any other books than the Jewish Scriptures.

He was not a subtile reasoner. It is the fame of a few men that they have analyzed every thought & emotion of the human mind into its ⟨first⟩ elements that they have received nothing until it was proved, that they have shaken the evidence of the best authenticated facts & have introduced doubt under the foundation of every opinion. Others there are↑,↓ [added in pencil] who have applied the same ingenuity to better purpose↑,↓ [added in pencil] & have done what they could to fortify with impregnable reason every useful ⟨truth⟩ custom↑,↓ [added in pencil] & every important truth. Neither of these sorts of skill was the merit of Jesus, of whose instructions it is ↑one of↓ the most remarkable feature↑s↓ that he does not reason at all. He proves nothing by argument.

He simply asserts, ⟨& appeals to⟩ ↑on the ground of↓ his divine commission. Every one of his declarations is a naked appeal to every man's consciousness whether ⟨it⟩ ↑the fact↓ be so or not. Christianity could not be defended↑,↓ [added in pencil] if it looked to its author for a systematic account of its evidences arranged by the rules of logic.

Nor was it by powerful declamation, nor insinuating arts of address, that he attained this end. Nothing can be more simple than the style of his discourses. It is the style of conversation. Nor was it by means very acceptable to his countrymen, the charm of a great name, or the stately manners of a Rabbi. ⟨The⟩ He came among them the reputed son of Joseph↑,↓ [added in pencil] & the story of his life shows us how free were his habits of intercourse with men. It is true that many passages incidentally show the singular deference with which he was approached; yet so entirely did this spring from other causes than ⟨p⟩ such external accomplishments, that no pen has transmitted one syllable respecting the personal appearance, or yᵉ manners, or the voice of so remarkable a personage.

On these considerations, the enquiry returns with new force, how was it, if he was not learned, or subtile, or of noble family, or of popular arts, like many of his later disciples, that he spoke with an authority which they have never obtained?

I conceive it was because he taught truth, & the supreme kind of truth, ↑(↓that which relates to mans moral nature↑)↓ [parentheses added in pencil] with greater fidelity & distinctness than any other, because he taught more ⟨&⟩truth, & (if I may say so) more *truly,* because he did not as other teachers drop here & there a good hint, a valuable fragment, but ↑plainly↓ announced the leading principles by wh. whilst the soul exists, it must be governed; ⟨because, he taught ⟨as true⟩ what man recognized as true the moment it was declared⟩; because, speaking on his own convictions, he expressed with unexampled force, the great laws to which the human understanding must always bow, whilst it retains its own constitution; the great laws, which, after all our doubts, after running the round of skepticism, we return to acknowledge with new conviction.

He spoke of God in a new tongue, not as the philosophers had done, as an intellectual principle, nor as the vulgar had done, ↑as↓ a cruel or sensual ⟨idol⟩ ↑demon↓, but in terms of earnest affection as being best understood by us as the Father of the human soul, the grand object of all tho't, & that the end of life was a preparation of the soul to approach him by likeness of character.

Humility, ⟨benevolence, purity⟩ ↑love↓, [emendation in pencil] self denial, were the means of approaching him,↑—↓ [in pencil] were the true glories of ⟨hu⟩man ⟨character⟩. [cancellations in pencil] To have them was to have life. They make the natural felicity of a good mind the real heaven after which men should seek. And as these cannot die, the mind that was clothed in them should not die.

And he summed up his instructions in the rule Be ye perfect even as your father in heaven is perfect.

↑These sublime & salutary lessons found a willing entrance into such hearts as were not shut up against the truth by sin. The candid & virtuous were astonished at the gracious words that proceeded out of his mouth Their hearts burned within them as he opened to them the Scriptures↓ [addition on a half-sheet attached to MS p. 5 with brown sealing wax; verso blank]

⟨To⟩ ↑I would↓ speak a little more particularly of the nature & reason of this superiority of Jesus over other teachers. There are ⟨various ways of⟩ different sorts of truth & various ways of possessing it & of communicating ↑it↓; & it is quite important here to discriminate. You say the same truth is now possessed; we have the very words of Jesus, yet how ineffectual they prove from so many lips as utter them, & only rarely are they spoken in the spirit of our Common Teacher.

In the first place, then, it was in Jesus *living* truth. ⟨Who has not seen abundant reason for this distinction among men.⟩ There is a ⟨vast⟩ ↑wide↓ difference between the power of two teachers ordinarily classed under the same name & understood to teach the same faith. The reason is that in one his doctrine is to himself *living* truth, & he speaks it as he sees it; & in the other, it is dead truth, it is passively taken ⟨in⟩ & taught at second hand; it is like a lump of ⟨foreign⟩ ↑indigestible↓ matter in his ⟨intellectual⟩ ↑animal↓ system separate & ⟨inoperative⟩ ↑of no nourishment or use.↓

It is, compared with yᵉ same truth quickened in another mind, like a fact in a Child's lesson in geography, as it lies unconnected & useless in his memory, compared with the same fact as it enters into the knowledge of the surveyor or the shipmaster.

This is a distinction which I apprehend every one at all attentive to his own tho'ts will readily understand. Every one will remember how often he heard in youth without heeding it any one of the common proverbs that pass from mouth to mouth & the lively satisfaction he derived from the perception of its truth the first time that his own experience led him to express the same fact in similar language. And he smiled ⟨at saying a⟩ ↑when he thot he was saying something↓ new [canceled "a" is part of the word "anew"] ↑at↓ so trite a sentence. Hence too the common remark upon the new force which a man gives to a trivial tho't when it is the fresh result of his own observation. Truth is always new from the mind that perceives it.

But much more ⟨striking is⟩ impressive is this property in the case of moral than of intellectual or physical ⟨nature⟩ ↑facts.↓

First then it was living truth.

In the next place this truth which lived in him was *moral* truth. That truth whose distinguishing mark is that as soon as it is perceived, it commands. This introduces us into a new world. What is moral truth? moral law? or the authority of Virtue?

"It is that which all ages & all countries have made profession of in public it is that which every man you meet puts on the show of; it is that which the primary & fundamental laws of all civil constitutions over the face of the earth make it their business & endeavor to ⟨f⟩ enforce the practice of upon mankind viz. Justice veracity & a regard to common good." (Butler.)

It is Gods mark upon every moral act that it tends to produce good; upon every immoral act that it tends to produce harm.

Obedience to it is that way of life to which all good is promised & the contrary of which all nature fights against. But what more concerns us at this time is that it is essential to the perfection of the ⟨faculties. It opens the eye It sharpens the sight.⟩ faculties. It opens the eye it sharpens the sight It is the door to wisdom; it is the cause of love; it is the means of power.

"Since the world, (says Hartley) is a system of benevolence & consequently its author the object of unbounded love love & adoration benevolence & piety are the only true guides in our inquiries into it, the only ⟨true⟩ keys which will unlock the mysteries of nature & clues which will lead through her labyrinths."

And certainly every man will admit that a good man is a better judge ↑of truth↓ in any question than a bad man of the same abilities.

But in the next place there is a vital connexion between moral truth & right action that where ⟨it⟩ ↑the truth↓ is vividly seen, it leads directly to action, & when the actions are done, they lead directly to better knowledge & so there is a constant reciprocal action of the opinions on the will, & of the will on the opinions. So that they cannot be separated in the thought of the observer, but the words are enforced by his veneration for the character, & the character is exalted by the dignity of the sentiments it is accustomed to express. This is what we mean to say by the expression *living truth,* when applied to morals. And this it will be admitted was true (if then only) in the character of Christ. His character was consistent, part with part, & the mighty work of his hand was justified by the ⟨mighty⟩ ↑gracious↓ word of his mouth. ↑We may even say↓ His miraculous powers were not separate but harmonized into his character. ²Rather ¹say his hand was strong because his soul was filled ↑with↓ angelic virtue.

In the third place, a necessary accompaniment of moral truth is ⟨a tone of⟩ ↑its↓ authority. This belongs to it in the nature of man. It always speaks with a voice of command which all other desires feel it right to obey. ↑This is not a rhetorical expression but a scientific fact.↓ ↑{Insert X} [On a slip of paper attached to MS p. 13 with red sealing wax, a passage marked "X"; verso blank:] {There is no man but perceives a difference between the natural reverence that belongs to this & to any other. The feeling is very different with which we hear that the sky is blue the earth is a globe $3 + 2 = 5$ or any speculative opinion or mathematical law & yᵗ with which we hear Blessed are the meek, Love God, Serve all men, Judge not, & yᵉ like for here comes in the new relation *I* ⟨oght⟩ ↑ought↓ *& I ought not.* Here comes in yᵉ new relation of command & obedience}↓ Thus I want food, or power, or praise, or society, but the moral faculty forbids me to seek them at my neighbors expense—and all those desires feel the right of that command & the propriety of their obedience. "Had it strength as it has right it wd govern the world." (Butler) Whosoever therefore teaches this truth participates of its authority. ⟨Whosoever speaks it worthily,⟩ ↑Whosoever↓ speaks it ⟨from his own⟩ ↑out of a↓ soul over which it has full dominion, must speak as a God unto men, for he utters the word of God.

It is remarkable how this mastery wh. belongs to it shows itself in the tone that is taken by its teacher as much as in the facts that are presented. A tone of authority cannot be taken without truths of authority. It is impossible to mimick it. It proceeds directly from ye perception of great principles. It is powerful because truth always convinces, & people always know whether they have been convinced or not. There is therefore no artifice possible in dealing with truth. He that hath it in himself will move you. He will speak with authority. He that hath it not will labor with his rhetoric & his learning in vain.

It is this truth more than miracles that moves the whole frame of human nature. It is not the power to make surprising changes in matter to heal the sick to wake the dead that can act on the soul of man with most effect. These things wd. be prodigious indeed, but what then? ↑Beyond the temporary convenience afforded to the individual↓ they wd. effect nothing but a blind wonder.—No; real power is in that command of truth which can pour light ⟨in a flood⟩ thro' the soul. He that can reveal to me the great secrets of my own nature which I see to be true the moment they are disclosed will have a ⟨more lasting⟩ ↑deeper↓ influence on me than he who chains my limbs or feeds me or ⟨hurts me.⟩ ↑who heals my disease.↓ Because he holds the lamp by which I walk, he determines the course of my tho'ts and actions and all the happiness I attain looks back to him under God as its author. This is what is meant by saying that Jesus is the Author & Finisher of our salvation.

Jesus then was distinguished from other teachers by the possession of living moral truth which he held ⟨under⟩ according to its just conditions, that of being the principle of his own life

1. ⟨But what is most important⟩ ↑⟨I wish to⟩The subject suggest two general considerations. A great↓ error ↑to which we are liable↓ on this subject, is, that we are apt to separate the truth taught by Jesus from his office, & suppose that it was his divine authority, his peculiar designation to the office of Messiah that give↑s↓ authority to his words, & not his words that mark him out as the Messiah. ↑The utterance of that Truth is his office↓ It is his Truth that made him Messiah. (And it is his goodness that revealed to him so much truth.) He is our Saviour or Redeemer not because oil was poured on his head, nor because he descended by his mother of the line of David, nor because prophets predicted him or miracles attended him nor for all of these reasons but because he declared for the first time fully & intelligibly those truths on which the welfare of the human soul depends, because he declared them not as formal propositions ↑but↓ in a full apprehension of their commanding importance. He lived by them, because in short they were so vitally his own that he has identified his own memory almost with the conscience of ⟨all⟩ good men from that day to this

Now there had been many other moral teachers before him yet had no one devoted himself with this entireness to the highest interests of the human race or expressed the rule of life in anything like so just & comprehensive & significant a manner. Filled & empowered by this ⟨spirit⟩ truth, his words have gone through the whole earth & his spirit has moved & continues to move the human family to the renouncement of their sin & conversion to God. And therefore & thus is he the Messiah the Saviour of men.

2. The next consideration of much importance is that as this authority belonged to this truth & not to any person, so it is not confined to the pure & benevolent Founder of Christianity but may & must belong to all his disciples in that measure in which they

possess themselves of the truth which was in him. Jesus has not monopolized it. His mission was to communicate it & precisely in the same measure with it he communicates his power over men. There is no stint or jealousy or grudge in the divine bounty. Gods thots are not like mans tho'ts. Jesus is loved & followed in proportion ⟨as⟩ not as men cower at his name & obey ⟨his⟩ the letter of his commands in a slavish spirit, but as they generously embark in the same cause ↑by word & by act;↓ open the ↑elementary↓ truth he gave them; carry it out to farther conclusions; & ↑each↓ be to their own age & circumstances as nearly as they can the excellent benefactor⟨s⟩ which he has been to so many ages & nations. ⟨And they receive it & understand it & impart it who keep his commandments.⟩

And thus many a disciple in different ages of the Church hath learned of Christ so much of his truth, hath had infused into his soul so much of his masters spirit that he hath spoken with a large measure of his masters authority And these are they who have been the lights of the world & whose precepts & memory prompt all men to virtue

And all of us receive & understand & & impart the same truth as we keep his commandments.

My friends, let us not be the last to receive this instruction. We can do nothing against his truth. It is the law & mould wherein God made the heavens & the earth & them that dwell therein Let us not be slower than yᵉ multitude who first heard him, but let us pluck out of ourselves the only enemies his words can find in the human heart our own sins; our false estimates of earthly good; our sensual, selfish, uncharitable tho'ts; & we shall find, that, as we do this, yᵉ voice of our Saviour becomes yᵉ voice of a Friend;—sounds ↑to↓ us full of consolation, of promise, of praise. At last when truth has had its ⟨f⟩ whole effect on our minds, it will gain its fulness of authority by becoming to us simply yᵉ echo of our own thought. We shall find we think as Christ tho't. Thus we shall be one with him & with him one with the Father

30 May 1830
rewritten March 31 1832.

Sermon LXXVII

Manuscript A: Six sheets folded to make four pages each; folios stacked and sewn along the left margin with black thread, only traces of which remain; pages measure 25 x 20.3 cm (folios 1–3) and 23.9 x 19.5 cm (folios 4–6). Affixed to the right margin of MS p. 18 with red sealing wax is an irregular scrap of paper, approximately 6 x 11 cm, containing unlabeled Insert "X."

[Above Bible text] Charity Lecture at Old South June 1830

Lines	Page 196
4–5	uttered ⟨ & charity has been upon its lips wherever it has gone.⟩ ↑and . . . country.↓
13	these ⟨exal⟩ generous
15	i.e. ⟨kindness⟩ ↑assistance↓
19	brings ⟨the⟩ an
22–24	↑unhappy↓ suffer⟨ing⟩↑ers↓ ⟨families⟩ ↑in our community↓ . . . showing ⟨that⟩ first

	Page 197
2	urge the [end of line] the

8–10   ↑the soul of↓ . . . much ⟨h⟩as . . . ↑his knowledge . . . goodwill↓,

13   lives ⟨for the largest number⟩ to

16   in ⟨the Universe⟩ existence

28   exercises /a/the/ deep⟨&⟩est &

30   every where

31–37   ↑shd . . . good↓ . . . times ⟨now⟩ ↑and↓ . . . ↑now . . . . perished↓ . . . ↑it will be ⟨m⟩far more truly mourned↓

Page 198

1   from ⟨their⟩ action ↑of such men↓

2–4   ↑The world wd. . . . but↓ . . . never ⟨poor⟩ [canceled in pencil] ↑exhausted↓.

10   so he he

13–15   men ↑⟨&⟩And . . . Gods ⟨m⟩energy . . . joy.↓

16–17   ever /merely intellectual superiority/external distinc/ [variant in pencil]

18   greatness i⟨t⟩s to

28   they ⟨they⟩ tempt . . . out-⟨working powers⟩↑stretching branches↓,

36   is ⟨writte⟩ set . . . on ⟨l⟩all parts

38–39   use /Once/Try to/ . . . exclusive ⟨use⟩ ↑benefit. It . . . can↓ &

Page 199

4   ↑it↓

8   burned; And

13–19   ↑¶ He . . . blessings [in pencil] And . . . well⟨s⟩ as . . . laws↓ ↑¶ Thus . . . charity.↓ [in pencil]

20   views ⟨of Charity⟩ ↑thus generally stated↓ [emendation in pencil]

28–36   ↑tis↓ for ⟨ch⟩the . . . charity. ⟨These are words but not reason. God never authorized them. God never made the heart of flint.⟩ ↑Insert A A{These . . . ↑actions↓ [addition in pencil] . . . to ⟨every⟩ all . . . statesman.}↓

37   wrong. ⟨It⟩ Suppose

40   The ⟨dangers of injudicious⟩ ↑abuses of↓

Page 200

1–2   Man ↑wh⟨o⟩ich refuses to give↓ . . . as ⟨much⟩ ↑genuine↓

3–4   you /give to the best/chuse between them/, But . . . that ⟨in⟩ ↑out of your aid to↓

6   or ⟨for⟩ absurd

7–8   on ⟨on⟩ public . . . ↑conspicuous↓

10   bro't ⟨nearer⟩ to

12   deni↑e↓d

13   some↑thing↓ ⟨motion⟩ must be ⟨made⟩ ↑done↓

14   ↑expedients to adopt↓?

15–20   be ⟨an⟩one experiment, ⟨a⟩ ↑one↓ step, not to be ⟨repeated.⟩ ↑gone over.↓ /It/Every charitable institution, the least useful of all/ . . . consequence. ↑{Insert X} [On a slip of paper affixed by red sealing wax to the right margin of the facing page at this point, verso blank, is

	the following passage:] Because . . . greatest ⟨s⟩ evils . . . the ⟨absence from all⟩ ↑privation↓ many . . . woes↓
23	A ⟨munificent charity⟩ ↑great . . . want↓
26	educating ⟨us⟩its
31–38	¶ Therefore . . . altogether. [entire paragraph in pencil with emendations in ink as noted below]
32–33	us be- [end of line] ↑clothed with ⟨the⟩ beauty of this eldest grace. [end of line] Be↓ware . . . of ²{Want & ¹{Misfortune
34	to us↑,↓
37	help↑,↓ . . . ↑bestow it somewhere else↓ do
40	bestow. ⟨If [to this point paragraph in pencil] you are poor⟩ ↑If↓ [emendation in pencil]
41	disasters of [Emerson wrote "broken fortunes" as a variant for "bankruptcy" and then "credit" as a variant for "fortunes"; variants in pencil]
45	your own . . . reward [in pencil]

Manuscript B: Five sheets folded to make four pages each; folios stacked, with a single half-sheet inserted before the fifth folio, the whole sewn along the left margin with white thread; pages measure 25 x 20.3 cm.

LXXVII.
Evangelical Treasury 1831
⟨Charity Lecture⟩
⟨Old South⟩
Let no man seek his own but every man
anothers wealth I Cor. 10.24.

It is a distinguishing feature of Christianity & so has been a great commendation of it that it enforced the social duties with stronger emphasis than any moral code had done before. Peace & good will were the first words it uttered & alms giving & charitable institutions have attended the establishment of Christianity in every country

But it is an exaggeration to say that Christianity first taught the law of benevolence God taught it to the first man↑,↓ [addition in pencil] & to every man in the Constitution of his own mind & in the Constitution of society. The law of love, the duty of seeking the good of others, & postponing our own to it, is no obscure or local doctrine. It hath gone out into the ends of the earth It hath teachers & examples in every savage tribe.

To die for friendship, for love, for the protection of the innocent, or for our country, was always accounted noble. It is an universal sentiment

To shrink from these generous impulses & ↑steadily↓ prefer the present good of self ↑& the least good of self to the greatest public good↓ was always reckoned Cowardly & infamous.

And so the duty of Charity in its peculiar sense, i.e. assistance to the indigent, is very plain. And no man denies the obligation. It would argue a man of ferocious temper to deny it broadly. But how little is the duty felt! how little understood! how imperfectly discharged! ↑Men admit the duty in general but cavil at particular claims.↓ [addition in pencil]

I embrace with pleasure the opportunity offered me by the returning anniversary of the Charitable association of this Society to speak a few words to the general subject. Perhaps you may & perhaps you may not feel it be your duty to ⟨assist⟩ supply the wants we shall present, but I wish to remind you that there is a sovereign obligation on us all, to be, to the extent of our means, charitable ⟨souls.⟩ ↑persons.↓ [emendation in pencil] Particular wants may be neglected perhaps /without fatal consequence/or relieved according to your discretion/ [variant in pencil] but the habit of imparting to others must be as extensive as are our means, the spirit of love must pervade the whole soul or the soul is departing from its good.

There are two great facts that force themselves upon the mind which considers attentively the subject of Charity,—*first;* that Nature teaches it; *secondly;* that Revelation enjoins it. And this surely is all the authority we need to bind our actions. I shall attempt to show these facts

I. ↑I observe yᵗ↓ [addition in pencil] The law of nature teaches charity. Man is constituted to be a beneficent being, & injures himself by every attempt to confine his advantages to himself. It is customary to urge on men the claims of a particular object that needs help. We ought rather ↑as I have said↓ [addition in pencil] to dwell on the necessity to the soul itself—of being charitable Men should know how much it is necessary to their own happiness, how indispensable it is to the progress, to the salvation of the soul, that it comply with this law of universal nature. All education should show the fact that he who withholds his ↑needed↓ aid from his fellow man is more a loser than his fellow man from whom he withholds it; that the soul of man was made to act for others, as much as his body was made to breathe the air; that it is the natural action of man to *impart* his knowledge, his labor, his possessions, his virtue,—↑{(↓the [addition in pencil] way in which he grows great,↑)↓ [addition in pencil] the way in which he moves toward the perfection of his being.↑}↓ [addition in pencil] We were made to communicate. The greatest man is the greatest giver. ⟨A⟩ The most useful man the man who lives most for all others is most like God.—God is God because he is the great Giver of all things. It is an exclamation of the devout Thomas A Kempis, "Lord! all that I have, all the ability by which I am made capable of serving thee is thine; & thou therefore ⟨se⟩ rather servest me." And as we are made in the divine image, whatever tends to increase the real power & dignity of man, to raise him towards the perfection of his nature,—in any true sense,—to make him greater in physical, ⟨mor⟩ intellectual, or moral capacity, tends to the same degree ⟨toward communication, serving⟩ to make him more serviceable to others Our least excellent faculties are those which are most exclusively employed for self, & the nobler is the faculty the more extensive is the ⟨participation⟩ ↑communication of good↓. Our hands & feet ⟨and bodily faculties⟩ work for ourselves [over "our se"] but the tongue the /communicator/organ/ of thought is for society; & reason & truth is not mine or thine. ⟨It is⟩They are shared by the ⟨whole Universe.⟩ great society of intelligent beings.

↑Indeed see how poor were the richest endowments without society↓ [addition in pencil] What is speech ↑good↓ for? What is genius ↑good↓ for? What is your grace, your learning↑,↓ [addition in pencil] your industry your wealth, power, wit; much more What is your moral nature—your courage justice benevolence what are these for—if once they are put out of use to others—if you are shut up in a lonely cell far from the pleasing tumult of society—or if you shut up yourself in the loneliest cell of a thorough selfishness. Try to separate them to your own exclusive benefit. It is impossible. Do it as far as you can,—& you become a burden to the earth, & a burden to yourself.

On the contrary, the very way as all men know in which human powers increase is by *use* i.e. by communication of their virtue. What is the way in which ⟨the Memory ardent scholar⟩ a man most rapidly & effectually acquires knowledge? ⟨Is it not by the effort to impart it⟩ by the effort to apply what he knows to some useful end; or by the effort to impart what he knows to other minds, his own tho'ts are drawn out of their confusion into order & clearness & new truth is suggested. It is a maxim yᵗ yᵉ more ↑information↓ a man gives, the more he gets. What is the way in which the physician would make progress in his art, ⟨to⟩ wd. acquire new skill in the treatment of disease? Is it not by devoting all his art & time to the healing of the sick?—How shall the orator learn the art of persuading & convincing but by giving up his whole mind to the attempt to persuade & convince his fellow men? What is the secret of *happiness* as far as wisest men have found it out? Is it not to be found, & only found in producing the happiness of others? And how is *virtue* to be acquired? Is it not by giving up the whole man to the promotion of the cause of virtue in the world, as did Socrates or St Paul or Jesus of Nazareth.

Simple & manifest as I trust these views are↑,↓ [addition in pencil] they have been wofully neglected or unknown to men in past ages. It has been a sort of recommendation of a pleasure that it was shared by few, instead of enhancing the delight by the feeling that it ran thro a thousand bosoms. A king, according to the theory of ages & nations, instead of being the servant of his people, was the pampered cosset for whose pleasure the people—(thousands & thousands of wiser & better men than himself,) lived & toiled. What ⟨w⟩ has been the consequence? That the king ↑by being the most useless,↓ became the most worthless person in his dominions.

What if his name & power were known & felt throughout the world, because his treasury drained the wealth of a great country. What if the wheat grew on the plains, & the sheep grazed on the hills, & the ships ploughed the sea, for him.↑—↓All this nominal majesty served only to render more manifest his real insignificance He dies in his place, which is filled instantly by a successor & his departure ⟨shall⟩ ↑doth↓ not cause one pang in any community, or in any family, scarcely in one individual.

But if there should be within the dominions of that King a mind which is not more its own property than it is the property of the country & the age in which it acts, a mind which is nearly allied to God by the love of Him & so a love of mankind & which by its ⟨labors to⟩ ↑piety & benevolence↓ [emendation in pencil] ⟨&⟩ [canceled in pencil] exercises the deepest & most salutary influence on all surrounding minds & thro' them on all society and further if this mind shd. apply itself in all its extent to the public good; shd be the instructor of his country, shd. be the ⟨defender⟩ expounder & defender of its rights, the central spring of all the great beneficent enterprizes of the times↑,↓ [addition in pencil] this man is the real king the legitimate sovereign ↑whoever wd. forward a good work looks up to him, whoever wd. have counsel a asks him↓ [addition in pencil] and if ⟨su⟩ this man die↑,↓ [addition in pencil] if this amount of good influence be withdrawn from the community↑,↓ then↑—↓& [additions in pencil] not before is greatness perished↑,↓—⟨l⟩Let [added comma and capital "L" in pencil] the forms of mourning be more or less, it will be far more deeply mourned—a severe loss is felt—a torch has been extinguished that rayed out knowledge & safety far & wide & made the earth light with its beams.

The world is the gainer by the talents & virtues of such a man but not the less has the individual been the gainer. How is he exalted & ennobled by this development of his powers! What instruction has he not gained!—what vigor by use to every faculty! All that interests man interests him. He identifies himself with th⟨is⟩e cause ↑he pleads↓—. The progress of science is *his* progress. The increase of Liberty is *his* increase. The advancement of virtue is *his* advancement. So that no good can happen throughout the ⟨Universe⟩ ↑world↓ [emendation in pencil] but he hath his share in it by means of boundless charity. ↑X X{In this manner in proportion to the elevation of every mind is its property in the general good. Thus Jesus Christ saith to God And all mine are thine & ↑all↓ thine are mine.↓ [addition in pencil]

Thus brethren the more it is considered the more it will appear that man's natural greatness is to do good. All the seeds of weakness in his constitution are those tendencies which draw him from the good of others to his own. His appetites oppose his greatness How? Because they seduce him to seek a good that begins & ends in self. His passions are injurious to him↑,↓ only↑,↓ [additions in pencil] when like Avarice, Envy, Ambition, Pride, Revenge, they tempt him to contract his outstretching branches & tie them inward to himself

He seeks the good of the Universe & enlarges himself to the vast objects⟨:⟩ he contemplates↑;↓ [colon canceled and semicolon added in pencil] or he prefers a solitary selfish enjoyment & shuts up one door of the soul after another; kills by disuse one power after another, till like the miser or the sensualist, he becomes less than man, and dies the second death.

II Secondly. Not only doth Nature teach man the lesson of beneficence but Revelation enjoins it. As far as Christianity is a Moral Law—as far as it represents man as a sinner in need of salvation—it teaches one great truth the necessity of Regeneration or a change of heart. But what is that change—Simply a change from the love of self to the love of God—or from the love of those advantages that terminate in ourselves as the love of animal pleasure & of wealth & power to that end—⟨and an adoption of⟩ ↑to↓ [emendation in pencil] the love of those advantages which may be equally shared by all Gods moral creatures as truth & virtue—↑,↓ in short↑,↓ [additions in pencil] a change from ⟨th⟩ selfishness to Chari⟨ty.⟩↑tableness.↓ This is the lesson one in substance tho' taught in many forms by Jesus Christ, ⟨teaching men⟩ ↑& wh. may be shortly summed up in his precept↓ [emendation in pencil] that whoso would be greatest among them let him be the servant of all.

In this manner Reason & Revelation conspire to teach us that then only we truly seek our own good, when we seek it in connexion with or rather for the end of the good of the whole. This should incline our ear to every appeal of want. We should look upon every occasion of charity not as a disagreeable importunity, but as an opportunity of self improvement as an opportunity to be embraced with cheerful alacrity of serving at once God & the creation & ourselves.

I wish to ask your attention a few moments to the Report of the Evangelical Treasury. It may not be known to all to whom I speak that the Evang Treas. is a Charitable association formed ⟨of ⟨members⟩⟩ ↑persons↓ in this Religious Society who become members by paying one dollar a year. There are now eighty five Subscribers. In addition to the sum thus raised the ⟨An⟩ standing Committee of the Church permit an annual contribution to be collected /in/on/ the Lords Day in aid of the funds

These sums are expended for various purposes by a body of twenty directors.

In the last year the whole expenditure of the Treasury has been $125.30. Of this sum $25.00 were given to the Evang. Missionary Society the object of which is to aid feeble societies in the support of public worship & wh. for some years has been accustomed to look to us for a part of its means $30.30 have been appropriated to the use of the Library of the Church. This sum is to expended immediately to purchase books. ↑It is regretted that some unfavorable circumstances↓ [addition in pencil]

The Hancock Sunday School looks to this society alone for the payment of its expenses—$45.00 have been paid on its account the last year.

$25.00 have been expended in alms to indigent persons within the parish.

These & such as these are the objects of the Evang. Treasury, & this the aid, small, but it is hoped, effectual, wh. it has afforded them. You see plainly that from the limits of its subscription list, it relies much on the annual contribution. If you think these objects important, if you feel that the cause of ⟨m⟩ domestic missions; the ⟨cause⟩ circulation of good books among ourselves; the interests of the Sunday School; & the pressing wants of the hungry & the half clothed if these are causes that you feel have any claim upon you—then give in aid of them

But strong as these claims are, I pray you remember ⟨they are⟩ their wants are not so pressing ⟨as the necessity⟩ as your own, in this matter.. their necessities not so great, as the necessity of being charitable is to yourself. Give to these claims, because God gave you all. Give, because God loveth a cheerful giver [II Corinthians 9:7]. Give because by the constitution of your nature, & by the law of the gospel ⟨according to⟩ your bounty becomes the measure of your powers & as you gi⟨w⟩ve so shall you receive.

Sermon LXXVIII

Manuscript: Five sheets folded to make four pages each; folios nested and sewn along the left margin with white thread; pages measure 24.1 x 19.9 cm. The lower outside corners of leaves bearing pp. 11–12 and 13–14 were torn away before inscription. There is no loss of text.

["Salem" in pencil below the biblical text]

Lines	Page 201
5–6	we⟨e⟩akness . . . beneficence. in
10–11	↑soul↓ . . . to ⟨all⟩ ↑every soul↓ to be obtained by ⟨their⟩ ↑its↓ [all emendations in ink over pencil]
14	is / appointed / indulged /
17	↑& the importance↓
18–(202)3	made. ¶ ⟨It is o⟩One . . . past, ⟨to conceive⟩ ↑We are accustomed to speak↓ [ink over pencil] ↑of↓ . . . if ⟨we⟩ ↑one individual↓ . . . was ⟨not new⟩ ↑trite↓ on earth, was ⟨not new⟩ ↑trite↓ to us. ⟨Why should men class⟩ ↑It . . . group↓ . . . gospel has [end of page] proclaimed

	Page 202
4–8	we ⟨say⟩ ↑slight . . . say↓ . . . reason ↑why↓ . . . ↑if . . . life↓?
8–9	↑The . . . time.↓
10	now⟨.⟩ ↑to any individual?↓
11–13	new. ⟨↑Old things are passed away↓⟩ [In erased pencil, written over by the following in ink:] ↑In . . . new↓
13	↑now↓ exhaled ⟨in⟩ ↑from↓
17–21	life ⟨today.⟩ ↑for another hour. So for↓ The . . . animal⟨s⟩ ↑remains↓ are now ↑undergoing↓ decomposi⟨ng⟩tion . . . enliven, / heat / warm /, moisten, & nourish the ↑green↓ herb that Providence ⟨is providing⟩ ↑has set apart↓

23–26   mind. ⟨What⟩ The . . . vice, kowledge,
28   ↑until I perceive it↓ . . . helping ⟨or hurting⟩ me
30   ¶ What ⟨is⟩ ↑matters↓
31–32   influences; ⟨to⟩ ↑exists in↓ . . . unexampled. ⟨{The same event has
          different faces to different men. The same man is ⟨pleas⟩ loved by
          one, & hated by another.}⟩ [bracketed and canceled in pencil] Men
34–35   ↑whose habits . . . remote↓
41–(203)3 another. ¶ ⟨Men dont think or each of us does not think he is
          addressed by⟩ It . . . ↑the work you do↓ . . . ↑the hope . . . you↓
          these [addition in ink over pencil; pencil layer reads: "the hope yᵗ
          cheers the pain that crushes you"]

Page 203

7–9   ↑These . . . commandment.↓
10–11   unheeded, ⟨in⟩days, . . . mind. ⟨They⟩ Men
12–15   ↑& wisdom↓ . . . cannot; ↑They s⟨ay⟩peak or they act if↓
16   ↑Because . . . fails.↓
18–25   than ⟨for an hour⟩ ↑it would for↓ . . . hour? ⟨d⟩Does . . . ↑vast &↓
          . . . you a⟨n occasional⟩ ↑special↓ . . . revelation⟨?⟩ ↑for your
          instruction?↓ ¶ ⟨Why not believe then that⟩ ↑It . . . ↑as↓ . . . believe↓
          ["It . . . believe" is in ink over pencil; "as" appears only in ink layer.]
          the present moment ⟨& each moment is the accepted time⟩ ↑contains
          . . . moment↓ bring⟨ing⟩s to you ↑⟨with⟩ ↑in↓ its peculiar trial or
          lesson↓
27   ↑For↓ [in pencil] Do
29   ↑or any part of it↓
34   ↑probably↓ never. ⟨It must *now,*⟩ ↑I say probably never↓ [emenda-
          tions in ink over pencil]
37   evil ⟨of t⟩effect
39   ↑What . . . for?↓
43–45   ↑Something . . . end;↓ [in ink over pencil; pencil layer identical except
          for last word: ". . . its ⟨end⟩ ↑term↓."] ↑↑Many↓ Men . . .
          apprehending ⟨the truth of⟩ its meaning↓ ¶ ⟨No⟩; this salvation is
          no↑t↓ . . . as ⟨action⟩ ↑intelligent being↓ [emendation in ink over
          pencil]

Page 204

1–2   moral ⟨action⟩ ↑perception↓ [emendation in ink over pencil] in the
          soul↑,↓ [in pencil] . . . ↑and . . . progress↓ [ink over pencil]
4   hour↑,↓ [in pencil] . . . ↑as long as you exist,↓
5   And ⟨now⟩ ↑the present time,↓
11   him. ↑in a crowd.↓
12   fly ⟨from the past⟩ to
12–13   ↑I . . . itself.↓
14–17   future. ⟨The present is the soil in which all the seeds of time are sown,
          & are watered, & are ripening.⟩ O . . . compound ²{for this one
          indulgence that is near your heart, & involves no great transgression,}
          ¹{by sternest self-denial in time to come},—o consider, how truly /
          one/this/ . . . the ⟨former⟩ ↑last↓,

18   failed ⟨of⟩ ↑to keep↓
22   vain. ⟨Here⟩ ↑This experience↓ [emendation in pencil]
24–26   that ⟨perhaps⟩ the . . . to /Virtue/God/ [variant in pencil] . . .
                ↑they↓
33   todays ⟨undone duties⟩ ↑neglected work↓. ["work" in ink over
                pencil]
37   consc⟨e⟩ience
40–41   ↑"If . . . him.↓

Page 205

1–3   ↑then . . . eye↓ . . . you↑;↓ [ink over pencil] ⟨t⟩They [capitalized in
                pencil] . . . meaning↑,↓ [in pencil] . . . the ⟨e⟩watchful

Sermon LXXIX

Manuscript A: Six sheets folded to make four pages each; folios nested and sewn along
the left margin with white thread; a half-sheet, 24.1 x 20.2 cm, inscribed on both sides, is
laid in before the last leaf of the outermost folio; pages measure 25 x 20.3 cm.

[Above Bible text] Evangelical Treasury. 1830. June.
                Charity Lecture. Old South June 1832

Lines   *Page 206*
8   so /I shall rather use this occasion/it becomes me/ [variant in pencil]
16   ↑appearances of the↓
18–19   ↑To select a single instance;↓ A
24   the ⟨restless⟩ eye

Page 207

11–12   fall, ⟨it⟩they suppl⟨ies⟩y
13   exami⟨m⟩nes
17–18   ↑in its cavities↓
19–20   ↑& on every bough↓
24   us, ⟨wh⟩ all . . . uses ⟨as⟩ more
26   limited. ⟨Every⟩ The
32–33   indispesable to us wh⟨o⟩ich devour the vast ⟨mass⟩ excess of
                corrupting ⟨&⟩ animal
40   Providence ⟨whilst⟩ there

Page 208

2   no ⟨coffin⟩ tomb
6   ↑does↓
21–22   kindness. ⟨But what⟩ All
24–25   good ⟨for good's sake⟩ [canceled in pencil] ↑& . . . it,↓
27   capacity ⟨their maker⟩ ↑He↓ . . . power↑s↓
37–38   physician, ⟨the teacher⟩ ↑the jurist, the historian,↓ the man of
                ⟨learning⟩ ↑science↓,

Page 209

3–4   men ⟨is⟩ ↑has↓ obviously ⟨not a⟩ ↑no pretensions to↓ high ⟨kind of⟩
                virtue,

6   ↑a↓
9   without ⟨leas⟩ discovering
16   yet ⟨need not seek⟩ ↑may not proceed from↓
20-23   who ⟨smitten⟩ ↑moved↓ . . . fame ⟨does⟩ ↑renders↓ . . . most
                     ⟨generous & successful⟩ ↑daring↓ . . . humanity; The ↑man of↓
                     genius, that, in ⟨his efforts to distinguish himself⟩ ↑⟨devotion to⟩
                     ↑aiming at↓ . . . tastes↓,
28-29   Charity; ⟨T⟩the . . . cost. ⟨to⟩ ⟨There are⟩ And
33-35   day, i⟨n⟩f they . . . them ⟨this way⟩ ↑here↓
40-41   gran [end of line] deur. [end of page] deur. ⟨The⟩ ↑And not only↓
                     blessing . . . perish ⟨is⟩ ↑rests↓

Page 210

5   ↑material↓
7   us ⟨his will⟩ that
11   the ⟨good⟩ ↑comfort↓
12   who ⟨would make⟩ manifests . . . of ⟨many⟩ ↑his↓
17-19   that ⟨loves⟩ makes . . . all ⟨who⟩ the
21-22   ↑men . . . himself,↓,
29   death ⟨t⟩an
40   uses ⟨to⟩ ↑on↓

Page 211

3   appointed ⟨f⟩ to solicit subscriptions. ⟨The present number of
                     subscribers is ninety five. By⟩ It
5   ↑are the↓
8-9   ↑¶ The . . . chosen.↓
10   of $⟨2⟩35.00 to
17   ↑by the Treasury↓ [in pencil]
23   & ⟨these the sums⟩ ↑this . . . effectual↓ [emendation in pencil]
28   which ⟨in one⟩ ↑in↓ such ↑a↓ [emendation and addition in pencil]
33-35   care. [Laid in at this point is a single half-sheet, not included in the
                     sewing, on which Emerson wrote a paragraph almost certainly
                     intended for the sermon's second delivery, the Charity Lecture at the
                     Old South, June 3, 1832:] ⟨↑It remains to ask your contribution in aid
                     of the indigent persons in our Churches for whose benefit this Lecture
                     was appointed. Spare a little out of your abundance, spare something
                     out of your savings to assist the unfortunate the sick the old & the
                     very young persons whom their poverty & their worth has recom-
                     mended to the discreet overseers of this Charity↓⟩ [Emerson canceled
                     this passage in ink, then wrote the following (upside down in relation
                     to the canceled text) for one or more deliveries subsequent to the
                     second:] ↑¶ There is no one of us who has not the power to serve many
                     individuals by ⟨personal sacrifices⟩ ↑this time, his substance,↓ by
                     active cooperation, by ⟨advice⟩ instruction, by prayers & good
                     wishes, which↑, when true,↓ are no mean helps, & may be followed
                     by all the rest. Let the voice of reason & of scripture call our earnest
                     attention to our social duties. ⟨At least⟩ Are they many & endless. At

least let us begin to fulfil them. Let us not, in flat contradiction to their commands, ↑neglect yᵉ rights nor↓ [addition in pencil] hurt the feelings by our wanton tongue of those of our household. Let us not ⟨backbite⟩ ↑traduce↓ [emendation in pencil] the absent. ↑Let us not ⟨feel⟩ think all our duty done when we have performed our promises.↓

Let us feel that ⟨an⟩ ↑other⟨s⟩↓ obligation↑s↓ may exist of duty to a brother as valid as a note of hand, that we truly owe him nothing less than all the service we can ↑justly↓ render him. Let us do what we can, not with a grudging but a thankful mind, thankful that God has made the communication of his gifts the way of all ⟨true⟩ real increase of our own powers & happiness.

I do not think fit to enjoin this duty or awaken this ⟨feel⟩ sentiment by a strong representation of the wants the sufferings that may be found within a short distance of every dwelling within the immediate knowledge of every individual. For I am now looking at i⟨n⟩t in the light of a duty to ourselves not as a want of others. ↑Be assured my brother↓ Sore as are the sufferings of ↑the↓ wretched among us ⟨I would yet have you to be assured⟩ that ⟨the⟩ no ⟨distresses⟩ ↑evils↓ of poverty of pain of fear are so hard to bear or hard to cure as ↑the evil of↓ your own selfishness. Moreover if you fail them they will not yet be wholly friendless God will provide them aid himself↓

↑You may make of these reflexions what application you will. An appeal is now made to you in behalf of a large number of destitute families & individuals sorely reduced by the late calamity in our vicinity. Here is an oppʸ offered of exercising your love to these fellowmen & neighbors according to your ability↓ [this paragraph in pencil; end of insert]

⟨But, . . . himself.⟩ [canceled in pencil, undoubtedly in conjunction with the insert above and therefore for a late delivery]

36   comfort ⟨yᵉ⟩the

39–40   Therefore ⟨if you think this charity has no call upon you⟩ ↑use your own judgment in determining what objects ha⟨s⟩ve a ↑rightful↓ claim upon you↓, [emendations in pencil, probably for a late delivery and therefore not adopted]

Manuscript B: Eight sheets folded to make four pages each; five folios are nested and sewn along the left margin with white thread; following this gathering are two stacked folios, the whole tucked into the outermost folio. The pinholes in the two stacked folios differ from each other and from those of the sewn gathering; the outer folio has no pinholes. Pages measure 23.8 x 20 cm, except for those of the two stacked folios, which measure 25 x 20.3 cm. The leaf bearing MS pp. 13-14 has been cut out, leaving stubs bearing evidence of writing on both sides.

As we have therefore opportunity, let us do
good unto all men. Galatians 6.10

It is a distinguishing feature of Christianity & so has been a great commendation of it, that it enforced the social duties with stronger emphasis than any moral code had done before. Peace & good will were the first words it uttered; & alms-giving & charitable institutions have ↑been observed to↓ attend⟨ed⟩ the establishment of Christianity in every country. [end of page]

Copied elsewhere

⟨It is my duty ⟨my⟩ to bring before you this day the claims of the ancient association for Charitable purposes in this Society called the Evangelical Treasury upon your bounty. In a Christian Church a plea for charity is always seasonable. A Christian Church should have a heart as large as the family of man, a hand always open whilst any wants & any ability to relieve them remain.

But as God rather seeks in us the developement of the will than our aid in any particular work so I shall rather ⟨seek to open the great law⟩ ↑use the opportunity to press from reason & revelation the general duty↓ of Charity than to urge the claims of a single institution⟩

When we inspect the works of God we find that every thing is made to answer some purpose ⟨out of its own being⟩ beyond the Continuance of its own being. A tree of the forest when it is minutely examined is found to have an organization of consummate art Capable of performing within itself from year to year all the delicate & varied processes that are essential to its perfection & though every part is of the frailest beginnings, yet is it able to resist the cold, & the wind, & to repair the injuries it receives, & to outlast many of mans generations. But how soon would the covetous eye of man weary of the microscope if his examination of its parts only detected means of promoting the good of the vegetable itself, if nothing was in a tree, but the means of enlarging continuing or propagating a tree. It is the usefulness of this being & mainly its usefulness to man, that gives it so much regard. It is the ornament of the earth. It gives hospitable shade to man & beast. It yields its fruit after its kind for food. It is timber for towns & for navies. But when this has been said is all known?

It hath abundantly more to accomplish by its existence in nature. ⟨Every leaf⟩ Its roots grasp the ⟨soil⟩ ↑earth↓ & prevent the inroads of sand upon the soil. ↑Under its shade plants arise that could not grow in the sun.↓ [in ink over pencil] Every leaf hath its functions to perform to the atmosphere. Its evaporation cools the air. It exhales new & healthful elements When its leaves fall, they supply rich nourishment to the new plants.

Yet here is but a portion of its uses. As the observer more nearly examines it, he finds it to be a world by itself peopled with a vast mass of life. It is the residence of countless animals of various forms & habits,—both social & solitary ⟨speeches⟩ species,—to which it affords habitation & food. The bird builds its nest, & sings in its branches: the ⟨caterpill⟩ squirrel lays up in ⟨a hole⟩ ↑its cavities↓ ⟨its⟩his winter store; the caterpillar weaves his web, & then spins his shroud, & waits his resurrection in a summer morn; the worm & the fly find their mansion, down to the minute herds of insects who take their colour from the leaf which is the pasture over which they roam.

This is but one of the countless forms of matter around us, which all have their uses, but of which our knowledge is only in its infancy. Every vegetable, every mineral, every animal has its part assigned ⟨it⟩to it in the general economy. Animals

Not those only serve man & nature wh⟨o⟩ich are our bondservants, the camel, the reindeer, the horse, & the domestic animals generally, ⟨but⟩ but birds & beasts of prey & the small communities of insects ants not less serve him by devouring ⟨on⟩ the vast mass of corrupting animal & vegetable matter that else mt. taint the atmosphere. The bee carries the fertilizing dust from flower to flower

So is it with all. God has made nothing in vain. The waters /do their part in the great economy/do not limit their beneficence to bearing our frail ships/. The broad basin of the sea cools the world by its evaporation & forms the clouds, ⟨& bears the ship on its bosom⟩ & ↑conceals↓ another kingdom of life ⟨under its surface⟩ ↑within its bosom↓

In all the arrangements of ⟨nature⟩ ↑Providence↓ whilst there is no prodigality ⟨there is⟩ [canceled in pencil] no ↑selfish↓ hoarding ↑is permitted↓ [additions in pencil] Nothing is separated from the general good Every thing is made to minister to the ⟨greatest⟩ ↑widest↓ [emendation in pencil] good. It is wonderful the strict economy with which all atoms are taken up. There is no graveyard in nature, no urn of useless decay. The mouldering forms from which life is departed are immediately converted into new forms of strength & beauty, they live again, again they minister to power & happiness.

Nor do the sun & moon & the stars burn for their own pleasure. Nor the earth roll in ⟨useless⟩ ↑unprofitable↓ light through space. For use, they shine, for the good of intelligent beings they revolve for times & seasons, for months & years for health & life, for mind, for moral nature, for virtue for truth.

{Thus it is in these obvious instances & yet more striking as it is pursued in detail the great purpose of Nature, throughout all her order, to produce a general not a particular good. ⟨It⟩ The ↑creation↓ seems to teach this moral through every race & man as well as brute since in all the race never dies, the individual never is spared}

But all these great agents of mercy are involuntary benefactors. It is conscience in man that gives them a tongue. It is we who by our nature read the moral & not they who intelligently say it. The bee⟨r⟩ bears you no good will whilst he separates the honey & kneads the wax ⟨for your service.⟩ which you shall use. The world enkindling sun in his cloudy tabernacle is inert & brute as the dust we tread upon. It is not they who bless us, it is the beneficence of God working through them that we feel it is the goodness of Him who makes the winds his wings & the clouds his servants & the sun his minister. He breathes the life of his love through their silent frame He impresses his purpose on the clod & it teems with life and through the Universe as through the mouth of a prophet he speaks to the heart of his children.

It is God whom we perceive ⟨but we thank⟩ ↑&↓ not the /means/ ⟨forms of outward nature⟩/ ⟨for their advantages⟩ ↑he uses The powers of nature have no purpose of kindness.↓ But what they fail to show us, it is given to man the likeness of God to unfold. We know there is a higher stage of being than theirs a better beneficence. It is the glory of man to do good for good's sake, to ⟨do well⟩ confer benefits on others [Here the end of MS p. 11 is followed by a page canceled with a large "X" in ink:] ⟨with understanding & the intent to produce good as an end. ↑God has made men to be voluntary benefactors↓ And to this capacity his Maker has added the richest powers of producing happiness.

↑I   Those who do good at no cost to themselves
II   at a sacrifice↓ [in pencil]
But there are two classes of voluntary benefactors. ↑I. those who do good at no cost II. those who do good at a sacrifice↓ Not all men who do good with ⟨like⟩ ↑equal↓ success, ⟨& equal amount⟩ do it with like motive or like merits. God has made good the natural fruit of all innocent exertions, of all ⟨di⟩ the innocent exercise of our natural powers. So that if merely you keep in the course which nature has marked out for you; if, guided by a wise self-interest, you seek to develope all your powers of body & mind in the best way, you cannot help being a benefactor of society. The ↑honest↓ merchant whose principle of action is the obtaining his own estate is a public benefactor⟩ [end of MS p. 12; next leaf has been cut out, leaving a half-inch stub with traces of writing on both sides]

But the Second class is those who do good at a sacrifice. And ⟨this⟩ herein is the duty of Charity There are those who feel it to be their daily vocation their indispensable duty to do good, not as a flourish & commendation to their own bye ends, but as itself the highest end, who cannot eat their bread in peace, unless they have earned it by removing a portion of evil; who count that they have lost a day, if they have not done man a ⟨service⟩ a good office; who espouse the cause which others forsake, who see the hand which others cannot see, beckoning them here to the hungry, & there to the ignorant; who submit to privation that others may abound, who prefer the useful to the honoured place, who are ministering angels sent forth to ⟨minister⟩ multiply those who shall be heirs of salvation.

These are not the inert laborers the unconscious ⟨benefactors⟩ distributors of Gods bounty we considered before these are of God; his spirit is in them they act on principles of infinite grandeur. The merit of Charity is always exactly commensurate with the sacrifice.

↑4 Ephes[ians]. 32↓ [in pencil; end of MS p. 16]

Brethren, I have endeavoured to set before you the fact that the lesson of Charity is taught us in the strongest possible manner in the works of God in the moral economy of man. I know not how God could more distinctly teach us than he does by the ordinary operation of his laws, what manner of persons we ought to be. For precisely as a man separates his good from the whole he becomes hateful. As he finds his good in the common good he ⟨h⟩becomes beloved. To a man kind to his family seeking ⟨a⟩the comfort of self & wife & children we feel a low degree of regard. The man who wd. make his friends or town happy & contemns yᵉ rest of yᵉ world has made a higher advancement Still he makes by his exclusion all who are out of yᵉ Circle he has chalked his natural enemies. He that loves his country will be loved by that country. But he that makes the world his country & beholds a brother in man cannot help being loved & reverenced by all the good. And must not /that/his/ be the highest & surest happiness wh⟨o⟩ich that every event obliges some whom he loves whose good feelings are reflected to him by every object in the Universe.

But he has added to all this instruction of nature the explicit instruction of his word. It is with reason that a religion coming from God insists chiefly on love to man. It is what we might expect that the bearer of that message should have been one who counted not poverty or reproach or death ⟨&⟩an evil so that he might ⟨o⟩redeem his brethren from the greatest evil.

Therefore brethren let us take heed that these loud lessons are not lost on us. Let us feel the direct appeal to our consciences that comes from all. God does not want our aid to remove evils but he wishes that we shd. have the disposition to do well. We continually fail in our well meant endeavours to do good. The success of a charity is a measure of the wisdom that directed it but by no means of its moral merit.

It remains to state briefly the expenditure of our humble fund for the last year & to solicit your aid to it.

It is known to most of you that the E.T. is an charitable association of members of this religious Society who become members of yᵉ Treasury by the payment of one dollar The present number of Subscribers is 95. ↑& it is proper to mention yᵗ a committee has been formed to solicit subscriptions.↓

During the last year ⟨one⟩ $139.00 have been expended, ↑$35.00↓ for the increase & support of the Parish Library ⟨35.00⟩ which has no other aid except a trifling sum from the church & which is an object that should never be neglected by any

To the Hancock Sunday School more immediately under the care of this Church $40.00 have been given.

To aid ⟨the⟩ sick & indigent persons within the Parish small sums have been expended not exceeding 14.00

To the Evangelical Missionary Society which object is to aid feeble societies in the support of public Worship it has been accustomed to look to our Treasury for a part of its means. Fifty dollars have been appropriated for this purpose.

These, brethren, are the objects which our Treasury desires should prosper, & these the sums it has afforded them. You see plainly that from the limits of its subscription list, it relies much upon the annual public Contribution. If you think these ⟨subs⟩ objects important if you desire that these & such as these should prosper, if there is so much light in your understanding & so much love in your heart that you can feel the solemnity of this simple petition which the Providence of God brings this day to your ears if you will that the sorrows of indigence & sickness should be alleviated, that the Sunday School should not go down that good books should be circulated amongst us & that the poor should have yᵉ gospel preached to them then out of your abundance give freely or out of your frugal savings give a part that the Cause of Mercy many not halt in our care.

But oh my brother be sure that the greatest want in the case is not the necessities we plead but your own. God can provide an offering for himself God can instruct the ignorant & comfort the poor & heal the sick by others than by you. But no otherwise than by your own mercy can he render unto you mercy. Only by the love that is in your own heart to others can ⟨his⟩ the love of the Father be shed abroad in you Therefore if you think this charity has no call upon you I beseech you do not neglect that which has as surely there is one wherever it may be.

6 years.

in 1829   175.00   no. of subs. in 1830...95

sum spent per ann. 139.00 [end of MS p. 22]

I. The lowest use subserved to us by our fellow men, is one which is demanded by the natural necessities of man—a creature who must be fed, & clothed, ⟨&⟩ & armed, & cheered—⟨and is a quite mercenary aid⟩ the supply of the animal wants. Thus parents feed & clothe & protect their children. Thus every man in society devotes himself to the service of the community in some one occupation, that they in return may serve him in others. Thus the rich feed the poor; the strong protect the weak. Thus men continally cultivate the good will of their neighbors, with an eye to the advantages of good neighborhood—that is, of mutual hospitality, mutual preference, gifts, feasts, protection from fire & violence. We join ourselves to certain individuals that we may have whom to eat our bread with. Society is necessary to health.

This is the lowest but a quite indispensable service of man to man. The good man regards it with satisfaction & gratitude as the beneficent order of Providence & sees ⟨how⟩ ↑the occasion↓ it gives ⟨occasion⟩ [emendations in pencil] to the virtues of justice & generosity. But it is obvious that these are goods which the sensual & selfish can also covet & enjoy. The evil & unthankful think that society exists for the supply of our mutual outward wants. There are persons who think the mercenary advantages afforded us by our friends to be the main design for which friends should be sought. They applaud great sacrifices made by men for the sake of a friend↑'s↓ ⟨as the risk of⟩ property or ⟨of⟩ [emendations in pencil] life with excessive praise as the utmost service possible to friendship. They have yet to learn that there are infinitely higher services which a man is to receive from his friends, & which he is to render to them.

II. A higher good ⟨derives⟩ which we receive from our fellowmen is their cooperation with us for the sake of effecting various beneficent results which solitary men could not effect A society of men possesses a power very much greater than the added power of all the individuals. Association has subdued the world, ⟨&⟩ & holds all the fierce evils in it, in check. Safety, order, convenience, pleasure, the advancement of science, of art, & of intercourse, are secured by union with our fellow men. The legislator, therefore, strengthens these bonds. It must however be seen that these are temporal advantages— ⟨which⟩of a higher character, but still temporal;—are sought from a regard to our present convenience, & that of those who belong to us. they have reference to our present circumstances & are not yet the purest ⟨highest⟩ fruit of society

On behalf of the Society whose organ I am, it is, I trust, wholly needless to show its absolute necessity in a town like this. The society ⟨will find those who will give⟩ ↑in addition to their subscriptions promise↓ the⟨ir⟩ time & attention ⟨to⟩ ↑of discreet & benevolent agents↓ carrying what sums their fellow citizens can spare to those who are most in need, & to the most deserving of the needy.

It ought to be known however that the receipts of the Treasury of the Society for the last year are less by a considerable amount than in former years. ⟨We⟩ The ↑Society↓ now ask you⟨r aid⟩ fellow Christians ↑in behalf of their beneficiaries. We ask you↓ to give what you can spare to many persons in extreme distress. ⟨They want food [illegible word] & fuel⟩. Some of them are ⟨laborious⟩ ↑hardworking↓ persons who cannot with all their labor quite make up their rent on the quarter day. ↑[sketch of a hand pointing left] To others a few necessary stores wh. they cannot procure are furnished↓ A large number are the cases of sickness, & ⟨the S⟩ much of the assistance that is given, is a quantity of fuel to keep ⟨the⟩ families from going to bed, to avoid suffering from the cold.

My friends, if you will go into the cold chambers where the kindness of this Society does what it can, in the spirit of the New Testament, you will not dare to question the claim. God shall speak to you for his child & your brother. Your Makers image will meet you there. If you are wise if you know your own nature & destiny if you are not so estranged from God that you cannot understand the principle of your social duty—let this plea have weight with you now, that for God's sake we ask your charity.

⟨Let me remind you of the inscription on the tomb of the benevolent man. What I have given away is all I now possess [Rabirius, quoted by Seneca; see Sermon XL (1:306)] The day will shortly come to close the mortal account of all, the day wh. takes all we have out of our hand.⟩

⟨Our earthly comforts & the pleasures & luxuries which money can buy can please us but a few months or a few days but by their sacrifice the character which is eternal shall be enriched shall be exalted shall be united to its source. Thus has God put it into our power with our earthly wealth to buy us bags of treasure which wax not old a treasure in the heavens that shall forever accumulate.⟩ [cf. Luke 12:33]

Sermon LXXX

Manuscript: Five sheets folded to make four pages each; folios nested and sewn through the center fold with white thread; pages measure 25 x 20.3 cm. A slip of paper, 9.8 x 20 cm, containing Insert "A" is affixed with red sealing wax to the right margin of MS p. 4.

Lines   *Page 212*
Bible Text   We . . . old Ps 44 [in pencil]

3   ↑No . . . country.↓ [in pencil]
4–5   that /touch/call out/ [variant in pencil] the loftiest ⟨springs in man⟩
            ↑sentiments in our nature↓. [emendation in pencil]
6–8   ↑in God's Providence↓ . . . ↑to arrest the attention↓ of one⟨,⟩
            ↑mind,↓ . . . deeper ⟨delight⟩ admiration
10   ↑in its origin . . . effect↓, [in pencil]
13   We ⟨a⟩own
17   ↑together↓
21   the ²{assertion or ¹{defence

                            Page 213

2   of ↑our↓
3–5   us. ¶ ⟨It is⟩ ↑We . . . that↓ . . . thought the power ⟨inf⟩ of a ↑great
            &↓
7   become ⟨almost⟩ proverbial
8–9   ↑The . . . mankind↓ [in pencil]
10   ↑tribute of↓
15–17   name↑,↓ . . . sound↑,↓ . . . dead↑,↓ . . . batteries or ⟨kingdoms⟩
            ↑princes↓. [additions and emendation in pencil]
19–24   name. ⟨For the most simple & obvious reasons, the⟩ ↑It . . . of↓
            cannon↑;↓ ⟨cannot⟩ ⟨↑is silenced↓⟩ & ↑overcomes↓ the ⟨m⟩ great-
            est armies↑,↓ ⟨are vanquished⟩ ↑& changes /the oldest/powerful/
            [variant in pencil] kingdoms. And . . . reasons;↓ . . . ↑the breast of↓
            every ⟨hu⟩man↑,↓ ⟨breast⟩ in
25–37   Now ⟨when⟩ ↑Let↓ it ⟨is⟩be . . . ↑yᵉ cause of human↓ right↑s↓ ⟨&
            so contributing every day to the final victory of right over wrong⟩ ⟨is
            it⟩ ↑Insert A. [On a slip of paper affixed with red sealing wax to the
            right margin of the preceeding (facing) page, verso blank, a passage
            marked "A":] {Thus . . . ↑far↓ [addition in pencil] . . . constitution
            they . . . Andes, i⟨t⟩n France, in Greece ↑& throughout Europe↓
            they . . . mankind. ↑& so . . . wrong↓↓ [end of Insert "A"] does it not
            ↑this influence↓ amount to such ⟨a⟩puissant ⟨virtue⟩ ↑force↓ . . .
            men ↑& who . . . failure↓

                            Page 214

1–2   it ⟨is⟩ ↑hath a↓ different ↑form↓
5   ↑a man of miserable condition↓ [in pencil]
12–13   same ⟨country⟩ ↑land↓ . . . ↑but not ⟨otherwise⟩ of more generous
            sentiments↓
15–17   his ⟨love of⟩ country . . . signs he . . . he ⟨reckons in to⟩ ↑enriches↓
20   intellectual ⟨distinction⟩ excellence
25–27   men & ⟨p⟩ to . . . imagination ⟨fills⟩ enters
29–30   of ⟨patriotism⟩ ↑fellow countryman↓
36–41   wishes; ↑Insert X [At the bottom of the preceeding (facing) page, a
            passage marked "X":] The America . . . ↑more↓ fair or noble ⟨place⟩
            ↑abode↓ . . . ↑turbulent↓ vanity↓ [insert in pencil] . . . as ⟨holy⟩
            ↑precious↓

42-(215)2   ↑covetous↓ [in pencil] of money, prizes the /ground/soil/ [variant in pencil] . . . market [end of page] he . . . ↑no greatness in its ⟨cultivated⟩ ↑ample↓ regions↓ [addition and emendation in pencil] . . . ↑no honor↓

Page 215

7-9   of ⟨men⟩the . . . then ⟨t⟩all . . . it⟨s shores⟩ beyond
13   ↑the cities of↓
15   to ⟨emancipate⟩ ↑save↓.
16   the ⟨stirring⟩ ↑thrilling↓
30-31   Righteousness ⟨where good men abound⟩ where
35   never be⟨e⟩ too
36-37   do /much/all/ . . . all to ⟨avert the⟩ remove

Sermon LXXXI

Manuscripts: Sermon LXXXI is represented in two manuscripts, each incomplete: the earlier of the two, in the Houghton Library, consists of a single folio into which three leaves torn from a sewn gathering have been inserted; pages measure 25 x 20.3 cm. The second and later manuscript, owned by Professor Eleanor M. Tilton, consists of four separate leaves, disbound from volumes 1-4 of a set of the large paper edition of *The Journals of Ralph Waldo Emerson* (Cambridge, 1909), No. 7 of 600 "signed and numbered copies." The pages measure 25 x 20.3 cm. It is evident that the Tilton manuscript represents a revised version of Sermon LXXXI.

[Below Bible text] ↑{I would write as a man who writes for his own eye only.}

Lines
Bible Text   *Page 216*
          ↓Matt 7.20 [in pencil, below "Matt 2.20." in ink]
3-4   explain ⟨two important⟩ ⟨senses⟩ ↑in the following remarks the import↓ which I underst[MS torn] our
6-8   as ⟨th⟩ every . . . every ⟨man⟩ ↑mind↓ hath his mark ↑of his character↓ [addition in pencil]

Page 217

8   pains [end of Houghton MS p. 2; text discontinuous at this point]
11   need an ⟨assiduity of⟩ ⟨↑an↓⟩ ⟨imitation⟩ ↑simulation↓ of virtue ↑so assiduous↓ that would
16   truths ⟨produce⟩ prevent.
24-26   these ⟨it will give us⟩ the . . . ↑past↓ . . . ↑past↓ . . . to ⟨desire⟩ ↑seek↓ ⟨& the ⟨desire of his favor⟩ ↑conviction that↓ who is greater than our hearts & will measure his sentence by their sentence on our merits⟩ the law ⟨&⟩of
28-31   us. ¶ ⟨It should n⟩ The . . . to ⟨n⟩ bring
35   fruit if you [end of Houghton MS p. 5] by which [Emerson apparently neglected to cancel "if you".]
36   but ⟨ou⟩the

43   blind. ⟨They are leaning on others t⟩They

Page 218

7   Society ↑to↓
8–12   that ⟨every man⟩ there . . . men but I believe th⟨is⟩at . . . namely,
                            ⟨that this credit rests upon fact & that eve⟩ Every man's /influence/
                            power/ is ↑exactly↓ . . . ↑the eye of↓ God⟨'s eye⟩ ↑& of enlarged
                            minds↓ as plain & ⟨consecutive⟩ ↑closely connected↓ as physical
                            causes ↑& effects↓
13   lea⟨f⟩ves
16   say ⟨there is not⟩ in
18   mind↑. Your present mind is yᵉ average of all↓ & to [incomplete
                            emendation]
23–24   happiness ⟨& they⟩ your self esteem. ¶ & every . . . to [end of
                            Houghton MS p. 8; text discontinuous at this point]
26   before ⟨its⟩ half
34   but /uncharitable/jealous/ [variant in pencil]
35–36   ↑Does . . . condition↓ [in pencil]

[The following notations appear by themselves on the last inscribed page (Houghton MS
p. 10):] ¶ If you take a drop from the bottom of the cask it will be missing from the top. ¶
The conduct cannot be higher than the principles any more than the waters of a fountain
can rise higher than the level of the reservoir. [end of Houghton MS]

Page 219

5–6   that ⟨self-conceit⟩ ↑integrity & independence are coupled↓ [addition
                            in pencil] ↑servility↓ is apt to be accompanied by ⟨servility⟩ ↑back-
                            biting↓;
9   smoke; we
13   the ⟨issues⟩ habits
14   its ⟨own food⟩ ↑proper nourishment↓
25   large. ⟨Each⟩ Paul . . . & a [end of Tilton MS p. 2] an
34–35   the ⟨event⟩ ↑fruit↓ . . . us. /As/because/ there

Page 220

4   are, ⟨&⟩ what
8   shall [end of Tilton MS p. 4; text discontinuous at this point]
10   ↑all↓
13   forehead ⟨a brand⟩ ↑the . . . offence↓,
16   exist. ⟨{If we know without possibility of mistake an oak or an apple
                            which have but single modes of exhibiting their properties, how then
                            can there be concealment of the properties of rational nature, every
                            act & habit of which ex⟨hibits⟩presses the inward will}.⟩ [brackets
                            in pencil] A
20   ¶ ↑I say . . . character.↓
23   that ⟨a⟩ we . . . opinions ⟨of⟩ concerning

30-31   And ⟨the more strong the impression created by the energy of his
             benevolence ⟨⟨or⟩of⟩ ⟨↑or↓⟩ of his malevolence⟩ ↑if . . . extraordi-
             nary,↓
40-(221)1   that↑, take our life through,↓ . . . true ⟨merit⟩ ↑value↓, [emendations
             in pencil]

                              Page 221

3-4   action I . . . imagined I
7   ↑We . . . deception↓
8   to better
12-17   ↑As . . . that↓ Light . . . & ⟨we feel⟩ that . . . Heavens↑; that . . .
             felicity.↓

                           Sermon LXXXII

Manuscript: Five sheets folded to make four pages each; folios nested and sewn through
the center fold with white thread; a single half-sheet, inserted before the last leaf of the
outer folio, contains the pencil version of Emerson's notes from Goethe on St. Philip
Neri. Pages measure 25 x 20.3 cm.

Lines   *Page 222*
1   ¶ It ⟨is observable⟩ can
9-10   high ⟨pretensions.⟩ ↑merit↓
10   in its⟨elf⟩ importance
12   world but . . . of ⟨↑direct↓⟩ ↑specific↓

                              Page 223

1-3   ¶ ↑Those who ↑are↓ . . . in N. T?↓
5-12   *worth.* ↑¶ {We . . . of ⟨such⟩ ↑fragments of Christians↓. . . .
             ↑called↓ . . . the ⟨presence⟩ moral health}↓
14-20   oak. ¶ ⟨What then is it the sign of?⟩ ¶ What . . . ↑truly↓ . . . ↑&
             naturally↓ . . . of ⟨little⟩ inferior . . . has ⟨sore⟩ failed
24-25   those ⟨t⟩objects.
25-26   spirit, ⟨ & can only be ⟨assumed⟩ ⟩ [cancellations in pencil] ↑taken↓
             by a good ⟨spirit.⟩ mind.
27   that ⟨art is long⟩ much
28   humble, ⟨struck⟩ because
31   thoughts. ⟨th⟩He then
32-35   ↑A haughty . . . creatures.↓
38   of ⟨sensations⟩ ↑sense↓ & ⟨perceptions⟩ ↑thots↓
40-41   Even ⟨my⟩ virtue, . . . guards ⟨my⟩ ↑our↓ freedom, ↑in some sort↓
             ⟨he⟩God must ⟨for⟩ originate.
41-(224)5   perceive⟨d⟩s it, ↑& . . . perceived↓ are ⟨his⟩ ↑constituted . . . ↑It is↓
             We ⟨choose right⟩ do . . . the ⟨clear⟩ ↑irresistible↓ . . . in all↓

                              Page 224

6-8   sin ⟨a⟩ not . . . I ⟨measure myself with Him⟩ ↑contend . . . merits↓?
13-14   thanks? ¶ ⟨Faith in⟩ ↑An acknowledgment of↓

18	↑natural↓
22–23	independance ⟨in⟩ ↑to pay↓ the least ⟨tribute of homage⟩ ↑grain of incense↓
23–24	↑No . . . so ⟨slow⟩ far . . . man↓
25–28	It ⟨is plain⟩ ↑must sometimes happen↓ that we shall ⟨often⟩ be embarrassed when the ⟨idea⟩ ↑claim↓ . . . humility. ↑that is when ⟨humility⟩ an . . . dishonest.↓
29–30	duty. ⟨The⟩ ↑If our↓ humility ⟨that⟩ grows ⟨continually⟩ ↑on the true stock grows↓ . . . him, ↑it↓
32–(225)7	would ⟨labor⟩ ↑try↓ . . . exhibit ⟨p⟩ in . . . the ⟨crisis⟩ occasion. ¶ {And . . . humility, ⟨which⟩ ↑&↓ . . . unexpected ⟨proof⟩ presumption . . . the ⟨applicability⟩ ↑natural suitableness↓ . . . mind.} ¶ ⟨{It is important to us to know & ponder these things & apply to our own characters this test of our progress in true wisdom. ⟨The⟩ ⟨book⟩ ↑No↓ writings ⟨that⟩ have had ⟨the greatest⟩ ⟨↑perhaps↓⟩ ↑a greater↓ currency in our times is a ⟨description in⟩ ↑than those of the poet who has described in↓ many forms ⟨of a⟩ ↑the same character↓ certain /Satanic/diabolical/ pride. It is popular ⟨in⟩ reading because it is an exaggerated image of popular feeling. Men affect pride. The word *pride* is equivocal & is continually applied in a good sense, as a commendation.⟩ ¶ ↑It . . . pride'↓

Page 225

8–11	by ⟨it⟩ ↑this reading↓ . . . found ⟨in books⟩ & . . . a ⟨kind⟩ ↑sort↓ . . . selfreliance ⟨& gloom⟩ &
13	desireable quality, but it ⟨is⟩ rightly
14–15	hero⟨.⟩ ↑of . . . world.↓
17	which ⟨fascinate⟩ ↑engage↓
18–20	qualities, ⟨sh⟩ and, . . . mankind↑,↓ . . . imposing ⟨character⟩ ↑ruffians↓ they would lose all their /lustre/honor/.
22–23	↑But ⟨f⟩courage . . . pride.↓
25–26	when ⟨w⟩I . . . feel ⟨n⟩that
28	↑sorely↓
34–38	↑an↓ angry maint⟨enance⟩aining . . . ↑good↓ . . . towards us, ⟨I am afraid we shall find that⟩ ↑let . . . that↓ . . . used.' let . . . the ⟨great idea⟩ ↑thought↓ of God ⟨out of⟩ which

Page 226

1	motives ⟨actions⟩ of
9–10	they ⟨need⟩ ↑ought↓ . . . that ⟨no⟩ he

[After the end of the sermon, in pencil on a loose half-sheet laid in, the following passage:] St Philip Neri went one day into the presence of the Pope just after his holiness had been informed of that in the neghborhd of Rome was a nun who had exhibited miraculous gifts. St Philip received from the holy father the charge to investigate the truth of these tales. ¶ He mounted his mule & through very foul roads arrived soon at the Cloister. Being ⟨introduced⟩ admitted he conversed with the Abbess who gave him a circumstantial account of the gifts of the nun. The nun being sent for entered the apartment & he without further greeting stretched out to her his muddy boot with intimations that she shd. draw it off. The holy pure maiden drew back much shocked & let her indignation at this purpose be known with violent words. Neri rose all tired as he was mounted his beast & returned to the Pope ⟨be⟩ sooner than he was expected; since for the proof of such spiritual gifts very exact /rules/methods/ are prescribed by the Catholic fathers because the Ch. certainly admits the possibility of such powers but does not admit their presence without close scrutiny. ↑To↓ The wondering Pope he quickly opened yᵉ report She is no saint She works no miracles since the crowning grace she wants Hum

[After the end of the sermon, the following passage in ink:] One of the pious & remarkable men of the Catholic Church who most deserved the name of Saint was Philip Neri (born 1515 at Florence) who dedicated himself to a life of self denial & benevolence. ¶ The Pope say ↑St↓ Philips biographers was informed that in a certain Cloister in the Country a Nun had appeared endowed with miraculous gifts. He committed to Philip the charge of investigating the facts. He mounted his mule to perform his commission but came back quicker than the holy father expected him. Philip addressed him in these words "Holiest Father! This person works no miracle since the first Christian grace is lacking, namely, Humility. I went through bad roads & bad weather to the Cloister I inquired for her in your name. She appeared, & I instead of a greeting, reached out to her my boot intimating that she should draw it off. Angry she drew back & re⟨sisted⟩plied to my desire with ⟨anger &⟩ sharpness 'For what do you hold me? she said, she was the maid of the Lord, but not for every one who came hither to put her upon a groom's work." I got up immediately; mounted my beast; came hither and I am sure you will ask no further proof." ¶ Goethe vol 24 p 201

[The following outline is in pencil:]

> Humility praised in SS
> Yet Humility not ⟨itself⟩ a virtue like Industry or Charity
> But a *sign*
> Sign of moral health
>   of knowledge
>   of hope
>   of seeing God
> Knowledge of God then is the cause of true Humility
>   also—the measure of it
> Popular mistake yᵗ pride is good—Byron
> All pride is false
> Exhortation to be humble

Sermon LXXXIII

Manuscript: Seven sheets folded to make four pages each; five nested folios followed by two stacked folios, the whole sewn along the left margin with black thread; pages measure 25 x 20.3 cm.

Lines	Page 227
Bible Text	Add . . . II Peter 1.5. [In ink over the following in pencil:] Add to your faith knowledge

2–4	own /actions/frame of mind,/ . . . met. ⟨I⟩ Whatever . . . our / minds/thot's/ [variant in pencil]
6	conscience↑,↓ ⟨is sounding a monitory⟩ ↑if we listen,↓
9–10	↑any↓ . . . ↑apart↓,
16–17	↑not . . . ones↓.
17	behold ⟨the neighbors⟩—the
19–20	are! ⟨how fe⟩ what . . . weakness ⟨out⟩ to
26	for ⟨active⟩ business
28–(228)1	who ⟨was⟩ ↑is↓ . . . who ⟨was⟩ ↑is↓

Page 228

9	a ⟨blind⟩ covert
12	countenance ⟨which they⟩ ↑& . . . he↓ would ⟨not⟩ have ⟨done⟩ ↑been↓ in ↑a↓
13–14	calls ⟨the⟩ experience . . . virtue, he
14–15	vain would . . . rate the . . . deal, it
20	↑an appeal to↓
25–26	vice is the . . . ↑stands good↓
27	has ⟨has⟩ ⟨set us down⟩ here
30	immeasureable
31	practical ⟨question⟩ ↑duty↓
33–34	↑Another . . . himself↓
39	¶ ↑In↓ What ⟨is⟩ does
41–(229)1	↑Apart . . . sake,↓

Page 229

7–10	who ⟨would be shocked at the⟩ think . . . as ⟨a part of religious⟩ objects
15–16	reading. ¶ ⟨There is much said occasionally⟩ ↑But . . . mind↓
17	↑next to vice↓
23	accompan⟨ies⟩y
24–25	immortal ⟨soul⟩ ↑being↓.
29	at ⟨the⟩ ↑a↓
32	It is the eye of your soul [end of page] It is the eye of your soul,
33–34	Universe. ↑of matter.↓
39–40	↑It . . . body↓

Page 230

2	me ⟨to have been provided⟩ the [Pencil notation on otherwise blank facing page:] study of the principles of useful arts
4–5	minerals ⟨of⟩ the history of beast [end of line] birds
10–11	unremitted ⟨labour⟩ ↑toil↓ . . . leave ⟨all⟩ providing
12–14	answer, ⟨Certainly not⟩ in . . . to ⟨affect his⟩ modify . . . place, ⟨his⟩ he
19–22	needs th⟨is⟩e perception . . . work ⟨the⟩ ↑a↓ strong sense of ⟨his⟩ the
28	abundance [end of line] light
33	second /condition/element/

Sermon LXXXIV

Manuscript: Six sheets folded to make four pages each; folios nested and sewn along left margin with white thread; pages measure 24.2 x 20.6 cm. Text is incomplete, breaking off in mid-sentence at the bottom of MS p. 24.

Lines

Page 232

3–4 these ⟨su⟩ topics . . . for ⟨s⟩ acquiring
5–7 ↑Mere . . . know.↓
11–12 mankind↑, it is commonly said,↓
15–16 & ⟨so⟩ ↑therefore↓ . . . power / resides / there is /
22–(233)10 use ⟨& bade⟩ ↑ordaining↓ . . . sown. ¶ ²{To say that ⟨this⟩ ↑great degrees of improvement↓ cannot be / done / attained / . . . themselves.} ¶ ¹{⟨Then again⟩ ↑Now↓ . . . multitude ⟨have no⟩ ↑cannot acquire↓ . . . of ⟨wisdom⟩ ↑intelligence↓ . . . that ⟨of Newton⟩ ↑which touches wisdom↓ ↑down↓ . . . ↑valuable↓ knowledge} ¶ The fact

Page 233

15 man. ↑as . . . blood↓
16 data. the
19 ↑at last↓
26–27 but ⟨that⟩ the . . . in [end of line] in
37–(234)2 ¶ ↑There . . . out↓ [in pencil]

Page 234

4 tho'ts ⟨ & scrutiny of them⟩ with [Pencil notation on otherwise blank facing page:] ↑Humble life possesses some advantages for the acquisition of truth over other conditions. Make his speculations tally with facts, for gross habits will correct futile theories↓
12 work⟨,⟩ of
29 world ⟨w⟩ no
37 accurately ⟨known⟩ described,
39 & ⟨action⟩ duty

Page 235

2–6 ↑And so . . . shall / see / know / as we are / seen / known / . . . state.↓ ↑prod. facilities↓ [last addition in pencil]
7 which ⟨leads us⟩ ↑relates↓
9 less ⟨one⟩ does
13–14 ¶ ↑IV.↓ . . . I ⟨n⟩ have to . . . paramount ⟨consider⟩ importance
14 to wisdom
22 this ⟨sense⟩ ↑definition↓
24–32 more ⟨just⟩ certain . . . observation it . . . places. [end of page] & . . . ↑a↓ person⟨s⟩ of . . . who ha⟨ve⟩s a . . . & ⟨it⟩ ↑the↓ . . . for ⟨its⟩his

Page 236

8 *style* [underlined twice]
9–10 agitations ⟨Its⟩ The . . . longer ⟨disturb it⟩ warp

Sermon LXXXV

Manuscript (earlier version): Six sheets folded to make four pages each; two nested folios, followed by a single folio, followed by three nested folios, with a single half-sheet, 23.9 x 19.8 cm, containing Insert "A" loosely inserted after the innermost folio; sewn along left margin with white thread; pages measure 25 x 20.3 cm. A half-sheet is affixed with red sealing wax to the upper and lower left margins of MS p. 13 (now detached). MS p. 1 headed "LXXXV" in green pencil, possibly not in RWE's hand.

[Above Bible text:] ↑Princeps Edit.↓

Lines	Page 237
6	feeling ⟨a⟩we
15	if h⟨e⟩is ⟨does not know⟩ ↑acquaintance does not lie in↓ one we presume ⟨he⟩ ↑it↓ does ⟨know⟩ ↑in↓
16	of a ⟨man⟩ ↑person↓
18–19	↑Every . . . bad man↓
25–(238)4	but↑, when↓ present⟨ing⟩ed to my mind↑,↓ . . . me; ⟨a⟩ truth . . . all ⟨my⟩ ↑the↓ wants ↑of my nature↓ [last addition in ink over pencil]

	Page 238
6	¶ The ⟨Apostle⟩ ↑Scripture↓
7	every ⟨one of us in our best hours⟩ ↑Christian↓
12	practical ↑difficulty↓
13–14	true. ¶ ↑To illustrate in the first place its↓ [incomplete addition] I conceive that our ⟨views of our relation to⟩ ↑belief in↓ God stand in
17–18	↑wh. . . . reason↓ contradicted . . . for ⟨↑earth↓ the sun seems to go round⟩ the
21	which ⟨it cannot explain.⟩ is
25	of ⟨the⟩ all
29	explanation of [end of line] of
31	of ⟨lif⟩ condition
32–33	value. ¶ ⟨When this knowledge of God enters into the mind not only is it felt to be valuable but it is itself the best witness of its truth, that is to say its applicability to human nature is the strongest evidence of our faith in God⟩ If
37–38	understand ⟨t⟩ how . . . he ⟨sees⟩ himself ↑finds↓

	Page 239
1	enthusiast he
5	soul it
9–10	↑The . . . God.↓
16	of /their/its/ great sanction ↑i.e.↓ /their/its/
18	solitude ⟨w⟩in
20–22	↑In my prosperity . . . downfall?↓ . . . ↑In my fear . . . me?↓
24	him, an⟨y⟩d
26–39	life. ↑an↓ ⟨In teaching the omnipresence of God, we learn something that is made perfectly natural by this moral nature for when we think

of right & wrong we think of some thing which has no relation to space or matter⟩ [On a half-sheet affixed with red sealing wax to MS p. 13, verso blank:] ¶ ↑And . . . a ⟨measure⟩ rule . . . of ⟨d⟩every . . . truth.↓ ¶ ↑In . . . action.↓ ¶ ⟨We were searching for something better & greater & that something is supplied. In our nature we are insufficient to ourselves We are orphans who have found their Father.⟩ ¶ Look

Page 240

2	↑See . . . poor↓
7-8	to /him/that fainting wretch/ . . . condition a⟨re⟩ll
22	was ⟨wronged⟩ wretched
25	↑chosen↓
28	heights excellence
31	year a ⟨day⟩ an hour
33-35	felt. ⟨And when⟩ Not . . . moment ⟨with⟩ defeats

Page 241

6	also It
11-14	privelege . . . ↑removing . . . actions↓ . . . away ⟨has⟩ is

[The following notation appears after the end of the sermon:] Every human mind has some obscure notion of God even those who grossly disobey his laws & those who deny him. ↑The regard paid to↓ The law of honor, the received ⟨opinion⟩ ↑usage↓ of the most reputable men among whom we associate are clear marks of obscure perceptions of religion that are never quite obliterated

[On a loose half-sheet, verso blank, is the following passage in pencil marked "A":] There is a period of life in which just views of our relation to the Divine Providence & of its modes of discipline ⟨are⟩ ↑always↓ of great importance ↑seem peculiarly necessary↓. Men in mature or in old age are not so much exposed ↑to↓ the extremes of enjoyment nor of dejection as those in earlier life. Their pulse is regular their habits are fixed & whatever may be their spiritual ⟨condition⟩ ↑state↓, they have learned to accommodate their desires to their condition.

But to the young occur moments which fix the fate of years. To them occur thoughts that determine often the colour of their life & it behooves them ⟨the⟩ to give the more earnest heed to the silent but not insignificant workings of Providence in their behalf. In young persons, especially in those of active mind & a sympathetic temper when the ardor of their hopes is checked by the straitness of their circumstances a chilling discontent is apt to appear.

Manuscript (later version): Five sheets folded to make four pages each; four nested folios with a fifth, containing Insert "A," inserted after the innermost folio; sewn through the center fold (between MS pp. 8 and 9) in such a way as to include the inserted folio, the second leaf of which has been torn out. Pages measure 25 x 20.3 cm, except for the inserted folio, the remaining leaf of which measures 25 x 17.5 c.m. The manuscript is incomplete, lacking the conclusion.

Palimpsest
It is not a vain thing for you because it is
your life Deut. 32. 47.
To be spiritually minded is life & peace
Romans 8. 6

[Pencil sketch of a woman]

However true it may be that ⟨to⟩by most men the religious character is ⟨unkno⟩ neglected ⟨or despised⟩ it is quite as true that the consideration of it is & always will be the most important concern of every one of us. And however ignorant we may be in our own experience of the power & the sweetness of religious feeling, we all, in some ⟨manner⟩ measure, acknowledge this fact. If a man be brought into the company of a scholar learned in the languages, he may value this accomplishment at a high rate, he may wish he possessed it, but he feels no necessary shame at his ignorance. Nor if one is known to be a skilful chemist, is his science felt to be any rebuke upon those who do not know the laws of chemistry; nor if a man can build a house, or forge an anchor, does he by his knowledge cast any shame upon those who cannot,—because we know that life is insufficient to enable one man to acquire more than a very limited acquaintance with more than one or two departments of knowledge, & if his acquaintance do not lie in one, we presume it does in another. But if a man is thrown into the company of a person distinguished for his attainments in a religious life, & he himself be deficient in that respect, he feels this deficiency to be culpable. Every virtue in the good man reflects dishonour on the want of it in the bad man. This is a knowledge of which all are capable & to which all are bound. Religion does not take any inferior or even equal ground among the objects of human pursuit. It is the head & the censor of them all.

And what is ⟨r⟩Religion? It is the knowledge of God. It is to every mind the knowledge of God in his connexion with itself. Not surely a system of doctrines asserting incomprehensible facts which it cannot explain, & whose truth or falsehood it really does not concern me to know, but when presented to my mind something which I instantly feel to be true, & not after the common order of truths; something which comes secretly into me, *but has a rightful dominion over me;* truth of which the soul is not the parent, but the child; by which all my being is affected & all the wants of my nature are supplied.

The Scripture says, /It is not a vain thing but it is your life/ To be spiritually minded is life & peace/; [variant in pencil] and this expresses very nearly the sentiment which I apprehend every Christian entertains respecting our faith. When this knowledge of God enters into the mind, it is not only felt to be valuable, but it is itself the best witness of its truth.

And this is the fact to which I wish to call your attention, *that the applicability of the great idea of God to the mind, its suitableness to all the real wants of human nature, is the very strongest evidence of its truth.* A miracle will not add any strength to the convictions of a religious man. The belief in God solves every speculative difficulty, & meets every practical difficulty with a perfect remedy. No other belief will do this, and therefore I hold this to be true.

↑I.↓ Now here are two considerations; first, *that it solves every speculative difficulty.*

To illustrate this briefly. I conceive that our belief in God stands in this respect on the same foundation of evidence as our belief in the Copernican System does in Astronomy.

The Copernican System asserts that the sun is stationary, & that the Earth moves round it;—an opinion which though confirmed by our reason, is contradicted by our senses, for the earth seems to stand still & the sun to go round it every day. Now the ground on which this theory stands, is, that it furnishes a complete solution of all the movements which we observe in the planets, as no other theory does, & nothing has ever been observed which is inconsistent with the supposition of its truth & therefore all ↑learned↓ men have acquiesced in its correctness.

Apply this to the cause of religion. The unbeliever says; My senses do not teach me as you say. I see the world of matter, but I see no God. I behold no miracle. I behold neither angel nor spirit, & I believe in none. The Christian says, Some account there must be of all I behold & feel. Here is one offered me which on trial I find will give me a satisfactory explanation of every ⟨fact⟩ doubt, & I accept it.

Consider this a little. If I could bring myself to doubt the being of God, I should be left in a state of absolute perplexity as to the origin of man & of the world, & as to every event that occurred within & without me; & I should be left in a state of miserable apprehension as to all the future, for I should have no security whatever for the permanence of my own being or any other object

And though I might perceive the general good consequences of virtuous conduct, I should feel that it had been bereft of its great sanction, its agreement with the nature of Him who is the maker & the Soul of the Universe

But restore to me my faith in God & you give me a rational & consistent account of the origin & destination of our race. You give a source & a government & an object to human life. I see whence I came. I understand why I am here I see a reason for the evils of life; a reward for the afflictions of the righteous; & an end to death.

II. The second consideration was that it furnishes *a remedy to every practical difficulty*. It proves itself by actually supplying our wants. ⟨{Moral truth has this advantage over material facts that it is recognized by the mind}⟩

If a savage is shown a watch, & told that it will measure the passage of time, probably he will not believe it. It is of no use ↑in order↓ to convince him of the fact, that you show him the elegance & exquisite contrivance of the machine,—it is only an object of stupid wonder ↑to him↓. But make him acquainted with your artificial division of time, & then make him understand how this is adapted to it so that he himself finds the time of day, & he not only believes you, but he becomes perfectly convinced that this ↑machine↓ was made for that very purpose. So you may tell a man of God, of his nature, his perfections, & his relation to the human soul. He thinks you are an enthusiast. He does not believe you, because he does not understand you. But once let him apply his own heart to the seeking of God, let the sentiment of devotion get possession of his breast, & the idea of God will explain & vindicate itself. He has that evidence in him that all the external evidences of religion that were ever accumulated, may fall in with, but cannot i⟨c⟩ncrease. I called it the *idea* of God—but it is not any longer an idea, a theory, a sentiment; it is in itself a living soul; it is a life within life. It is, as it has been truly called, the life of God in the soul of man. He perceives how naturally this belief not only harmonizes with all that he knows & explains all, but ⟨but⟩ it comes into the inner nature of man & speaks directly to the soul, & commands in a voice that must be obeyed, issuing laws which are truths; consoling, encouraging, forbidding, by considerations which the soul feels to be a part of its own nature. And this perfect congruity of ⟨our⟩ ↑this↓ belief in God to man, & human life, convinces ↑him↓ of its truth, that is, convinces him of the being of God. This is what I understand the apostle to declare, when he says, *The Spirit bearth witness with our Spirit, that we are the Children of God.*

Indeed, brethren, I need hardly tell you how indispensable is the sense of God's presence to a thoughtful mind. Without it, man is affrighted at the solitude in which he is left, & is wholly without Consolation for the evils of his present condition I am left without support against human injustice or human neglect. In my prosperity, who shall secure me from a downfall? In my extreme sorrow, who shall hear my moanings? In my fear, who shall avert the danger that menaces me? ↑But this subject divides itself into two parts.↓

1. ⟨But ⟨ther⟩ un⟩Under this view of the perfect fitness of ⟨the⟩ religion, or the belief in God to supply the wants of human nature, there is one consideration of great importance which I do not think has received so much attention as it ought; and that is, that it gives us a rule of life, an unerring standard by which to measure the value of every object & the claim of every duty upon us. ⟨Cases continually occur in every man's experience where if this rule were set aside he would distrust himself, whilst at the⟨e⟩ same time it is necessary to act at once. Duty strives with duty & the more they are compared the more difficult the question becomes. The life of many men for want of a more clear perception of God is distracted by these waverings. They have taken fallacious standards—the law of honor—the received opinion of reputable men, & they are embarrassed always by doubts.⟩ ↑{Insert A} [The following passage is inscribed on both sides of the first leaf of an inserted folio, included in the sewing, the second leaf of which has been torn out, leaving stubs bearing no evidence of writing:] A {Cases continually occur in the experience of every man who aims to do right, in which if this principle be left out, he would hesitate how to act, whilst at the same time it is necessary to act at once. Duty contends in his mind with duty, & the more they are compared the more difficult the question becomes. The life of many men who without being religious men, that is to say, without having very clear views of God, yet wish, in general, to do right, is ⟨distracted⟩ embarassed by these waverings. Every human mind has some obscure notion of God, even those who grossly disobey his laws & deny his name. The regard paid to the law of honor, the regard paid to the received usage of the most reputable men among whom we associate, however high or low our associates may be, are ⟨evident⟩ indications ↑of obscure ⟨o⟩perceptions↓ of religion that are never quite obliterated. Men who act on these fallacious standards, the law of honor, or the law of respecting one's self, will find their rule imperfect in a thousand cases.↓

↑By fixing his eye on God he will not only do relatively right but the wonder is he will do absolutely right↓ [addition in pencil]

Take, for instance, the case of a man who would strike the balance between humility on the one hand, & that unbending independence which it is the first duty of every mind to cherish, on the other. Let him honestly try to keep the golden mean that shall unite these virtues in all his conduct. He will be continually in danger in every effort to surrender himself, of ⟨betraying⟩ being betrayed into a slavish deference to others & in every assertion of himself, of being foolhardy & conceited.⟨.⟩ I apprehend a man of very acute intellect will find extreme difficulty in defining by any rules, the boundaries of these virtues. Now a reference to God is always a certain & instantaneous answer to every doubt. In every doubt let a man throw his soul at once into the attitude of devotion, consider himself ⟨in the relation⟩ as religion places him, in his relation to God, & all darkness will be scattered & his duty will be plain. He will exhibit in his conduct precisely that combination of humility & of spirit which the most enlightened mind would approve.

As it is with these virtues so it is with all. Would a man know what is the limit of his charity & ⟨what it means⟩ ↑where the command↓ to give all his goods to the poor trenches on his duty to his family & friends? Here also, by ⟨conceiving⟩ fixing his eye upon God, his Benefactor, & so recognizing his bounty to him, he will learn to hold all he has, in trust for others,—never to live for himself.

Would he distinguish in his own mind the love of truth from the zeal for his party? The acknowledgment of God's presence will be a faithful guide.

And so it is with every question ↑that↓ can be proposed to the mind. Now brethren is not this fact if you separate it from its union with familiar & ordinary facts is not this fact that every human mind is provided in this infinite tho't of a Deity not only with a perpetual commandment but with a perfect regulator of duty, something very admirable & does it not afford a very strong proof of the adaptation of our minds to that thought & so testify to its truth.

2. In the next place, it suits the changes of life, as well as the habits of action. Consider the strange inequality of human condition as we behold it every day. See, with all this indwelling consciousness that they were made for all that is great & good, into what sad extremities they fall. See the tears of the miserable. See the soiled & swollen hands of the poor whose industry never avails to procure their comfort. Think of the wretched pittance of bread for which so much labour is performed, & all their time taken up & all the delights of thought & conversation forgone. All refinement, all the elevation which comes from consulting & administering great interests, is denied to them. What is left to them? Faith in God; and this faith more than compensates for every want. It speaks to the obscure & the wretched. It reveals to him a Being before whom the differences of condition all disappear. With Him is no high, no low, no great, no small. These distinctions were of the body. This speaks to his moral nature. He is not the equal of rich & powerful men. He is the equal of angels, of seraphim, formed of the same spiritual body subject to the same laws capable of their knowledge & of their pleasures, comprehending what they comprehend, a spark of the same fire, a ray of the same source of light from which they came, mean as he may be not too low for the power & the love of God to stoop nor too far from him to inhale the breath of an immortal life. These great views are not more grand than true. They do not sound like a fable to him. He understands what you mean. He feels their fitness to him. He feels that his miseries, his poverty his disadvantages, do not exclude him, but qualify him rather for this spiritual kingdom that he is capable of acting on principles that dignify his rags & straw into the discipline of a moral agent, & the means & occasions of heavenly virtue. What change has not this produced in his mind. He felt before that he was wretched & that he was wronged—wronged by being shut out from enjoyments to which others were admitted & of which he was as capable as they. Now he feels that he may walk in his lowly place with the meekness yet with the dignity of an angel. He understands how the dignity of the other world may be consistent with offence & degradation of this. He reads in his bible that the chosen Son of God was born in a manger was despised by men & died on a cross ⟨with⟩ between thieves.

Thus Religion shows its suitableness to man in smoothing down the great differences of condition in showing what excellence is within reach of those whose external condition is lowest. But brethren all are poor & low enough in our external nature. What shall guard the most robust frame a year an hour from the inroads of decay. Time every moment is undermining our health & our life. Not only Time but sickness assails us— not virtue not youth not wisdom can save you though they make the blow more exquisitely felt—It cuts down our brightest hopes in a moment; defeats instantly every purpose, paralyzes your strength, & embitters your languid hours as they slowly waste, with advertisements of your mortality.

What balm is provided for this common grief? I believe there is no Consideration but this we speak of that can render any adequate Comfort to the bed of sickness & the fear of death. But the firm persuasion that God is with us, that our friend has done this, & that by our place in his love it is made a matter of indifference whether our days on earth are few or many & whether they are passed in action or in confinement, will brighten the

Sermon LXXXVI

Manuscript: Five sheets folded to make four pages each; folios nested and sewn along the left margin with white thread; pages measure 25 x 20.3 cm.

Lines	Page 242
5	them. &
6	↑so . . . religion↓
10	offered. ⟨the consideration⟩ Before
11	↑The Spirit says↓
13	↑in . . . God↓ may be our ⟨ignorance⟩ ↑want of knowledge↓ of o⟨n⟩ur
15	↑on good grounds↓
19–22	¶ ↑I . . . ↑general↓ . . . efficacy. ⟨Prayer in its widest sense imports more than petition It signifies Communion with God.⟩ but in its more limited sense↓ [in pencil] ¶ Prayer
23–(243)8	address. ⟨Manifestly the most pure & elevated conception that my mind is capable of forming. It is the individuals own soul / carried out to perfection/ stript of all infirmity/. [variant in pencil] ↑but aided↓ [in pencil] ↑aided by all the images of power & majesty that the sight of his works can give.↓ For no other Deity can he conceive.⟩ ↑{Insert X} X {⟨It is most true that I cannot see God as he is⟩ Behold . . . irres⟨is⟩istible . . . to ⟨form any⟩ comprehend . . . capable. ⟨The God we worship⟩ When . . . is ⟨yᵉ ind⟩ our . . . ↑made↓ . . . worship.↓ [end of insert]

	Page 243
12–13	sovereign ⟨idea⟩ ↑object↓, . . . to ⟨bring home to the thoughts so grand a⟩ ↑carry . . . greater↓
14	what ⟨is likely to be the effect⟩ ↑will . . . effect↓
17	being th⟨is⟩e habit
24–25	must ⟨make him⟩ bring . . . ↑both↓
29	higher, ⟨o⟩raises
33	↑Him who is↓
35–36	faces ⟨become⟩ shine . . . his ⟨glory⟩ ↑light↓?

Page 244

2   fact / according / agreeable /
6   prayer ⟨according to the old expression as the key to unlock the morn
                 & t⟨he⟩o lock the night⟩ without [A small, irregular scrap of paper
                 inscribed "Vide serm CV." is attached with red sealing wax to the
                 bottom right margin of the page below the conclusion of this
                 paragraph.]
10   But /I see no reason for such/this seems to be too/ close
                 restrict⟨r⟩ion.
13-15   nourish↑es↓ . . . delivered ⟨acknowledging⟩ pouring
16-18   the ⟨his⟩ mode . . . more ⟨freely⟩ ↑sensibly↓ . . . every ⟨passage⟩
                 ↑action↓ . . . every ⟨moment⟩ ↑shade↓
20   prayer ↑are↓
21-22   There ⟨is⟩ ↑are↓ . . . ↑friends↓
24   is ⟨bound up⟩ ↑engaged↓
31-33   ¶ If ⟨I⟩ ↑a man↓ . . . loathsome↑—if . . . cheerful [end of line] If . . .
                 love↓ [end of page] if life seems to ⟨me⟩him desireable
39   ↑his↓

Page 245

3   as ⟨a⟩one man
4   ↑very↓
15-17   sick. & . . . much. ⟨Certainly I think they may procure the good they
                 seek.⟩ ↑And . . . considerations.↓
18   a↑n↓ empty name [end of line] Unless

Sermon LXXXVII

Manuscript: Five sheets folded to make four pages each; folios nested and sewn along the
left margin with white thread; a single leaf (apparently from a journal or notebook) is
loosely inserted after the innermost folio. Folio pages measure 25 x 20.3 cm, and the
inserted leaf measures 25.3 x 20.6 cm.

The evidence of the manuscript alterations suggests that the sermon was begun with
an expectation that the now canceled first Bible text, from Romans 2:7, would be used,
that it was perhaps put aside for a time unfinished, then completed on the theme of the
second Bible text, Romans 12:1. Interlined additions in the early part of the manuscript—all in ink—show Emerson incorporating allusions to this second text. It is likely
that these additions were done before the first delivery, since the material on MS pp. 12
and 13, alluding to the second Bible text, is not added, but belongs to the original
inscription. The same cannot be said for the paragraph added in pencil to the beginning
of the sermon, which seems to refer to a specific incident; if the reference is to the
convalescence of the church's minister, the passage would date to 1838 or 1839.

[Below Bible text:] ↑I cong you that we come up again with in circ so pleasing that we see
the face of our brother in the house of God, that we have this new testimony of Gods care
⟨of⟩ & love of his children. It is a new call where all things are calls to acknowledge and
serve him with our bodies & our spirits. ⟨Th⟩His trials wh. have been yr trials and those
in which every one of us are called to pass ought to stir our minds. I repeat then the
words of the Apostle↓ [late addition, in pencil]

Lines	Page 246
Bible Text	⟨To them who by patient continuance in well doing seek for glory & honour & immortality, eternal life II Chap ROM. 7.⟩ ↑I . . . Rom XII. 1.↓
4	well-being, ⟨in t⟩but
11-13	shall /go/attend us/ [variant in pencil] . . . the ⟨fac⟩ factory; . . . favours., We . . . shall ⟨select⟩ ↑direct↓ our ⟨profession⟩ ↑education↓
20-21	¶ ↑The . . . Christ ⟨supplies⟩ discovers in us↓ ⟨S⟩such principles ⟨religion supplies.⟩ ↑& appeals to them↓.

Page 247

1	↑fixed↓ . . . commands ⟨with⟩ a
5	↑of God↓
10-11	nature, ⟨to obtain⟩ it . . . ↑(I . . . reverence)↓
16-17	¶ ↑Blessed . . . history!↓
17-19	his ²low, ¹capricious, . . . God, ⟨comes⟩ ↑is suggested↓ . . . from ⟨the⟩ ↑this↓ gospel↑.↓ ⟨of Jesus Christ.⟩ He
20-23	↑In a degenerate age,↓ In . . . to ⟨establish forever⟩ ↑exemplify to all time↓
24-27	¶ ↑↑It . . . apostle↓ ⟨We are⟩Paul enjoin⟨ed⟩↑s↓ ⟨by⟩us ⟨the apostle⟩ to present ourselves living sacrifices↓ ¶ The ⟨great & comprehensive⟩ duty ⟨which we learn from the gospel⟩ ↑to . . . called↓ is ↑nothing less↓ an . . . self ⟨improvement⟩ ↑culture↓,
29-30	present ⟨gr⟩ condition, . . . this ⟨vast⟩ height . . . ↑towards↓
32	¶ ↑We . . . sacrifices.↓
33-36	↑I . . . an /instant/immediate/ [variant in pencil] . . . better.↓

Page 248

3	are ⟨infi⟩ eternal,
3-5	↑When . . . enter↓ [in pencil]
8	of ⟨our character.⟩ ↑the man.↓
8-10	will, you⟨r⟩ shall . . . effect. ↑make . . . fruits↓ [addition in pencil]
10	↑shall↓ hold⟨s⟩ a
13	which ⟨the⟩ ↑every↓ mind sees its⟨elf⟩ ↑own image↓ [emendations in pencil]
16	↑As . . . receives↓
17-18	↑Let . . . confirmation↓
19-20	↑of the tender love of the ²Father ¹Universal↓
22-23	↑brethren of other persuasions↓ . . . ↑in the temple of heathen↓
26-28	↑And . . . creation.↓ [added in pencil at the bottom of the page; position indicated by caret] ↑And . . . world.↓
32-33	¶ ↑A↓ Retribution . . . nor ⟨r⟩adversity
38-(249)3	↑Every . . . Watch↓ We must ⟨p⟩ have . . . manners, ⟨intention in⟩ ↑we must watch our↓ conversation ⟨intention in⟩ ↑watch↓ pleasure ⟨intention⟩ ↑watch↓ in the street ⟨intention⟩ ↑watch↓ in the closet. ↑in . . . maker.↓

Page 249

4-5	to ⟨be intent on improving the time⟩ ↑to hasten . . . sacrifice↓ . . . ↑to changes & care↓
7-12	↑A thousand . . . time.↓ ¶ ⟨Well⟩ then [cancellation in pencil]
17	bones. ↑& . . . deferred.↓
20-22	draft of [end of line] of . . . ↑on earth↓.
26-28	two /must/will/ suffice ↑to the wise↓ . . . that ⟨our⟩ we
31	perfection. ↑surrender of [end of line] of ourselves to God.↓
33-34	has↑.↓ the way is plain↑—↓the work is simple↑—↓ [additions in pencil]
35	have. ⟨w⟩We
36	↑We must give↓ not what we would↑,↓ [additions in pencil]
39	↑of↓ [in pencil]
40-41	the ⟨hour of sickness⟩ loitering . . . sickness, ⟨patiently⟩ ↑to bring the reluctant spirit↓

Page 250

10	↑eternal↓
11	customs & ⟨spe⟩ think

[On a loose leaf are the following notations, unrelated to the present sermon:]

The truth is the soul of man is instructed in the signs of character by the presence to his consciousness of the selfsame spirit which made which makes the law our souls live in God. What wisdom what ↑inward↓ light we have we have from him. Our very perception is nothing but his perception through us; & thus are the marks of ⟨action⟩ character significant to us. But without further stopping to consider this wonderful insight of souls, it will not be questioned by any experienced man that vice does thus ↑secretly↓ discolor ⟨&⟩the whole man & betray itself [end of page]

Shun manufacture &c B 102 [*JMN* 5:92]

Mme. de Stael's writer. Ibid. [*JMN* 5:92; used in "Ben Jonson, Herrick, Herbert, Wotton," *EL* 1:341]

Every work of genius makes us for the moment idealists Genius dissipates this block of earth into shining ether [*JMN* 5:123; used in "Genius," *EL* 3:79]

———

To believe your own tho't, that is Genius. [*JMN* 5:163 and 6:229; used in "Ethics," *EL* 2:152, "Genius," *EL* 3:77, and "Self-Reliance," *CW* 2:27]

———

Humanity characterises the highest class of genius. [*JMN* 5:192, 6:196 and 6:229; used in "Literature," *EL* 2:62]

The man of genius apprises us not so much of his wealth as of yᵉ commonwealth [*JMN* 5:232; used in "Society," *EL* 2:99, "Genius," *EL* 3:81, and "The Poet," *CW* 3:4]

Genius always situated alike C 3 [entry in pencil; see *JMN* 5:280]

If ⟨Milton⟩ ↑Collins↓ if Burns if Bryant is in the world we have more tolerance & more love for the changing sky the mist the rain the black overcast day, the indescribable sunrise & the immortal stars. If we believed no poet survived on the planet nature wd. be tedious. B 16 [*JMN* 5:16]

Genius is representative. [The first six and the last two entries on the page are struck through with a vertical use mark in ink.]

Sermon LXXXVIII

Manuscript: Five sheets folded to make four pages each; folios nested and sewn through the center fold with white thread; a single half-sheet is laid in before the second leaf of the outermost folio. Pages, including the insert, measure 25 x 20.3 cm.

Lines	*Page 251*
Bible Text	own. for . . . which ⟨is⟩are God's.
1	¶ ⟨There is matter for much consideration, brethren, in these words of the apostle & in the kindred passage in the third chapter of this epistle. They teach us a doctrine that should either fill us with consternation or a joyful peace. They teach with great distinctness by far the most affecting & most fruitful truth that can be announced to us that God dwells with us⟩ ¶ We . . . for ⟨works⟩ ↑particular rules↓
10–15	his ↑removal to a new country↓ obtaining . . . government, ⟨or in a good age⟩ ↑⟨his good⟩ a happy marriage↓, his long life ⟨his⟩ the ⟨virtue⟩ ↑merit↓ of his children. ¶ ↑These are good ↑to . . . are↓ consequences of good actions, but↓ The . . . perform↑.↓ ⟨can be.⟩ Because th⟨i⟩ese
19–20	being ⟨controlling all his issues.⟩ ¶ It
22–(252)1	selflove & ⟨enrich⟩ augmenting

	Page 252
3–7	↑because . . . larger↓ . . . are ⟨princely⟩ ↑liberal↓ . . . pity. ⟨↑The height of the tower must depend on the breadth of the base↓⟩ ¶ And . . . exertion ⟨to a soul of high motives⟩ than
10	to /those/a great/ principle⟨s⟩ of
13–14	own. for . . . which ⟨are⟩ ↑is↓
16	us ⟨with⟩ either
21–23	joy if . . . ↑not↓ wronging ⟨our own souls⟩ ↑a being . . . works↓. [emendations in pencil]
24	chapter ⟨& very probably in this passage⟩ is
26–28	this ⟨only removes the sense⟩ is . . . ↑made up of↓ . . . God⟨. It is only as the individuals commune with God that the church communes with him⟩ ↑and . . . individual⟨s⟩ members . . . church↓.
30–31	temple. ¶ ↑Ought to obey & what does *ought* mean Why only that we have an inward instruction a law of the mind.↓ ¶ Now [notation in pencil]
31–37	the ⟨principle which we get from⟩ ↑doctrine of↓ . . . ↑however . . . developed,↓ . . . we /would/please/, [variant in pencil] but ⟨must⟩ ↑ought to↓ . . . power, ⟨that this is the spirit of God within us,⟩ that . . . drawing, ⟨f⟩but
38–39	↑spiritual↓ . . . him & ⟨the⟩ a

Page 253

3–4	humble. ↑& . . . gift.↓
5	saith, "⟨i⟩If
12	himself,—⟨No man ever did wrong⟩ without
15	↑¶ Let . . . principle↓
16–18	¶ ↑1.↓ Here↑in↓ . . . every ⟨worldly⟩ evil . . . conscience. When
21	by ⟨a different⟩ ↑an opposite↓
23	for ⟨far mightier⟩ ↑sorer↓ [emendation in ink over pencil]
24	on ⟨an infinite ⟨bas⟩ breadth.⟩ ↑a Rock ⟨of⟩ broader than the world.↓
25	¶ ↑2.↓ Here↑in↓ . . . ↑a↓ ⟨a⟩bad
27	falls. it . . . no ⟨foundation⟩ depth
28–29	external ⟨strength⟩ ↑helps↓.
31	¶ ↑3.↓ Here
33	hour ⟨sh⟩ would
35–37	we ⟨are interested⟩ have . . . ↑& shut up our eyes↓ . . . ↑it is because↓

Page 254

4	¶ ↑4.↓ It
10–11	also. [end of page] & whilst . . . ↑I know that↓
15–18	↑soever↓, . . . us, ⟨that⟩ ↑and ponder well what those words mean↓ ⟨t⟩The . . . man ⟨hold his nature in a reverential awe⟩ seeing
19	Let ⟨a⟩every
24–31	↑nothing false,↓ . . . him, ¶ ⟨Let him not tamper with himself. Having ⟨Ch⟩ a foundation of this etherial nature let him ⟨be⟩ take heed how he buildeth thereupon & not bring wood hay or stubble lest the⟩ ¶ If ever⟨s⟩ you . . . ↑from . . . parts↓ may come ⟨in⟩forth
34–35	midst of ⟨business⟩ the . . . table, ⟨of conversation⟩ ↑solitude,↓

Page 255

7–11	it? ↑or will . . . God↓ [in pencil] ¶ ↑Finally↓ Let
21	off ⟨of⟩ from
22	never-ending ⟨progress⟩ ↑growth↓
23	you, ⟨which ye have of God⟩ that

[On a half-sheet laid in at the end of the sermon, verso blank:] My friends, I have no hope of giving anything like accuracy or great distinctness to this tho't. In our ignorance & sin we must dimly see it. I cannot find out the Almighty unto Perfection. I cannot tell *how* he is present to me, & yet I can feel that he is present—that in him ⟨we⟩I live & move, & have my being. ⟨It was⟩ The best & greatest men have in every age labored to give utterance to the same conviction as this of Paul. Fenelon saith, God is in our soul as our soul is in our body not to be ⟨con⟩↑de↓fined, but every where present. We feel that tho' he is present it is very darkly present, and that our ignorance & sins are clouds & obstructions thro' which he ⟨sends⟩ ↑speaks in↓ a stifled f voice but every effort to do his will to obey this voice does something to remove these obstructions. ↑It will benefit us, if we / are good/ seek/ to meditate upon it until more of its meaning is apparent.↓

Sermon LXXXIX

Manuscript: Ten sheets folded to make four pages each; the first four folios are stacked and sewn along the left margin with white thread; followed by a single folio, now loose, which may originally have been included in the sewing; followed by two nested folios, each with the first leaf cut out (MS pp. 21–24); followed by three nested folios; the entire gathering sewn together along the left margin with black thread. Pages measure 25 x 20.3 cm.

Lines	Page 256
1	¶ ⟨In⟩ The
3	Though ⟨I dispute not that⟩ there . . . ignorance ⟨that still darken-s⟩in mens minds ⟨in all that⟩ concern⟨s⟩ing
7–9	natural The⟨y⟩ truth . . . only ⟨because⟩ ↑inasmuch↓ he
10	that /he/God/ [variant in pencil]
12–14	it. ¶ ⟨Ever⟩ One . . . of ⟨small wit & youthful argument⟩ ↑flippant objection & ridicule↓ . . . the ⟨a⟩unphilosophical
16	no ⟨better⟩ inspiration, ⟨no⟩ ↑nothing↓
18	¶ Now ↑that↓

	Page 257
1–5	had ⟨lips⟩ ↑spread a feast [ink over pencil] or stood at gates↓ . . . hands ¶ ⟨But what I want to say about⟩ ↑One remark as to↓ this ⟨railing⟩ ↑cavilling↓ [addition in ink over pencil] at the Old Testa-ment⟨,⟩; ⟨is, that⟩ those . . . means. ⟨w⟩The
12	the⟨y⟩ disposition
16–21	¶ ↑One . . . in O.T. is that in text ⟨calling⟩ yᵉ . . . anger.↓ ¶ ⟨But I do not mean to vindicate the language or the theology of the ancient Jews which tho' sincere & containing truth in the seed ⟨rather than⟩ was yet hurtful.⟩ The . . . language. ⟨It⟩ ↑Christ has taught us better.↓
24	angry ⟨they⟩ magnify
27–32	↑& mildew↓; ⟨storms⟩ ↑drought↓ . . . occasions. ⟨Smit⟩ If . . . order, ⟨mea⟩ [canceled in pencil] these . . . a⟨s⟩ccomplished.
32–35	the ⟨mighty chain⟩ ↑invisible link↓ . . . ruin; ⟨all matter⟩ ↑the . . . iron↓
37–41	let ⟨unchain⟩ ↑snap↓ the ⟨great tie⟩ ↑old chain↓ . . . revolution. ⟨let it⟩ loose ⟨snap the invisible⟩ the

	Page 258
3	why ⟨name⟩ ↑prescribe↓
6	unreason [end of page] ble
8	the ⟨author⟩ all
13–18	of ⟨g⟩God . . . selves. ⟨It is the sin of man that makes the wrath of God⟩ ↑Gods wrath is man's sin↓ [cancellation and addition in pencil] ¶ ⟨Thus what we call his judgments ¶ All our sufferings are either our own work or the work of God.⟩ ¶ Thus . . . the ⟨region⟩ harvest, . . . ↑if an . . . nation↓
24	paints ⟨a⟩the

29–35   ↑{It . . . occasions of ⟨It⟩ ⟨ne⟩ immediately . . . text}↓ [addition in
                   pencil]
39   momen[t] but [inscription runs off the page]

                                    Page 259
3   ¶ ↑Let . . . particulars.↓
5   have ⟨summed⟩ enumerated
10   ↑yᵉ want of↓
14–16   affections. ⟨What a glorious panorama do not these make and if each
                   one how much more all.⟩ ¶ There . . . the [end of line] the threescore
25–27   {The . . . disagreeable.}
33   to ⟨provide for ourselves⟩ draw
38–40   dependant . . . rejoice ↑in↓

                                    Page 260
6–9   him. [Here after the end of MS p. 19, p. 20 is blank and pp. 21–24
                   have been cut out, with stubs bearing evidence of writing, though no
                   text has been recovered. The text resumes on MS p. 25:] ¶ ⟨I shall
                   endeavour to ⟨explain the⟩ offer some remarks in illustration of this
                   truth.⟩ ¶ II. In . . . dependant
13   him [end of line] at . . . cooperation ⟨in⟩ with
14–17   ↑a↓ good ⟨pare⟩ country, . . . these, ⟨or⟩and,
18–19   ↑of themselves↓
21–23   might. ↑⟨The whole spirit⟩ ↑All the language o↓ of . . . joy.↓
27   than ⟨not appear⟩ be
30–32   noticed ⟨perhaps we have sometimes⟩ in . . . ↑we↓ relish
35–(261)15   ¶ {As . . . position.}
37–38   querulous ⟨discontented⟩ temper, . . . to ⟨s⟩content

                                    Page 261
10   be ⟨happy⟩ ↑happy,↓
18–19   find ⟨a⟩ precisely . . . asked "⟨a⟩Am I ↑without↓ sin⟨less⟩?"
21–31   dependant . . . right. ¶ ↑The ⟨o⟩reservation of the Deitys necessity of
                   originating virtue↓ [notation in pencil] ¶ ↑It . . . that all ⟨behind⟩ us
                   all our past . . . ↑& so in happiness↓ . . . dependance ⟨& are
                   disposed to say not⟩ that . . . this—↓ [in pencil]
33–34   the ⟨spiritual⟩ blessings ↑that belong to piety to living with God↓
                   [Insertion is in ink over pencil; the pencil layer reads:] ↑that belong to
                   piety ⟨to it⟩ living with God↓
39   this ⟨mighty⟩ ↑spiritual↓

                                    Page 262
4   to ⟨on⟩ a
10   sent. ⟨God⟩ We
16   and his supper, [circled in pencil]
27–28   ↑never . . . shall↓

[Following the end of the sermon, at the bottom of MS p. 34:] pluviosa

Sermon XC

Manuscript: Seven sheets folded to make four pages each; folios stacked and sewn along the left margin with white thread; pages measure 25 x 20.3 cm.

Lines	Page 263
Bible Text	profited; if [Below the text a capital "S" is written twice in pencil, once in print-writing, once in script.]
1–3	man ⟨proceed on the supp⟩ imply . . . acting ⟨b⟩ upon
8	must ⟨be of ⟨the⟩⟩ ↑have↓
9–10	small /thing/trust/ to have ↑the keeping [in ink over pencil] of↓ a soul. And ⟨there are no such⟩ ↑compared with their capacity↓ men ↑are not such↓ as there ought
18	its ⟨conditions⟩ /contigences/nature & connexions./
20–(264)1	there ⟨is⟩ ↑are↓ . . . of ⟨a perfect character⟩ ↑moral & intellectual excellence↓, . . . a ⟨noble⟩ ↑perfect↓ character. ⟨What⟩ ⟨The lesson then that I gather from [illegible word] ↑this Scripture↓ is⟩ ⟨↑It should teach us↓⟩ ↑{Insert A} A {Our . . . ↑his↓ instructions supposed in ⟨the⟩ human . . . souls. to . . . them. & . . . discourse}↓ [end of Insert "A"] ↑I wish to enforce the doctrine↓

	Page 264
5–7	↑probably↓ . . . is ⟨appar⟩ manifest . . . cultivate ⟨his⟩ some
10	own ⟨character⟩ ↑soul↓ by ⟨im⟩ an
11–18	God ⟨intended⟩ gave . . . a ⟨perfect but of a⟩ peculiar character. ¶ ⟨It⟩The . . . various. ↑{Insert B} *below*↓ [The passage marked "B" and set off with square brackets is part of the original inscription following "wholly unlike. ⟨cast your⟩":] {As . . . is ⟨this⟩ ↑its↓ /peculiarity/individuality/.}
19–24	purposes. ⟨↑{Insert B}↓⟩ If . . . have ⟨created⟩ the most decided ⟨character⟩ ↑greatness↓ ["greatness" struck through twice in pencil, but no term replaces it] you . . . tho't. ⟨Socrates⟩ Abraham, . . . unlike. ⟨Cast your⟩ [followed by bracketed passage marked "B"; see previous note] ¶ ⟨But now⟩ ↑But . . . mind↓ there ⟨is⟩ ↑may be noticed everywhere↓
25–28	The ⟨vines⟩ gardeners . . . ↑tried . . . another soil↓ . . . when ⟨commonly⟩ ↑often↓ the ⟨grape⟩ ↑fruit↓ [last addition in ink over pencil]
31	inborn ⟨genius⟩ ↑intelligence↓
36–(265)5	vain. ↑{Insert C} C {It . . . that ⟨his⟩ he possesses some ⟨shade⟩ ⟨degree⟩ ↑particular manner↓ . . . ↑tho' reckoned advantages↓ he thinks ⟨prevent him⟩ rather . . . is ⟨the height of folly⟩ ↑ungrateful & injurious↓ [emendation in ink and pencil] He thinks ⟨they are⟩ ↑this quality is↓ . . . have ⟨them⟩ ↑it.↓. . . . good.}↓

	Page 265
5	look ⟨at the inferior natures⟩ at
9–10	resemble ⟨every⟩ ↑any↓ other one. ↑and . . . kind.↓

13–14   him ⟨ou⟩ from . . . ↑the complexion↓ of his mind & ⟨he is a fool⟩ ↑it
          . . . folly↓ [Last addition is in ink over pencil; the pencil version
          reads:] it is the hextreme of folly
16   secondary ⟨being⟩ man.
18–19   Mind. ¶ ⟨If any⟩ ⟨The⟩ ↑One↓ measure of a mans ⟨power⟩
          ↑character↓
20   ↑I think↓
24–26   ta↑l↓king, from his brother⟨.⟩, ↑& . . . respect.↓
30   floating [end of page] ⟨parlance of the time they think what is
          expected to be said what others have said⟩ [end of page] parlance [At
          the bottom of the page containing the canceled passage is a large
          question mark in pencil.]
31–33   said,—What ²others ¹have said,— . . . true. ⟨Well now it i⟩Is ↑it not↓
34–36   I ⟨↑cannot↓⟩ think this ⟨may⟩ ↑cannot↓ be illustrate⟨d⟩ ⟨by consid-
          ering⟩ ↑better . . . with↓ . . . the↑ir↓ talk ⟨of common men⟩ in
37–38   truth ⟨in⟩ ⟨common affairs⟩ ↑↑in things concerning↓ his ordinary
          business↓
40–(266)1 ↑the learning or eloquence of↓

                              Page 266

2–3   ↑when↓ men ⟨engaged in⟩ ↑converse on↓ their pressing affairs
          ⟨become mere organs⟩ ↑they↓ . . . speak ⟨themselves⟩ as
7   & ⟨through them it is the Universe that⟩ are
8   as ⟨these⟩ men
12   observe ⟨that⟩ that
14–17   ↑Some will say↓ To press on ⟨men⟩ ↑a man↓ the necessity of ⟨only
          considering⟩ guiding . . . the ⟨dim⟩ ↑unaided↓ . . . to ⟨neglect⟩
          shun . . . men ⟨may⟩ seem↑s↓ . . . commandments of ⟨lowliness⟩
          ↑that enjoin↓
20–29   & ⟨always⟩ gratefully . . . our↑s↓ ⟨own⟩, but ↑the . . . plain↓ . . .
          ↑we ought↓ . . . own. ⟨A man who⟩ ↑Breth⟨e⟩ren, . . . instance↓
          forsake⟨s⟩n ⟨his⟩your . . . adopt⟨s⟩ed new ones from complai-
          sance↑,↓ ⟨is likely⟩ ↑you have not↓ by & by ⟨to⟩ be↑en↓ compelled
          to receive ⟨his⟩ ↑your↓ . . . by ⟨his⟩ ↑your↓ own weapons. ↑Cer-
          tainly . . . respect↓
29–30   the ⟨ingenuous⟩ modesty . . . worth & ⟨to all their⟩ thinks
32–33   is ⟨beyond⟩ ↑above↓ . . . excellence. ⟨The⟩ ↑Every . . . realized.↓
35–37   the ⟨meanest⟩ ↑most obscure & ignorant↓ . . . ↑you shall find that↓
          . . . in ⟨their⟩ ↑that↓
41   dependen⟨t⟩ce

                              Page 267

4   it ⟨is⟩ contains
6   himself. ⟨To be wholly⟩ An
9   ↑can↓
16–17   the ⟨sensualist⟩ voluptuary . . . unknown ⟨tongue⟩ ↑language↓ as in
          their ⟨own⟩ ↑mother tongue↓.

18–21   Thyself. ⟨In⟩ To ⟨view of this⟩ ↑him . . . wisdom↓ . . . Cesar . . .
               ↑almost↓
33   us ⟨r⟩hear

[Following the end of the sermon:] {"In every good work trust thy own soul; for this is
the keeping of the Commandment." Eccl[esiastic]us. 32. 23

[On the page facing the conclusion of the sermon, the following passage in pencil:] The
sense of the worth of a human soul may well be urged on the consciences of those to
whom it is committed the charge of instructing you. We may well tremble at the
greatness of the office we assume. But ↑it is little tha⟨n⟩t we can do for you↓ the minister
passes away to the world of spirits ⟨&⟩ ↑or↓ to other duties on earth & the care of your
soul must always rest on yourself. Let me then exhort you in the words of the apostle Let
every man prove his own work then shall he have rejoicing in himself alone [Galatians
6:4]

INDEX

A

Abraham, 219*n4*, 264
Abstinence, 154
Achan, 164*n2*
Actions, 19, 20, 120, 128, 153, 186, 189, 217–18, 220–21, 230, 241, 245, 247, 251–54. *See also* Principles; Works, Good
Adam, 76
Affection, 193; and reason, 49; for Christ, 118–19, 120
Affections, 20, 21, 23, 76, 98–99, 110, 166–70, 187, 193, 200, 203, 215, 235, 247; development of, 157; in children, 173
Afterlife, 19, 176–80, 181, 183, 188, 136, 137, 150. *See also* Heaven
Alfred, 29
Ambition, 39, 41, 44, 127, 198
America, God's feeling for, 212; duties of, 213–15; as Zion, 215; and religious liberty, 215
American Indian. *See* Native American
American Revolution, leaders of, 213
American Sunday School Union, 95*n7*
Amsdorff, Nicholas von, 48
Anniversary Sermon, Second Church, Boston (LXIX), 156–61
Antinomianism, 148
Arethusa, 79*n3*
Arianism, 187–88
Arius, 187*n3*
Astronomy, 29, 140
Atheism, 63, 87, 90. *See also* Skepticism
Atonement, 187
Avarice, 37, 44, 145, 198; as perversion of duty, 39. *See also* Sin

B

Baal, 138
Bacchus, 145
Bacon, Sir Francis: "Of Friendship," quoted, 67
Baptism, 148
Beauty: and spiritual nature of man, 146
Beneficence, 133–34, 153, 197, 201, 207–8, 223
Benevolence, 31, 34, 116, 133–36, 150, 159, 168, 169, 183, 184, 187, 193, 196, 209, 210, 249, 259, 266. *See also* Virtue
Bible, Emerson's views of, 19, 187–88, 201
—Genesis, *1:3*, 258; *1:11*, 207; *1:11–12*, 265; *1:20*, 207; *1:24*, 207; *1:26*, 56, 113, 120, 208, 218, 252, 256; *1:31*, 92; *2:7*, 208; *2:18*, 84; *3:19*, 115, 144; *4:7*, 59; *6:3*, 80; *35:39*, 160; *49:24*, 246
—Exodus, 7, 164; *12:8*, 156; *15:8*, 257; *19:5*, 168; *20:1–17*, 124; *20:13*, 124; *23:22*, 168
—Numbers, *9:11*, 156
—Deuteronomy, *5:7–21*, 124; *5:17*, 124; *14:2*, 165; *28:23*, 258; *32:47*, 237
—Joshua, *9:23–27*, 229; *24:15*, 201
—I Samuel *5*, 48
—II Samuel, *22:10*, 256; *22:11*, 208
—I Kings, *17:4–6*, 142
—I Chronicles, *28:2*, 256
—II Chronicles, *32:8*, 248
—Esther, *5:13*, 261
—Job, *1:21*, 51; *23:8–9*, 242; *29:13*, 209; *31:40*, 248; *32:8*, 144; *38:11*, 105; *42:5*, 21, 180;
—Psalms, *2:4*, 256; *2:11*, 190; *11:4*, 257; *12:1*, 114; *13:43*, 215; *14:1*, 63; *14:3*, 152; *18:10*, 208; *18:26*, 136; *19:8*, 30; *24:3–5*, 46; *37:3*, 256; *42:5*, 157; *42:11*, 157; *43:5*, 157; *44:1*, 212; *49:7*, 72; *53:3*, 152; *55:14*, 160; *78:25*, 147; *90:10*, 259; *95:4–5*, 256; *98:8*, 146; *99:5*, 256; *103:2*, 92; *104:8*, 208; *139:6*, 24; *144:15*, 162
—Proverbs, *3:6*, 24; *4:18*, 55; *4:23*, 166, 167; *8:3*, 257; *9:1–5*, 257; *10:7*, 111; *10:9*, 216; *11:2*, 222; *13:12*, 139; *14:10*, 142; *14:14*, 267; *16:18–19*, 222; *16:32*, 41; *19:8*, 232; *23:7*, 248; *27:19*, 219
—Ecclesiastes, *2:2*, 169; *9:10*, 107; *11:40*, 28; *12:13*, 41
—Isaiah, *3:15*, 37; *7:14*, 24; *10:13*, 255; *10:14*, 261; *29:13*, 257; *53:3*, 23, 110, 195, 240; *54:8*, 256, 262; *55:8*, 317; *55:12*, 146, 257; *60:11*, 36; *66:24*, 19
—Jeremiah, *8:22*, 240; *13:23*, 76; *18:8*, 256
—Ezekiel, *12:19*, 116
—Daniel, *12:4*, 74
—Jonah, *3:9*, 256
—Micah, *6:8*, 159, 169
—Nahum, *1:3*, 256
—Habakkuk *2:2*, 38
—Ecclesiasticus, *32:23*, 400; *42:24*, 198, 248
—Matthew, *1:23*, 24, 240; *4:17*, 169; *5–7*, 97–101; *5:3*, 99, 180; *5:3–6*, 255; *5:7*, 199, 211; *5:8*, 30, 61, 65, 99, 180, 222; *5:9*, 144; *5:14*, 53, 97, 165; *5:39*, 90; *5:44*, 199; *5:45*,

110, 182; *5:46*, 53; *5:48*, 90; *6:2*, 97, 154; *6:6*,
82, 84; *6:9-10*, 62; *6:10*, 244; *6:19*, 97;
6:20, 98; *6:21*, 97; *6:26*, 97; *6:28*, 97, 265;
7:1-2, 199; *7:7-8*, 149, 245; *7:12*, 41, 209;
7:16, 46, 48, 97; *7:20*, 216, 255; *7:21*, 49;
7:26, 50; *7:28*, 357; *7:29*, 192; *8:20*, 110;
9:13, 59; *10:42*, 152, 199; *11:5*, 211; *11:28*,
36, 262; *11:29*, 222; *12:33*, 251; *13:12*, 234;
13:24-30, 34; *13:37-43*, 34; *13:46*, 152;
15:11-20, 166; *16:24*, 129; *16:26*, 263, 267;
17:2, 243; *18:3*, 171, 173; *18:10*, 171; *18:22*,
107; *19:17*, 74; *19:19*, 259; *19:21*, 90, 239;
19:26, 126; *21:44*, 148; *22:30*, 147; *22:37*,
34; *22: 37-39*, 29, 190, 254; *23:12*, 222;
24:35, 111; *25:14-30*, 54, 73; *25:21*, 260;
25:23, 151, 155; *25:25*, 19; *26:18*, 57; *26:41*,
44; *27:38*, 240; *28:20*, 240
—Mark, *2:17*, 59; *4:22*, 220; *4:25*, 234; *4:26-
29*, 113; *8:18*, 189; *8:34*, 129, 326; *10:14*, 171,
174; *10:16*, 171; *10:17-18*, 110; *10:21*, 90,
239; *10:27*, 126; *12:25*, 147; *12:30*, 34, 148;
12:30-31, 29, 190, 254; *12:31*, 159; *12:42*,
152; *12:42-44*, 33; *13:31*, 111; *14:38*, 44
—Luke, *2:7*, 240; *2:10*, 110; *2:14*, 196; *2:29*,
181; *5:32*, 59; *6:25*, 19; *6:27-28*, 111, 199;
6:29, 90; *6:31*, 41, 132, 137, 209; *6:35*, 199;
6:37-38, 248; *8:18*, 234; *9:54-56*, 59; *9:55*,
229; *10:27*, 29, 34, 148, 190, 204; *10:30-37*,
33; *10:41-42*, 25; *10:42*, 41, 178; *11:2*, 244;
11:9-10, 149, 245; *12:6-7*, 138; *12:27*, 254,
265; *12:33*, 380; *12:48*, 149; *16:19-31*, 133;
16:31, 179; *17:10*, 199; *17:21*, 24, 99; *17:24*,
83; *18:1*, 242; *18:14*, 34; *18:17*, 171; *18:22*,
90-91, 239; *20:18*, 148; *20:35*, 147; *20:36*,
14; *21:2*, 152; *21:2-4*, 33; *21:33*, 111; *22:17-
19*, 53; *22:19*, 56; *22:42*, 23; *23:4*, 357
—John, *1:3*, 21; *1:10*, 256; *1:14*, 109; *3:6*, 148;
3:19, 113; *4:14*, 74, 262; *5:24*, 147; *6:12*, 113;
8:7, 261; *8:12*, 167, 239; *8:32*, 221; *11:25*, 57,
74; *11:33*, 58; *11:33-44*, 184; *11:35*, 169;
11:52, 144; *14:6*, 170; *14:10*, 253; *14:15*,
204; *14:23*, 253; *15:5-6*, 64; *15:10*, 65, 122;
15:14, 118; *15:15*, 118, 119; *17:1-5*, 57; *17:3*,
187; *17:21*, 195; *17:21-22*, 255; *17:21-23*, 90;
19:34, 120; *20:21*, 110
—Acts, *2:3*, 49; *5:29*, 86; *7:57*, 111; *9:18*, 132;
14:12, 219; *16:25*, 22; *16:30*, 187; *17:28*, 9,
22; *20:35*, 135; *24:26*, 219; *28:1-6*, 219
—Romans, *1:14-15*, 110; *2:4*, 80; *2:7*, 247;
6:5, 128; *6:23*, 241; *7:23*, 44; *8:16*, 144, 239;
8:17, 122; *8:28*, 143; *9:26*, 144; *12:1*, 246;
12:2, 124, 128, 250; *12:19*, 70; *13:9*, 124;
13:11, 75; *13:12*, 112; *13:34*, 124; *14:5*, 138;
14:7, 170; *14:12*, 71, 72, 254
—I Corinthians, *1:21*, 157; *2:10*, 337; *2:14*,
180; *3:7*, 158; *3:16*, 144, 145, 148, 252; *3:21*,
149; *6:2*, 25; *6:19-20*, 251, 255; *7:31*, 24;
8:28, 176; *10:4*, 253; *10:12*, 51, 54; *10:24*,
196; *10:31*, 244; *11:29*, 57; *12:26*, 118; *12:27*,

302; *13:1*, 72; *13:3*, 199; *13:12*, 176, 235, 185;
15:19, 62; *15:26*, 181; *15:41*, 235
—II Corinthians, *3:6*, 188; *3:18*, 243-44; *4:3-4*,
87; *4:9*, 190; *4:18*, 51; *6:1*, 90, 156; *6:2*, 201,
203; *9:7*, 371
—Galatians, *2:7-8*, 110; *3:26*, 144; *4:4*, 108;
4:8-10, 138; *5:1*, 190; *5:13*, 134; *6:4*, 405;
6:4-5, 186; *6:5*, 82; *6:7*, 232; *6:9*, 102, 104,
106; *6:10*, 198; *6:14*, 119
—Ephesians, *2:1*, *2:5*, 64; *4:22-24*, 247; *5:15*,
51
—Philippians, *3:7-8*, 119; *3:13*, 51; *3:14*, 249;
4:13, 107
—Colossians, *1:12*, 245; *2:2*, 84; *2:13*, 64; *2:19*,
84; *3:17*, 244; *4:11*, 90
—I Thessalonians, *5:17*, 244; *5:21*, 158
—I Timothy, *4:8*, 165; *6:7*, 179
—II Timothy *3:17*, 24; *4:2*, 158
—Titus, *1:15*, 129; *2:14*, 165
—Hebrews, *1:14*, 209; *3:12*, 37, 168; *4:1*, 180;
4:3-11, 241; *6:18-19*, 36; *6:19*, 35; *11:16*,
165; *12:22*, 126; *13:16*, 206
—James, *1:13*, 258; *1:27*, 254; *2:10*, 223; *2:23*,
219; *3:2*, 66, 70; *4:14*, 61, 112; *5:12*, 172;
5:15-16, 245
—I Peter, *4:7*, 170
—II Peter, *1:4*, 144; *1:5*, 227, 231; *1:8*, 231; *3:8*,
117
—I John, *1:5*, 22; *3:14*, 147; *3:17*, 199; *4:8*, 41;
4:11, 123; *4:12*, 253; *4:18*, 122, 190; *5:2*, 144
—Revelation, *2:10*, 111; *4:9*, 202; *21:4-5*, 202;
21:8, 135; *21:23*, 231; *21:25*, 36
Body: versus Spirit, 144-50
Bonaparte, Napoleon, 39, 267
Book of Common Prayer, 24
Boston Prison Disciple Society, 68*n3*
Brahma, 138
Browne, Sir Thomas, 30*n1*
Burke, Edmund, 168; quoted, 120, 243
Butler, Joseph, quoted, 151, 363
Byron, Admiral John, 93, 222
Byron, Lord, 169*n12*

C
Caesar, 267
Caiaphas, 120
Calumny, 155, 164
Calvin, John, 19, 20
Calvinist-Trinitarian sect, 186, 189. *See also*
Trinitarian
Calvinists, 248; materialism of, 19
Cameron, Kenneth W., 216, 235*n5*, 238*n1*
Castlereagh, Robert Stewart, 128*n8*
Catholic Church, 248
Cato, 32
Change, fear of, 127-28
Channing, William Ellery, 186, 213*n1*, 243*n2*,
247*n2*, 263
Character, 216; improvement of, 119, 125, 128,

153, 165, 227; standard of, 266. *See also* Man: improvement of

Charity, 90–91, 116, 178, 183, 196–200, 206, 209–11, 222, 239

Chesterfield, Lord. *See* Stanhope, Philip Dormer

Children: education of, 28–29, 172–74; instilling virtue in, 29; virtues of, 171–75; conscience of, 173

Chilo (Chilon), quoted, 41

Christian: conception of God, 22; definition of, 22–23, 28; contempt of trifles, 28; province of, 42

Christianity, 192, 206, 209, 223, 238, 244, 254; divisions within, 19–20, 186–91; and Jewish Law, 56, 58; and paganism, 57, 58, 119; teachings of 82, 90, 263; excellence of, 90; influence of, 111, 123; as majestic principle, 122; obedience to laws of, 152–53; and social code, 196; and ideas of God, 256

Christmas, festival of: moral interest of, 108–111

Church: as temple of God, 252

Civilization, 25, 234; good of, 93–94

Cleobulus, quoted, 41

Cole, Arthur H., 114*n7*

Coleridge, Samuel Taylor: *Biographia Literaria,* quoted, 95; *Aids to Reflection,* 126*n3,* 228*n3; The Friend,* 183*n5,* 349, 360

Columbus, Christopher, 27, 109, 233*n2*

Commandments, 55, 124, 159, 164, 165, 169, 171, 180, 201, 203, 204–5, 221, 241, 254, 262, 266; obedience to, 40, 47, 249; practice of, 120, 123. *See also* Law

Conscience, 21, 80, 193, 195, 204, 208, 222, 224, 225, 228, 253, 254; versus action, 45; in children, 173

Conversation. *See* Speech

Cook, Captain James, 93

Cooperation: of Soul and God, 90

Copernican System, 238

Crucifixion, 106

D

David, 152

Death, 30, 35, 112, 128, 129, 177, 179, 190, 193, 210, 240, 241; preparation for, 24, 181, 185; second, 135; fear of, 182–85

Deception, practice of among men, 216–17

Declaration of Independence, 215*n3*

Diligence, 178, 187

Doubt, 239. *See also* Skepticism

Duty, 26, 30–32, 34–35, 39, 41–42, 45, 55, 91, 134, 150, 152, 153, 156, 158–60, 167, 183, 188, 196, 199, 204, 206, 209, 224, 228, 231, 233–34, 239, 242, 245, 246, 247, 250, 263, 266; as love of virtue, 31; in relation to Doctrines of Faith and Good Works, 47. *See also* Virtue

Duty, social. *See* Responsibility, social

E

Echo, 79*n3*

Economy, political, 126*n5,* 133; law of, 78, 142

Education, 188

Emerson, Mary Moody, 20*n5,* 24*n17,* 332, 334

Emerson, Ralph Waldo: theology of, 46–50, 159, 186–91; views of Doctrines of Faith and Good Works, 46–50; first anniversary as pastor of Second Church, 156; on teaching of commandments, 159.

—Works: "Ben Jonson, Herrick, Herbert, Wotton," 398; Blotting Book Psi, 150*n22;* "Compensation," 198*n4,* 248*n5;* "The Divinity School Address," 149*n18;* "Doctrine of Hands," 126*n5;* Essays and Lectures, 128*n9;* "Ethical Writers," 90*n2,* 103*n1;* "Ethics," 198*n4,* 220*n5,* 248*n5,* 253*n7,* 398; "General Views," 151*n1;* "Genius," 398; "George Fox," 235*n8;* "Historic Notes of Life and Letters in New England," 186; "Immortality," 151*n1; Journals,* 20*n5,* 24*n17;* "Introductory," Human Culture Series, 105*n4;* "Literature," 398; "Martin Luther," 48*n2;* *Nature,* 146*n7,* 151*n1,* 201, 206, 235*n5;* "Old Age," 103*n2;* "Plutarch," 90*n2;* "The Poet," 398; "Politics," 162*n1;* "Reforms," 42*n4;* "The Relation of Man to the Globe," 140*n3;* "Religion," 218*n2;* "Self-Reliance," 398; "Society," 186, 195*n3;* "Spiritual Laws," 218*n2;* "The Superlative," 155*n8;* "The Transcendentalist," 186; "The Uses of Natural History," 140*n3,* 195*n3;* "The Young American," 38*n7*

Envy, 198

Erie Canal, 114*n7*

Evangelical Missionary Society, 211

Evangelical Treasury, 206, 210, 211

Evil, 29, 119, 147, 164, 182–83, 187, 193, 199, 200, 203, 204, 209, 210, 217, 218, 239, 241, 245, 253, 264; source of, 144

F

Faith, 20, 23, 176, 182, 184, 185, 187, 223, 224, 225, 227, 238, 240, 243, 254; doctrine of, opposed to doctrine of good works, 46–50; advantage of, 61; reasonableness of, 92

Fame, pursuit of, 123

Fast Day sermon (LXX), 162–65

Fear, 130, 187, 190, 191, 203

Felix, 219

Fénelon, François de Selignac de La Mothe-, 20, 210, 229, 264, 400

Flattery, 155

Fontenelle, Bernard le Bovier de, 28*n5;* quoted, 195

Fourth of July Sermon (LXXX), 212–15

Fox, George, 235*n8*

Franklin, Benjamin, 266
Frederic of Prussia, 26
Free agency. *See* Free Will
Freedom, 245, 247. *See also* Independence
Free will, 34, 52, 71–75, 79, 84–85, 120, 178, 261
Friendship, 118, 120, 123
Future, 125–26, 204

G
Genius, 146–47
Geology, 140
Gilead, 240
God: and Nature, 21; effects on mind, 21, 197; manifestations of, 21, 22; man's relationship to, 21–24; as Energetic Benefactor, 22; within, 24; as highest theology, 61; idea of, 61–65, 138–40, 238–39, 241, 242, 243, 256–58; belief in, 138–43, 224, 238–39; pagan, 139; Xenophon's proof for existence of, 141; offenses to, 187; purposes of, 188; knowledge of, 222, 237–41; anger of, 257–58, 261–62; Old Testament representations of, 256–57, 261
Goethe, Johann Wolfgang von: on St. Philip Neri, 385–86
Golden Rule, 136, 209. *See also* Bible: Luke 6:31
Goldsmith, Oliver: "Retaliation: A Poem," quoted, 189
Government, influence of, 162; description of good, 162; and virtue, 162–64; American, 162, 165; and religious character, 163
Grace, 201, 223
Gratitude, 187
Guilt, 125, 187, 258

H
Habit, 28, 76–81, 85, 98, 100, 107, 160, 166, 168, 203, 233, 239, 243; evil, 120, 190, 262
Haman, 261*n14*
Hancock Sunday School, 95, 211
Happiness, 86, 101, 155, 218, 259–62
Harrington, James, 166*n3*
Hastings, James, 188*n3*
Hazlitt, William, 235*n7*
Heaven, 99–101, 180, 184, 193, 225, 235, 259, 261; as state of mind, 99. *See also* Afterlife
Hell, 184
Herbert, George, "Sinne," quoted, 126
Heroes, interest in, 225
Hobbes, Thomas, 30*n1*
Holbrook, Josiah, 95*n7*
Holy Ghost, body as temple of, 252–55
Honesty, 178, 183
Hopkins, Samuel, 33
Horace, quoted, 258
Humboldt, Baron Alexander von, 93
Hume, David, 50
Humility, 90–91, 99, 222–26

Hutcheson, Francis, 197*n2*
Hypocrisy, 148, 220, 223

I
Imitation, dangers of, 264–67
Immortality, 19, 23, 74, 88, 90, 145, 147, 176, 178, 193, 255, 263. *See also* Afterlife
Improvement, 25, 28, 38, 40, 228, 230, 232–34, 246, 249. *See also* Man: improvement of
Independence, 127–29, 190, 224; and imitation, 73
Individuality, 264
Industry, 222
Intemperance, 145
Irving, Washington, 233*n2*

J
James 48, 70, 245
Jealousy, 190
Jefferson, Thomas, 162*n1*, 212, 215*n3*, 215*n4*
Jesus Christ, 23, 28, 57–58, 108–111, 141, 169, 185, 222, 247, 253, 255; and Sermon on the Mount, 97; example of, 109, 217; as friend, 118–23, 217; teachings of, 122, 129, 136, 157, 171–75, 192–95, 204, 217, 257, 262; fellowship with, 123; authority of, 192–95, 247; and Salvation, 201
John, 253
Johnson, Samuel: *The Rambler,* 263; quoted, 102–3, 316, 354
Jonson, Ben, 66*n1*
Jove, 138
Judas, 106
Justice, 125, 222
Jupiter, 219

K
Knowledge, 22, 26, 126–29, 177, 179, 194, 207, 222, 227, 231, 237, 242; acquisition of, 132, 228, 232–36; and improvement, 228–30. *See also* Wisdom
Knox, Vicesimus, 42*n4*

L
Laertius, Diogenes, 42*n4*
Lafayette, 68*n3*
Last Judgment, 30*n2*
Law: Christian, 121–22, 193, 206, 210; of God, 127, 134, 187, 248, 154; of nature, 139, 141, 142; perfection of, 148; and mercy, 152; civil, 163; Jewish, 192; of Love, 196
Lazarus, 74
Leonidas, 32
Liberty. *See* Independence; Free Will
Lodestone, 20
Lord's Prayer, 244
Lord's Supper, 56–60, 148, 242, 262
Love, 23, 41, 122, 123, 136, 187, 190, 191, 196,

200, 203, 209, 210, 211, 231, 241, 243, 247, 248, 258, 260. *See also* Virtue
Lust, 145
Luther, Martin, 29, 48
Lyceum, 95

M
Mackenzie, Sir Alexander, 93
Man: perfection of, 38, 49; improvement of, 51–55, 58–60, 61–63, 66, 76, 119–20, 141, 175, 183, 223; nature of, 56, 144–50, 198, 208; standard idea of, 69
Martha, 25, 28
Mary, 28, 74
Materialists, 30
Meditation, 120
Mercy, 19, 152, 169, 208, 211, 258, 262
Milton, John, 229, 264; *Areopagitica,* quoted, 86; "Of Reformation in England," quoted, 91; *Paradise Lost,* quoted, 157; "To Mr. Cyriack Skinner upon His Blindness," quoted, 157; Sonnet XIX, quoted, 250
Mind, 145, 146, 147; and perception of God, 19, 20, 64; versus matter, 30; changes in, 103; power of, 149
Minister, duties of, 156–61, 196; relation to congregation, 156; as preacher and pastor, 158
Moderation, 125, 244
Modesty, 125, 135, 266
Moore, George, 216
Moral design, 142. *See also* Providence, design of
Moral economy, 210
Moral excellence, 27, 41, 109, 263
Moral law, 86; obedience to, 47
Moral nature: and habit, 78; law of, 79, 193
Moral perception, 204
Moral slavery, 201
Moral truth, 194
Moral world, 202, 208
Mordecai, 261
Mortalist heresy, 30n1
Moses, 141, 264
Murder, 145

N
Native American, 95
Natural religion. *See* Religion: natural
Nature 202, 208; laws of, 21; kingdom of, 139; order of, 141; as mirror of soul, 146, 219, 248
Neri, St. Philip, 385–86
Newton, Sir Isaac, 28, 29, 229, 233, 266; quoted, 151
New Year's Eve Sermon (LXI), 112–17
Niles, Hezekiah, 106n6
Numa. *See* Pompilius

O
Overton, Richard, 30n1
Ovid, 79

P
Paley, William: *Natural Theology,* 238n1; quoted, 71
Parnassus, 126n3
Pascal, Blaise: *Pensées,* quoted, 167–68
Past, man's relation to, 201–2, 204
Patriotism, 213–15; duty of, 165
Paul, 22, 39, 57, 90, 107, 119, 157, 170, 180, 192, 219, 229, 247, 252
Penitence, 187
Perfection, 106, 111, 129, 132, 145, 147, 148, 151, 168, 170, 188, 197, 217, 227, 230, 243, 249, 263, 265; idea of, 22. *See also* Man: improvement of
Periander, quoted, 41
Perseverance, 102–7
Peter, 170n14
Pittacus, quoted, 41
Plato, 229
Plutarch, 50; "How a Man May Be Sensible of His Progress in Virtue," quoted, 43
Politicians, as measure of virtue of country, 164
Politics, doctrine of modern, 94
Polytheism, 139
Pompilius, Numa, 29
Pope, Alexander: "Elegy to the Memory of an Unfortunate Lady," quoted, 113
Prayer, 22, 28, 61–62, 120, 126, 148–50, 159, 170, 185, 187, 190, 217; efficacy of, 23, 245; natural, 139; duty of, 242–45; use of, 242–44; objects of, 244–45
Preparation, 127, 147, 178, 179, 190, 202; of soul, 90
Press, 163–64
Pride, 135, 136, 183, 198, 222, 225
Priestley, Joseph, 28
Principles, 26, 128, 130, 209, 246, 247, 251–55, 263; as separate from actions, 46
Property. *See* Wealth
Providence, 22, 23, 34, 43, 75, 83, 85, 96, 114, 149, 159, 162, 168, 177, 178, 184, 187, 200, 201–2, 205, 207, 211, 212, 215, 230, 233, 244, 252, 258, 260, 261; doctrine of, 139, 142; design of, 141–42
Puritans, 215

Q
Quakers, 235n8

R
Rabirius, 380
Reason, 98, 126, 129, 145, 166, 192, 206, 235, 265; in struggle with vice, 44–45; and affection, 49; in relation to Good Works, 49; and

idea of God, 49, 138, 142; purposes of, 203; and virtue, 224; and senses, 238

Reckoning of moral accounts: importance of at year's end, 112–17

Reed, Sampson, 238n1; quoted, 235

Reformation, 48

Regeneration, Doctrine of, 46

Religion, 22, 24, 122, 125, 138, 145, 151, 152, 157, 160, 183, 199, 237, 246, 260, 263, 267; practical, 20; natural, 20, 138–39, 196; desires of, 44; purposes of, 52–55, 88–90; essence of, 54; substance of, 61; and views of God, 62–63, 237–41; teachings of, 82; advantages of, 88; as theory of life, 88; opposed to worldliness, 88; false, 119; foundation of, 144; and virtuous soul, 168; divisions within, 186–91; and intellect, 229–30; defined, 237; practical value of, 238; and equality of men, 240; and prayer, 242

Repentance, 169

Reputation, 220

Responsibility, social, 83; opposed to self-ishness, 132–37

Resurrection, 106, 183

Revelation, 22, 23, 24, 109, 115, 121, 122, 141, 142, 149, 176, 179, 182, 188, 203, 204, 206, 231, 246, 261

Romulus, 29n6

S

Sabbath, 38, 40, 160, 254, 262

Sacrifice: of self to God, 246–50

Salvation, 201–5, 209, 230, 255, 267; importance of Faith and Good Works to, 46, 48; and obedience to moral law, 47; defined, 201; time of, 201

Science, 29, 93–94, 139–40, 207, 230, 236, 251

Scriptures. See Bible; Law

Scougal, Henry, 239n2

Second Church, Boston, 56

Sects, 253; differences between, 19, 20, 186–91

Self, claims of, 132–34

Self-command, 42–45, 82, 100, 107, 190, 225; defined, 43

Self-control. See Self-command

Self-denial, 129–30, 204

Self-indulgence, 129

Self-interest, 163, 209

Selfishness, 27, 29, 133–37, 150, 154, 164, 167, 168, 169, 193, 196, 198, 199, 200, 262

Self-knowledge, 267. See also Wisdom

Self-love, 132, 134, 136, 251. See also Selfishness

Self-reliance, 263–67

Self-restraint, 154

Self-sufficiency, 157

Seneca, 50; "De Providentia," quoted, 90; "On the Renown Which My Writings Will Bring You," 115n22

Sermon on the Mount, 97–101. See also Bible: Matthew 5–7

Seven Sages, 42n4; quoted, 41–42

Sexes, distinctions between, 147

Shakespeare, William: Hamlet, 147n10; The Tempest, quoted, 105

Silas, 22

Sin, 23, 126, 129–30, 136, 142, 144, 145, 148, 153, 154, 187, 190, 191, 193, 195, 201, 203, 204, 224, 225, 226, 241, 253, 254, 255, 257, 258, 261; and selfishness, 134

Skepticism, 44, 87, 90, 110, 124–25, 176, 193. See also Atheism

Smith, Adam: 69n4

Smith, Walter B., 114n7

Society, 23, 196, 197, 217, 218, 232, 246; advantages of, 25, 83–84; evils of, 25–26; and individual, 82–86, 134; order of, 142

Socrates, 29, 39, 141, 229, 264

Solitude: advantages of, 25, 77, 121; as preparation for social discourse, 84–86

Solomon, 42, 166, 167, 169, 222, 267

Solon, quoted, 41

Soul, 20, 27, 28, 39, 106, 117, 194, 197, 218, 219, 228, 229, 239, 245, 247, 248, 254, 258, 263, 264, 266, 267; awareness of God, 20; and relation to God, 21, 22, 23, 89, 199; death of, 30n1; as another world, 88; education of, 88–91, 155, 223; virtue of, 89; as colony of Heaven, 99; immortality of, 193; salvation of, 201–5; health of, 224; in union with God, 236. See also Spirit

Speech, 66–70; and knowledge, 68, 70; and duty, 69; truth as aim of, 69

Spence, Joseph, 128, 151, 210

Spirit, 252–53; versus body, 144–50; attributes of, 145–49

Stabler, Edward, 149n18

Staël, Madame de: Germany, quoted, 195

Stanhope, Philip Dormer, Lord Chesterfield, quoted 155

Stewart, Dugald, 260n13

Stoddard, Solomon, 59n8

Stoics, 29

Suffering, 101

Suicide, 128

Swift, Jonathan, quoted, 128

Sympathy, 101; with Christ, 120; with men, 235, 261

T

Tamur, destroyed by Vishnu, 32

Taylor, Jeremy, 20

Temperance, 31, 154, 178, 193, 222. See also Virtue

Thanksgiving Day sermon (LVII), 92–96

Thought, 126–27. See also Knowledge; Reflection

Timothy, 219
Transfiguration, 243*n5*
Transubstantiation, Doctrine of, 57
Trinitarian-Unitarian Conflict, 186–91
Trinity, 187
Truth, 26, 109, 123, 127, 141, 147, 155, 179, 190, 193–95, 202, 216, 217, 221, 224, 225, 230, 234–36, 238, 243, 247, 248, 252, 253, 254, 265, 267; scientific, 251

U
Unitarian Church: critics of, 19
Unitarian-Trinitarian Conflict, 186–91
Unitarians, 187*n3,* 189

V
Vanity, 138, 155
Venus, 145
Vice, 19, 22, 26, 106, 120, 135, 137, 138, 145, 152, 164, 165, 183, 193, 200, 202, 217, 219, 224, 225, 229, 248, 254
Virgin, Holy, 138
Virtue, 21, 22, 23, 24, 29, 31–34, 37, 40, 41, 49–50, 54, 89, 91, 106–7, 109, 111, 120–24, 125–28, 130, 132–34, 136–37, 143, 146–48, 178, 179, 183, 185, 187, 189–91, 192, 193, 194, 196–97, 199, 202, 206, 209, 217–21, 222–26, 227–31, 232, 239, 240, 244, 248, 254, 261, 265; advantages of, 31; as law of love, 41, 136; and Good Works, 48; and free will, 72–75; differences in among men, 151; standards of, 153–54; and government, 164–65; and good-heartedness, 166–70

Vishnu, destruction of Tamur, 32
Voltaire, 50

W
Ward, Robert Plummer, 151*n1*
Ware, Henry, Jr., 114
Ware, Henry, Sr., 186
Washington, George, 215*n4,* 266
Watts, Isaac: "An Hymn for the Lord's Day Evening," quoted, 36
Wealth, 127–29, 134, 229; pursuit of, 123
Webster, Daniel, 95*n7*
Will, 102, 104, 105, 106, 126. *See also* Free Will
Wisdom, 28, 110, 125, 127, 210, 217, 218, 232, 234–35, 242, 243, 252, 258. *See also* Knowledge; Self-knowledge
"Wood 'n' Ware Debate," 186
Woods, Leonard, 186
Worcester, Samuel, 186
Worldliness, 87–88, 91
Works, Good, 165, 188, 197; Doctrine of opposed to Doctrine of Faith, 46–50; defined, 47; as signs of God's presence, 48. *See also* Actions

X
Xenophon, 141

Y
Young, Edward: *Night Thoughts,* quoted, 38, 54, 84, 181, 225